CHILTON'S 1994 QUICK SPECS MANUAL

Publisher and Editor-In-Chief Kerry A. Freeman, S.A.E.
Managing Editors Peter M. Conti, Jr. □ W. Calvin Settle, Jr., S.A.E
Assistant Managing Editor Nick D'Andrea
Senior Editors Debra Gaffney □ Ken Grabowski, A.S.E., S.A.E.
Michael L. Grady □ Richard J. Rivele, S.A.E.
Richard T. Smith □ Jim Taylor □ Ron Webb
Project Managers Ben Greisler, S.A.E. □ Martin J. Gunther
Jeffrey M. Hoffman □ Steven Morgan □ James B. Steele
Service Editors Peter A. Bilotta, A.S.E. □ Lawrence C. Braun, S.A.E., A.S.C.
Thomas P. Browne III □ Hugh J. Brulliea □ Dean G. Callahan
Michael M. Carroll □ William C. Cottman, A.S.E. □ Robert B. Day, Jr.
Paul DeGuiseppi, A.S.E. □ Robert F. Dougherty, Jr. □ Robert E. Doughten
Sam Fiorani □ Andrew J. Folz, A.S.E. □ Edward J. Giacomucci, A.S.E.
Jacques Gordon □ Neil Leonard, A.S.E. □ Kevin Maher
Robert McAnally □ Raymond K. Moore □ Craig P. Nangle, A.S.E.
Roy Ripple, A.S.E. □ John H. Rutter □ Don Schnell, A.S.E., S.A.E.
Larry E. Stiles □ Anthony Tortorici, A.S.E., S.A.E. □ Thom Young

Director of Manufacturing Mike D'Imperio
Assistant Production Manager Andrea Steiger
Production Assistants Marsha Park Herman □ Monica Santa Maria □ Margaret Stoner
Mechanical Artists Lisa Gressen □ Kim Hayes

National Sales Manager Lawrence Rufo
National Administrator, Sales Benjamin Tatta

OFFICERS
President, Chilton Enterprises David S. Loewith
Senior Vice President Ronald A. Hoxter

CHILTON PROFESSIONAL AUTOMOTIVE
ONE OF THE *DIVERSIFIED PUBLISHING COMPANIES*,
A PART OF *CAPITAL CITIES/ABC, INC.*
Manufactured in USA ©1993 Chilton Book Company • Chilton Way, Radnor, Pa. 19089
ISBN 0-8019-8469-6   1234567890 2109876543

SAFETY NOTICE

Proper service and repair procedures are vital to the safe, reliable operation of all motor vehicles, as well as the personal safety of those performing repairs. This manual outlines procedures for servicing and repairing vehicles using safe, effective methods. The procedures contain many NOTES, CAUTIONS and WARNINGS which should be followed along with standard safety procedures to eliminate the possibility of personal injury or improper service which could damage the vehicle or compromise its safety.

It is important to note that the repair procedures and techniques, tools and parts for servicing motor vehicles, as well as the skill and experience of the individual performing the work vary widely. It is not possible to anticipate all of the conceivable ways or conditions under which vehicles may be serviced, or to provide cautions as to all of the possible hazards that may result. Standard and accepted safety precautions and equipment should be used when handling toxic or flammable fluids, and safety glasses or other protection should be used during cutting, grinding, chiseling, or any other process that can cause material removal or projectiles.

Some procedures require the use of tools specially designed for a specific purpose. Before substituting another tool or procedure, you must be completely satisfied that neither your personal safety, nor the performance of the vehicle will be endangered.

PART NUMBERS

Part numbers listed in this reference are not recommendations by Chilton for any product by brand name. They are references that can be used with interchange manuals and aftermarket supplier catalogs to locate each brand supplier's discrete part number.

Although information in this manual is based on industry sources and is complete as possible at the time of publication, the possibility exists that some vehicle manufacturers made later changes which could not be included here. While striving for total accuracy, Chilton Book Company cannot assume responsibility for any errors, changes or omissions that may occur in the compilation of this data.

Contents

AMERICA'S AUTOMOTIVE AUTHORITY

THE BUSINESSMAN/TECHNICIAN'S TOTAL INFORMATION LIBRARY FOR PROFESSIONAL TECHNICIAN'S ONLY

8470	Auto Service Manual 90-94	8468	Chassis Electronic Service 91-93 — European
8290	Auto Service Manual 89-93	8450	Chassis Electronic Service 91-93 — Asian, M-Z
8178	Auto Service Manual 88-92	8449	Chassis Electronic Service 91-93 — Asian, A-L
7690	Auto Service Manual 83-87	8440	Chassis Electronic Service 91-93 — Chrysler
7526	Auto Service Manual 76-82	8439	Chassis Electronic Service 91-93 — Ford
8448	Import Auto Service Manual 89-93	8289	Chassis Electronic Service 91-93 — GM
8133	Import Auto Service Manual 87-91	8152	Chassis Electronic Service 89-91 — Asia
8149	Import Auto Service Manual 80-87	8188	Chassis Electronic Service 89-91 — European
8547	Truck & Van Service Manual 90-94	8078	Chassis Electronic Service 89-91 — Ford/Chrysler
8281	Truck & Van Service Manual 88-92	8077	Chassis Electronic Service 89-91 — GM
8048	Truck & Van Service Manual 86-90	7857	Chassis Electronic Service 87-89
7688	Truck & Van Service Manual 80-86	8447	Emission Control Manual 93
8443	Heavy Duty Truck Service Manual 89-92	8288	Emission Control Manual 92
8282	Medium Truck Service Manual 89-92	8154	Emission Control Manual 90-91
8471	Domestic Labor Guide & Parts Manual 90-94	8121	Domestic Emission Diagnostic Manual 89
8179	Domestic Labor Guide & Parts Manual 88-92	8049	Import Emission Diagnostic Manual 89
8446	Import Labor Guide & Parts Manual 89-93	7974	Domestic Emission Diagnostic Manual 88
8132	Import Labor Guide & Parts Manual 87-91	7973	Import Emission Diagnostic Manual 88
8472	Domestic & Import Labor Guide Manual 80-94	7774	Domestic Emission Service Manual 84-87
8280	Component Locator Manual 89-91	7775	Import Emission Service Manual 84-87
8045	Component Locator Manual 82-89	7280	Domestic Emission Diagnostic Manual 75-83
8285	Diagnostic Trouble Code 90-91	7281	Import Emission Diagnostic Manual 75-83
8284	Diagnostic Trouble Code 87-89	8442	Domestic Wiring Diagrams Manual 91
8283	Diagnostic Trouble Code 80-86	8441	Import Wiring Diagrams Manual 91
8474	Driveability Manual 92-94 — GM Cars	8071	Domestic Wiring Diagrams Manual 90
8501	Driveability Manual 92-94 — GM Trucks/Geo/Saturn	8072	Import Wiring Diagram Manual 90
8273	Electronic Engine Controls 90-92 — Asian, A-M	7937	Domestic Wiring Diagrams Manual 89
8274	Electronic Engine Controls 90-92 — Asian, N-Z	7938	Import Wiring Diagram Manual 89
8275	Electronic Engine Controls 90-92 — European	7959	Domestic Transmission Manual 84-89
8272	Electronic Engine Controls 90-92 — Ford/Chrysler	7960	Import Transmission Manual 84-89
8181	Electronic Engine Controls 90-92 — GM	7390	Automatic Transmission Manual 80-84
8046	Electronic Engine Controls 88-90 — Asian, A-M	6927	Automatic Transmission Manual 74-80
8047	Electronic Engine Controls 88-90 — Asian, N-Z	8473	Automatic Transmission Diagnostic Manual 88-93
8112	Electronic Engine Controls 88-90 — European	8444	Air Conditioning & Heating 91-93
8017	Electronic Engine Controls 88-90 — Ford/Chrysler	8151	Air Conditioning & Heating 89-91
7957	Electronic Engine Controls 88-90 — GM	7963	Air Conditioning & Heating 87-89
7781	Domestic Electronic Engine Controls 84-88	8482	Air Conditioning & Heating labor 91-93
7800	Import Electronic Engine Controls 84-88	8222	Air Conditioning & Heating Labor 89-91

HOW TO USE CHILTON'S QUICK SPECS

General Information

The increased complexity of today's vehicles and high cost of both parts and repair labor means that a shop needs to do fast and accurate maintenance and service work to ensure customer satisfaction and repeat service business. **Chilton's Quick Specs** is designed for fast and easy access to the most important information and specifications required by today's professional service technicians.

HOW CHILTON'S QUICK SPECS IS ARRANGED

This book covers 1990–94 domestic automobiles. An extensive index and table of contents is provided to help locate the exact vehicle listing for which service information is needed.

Chilton's Quick Specs is divided by vehicle manufacturer, **Chrysler Corporation, Ford Motor Company** and **General Motors Corporation**. With each vehicle section there will be information covering:

- **VEHICLE IDENTIFICATION NUMBER:** Vehicle VIN charts help the technician accurately determine the vehicle's identity. This is more and more important as vehicles are becoming "world class." Today's vehicles are built with parts and components from all over the globe and most vehicle lines use components from many different companies. Ordering correct service parts can be difficult without an accurate VIN code for the model year and engine identification.
- **ENGINE IDENTIFICATION:**
Engine identification charts are valuable because a number of different engines may be available for the same model vehicle. These engines may appear similar, differing only in unseen internal parts or emission calibration. Even country of origin may vary among engines of a vehicle manufacturer. Getting the engine identified correctly is of utmost importance when looking up specifications, ordering service parts and performing repairs.
- **GENERAL ENGINE SPECIFICATIONS:**
This information gives the technician a baseline of factory-specified basic performance parameters as well as the bore and stroke, compression ratio and base oil pressure where applicable.
- **GASOLINE ENGINE TUNE-UP SPECIFICATIONS:**
A vehicle's performance and emission levels are dependent on the engine's conformance to factory tune-up specifications. This section gives charts of specifications based on model year and engine VIN. Spark plug gap, ignition timing, fuel pressure, idle speed and valve clearance may all be found in this section.
- **CAPACITIES:** All service facilities will find these charts especially useful as they give, by model year and engine VIN, the crankcase capacity, transmission/transaxle/transfer case capacity as well as the drive axle, fuel tank and cooling system capacities.
- **CAMSHAFT SPECIFICATIONS:** When troubleshooting a performance problem, its helpful to check camshaft lift. Worn cam lobes affect engine performance, fuel use and emission levels. The specifications are listed by engine VIN and allow the technician to compare published camshaft specifications against the actual engine's camshaft lift, usually measured with a dial indicator.

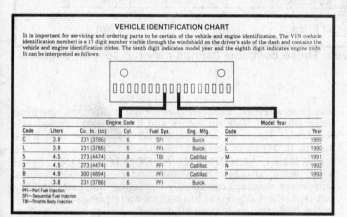

Example of a Vehicle Identification chart as used in this book. Note how engine manufacturer varies making accurate identification mandatory for ordering correct replacement parts

TORQUE SPECIFICATIONS
All readings in ft. lbs.

Year	Engine ID/VIN	Engine Displacement Liters (cc)	Cylinder Head Bolts	Main Bearing Bolts	Rod Bearing Bolts	Crankshaft Damper Bolts	Flywheel Bolts	Manifold Intake	Manifold Exhaust	Spark Plugs	Lug Nut
1990	8	5.7 (5733)	67	80	45	70	74	35②	19	22	100
	J	5.7 (5727)	③	⑤	22⑥	148	74	④	22①	15	100
1991	8	5.7 (5733)	67	80	45	70	74	35②	19	22	100
	J	5.7 (5727)	③	⑤	22⑥	148	74	④	22①	19	100
1992–93	P	5.7 (5733)	65	68⑦	47	60	74	35⑧	26	11	100
	J	5.7 (5727)	③	⑤	22⑥	148	74	④	22⑨	15	100

① Manifold studs only, all others; 11 ft. lbs.
② All except Nos. 1 and 4; 1 and 4, 45 ft. lbs.
③ Torque bolts in 3 steps: 1st at 45 ft. lbs.; 2nd at 74 ft. lbs.; and final at 118 ft. lbs.
④ Injector Housing Bolts & Fuel Rail Bolts; 20 ft. lbs.
⑤ Torque bolts on No. 1, 3 and 5 to 30 ft. lbs. (40 Nm) plus 45–50° turn
Torque bolts on No. 2 and 4 to 15 ft. lbs. (20 Nm), plus 77.5–82.5° turn
⑥ Plus 80–85° turn
⑦ Inboard bolts on 4-bolt cap—78 ft. lbs.
⑧ Tighten in 2 passes. 1st pass torque to 71 inch lbs.
⑨ Studs only, tigthen bolts to 18 ft. lbs.

Basic torque specifications are quickly available including footnotes with special instructions

HOW TO USE CHILTON'S QUICK SPECS

TORQUE SPECIFICATIONS

Component	English	Metric
Clutch housing-to-engine		
5.7L (VIN 8) engine	30 ft. lbs.	40 Nm
5.7L (VIN J and VIN P) engines	37 ft. lbs.	50 Nm
Camshaft sprocket bolt		
5.7L (VIN 8) engine	20 ft. lbs.	27 Nm
5.7L (VIN P) engine	21 ft. lbs.	28 Nm
5.7L (VIN J) engine		
Idler sprocket:	19 ft. lbs.	26 Nm
Connecting rod bearing cap bolts		
5.7L (VIN 8) engine	45 ft. lbs.	60 Nm
5.7L (VIN P) engine	47 ft. lbs.	64 Nm
5.7L (VIN J) engine		
Step 1:	22 ft. lbs.	30 Nm
Step 2:	+ 80–85 degrees turn	+ 80–85 degrees turn
Crankshaft damper bolt		
5.7L (VIN 8) engine	70 ft. lbs.	95 Nm
5.7L (VIN P) engine	60 ft. lbs.	81 Nm
5.7L (VIN J) engine	148 ft. lbs.	200 Nm
Crankshaft pulley bolt		
5.7L (VIN 8) engine	32 ft. lbs.	43 Nm

More complete engine torque specifications are also given. These complete listings may run several pages covering most engine fasteners.

• **CRANKSHAFT AND CONNECTING ROD SPECIFI-CATIONS:** A complete engine overhaul means the crankshaft and connecting rods are measured and inspected. If necessary, they will be replaced or reconditioned. The specifications in this chart gives the technician standard crankshaft size, endplay specification and the all-important bearing oil clearances. Skilled technicians know that even a fresh aftermarket remanufactured crankshaft must be thoroughly checked against factory specification before assembly, as insurance against incorrect parts causing a costly "come-back" failure.

• **VALVE SPECIFICATIONS:** Unleaded fuel and hot running, high revving small engines with overhead cam aluminum heads are naturally going to need valve, seat and guide work as the vehicle ages. Rubber timing belts which strip and snap are bending countless valves. Valve specifications are becoming more and more important to the general repair shop which are seeing increasing amounts of top-engine work.

• **PISTON AND RING SPECIFICATIONS:** These specifications are valuable because today's engines are running with tighter clearances. Parts must be right on specification if the engine is to deliver rated power and specified emission levels while delivering the life expectancy customers demand.

• **TORQUE SPECIFICATIONS:**
Of all the charts and specifications available, technicians turn to torque specifications most often. The widespread use of light alloy parts in many areas of an engine assembly demand the proper clamping forces that can only result from correct torque specifications and tightening practices.

There are 2 Torque Specification charts. The first is a short chart whose focus in on the primary engine torque specifications: head bolts, main bearing caps bolts, connecting rod bearing cap bolts, crankshaft damper and flywheel bolts as well as manifold and spark plug torque.

The second chart is much more extensive. This chart lists most parts, large and small, that comprise an engine assembly and their factory recommended torque specifications. Remember that all bolts hold by stretching just a little when tightened. Therefore all bolts have a specific recommended torque required to provide designed clamp loads.

• **BRAKE SPECIFICATIONS:** Both brake specialty shops and general repair facilities need brake component specifications. Machine work on rotors and drums could exceed safe standards. These factory specifications are important when making a "repair or scrap" decision.

• **WHEEL ALIGNMENT SPECIFICATIONS:** Front wheel drive, all-wheel drive, fully independent suspensions, four-wheel steering, continually escalating tire costs and the fact that wheel alignment has become an important component in the fuel-saving equation all mean that alignment specifications are more vital than ever. These charts give alignment specifications for both front and rear, where required.

• **AIR CONDITIONING BELT TENSION SPECIFICATIONS:** Small compressors build up extremely high head pressures, especially on unusually hot days. Customer complaints of belt squeal can be avoided with proper belt tension. These are the factory specifications.

• **AIR CONDITIONING REFRIGERANT CAPACITY SPECIFICATIONS:** The entire industry is in the midst of changing to new refrigerants with different characteristics than those previously used. Precise fill quantities are more important than ever before.

Use care when servicing late model vehicles which may be equipped with the new R-134a refrigerant. R-12 (the old refrigerant, usually called Freon) is not compatible or interchangeable with R-134a under any circumstances. No blend is acceptable. These refrigerants use different lubricants. Any R-12 in an R-134a system will destroy the entire system requiring complete system replacement. No R-12 system can be flushed well enough to be thoroughly clean; the oil residue will still hold some R-12 and will contaminate R-134a if any attempt is made to charge an "old" system with the "new" refrigerant. Even so-called "soft parts" such as hoses and seals are different and must not be interchanged. Some manufacturers claim to be working on a "drop-in" R-12 replacement to service the millions of vehicles using R-12. To date, no factory approved substitute is available.

A standard specification for refrigerant oil for the new R-134a systems is still a source of confusion with different specifications from the major automobile manufacturers. Make sure that the proper oil and refrigerant is used when servicing an R-

134a system. Mistakes could be very costly for the independent shop since it appears that at least some manufacturers may adopt the position that repairs to an R-134a system contaminated with R-12 would not be considered a warranty matter.

To avoid system contamination, some manufacturers are using different size service valve fittings. This means that a shop's existing R-12 gauges, recyclers, storage and recovery units, vacuum pumps, etc. may need to be duplicated to service R-134a systems. Too, electronic leak detectors for the 2 systems are different. An R-12 sensor is likely not sensitive enough to detect R-134a. An R-134a sensor is very sensitive to R-12 and will signal its presence in the smallest quantities, even if the wand is not next to a component. The R-134a sensor is somewhat slow to sense R-134a and may need to be held in place for several seconds before the alarm sounds.

More precision in charging R-134a systems will be required. Charge volumes are slightly less than R-12 but the margin of error may be as close as "specification + 1 oz. and − 0 oz." The system will be inefficient if undercharged and damaged if overcharged. R-134a can be recovered, reused and recycled if the correct equipment is used. Look for a label on or near the compressor indicating refrigerant charge and lubrication type.

The same personal safety cautions used when working with R-12 still apply when working with R-134a. Avoid breathing the refrigerant and lubricant vapor or mist. Exposure may irritate eyes, nose and throat. Use only approved service equipment. If accidental system discharge occurs, ventilate the work area before resuming service. Too, never pressure test an R-134a system with compressed air. Although R-134a is designed to be non-flammable, some mixtures of air/R-134a have been shown

MAINTENANCE INTERVALS—TYPE A: NORMAL SERVICE
Cutlass Supreme • Grand Prix • Lumina • Regal

TO BE SERVICED	TYPE OF SERVICE	VEHICLE MILEAGE INTERVAL (X1000)							
		7.5	15	22.5	30	37.5	45	52.5	60
Oxygen Sensor	I				✔				✔
Vacuum Lines and Hoses	I		✔		✔		✔		✔
Ignition Wires	I				✔				✔
Spark Plugs	R				✔				✔
Engine Oil	R	✔	✔	✔	✔	✔	✔	✔	✔
Engine Air Cleaner Element	R				✔				✔
PCV Valve	R				✔				✔
Fuel Filter	R				✔				✔
Engine Oil Filter	R①	✔		✔		✔		✔	
Fuel/Vapor Return Lines	I				✔				✔
Fuel Tank Cap and Restrictor	I				✔				✔
Coolant System Service	R				✔				✔
Exhaust Pipe and Muffler	I				✔				✔
Tire Rotation	I②	✔		✔		✔		✔	
Catalytic Converter and Shield	I				✔				✔
EGR System	I				✔				✔
Automatic Transaxle Fluid	R③								
Battery Connections	I		✔		✔		✔		✔
Chassis Lubrication	L	✔	✔	✔	✔	✔	✔	✔	✔
CV-Joints and Boots	I	✔	✔	✔	✔	✔	✔	✔	✔
Idle Speed System	I				✔				✔
Throttle Body Mounting Torque	I	✔							
Drive Belts	I				✔				✔
Brake Linings	I		✔		✔		✔		✔
Parking Brake	I		✔		✔		✔		✔
Coolant Hoses and Clamps	I		✔		✔		✔		✔
Seat Belt Operation	I		✔		✔		✔		✔

FOR COMPLETE WARRANTY COVERAGE CONSULT INDIVIDUAL VEHICLE MANUFACTURER'S WARRANTY MAINTENANCE GUIDE.

I—Inspect
L—Lubricate
R—Replace
① Replace oil filter at first and every other oil change
② Rotate tires at 7,500 miles, then every 15,000 miles
③ Replace automatic transmission fluid and filter at 100,000 miles

Charts indicating factory recommended maintenance intervals make service bay work easier and more accurate. Charts are given for both NORMAL SERVICE and SEVERE SERVICE. Always inquire with the vehicle's operator what type of driving is done. If the vehicle fits the profile of SEVERE SERVICE, maintenance should be more often.

HOW TO USE CHILTON'S QUICK SPECS

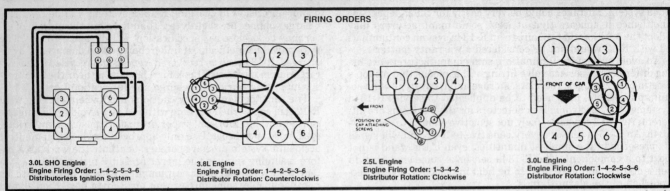

FIRING ORDERS

3.0L SHO Engine
Engine Firing Order: 1–4–2–5–3–6
Distributorless Ignition System

3.8L Engine
Engine Firing Order: 1–4–2–5–3–6
Distributor Rotation: Counterclockwis

2.5L Engine
Engine Firing Order: 1–3–4–2
Distributor Rotation: Clockwise

3.0L Engine
Engine Firing Order: 1–4–2–5–3–6
Distributor Rotation: Clockwise

Firing order diagrams are always important, especially when a number of different engines are used in a single car line as this example of Continental, Sable and Taurus

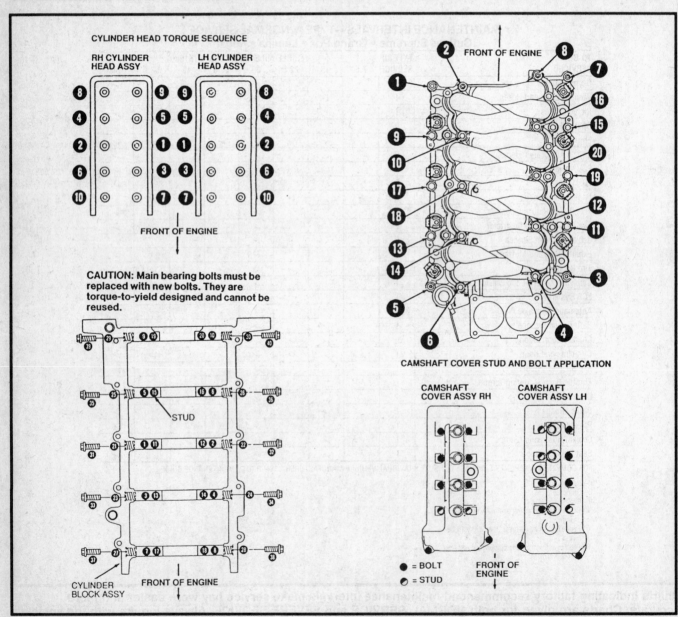

CYLINDER HEAD TORQUE SEQUENCE

RH CYLINDER HEAD ASSY   LH CYLINDER HEAD ASSY

FRONT OF ENGINE

CAUTION: Main bearing bolts must be replaced with new bolts. They are torque-to-yield designed and cannot be reused.

STUD

CYLINDER BLOCK ASSY   FRONT OF ENGINE

FRONT OF ENGINE

CAMSHAFT COVER STUD AND BOLT APPLICATION

CAMSHAFT COVER ASSY RH   CAMSHAFT COVER ASSY LH

● = BOLT
◐ = STUD

FRONT OF ENGINE

Cylinder head torque sequence has become even more important, especially with complex engines such as this all-aluminum 4.6L (32 valve) V8 engine as used in the 1993–94 Lincoln Mark VIII

to be combustible at elevated pressures. These mixtures are potentially dangerous and may result in fire or explosion causing injury or property damage.

NOTE: At the time of publication, refrigerant capacity information relating to R-134a may not be available from all manufacturers.

- **MAINTENANCE INTERVAL CHARTS:**
These charts are designed around the official factory recommended maintenance intervals. Two versions are given: **Normal Service** and **Severe Service**. These can be most helpful when explaining the importance of regular maintenance to your customers.

- **FIRING ORDERS:**
These illustrations can be real problem solvers, especially when troubleshooting an ignition secondary problem after the ignition system has been disturbed or has seen tampering.

- **CYLINDER HEAD TORQUE SEQUENCES:**
Since the early days of the flathead engine, proper torque sequence has been vital to getting a good head gasket seal. Today's engines with electronic knock sensors control detonation well enough that compression ratios are creeping upwards again. High compression teamed up with alloy heads and higher temperature cooling systems means proper cylinder head torque and torque sequence is more important than ever.

Be alert for any direction as to head bolt replacement. Some, though not all, manufacturers recommend new, replacement cylinder head bolts whenever a cylinder head has been removed and installed. All bolts hold by stretching. Torque wrenches and angle indicators help make sure that torque, and consequently bolt stretch, is applied evenly. Used bolts have already been stretched at least once. A technician may have no way of knowing if the head has been removed once or more before, and has no idea how close the bolts are to their fatigue limit breaking point. Too, replacement head bolts will likely be the latest design and strength as head bolts are often revised as field problems are reported. Replacement bolts may be a cheap form of insurance for the technician, avoid the headache and expense of a head bolt breaking just as the job is being completed and adds little to the overall price of a valve job or head gasket replacement.

- **TIMING MARK LOCATIONS:**
One of the most important factors in low engine emissions is proper spark timing. Most state-mandated emission programs require an ignition timing check. The problem is finding the timing marks in a crowded engine compartment. These illustrations are most helpful in showing where to look. Remember, even if the engine does not have adjustable ignition timing, checking the spark against specification can be most useful in pointing to a problem in the electronic control system.

- **TIMING CHAIN/BELT MARK LOCATIONS:**
Complex camshaft drives and unforgiving non-freewheeling engine designs mean camshaft timing marks are vital. Multiple camshafts and automatic tensioners compound the problem where a mistake could cost an engine. These diagrams show factory camshaft timing marks.

- **AIR CONDITIONING SERVICE VALVE LOCATIONS:**
Crowded engine compartments means air conditioning service can be more difficult. Accounts of technicians accidently connecting air conditioning evacuation equipment to fuel injection service ports with disastrous results means this once simple operation now requires the utmost in care. This section shows air conditioning service ports.

- **WHEEL ALIGNMENT ADJUSTMENT LOCATIONS:**
Having the wheel alignment specifications is fundamental. Knowing where to make the adjustment is just as important. Shim or cam? Upper or lower arm? Strut or A-arms? Save time by knowing the adjustment location.

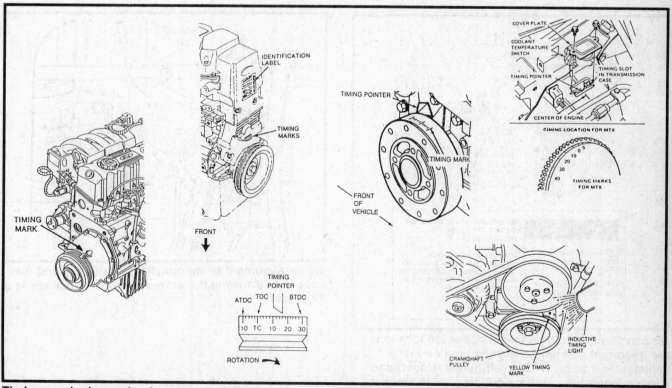

Timing marks have also become more important and part of most state-mandated emission tests. Timing locations may vary between harmonic balancer and flywheel. Save time by looking up the correct location

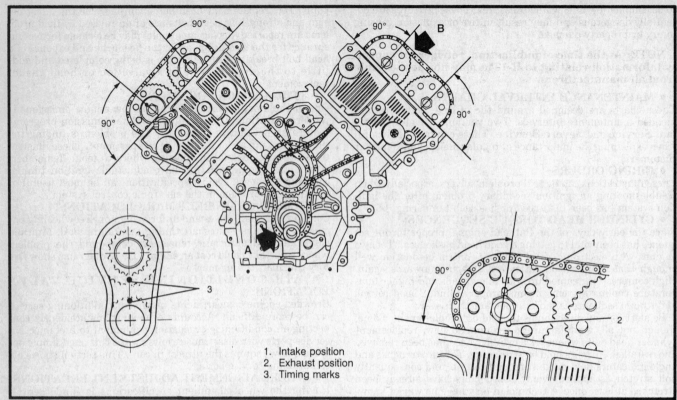

1. Intake position
2. Exhaust position
3. Timing marks

Camshaft timing has always been important. New engines such as this 4.6L Northstar engine used in the 1993–94 Eldorado and Seville make it even more critical as both primary and secondary DOHC chains must be precisely positioned

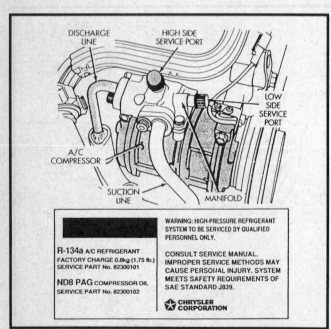

Air conditioning refrigerant service valve locations are important and have been changed on many vehicles now using R-134a refrigerant. Underhood service labels also indicate critical charge amount and special oil type that must be used—1993–94 Chrysler LH series shown

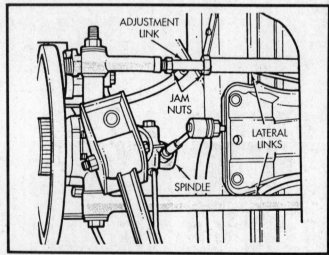

Wheel alignment is important to both safety and fuel economy. Knowing the correct adjuster locations is a time-saver

SPECIFICATION CHARTS

VEHICLE IDENTIFICATION CHART

It is important for servicing and ordering parts to be certain of the vehicle and engine identification. The VIN (vehicle identification number) is a 17 digit number visible through the windshield on the driver's side of the dash and contains the vehicle and engine identification codes. The tenth digit indicates model year and the eighth digit indicates engine code. It can be interpreted as follows:

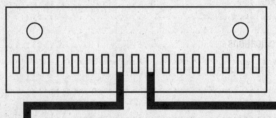

Engine Code						Model Year	
Code	**Liters**	**Cu. In. (cc)**	**Cyl.**	**Fuel Sys.**	**Eng. Mfg.**	**Code**	**Year**
A	1.5	90 (1468)	4	MPI	Mitsubishi	L	1990
B (1990–92)	3.0	181 (2972)	4	MPI	Mitsubishi	M	1991
B (1993–94)	1.8	107 (1753)	4	MPI	Mitsubishi	N	1992
C (1990–92)	3.0	181 (2972)	4	MPI-Turbo	Mitsubishi	P	1993
C (1993–94)	1.8	112 (1834)	4	MPI	Mitsubishi	R	1994
D	1.8	112 (1834)	4	MPI	Mitsubishi		
E	2.0	122 (1999)	4	MPI	Mitsubishi		
F	2.0	122 (1999)	4	MPI-Turbo	Mitsubishi		
G	2.4	146 (2393)	4	MPI	Mitsubishi		
H	3.0	181 (2972)	6	MPI	Mitsubishi		
J	3.0	181 (2972)	6	MPI	Mitsubishi		
K	3.0	181 (2972)	6	MPI-Turbo	Mitsubishi		
R	2.0	122 (1999)	4	MPI	Mitsubishi		
S	3.0	181 (2972)	6	MPI	Mitsubishi		
T	1.8	107 (1753)	4	MPI	Mitsubishi		
U	2.0	122 (1999)	4	MPI-Turbo	Mitsubishi		
W	2.4	143 (2350)	4	MPI	Mitsubishi		
X	1.5	90 (1468)	4	MPI	Mitsubishi		
Y	1.6	97 (1595)	4	MPI	Mitsubishi		

MPI—Multi Point Fuel Injection
Turbo—Turbocharged

ENGINE IDENTIFICATION

Year	Model	Engine Displacement Liters (cc)	Engine Series (ID/VIN)	Fuel System	No. of Cylinders	Engine Type
1990	Summit	1.5 (1468)	X	MPI	4	SOHC
	Summit	1.6 (1595)	Y	MPI	4	DOHC
	Laser/Talon	1.8 (1753)	T	MPI	4	SOHC
	Laser/Talon	2.0 (1999)	R	MPI	4	DOHC
	Laser/Talon	2.0 (1999)	U	MPI-Turbo	4	DOHC

ENGINE IDENTIFICATION

Year	Model	Engine Displacement Liters (cc)	Engine Series (ID/VIN)	Fuel System	No. of Cylinders	Engine Type
1991	Summit	1.5 (1468)	A	MPI	4	SOHC
	Laser/Talon	1.8 (1753)	T	MPI	4	SOHC
	Laser/Talon	2.0 (1999)	R	MPI	4	DOHC
	Laser/Talon	2.0 (1999)	U	MPI-Turbo	4	DOHC
	Stealth	3.0 (2972)	S	MPI	6	SOHC
	Stealth	3.0 (2972)	B	MPI	6	DOHC
	Stealth	3.0 (2972)	C	MPI-Turbo	6	DOHC
1992	Summit	1.5 (1468)	A	MPI	4	SOHC
	Summit Wagon	1.8 (1834)	D	MPI	4	SOHC
	Summit Wagon	2.4 (2350)	W	MPI	4	SOHC
	Laser/Talon	1.8 (1753)	T	MPI	4	SOHC
	Laser/Talon	2.0 (1999)	R	MPI	4	DOHC
	Laser/Talon	2.0 (1999)	U	MPI-Turbo	4	DOHC
	Stealth	3.0 (2972)	S	MPI	6	SOHC
	Stealth	3.0 (2972)	B	MPI	6	DOHC
	Stealth	3.0 (2972)	C	MPI-Turbo	6	DOHC
1993–94	Summit	1.5 (1468)	A	MPI	4	SOHC
	Summit	1.8 (1834)	C	MPI	4	SOHC
	Summit Wagon	1.8 (1834)	C	MPI	4	SOHC
	Summit Wagon	2.4 (2350)	G	MPI	4	SOHC
	Laser/Talon	1.8 (1753)	B	MPI	4	SOHC
	Laser/Talon	2.0 (1999)	E	MPI	4	DOHC
	Laser/Talon	2.0 (1999)	F	MPI-Turbo	4	DOHC
	Stealth	3.0 (2972)	H	MPI	6	SOHC
	Stealth	3.0 (2972)	J	MPI	6	DOHC
	Stealth	3.0 (2972)	K	MPI-Turbo	6	DOHC

MPI—Multi Point Fuel Injection
SOHC—Single Overhead Camshaft
DOHC—Double Overhead Camshaft
Turbo—Turbocharged

GENERAL ENGINE SPECIFICATIONS

Year	Engine ID/VIN	Engine Displacement Liters (cc)	Fuel System Type	Net Horsepower @ rpm	Net Torque @ rpm (ft. lbs.)	Bore × Stroke (in.)	Compression Ratio	Oil Pressure @ rpm
1990	X	1.5 (1468)	MPI	81 @ 5500	91 @ 3000	2.972 × 3.228	9.4:1	54 @ 2000
	Y	1.6 (1595)	MPI	113 @ 6500	99 @ 5000	3.243 × 2.955	9.2:1	54 @ 2000
	T	1.8 (1753)	MPI	92 @ 5000	105 @ 3500	3.172 × 3.388	9.0:1	41 @ 2000
	R	2.0 (1999)	MPI	135 @ 6000	125 @ 5000	3.349 × 3.467	9.0:1	41 @ 2000
	U	2.0 (1999)	Turbo	190 @ 6000	203 @ 3000	3.349 × 3.467	7.8:1	41 @ 2000

GENERAL ENGINE SPECIFICATIONS

Year	Engine ID/VIN	Engine Displacement Liters (cc)	Fuel System Type	Net Horsepower @ rpm	Net Torque @ rpm (ft. lbs.)	Bore × Stroke (in.)	Compression Ratio	Oil Pressure @ rpm
1991	A	1.5 (1468)	MPI	92 @ 6000	93 @ 3000	2.97 × 3.23	9.2:1	54 @ 2000
	T	1.8 (1753)	MPI	92 @ 5000	105 @ 3500	3.17 × 3.39	9.0:1	41 @ 2000
	R	2.0 (1999)	MPI	135 @ 6000	125 @ 5000	3.35 × 3.47	9.0:1	41 @ 2000
	U	2.0 (1999)	Turbo	190 @ 6000	203 @ 3000	3.35 × 3.47	7.8:1	41 @ 2000
	S	3.0 (2972)	MPI	164 @ 5500	185 @ 4000	3.58 × 2.99	8.9:1	30–80 @ 2000
	B	3.0 (2972)	MPI	222 @ 6000	201 @ 4500	3.58 × 2.99	10.0:1	30–80 @ 2000
	C	3.0 (2972)	Turbo	300 @ 6000	307 @ 2500	3.58 × 2.99	8.0:1	30–80 @ 2000
1992	A	1.5 (1468)	MPI	92 @ 6000	93 @ 3000	2.97 × 3.23	9.2:1	54 @ 2000
	T	1.8 (1753)	MPI	92 @ 5000	105 @ 3500	3.17 × 3.39	9.0:1	41 @ 2000
	R	2.0 (1999)	MPI	135 @ 6000	125 @ 5000	3.35 × 3.47	9.0:1	41 @ 2000
	U	2.0 (1999)	Turbo	190 @ 6000	203 @ 3000	3.35 × 3.47	7.8:1	41 @ 2000
	S	3.0 (2972)	MPI	164 @ 5500	185 @ 4000	3.58 × 2.99	8.9:1	30–80 @ 2000
	B	3.0 (2972)	MPI	222 @ 6000	201 @ 4500	3.58 × 2.99	10.0:1	30–80 @ 2000
	C	3.0 (2972)	Turbo	300 @ 6000	307 @ 2500	3.58 × 2.99	8.0:1	30–80 @ 2000
	D	1.8 (1834)	MPI	113 @ 6000	116 @ 4500	3.19 × 3.50	9.5:1	①
	W	2.4 (2350)	MPI	116 @ 5000	136 @ 3500	3.41 × 3.94	8.5:1	①
1993–94	A	1.5 (1468)	MPI	92 @ 6000	93 @ 3000	2.97 × 3.23	9.2:1	54 @ 2000
	B	1.8 (1753)	MPI	92 @ 5000	105 @ 3500	3.17 × 3.39	9.0:1	41 @ 2000
	C	1.8 (1834)	MPI	113 @ 6000	116 @ 4500	3.19 × 3.50	9.5:1	①
	E	2.0 (1999)	MPI	135 @ 6000	125 @ 5000	3.35 × 3.47	9.0:1	41 @ 2000
	F	2.0 (1999)	MPI-Turbo	190 @ 6000	203 @ 3000	3.35 × 3.47	7.8:1	41 @ 2000
	G	2.4 (2350)	MPI	136 @ 5500	145 @ 4250	3.41 × 3.94	9.5:1	①
	H	3.0 (2972)	MPI	164 @ 5500	185 @ 4000	3.58 × 2.99	8.9:1	30–80 @ 2000
	J	3.0 (2972)	MPI	222 @ 6000	201 @ 4500	3.58 × 2.99	10.0:1	30–80 @ 2000
	K	3.0 (2972)	MPI-Turbo	300 @ 6000	307 @ 2500	3.58 × 2.99	8.0:1	30–80 @ 2000

MPI—Multi Point Fuel Injection
① 11.4 psi or more at curb idle speed

GASOLINE ENGINE TUNE-UP SPECIFICATIONS

Year	Engine ID/VIN	Engine Displacement Liters (cc)	Spark Plugs Gap (in.)	Ignition Timing (deg.) MT	Ignition Timing (deg.) AT	Fuel Pump (psi)	Idle Speed (rpm) MT	Idle Speed (rpm) AT	Valve Clearance In.	Valve Clearance Ex.
1990	X	1.5 (1468)	0.039–0.043	5B	5B	38	750	750	0.006	0.010
	Y	1.6 (1595)	0.039–0.043	5B	5B	38	750	750	Hyd.	Hyd.
	T	1.8 (1753)	0.039–0.043	5B	5B	38	700	700	Hyd.	Hyd.
	R	2.0 (1999)	0.039–0.043	5B	5B	38	700	700	Hyd.	Hyd.
	U	2.0 (1999)	0.028–0.031	5B	5B	27①	750	750	Hyd.	Hyd.
1991	A	1.5 (1468)	0.039–0.043	5B	5B	38	750	750	0.006	0.010
	T	1.8 (1753)	0.039–0.043	5B	5B	38	750	750	Hyd.	Hyd.
	R	2.0 (1999)	0.039–0.043	5B	5B	38	700	700	Hyd.	Hyd.
	U	2.0 (1999)	0.028–0.031	5B	5B	27①	750	750	Hyd.	Hyd.
	S	3.0 (2972)	0.039–0.043	5B	5B	38	750	750	Hyd.	Hyd.
	B	3.0 (2972)	0.039–0.043	5B	5B	38	750	750	Hyd.	Hyd.
	C	3.0 (2972)	0.035	5B	5B	34	700	700	Hyd.	Hyd.

GASOLINE ENGINE TUNE-UP SPECIFICATIONS

Year	Engine ID/VIN	Engine Displacement Liters (cc)	Spark Plugs Gap (in.)	Ignition Timing (deg.) MT	AT	Fuel Pump (psi)	Idle Speed (rpm) MT	AT	Valve Clearance In.	Ex.
1992	A	1.5 (1468)	0.039–0.043	5B	5B	38	750	750	0.006	0.010
	T	1.8 (1753)	0.039–0.043	5B	5B	38	750	750	Hyd.	Hyd.
	R	2.0 (1999)	0.039–0.043	5B	5B	38	700	700	Hyd.	Hyd.
	U	2.0 (1999)	0.028–0.031	5B	5B	27①	750	750	Hyd.	Hyd.
	S	3.0 (2972)	0.039–0.043	5B	5B	38	750	750	Hyd.	Hyd.
	B	3.0 (2972)	0.039–0.043	5B	5B	38	750	750	Hyd.	Hyd.
	C	3.0 (2972)	0.035	5B	5B	34	700	700	Hyd.	Hyd.
	D	1.8 (1834)	0.039–0.043	5B	5B	38	750	750	0.004	0.008
	W	2.4 (2350)	0.039–0.043	5B	5B	38	750	750	Hyd.	Hyd.
1993	A	1.5 (1468)	0.039–0.043	5B	5B	38	750	750	0.006	0.010
	B	1.8 (1753)	0.039–0.043	5B	5B	38	750	750	Hyd.	Hyd.
	C	1.8 (1834)	0.039–0.043	5B	5B	38	750	750	Hyd.	Hyd.
	E	2.0 (1999)	0.039–0.043	5B	5B	38	700	700	Hyd.	Hyd.
	F	2.0 (1999)	0.028–0.031	5B	5B	27①	750	750	Hyd.	Hyd.
	G	2.4 (2350)	0.039–0.043	5B	5B	38	750	750	Hyd.	Hyd.
	H	3.0 (2972)	0.039–0.043	5B	5B	38	700	700	Hyd.	Hyd.
	J	3.0 (2972)	0.039–0.043	5B	5B	38	700	700	Hyd.	Hyd.
	K	3.0 (2972)	0.039–0.043	5B	5B	34	700	700	Hyd.	Hyd.
1994	SEE UNDERHOOD SPECIFICATIONS STICKER									

NOTE: The lowest cylinder pressure should be within 75% of the highest cylinder pressure reading. For example, if the highest cylinder is 134 psi, the lowest should be 101. Engine should be at normal operating temperature with throttle valve in the wide open position.
The underhood specifications sticker often reflects tune-up specification changes in production. Sticker figures must be used if they disagree with those in this chart.
Hyd.—Hydraulic
B—Before Top Dead Center—BTDC
① Fuel pressure for automatic transmission model
   is 33 psi

CAPACITIES

Year	Model	Engine ID/VIN	Engine Displacement Liters (cc)	Engine Crankcase with Filter④	Transmission (pts.) 4-Spd	5-Spd	Auto.	Transfer case (pts.)	Drive Axle Front (pts.)	Rear (pts.)	Fuel Tank (gal.)	Cooling System (qts.)
1990	Summit	X	1.5 (1468)	3.6①	3.6	3.8②	13③	—	—	—	13.2	5.3
	Summit	Y	1.6 (1595)	4.6①	3.6	3.8	13③	—	—	—	13.2	5.3
	Laser	T	1.8 (1753)	4.1①	—	3.8	13③	—	—	—	16.0	6.6
	Laser	R	2.0 (1999)	4.6①	—	4.6⑤	13③	—	—	—	16.0	7.6
	Laser	U	2.0 (1999)	4.6①	—	4.8⑥	13③	1.25	—	⑦	16.0	7.6
	Talon	R	2.0 (1999)	4.6①	—	4.6⑤	13③	—	—	—	16.0	7.6
	Talon	U	2.0 (1999)	4.6①	—	4.8⑥	13③	1.25	—	⑦	16.0	7.6
1991	Summit	A	1.5 (1468)	3.6⑧	3.6	3.8	13③	—	—	—	13.2	5.3
	Laser	T	1.8 (1753)	4.1⑧	—	3.8	13③	—	—	—	16.0	6.6
	Laser	R	2.0 (1999)	4.6⑧	—	4.6⑤	13③	—	—	—	16.0	7.6
	Laser	U	2.0 (1999)	4.6⑧	—	4.8⑥	13③	1.25	—	⑦	16.0	7.6

CAPACITIES

Year	Model	Engine ID/VIN	Engine Displacement Liters (cc)	Engine Crankcase with Filter④	Transmission (pts.)			Transfer case (pts.)	Drive Axle		Fuel Tank (gal.)	Cooling System (qts.)
					4-Spd	5-Spd	Auto.		Front (pts.)	Rear (pts.)		
	Talon	R	2.0 (1999)	4.6⑧	—	4.6⑤	13③	—	—	—	16.0	7.6
	Talon	U	2.0 (1999)	4.6⑧	—	4.8⑥	13③	1.25	—	⑦	16.0	7.6
	Stealth	S	3.0 (2972)	4.7⑧	—	5	15.8③	—	—	—	19.8	8.5
	Stealth	B	3.0 (2972)	4.7⑧	—	5	15.8③	—	—	⑨	19.8	8.5
	Stealth	C	3.0 (2972)	5.2⑧	—	5	—	1.25	—	⑨	19.8	8.5
1992	Summit	A	1.5 (1468)	3.6⑧	3.6	3.8	13③	—	—	—	13.2	5.3
	Laser	T	1.8 (1753)	4.1⑧	—	3.8	13③	—	—	—	16.0	6.6
	Laser	R	2.0 (1999)	4.6⑧	—	4.6⑤	13③	—	—	—	16.0	7.6
	Laser	U	2.0 (1999)	4.6⑧	—	4.8⑥	13③	1.25	—	⑦	16.0	7.6
	Talon	R	2.0 (1999)	4.6⑧	—	4.6⑤	13③	—	—	—	16.0	7.6
	Talon	U	2.0 (1999)	4.6⑧	—	4.8⑥	13③	1.25	—	⑦	16.0	7.6
	Stealth	S	3.0 (2972)	4.7⑧	—	5	15.8③	—	—	—	19.8	8.5
	Stealth	B	3.0 (2972)	4.7⑧	—	5	15.8③	—	—	—	19.8	8.5
	Stealth	C	3.0 (2972)	5.2⑧	—	5	—	1.25	—	⑨	19.8	8.5
	Summit Wagon	D	1.8 (1834)	4.0⑧	—	3.8	13③	1.25	—	⑦	14.5	6.3
	Summit Wagon	W	2.4 (2350)	4.1⑧	—	4.8	13③	1.25	—	⑦	16.0	6.8
1993–94	Summit	A	1.5 (1468)	3.0⑧	—	3.8	13③	—	—	—	13.2	5.3
	Summit	C	1.8 (1834)	4.0⑧	—	3.8	13③	—	—	—	13.2	6.3
	Laser	B	1.8 (1753)	4.1⑧	—	3.8	13③	—	—	—	16.0	6.6
	Laser	E	2.0 (1999)	4.6⑧	—	4.6⑤	13③	—	—	—	16.0	7.6
	Laser	F	2.0 (1999)	4.6⑧	—	4.6⑥	13③	1.25	—	⑦	16.0	7.6
	Talon	E	2.0 (1999)	4.6⑧	—	4.6⑤	13③	—	—	—	16.0	7.6
	Talon	F	2.0 (1999)	4.6⑧	—	4.8⑥	13③	1.25	—	⑦	16.0	7.6
	Stealth	H	3.0 (2972)	4.7⑧	—	5	15.8③	—	—	2.4	19.8	8.5
	Stealth	J	3.0 (2972)	4.7⑧	—	5	15.8③	—	—	2.4	19.8	8.5
	Stealth	K	3.0 (2972)	5.2⑧	—	5	15.8③	1.25	—	⑨	19.8	8.5
	Summit Wagon	C	1.8 (1834)	4.0⑧	—	3.8	13③	1.25	—	⑦	14.5	6.3
	Summit Wagon	G	2.4 (2350)	4.1⑧	—	4.8	13③	1.25	—	⑦	16.0	6.8

① Use API class SF or SF/CC engine oil
② 3.8 pts. for transaxle models KM201, KM206.
4.4 pts. for transaxle model KM210
See Vehicle Information Code Plate on firewall for transaxle number. Manual transaxles, use API class GL-4 or higher Hypoid Gear oil
③ Automatic—Use Dexron II type fliud. Quantity shown includes converter. Check when hot.
④ Add 0.5 qt. for oil cooler on Turbo models.
⑤ 2WD-Turbo
⑥ 4WD-Turbo
⑦ Rear axle—with 4WD, capacity 0.75 qt. plus 0.63 qt. in transfer case.
⑧ Use API class SG or SG/CD engine oil.
⑨ Rear axle with 4WD capacity 1.16 qts. plus 0.69 qt. in transfer case.

CAMSHAFT SPECIFICATIONS
All measurements given in inches.

Year	Engine ID/VIN	Engine Displacement Liters (cc)	Journal Diameter					Elevation		Bearing Clearance	Camshaft End Play
			1	2	3	4	5	In.	Ex.		
1990	X	1.5 (1468)	1.8110	1.8110	1.8110	—	—	1.5318	1.5344	0.0015–0.0031	0.002–0.008
	Y	1.6 (1595)	1.0200	1.0200	1.0200	1.0200	1.0200 ①	1.3858	1.3743	0.0020–0.0035	0.004–0.008
	T	1.8 (1753)	1.3360–1.3366	1.3360–1.3366	1.3360–1.3366	1.3360–1.3366	1.3360–1.3370	1.4138	1.4138	0.0020–0.0035	0.004–0.008
	R	2.0 (1999)	1.0217–1.0224	1.0217–1.0224	1.0217–1.0224	1.0217–1.0224	1.0217–1.0224 ①	1.3974	1.3858	0.0020–0.0035	0.004–0.008
	U	2.0 (1999)	1.0217–1.0224	1.0217–1.0224	1.0217–1.0224	1.0217–1.0224	1.0217–1.0224 ①	1.3974	1.3858	0.0020–0.0035	0.004–0.008
1991	A	1.5 (1468)	1.8110	1.8110	1.8110	1.8110	—	1.5059–1.5256	1.5197–1.5394	0.0024–0.0055	NA
	T	1.8 (1753)	1.3360–1.3366	1.3360–1.3366	1.3360–1.3366	1.3360–1.3366	1.3360–1.3366	1.4138	1.4138	0.0020–0.0035	0.004–0.008
	R	2.0 (1999)	1.0217–1.0224	1.0217–1.0224	1.0217–1.0224	1.0217–1.0224	1.0217–1.0224 ①	1.3974	1.3858	0.0020–0.0035	0.004–0.008
	U	2.0 (1999)	1.0217–1.0224	1.0217–1.0224	1.0217–1.0224	1.0217–1.0224	1.0217–1.0224–	1.3974	1.3858	0.0020–0.0035	0.004–0.008
	S	3.0 (2972)	1.3400	1.3400	1.3400	1.3400	—	1.6430–1.6440	1.6430–1.6440	0.0020–0.0035	0.004–0.008
	B	3.0 (2972)	1.0200	1.0200	1.0200	1.0200	1.0200	1.3776–1.3972	1.3661–1.3858	0.0020–0.0035	0.004–0.008
	C	3.0 (2972)	1.0200	1.0200	1.0200	1.0200	1.0200	1.3776–1.3972	1.3661–1.3858	0.0020–0.0035	0.004–0.008
1992	A	1.5 (1468)	1.8110	1.8110	1.8110	1.8110	—	1.5059–1.5256	1.5197–1.5394	0.0024–0.0055	NA
	T	1.8 (1753)	1.3360–1.3366	1.3360–1.3366	1.3360–1.3366	1.3360–1.3366	1.3360–1.3366	1.4138	1.4138	0.0020–0.0035	0.004–0.008
	R	2.0 (1999)	1.0217–1.0224	1.0217–1.0224	1.0217–1.0224	1.0217–1.0224	1.0217–1.0224 ①	1.3974	1.3858	0.0020–0.0035	0.004–0.008
	U	2.0 (1999)	1.0217–1.0224	1.0217–1.0224	1.0217–1.0224	1.0217–1.0224	1.0217–1.0224 ①	1.3974	1.3858	0.0020–0.0035	0.004–0.008
	S	3.0 (2972)	1.3400	1.3400	1.3400	1.3400	—	1.6430–1.6440	1.6430–1.6440	0.0020–0.0035	0.004–0.008
	B	3.0 (2972)	1.0200	1.0200	1.0200	1.0200	1.0200	1.3776–1.3972	1.3661–1.3858	0.0020–0.0035	0.004–0.008
	C	3.0 (2972)	1.0200	1.0200	1.0200	1.0200	1.0200	1.3776–1.3972	1.3661–1.3858	0.0020–0.0035	0.004–0.008
	D	1.8 (1834)	1.7689–1.7693	1.7689–1.7693	1.7689–1.7693	1.7689–1.7693	1.7689–1.7693	1.4670–1.4880	1.4800–1.4990	0.0020–0.0035	NA
	W	2.4 (2350)	1.3362–1.3366	1.3362–1.3366	1.3362–1.3366	1.3362–1.3366	1.3362–1.3366	1.7335–1.7531	1.7335–1.7531	0.0020–0.0035–	NA

CAMSHAFT SPECIFICATIONS
All measurements given in inches.

Year	Engine ID/VIN	Engine Displacement Liters (cc)	Journal Diameter					Elevation		Bearing Clearance	Camshaft End Play
			1	2	3	4	5	In.	Ex.		
1993-94	A	1.5 (1468)	1.8110	1.8110	1.8110	1.8110	—	1.5059–1.5256	1.5197–1.5394	0.0024–0.0055	NA
	B	1.8 (1753)	1.3360–1.3366	1.3360–1.3366	1.3360–1.3366	1.3360–1.3366	1.3360–1.3366	1.4138	1.4138	0.0020–0.0035	0.004–0.008
	C	1.8 (1834)	1.7689–1.7693	1.7689–1.7693	1.7689–1.7693	1.7689–1.7693	1.7689–1.7693	1.4670–1.4880	1.4800–1.4490	0.0020–0.0035	NA
	E	2.0 (1999)	1.0217–1.0224	1.0217–1.0224	1.0217–1.0224	1.0217–1.0224	1.0217–1.0224 ①	1.3974	1.3858	0.0020–0.0035	0.004–0.008
	F	2.0 (1999)	1.0217–1.0224	1.0217–1.0224	1.0217–1.0224	1.0217–1.0224	1.0217–1.0224	1.3974	1.3858	0.0020–0.0035	0.004–0.008
	G	2.4 (2350)	1.7689–1.7693	1.7689–1.7693	1.7689–1.7693	1.7689–1.7693	1.7689–1.7693	1.4720	1.4752	0.0020–0.0035	NA
	H	3.0 (2972)	1.3400	1.3400	1.3400	1.3400	—	1.6430–1.6440	1.6430–1.6440	0.0020–0.0035	0.004–0.008
	J	3.0 (2972)	1.0200	1.0200	1.0200	1.0200	1.0200	1.3776–1.3972	1.3661–1.3858	0.0020–0.0035	0.004–0.008
	K	3.0 (2972)	1.0200	1.0200	1.0200	1.0200	1.0200	1.3776–1.3972	1.3661–1.3858	0.0020–0.0035	0.004–0.008

NA—Not available
① 6 journals are used.
Bearing caps Nos. 2–5 are the same shape.
''L'' or ''R'' is stamped on No. 1 bearing cap.
L=Intake side, R=Exhaust side. Bearing caps
should be reinstalled at their original locations.

CRANKSHAFT AND CONNECTING ROD SPECIFICATIONS
All measurements are given in inches.

Year	Engine ID/VIN	Engine Displacement Liters (cc)	Crankshaft				Connecting Rod		
			Main Brg. Journal Dia.	Main Brg. Oil Clearance	Shaft End-play	Thrust on No.	Journal Diameter	Oil Clearance	Side Clearance
1990	X	1.5 (1468)	1.890	0.0008–0.0018	0.0020–0.0071	3	1.6500	0.0006–0.0017	0.0039–0.0098
	Y	1.6 (1595)	2.240	0.0008–0.0020	0.0020–0.0071	3	1.7700	0.0008–0.0020	0.0039–0.0098
	T	1.8 (1753)	2.240	0.0008–0.0020	0.0020–0.0070	3	1.7700	0.0008–0.0020	0.0039–0.0098
	R	2.0 (1999)	2.243–2.244	0.0008–0.0020	0.0020–0.0070	3	1.7709–1.7715	0.0008–0.0020	0.0040–0.0098
	U	2.0 (1999)	2.243–2.244	0.0008–0.0020	0.0020–0.0070	3	1.7709–1.7715	0.0008–0.0020	0.0040–0.0098
1991	A	1.5 (1468)	1.890	0.0008–0.0028	0.0020–0.0071	3	1.6500	0.0008–0.0024	0.0039–0.0098
	T	1.8 (1753)	2.240	0.0008–0.0020	0.0020–0.0070	3	1.7700	0.0008–0.0020	0.0039–0.0098
	R	2.0 (1999)	2.243–2.244	0.0008–0.0020	0.0020–0.0070	3	1.7709–1.7715	0.0008–0.0020	0.0040–0.0098
	U	2.0 (1999)	2.243–2.244	0.0008–0.0020	0.0020–0.0070	3	1.7709–1.7715	0.0008–0.0020	0.0040–0.0098

CRANKSHAFT AND CONNECTING ROD SPECIFICATIONS

All measurements are given in inches.

Year	Engine ID/VIN	Engine Displacement Liters (cc)	Crankshaft Main Brg. Journal Dia.	Crankshaft Main Brg. Oil Clearance	Crankshaft Shaft End-play	Thrust on No.	Connecting Rod Journal Diameter	Connecting Rod Oil Clearance	Connecting Rod Side Clearance
	S	3.0 (2972)	2.358	0.0008–0.0019	0.0020–0.0098	3	1.9650	0.0006–0.0018	0.0040–0.0098
	B	3.0 (2972)	2.358	0.0007–0.0017	0.0020–0.0098	3	1.9650	0.0006–0.0018	0.0040–0.0098
	C	3.0 (2972)	2.358	0.0007–0.0017	0.0020–0.0098	3	1.9650	0.0006–0.0018	0.0040–0.0098
1992	A	1.5 (1468)	1.890	0.0008–0.0028	0.0020–0.0071	3	1.6500	0.0008–0.0024	0.0039–0.0098
	T	1.8 (1753)	2.240	0.0008–0.0020	0.0020–0.0070	3	1.7700	0.0008–0.0020	0.0039–0.0098
	R	2.0 (1999)	2.243–2.244	0.0008–0.0020	0.0020–0.0070	3	1.7709–1.7715	0.0008–0.0020	0.0040–0.0098
	U	2.0 (1999)	2.243–2.244	0.0008–0.0020	0.0020–0.0070	3	1.7709–1.7715	0.0008–0.0020	0.0040–0.0098
	S	3.0 (2972)	2.358	0.0008–0.0019	0.0020–0.0098	3	1.9650	0.0006–0.0018	0.0040–0.0098
	B	3.0 (2972)	2.358	0.0007–0.0017	0.0020–0.0098	3	1.9650	0.0006–0.0018	0.0040–0.0098
	C	3.0 (2972)	2.358	0.0007–0.0017	0.0020–0.0098	3	1.9650	0.0006–0.0018	0.0040–0.0098
	D	1.8 (1834)	1.968	0.0008–0.0016	0.0020–0.0070	3	1.7709–1.7715	0.0008–0.0020	0.0040–0.0098
	W	2.4 (2350)	2.243–2.244	0.0008–0.0020	0.0020–0.0070	3	1.7709–1.7717	0.0008–0.0020	0.0039–0.0098
1993–94	A	1.5 (1468)	1.890	0.0008–0.0028	0.0020–0.0071	3	1.6500	0.0008–0.0024	0.0039–0.0098
	B	1.8 (1753)	2.240	0.0008–0.0020	0.0020–0.0070	3	1.7700	0.0008–0.0020	0.0039–0.0098
	C	1.8 (1834)	1.968	0.0008–0.0016	0.0020–0.0070	3	1.7709–1.7715	0.0008–0.0020	0.0040–0.0098
	E	2.0 (1999)	2.243–2.244	0.0008–0.0020	0.0020–0.0070	3	1.7709–1.7715	0.0008–0.0020	0.0040–0.0098
	F	2.0 (1999)	2.243–2.244	0.0008–0.0020	0.0020–0.0070	3	1.7709–1.7715	0.0008–0.0020	0.0040–0.0098
	G	2.4 (2350)	2.243–2.244	0.0008–0.0020	0.0020–0.0070	3	1.7709–1.7717	0.0008–0.0020	0.0039–0.0098
	H	3.0 (2972)	2.358	0.0008–0.0019	0.0020–0.0098	3	1.9650	0.0006–0.0018	0.0040–0.0098
	J	3.0 (2972)	2.358	0.0007–0.0017	0.0020–0.0098	3	1.9650	0.0006–0.0018	0.0040–0.0098
	K	3.0 (2972)	2.358	0.0007–0.0017	0.0020–0.0098	3	1.9650	0.0006–0.0018	0.0040–0.0098

VALVE SPECIFICATIONS

Year	Engine ID/VIN	Engine Displacement Liters (cc)	Seat Angle (deg.)	Face Angle (deg.)	Spring Test Pressure (lbs. @ in.)	Spring Installed Height (in.)	Stem-to-Guide Clearance (in.) Intake	Stem-to-Guide Clearance (in.) Exhaust	Stem Diameter (in.) Intake	Stem Diameter (in.) Exhaust
1990	X	1.5 (1468)	44–44.5	45–45.5	53②	1.756①	0.0008–0.0020	0.0020–0.0035	0.2600	0.2600
	Y	1.6 (1595)	44–44.5	45–45.5	66②	1.902④	0.0008–0.0019	0.0020–0.0033	0.2585–0.2586	0.2571–0.2579
	T	1.8 (1753)	44–44.5	45–45.5	62②	1.937⑦	0.0012–⑤0.0024	0.0020–⑥0.0035–	0.3100	0.3100
	R	2.0 (1999)	44–44.5	45–45.5	66②	1.902⑧	0.0008–⑤0.0019	0.0020–⑥0.0033	0.2585–0.2591	0.2571–0.2579
	U	2.0 (1999)	44–44.5	45–45.5	66②	1.902⑧	0.0008–⑤0.0019	0.0020⑥0.0033	0.2585–0.2591	0.2571–0.2579
1991	A	1.5 (1468)	44–44.5	45–45.5	② ⑨	⑩	0.0008–0.0020	0.0020–0.0035	0.2585–0.2591	0.2571–0.2579
	T	1.8 (1753)	44–44.5	45–45.5	62②	1.937⑦	0.0012–⑤0.0024	0.0020–⑥0.0035	0.3100	0.3100
	R	2.0 (1999)	44–44.5	45–45.5	66②	1.902⑧	0.0008–⑤0.0019	0.0020–⑧0.0033	0.2585–0.2591	0.2571–0.2579
	U	2.0 (1999)	44–44.5	45–45.5	66②	1.902⑧	0.0008–⑤0.0019	0.0020–⑥0.0033	0.2585–0.2591	0.2571–0.2579
	S	3.0 (2972)	44–44.5	45–45.5	74②	1.600–1.630	0.0012–0.0039	0.0020–0.0059	0.3140	0.3140
	B	3.0 (2972)	44–44.5	45–45.5	62②	1.500–1.530	0.0008–0.0039	0.0020–0.0047	0.2600	0.2600
	C	3.0 (2972)	44–44.5	45–45.5	62②	1.500–1.530	0.0008–0.0039	0.0020–0.0047	0.2600	0.2600
1992	A	1.5 (1468)	44–44.5	45–45.5	② ⑨	⑩	0.0008–0.0020	0.0020–0.0035	0.2585–0.2591	0.2571–0.2579
	T	1.8 (1753)	44–44.5	45–45.5	62②	1.937⑦	0.0012–⑤0.0024	0.0020–⑥0.0035	0.3100	0.3100
	R	2.0 (1999)	44–44.5	45–45.5	66②	1.902⑧	0.0008–⑤0.0019	0.0020–⑧0.0033	0.2585–0.2591	0.2571–0.2579
	U	2.0 (1999)	44–44.5	45–45.5	66②	1.902⑧	0.0008–⑤0.0019	0.0020–⑥0.0033	0.2585–0.2591	0.2571–0.2579
	S	3.0 (2972)	44–44.5	45–45.5	74②	1.600–1.630	0.0012–0.0039	0.0020–0.0059	0.3140	0.3140
	B	3.0 (2972)	44–44.4	45–45.5	62②	1.500–1.530	0.0008–0.0039	0.0020–0.0047	0.2600	0.2600
	C	3.0 (2972)	44–44.5	45–45.5	62②	1.500–1.530	0.0008–0.0039	0.0020–0.0047	0.2600	0.2600
	D	1.8 (1834)	43.5–44	45–45.5	132②	⑪	0.0008–0.0020	0.0020–0.0035	0.2350–0.2354	0.2343–0.2350
	W	2.4 (2350)	44–44.5	45–45.5	73②	③	0.0012–0.0024	0.0020–0.0035	0.3100	0.3100
1993-94	A	1.5 (1468)	44–44.5	45–45.5	② ⑨	⑩	0.0008–0.0020	0.0020–0.0035	0.2585–0.2591	0.2571–0.2579
	B	1.8 (1753)	44–44.5	45–45.5	62②	1.937⑦	0.0012–⑤0.0024	0.0020–⑥0.0035	0.3100	0.3100
	C	1.8 (1834)	43.5–44	45–45.5	132②	⑪	0.0008–0.0020	0.0020–0.0035	0.2350–0.2354	0.2343–0.2350

VALVE SPECIFICATIONS

Year	Engine ID/VIN	Engine Displacement Liters (cc)	Seat Angle (deg.)	Face Angle (deg.)	Spring Test Pressure (lbs. @ in.)	Spring Installed Height (in.)	Stem-to-Guide Clearance (in.) Intake	Stem-to-Guide Clearance (in.) Exhaust	Stem Diameter (in.) Intake	Stem Diameter (in.) Exhaust
1993–94	E	2.0 (1999)	44–44.5	45–45.5	66②	1.902⑧	0.0008–⑤ 0.0019	0.0020–⑧ 0.0033	0.2585–0.2591	0.2571–0.2579
	F	2.0 (1999)	44–44.5	45–45.5	66②	1.902⑧	0.0008–⑤ 0.0019	0.0020–⑥ 0.0033	0.2585–0.2591	0.2571–0.2579
	G	2.4 (2350)	44–44.5	45–45.5	60②	1.740	0.0008–0.0020	0.0012–0.0028	0.2350–0.2354	0.2343–0.2350
	H	3.0 (2972)	44–44.5	45–45.5	74②	1.600–1.630	0.0012–0.0039	0.0020–0.0059	0.3140	0.3140
	J	3.0 (2972)	44–44.4	45–45.5	62②	1.500–1.530	0.0008–0.0039	0.0020–0.0047	0.2600	0.2600
	K	3.0 (2972)	44–44.5	45–45.5	62②	1.500–1.530	0.0008–0.0039	0.0020–0.0047	0.2600	0.2600

NA—Not available
① Free length, not installed height
  Used limit = 1.717
② At installed height
③ Free length, not installed height—1.961
④ Free length, not installed height
  Used limit = 1.862

⑤ Used limit = 0.004
⑥ Used limit = 0.006
⑦ Free length, not installed height
  Used limit = 1.898
⑧ Free length, not installed height
  Used limit = 1.862

⑨ Intake: 51
  Exhaust: 64
⑩ Free length, not installed height
  Intake: 1.776–1.815
  Exhaust: 1.803–1.843
⑪ Free length, not installed height—2.004

PISTON AND RING SPECIFICATIONS
All measurements are given in inches.

Year	Engine ID/VIN	Engine Displacement Liters (cc)	Piston Clearance	Ring Gap Top Compression	Ring Gap Bottom Compression	Ring Gap Oil Control	Ring Side Clearance Top Compression	Ring Side Clearance Bottom Compression	Ring Side Clearance Oil Control
1990	X	1.5 (1468)	0.0008–0.0016	0.0079–0.0138	0.0079–0.0138	0.0079–0.0276	0.0012–0.0028	0.0008–0.0024	NA
	Y	1.6 (1595)	0.0008–0.0016	0.0098–0.0157	0.0138–0.0197	0.0079–0.0276	0.0012–0.0028	0.0012–0.0028	NA
	T	1.8 (1753)	0.0004–0.0012	0.0118–0.0177	0.0079–0.0138	0.0080–0.0280	0.0018–0.0033	0.0008–0.0024	NA
	R	2.0 (1999)	0.0008–0.0016	0.0098–0.0157	0.0138–0.0197	0.0079–0.0276	0.0012–0.0028	0.0012–0.0028	NA
	U	2.0 (1999)	0.0012–0.0020	0.0098–0.0177	0.0138–0.0197	0.0079–0.0276	0.0012–0.0028	0.0012–0.0028	NA
1991	A	1.5 (1468)	0.0008–0.0016	0.0079–0.0157	0.0079–0.0138	0.0079–0.0276	0.0012–0.0028	0.0008–0.0024	NA
	T	1.8 (1753)	0.0004–0.0012	0.0118–0.0177	0.0079–0.0138	0.0080–0.0280	0.0018–0.0033	0.0008–0.0024	NA
	R	2.0 (1999)	0.0008–0.0016	0.0098–0.0157	0.0138–0.0197	0.0079–0.0276	0.0012–0.0028	0.0012–0.0028	NA
	U	2.0 (1999)	0.0012–0.0020	0.0098–0.0177	0.0138–0.0197	0.0079–0.0276	0.0012–0.0028	0.0012–0.0028	NA
	S	3.0 (2972)	0.0012–0.0020	0.0118–0.0177	0.0098–0.0157	0.0118–0.0154	0.0020–0.0035	0.0008–0.0024	NA
	B	3.0 (2972)	0.0012–0.0020	0.0118–0.0177	0.0177–0.0236	0.0079–0.0236	0.0012–0.0028	0.0008–0.0024	NA
	C	3.0 (2972)	0.0012–0.0020	0.0118–0.0177	0.0177–0.0236	0.0079–0.0236	0.0012–0.0028	0.0008–0.0024	NA

PISTON AND RING SPECIFICATIONS
All measurements are given in inches.

Year	Engine ID/VIN	Engine Displacement Liters (cc)	Piston Clearance	Ring Gap Top Compression	Ring Gap Bottom Compression	Ring Gap Oil Control	Ring Side Clearance Top Compression	Ring Side Clearance Bottom Compression	Ring Side Clearance Oil Control
1992	A	1.5 (1468)	0.0008–0.0016	0.0079–0.0157	0.0079–0.0138	0.0079–0.0276	0.0012–0.0028	0.0008–0.0024	NA
	T	1.8 (1753)	0.0004–0.0012	0.0118–0.0177	0.0079–0.0138	0.0080–0.0280	0.0018–0.0033	0.0008–0.0024	NA
	R	2.0 (1999)	0.0008–0.0016	0.0098–0.0157	0.0138–0.0197	0.0079–0.0276	0.0012–0.0028	0.0012–0.0028	NA
	U	2.0 (1999)	0.0012–0.0020	0.0098–0.0177	0.0138–0.0197	0.0079–0.0276	0.0012–0.0028	0.0012–0.0028	NA
	S	3.0 (2972)	0.0012–0.0020	0.0118–0.0177	0.0098–0.0157	0.0118–0.0154	0.0020–0.0035	0.0008–0.0024	NA
	B	3.0 (2972)	0.0012–0.0020	0.0118–0.0177	0.0177–0.0236	0.0079–0.0236	0.0012–0.0028	0.0008–0.0024	NA
	C	3.0 (2972)	0.0012–0.0020	0.0118–0.0177	0.0177–0.0236	0.0079–0.0236	0.0012–0.0028	0.0008–0.0024	NA
	D	1.8 (1834)	0.0008–0.0016	0.0098–0.0157	0.0157–0.0217	0.0079–0.0236	0.0012–0.0028	0.0008–0.0024	NA
	W	2.4 (2350)	0.0004–0.0012	0.0098–0.0157	0.0079–0.0157	0.0079–0.0276	0.0012–0.0028	0.0008–0.0024	NA
1993–94	A	1.5 (1468)	0.0008–0.0016	0.0079–0.0157	0.0079–0.0138	0.0079–0.0276	0.0012–0.0028	0.0008–0.0024	NA
	B	1.8 (1753)	0.0004–0.0012	0.0118–0.0177	0.0079–0.0138	0.0080–0.0280	0.0018–0.0033	0.0008–0.0024	NA
	C	1.8 (1834)	0.0008–0.0016	0.0098–0.0157	0.0157–0.0217	0.0079–0.0236	0.0012–0.0028	0.0008–0.0024	NA
	E	2.0 (1999)	0.0008–0.0016	0.0098–0.0157	0.0138–0.0197	0.0079–0.0276	0.0012–0.0028	0.0012–0.0028	NA
	F	2.0 (1999)	0.0012–0.0020	0.0098–0.0177	0.0138–0.0197	0.0079–0.0276	0.0012–0.0028	0.0012–0.0028	NA
	G	2.4 (2350)	0.0004–0.0012	0.0098–0.0157	0.0079–0.0157	0.0079–0.0276	0.0012–0.0028	0.0008–0.0024	NA
	H	3.0 (2972)	0.0012–0.0020	0.0118–0.0177	0.0098–0.0157	0.0118–0.0154	0.0020–0.0035	0.0008–0.0024	NA
	J	3.0 (2972)	0.0012–0.0020	0.0118–0.0177	0.0177–0.0236	0.0079–0.0236	0.0012–0.0028	0.0008–0.0024	NA
	K	3.0 (2972)	0.0012–0.0020	0.0118–0.0177	0.0177–0.0236	0.0079–0.0236	0.0012–0.0028	0.0008–0.0024	NA

NA—Not available

TORQUE SPECIFICATIONS
All readings in ft. lbs.

Year	Engine ID/VIN	Engine Displacement Liters (cc)	Cylinder Head Bolts	Main Bearing Bolts	Rod Bearing Bolts	Crankshaft Damper Bolts	Flywheel Bolts	Manifold Intake	Manifold Exhaust	Spark Plugs	Lug Nut
1990	X	1.5 (1468)	①	36–40	⑥	51–72②	94–101	11–14	11–14	15–21③	65–80
	Y	1.6 (1595)	④	47–51	36–38	80–94⑤	94–101	18–22	18–22	15–21③	65–80
	T	1.8 (1753)	51–54	37–39	24–25	80–94	94–101	13–18	18–22	15–21③	87–101
	R	2.0 (1999)	65–72	47–51	36–38	80–94	94–101	18–22	18–22	15–21③	87–101
	U	2.0 (1999)	65–72	47–51	36–38	80–94	94–101	18–22	18–22	15–21③	87–101

TORQUE SPECIFICATIONS
All readings in ft. lbs.

Year	Engine ID/VIN	Engine Displacement Liters (cc)	Cylinder Head Bolts	Main Bearing Bolts	Rod Bearing Bolts	Crankshaft Damper Bolts	Flywheel Bolts	Manifold Intake	Manifold Exhaust	Spark Plugs	Lug Nut
1991	A	1.5 (1468)	①	47–51	36–38	51–72 ②	94–101	11–14	11–14	15–21 ③	65–80
	T	1.8 (1753)	51–54	37–39	24–25	80–94	94–101	13–18	18–22	15–21 ③	87–101
	R	2.0 (1999)	65–72	47–51	36–38	94	94–101	18–22	18–22	15–21 ③	87–101
	U	2.0 (1999)	65–72	47–51	36–38	94	94–101	18–22	18–22	15–21 ③	87–101
	S	3.0 (2972)	76–83	58	38	108–116	55	13	13	18 ③	87–101
	B	3.0 (2972)	76–83	58	38	130–137	55	14	33	18 ③	87–101
	C	3.0 (2972)	87–94 ⑨	58	38	130–137	55	9–11	22 ⑧	18 ③	87–101
1992	A	1.5 (1468)	①	47–51	36–38	51–72 ②	94–101	11–14	11–14	15–21 ③	65–80
	T	1.8 (1753)	51–54	37–39	24–25	80–94	94–101	13–18	18–22	15–21 ③	87–101
	R	2.0 (1999)	65–72	47–51	36–38	94	94–101	18–22	18–22	15–21 ③	87–101
	U	2.0 (1999)	65–72	47–51	36–38	94	94–101	18–22	18–22	15–21 ③	87–101
	S	3.0 (2972)	76–83	58	38	108–116	55	13	13	18 ③	87–101
	B	3.0 (2972)	76–83	58	38	130–137	55	14	33	18 ③	87–101
	C	3.0 (2972)	87–94 ⑨	58	38	130–137	55	9–11	22 ⑧	18 ③	87–101
	D	1.8 (1834)	⑦	14	14.5	134	72	13	13	18	65–80
	W	2.4 (2350)	⑦	38	38	—	98	13	13	18	65–80
1993–94	A	1.5 (1468)	①	47–51	36–38	51–72 ②	94–101	11–14	11–14	15–21 ③	65–80
	B	1.8 (1753)	51–54	37–39	24–25	80–94	94–101	13–18	18–22	15–21 ③	87–101
	C	1.8 (1834)	⑦	14	14.5	134	72	13	13	18	65–80
	E	2.0 (1999)	65–72	47–51	36–38	94	94–101	18–22	18–22	15–21 ③	87–101
	F	2.0 (1999)	65–72	47–51	36–38	94	94–101	18–22	18–22	15–21 ③	87–101
	G	2.4 (2350)	⑦	38	38	—	98	13	13	18	65–80
	H	3.0 (2972)	76–83	58	38	108–116	55	13	13	18 ③	87–101
	J	3.0 (2972)	76–83	58	38	130–137	55	14	33	18 ③	87–101
	K	3.0 (2972)	87–94 ⑨	58	38	130–137	55	9–11	22 ⑧	18 ③	87–101

① 51–54 COLD
58–61 HOT
② Pulley to crankshaft sprocket—9–11
③ Spark plugs used in aluminum heads should always have lubricated threads
④ 65–72 COLD
72–80 HOT
⑤ Pulley to crankshaft sprocket—14–22
⑥ Torque to 14.5 ft. lbs., back off, torque again to 14.5 ft. lbs., then turn additional ¼ turn

⑦ Step 1: 54 ft. lbs.
Step 2: Fully loosen
Step 3: 14 ft. lbs.
Step 4: + 90 degrees turn
Step 5: + 90 degrees turn
⑧ See text for special torque sequence
⑨ Loosen all bolts and retorque in proper sequence

TORQUE SPECIFICATIONS

Component	English	Metric
Camshaft sprocket bolt		
1.5L engine:	47–54 ft. lbs.	65–75 Nm
1.6L, 1.8L (Laser) and 2.0L engines:	58–72 ft. lbs.	80–100 Nm
1.8L (Summit Wagon) and 2.4L engines:	65 ft. lbs.	90 Nm
3.0L engine:	65 ft. lbs.	90 Nm

TORQUE SPECIFICATIONS

Component	English	Metric
Connecting rod bearing cap bolts		
1.8L (Laser) and 1989 1.5L engines:	23–25 ft. lbs.	32–35 Nm
1.8L (Summit Wagon) engine:	15 ft. lbs.	20 Nm
1990–94 1.5L engine		
Step 1:	14.5 ft. lbs.	20 Nm
Step 2:	fully loosen	fully loosen
Step 3:	14.5 ft. lbs.	20 Nm
Step 4:	+ 90 degrees turn	+ 90 degrees turn
1.6L and 2.0L engines:	36–38 ft. lbs.	50–53 Nm
2.4L and 3.0L engines:	38 ft. lbs.	52 Nm
Crankshaft damper bolt		
1.5L engine:	51–72 ft. lbs.	70–100 Nm
1.6L, 1.8L (Laser) and 2.0L engines:	89–94 ft. lbs.	110–130 Nm
3.0L SOHC engine:	108–116 ft. lbs.	150–160 Nm
3.0L DOHC engine:	130–137 ft. lbs.	180–190 Nm
Crankshaft pulley bolt		
1.5L engine:	108–132 inch lbs.	12–15 Nm
1.8L (Laser) engine:	132–156 inch lbs.	15–18 Nm
1.8L (Summit Wagon) engine:	134 ft. lbs.	185 Nm
1.6L and 2.0L engines:	14–22 ft. lbs.	20–30 Nm
2.4L engine:	18 ft. lbs.	25 Nm
* Note: The 3.0L engine crankshaft pulley is an integral part of the damper.		
Cylinder head bolt		
1.5L and 1.8L (Laser/Talon) engines:	51–54 ft. lbs.	70–75 Nm
1.8L (Summit Wagon), 2.0L (Laser/Talon) and 2.4L engines		
Step 1:	54 ft. lbs.	75 Nm
Step 2:	fully loosen	fully loosen
Step 3:	14 ft. lbs.	20 Nm
Step 4:	+ 90 degrees turn	+ 90 degrees turn
Step 5:	+ 90 degrees turn	+ 90 degrees turn
1.6L and 2.0L engines:	65–72 ft. lbs.	90–100 Nm
3.0L engine:	76–83 ft. lbs.	105–115 Nm
3.0L (turbo) engine:	87–94 ft. lbs.	120–130 Nm
EGR valve-to-intake plenum		
1.5L and 1.8L (Laser) engines:	84–132 inch lbs.	10–15 Nm
1.8L (Summit Wagon) engine:	9 ft. lbs.	13 Nm
1.6L and 2.0L engines:	132–192 inch lbs.	15–22 Nm
2.4L engine:	9 ft. lbs.	13 Nm
3.0L engine:	13 ft. lbs.	19 Nm
Engine-to-transaxle		
Except Stealth		
Upper bolts:	31–40 ft. lbs.	43–55 Nm
Lower bolts:	22–25 ft. lbs.	30–35 Nm
Stealth		
Upper bolts:	54 ft. lbs.	75 Nm
Lower bolts:	65 ft. lbs.	90 Nm
Exhaust manifold		
1.5L and 1.8L (Laser) engines:	11–14 ft. lbs.	15–20 Nm
1.6L and 2.0L engines:	18–22 ft. lbs.	25–30 Nm
1.8L (Summit Wagon) and 2.4L engines:	13 ft. lbs.	18 Nm
3.0L SOHC engine:	13 ft. lbs.	18 Nm
3.0L DOHC engine:	33 ft. lbs.	45 Nm
Exhaust pipe-to-exhaust manifold nuts		
Except 1991–93 1.5L engine, Summit Wagon and 3.0L engines:	22–29 ft. lbs.	30–40 Nm
1.8L and 2.4L (Summit Wagon) engines:	33 ft. lbs.	45 Nm
1991–93 1.5L engine:	14–22 ft. lbs.	20–30 Nm
3.0L engine:	36 ft. lbs.	50 Nm

TORQUE SPECIFICATIONS

Component	English	Metric
Flywheel/flexplate-to-crankshaft bolts		
Except 1.8L (Summit Wagon), 2.4L and 3.0L engines:	94–101 ft. lbs.	130–140 Nm
1.8L (Summit Wagon) and 2.4L engines:	72 ft. lbs.	100 Nm
3.0L engine:	55 ft. lbs.	75 Nm
Flywheel-to-converter bolts		
Except 3.0L engine:	34–38 ft. lbs.	46–53 Nm
3.0L engine:	55 ft. lbs.	75 Nm
Engine mount bracket through bolt		
Except 1.8L (Summit Wagon), 2.4L and 3.0L engines:	36–47 ft. lbs.	50–65 Nm
1.8L (Summit Wagon), 2.4L and 3.0L engines:	51 ft. lbs.	70 Nm
Intake manifold		
1.5L and 1.8L (Laser/Talon) engines:	11–14 ft. lbs.	15–20 Nm
1.6L and 2.0L engines		
M8 bolt:	11–14 ft. lbs.	15–20 Nm
M10 bolt and nut:	22–30 ft. lbs.	30–42 Nm
1.8L (Summit Wagon), 2.4L and 3.0L engines:	13 ft. lbs.	18 Nm
3.0L (turbo) engine		
Step 1 tigten front bank:	24–36 inch lbs.	3–5 Nm
Step 2 tighten rear bank:	108–132 inch lbs.	12–15 Nm
Step 3 tighten front bank:	108–132 inch lbs.	12–15 Nm
Step 4 tighten all bolts:	108–132 inch lbs.	12–15 Nm
Main bearing cap bolts		
1.8L and 1989–90 1.5L engines:	36–40 ft. lbs.	50–55 Nm
1.6L, 2.0L and 1991–93 1.5L engines:	47–51 ft. lbs.	65–70 Nm
1.8L (Summit Wagon) engine:	14 ft. lbs.	20 Nm
2.4L engine:	38 ft. lbs.	53 Nm
3.0L engine:	38 ft. lbs.	53 Nm
MPI throttle body		
Except 3.0L engine:	11–16 ft. lbs.	15–22 Nm
3.0L engine:	84–108 inch lbs.	10–13 Nm
MPI fuel rail:	84–108 inch lbs.	10–13 Nm
Oil pan		
1.5L and 1.6L engines:	48–72 inch lbs.	6–8 Nm
1.8L (Laser/Talon) and 2.0L engines		
Bolts:	48–72 inch lbs.	6–8 Nm
Nuts:	48–60 inch lbs.	5–7 Nm
1.8L (Summit Wagon) and 2.4L engines:	5 ft. lbs.	7 Nm
3.0L engine:	60 inch lbs.	6 Nm
Oil pan drain plug		
Except 1.8L (Summit Wagon), 2.4L and 3.0L engines:	25–33 ft. lbs.	35–45 Nm
1.8L (Summit Wagon) and 2.4L engines:	29 ft. lbs.	40 Nm
3.0L engine:	29 ft. lbs.	40 Nm
Oil pump cover screws		
1.5L engine:	72–84 inch lbs.	8–10 Nm
1.8L (Summit Wagon) and 2.4L engines:	7 ft. lbs.	10 Nm
1.6L, 1.8L (Laser/Talon) and 2.0L engines:	11–13 ft. lbs.	15–18 Nm
3.0L engine:	60 inch lbs.	6 Nm

TORQUE SPECIFICATIONS

Component	English	Metric
Rocker arm shaft bolt		
1.5L engine:	14–20 ft. lbs.	19–27 Nm
1.8L (Laser/Talon) engine		
Short bolts:	14–15 ft. lbs.	19–21 Nm
Long bolts:	14–20 ft. lbs.	19–27 Nm
1.8L (Summit Wagon) engine:	21–25 ft. lbs.	29–35 Nm
2.4L and 3.0L SOHC engines:	15 ft. lbs.	20 Nm
Rocker (valve) cover		
1.5L engine:	12–18 inch lbs.	1.5–2.0 Nm
1.6L and 2.0L engine:	24–36 inch lbs.	3-4 Nm
1.8L (Laser/Talon) engine:	48–60 inch lbs.	5–7 Nm
1.8L (Summit Wagon) engine:	2.5 ft. lbs.	3.5 Nm
2.4L engine:	4 ft. lbs.	6 Nm
3.0L SOHC engine:	84 inch lbs.	9 Nm
3.0L DOHC engine:	36 inch lbs.	4 Nm
Spark plug		
Except 3.0L engine:	15–21 ft. lbs.	20–30 Nm
3.0L engine:	15 ft. lbs.	20 Nm
Starter-to-transaxle bolts:	20–25 ft. lbs.	27–34 Nm
Thermostat housing:	12–14 ft. lbs.	17–20 Nm
Timing cover:	7–9 ft. lbs.	10–12 Nm
Turbocharger-to-exhaust pipe		
2.0L engine:	29–43 ft. lbs.	40–60 Nm
3.0L engine:	36 ft. lbs.	60 Nm
Water pump		
Except 3.0L engine		
Long bolt:	14–20 ft. lbs.	20–27 Nm
Short bolt:	9–11 ft. lbs.	12–15 Nm
3.0L engine:	17 ft. lbs.	24 Nm
Water pump pulley:	6–7 ft. lbs.	8–10 Nm

NOTE: On the 3.0L engine the water pump pulley is integral with the pump assembly.

BRAKE SPECIFICATIONS
All measurements in inches unless noted.

Year	Model	Axle	Master Cylinder Bore	Brake Disc Original Thickness	Brake Disc Minimum Thickness	Brake Disc Maximum Runout	Brake Drum Diameter Original Inside Diameter	Brake Drum Diameter Max. Wear Limit	Brake Drum Diameter Maximum Machine Diameter	Minimum Lining Thickness Front	Minimum Lining Thickness Rear
1990	Summit①	—	13/16	0.510	0.449	0.006	7.10	7.2	NA	0.080	0.040
	Summit②	front	7/8	0.940	0.882	0.006	—	—	—	0.080	0.080
		rear	—	0.390	0.331	0.006	—	—	—	0.080	0.080
	Laser	front	③	0.940	0.882	0.003	—	—	—	0.080	0.080
		rear	—	0.390	0.331	0.003	—	—	—	0.080	0.080
	Talon	front	③	0.940	0.882	0.003	—	—	—	0.080	0.080
		rear	—	0.390	0.331	0.003	—	—	—	0.080	0.080

BRAKE SPECIFICATIONS
All measurements in inches unless noted.

Year	Model	Axle	Master Cylinder Bore	Brake Disc Original Thickness	Brake Disc Minimum Thickness	Brake Disc Maximum Runout	Brake Drum Diameter Original Inside Diameter	Brake Drum Diameter Max. Wear Limit	Brake Drum Diameter Maximum Machine Diameter	Minimum Lining Thickness Front	Minimum Lining Thickness Rear
1991	Summit ④	—	13/16	0.510	0.449	0.006	7.10	7.2	NA	0.080	0.040
	Summit ⑤	—	7/8	0.710	0.646	0.006	7.10	7.2	NA	0.080	0.040
	Laser	front	⑥	0.940	0.882	0.003	—	—	—	0.080	0.080
		rear	—	0.390	0.331	0.003	—	—	—	0.080	0.080
	Talon	front	⑥	0.940	0.882	0.003	—	—	—	0.080	0.080
		rear	—	0.390	0.331	0.003	—	—	—	0.080	0.080
	Stealth ⑦	front	⑨	0.940	0.880	0.003	—	—	—	0.080	0.080
		rear	—	0.710	0.650	0.003	—	—	—	0.080	0.080
	Stealth ⑧	front	1 1/16	1.180	1.120	0.003	—	—	—	0.080	0.080
		rear	—	0.790	0.720	0.003	—	—	—	0.080	0.080
1992	Summit ④	—	13/16	0.510	0.449	0.006	7.10	7.2	NA	0.080	0.040
	Summit ⑤	—	7/8	0.710	0.646	0.006	7.10	7.2	NA	0.080	0.040
	Laser	front	⑥	0.940	0.882	0.003	—	—	—	0.080	0.080
		rear	—	0.390	0.331	0.003	—	—	—	0.080	0.080
	Talon	front	⑥	0.940	0.882	0.003	—	—	—	0.080	0.080
		rear	—	0.390	0.331	0.003	—	—	—	0.080	0.080
	Stealth ⑦	front	⑨	0.940	0.880	0.003	—	—	—	0.080	0.080
		rear	—	0.710	0.650	0.003	—	—	—	0.080	0.080
	Stealth ⑧	front	1 1/16	1.180	1.120	0.003	—	—	—	0.080	0.080
		rear	—	0.790	0.720	0.003	—	—	—	0.080	0.080
	Summit Wagon	front	⑩	0.945	0.882	0.003	—	—	—	0.080	0.040
		rear	—	0.394	0.331	0.003	⑪	⑫	—	0.080	0.040
1993-94	Summit ④	—	13/16	0.510	0.449	0.006	7.10	7.2	NA	0.080	0.040
	Summit ⑤	—	7/8	0.710	0.646	0.006	7.10	7.2	NA	0.080	0.040
	Laser	front	⑥	0.940	0.882	0.003	—	—	—	0.080	0.080
		rear	—	0.390	0.331	0.003	—	—	—	0.080	0.080
	Talon	front	⑥	0.940	0.882	0.003	—	—	—	0.080	0.080
		rear	—	0.390	0.331	0.003	—	—	—	0.080	0.080
	Stealth ⑦	front	⑨	0.940	0.880	0.003	—	—	—	0.080	0.080
		rear	—	0.710	0.650	0.003	—	—	—	0.080	0.080
	Stealth ⑧	front	1 1/16	1.180	1.120	0.003	—	—	—	0.080	0.080
		rear	—	0.790	0.720	0.003	—	—	—	0.080	0.080
	Summit Wagon	front	⑩	0.945	0.882	0.003	—	—	—	0.080	0.040
		rear	—	0.394	0.331	0.003	⑪	⑫	—	0.080	0.040

NA—Not available
① 1.5L engine
② 1.6L engine
③ Non-turbocharged engine: 7/8
   Turbocharged engine: 15/16
④ Hatchback
⑤ Sedan
⑥ Non-turbocharged without ABS: 7/8
   Non-turbocharged with ABS: 15/16
   Turbocharged with FWD: 15/16
   Turbocharged with AWD: 1

⑦ FWD—Front Wheel Drive
⑧ AWD—All Wheel Drive
⑨ Without ABS: 1
   With ABS: 1 1/16
⑩ Without ABS: 15/16
   With ABS: 1
⑪ 8 in. drum: 7.992
   9 in. drum: 9.0
⑫ 8 in. drum 8.071
   9 in. drum 9.079

WHEEL ALIGNMENT

Year	Model	Axle	Caster Range (deg.)	Caster Preferred Setting (deg.)	Camber Range (deg.)	Camber Preferred Setting (deg.)	Toe-in (in.)	Steering Axis Inclination (deg.)
1990	Summit	front	2P–3P	$2\frac{1}{3}$P	$\frac{1}{2}$N–$\frac{1}{2}$P	0	0	—
		rear	—	—	1N–0	$\frac{2}{3}$N	0	—
	Laser [1]	front	$1\frac{5}{16}$P–$2\frac{5}{6}$P	$2\frac{1}{3}$P	$\frac{4}{15}$N–$\frac{11}{15}$P	$\frac{7}{30}$P	0	—
		rear	—	—	$1\frac{1}{4}$N–$\frac{1}{4}$N	$\frac{3}{4}$N	0	—
	Laser [2]	front	$1\frac{9}{10}$P–$2\frac{9}{10}$P	$2\frac{2}{5}$P	$\frac{5}{12}$N–$\frac{7}{12}$P	$\frac{1}{12}$P	0	—
		rear	—	—	$1\frac{1}{4}$N–$\frac{1}{4}$N	$\frac{3}{4}$N	0	—
	Laser [3]	front	$1\frac{4}{5}$P–$2\frac{4}{5}$P	$2\frac{3}{10}$P	$\frac{1}{3}$N–$\frac{2}{3}$P	$\frac{1}{6}$P	0	—
		rear	—	—	$2\frac{1}{20}$N–$1\frac{1}{20}$N	$1\frac{11}{20}$N	0.14	—
	Talon [2]	front	$1\frac{9}{10}$P–$2\frac{9}{10}$P	$2\frac{2}{5}$P	$\frac{5}{12}$N–$\frac{7}{12}$P	$\frac{1}{12}$P	0	—
		rear	—	—	$1\frac{1}{4}$N–$\frac{1}{4}$P	$\frac{3}{4}$N	0	—
	Talon [3]	front	$1\frac{4}{5}$P–$2\frac{4}{5}$P	$2\frac{3}{10}$P	$\frac{1}{3}$N–$\frac{2}{3}$P	$\frac{1}{6}$P	0	—
		rear	—	—	$2\frac{1}{20}$N–$1\frac{1}{20}$P	$1\frac{11}{20}$N	0.14	—
1991	Summit	front	$1\frac{5}{6}$P–$2\frac{5}{6}$P	$2\frac{1}{3}$P	$\frac{1}{2}$N–$\frac{1}{2}$P	0	0	—
		rear	—	—	$1\frac{1}{6}$N–$\frac{1}{6}$N	$\frac{2}{3}$N	0	—
	Laser [1]	front	$1\frac{5}{16}$P–$2\frac{5}{6}$P	$2\frac{1}{3}$P	$\frac{4}{15}$N–$\frac{11}{15}$P	$\frac{7}{30}$P	0	—
		rear	—	—	$1\frac{1}{4}$N–$\frac{1}{4}$N	$\frac{3}{4}$N	0	—
	Laser [2]	front	$1\frac{9}{10}$P–$2\frac{9}{10}$P	$2\frac{2}{5}$P	$\frac{5}{12}$N–$\frac{7}{12}$P	$\frac{1}{12}$P	0	—
		rear	—	—	$1\frac{1}{4}$N–$\frac{1}{4}$N	$\frac{3}{4}$N	0	—
	Laser [3]	front	$1\frac{4}{5}$P–$2\frac{4}{5}$P	$2\frac{3}{10}$P	$\frac{1}{3}$N–$\frac{2}{3}$P	$\frac{1}{6}$P	0	—
		rear	—	—	$2\frac{1}{20}$N–$1\frac{1}{20}$N	$1\frac{11}{20}$N	0.14	—
	Talon [2]	front	$1\frac{9}{10}$P–$2\frac{9}{10}$P	$2\frac{2}{5}$P	$\frac{5}{12}$N–$\frac{7}{12}$P	$\frac{1}{12}$P	0	—
		rear	—	—	$1\frac{1}{4}$N–$\frac{1}{4}$P	$\frac{3}{4}$N	0	—
	Talon [3]	front	$1\frac{4}{5}$P–$2\frac{4}{5}$P	$2\frac{3}{10}$P	$\frac{1}{3}$N–$\frac{2}{3}$P	$\frac{1}{6}$P	0	—
		rear	—	—	$2\frac{1}{20}$N–$1\frac{1}{20}$P	$1\frac{11}{20}$N	0.14	—
	Stealth	front	$3\frac{5}{12}$P–$4\frac{5}{12}$P	$3\frac{11}{12}$P	$\frac{1}{2}$N–$\frac{1}{2}$P	0	0.12	—
		rear	—	—	[4]	[5]	0.01	—
1992	Summit	front	$1\frac{5}{6}$P–$2\frac{5}{6}$P	$2\frac{1}{3}$P	$\frac{1}{2}$N–$\frac{1}{2}$P	0	0	—
		rear	—	—	$1\frac{1}{6}$N–$\frac{1}{6}$N	$\frac{2}{3}$N	0	—
	Laser [1]	front	$1\frac{5}{16}$P–$2\frac{5}{6}$P	$2\frac{1}{3}$P	$\frac{4}{15}$N–$\frac{11}{15}$P	$\frac{7}{30}$P	0	—
		rear	—	—	$1\frac{1}{4}$N–$\frac{1}{4}$N	$\frac{3}{4}$N	0	—
	Laser [2]	front	$1\frac{9}{10}$P–$2\frac{9}{10}$P	$2\frac{2}{5}$P	$\frac{5}{12}$N–$\frac{7}{12}$P	$\frac{1}{12}$P	0	—
		rear	—	—	$1\frac{1}{4}$N–$\frac{1}{4}$N	$\frac{3}{4}$N	0	—
	Laser [3]	front	$1\frac{4}{5}$P–$2\frac{4}{5}$P	$2\frac{3}{10}$P	$\frac{1}{3}$N–$\frac{2}{3}$P	$\frac{1}{6}$P	0	—
		rear	—	—	$2\frac{1}{20}$N–$1\frac{1}{20}$N	$1\frac{11}{20}$N	0.14	—
	Talon [2]	front	$1\frac{9}{10}$P–$2\frac{9}{10}$P	$2\frac{2}{5}$P	$\frac{5}{12}$N–$\frac{7}{12}$P	$\frac{1}{12}$P	0	—
		rear	—	—	$1\frac{1}{4}$N–$\frac{1}{4}$P	$\frac{3}{4}$N	0	—
	Talon [3]	front	$1\frac{4}{5}$P–$2\frac{4}{5}$P	$2\frac{3}{10}$P	$\frac{1}{3}$N–$\frac{2}{3}$P	$\frac{1}{6}$P	0	—
		rear	—	—	$2\frac{1}{20}$N–$1\frac{1}{20}$P	$1\frac{11}{20}$N	0.14	—
	Stealth	front	$3\frac{5}{12}$P–$4\frac{5}{12}$P	$3\frac{11}{12}$P	$\frac{1}{2}$N–$\frac{1}{2}$P	0	0.12	—
		rear	—	—	[4]	[5]	0.01	—
	Summit Wagon [10]	front	[6]	[7]	[8]	[9]	0.12	—
		rear	—	—	1N–0	$\frac{1}{2}$N	0.08	—

WHEEL ALIGNMENT

Year	Model	Axle	Caster Range (deg.)	Caster Preferred Setting (deg.)	Camber Range (deg.)	Camber Preferred Setting (deg.)	Toe-in (in.)	Steering Axis Inclination (deg.)
1993-94	Summit	front	1⅚P–2⅚P	2⅓P	½N–½P	0	0	—
		rear	—	—	1⅙N–⅙N	⅔N	0	—
	Laser ①	front	1$\frac{5}{16}$P–2⅚P	2⅓P	$\frac{4}{15}$N–$\frac{11}{15}$P	$\frac{7}{30}$P	0	—
		rear	—	—	1¼N–¼N	¾N	0	—
	Laser ②	front	1$\frac{9}{10}$P–2$\frac{9}{10}$P	2⅖P	$\frac{5}{12}$N–$\frac{7}{12}$P	$\frac{1}{12}$P	0	—
		rear	—	—	1¼N–¼N	¾N	0	—
	Laser ③	front	1⅘P–2⅘P	2$\frac{3}{10}$P	⅓N–⅔P	⅙P	0	—
		rear	—	—	2$\frac{1}{20}$N–1$\frac{1}{20}$N	1$\frac{11}{20}$N	0.14	—
	Talon ②	front	1$\frac{9}{10}$P–2$\frac{9}{10}$P	2⅖P	$\frac{5}{12}$N–$\frac{7}{12}$P	$\frac{1}{12}$P	0	—
		rear	—	—	1¼N–¼P	¾N	0	—
	Talon ③	front	1⅘P–2⅘P	2$\frac{3}{10}$P	⅓N–⅔P	⅙P	0	—
		rear	—	—	2$\frac{1}{20}$N–1$\frac{1}{20}$P	1$\frac{11}{20}$N	0.14	—
	Stealth	front	3$\frac{5}{12}$P–4$\frac{5}{12}$P	3$\frac{11}{12}$P	½N–½P	0	0.12	—
		rear	—	—	④	⑤	0.01	—
	Summit Wagon ⑩	front	⑥	⑦	⑧	⑨	0.12	—
		rear	—	—	1N–0	½N	0.08	—

N—Negative
P—Positive
① 1.8L engine
② 2.0L engine with FWD
③ AWD—All Wheel Drive
④ FWD: ½N–½P
   AWD: ⅔N–⅓P
⑤ FWD: 0
   AWD: ⅙N
⑥ FWD: 1½P–2⅚P
   AWD: 1$\frac{5}{12}$P–2¾P

⑦ FWD: 2⅙P
   AWD: 2½P
⑧ FWD: $\frac{1}{16}$N–$\frac{5}{16}$P
   AWD: ⅙P–1$\frac{1}{16}$P
⑨ FWD: ⅓P
   AWD: ⅔P
⑩ Camber & Caster are preset and cannot be adjusted. If Camber is not within specifications, check for bent or damaged parts.

AIR CONDITIONING BELT TENSION

Year	Model	Engine Displacement Liters (cc)	Belt Type	Specifications (lbs.) New	Specifications (lbs.) Used
1990	Summit	1.5 (1468)	Poly-V	0.23	0.25
	Summit	1.6 (1597)	Poly-V	0.21	0.25
	Laser	1.8 (1754)	Poly-V	0.18	0.23
	Laser	2.0 (2000)	Poly-V	0.20	0.23
	Talon	2.0 (2000)	Poly-V	0.20	0.23
1991	Laser	1.8 (1754)	Poly-V	0.16–0.20①	0.22–0.24①
	Talon	1.8 (1754)	Poly-V	0.16–0.20①	0.22–0.24①
	Laser	2.0 (2000)	Poly-V	0.18–0.20①	0.22–0.24①
	Talon	2.0 (1754)	Poly-V	0.18–0.20①	0.22–0.24①
	Stealth	3.0 (2967) ③	Poly-V	0.26–0.27①	0.27–0.33①
	Stealth	3.0 (2967) ④	Poly-V	0.14–0.16①	0.16–0.20①
	Summit	1.5 (1468)	Poly-V	0.20–0.23①	0.23–0.28①

AIR CONDITIONING BELT TENSION

Year	Model	Engine Displacement Liters (cc)	Belt Type	Specifications (lbs.) New	Used
1992	Laser	1.8 (1754)	Poly-V	0.16–0.20①	0.22–0.24①
	Talon	1.8 (1754)	Poly-V	0.16–0.20①	0.22–0.24①
	Laser	2.0 (2000)	Poly-V	0.18–0.20①	0.22–0.24①
	Talon	2.0 (1754)	Poly-V	0.18–0.20①	0.22–0.24①
	Stealth	3.0 (2967)③	Poly-V	0.26–0.27①	0.27–0.33①
	Stealth	3.0 (2967)④	Poly-V	0.14–0.16①	0.16–0.20①
	Summit	1.5 (1468)	Poly-V	0.20–0.23①	0.23–0.28①
	Summit	1.8 (1834)	Poly-V	0.20–0.23①	0.23–0.28①
	Summit Wagon	1.8 (1834)	Poly-V	0.22–0.24①	0.27–0.30①
	Summit Wagon	2.4 (2350)	Poly-V	0.15①	0.17①
1993–94	Laser	1.8 (1754)	Poly-V	0.16–0.20①	0.22–0.24①
	Talon	1.8 (1754)	Poly-V	0.16–0.20①	0.22–0.24①
	Laser	2.0 (2000)	Poly-V	0.18–0.20①	0.22–0.24①
	Talon	2.0 (1754)	Poly-V	0.18–0.20①	0.22–0.24①
	Stealth	3.0 (2967)③	Poly-V	0.26–0.28①	0.28–0.33①
	Stealth	3.0 (2967)④	Poly-V	0.14–0.16①	0.16–0.20①
	Summit	1.5 (1468)	Poly-V	0.20–0.24①	0.24–0.28①
	Summit	1.8 (1834)	Poly-V	0.20–0.24①	0.24–0.28①
	Summit Wagon	1.8 (1834)	Poly-V	0.22–0.24①	0.27–0.30①
	Summit Wagon	2.4 (2350)	Poly-V	0.15①	0.17①

① Except where noted, specification is inches of deflection at center of longest run of belt with standard deflection gauge

② Equipped with automatic tensioner
③ SOHC—Single Overhead Cam
④ DOHC—Dual Overhead Cam

REFRIGERANT CAPACITIES

Year	Model	Refrigerant (oz.)	Oil (fl. oz.)	Compressor Type
1990	Summit	36.0	9.8①	10PA17
	Laser	32.0	6.0①	10PA17
	Talon	32.0	6.0①	R-12
1991	Laser	33.0	2.7	10PA17
	Talon	33.0	2.7	10PA17
	Stealth	34.0	5.4	FX-105VS
	Summit	36.0	5.1	FX-105V
1992	Laser	33.0	2.7	10PA17
	Talon	33.0	2.7	10PA17
	Stealth	34.0	5.4	FX-105VS
	Summit	36.0	5.1	FX-105V
	Summit Wagon	30.0	2.7	10PA17
1993	Laser	33.0	2.7	10PA17
	Talon	33.0	2.7	10PA17
	Stealth	29.0	5.4	FX-105VS
	Summit	26.0–30.0	4.4	FX-105VS or VL
	Summit Wagon	30.0	2.7	10PA15

NOTE: At the time of publication, refrigerant capacity information relating to R-134a was not available from the manufacturer.
① Cubic inches

MAINTENANCE INTERVALS—TYPE A: NORMAL SERVICE
Laser • Stealth • Summit • Summit Wagon • Talon

TO BE SERVICED	TYPE OF SERVICE	VEHICLE MILEAGE INTERVAL (X1000)							
		7.5	15	22.5	30	37.5	45	52.5	60
Oxygen Sensor	I				✔				✔
Vacuum Lines and Hoses	I		✔		✔		✔		✔
Ignition Wires	I				✔				✔
Spark Plugs	R①				✔				✔
Engine Oil	R②	✔	✔	✔	✔	✔	✔	✔	✔
Engine Air Cleaner Element	R				✔				✔
Crankcase Emission Filter	R				✔				✔
PCV Valve	I				✔				✔
Fuel Filter	R			✔			✔		✔
Charcoal Canister	I				✔				✔
Fuel/Vapor Return Lines	I				✔				✔
Fuel Tank Cap and Restrictor	I				✔				✔
Coolant System	R				✔				✔
Exhaust Pipe and Muffler	I				✔				✔
Engine Oil Filter	R③		✔		✔		✔		✔
Catalytic Converter and Shield	I				✔				✔
EGR System	I				✔				✔
Chassis Lubrication	L	✔	✔	✔	✔	✔	✔	✔	✔
CV-Joints and Boots	I		✔		✔		✔		✔
Battery Connections	I		✔		✔		✔		✔
Timing Belt	R④								
Idle Speed System	I				✔				
Throttle Body Mounting Torque	I	✔							
Drive Belts	I				✔				✔
Automatic Transaxle Fluid	R								✔
Manual Transaxle Fulid	I				✔				✔
Brake Linings	I		✔		✔		✔		✔
Parking Brake	I		✔		✔		✔		✔
Seat Belt Operation	I				✔				✔

FOR COMPLETE WARRANTY COVERAGE CONSULT INDIVIDUAL VEHICLE MANUFACTURER'S WARRANTY MAINTENANCE GUIDE.

I—Inspect
L—Lubricate
R—Replace
① On Stealth with Platinum spark plugs, replace at 60,000 miles
② On turbo engines, change oil every 5,000 miles
③ On turbo engines, change oil filter every 10,000 miles
④ Replace timing belt at 60,000 miles

MAINTENANCE INTERVALS—TYPE B: SEVERE SERVICE
Laser • Stealth • Summit • Summit Wagon • Talon

TO BE SERVICED	TYPE OF SERVICE	VEHICLE MILEAGE INTERVAL (X1000)									
		3	6	9	12	15	18	21	24	27	30
Oxygen Sensor	I										✔
Vacuum Lines and Hoses	I					✔					✔
Ignition Wires	I										✔
Spark Plugs	R①					✔					✔
Engine Oil	R②	✔	✔	✔	✔	✔	✔	✔	✔	✔	✔
Engine Air Cleaner Element	R					✔					✔
Crankcase Emission Filter	R					✔					✔
PCV Valve	R										✔
Fuel Filter	R					✔					✔
Fuel/Vapor Return Lines	I										✔
Fuel Tank Cap and Restrictor	I										✔
Coolant System	R					✔					✔
Exhaust Pipe and Muffler	I										✔
Engine Oil Filter	R②		✔		✔		✔		✔		✔
Catalytic Converter and Shield	I										✔
EGR System	I										✔
Chassis Lubrication	L		✔		✔		✔		✔		✔
CV-Joints and Boots	I	✔	✔	✔	✔	✔	✔	✔	✔	✔	✔
Battery Connections	I					✔					✔
Timing Belt	R③										
Idle Speed System	I										✔
Throttle Body Mounting Torque	I		✔								
Drive Belts	I					✔					✔
Automatic Transaxle Fluid	R					✔					✔
Manual Transaxle Fluid	I					✔					✔
Brake Linings	I					✔					✔
Parking Brake	I					✔					✔
Seat Belt Operation	I										✔

FOR COMPLETE WARRANTY COVERAGE CONSULT INDIVIDUAL VEHICLE MANUFACTURER'S WARRANTY MAINTENANCE GUIDE.

I—Inspect
L—Lubricate
R—Replace
① On Stealth vehicles with Platinum spark
   plugs—replace at 60,000 miles
② On Turbo engines change oil and filter every
   3,000 miles
③ Replace timing belt at 60,000 miles

FIRING ORDERS

NOTE: To avoid confusion, always replace spark plugs and wires one at a time.

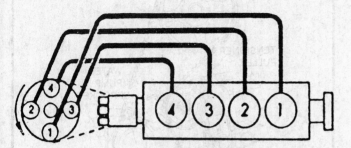

1991–94 1.5L and 1992–94 1.8L Engines
Engine Firing Order: 1-3-4-2
Distributor Rotation: Counterclockwise

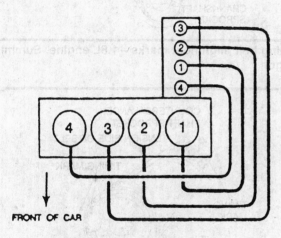

1.6L and 2.0L Engines
Engine Firing Order: 1-3-4-2
Distributorless Ignition System

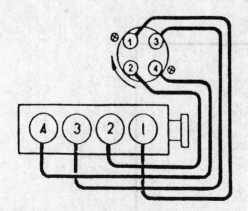

1990 1.5L, 1.8L and 1992–94 2.4L Engines
Engine Firing Order: 1-3-4-2
Distributor Rotation: Clockwise

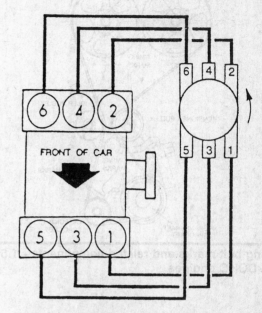

3.0L SOHC Engine
Engine Firing Order: 1-2-3-4-5-6
Distributor Rotation: Counterclockwise

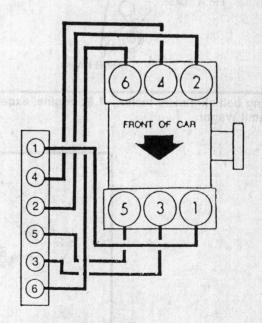

3.0L DOHC Engine
Engine Firing Order: 1-2-3-4-5-6
Distributorless Ignition System

TIMING BELT ALIGNMENT MARKS

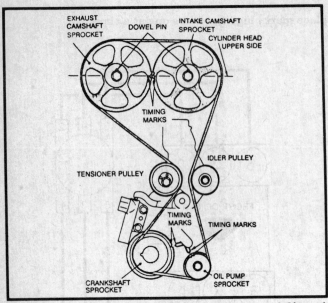

Timing belt marks and related components—1.6L and 2.0L DOHC engines

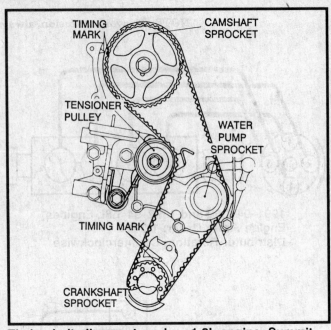

Timing belt alignment marks—1.8L engine, Summit Wagon

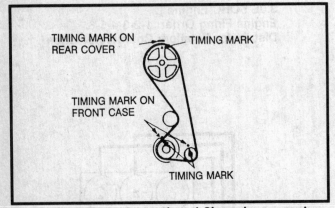

Timing belt alignment marks—1.8L engine, except Summit Wagon

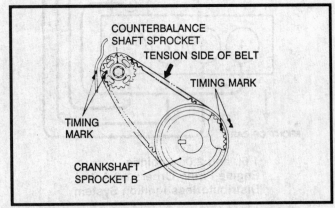

Inner timing belt alignment marks—2.4L engine

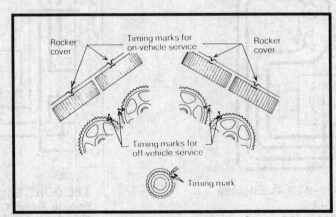

Timing belt alignment marks—3.0L engine

TIMING BELT ALIGNMENT MARKS

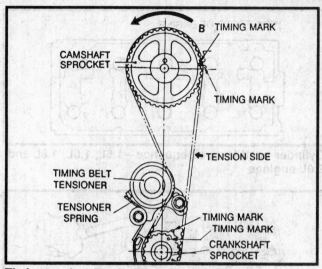

Timing marks alignment—1.5L engine

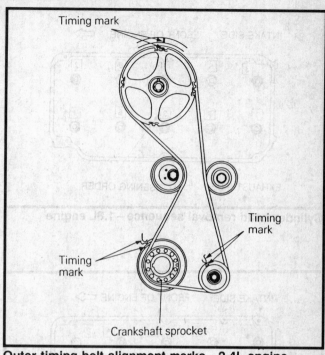

Outer timing belt alignment marks—2.4L engine

AIR CONDITIONING SERVICE VALVE LOCATIONS

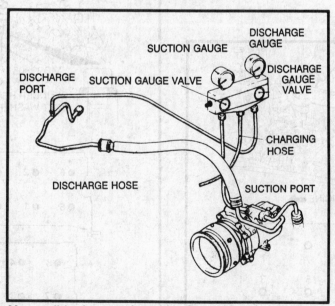

Air conditioning service valve location

CYLINDER HEAD TORQUE SEQUENCES

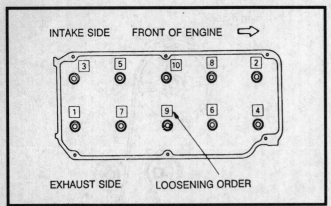

Cylinder head removal sequence—1.8L engine

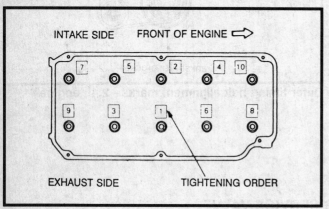

Cylinder head torque sequence—1.8L engine

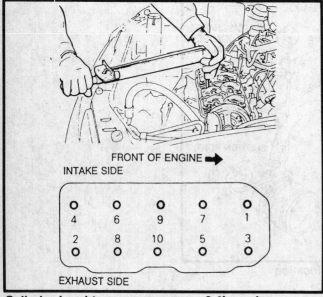

Cylinder head torque sequence—2.4L engine

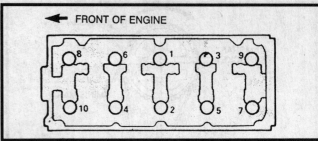

Cylinder head torque sequence—1.5L, 1.6L, 1.8L and 2.0L engines

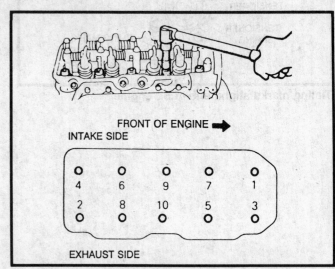

Cylinder head removal sequence—2.4L engine

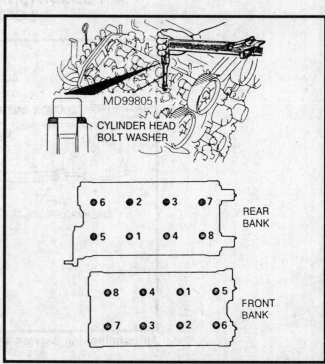

Cylinder head torque sequence—3.0L engine

TIMING MARK LOCATIONS

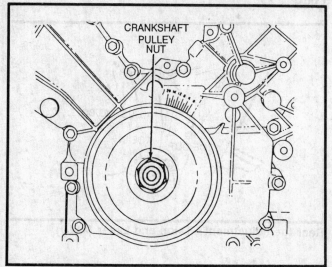

Timing mark location—2.0L engine

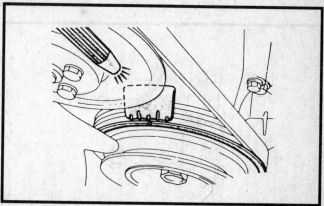

Timing mark location—1.5L, 1.8L and 2.4L engines

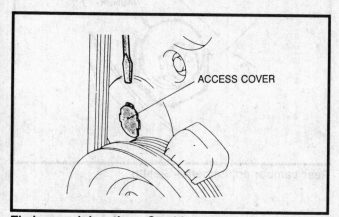

Timing mark location—Stealth

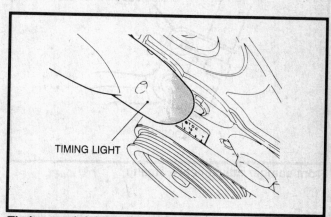

Timing mark location—1.8L engine

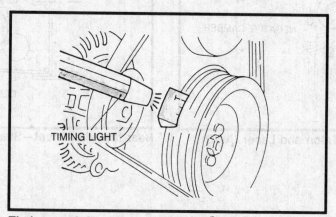

Timing mark location—2.4L engine

WHEEL ALIGNMENT ADJUSTMENT
LOCATIONS

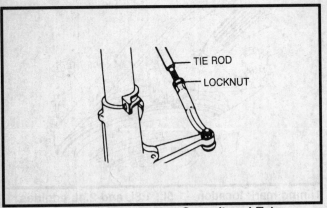

Front toe adjustment—Laser, Summit and Talon

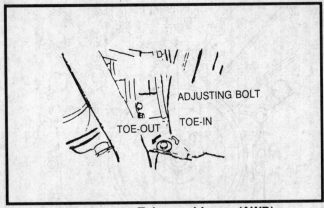

Rear toe adjustment—Talon and Laser (AWD)

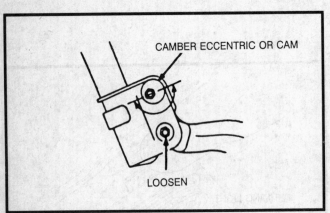

Front camber adjustment—Stealth

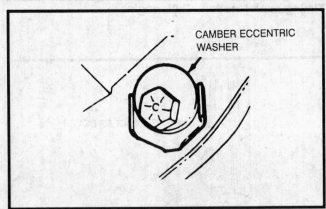

Rear camber adjustment—Stealth

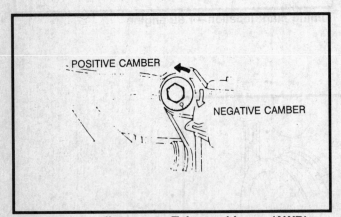

Rear camber adjustment—Talon and Laser (AWD)

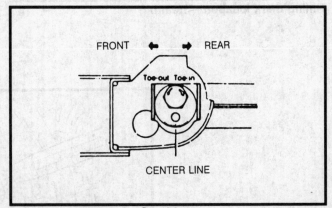

Rear toe adjustment—Stealth

SPECIFICATION CHARTS

VEHICLE IDENTIFICATION CHART

It is important for servicing and ordering parts to be certain of the vehicle and engine identification. The VIN (vehicle identification number) is a 17 digit number visible through the windshield on the driver's side of the dash and contains the vehicle and engine identification codes. The tenth digit indicates model year and the eighth digit indicates engine code. It can be interpreted as follows:

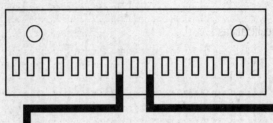

Engine Code							Model Year	
Code	Liters	Cu. In. (cc)	Cyl.	Fuel Sys.	Eng. Mfg.		Code	Year
U	3.0	180 (2950)	6	MPI	Renault		L	1990
							M	1991
							N	1992

MPI—Multi Port Injection

ENGINE IDENTIFICATION

Year	Model	Engine Displacement Liters (cc)	Engine Series (ID/VIN)	Fuel System	No. of Cylinders	Engine Type
1990	Premier	3.0 (2950)	U	MPI	6	SOHC
	Monaco	3.0 (2950)	U	MPI	6	SOHC
1991	Premier	3.0 (2950)	U	MPI	6	SOHC
	Monaco	3.0 (2950)	U	MPI	6	SOHC
1992	Premier	3.0 (2950)	U	MPI	6	SOHC
	Monaco	3.0 (2950)	U	MPI	6	SOHC

MPI—Multi-Point Fuel Injection
SOHC—Single Overhead Camshaft

GENERAL ENGINE SPECIFICATIONS

Year	Engine ID/VIN	Engine Displacement Liters (cc)	Fuel System Type	Net Horsepower @ rpm	Net Torque @ rpm (ft. lbs.)	Bore × Stroke (in.)	Compression Ratio	Oil Pressure @ rpm
1990	U	3.0 (2950)	MPI	150 @ 5000	171 @ 3750	3.66 × 2.87	9.3:1	60 @ 4000
1991	U	3.0 (2950)	MPI	150 @ 5000	171 @ 3750	3.66 × 2.87	9.3:1	60 @ 4000
1992	U	3.0 (2950)	MPI	150 @ 5000	171 @ 3750	3.66 × 2.87	9.3:1	60 @ 4000

MPI—Multi-Point Fuel Injection

GASOLINE ENGINE TUNE-UP SPECIFICATIONS

Year	Engine ID/VIN	Engine Displacement Liters (cc)	Spark Plugs Gap (in.)	Ignition Timing (deg.) MT	Ignition Timing (deg.) AT	Fuel Pump (psi)	Idle Speed (rpm) MT	Idle Speed (rpm) AT	Valve Clearance In.	Valve Clearance Ex.
1990	U	3.0 (2950)	0.035	①	①	28–30	700	700	Hyd.	Hyd.
1991	U	3.0 (2950)	0.035	①	①	②	①	①	Hyd.	Hyd.
1992	U	3.0 (2950)	0.035	①	①	43	①	①	Hyd.	Hyd.

NOTE: The lowest cylinder pressure should be within 75% of the highest cylinder pressure reading. For example, if the highest cylinder is 134 psi, the lowest should be 101. Engine should be at normal operating temperature with throttle valve in the wide open position.

The underhood specifications sticker often reflects tune-up specification changes in production. Sticker figures must be used if they disagree with those in this chart.

Hyd.—Hydraulic

① Refer to Underhood Specifications Sticker

② Vehicles built before 10-9-91: 28–31 psi
   Vehicles built after 10-9-91: 43 psi

CAPACITIES

Year	Model	Engine ID/VIN	Engine Displacement Liters (cc)	Engine Crankcase with Filter (qts.)	Transmission (pts.) 4-Spd	Transmission (pts.) 5-Spd	Transmission (pts.) Auto.	Drive Axle Front (pts.)	Drive Axle Rear (pts.)	Fuel Tank (gal.)	Cooling System (qts.)
1990	Premier	U	3.0 (2950)	6.0	—	—	14.7②	1.32①	—	17	8.6
	Monaco	U	3.0 (2950)	6.0	—	—	14.7②	1.32①	—	17	8.6
1991	Premier	U	3.0 (2950)	6.0	—	—	14.7②	1.32①	—	17	9.5
	Monaco	U	3.0 (2950)	6.0	—	—	14.7②	1.32①	—	17	9.5
1992	Premier	U	3.0 (2950)	6.0	—	—	14.7②	1.32①	—	17	9.5
	Monaco	U	3.0 (2950)	6.0	—	—	14.7②	1.32①	—	17	9.5

① The differential requires a synthetic-type SAE grade 75W-140 gear lubricant. It is the only recommended lubricant. It is factory filled and designed to last the life of the differential under normal conditions.

② The ZF-4 transaxle requires Mopar Mercon automatic transmission fluid only. No substitutions are to be made.

CAMSHAFT SPECIFICATIONS

All measurements given in inches.

Year	Engine ID/VIN	Engine Displacement Liters (cc)	Journal Diameter 1	2	3	4	5	Elevation In.	Elevation Ex.	Bearing Clearance	Camshaft End Play
1990	U	3.0 (2950)	NA	NA	NA	NA	—	NA	NA	NA	0.003–0.005
1991	U	3.0 (2950)	NA	NA	NA	NA	—	NA	NA	NA	0.003–0.005
1992	U	3.0 (2950)	NA	NA	NA	NA	—	NA	NA	NA	0.003–0.005

NA—Not available

CRANKSHAFT AND CONNECTING ROD SPECIFICATIONS

All measurements are given in inches.

			Crankshaft				Connecting Rod		
Year	Engine ID/VIN	Engine Displacement Liters (cc)	Main Brg. Journal Dia.	Main Brg. Oil Clearance	Shaft End-play	Thrust on No.	Journal Diameter	Oil Clearance	Side Clearance
1990	U	3.0 (2950)	2.7576–2.7583	0.0015–0.0035	0.003–0.010	1	2.3611–2.3618	0.0008–0.0030	0.008–0.015
1991	U	3.0 (2950)	2.7576–2.7583	0.0015–0.0035	0.003–0.010	1	2.3611–2.3618	0.0008–0.0030	0.008–0.015
1992	U	3.0 (2950)	2.7576–2.7583	0.0015–0.0035	0.003–0.010	1	2.3611–2.3618	0.0008–0.0030	0.008–0.015

VALVE SPECIFICATIONS

							Stem-to-Guide Clearance (in.)		Stem Diameter (in.)	
Year	Engine ID/VIN	Engine Displacement Liters (cc)	Seat Angle (deg.)	Face Angle (deg.)	Spring Test Pressure (lbs. @ in.)	Spring Installed Height (in.)	Intake	Exhaust	Intake	Exhaust
1990	U	3.0 (2950)	45	45	155 @ 1.220	1¹³⁄₁₆	NA	NA	0.315	0.315
1991	U	3.0 (2950)	45	45	155 @ 1.220	1¹³⁄₁₆	NA	NA	0.315	0.315
1992	U	3.0 (2950)	45	45	155 @ 1.220	1¹³⁄₁₆	NA	NA	0.315	0.315

NA—Not available

PISTON AND RING SPECIFICATIONS

All measurements are given in inches.

				Ring Gap			Ring Side Clearance		
Year	Engine ID/VIN	Engine Displacement Liters (cc)	Piston Clearance	Top Compression	Bottom Compression	Oil Control	Top Compression	Bottom Compression	Oil Control
1990	U	3.0 (2950)	NA	0.016–0.022	0.016–0.022	NA	0.0010–0.0020	0.0010–0.0020	0.0015–0.0035
1991	U	3.0 (2950)	NA	0.016–0.022	0.016–0.022	NA	0.0010–0.0020	0.0010–0.0020	0.0015–0.0035
1992	U	3.0 (2950)	NA	0.016–0.022	0.016–0.022	NA	0.0010–0.0020	0.0010–0.0020	0.0015–0.0035

NA—Not available

TORQUE SPECIFICATIONS

All readings in ft. lbs.

								Manifold			
Year	Engine ID/VIN	Engine Displacement Liters (cc)	Cylinder Head Bolts	Main Bearing Bolts	Rod Bearing Bolts	Crankshaft Damper Bolts	Flywheel Bolts	Intake	Exhaust	Spark Plugs	Lug Nut ③
1990	U	3.0 (2950)	①	②	35	133	48–54	11	13	11	90
1991	U	3.0 (2950)	①	②	35	133	48–54	11	13	11	90
1992	U	3.0 (2950)	①	②	35	133	48–54	11	13	11	90

① See text
② Tighten in 2 steps, in sequence:
  1st—20 ft. lbs.
  2nd—Angular torque 75 degrees
③ Specification given for aluminum wheels.
  Tighten steel wheels to 63 ft. lbs.

TORQUE SPECIFICATIONS

Component	English	Metric
Camshaft sprocket bolt:	59 ft. lbs.	80 Nm
Camshaft thrust plate mounting bolt:	9 ft. lbs.	12 Nm
Connecting rod bearing cap bolts:	35 ft. lbs.	48 Nm
Crankshaft pulley bolt:	133 ft. lbs.	180 Nm
Crankshaft rear seal housing bolts:	9 ft. lbs.	12 Nm
Cylinder head bolt		
Step 1:	44 ft. lbs.	60 Nm
Step 2:	Loosen all bolts	Loosen all bolts
Step 3:	30 ft. lbs.	40 Nm
Step 4:		
1990 vehicles	70 ft. lbs.	95 Nm
1991–92 vehicles	80 ft. lbs.	108 Nm
EGR valve-to-intake plenum:	20 ft. lbs.	27 Nm
Engine cradle mounting bolt:	92 ft. lbs.	125 Nm
Engine damper bottom locknut:	20 ft. lbs.	27 Nm
Engine damper top nut:	32 ft. lbs.	43 Nm
Engine mount nut:	48 ft. lbs.	65 Nm
Engine mount stud locknut:	48 ft. lbs.	65 Nm
Engine-to-transaxle:	32 ft. lbs.	43 Nm
Exhaust manifold	13 ft. lbs.	17 Nm
Exhaust pipe-to-exhaust manifold nuts:	25 ft. lbs.	34 Nm
Flexplate-to-converter bolts:	24 ft. lbs.	33 Nm
Front engine mount through bolt:	48 ft. lbs.	65 Nm
Idler pulley-to-timing cover bolt:	30 ft. lbs.	40 Nm
Intake manifold:	11ft. lbs.	15 Nm
Main bearing cap bolts		
Step 1:	20 ft. lbs.	30 Nm
Step 2:	+ 75 degrees turn	+ 75 degrees turn
Oil pan:	9 ft. lbs.	12 Nm
Oil pan drain plug:	22 ft. lbs.	30 Nm
Oil pump attaching bolts:	9 ft. lbs.	12 Nm
Oil pump cover bolts:	9 ft. lbs.	12 Nm
Oil pump sump-to-block bolts:	9 ft. lbs.	12 Nm
Rocker arm shaft bolt:	53 inch. lbs.	6 Nm
Rocker (valve) cover:	9 ft. lbs.	12 Nm
Spark plug:	11 ft. lbs.	15 Nm
Starter-to-block bolts:	31 ft. lbs.	42 Nm
Thermostat housing:	20 ft. lbs.	27 Nm
Throttle body-to-manifold bolts:	13 ft. lbs.	18 Nm
Timing case cover bolt:	9 ft. lbs.	12 Nm
Timing chain guide mounting bolts:	53 inch lbs.	6 Nm
Timing chain tensioner mounting bolts:	53 inch lbs.	6 Nm
Timing chain tensioner shoe bolts:	9 ft. lbs.	12 Nm
Torque converter-to-flexplate bolts:	24 ft. lbs.	33 Nm
Water pump:	20 ft. lbs.	27 Nm

BRAKE SPECIFICATIONS
All measurements in inches unless noted.

Year	Model		Master Cylinder Bore	Brake Disc Original Thickness	Brake Disc Minimum Thickness	Brake Disc Maximum Runout	Brake Drum Diameter Original Inside Diameter	Brake Drum Diameter Max. Wear Limit	Brake Drum Diameter Maximum Machine Diameter	Minimum Lining Thickness Front	Minimum Lining Thickness Rear
1990	Premier	front	0.945	0.866	0.807	0.003	—	—	NA	0.236	0.236
		rear	—	0.393	0.374	0.003	8.858	8.917	NA	0.132	0.132
	Monaco	front	0.945	0.866	0.807	0.003	—	—	NA	0.236	0.236
		rear	—	0.393	0.374	0.003	8.858	8.917	NA	0.132	0.132
1991	Premier	front	0.945	0.950	0.890	0.003	—	—	NA	0.160	0.160
		rear	—	0.393	0.374	0.003	8.858	8.917	NA	0.060	0.060
	Monaco	front	0.945	0.950	0.890	0.003	—	—	NA	0.160	0.160
		rear	—	0.393	0.374	0.003	8.858	8.917	NA	0.060	0.060
1992	Premier	front	0.945	0.950	0.890	0.003	—	—	NA	0.160	0.160
		rear	—	0.393	0.374	0.003	8.858	8.917	NA	0.060	0.060
	Monaco	front	0.945	0.950	0.890	0.003	—	—	NA	0.160	0.160
		rear	—	0.393	0.374	0.003	8.858	8.917	NA	0.060	0.060

NA—Not available

WHEEL ALIGNMENT

Year	Model	Caster Range (deg.)	Caster Preferred Setting (deg.)	Camber Range (deg.)	Camber Preferred Setting (deg.)	Toe-out (in.)	Steering Axis Inclination (deg.)
1990	Premier	$1\frac{1}{2}P$–$2\frac{1}{2}P$	2P	$\frac{9}{16}N$–$\frac{1}{16}N$	$\frac{5}{16}N$	0	NA
	Monaco	$1\frac{1}{2}P$–$2\frac{1}{2}P$	2P	$\frac{9}{16}N$–$\frac{1}{16}N$	$\frac{5}{16}N$	0	NA
1991	Premier	$1\frac{1}{2}P$–$2\frac{1}{2}P$	2P	$\frac{9}{16}N$–$\frac{1}{16}N$	$\frac{5}{16}N$	0	NA
	Monaco	$1\frac{1}{2}P$–$2\frac{1}{2}P$	2P	$\frac{9}{16}N$–$\frac{1}{16}N$	$\frac{5}{16}N$	0	NA
1992	Premier	$1\frac{1}{2}P$–$2\frac{1}{2}P$	2P	$\frac{9}{16}N$–$\frac{1}{16}N$	$\frac{5}{16}N$	0	NA
	Monaco	$1\frac{1}{2}P$–$2\frac{1}{2}P$	2P	$\frac{9}{16}N$–$\frac{1}{16}N$	$\frac{5}{16}N$	0	NA

NA—Not applicable
N—Negative
P—Positive

AIR CONDITIONING BELT TENSION

Year	Model	Engine Displacement Liters (cc)	Belt Type	Specifications New	Specifications Used
1990	Monaco	3.0 (2950)	Serpentine	180–200 lbs.	140–160 lbs.
	Premier	3.0 (2950)	Serpentine	180–200 lbs.	140–160 lbs.
1991	Monaco	3.0 (2950)	Serpentine	180–200 lbs.	140–160 lbs.
	Premier	3.0 (2950)	Serpentine	180–200 lbs.	140–160 lbs.
1992	Monaco	3.0 (2950)	Serpentine	180–200 lbs.	140–160 lbs.
	Premier	3.0 (2950)	Serpentine	180–200 lbs.	140–160 lbs.

REFRIGERANT CAPACITIES

Year	Model	Refrigerant (oz.)	Oil (fl. oz.)	Compressor Type
1990	Monaco	36.0	8.1	SD-709
	Premier	36.0	8.1	SD-709
1991	Monaco	36.0	8.1	SD-709
	Premier	36.0	8.1	SD-709
1992	Monaco	36.0	8.1	SD-709
	Premier	36.0	8.1	SD-709

MAINTENANCE INTERVALS—TYPE A: NORMAL SERVICE
Monaco • Premier

TO BE SERVICED	TYPE OF SERVICE	VEHICLE MILEAGE INTERVAL (X1000)							
		7.5	15	22.5	30	37.5	45	52.5	60
Oxygen Sensor	I				✔				✔
Tire Rotation	I	✔		✔		✔		✔	
Vacuum Lines and Hoses	I				✔				✔
Ignition Wires	I				✔				✔
Spark Plugs	R				✔				✔
Engine Oil and Filter	R	✔	✔	✔	✔	✔	✔	✔	✔
Engine Air Cleaner Element	R				✔				✔
Crankcase Emission Filter	R				✔				✔
PCV Valve	R				✔				✔
Fuel Filter	R				✔				✔
Engine Oil Filter	R	✔		✔		✔		✔	
Fuel/Vapor Return Lines	I				✔				✔
Fuel Tank Cap and Restrictor	I				✔				✔
Coolant System	R				✔				✔
Exhaust Pipe and Muffler	I				✔				✔
Catalytic Converter and Shield	I				✔				✔
EGR System	I				✔				✔
Coolant Hoses and Clamps	I				✔				✔
Chassis Lubrication	L	✔		✔		✔		✔	
CV-Joints and Boots	I	✔	✔	✔	✔	✔	✔	✔	✔
Automatic Transaxle Fluid	R								✔
Battery Connections	I		✔		✔		✔		✔
Throttle Body Mounting Torque	I	✔							
Drive Belts	I				✔				✔
Brake Linings	I				✔				✔
Parking Brake	I		✔		✔		✔		✔
Seat Belt Operation	I		✔		✔		✔		✔

FOR COMPLETE WARRANTY COVERAGE CONSULT INDIVIDUAL VEHICLE MANUFACTURER'S WARRANTY MAINTENANCE GUIDE.

I—Inspect
L—Lubricate
R—Replace

MAINTENANCE INTERVALS—TYPE B: SEVERE SERVICE
Monaco • Premier

TO BE SERVICED	TYPE OF SERVICE	VEHICLE MILEAGE INTERVAL (X1000)									
		3	6	9	12	15	18	21	24	27	30
Oxygen Sensor	I										✔
Tire Rotation	I		✔		✔		✔		✔		✔
Vacuum Lines and Hoses	I					✔					✔
Ignition Wires	I										✔
Spark Plugs	R										✔
Engine Oil and Filter	R	✔	✔	✔	✔	✔	✔	✔	✔	✔	✔
Engine Air Cleaner Element	R					✔					✔
Crankcase Emission Filter	R										✔
PCV Valve	R										✔
Fuel Filter	R					✔					✔
Fuel/Vapor Return Lines	I										✔
Fuel Tank Cap and Restrictor	I										✔
Coolant System	R										✔
Exhaust Pipe and Muffler	I					✔					✔
Catalytic Converter and Shield	I					✔					✔
EGR System	I					✔					✔
Coolant Hoses and Clamps	I					✔					✔
Chassis Lubrication	L		✔		✔		✔		✔		✔
CV-Joints and Boots	I	✔	✔	✔	✔	✔	✔	✔	✔	✔	✔
Automatic Transaxle Fluid	R					✔					✔
Battery Connections	I					✔					✔
Throttle Body Mounting Torque	I		✔								
Drive Belts	I					✔					✔
Brake Linings	I					✔					✔
Parking Brake	I					✔					✔
Seat Belt Operation	I					✔					✔

FOR COMPLETE WARRANTY COVERAGE CONSULT INDIVIDUAL VEHICLE MANUFACTURER'S WARRANTY MAINTENANCE GUIDE.

I—Inspect
L—Lubricate
R—Replace

FIRING ORDERS

NOTE: To avoid confusion, always replace spark plug wires one at a time.

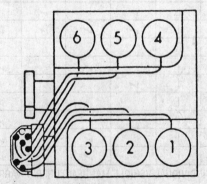

1990 3.0L Engine (Built before Oct. 9, 1991)
Engine Firing Order: 1-6-3-5-2-4
Distributor Rotation: Counterclockwise

FIRING ORDERS

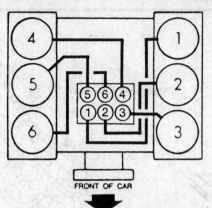

1991–94 3.0L Engine (Built on or after Oct. 9, 1991)
Engine Firing Order: 1-6-3-5-2-4
Distributorless Ignition System

CYLINDER HEAD TORQUE SEQUENCES

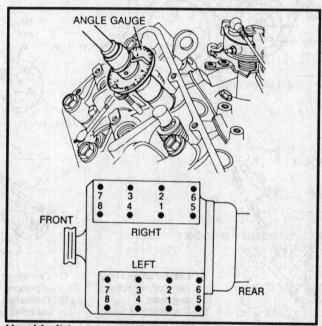

Head bolt torque sequence and torque angle gauge–
3.0L engine

TIMING MARK LOCATIONS

Timing scale near crankshaft pulley–3.0L engine

TIMING CHAIN ALIGNMENT MARKS

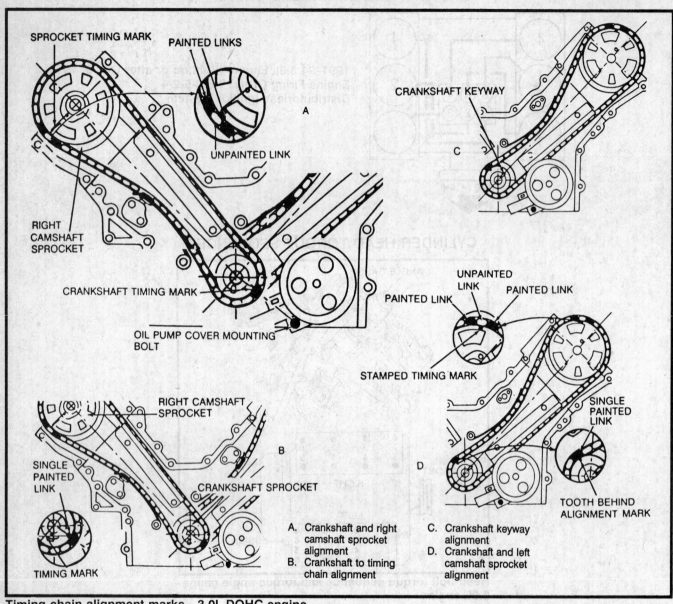

A. Crankshaft and right camshaft sprocket alignment
B. Crankshaft to timing chain alignment
C. Crankshaft keyway alignment
D. Crankshaft and left camshaft sprocket alignment

Timing chain alignment marks—3.0L DOHC engine

AIR CONDITIONING SERVICE VALVE LOCATIONS

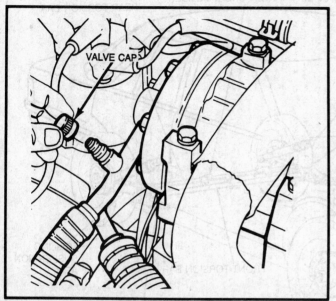

High pressure service valve location—Monaco and Premier

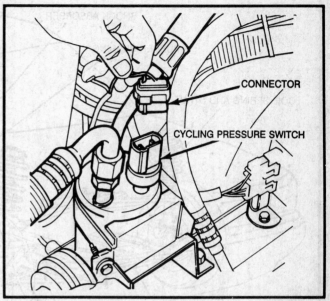

Low pressure service valve location—Monaco and Premier

WHEEL ALIGNMENT ADJUSTMENT LOCATIONS

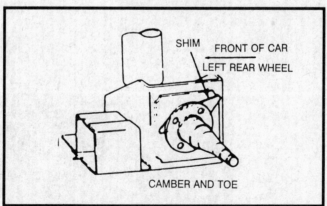

Rear camber and toe adjustment

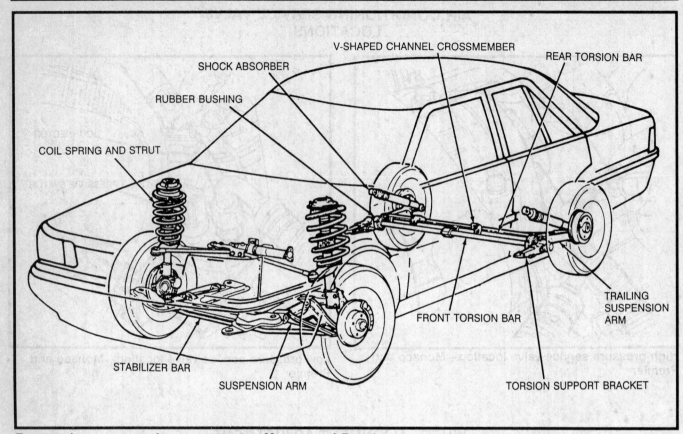

Front and rear suspension components—Monaco and Premier

SPECIFICATION CHARTS

VEHICLE IDENTIFICATION CHART

It is important for servicing and ordering parts to be certain of the vehicle and engine identification. The VIN (vehicle identification number) is a 17 digit number visible through the windshield on the driver's side of the dash and contains the vehicle and engine identification codes. The tenth digit indicates model year and the eighth digit indicates engine code. It can be interpreted as follows:

Engine Code						*Model Year*	
Code	Liters	Cu. In. (cc)	Cyl.	Fuel Sys.	Eng. Mfg.	Code	Year
A (1990)	2.2	135 (2213)	4	Turbo II	Chrysler	L	1990
A (1991–93)	2.2	135 (2213)	4	Turbo III	Chrysler	M	1991
C	2.2	135 (2213)	4	Turbo IV	Chrysler	N	1992
D	2.2	135 (2213)	4	EFI	Chrysler	P	1993
E	2.2	135 (2213)	4	Turbo	Chrysler	R	1994
B	2.5	153 (2507)	4	EFI	Chrysler		
J	2.5	153 (2507)	4	Turbo I	Chrysler		
K	2.5	153 (2507)	4	EFI	Chrysler		
V	2.5	153 (2507)	4	MPI-FFV	Chrysler		
3	3.0	181 (2966)	6	MPI	Mitsubishi		

EFI—Electronic Fuel Injection
FFV—Flexible Fuel Vehicle
MPI—Multi-Point Fuel Injection

VEHICLE IDENTIFICATION CHART
TC Maserati

It is important for servicing and ordering parts to be certain of the vehicle and engine identification. The VIN (vehicle identification number) is a 17 digit number visible through the windshield on the driver's side of the dash and contains the vehicle and engine identification codes. The tenth digit indicates model year and the fifth digit indicates engine code. It can be interpreted as follows:

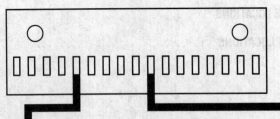

Engine Code						*Model Year*	
Code	Liters	Cu. In. (cc)	Cyl.	Fuel Sys.	Eng. Mfg.	Code	Year
A	2.2	135 (2213)	4	Turbo	Chrysler	L	1990
R	2.2	135 (2213)	4	Turbo	Chrysler①	M	1991
S	3.0	181 (2966)	6	EFI	Mitsubishi		

EFI—Electronic Fuel Injection
① Cylinder Head and Related Parts by Maserati

ENGINE IDENTIFICATION

Year	Model	Engine Displacement Liters (cc)	Engine Series (ID/VIN)	Fuel System	No. of Cylinders	Engine Type
1990	Daytona	2.5 (2507)	J	Turbo I	4	SOHC
	Daytona	2.2 (2213)	C	Turbo IV	4	SOHC
	Daytona	3.0 (2966)	3	MPI	6	SOHC
	LeBaron	2.5 (2507)	J	Turbo I	4	SOHC
	LeBaron	2.5 (2507)	K	EFI	4	SOHC
	LeBaron	2.2 (2213)	C	Turbo IV	4	SOHC
	LeBaron	3.0 (2966)	3	MPI	6	SOHC
	LeBaron Landau	3.0 (2966)	3	MPI	6	SOHC
	Shadow	2.2 (2213)	D	EFI	4	SOHC
	Shadow	2.2 (2213)	C	Turbo IV	4	SOHC
	Shadow	2.5 (2507)	J	Turbo I	4	SOHC
	Shadow	2.5 (2507)	K	EFI	4	SOHC
	Sundance	2.2 (2213)	D	EFI	4	SOHC
	Sundance	2.5 (2507)	J	Turbo I	4	SOHC
	Sundance	2.5 (2507)	K	EFI	4	SOHC
	Spirit	2.5 (2507)	J	Turbo I	4	SOHC
	Spirit	2.5 (2507)	K	EFI	4	SOHC
	Spirit	3.0 (2966)	3	MPI	6	SOHC
	Acclaim	2.5 (2507)	J	Turbo I	4	SOHC
	Acclaim	2.5 (2507)	K	EFI	4	SOHC
	Acclaim	3.0 (2966)	3	EFI	6	SOHC
	TC	2.2 (2213)	R	Turbo	4	DOHC
	TC	3.0 (2966)	S	EFI	6	SOHC
1991	Daytona	2.5 (2507)	J	Turbo I	4	SOHC
	Daytona	2.5 (2507)	K	EFI	4	SOHC
	Daytona	3.0 (2966)	3	MPI	6	SOHC
	LeBaron	2.5 (2507)	J	Turbo I	4	SOHC
	LeBaron	2.5 (2507)	K	EFI	4	SOHC
	LeBaron	3.0 (2966)	3	MPI	6	SOHC
	LeBaron Landau	3.0 (2966)	3	MPI	6	SOHC
	Shadow	2.2 (2213)	D	EFI	4	SOHC
	Shadow	2.5 (2507)	J	Turbo I	4	SOHC
	Shadow	2.5 (2507)	K	EFI	4	SOHC
	Sundance	2.2 (2213)	D	EFI	4	SOHC
	Sundance	2.5 (2507)	J	Turbo I	4	SOHC
	Sundance	2.5 (2507)	K	EFI	4	SOHC
	Spirit	2.5 (2507)	J	Turbo I	4	SOHC
	Spirit	2.5 (2507)	K	EFI	4	SOHC
	Spirit	3.0 (2966)	3	MPI	6	SOHC
	Spirit R/T	2.2 (2213)	A	Turbo III	4	DOHC
	Acclaim	2.5 (2507)	K	EFI	4	SOHC
	Acclaim	3.0 (2966)	3	MPI	6	SOHC
	TC	3.0 (2966)	S	EFI	6	SOHC

ENGINE IDENTIFICATION

Year	Model	Engine Displacement Liters (cc)	Engine Series (ID/VIN)	Fuel System	No. of Cylinders	Engine Type
1992	Daytona	2.5 (2507)	J	Turbo I	4	SOHC
	Daytona	2.5 (2507)	K	EFI	4	SOHC
	Daytona	3.0 (2966)	3	MPI	6	SOHC
	Daytona	2.2 (2213)	A	Turbo III	4	DOHC
	LeBaron	2.5 (2507)	J	Turbo I	4	SOHC
	LeBaron	2.5 (2507)	K	EFI	4	SOHC
	LeBaron	3.0 (2966)	3	MPI	6	SOHC
	Shadow	2.2 (2213)	D	EFI	4	SOHC
	Shadow	2.5 (2507)	J	Turbo I	4	SOHC
	Shadow	2.5 (2507)	K	EFI	4	SOHC
	Acclaim	2.5 (2507)	K	EFI	4	SOHC
	Acclaim	3.0 (2966)	3	MPI	6	SOHC
	Spirit R/T	2.2 (2213)	A	Turbo III	4	DOHC
	Spirit	2.5 (2507)	J	Turbo I	4	SOHC
	Spirit	2.5 (2507)	K	MPI	4	SOHC
	Spirit	3.0 (2966)	3	EFI	6	SOHC
	Sundance	2.2 (2213)	D	EFI	4	SOHC
	Sundance	2.5 (2507)	K	EFI	4	SOHC
1993–94	Daytona	2.5 (2507)	K	EFI	4	SOHC
	Daytona	3.0 (2966)	3	MPI	6	SOHC
	Daytona	2.2 (2213)	A	Turbo III	4	DOHC
	LeBaron	2.5 (2507)	K	EFI	4	SOHC
	LeBaron	3.0 (2966)	3	MPI	6	SOHC
	Shadow	2.2 (2213)	D	EFI	4	SOHC
	Shadow	2.5 (2507)	K	EFI	4	SOHC
	Shadow	3.0 (2966)	3	MPI	6	SOHC
	Acclaim	2.5 (2507)	K	EFI	4	SOHC
	Acclaim	3.0 (2966)	3	MPI	6	SOHC
	Spirit	2.5 (2507)	V	MPI-FFV	4	SOHC
	Spirit	2.5 (2507)	K	MPI	4	SOHC
	Spirit	3.0 (2966)	3	MPI	6	SOHC
	Sundance	2.2 (2213)	D	EFI	4	SOHC
	Sundance	2.5 (2507)	K	EFI	4	SOHC
	Sundance	3.0 (2966)	3	MPI	6	SOHC

DOHC—Double Overhead Camshaft
SOHC—Single Overhead Camshaft
EFI—Electronic Fuel Injection
FFV—Flexible Fuel Vehicle
MPI—Multi-Point Fuel Injection

GENERAL ENGINE SPECIFICATIONS

Year	Engine ID/VIN	Engine Displacement Liters (cc)	Fuel System Type	Net Horsepower @ rpm	Net Torque @ rpm (ft. lbs.)	Bore × Stroke (in.)	Compression Ratio	Oil Pressure @ rpm
1990	C	2.2 (2213)	Turbo	174 @ 5200	210 @ 2400	3.44 × 3.62	8.0:1	30–80 @ 3000
	D	2.2 (2213)	EFI	99 @ 5600	121 @ 3200	3.44 × 3.62	9.5:1	30–80 @ 3000
	K	2.5 (2507)	EFI	100 @ 4800	135 @ 2800	3.44 × 4.09	8.9:1	30–80 @ 3000
	J	2.5 (2507)	Turbo	150 @ 4800	180 @ 2000	3.44 × 4.09	7.8:1	30–80 @ 3000
	3	3.0 (2966)	EFI	141 @ 5000	171 @ 2000	3.59 × 2.99	8.9:1	30–80 @ 3000
	S	3.0 (2966)	EFI	141 @ 5000	170 @ 2800	3.59 × 2.99	8.9:1	30–80 @ 3000
	R	2.2 (2213)	Turbo	200 @ 5500	220 @ 3400	3.44 × 3.62	7.4:1	30–80 @ 3000
1991	D	2.2 (2213)	EFI	99 @ 5600	121 @ 3200	3.44 × 3.62	9.5:1	30–80 @ 3000
	K	2.5 (2507)	EFI	100 @ 4800	135 @ 2800	3.44 × 4.09	8.9:1	30–80 @ 3000
	J	2.5 (2507)	Turbo	150 @ 4800	180 @ 2000	3.44 × 4.09	7.8:1	30–80 @ 3000
	3	3.0 (2966)	EFI	141 @ 5000	171 @ 2000	3.59 × 2.99	8.9:1	30–80 @ 3000
	S	3.0 (2966)	EFI	141 @ 5000	170 @ 2800	3.59 × 2.99	8.9:1	30–80 @ 3000
	A	2.2 (2213)	Turbo	224 @ 2800	217 @ 6000	3.44 × 3.62	8.5:1	30–80 @ 3000
1992	D	2.2 (2213)	EFI	93 @ 4800	121 @ 3200	3.44 × 3.62	9.5:1	30–80 @ 3000
	A	2.2 (2213)	Turbo	224 @ 6000	217 @ 5600	3.44 × 3.62	8.5:1	30–80 @ 3000
	K	2.5 (2507)	EFI	100 @ 4800	135 @ 2800	3.44 × 4.09	8.9:1	30–80 @ 3000
	J	2.5 (2507)	Turbo	152 @ 4800	219 @ 2400	3.44 × 4.09	7.8:1	30–80 @ 3000
	3	3.0 (2966)	MPI	141 @ 5000	171 @ 2800	3.59 × 2.99	8.9:1	30–80 @ 3000
1993–94	D	2.2 (2213)	EFI	93 @ 4800	121 @ 3200	3.44 × 3.62	9.5:1	30–80 @ 3000
	A	2.2 (2213)	Turbo	224 @ 6000	217 @ 5600	3.44 × 3.62	8.5:1	30–80 @ 3000
	K	2.5 (2507)	EFI	100 @ 4800	135 @ 2800	3.44 × 4.09	8.9:1	30–80 @ 3000
	V	2.5 (2507)	MPI-FFV	106 @ 4400	145 @ 2400	3.44 × 4.09	9.0:1	30–80 @ 3000
	3	3.0 (2966)	MPI	141 @ 5000	171 @ 2800	3.59 × 2.99	8.9:1	30–80 @ 3000

EFI—Electronic Fuel Injection
FFV—Flexible Fuel Vehicle
MPI—Multi-Point Fuel Injection

GASOLINE ENGINE TUNE-UP SPECIFICATIONS

Year	Engine ID/VIN	Engine Displacement Liters (cc)	Spark Plugs Gap (in.)	Ignition Timing (deg.) MT	Ignition Timing (deg.) AT	Fuel Pump [2] (psi)	Idle Speed (rpm) MT	Idle Speed (rpm) AT	Valve Clearance In.	Valve Clearance Ex.
1990	C	2.2 (2213)	0.035	12B	—	55	900	—	Hyd.	Hyd.
	D	2.2 (2213)	0.035	12B	12B	14.5	850	850	Hyd.	Hyd.
	K	2.5 (2507)	0.035	12B	12B	14.5	850	850	Hyd.	Hyd.
	J	2.5 (2507)	0.035	12B	12B	55	900	720	Hyd.	Hyd.
	3	3.0 (2966)	0.040	—	12B	48	—	700	Hyd.	Hyd.
	S	3.0 (2966)	0.040	—	12B	48	—	700	Hyd.	Hyd.
	R	2.2 (2213)	0.030	12B	—	55	900	—	0.012	0.010
1991	D	2.2 (2213)	0.035	12B	12B	39	850	850	Hyd.	Hyd.
	K	2.5 (2507)	0.035	12B	12B	39 [1]	850	850	Hyd.	Hyd.
	J	2.5 (2507)	0.035	12B	12B	55	900	850	Hyd.	Hyd.
	3	3.0 (2966)	0.040	—	12B	48	—	700	Hyd.	Hyd.
	S	3.0 (2966)	0.040	—	12B	48	—	700	Hyd.	Hyd.
	A	2.2 (2213)	0.035	[3]	[3]	55	850	—	Hyd.	Hyd.

GASOLINE ENGINE TUNE-UP SPECIFICATIONS

Year	Engine ID/VIN	Engine Displacement Liters (cc)	Spark Plugs Gap (in.)	Ignition Timing (deg.) MT	Ignition Timing (deg.) AT	Fuel Pump② (psi)	Idle Speed (rpm) MT	Idle Speed (rpm) AT	Valve Clearance In.	Valve Clearance Ex.
1992	D	2.2 (2213)	0.035	12B	12B	39	850	850	Hyd.	Hyd.
	A	2.2 (2213)	0.035	③	③	55	850	—	Hyd.	Hyd.
	K	2.5 (2507)	0.035	12B	12B	39	850	850	Hyd.	Hyd.
	J	2.5 (2507)	0.035	12B	12B	55	900	850	Hyd.	Hyd.
	3	3.0 (2966)	0.040	—	12B	48	—	700	Hyd.	Hyd.
1993	D	2.2 (2213)	0.035	12B	12B	39	850	850	Hyd.	Hyd.
	A	2.2 (2213)	0.035	③	③	55	850	—	Hyd.	Hyd.
	K	2.5 (2507)	0.035	12B	12B	39	850	850	Hyd.	Hyd.
	V	2.5 (2507)	0.035	③	③	55	850	850	Hyd.	Hyd.
	3	3.0 (2966)	0.040	—	12B	48	—	700	Hyd.	Hyd.
1994	SEE UNDERHOOD SPECIFICATIONS STICKER									

NOTE: The lowest cylinder pressure should be within 75% of the highest cylinder pressure reading. For example, if the highest cylinder is 134 psi, the lowest should be 101. Engine should be at normal operating temperature with throttle valve in the wide open position.
Hyd.—Hydraulic
① Early 1991 Shadow Convertible: 14.5 psi
② The specifications listed reflect system pressures with the vacuum line at the pressure regulator disconnected
③ Refer to Emission Control Label on vehicle

CAPACITIES

Year	Model	Engine ID/VIN	Engine Displacement Liters (cc)	Engine Crankcase with Filter (qts.)	Transmission (pts.) 4-Spd	Transmission (pts.) 5-Spd	Transmission (pts.) Auto.	Transfer Case (pts.)	Drive Axle Front (pts.)	Drive Axle Rear (pts.)	Fuel Tank (gal.)	Cooling System (qts.)
1990	Daytona	J	2.5 (2507)	4	—	5	18	—	—	—	14	9
	Daytona	C	2.2 (2213)	4	—	5	—	—	—	—	14	9
	Daytona	3	3.0 (2966)	4	—	—	18	—	—	—	14	9.5
	LeBaron	J	2.5 (2507)	4	—	5	18	—	—	—	14	9
	LeBaron	K	2.5 (2507)	4	—	5	18	—	—	—	14	9
	LeBaron	C	2.2 (2213)	4	—	5	—	—	—	—	14	9.5
	LeBaron	3	3.0 (2966)	4	—	—	18	—	—	—	14	9.5
	LeBaron Landau	3	3.0 (2966)	4	—	—	18	—	—	—	14	9
	Shadow	D	2.2 (2213)	4	—	5	18	—	—	—	14	9
	Shadow	C	2.2 (2213)	4	—	5	—	—	—	—	14	9
	Shadow	J	2.5 (2507)	4	—	5	18	—	—	—	14	9
	Shadow	K	2.5 (2507)	4	—	5	18	—	—	—	14	9
	Sundance	D	2.2 (2213)	4	—	5	18	—	—	—	14	9
	Sundance	J	2.5 (2507)	4	—	5	18	—	—	—	14	9
	Sundance	K	2.5 (2507)	4	—	5	18	—	—	—	14	9
	Spirit	J	2.5 (2507)	4	—	5	18	—	—	—	14	9
	Spirit	K	2.5 (2507)	4	—	5	18	—	—	—	14	9
	Spirit	3	3.0 (2966)	4	—	—	18	—	—	—	14	9.5

CAPACITIES

Year	Model	Engine ID/VIN	Engine Displacement Liters (cc)	Engine Crankcase with Filter (qts.)	Transmission (pts.)			Transfer Case (pts.)	Drive Axle		Fuel Tank (gal.)	Cooling System (qts.)
					4-Spd	5-Spd	Auto.		Front (pts.)	Rear (pts.)		
1990	Acclaim	J	2.5 (2507)	4	—	5	18	—	—	—	14	9
	Acclaim	K	2.5 (2507)	4	—	5	18	—	—	—	14	9
	Acclaim	3	3.0 (2966)	4	—	—	18	—	—	—	14	9.5
	TC	R	2.2 (2213)	4.5	—	5	18	—	—	—	14	9.5
	TC	S	3.0 (2966)	4	—	5	18	—	—	—	14	9
1991	Daytona	J	2.5 (2507)	4.5	—	5	18	—	—	—	14	9
	Daytona	K	2.5 (2507)	4.5	—	5	—	—	—	—	14	9
	Daytona	3	3.0 (2966)	4.5	—	—	18	—	—	—	14	9.5
	LeBaron	J	2.5 (2507)	4.5	—	5	18	—	—	—	14	9
	LeBaron	K	2.5 (2507)	4.5	—	5	18	—	—	—	14	9
	LeBaron	3	3.0 (2966)	4.5	—	—	18	—	—	—	14	9.5
	LeBaron Landau	3	3.0 (2966)	4.5	—	—	18	—	—	—	16	9.5
	Shadow	D	2.2 (2213)	4.5	—	5	18	—	—	—	14	9
	Shadow	J	2.5 (2507)	4.5	—	5	18	—	—	—	14	9
	Shadow	K	2.5 (2507)	4.5	—	5	18	—	—	—	14	9
	Sundance	D	2.2 (2213)	4.5	—	5	18	—	—	—	14	9
	Sundance	J	2.5 (2507)	4.5	—	5	18	—	—	—	14	9
	Sundance	K	2.5 (2507)	4.5	—	5	18	—	—	—	14	9
	Spirit	J	2.5 (2507)	4.5	—	5	18	—	—	—	14	9
	Spirit	K	2.5 (2507)	4.5	—	5	18	—	—	—	16	9
	Spirit	3	3.0 (2966)	4.5	—	—	18	—	—	—	16	9.5
	Spirit R/T	A	2.2 (2213)	4.5	—	5	—	—	—	—	16	9.5
	Acclaim	K	2.5 (2507)	4.5	—	5	18	—	—	—	16	9
	Acclaim	3	3.0 (2966)	4.5	—	—	18	—	—	—	16	9.5
	TC	S	3.0 (2966)	4.5	—	—	18	—	—	—	14	9.5
1992	Daytona	J	2.5 (2507)	4.5	—	5	18	—	—	—	14	9
	Daytona	K	2.5 (2507)	4.5	—	5	18	—	—	—	14	9
	Daytona	3	3.0 (2966)	4.5	—	—	18	—	—	—	14	9.5
	Daytona	A	2.2 (2213)	4.5	—	5	—	—	—	—	14	9
	LeBaron	J	2.5 (2507)	4.5	—	5	18	—	—	—	14	9
	LeBaron	K	2.5 (2507)	4.5	—	5	18	—	—	—	14	9
	LeBaron	3	3.0 (2966)	4.5	—	—	18	—	—	—	16	9.5
	Shadow	D	2.2 (2213)	4.5	—	5	18	—	—	—	14	9
	Shadow	J	2.5 (2507)	4.5	—	5	18	—	—	—	14	9
	Shadow	K	2.5 (2507)	4.5	—	5	18	—	—	—	14	9
	Acclaim	K	2.5 (2507)	4.5	—	5	18	—	—	—	16	9
	Acclaim	3	3.0 (2966)	4.5	—	—	18	—	—	—	16	9.5
	Spirit R/T	A	2.2 (2213)	4.5	—	5	—	—	—	—	16	9
	Spirit	J	2.5 (2507)	4.5	—	5	18	—	—	—	16	9
	Spirit	K	2.5 (2507)	4.5	—	—	18	—	—	—	16	9
	Spirit	3	3.0 (2966)	4.5	—	5	18	—	—	—	16	9.5
	Sundance	D	2.2 (2213)	4.5	—	5	18	—	—	—	14	9
	Sundance	K	2.5 (2507)	4.5	—	5	18	—	—	—	14	9

CAPACITIES

Year	Model	Engine ID/VIN	Engine Displacement Liters (cc)	Engine Crankcase with Filter (qts.)	Transmission (pts.) 4-Spd	Transmission (pts.) 5-Spd	Transmission (pts.) Auto.	Transfer Case (pts.)	Drive Axle Front (pts.)	Drive Axle Rear (pts.)	Fuel Tank (gal.)	Cooling System (qts.)
1993-94	Daytona	K	2.5 (2507)	4.5	—	5	18	—	—	—	14	9
	Daytona	3	3.0 (2966)	4.5	—	—	18	—	—	—	14	9.5
	Daytona	A	2.2 (2213)	4.5	—	5	—	—	—	—	14	9
	LeBaron	K	2.5 (2507)	4.5	—	5	18	—	—	—	14	9
	LeBaron	3	3.0 (2966)	4.5	—	—	18	—	—	—	16	9.5
	Shadow	D	2.2 (2213)	4.5	—	5	18	—	—	—	14	9
	Shadow	3	3.0 (2966)	4.5	—	5	18	—	—	—	14	9
	Shadow	K	2.5 (2507)	4.5	—	5	18	—	—	—	14	9
	Acclaim	K	2.5 (2507)	4.5	—	5	18	—	—	—	16	9
	Acclaim	3	3.0 (2966)	4.5	—	—	18	—	—	—	16	9.5
	Spirit	V	2.5 (2507)	4.5	—	5	18	—	—	—	18	9
	Spirit	K	2.5 (2507)	4.5	—	—	18	—	—	—	16	9
	Spirit	3	3.0 (2966)	4.5	—	5	18	—	—	—	16	9.5
	Sundance	D	2.2 (2213)	4.5	—	5	18	—	—	—	14	9
	Sundance	K	2.5 (2507)	4.5	—	5	18	—	—	—	14	9
	Sundance	3	3.0 (2966)	4.5	—	5	18	—	—	—	14	9

CAMSHAFT SPECIFICATIONS

All measurements given in inches.

Year	Engine ID/VIN	Engine Displacement Liters (cc)	Journal Diameter 1	Journal Diameter 2	Journal Diameter 3	Journal Diameter 4	Journal Diameter 5	Elevation In.	Elevation Ex.	Bearing Clearance	Camshaft End Play
1990	C	2.2 (2213)	1.375–1.376	1.375–1.376	1.375–1.376	1.375–1.376	1.375–1.376	NA	NA	—	0.005–0.020
	D	2.2 (2213)	1.375–1.376	1.375–1.376	1.375–1.376	1.375–1.376	1.375–1.376	NA	NA	—	0.005–0.020
	K	2.5 (2507)	1.375–1.376	1.375–1.376	1.375–1.376	1.375–1.376	1.375–1.376	NA	NA	—	0.005–0.020
	J	2.5 (2507)	1.375–1.376	1.375–1.376	1.375–1.376	1.375–1.376	1.375–1.376	NA	NA	—	0.005–0.020
	3	3.0 (2966)	NA	NA	NA	NA	NA	①	①	—	NA
	S	3.0 (2966)	NA	NA	NA	NA	NA	①	①	—	NA
	R	2.2 (2213)	NA	NA	NA	NA	NA	NA	NA	—	NA
1991	D	2.2 (2213)	1.395–1.396	1.395–1.396	1.395–1.396	1.395–1.396	1.395–1.396	NA	NA	—	0.005–0.020
	K	2.5 (2507)	1.395–1.396	1.395–1.396	1.395–1.396	1.395–1.396	1.395–1.396	NA	NA	—	0.005–0.020
	J	2.5 (2507)	1.395–1.396	1.395–1.396	1.395–1.396	1.395–1.396	1.395–1.396	NA	NA	—	0.005–0.020
	3	3.0 (2966)	NA	NA	NA	NA	NA	①	①	—	NA
	S	3.0 (2966)	NA	NA	NA	NA	NA	①	①	—	NA
	A	2.2 (2213)	1.886–1.887	1.886–1.887	1.886–1.887	1.886–1.887	1.886–1.887	NA	NA	—	0.001–0.020

CAMSHAFT SPECIFICATIONS

All measurements given in inches.

Year	Engine ID/VIN	Engine Displacement Liters (cc)	Journal Diameter 1	2	3	4	5	Elevation In.	Ex.	Bearing Clearance	Camshaft End Play
1992	D	2.2 (2213)	1.395–1.396	1.395–1.396	1.395–1.396	1.395–1.396	1.395–1.396	NA	NA	—	0.005–0.013
	A	2.2 (2213)	1.886–1.887	1.886–1.887	1.886–1.887	1.886–1.887	1.886–1.887	NA	NA	—	0.001–0.020
	K	2.5 (2507)	1.395–1.396	1.395–1.396	1.395–1.396	1.395–1.396	1.395–1.396	NA	NA	—	0.005–0.013
	J	2.5 (2507)	1.395–1.396	1.395–1.396	1.395–1.396	1.395–1.396	1.395–1.396	NA	NA	—	0.001–0.020
	3	3.0 (2966)	NA	NA	NA	NA	NA	①	①	—	NA
1993–94	D	2.2 (2213)	1.395–1.396	1.395–1.396	1.395–1.396	1.395–1.396	1.395–1.396	NA	NA	—	0.005–0.013
	A	2.2 (2213)	1.886–1.887	1.886–1.887	1.886–1.887	1.886–1.887	1.886–1.887	NA	NA	—	0.001–0.020
	K	2.5 (2507)	1.395–1.396	1.395–1.396	1.395–1.396	1.395–1.396	1.395–1.396	NA	NA	—	0.005–0.013
	V	2.5 (2507)	1.395–1.396	1.395–1.396	1.395–1.396	1.395–1.396	1.395–1.396	NA	NA	—	0.001–0.020
	3	3.0 (2966)	NA	NA	NA	NA	NA	①	①	—	NA

NA—Not available
① Standard value: 1.624 in.
  Wear limit: 1.604 in.

CRANKSHAFT AND CONNECTING ROD SPECIFICATIONS

All measurements are given in inches.

Year	Engine ID/VIN	Engine Displacement Liters (cc)	Crankshaft Main Brg. Journal Dia.	Main Brg. Oil Clearance	Shaft End-play	Thrust on No.	Connecting Rod Journal Diameter	Oil Clearance	Side Clearance
1990	C	2.2 (2213)	2.362–2.363	0.0004–0.0040	0.002–0.014	3	1.9680–1.9690	0.0008–0.0040	0.005–0.013
	D	2.2 (2213)	2.362–2.363	0.0004–0.0040	0.002–0.014	3	1.9680–1.9690	0.0008–0.0040	0.005–0.013
	K	2.5 (2507)	2.362–2.363	0.0004–0.0040	0.002–0.014	3	1.9680–1.9690	0.0008–0.0040	0.005–0.013
	J	2.5 (2507)	2.362–2.363	0.0004–0.0040	0.002–0.014	3	1.9680–1.9690	0.0008–0.0040	0.005–0.013
	3	3.0 (2966)	2.361–2.362	0.0006–0.0020	0.002–0.010	3	1.9680–1.9690	0.0008–0.0028	0.004–0.010
	S	3.0 (2966)	2.361–2.363	0.0006–0.0020	0.002–0.010	3	1.9680–1.9690	0.0008–0.0028	0.004–0.010
	R	2.2 (2213)	2.362–2.363	0.0011–0.0031	0.002–0.007	3	1.9695–1.9705	0.0006–0.0016	0.006–0.009
1991	D	2.2 (2213)	2.362–2.363	0.0004–0.0040	0.002–0.014	3	1.9680–1.9690	0.0008–0.0040	0.005–0.013
	K	2.5 (2507)	2.362–2.363	0.0004–0.0040	0.002–0.014	3	1.9680–1.9690	0.0008–0.0040	0.005–0.013
	J	2.5 (2507)	2.362–2.363	0.0004–0.0040	0.002–0.014	3	1.9680–1.9690	0.0008–0.0040	0.005–0.013

CRANKSHAFT AND CONNECTING ROD SPECIFICATIONS

All measurements are given in inches.

Year	Engine ID/VIN	Engine Displacement Liters (cc)	Crankshaft				Connecting Rod		
			Main Brg. Journal Dia.	Main Brg. Oil Clearance	Shaft End-play	Thrust on No.	Journal Diameter	Oil Clearance	Side Clearance
1991	3	3.0 (2966)	2.361–2.362	0.0006–0.0020	0.002–0.010	3	1.9680–1.9690	0.0008–0.0028	0.004–0.010
	S	3.0 (2966)	2.361–2.363	0.0006–0.0020	0.002–0.010	3	1.9680–1.9690	0.0008–0.0028	0.004–0.010
	A	2.2 (2213)	2.362–2.363	0.0004–0.0040	0.002–0.014	3	1.9680–1.9690	0.0008–0.0034	0.005–0.013
1992	D	2.2 (2213)	2.362–2.363	0.0004–0.0040	0.002–0.014	3	1.9680–1.9690	0.0008–0.0030	0.005–0.013
	A	2.2 (2213)	2.362–2.363	0.0004–0.0040	0.002–0.014	3	1.9680–1.9690	0.0008–0.0030	0.005–0.013
	K	2.5 (2507)	2.362–2.363	0.0004–0.0040	0.002–0.014	3	1.9680–1.9690	0.0008–0.0030	0.005–0.013
	J	2.5 (2507)	2.362–2.363	0.0004–0.0040	0.002–0.014	3	1.9680–1.9690	0.0008–0.0030	0.005–0.013
	3	3.0 (2966)	2.361–2.362	0.0006–0.0020	0.002–0.010	3	1.9680–1.9690	0.0006–0.0020	0.004–0.010
1993–94	D	2.2 (2213)	2.362–2.363	0.0004–0.0040	0.002–0.014	3	1.9680–1.9690	0.0008–0.0030	0.005–0.013
	A	2.2 (2213)	2.362–2.363	0.0004–0.0040	0.002–0.014	3	1.9680–1.9690	0.0008–0.0030	0.005–0.013
	K	2.5 (2507)	2.362–2.363	0.0004–0.0040	0.002–0.014	3	1.9680–1.9690	0.0008–0.0030	0.005–0.013
	V	2.5 (2507)	2.362–2.363	0.0004–0.0040	0.002–0.014	3	1.9680–1.9690	0.0008–0.0030	0.005–0.013
	3	3.0 (2966)	2.361–2.362	0.0006–0.0020	0.002–0.010	3	1.9680–1.9690	0.0006–0.0020	0.004–0.010

VALVE SPECIFICATIONS

Year	Engine ID/VIN	Engine Displacement Liters (cc)	Seat Angle (deg.)	Face Angle (deg.)	Spring Test Pressure (lbs. @ in.)	Spring Installed Height (in.)	Stem-to-Guide Clearance (in.)		Stem Diameter ① (in.)	
							Intake	Exhaust	Intake	Exhaust
1990	C	2.2 (2213)	45	45	114 @ 1.65	1.65	0.001–0.003	0.0030–0.0047	0.3124	0.3103
	D	2.2 (2213)	45	45	114 @ 1.65	1.65	0.001–0.003	0.0030–0.0047	0.3124	0.3103
	K	2.5 (2507)	45	45	114 @ 1.65	1.65	0.001–0.003	0.0030–0.0047	0.3124	0.3103
	J	2.5 (2507)	45	45	114 @ 1.65	1.65	0.001–0.003	0.0030–0.0047	0.3124	0.3103
	3	3.0 (2966)	44.5	45.5	73 @ 1.59	1.59	0.001–0.002	0.0020–0.0030	0.3130–0.3140	0.3120–0.3130
	S	3.0 (2966)	44.5	45.5	180 @ 1.59	1.59	0.001–0.002	0.0020–0.0030	0.3130–0.3140	0.3120–0.3130
	R	2.2 (2213)	NA	NA	NA	NA	0.001–0.002	0.0010–0.0030	0.2750–0.2760	0.2750–0.2760

VALVE SPECIFICATIONS

Year	Engine ID/VIN	Engine Displacement Liters (cc)	Seat Angle (deg.)	Face Angle (deg.)	Spring Test Pressure (lbs. @ in.)	Spring Installed Height (in.)	Stem-to-Guide Clearance (in.)		Stem Diameter ① (in.)	
							Intake	Exhaust	Intake	Exhaust
1991	D	2.2 (2213)	45	45	114 @ 1.65	1.65	0.001–0.003	0.0030–0.0047	0.3124	0.3103
	K	2.5 (2507)	45	45	114 @ 1.65	1.65	0.001–0.003	0.0030–0.0047	0.3124	0.3103
	J	2.5 (2507)	45	45	114 @ 1.65	1.65	0.001–0.003	0.0030–0.0047	0.3124	0.3103
	3	3.0 (2966)	44.5	45.5	73 @ 1.59	1.59	0.001–0.002	0.0020–0.0030	0.3130–0.3140	0.3120–0.3130
	S	3.0 (2966)	44.5	45.5	180 @ 1.59	1.59	0.001–0.004	0.0020–0.0040	0.3130–0.3140	0.3120–0.3130
	A	2.2 (2213)	45	45	225 @ 1.34	1.34	0.001–0.004	0.0020–0.0040	0.2740	0.2730
1992	D	2.2 (2213)	45	45	114 @ 1.65	1.65	0.001–0.003	0.0030–0.0047	0.3124	0.3103
	A	2.2 (2213)	45	45	225 @ 1.34	1.34	0.001–0.004	0.0020–0.0040	0.2740	0.2730
	K	2.5 (2507)	45	45	114 @ 1.65	1.65	0.001–0.003	0.0030–0.0047	0.3124	0.3103
	J	2.5 (2507)	45	45	114 @ 1.65	1.65	0.001–0.003	0.0030–0.0047	0.3124	0.3103
	3	3.0 (2966)	44	45–45.5	73 @ 1.56	1.59	0.001–0.004	0.0020–0.0030	0.3130–0.3140	0.3120–0.3125
1993–94	D	2.2 (2213)	45	45	114 @ 1.65	1.65	0.001–0.003	0.0030–0.0047	0.3124	0.3103
	A	2.2 (2213)	45	45	225 @ 1.34	1.34	0.001–0.004	0.0020–0.0040	0.2740	0.2730
	K	2.5 (2507)	45	45	114 @ 1.65	1.65	0.001–0.003	0.0030–0.0047	0.3124	0.3103
	V	2.5 (2507)	45	45	114 @ 1.65	1.65	0.001–0.003	0.0030–0.0047	0.3124	0.3103
	3	3.0 (2966)	44	45–45.5	73 @ 1.56	1.59	0.001–0.004	0.0020–0.0030	0.3130–0.3140	0.3120–0.3125

NA—Not available
① If no range is given, the specification is the minimum allowable diameter.

SECTION 3

CHRYSLER/DODGE/PLYMOUTH
ACCLAIM • **ARIES** • **DAYTONA** • **LEBARON** • **SHADOW** • **SPIRIT** • **SUNDANCE** • **TC**

PISTON AND RING SPECIFICATIONS

All measurements are given in inches.

Year	Engine ID/VIN	Engine Displacement Liters (cc)	Piston Clearance	Ring Gap			Ring Side Clearance		
				Top Compression	Bottom Compression	Oil Control	Top Compression	Bottom Compression	Oil Control
1990	C	2.2 (2213)	0.0005–0.0027	0.010–0.039	0.009–0.037	0.015–0.074	0.0016–0.0030	0.0016–0.0035	0.0002–0.0080
	D	2.2 (2213)	0.0005–0.0027	0.010–0.039	0.011–0.039	0.015–0.074	0.0015–0.0040	0.0015–0.0040	0.0002–0.0080
	J	2.5 (2507)	0.0006–0.0030	0.010–0.039	0.009–0.037	0.015–0.074	0.0016–0.0030	0.0016–0.0035	0.0002–0.0080
	K	2.5 (2507)	0.0010–0.0027	0.010–0.039	0.011–0.039	0.015–0.074	0.0015–0.0040	0.0015–0.0040	0.0002–0.0080
	3	3.0 (2966)	0.0012–0.0020	0.012–0.018	0.010–0.016	0.012–0.035	0.0020–0.0035	0.0008–0.0020	NA
	S	3.0 (2966)	0.0012–0.0020	0.012–0.018	0.010–0.016	0.012–0.035	0.0020–0.0035	0.0008–0.0020	NA
	R	2.2 (2213)	0.0005–0.0015	0.010–0.039	0.010–0.039	0.012–0.035	0.0015–0.0031	0.0015–0.0016	0.0002–0.0080
1991	D	2.2 (2213)	0.0005–0.0027	0.010–0.039	0.011–0.039	0.015–0.074	0.0015–0.0040	0.0015–0.0040	0.0002–0.0080
	K	2.5 (2507)	0.0010–0.0027	0.010–0.039	0.011–0.039	0.015–0.074	0.0015–0.0040	0.0015–0.0040	0.0002–0.0080
	J	2.5 (2507)	0.0006–0.0030	0.010–0.039	0.009–0.037	0.015–0.074	0.0016–0.0030	0.0016–0.0035	0.0002–0.0080
	3	3.0 (2966)	0.0012–0.0020	0.012–0.018	0.010–0.016	0.012–0.035	0.0020–0.0035	0.0008–0.0020	NA
	S	3.0 (2966)	0.0012–0.0020	0.012–0.018	0.010–0.016	0.012–0.035	0.0020–0.0035	0.0008–0.0020	NA
	A	2.2 (2213)	0.0018–0.0039	0.014–0.039	0.014–0.039	0.010–0.039	0.0016–0.0030	0.0016–0.0030	0.0002–0.0040
1992	D	2.2 (2213)	0.0005–0.0027	0.010–0.039	0.011–0.039	0.015–0.074	0.0015–0.0040	0.0015–0.0040	0.0002–0.0080
	A	2.2 (2213)	0.0018–0.0039	0.014–0.039	0.014–0.039	0.010–0.039	0.0015–0.0040	0.0015–0.0040	0.0002–0.0080
	K	2.5 (2507)	0.0012–0.0020	0.012–0.018	0.010–0.016	0.012–0.035	0.0020–0.0035	0.0008–0.0020	NA
	J	2.5 (2507)	0.0006–0.0030	0.010–0.039	0.009–0.037	0.015–0.074	0.0016–0.0030	0.0016–0.0035	0.0002–0.0080
	3	3.0 (2966)	0.0012–0.0020	0.012–0.018	0.010–0.016	0.012–0.035	0.0020–0.0035	0.0008–0.0020	NA
1993–94	D	2.2 (2213)	0.0005–0.0027	0.010–0.039	0.011–0.039	0.015–0.074	0.0015–0.0040	0.0015–0.0040	0.0002–0.0080
	A	2.2 (2213)	0.0018–0.0039	0.014–0.039	0.014–0.039	0.010–0.039	0.0015–0.0040	0.0015–0.0040	0.0002–0.0080
	K	2.5 (2507)	0.0012–0.0020	0.012–0.018	0.010–0.016	0.012–0.035	0.0020–0.0035	0.0008–0.0020	NA
	V	2.5 (2507)	0.0006–0.0030	0.010–0.039	0.009–0.037	0.015–0.074	0.0016–0.0030	0.0016–0.0035	0.0002–0.0080
	3	3.0 (2966)	0.0012–0.0020	0.012–0.018	0.010–0.016	0.012–0.035	0.0020–0.0035	0.0008–0.0020	NA

NA—Not available

TORQUE SPECIFICATIONS

All readings in ft. lbs.

Year	Engine ID/VIN	Engine Displacement Liters (cc)	Cylinder Head Bolts	Main Bearing Bolts	Rod Bearing Bolts	Crankshaft Damper Bolts	Flywheel Bolts	Manifold Intake	Manifold Exhaust	Spark Plugs	Lug Nut
1990	C	2.2 (2213)	①	30③	40③	85	70	17	17	26	95
	D	2.2 (2213)	①	30③	40③	85	70	17	17	26	95
	K	2.5 (2507)	①	30③	40③	85	70	17	17	26	95
	J	2.5 (2507)	①	30③	40③	85	70	17	17	26	95
	3	3.0 (2966)	70	60	38	112	70	17	17	20	95
	S	3.0 (2966)	70	60	38	112	70	17	17	20	95
	R⑥	2.2 (2213)	②	④	⑤	80	70	17	18	13	95
1991	D	2.2 (2213)	①	30③	40③	85	70	17	17	26	95
	K	2.5 (2507)	①	30③	40③	85	70	17	17	26	95
	J	2.5 (2507)	①	30③	40③	85	70	17	17	26	95
	3	3.0 (2966)	80	60	38	112	70	17	17	20	95
	S	3.0 (2966)	80	60	38	112	70	17	17	20	95
	A	2.2 (2213)	①	④	48	80	70	17	17	18	95
1992	D	2.2 (2213)	①	30③	40③	85	70	17	17	26	95
	A	2.2 (2213)	①	30③	50	80	70	17	17	20	95
	K	2.5 (2507)	①	30③	40③	85	70	17	17	26	95
	J	2.5 (2507)	①	30③	40③	85	70	17	17	26	95
	3	3.0 (2966)	80	60	38	112	70	17	17	20	95
1993–94	D	2.2 (2213)	①	30③	40③	85	70	17	17	26	95
	A	2.2 (2213)	①	30③	50	80	70	17	17	20	95
	K	2.5 (2507)	①	30③	40③	85	70	17	17	26	95
	J	2.5 (2507)	①	30③	40③	85	70	17	17	26	95
	3	3.0 (2966)	80	60	38	112	70	17	17	20	95

① Sequence: 45, 65, 65, plus ¼ turn
② Sequence: 32, 50, 65, plus ¼ turn
③ Plus ¼ turn
④ Sequence: 32, 43, 76
⑤ Sequence: 32, 47
⑥ TC Turbo

TORQUE SPECIFICATIONS

Component	English	Metric
Camshaft bearing cap bolts		
2.2L and 2.5L engines:	18 ft. lbs.	25 Nm
3.0L engine:	15 ft. lbs.	20 Nm
Camshaft sprocket bolt		
2.2L and 2.5L engines:	65 ft. lbs.	88 Nm
2.2L turbo engine:	47 ft. lbs.	65 Nm
3.0L engine:	70 ft. lbs.	95 Nm
Connecting rod bearing cap bolts		
2.2L and 2.5L engines		
Step 1:	40 ft. lbs.	54 Nm
Step 2:	+ 90 degrees turn	+ 90 degrees turn
2.2L turbo engines:	50 ft. lbs.	68 Nm
3.0L engine:	38 ft. lbs.	52 Nm

TORQUE SPECIFICATIONS

Component	English	Metric
Crankshaft damper bolt		
2.2L and 2.5L engines:	85 ft. lbs.	115 Nm
2.2L turbo engine:	80 ft. lbs.	110 Nm
3.0L engine:	112 ft. lbs.	151 Nm
Crankshaft pulley bolt		
3.0L engine:	21 ft. lbs.	28 Nm
Cylinder head bolt		
2.2L and 2.5L engines		
Step 1:	45 ft. lbs.	61 Nm
Step 2:	65 ft. lbs.	89 Nm
Step 3:	65 ft. lbs.	89 Nm
Step 4:	+ 90 degrees turn	+ 90 degrees turn
3.0L engine:		
1990–91:	70 ft. lbs.	95 Nm
1992–94:	80 ft. lbs.	105 Nm
EGR valve-to-intake manifold/plenum:	17 ft. lbs.	22 Nm
Engine-to-transmission:	70 ft. lbs.	95 Nm
Exhaust manifold:	17 ft. lbs.	23 Nm
Exhaust pipe-to-exhaust manifold nuts:	25 ft. lbs.	33 Nm
Flywheel/flexplate-to-crankshaft bolts:	70 ft. lbs.	95 Nm
Flywheel-to-converter bolts:	55 ft. lbs.	74 Nm
Fuel injection		
MPI		
Intake plenum-to-cylinder head		
3.0L engine:	11 ft. lbs.	15 Nm
TBI		
Throttle body-to-manifold		
2.2L and 2.5L engines:	15 ft. lbs.	20 Nm
Intake manifold:	17 ft. lbs.	23 Nm
Main bearing cap bolts		
2.2L and 2.5L engines		
Step 1:	30 ft. lbs.	41 Nm
Step 2:	+ 90 degrees turn	+ 90 degrees turn
2.2L turbo engine		
Step 1:	32 ft. lbs.	44 Nm
Step 2:	43 ft. lbs.	59 Nm
Step 3:	76 ft. lbs.	103 Nm
3.0L engine:	60 ft. lbs.	80 Nm
Oil pan		
2.2L and 2.5L engines		
M8 bolts:	17 ft. lbs.	23 Nm
M6 bolts:	9 ft. lbs.	12 Nm
2.2L turbo engine		
M8 bolts:	22 ft. lbs.	29 Nm
M6 bolts:	18 ft. lbs.	25 Nm
3.0L engine:	50 inch lbs.	6 Nm
Oil pan drain plug		
Except 3.0L engine:	20 ft. lbs.	27 Nm
3.0L engine:	30 ft. lbs.	40 Nm
Oil pump attaching bolts		
2.2L and 2.5L engines:	17 ft. lbs.	23 Nm
3.0L engine:	115 inch lbs.	13 Nm
Rocker arm shaft bolt		
2.2L turbo engine:	18 ft. lbs.	24 Nm
3.0L engine		
Step 1:	7 ft. lbs.	10 Nm
Step 2:	15 ft. lbs.	20 Nm

TORQUE SPECIFICATIONS

Component	English	Metric
Rocker (valve) cover		
2.2L and 2.5L engines:	105 inch lbs.	12 Nm
2.2L turbo engine:	115 inch lbs.	13 Nm
3.0L engine:	88 inch lbs.	10 Nm
Spark plug		
2.2L and 2.5L engines:	26 ft. lbs.	35 Nm
2.2L turbo engine:	18 ft. lbs.	25 Nm
3.0L engine:	20 ft. lbs.	27 Nm
Starter-to-block bolts:	40 ft. lbs.	54 Nm
Turbocharger-to-exhaust manifold:	40 ft. lbs.	54 Nm
Thermostat housing		
2.2L and 2.5L engines:	21 ft. lbs.	28 Nm
2.2L turbo engine:	18 ft. lbs.	24 Nm
3.0L engine:	113 inch lbs.	12 Nm
Timing belt tensioner bolt		
2.2L and 2.5L engines:	45 ft. lbs.	61 Nm
3.0L engine:	21 ft. lbs.	28 Nm
Timing cover		
2.2L and 2.5L engines:	40 inch lbs.	4 Nm
2.2L turbo engine:	72 inch lbs.	8 Nm
3.0L engine:	115 inch lbs.	14 Nm
Water pump		
2.2L and 2.5L engines:		
Upper bolts:	21 ft. lbs.	28 Nm
Lower nuts:	50 ft. lbs.	68 Nm
3.0L engine:	20 ft. lbs.	27 Nm
Water pump pulley		
2.2L and 2.5L engines:	21 ft. lbs.	28 Nm

BRAKE SPECIFICATIONS

All measurements in inches unless noted.

Year	Model	Axle	Master Cylinder Bore	Brake Disc Original Thickness	Brake Disc Minimum Thickness	Brake Disc Maximum Runout	Brake Drum Diameter Original Inside Diameter	Brake Drum Diameter Max. Wear Limit	Brake Drum Diameter Maximum Machine Diameter	Minimum Lining Thickness Front	Minimum Lining Thickness Rear
1990	LeBaron Landau		0.827	0.861	0.803	0.005	7.87	NA	NA	0.30	0.06
	Shadow		0.827	0.935	0.882	0.005	7.87	NA	NA	0.30	0.06
	Sundance		0.827	0.861	0.803	0.005	7.87	NA	NA	0.30	0.06
	Spirit		0.827	0.935	0.882	0.005	7.87	NA	NA	0.30	0.06
	Acclaim		0.827	0.861	0.803	0.005	7.87	NA	NA	0.30	0.06
	Daytona	front	0.827	0.861	0.803	0.005	—	—	—	0.30	—
		solid rear disc	—	0.468	0.409	0.003	—	—	—	—	0.28
		vented rear disc		0.856	0.797	0.003	—	—	—	—	0.28
	LeBaron	front	0.827	0.861	0.803	0.005	—	—	—	0.30	—
		solid rear disc	—	0.468	0.409	0.003	—	—	—	—	0.28
		vented rear disc		0.856	0.797	0.003	—	—	—	—	0.28
	TC	front	NA	NA	0.882	0.005	—	—	—	0.30	—
		rear disc	—	NA	0.291	0.003	—	—	—	—	0.28

BRAKE SPECIFICATIONS

All measurements in inches unless noted.

Year	Model	Axle	Master Cylinder Bore	Brake Disc Original Thickness	Brake Disc Minimum Thickness	Maximum Runout	Brake Drum Diameter Original Inside Diameter	Max. Wear Limit	Maximum Machine Diameter	Minimum Lining Thickness Front	Rear
1991	LeBaron Landau	front	0.827	0.861	0.803	0.005	—	—	—	0.30	—
		rear disc	—	0.856	0.797	0.003	—	—	—	—	0.28
	Shadow		0.827	0.935	0.882	0.005	7.87	NA	NA	0.30	0.06
	Sundance		0.827	0.861	0.803	0.005	7.87	NA	NA	0.30	0.06
	Spirit	front	0.827	0.861	0.803	0.005	—	—	—	0.30	—
		rear disc	—	0.856	0.797	0.005	—	—	—	—	0.28
	Acclaim	front	0.827	0.861	0.803	0.005	—	—	—	0.30	—
		rear disc	—	0.856	0.797	0.005	—	—	—	—	0.28
	Daytona	front	0.827	0.861	0.803	0.005	—	—	—	0.30	—
		solid rear disc	—	0.468	0.409	0.003	—	—	—	—	0.28
		vented rear disc	—	0.856	0.797	0.003	—	—	—	—	0.28
	LeBaron	front	0.827	0.861	0.803	0.005	—	—	—	0.30	—
		solid rear disc	—	0.468	0.409	0.003	—	—	—	—	0.28
		vented rear disc	—	0.856	0.797	0.003	—	—	—	—	0.28
	TC	front	NA	NA	0.882	0.005	—	—	—	0.30	—
		rear disc	—	NA	0.291	0.003	—	—	—	—	0.28
1992	Shadow		0.827	0.935	0.882	0.005	7.87	NA	NA	0.30	0.06
	Sundance		0.827	0.861	0.803	0.005	7.87	NA	NA	0.30	0.06
	Spirit	front	0.827	0.861	0.803	0.005	—	—	—	0.30	—
		rear disc	—	0.856	0.797	0.005	—	—	—	—	0.28
	Acclaim	front	0.827	0.861	0.803	0.005	—	—	—	0.30	—
		rear disc	—	0.856	0.797	0.005	—	—	—	—	0.28
	Daytona	front	0.827	0.861	0.803	0.005	—	—	—	0.30	—
		solid rear disc	—	0.468	0.409	0.003	—	—	—	—	0.28
		vented rear disc	—	0.856	0.797	0.003	—	—	—	—	0.28
	LeBaron	front	0.827	0.861	0.803	0.005	—	—	—	0.30	—
		solid rear disc	—	0.468	0.409	0.003	—	—	—	—	0.28
		vented rear disc	—	0.856	0.797	0.003	—	—	—	—	0.28
1993-94	Shadow		0.827	0.930	0.882	0.005	7.87	NA	NA	0.30	0.06
		rear disc		0.468	0.409	0.005	—	—	—	—	0.28
	Sundance		0.827	0.861	0.882	0.005	7.87	NA	NA	0.30	0.06
		rear disc		0.468	0.409	0.005	—	—	—	—	0.28
	Spirit	front	0.827	0.930	0.882	0.005	—	—	—	0.30	—
		rear disc	—	0.856	0.468	0.409	—	—	—	—	0.28
	Acclaim	front	0.827	0.930	0.803	0.005	—	—	—	0.30	—
		rear disc	—	0.468	0.409	0.005	—	—	—	—	0.28
	Daytona	front	0.827	0.930	0.892	0.005	—	—	—	0.30	—
		solid rear disc	—	0.468	0.409	0.005	—	—	—	—	0.28
		vented rear disc	—	0.856	0.797	0.005	—	—	—	—	0.28
	LeBaron	front	0.827	0.930	0.882	0.005	—	—	—	0.30	—
		solid rear disc	—	0.468	0.409	0.005	—	—	—	—	0.28

NA—Not available

WHEEL ALIGNMENT

Year	Model		Caster Range (deg.)	Caster Preferred Setting (deg.)	Camber Range (deg.)	Camber Preferred Setting (deg.)	Toe-in (in.)	Steering Axis Inclination (deg.)
1990	Daytona	front	①	$1^3/_{16}$P	$^1/_4$N–$^3/_4$P	$^5/_{16}$P	$^1/_{16}$	$13^5/_{16}$
		rear	—	—	$1^1/_4$N–$^1/_4$N	$^1/_2$N	0	—
	LeBaron	front	①	$1^3/_{16}$P	$^1/_4$N–$^3/_4$P	$^5/_{16}$P	$^1/_{16}$	$13^5/_{16}$
		rear	—	—	$1^1/_4$N–$^1/_4$N	$^1/_2$N	0	—
	LeBaron Landau	front	①	$1^3/_{16}$P	$^1/_4$N–$^3/_4$P	$^5/_{16}$P	$^1/_{16}$	$13^5/_{16}$
		rear	—	—	$1^1/_4$N–$^1/_4$N	$^1/_2$N	0	—
	Shadow	front	①	$1^3/_{16}$P	$^1/_4$N–$^3/_4$P	$^5/_{16}$P	$^1/_{16}$	$13^5/_{16}$
		rear	—	—	$1^1/_4$N–$^1/_4$N	$^1/_2$N	0	—
	Sundance	front	①	$1^3/_{16}$P	$^1/_4$N–$^3/_4$P	$^5/_{16}$P	$^1/_{16}$	$13^5/_{16}$
		rear	—	—	$1^1/_4$N–$^1/_4$N	$^1/_2$N	0	—
	Spirit	front	①	$1^3/_{16}$P	$^1/_4$N–$^3/_4$P	$^5/_{16}$P	$^1/_{16}$	$13^5/_{16}$
		rear	—	—	$1^1/_4$N–$^1/_4$N	$^1/_2$N	0	—
	Acclaim	front	①	$1^3/_{16}$P	$^1/_4$N–$^3/_4$P	$^5/_{16}$P	$^1/_{16}$	$13^5/_{16}$
		rear	—	—	$1^1/_4$N–$^1/_4$N	$^1/_2$N	0	—
	TC	front	①	$1^3/_{16}$P	$^1/_4$N–$^3/_4$P	$^5/_{16}$P	$^1/_{16}$	$13^5/_{16}$
		rear	—	—	$1^1/_4$N–$^1/_4$N	$^1/_2$N	0	—
1991	Daytona	front	①	$2^3/_4$P	$^1/_4$N–$^3/_4$P	$^5/_{16}$P	$^1/_{16}$	$12^1/_2$
		rear	—	—	$1^1/_4$N–$^1/_4$N	$^1/_2$N	0	—
	LeBaron	front	①	$2^3/_4$P	$^1/_4$N–$^3/_4$P	$^5/_{16}$P	$^1/_{16}$	$12^1/_2$
		rear	—	—	$1^1/_4$N–$^1/_4$N	$^1/_2$N	0	—
	LeBaron Landau	front	①	$2^3/_4$P	$^1/_4$N–$^3/_4$P	$^5/_{16}$P	$^1/_{16}$	$12^1/_2$
		rear	—	—	$1^1/_4$N–$^1/_4$N	$^1/_2$N	0	—
	Shadow	front	①	$2^3/_4$P	$^1/_4$N–$^3/_4$P	$^5/_{16}$P	$^1/_{16}$	$12^1/_2$
		rear	—	—	$1^1/_4$N–$^1/_4$N	$^1/_2$N	0	—
	Sundance	front	①	$2^3/_4$P	$^1/_4$N–$^3/_4$P	$^5/_{16}$P	$^1/_{16}$	$12^1/_2$
		rear	—	—	$1^1/_4$N–$^1/_4$N	$^1/_2$N	0	—
	Spirit	front	①	$2^3/_4$P	$^1/_4$N–$^3/_4$P	$^5/_{16}$P	$^1/_{16}$	$12^1/_2$
		rear	—	—	$1^1/_4$N–$^1/_4$N	$^1/_2$N	0	—
	Acclaim	front	①	$2^3/_4$P	$^1/_4$N–$^3/_4$P	$^5/_{16}$P	$^1/_{16}$	$12^1/_2$
		rear	—	—	$1^1/_4$N–$^1/_4$N	$^1/_2$N	0	—
	TC	front	①	$1^3/_{16}$P	$^1/_4$N–$^3/_4$P	$^5/_{16}$P	$^1/_{16}$	$13^5/_{16}$
		rear	—	—	$1^1/_4$N–$^1/_4$N	$^1/_2$N	0	—
1992	Daytona	front	①	$2^3/_4$P	$^1/_4$N–$^3/_4$P	$^5/_{16}$P	$^1/_{16}$	$12^1/_2$
		rear	—	—	$1^1/_4$N–$^1/_4$N	$^1/_2$N	0	—
	LeBaron	front	①	$2^3/_4$P	$^1/_4$N–$^3/_4$P	$^5/_{16}$P	$^1/_{16}$	$12^1/_2$
		rear	—	—	$1^1/_4$N–$^1/_4$N	$^1/_2$N	0	—
	Shadow	front	①	$2^3/_4$P	$^1/_4$N–$^3/_4$P	$^5/_{16}$P	$^1/_{16}$	$12^1/_2$
		rear	—	—	$1^1/_4$N–$^1/_4$N	$^1/_2$N	0	—
	Sundance	front	①	$2^3/_4$P	$^1/_4$N–$^3/_4$P	$^5/_{16}$P	$^1/_{16}$	$12^1/_2$
		rear	—	—	$1^1/_4$N–$^1/_4$N	$^1/_2$N	0	—
	Spirit	front	①	$2^3/_4$P	$^1/_4$N–$^3/_4$P	$^5/_{16}$P	$^1/_{16}$	$12^1/_2$
		rear	—	—	$1^1/_4$N–$^1/_4$N	$^1/_2$N	0	—
	Acclaim	front	①	$2^3/_4$P	$^1/_4$N–$^3/_4$P	$^5/_{16}$P	$^1/_{16}$	$12^1/_2$
		rear	—	—	$1^1/_4$N–$^1/_4$N	$^1/_2$N	0	—

WHEEL ALIGNMENT

Year	Model		Caster Range (deg.)	Caster Preferred Setting (deg.)	Camber Range (deg.)	Camber Preferred Setting (deg.)	Toe-in (in.)	Steering Axis Inclination (deg.)
1993–94	Daytona	front	①	2³/₄P	¹/₄N–³/₄P	⁵/₁₆P	¹/₁₆	12¹/₂
		rear	—	—	1¹/₄N–¹/₄N	¹/₂N	0	—
	LeBaron	front	①	2³/₄P	¹/₄N–³/₄P	⁵/₁₆P	¹/₁₆	12¹/₂
		rear	—	—	1¹/₄N–¹/₄N	¹/₂N	0	—
	Shadow	front	①	2³/₄P	¹/₄N–³/₄P	⁵/₁₆P	¹/₁₆	12¹/₂
		rear	—	—	1¹/₄N–¹/₄N	¹/₂N	0	—
	Sundance	front	①	2³/₄P	¹/₄N–³/₄P	⁵/₁₆P	¹/₁₆	12¹/₂
		rear	—	—	1¹/₄N–¹/₄N	¹/₂N	0	—
	Spirit	front	①	2³/₄P	¹/₄N–³/₄P	⁵/₁₆P	¹/₁₆	12¹/₂
		rear	—	—	1¹/₄N–¹/₄N	¹/₂N	0	—
	Acclaim	front	①	2³/₄P	¹/₄N–³/₄P	⁵/₁₆P	¹/₁₆	12¹/₂
		rear	—	—	1¹/₄N–¹/₄N	¹/₂N	0	—

N—Negative
P—Positive
① Not adjustable; variation between sides should
not exceed 1.5°

AIR CONDITIONING BELT TENSION

Year	Model	Engine Liters (cc)	Belt Type	Specifications New	Specifications Used
1990	Daytona	2.2 (2213)	Poly-V	⁵/₁₆ ①	⁷/₁₆ ①
	Shadow	2.2 (2213)	Poly-V	⁵/₁₆ ①	⁷/₁₆ ①
	Sundance	2.2 (2213)	Poly-V	⁵/₁₆ ①	⁷/₁₆ ①
	LeBaron	2.2 (2213)	Poly-V	⁵/₁₆ ①	⁷/₁₆ ①
	TC	2.2 (2213)	Poly-V	⁵/₁₆ ①	⁷/₁₆ ①
	Acclaim	2.5 (2507)	Poly-V	⁵/₁₆ ①	⁷/₁₆ ①
	Daytona	2.5 (2507)	Poly-V	⁵/₁₆ ①	⁷/₁₆ ①
	Shadow	2.5 (2507)	Poly-V	⁵/₁₆ ①	⁷/₁₆ ①
	Sundance	2.5 (2507)	Poly-V	⁵/₁₆ ①	⁷/₁₆ ①
	LeBaron	2.5 (2507)	Poly-V	⁵/₁₆ ①	⁷/₁₆ ①
	TC	2.5 (2507)	Poly-V	⁵/₁₆ ①	⁷/₁₆ ①
	Acclaim	3.0 (2966)	Poly-V	⁵/₁₆ ①	⁷/₁₆ ①
	Daytona	3.0 (2966)	Poly-V	⁵/₁₆ ①	⁷/₁₆ ①
	Spirit	3.0 (2966)	Poly-V	⁵/₁₆ ①	⁷/₁₆ ①
	LeBaron	3.0 (2966)	Poly-V	⁵/₁₆ ①	⁷/₁₆ ①
	TC	3.0 (2966)	Poly-V	⁵/₁₆ ①	⁷/₁₆ ①

AIR CONDITIONING BELT TENSION

Year	Model	Engine Liters (cc)	Belt Type	Specifications New	Used
1991	Sundance	2.2 (2213)	Poly-V	5/16 ①	7/16 ①
	Spirit	2.2 (2213)	Poly-V	5/16 ①	7/16 ①
	LeBaron	2.2 (2213)	Poly-V	5/16 ①	7/16 ①
	TC	2.2 (2213)	Poly-V	5/16 ①	7/16 ①
	Shadow	2.2 (2213)	Poly-V	5/16 ①	7/16 ①
	Acclaim	2.5 (2507)	Poly-V	5/16 ①	7/16 ①
	Daytona	2.5 (2507)	Poly-V	5/16 ①	7/16 ①
	Spirit	2.5 (2507)	Poly-V	5/16 ①	7/16 ①
	Sundance	2.5 (2507)	Poly-V	5/16 ①	7/16 ①
	Shadow	2.5 (2507)	Poly-V	5/16 ①	7/16 ①
	LeBaron	2.5 (2507)	Poly-V	5/16 ①	7/16 ①
1992	Acclaim	2.2 (2213)	Poly-V	125 ②	80 ②
	Sundance	2.2 (2213)	Poly-V	125 ②	80 ②
	Spirit	2.2 (2213)	Poly-V	125 ②	80 ②
	Shadow	2.2 (2213)	Poly-V	125 ②	80 ②
	LeBaron	2.2 (2213)	Poly-V	125 ②	80 ②
	Acclaim	2.5 (2507)	Poly-V	125 ②	80 ②
	Shadow	2.5 (2507)	Poly-V	125 ②	80 ②
	Spirit	2.5 (2507)	Poly-V	125 ②	80 ②
	Sundance	2.5 (2507)	Poly-V	125 ②	80 ②
	LeBaron	2.5 (2507)	Poly-V	125 ②	80 ②
	Daytona	3.0 (2966)	Poly-V	125 ②	80 ②
	Acclaim	3.0 (2966)	Poly-V	125 ②	80 ②
	Spirit	3.0 (2966)	Poly-V	125 ②	80 ②
	Sundance	3.0 (2966)	Poly-V	125 ②	80 ②
	LeBaron	3.0 (2966)	Poly-V	125 ②	80 ②
1993	Daytona	2.2 (2213)	Poly-V	135 ②	80 ②
	Shadow	2.2 (2213)	Poly-V	135 ②	80 ②
	Sundance	2.2 (2213)	Poly-V	135 ②	80 ②
	Acclaim	2.5 (2507)	Poly-V	135 ②	80 ②
	Daytona	2.5 (2507)	Poly-V	135 ②	80 ②
	LeBaron	2.5 (2507)	Poly-V	135 ②	80 ②
	Sundance	2.5 (2507)	Poly-V	135 ②	80 ②
	Shadow	2.5 (2507)	Poly-V	135 ②	80 ②
	Spirit	2.5 (2507)	Poly-V	135 ②	80 ②
	Acclaim	3.0 (2966)	Poly-V	135 ②	80 ②
	Daytona	3.0 (2966)	Poly-V	135 ②	80 ②
	LeBaron	3.0 (2966)	Poly-V	135 ②	80 ②
	Shadow	3.0 (2966)	Poly-V	135 ②	80 ②
	Spirit	3.0 (2966)	Poly-V	135 ②	80 ②
	Sundance	3.0 (2966)	Poly-V	135 ②	80 ②

① Inches of deflection at the midpoint of the belt using 10 lbs. of force
② Specifications given in pounds are measured with appropriate belt tension gauge at midpoint of longest belt run

REFRIGERANT CAPACITIES

Year	Model	Refrigerant (oz.)	Oil (fl. oz.) ①	Compressor Type
1990	Acclaim, Shadow, Sundance, Spirit, Daytona, LeBaron	38.0	11.25	Fixed Displacement
	Acclaim, Spirit, LeBaron, Daytona, LeBaron Landau, TC	38.0	12.75	Variable Displacement
1991	Shadow	32.0	11.25	Fixed Displacement
	Sundance	32.0	11.25	Fixed Displacement
	Spirit	32.0	11.25	Fixed Displacement
	Spirit	32.0	12.80	Variable Displacement
	Acclaim	32.0	11.25	Fixed Displacement
	Acclaim	32.0	12.75	Variable Displacement
	LeBaron Landau	32.0	12.75	Variable Displacement
	Daytona	32.0	11.25	Fixed Displacement
	Daytona	32.0	12.75	Variable Displacement
	LeBaron	32.0	11.25	Fixed Displacement
	LeBaron	32.0	12.75	Variable Displacement
	TC	38.0	12.75	Variable Displacement
1992	Acclaim, Spirit, LeBaron, Daytona	32.0	11.25	Fixed Displacement 10PA17 or TR105
	Acclaim, Spirit, LeBaron, Daytona	32.0	11.25	Variable Displacement 6C17
1993	Acclaim, Spirit, LeBaron, Daytona	32.0	11.25	Fixed Displacement 10PA17, TR105, SD709P
	Acclaim, Spirit, LeBaron, Daytona	32.0	12.75	Variable Displacement 6C17

NOTE: At the time of publication, refrigerant capacity information relating to R-134a was not available from the manufacturer.
① System total capacity

MAINTENANCE INTERVALS—TYPE A: NORMAL SERVICE
Acclaim • Aries • Daytona • Lebaron • Shadow • Spirit • Sundance • TC

TO BE SERVICED	TYPE OF SERVICE	7.5	15	22.5	30	37.5	45	52.5	60
Oxygen Sensor	I				✔				✔
Ignition Timing	I				✔				✔
Vacuum Lines and Hoses	I		✔		✔		✔		✔
Ignition Wires	R								✔
Spark Plugs	R				✔				✔
Engine Oil	R	✔	✔	✔	✔	✔	✔	✔	✔
Engine Air Cleaner Element	R				✔				✔
Crankcase Emission Filter	R				✔				✔
PCV Valve	I	✔	✔	✔	✔	✔	✔	✔	✔
Fuel Filter	R				✔				✔
Engine Oil Filter	R②	✔		✔		✔		✔	
Fuel/Vapor Return Lines	I				✔				✔
Fuel Tank Cap and Restrictor	I				✔				✔
Coolant System	R				✔				✔

MAINTENANCE INTERVALS—TYPE A: NORMAL SERVICE
Acclaim • Aries • Daytona • Lebaron • Shadow • Spirit • Sundance • TC

TO BE SERVICED	TYPE OF SERVICE	VEHICLE MILEAGE INTERVAL (X1000)							
		7.5	15	22.5	30	37.5	45	52.5	60
Exhaust Pipe and Muffler	I				✔				✔
Coolant Hoses and Clamps	I		✔		✔		✔		✔
Catalytic Converter and Shield	I				✔				✔
EGR System	I				✔				✔
Chassis Lubrication	L	✔		✔		✔		✔	
CV-Joints and Boots	I	✔	✔	✔	✔	✔	✔	✔	✔
Tire Rotation	I	✔	✔	✔	✔	✔	✔	✔	✔
Timing Belt	R①								
Idle Speed System	I				✔				✔
Throttle Body	I				✔				✔
Drive Belts	I				✔				✔
Automatic Transaxle Fluid	R								✔
Battery Connections	I		✔		✔		✔		✔
Wheel Bearings	L				✔				✔
Brake Linings	I		✔				✔		✔
Parking Brake	I		✔		✔		✔		✔
Seat Belt Operation	I		✔		✔		✔		✔

FOR COMPLETE WARRANTY COVERAGE CONSULT INDIVIDUAL VEHICLE MANUFACTURER'S WARRANTY MAINTENANCE GUIDE.

I—Inspect
L—Lubricate
R—Replace
① Replace timing belt at 90,000 miles
② Replace oil filter at each oil change if mileage is less than 7,500 miles for 12 months, except turbocharged engine. Change oil and filter every 3,000 miles for turbocharged engine.

MAINTENANCE INTERVALS—TYPE B: SEVERE SERVICE
Acclaim • Aries • Daytona • Lebaron • Shadow • Spirit • Sundance • TC

TO BE SERVICED	TYPE OF SERVICE	VEHICLE MILEAGE INTERVAL (X1000)									
		3	6	9	12	15	18	21	24	27	30
Oxygen Sensor	I										✔
Ignition Timing	I										✔
Vacuum Lines and Hoses	I					✔					✔
Ignition Wires	R①										
Spark Plugs	R										✔
Engine Oil and Filter	R②	✔	✔	✔	✔	✔	✔	✔	✔	✔	✔
Engine Air Cleaner Element	R					✔					✔
Crankcase Emission Filter	R					✔					✔
PCV Valve	R					✔					✔
Fuel Filter	R					✔					✔
Fuel/Vapor Return Lines	I										✔
Fuel Tank Cap and Restrictor	I										✔
Coolant System	R										✔
Exhaust Pipe and Muffler	I										✔
Coolant Hoses and Clamps	I					✔					✔

MAINTENANCE INTERVALS—TYPE B: SEVERE SERVICE
Acclaim • Aries • Daytona • Lebaron • Shadow • Spirit • Sundance • TC

TO BE SERVICED	TYPE OF SERVICE	VEHICLE MILEAGE INTERVAL (X1000)									
		3	6	9	12	15	18	21	24	27	30
Catalytic Converter and Shield	I										✔
EGR System	I										✔
Chassis Lubrication	L		✔		✔		✔		✔		✔
CV-Joints and Boots	I	✔	✔	✔	✔	✔	✔	✔	✔	✔	
Tire Rotation	I		✔		✔		✔		✔		
Timing Belt	R ③										
Idle Speed System	I					✔					✔
Throttle Body	I					✔					✔
Drive Belts	I										✔
Automatic Transaxle Fluid	R					✔					✔
Battery Connections	I					✔					✔
Wheel Bearings	L					✔					✔
Brake Linings	I					✔					✔
Parking Brake	I					✔					✔
Seat Belt Operation	I					✔					✔

FOR COMPLETE WARRANTY COVERAGE CONSULT INDIVIDUAL VEHICLE MANUFACTURER'S WARRANTY MAINTENANCE GUIDE.

I—Inspect
L—Lubricate
R—Replace
① Replace wires at 60,000 miles
② On vehicles with turbocharged engines, change oil and oil filter every 3,000 miles
③ Replace timing belt at 90,000 miles

FIRING ORDERS

NOTE: To avoid confusion, always replace spark plug wires one at a time.

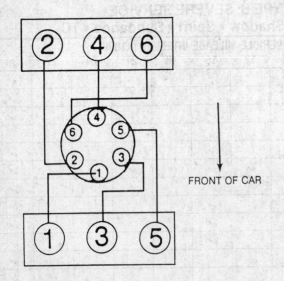

FRONT OF CAR

3.0L Engine
Engine Firing Order: 1–2–3–4–5–6
Distributor Rotation: Counterclockwise

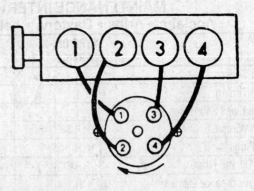

2.2L and 2.5L Engines (Except Turbo III)
Engine Firing Order: 1–3–4–2
Distributor Rotation: Clockwise

FIRING ORDERS

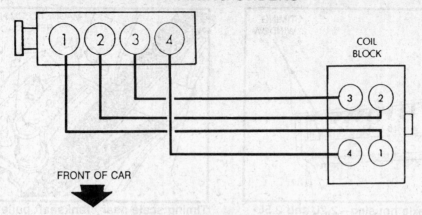

FRONT OF CAR

2.2L Turbo III Engine
Engine Firing Order: 1–3–4–2
Distributorless Ignition System

CYLINDER HEAD TORQUE SEQUENCES

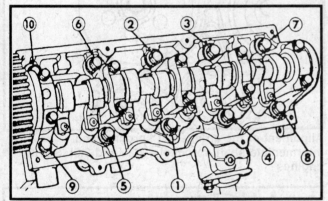

Cylinder head bolt torque sequence—2.2L and 2.5L SOHC engines

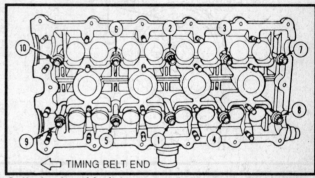

Cylinder head bolt torque sequence—2.2L DOHC engine—TC

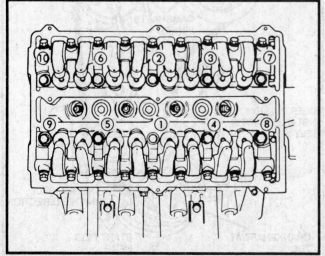

Cylinder head bolt torque sequence—2.2L Turbo III engine

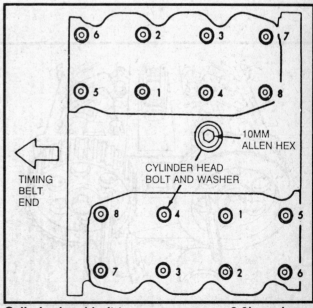

Cylinder head bolt torque sequence—3.0L engine

TIMING MARK LOCATIONS

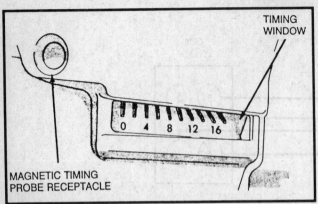

Timing scale on transaxle housing—2.2L and 2.5L engines

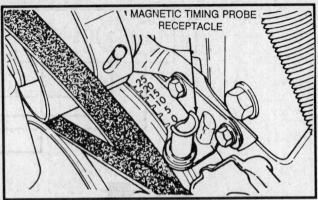

Timing scale near crankshaft pulley—3.0L engine

TIMING BELT ALIGNMENT MARKS

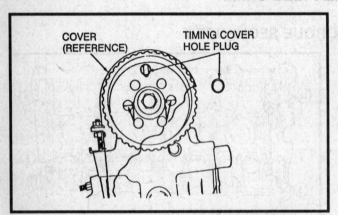

Alignment of arrows on the camshaft sprocket with the camshaft cap to cylinder head mounting line—2.2L and 2.5L SOHC engines

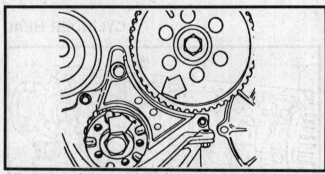

Alignment of the crankshaft sprocket and intermediate shaft sprocket—2.2L and 2.5L SOHC engines

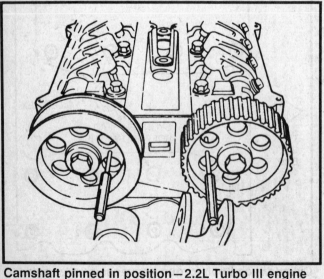

Camshaft pinned in position—2.2L Turbo III engine

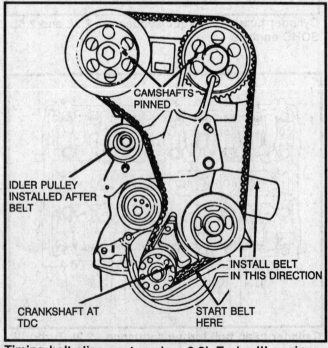

Timing belt alignment marks—2.2L Turbo III engine

TIMING BELT ALIGNMENT MARKS

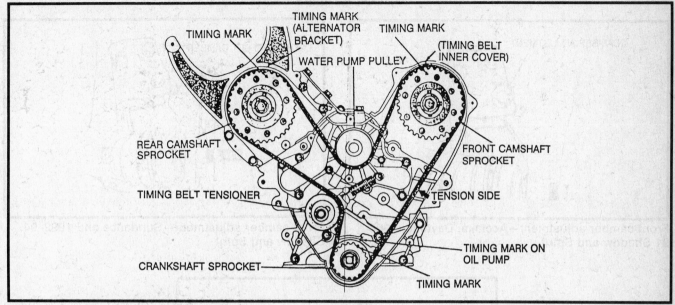

Timing belt alignment marks—3.0L engine

AIR CONDITIONING SERVICE VALVE LOCATIONS

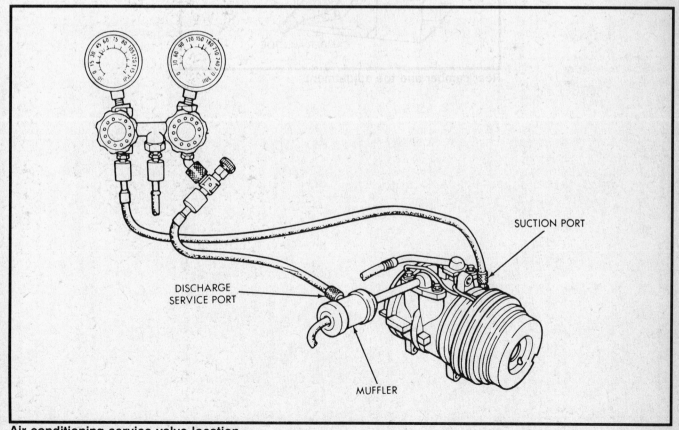

Air conditioning service valve location

WHEEL ALIGNMENT ADJUSTMENT LOCATIONS

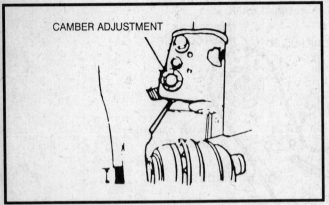

Front camber adjustment—Acclaim, Daytona, 1990–91 Shadow and Spirit

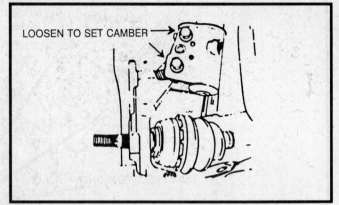

Front camber adjustment—Sundance and 1992–94 Shadow and Spirit

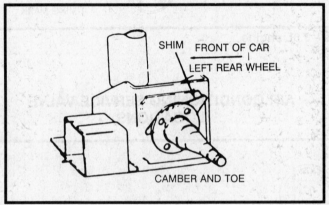

Rear camber and toe adjustment

SPECIFICATION CHARTS

VEHICLE IDENTIFICATION CHART

It is important for servicing and ordering parts to be certain of the vehicle and engine identification. The VIN (vehicle identification number) is a 17 digit number visible through the windshield on the driver's side of the dash and contains the vehicle and engine identification codes. The tenth digit indicates model year and the eighth digit indicates engine code. It can be interpreted as follows:

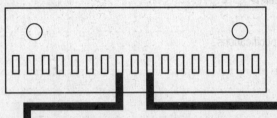

Engine Code						Model Year	
Code	Liters	Cu. In. (cc)	Cyl.	Fuel Sys.	Eng. Mfg.	Code	Year
K	2.5	153 (2507)	4	EFI	Chrysler	L	1990
3	3.0	181 (2966)	6	MPI	Mitsubishi	M	1991
R	3.3	201 (3294)	6	MPI	Chrysler	N	1992
L	3.8	231 (3786)	6	MPI	Chrysler	P	1993

EFI—Electronic Fuel Injection
MPI—Multipoint Fuel Injection

ENGINE IDENTIFICATION

Year	Model	Engine Displacement Liters (cc)	Engine Series (ID/VIN)	Fuel System	No. of Cylinders	Engine Type
1990	Dynasty	2.5 (2507)	K	EFI	4	OHC
	Dynasty	3.0 (2966)	3	MPI	6	OHC
	Dynasty	3.3 (3294)	R	MPI	6	OHV
	New Yorker Landau	3.0 (2966)	3	MPI	6	OHC
	New Yorker Landau	3.3 (3294)	R	MPI	6	OHV
	New Yorker Salon	3.0 (2966)	3	MPI	6	OHC
	New Yorker Salon	3.3 (3294)	R	MPI	6	OHV
	New Yorker 5th Avenue	3.3 (3294)	R	MPI	6	OHV
	Imperial	3.3 (3294)	R	MPI	6	OHV
1991	Dynasty	2.5 (2507)	K	EFI	4	OHC
	Dynasty	3.0 (2966)	3	MPI	6	OHC
	Dynasty	3.3 (3294)	R	MPI	6	OHV
	New Yorker Salon	3.3 (3294)	R	MPI	6	OHV
	New Yorker 5th Avenue	3.3 (3294)	R	MPI	6	OHV
	New Yorker 5th Avenue	3.8 (3786)	L	MPI	6	OHV
	Imperial	3.8 (3786)	L	MPI	6	OHV
1992	Dynasty	2.5 (2507)	K	EFI	4	OHC
	Dynasty	3.0 (2966)	3	MPI	6	OHC
	Dynasty	3.3 (3294)	R	MPI	6	OHV
	New Yorker Salon	3.3 (3294)	R	MPI	6	OHV
	New Yorker 5th Avenue	3.3 (3294)	R	MPI	6	OHV
	New Yorker 5th Avenue	3.8 (3786)	L	MPI	6	OHV
	Imperial	3.8 (3786)	L	MPI	6	OHV

ENGINE IDENTIFICATION

Year	Model	Engine Displacement Liters (cc)	Engine Series (ID/VIN)	Fuel System	No. of Cylinders	Engine Type
1993	Dynasty	2.5 (2507)	K	EFI	4	OHC
	Dynasty	3.0 (2966)	3	MPI	6	OHC
	Dynasty	3.3 (3294)	R	MPI	6	OHV
	New Yorker Salon	3.3 (3294)	R	MPI	6	OHV
	New Yorker 5th Avenue	3.3 (3294)	R	MPI	6	OHV
	New Yorker 5th Avenue	3.8 (3786)	L	MPI	6	OHV
	Imperial	3.8 (3786)	L	MPI	6	OHV

OHC—Overhead Camshaft
OHV—Overhead Valve
MPI—Multipoint Fuel Injection
EFI—Electronic Fuel Injection

GENERAL ENGINE SPECIFICATIONS

Year	Engine ID/VIN	Engine Displacement Liters (cc)	Fuel System Type	Net Horsepower @ rpm	Net Torque @ rpm (ft. lbs.)	Bore × Stroke (in.)	Compression Ratio	Oil Pressure @ rpm
1990	K	2.5 (2507)	EFI	100 @ 2800	135 @ 2800	3.44 × 4.09	8.9:1	30–80 @ 3000
	3	3.0 (2966)	MPI	141 @ 5000	171 @ 2800	3.59 × 2.99	8.9:1	30–80 @ 3000
	R	3.3 (3294)	MPI	147 @ 4800	183 @ 3600	3.66 × 3.19	8.9:1	30–80 @ 3000
1991	K	2.5 (2507)	EFI	100 @ 2800	135 @ 2800	3.44 × 4.09	8.9:1	30–80 @ 3000
	3	3.0 (2966)	MPI	141 @ 5000	171 @ 2800	3.59 × 2.99	8.9:1	30–80 @ 3000
	R	3.3 (3294)	MPI	147 @ 4800	183 @ 3600	3.66 × 3.19	8.9:1	30–80 @ 3000
	L	3.8 (3786)	MPI	150 @ 4400	203 @ 3200	3.78 × 3.42	9.0:1	30–80 @ 3000
1992	K	2.5 (2507)	EFI	100 @ 2800	135 @ 2800	3.44 × 4.09	8.9:1	30–80 @ 3000
	3	3.0 (2966)	MPI	141 @ 5000	171 @ 2800	3.59 × 2.99	8.9:1	30–80 @ 3000
	R	3.3 (3294)	MPI	147 @ 4800	183 @ 3600	3.66 × 3.19	8.9:1	30–80 @ 3000
	L	3.8 (3786)	MPI	150 @ 4400	203 @ 3200	3.78 × 3.42	9.0:1	30–80 @ 3000
1993	K	2.5 (2507)	EFI	100 @ 2800	135 @ 2800	3.44 × 4.09	8.9:1	30–80 @ 3000
	3	3.0 (2966)	MPI	141 @ 5000	171 @ 2800	3.59 × 2.99	8.9:1	30–80 @ 3000
	R	3.3 (3294)	MPI	147 @ 4800	183 @ 3600	3.66 × 3.19	8.9:1	30–80 @ 3000
	L	3.8 (3786)	MPI	150 @ 4400	203 @ 3200	3.78 × 3.42	9.0:1	30–80 @ 3000

NOTE: Horsepower and torque are SAE net figures. They are measured at the rear of the transmission with all accessories installed and operating. Since the figures vary when a given engine is installed in different models, some are representative rather than exact.
EFI—Electronic Fuel Injection
MPI—Multipoint Fuel Injection

GASOLINE ENGINE TUNE-UP SPECIFICATIONS

Year	Engine ID/VIN	Engine Displacement Liters (cc)	Spark Plugs Gap (in.)	Ignition Timing (deg.) MT	Ignition Timing (deg.) AT	Fuel Pump (psi)	Idle Speed (rpm) MT	Idle Speed (rpm) AT	Valve Clearance In.	Valve Clearance Ex.
1990	K	2.5 (2507)	0.035	—	12B	15	—	850	Hyd.	Hyd.
	3	3.0 (2966)	0.040	—	12B	48①	—	700	Hyd.	Hyd.
	R	3.3 (3294)	0.050	—	12B	48①	—	750	Hyd.	Hyd.
1991	K	2.5 (2507)	0.035	—	12B	15	—	850	Hyd.	Hyd.
	3	3.0 (2966)	0.040	—	12B	48①	—	700	Hyd.	Hyd.
	R	3.3 (3294)	0.050	—	12B	48①	—	750	Hyd.	Hyd.
	L	3.8 (3786)	0.050	—	12B	48①	—	750	Hyd.	Hyd.

GASOLINE ENGINE TUNE-UP SPECIFICATIONS

Year	Engine ID/VIN	Engine Displacement Liters (cc)	Spark Plugs Gap (in.)	Ignition Timing (deg.) MT	Ignition Timing (deg.) AT	Fuel Pump (psi)	Idle Speed (rpm) MT	Idle Speed (rpm) AT	Valve Clearance In.	Valve Clearance Ex.
1992	K	2.5 (2507)	0.035	—	12B	15	—	850	Hyd.	Hyd.
	3	3.0 (2966)	0.040	—	12B	48 ①	—	700	Hyd.	Hyd.
	R	3.3 (3294)	0.050	—	12B	48 ①	—	750	Hyd.	Hyd.
	L	3.8 (3786)	0.050	—	12B	48 ①	—	750	Hyd.	Hyd.
1993	K	2.5 (2507)	0.035	—	12B	15	—	850	Hyd.	Hyd.
	3	3.0 (2966)	0.040	—	12B	48 ①	—	700	Hyd.	Hyd.
	R	3.3 (3294)	0.050	—	12B	48 ①	—	750	Hyd.	Hyd.
	L	3.8 (3786)	0.050	—	12B	48 ①	—	750	Hyd.	Hyd.

NOTE: The lowest cylinder pressure should be within 75% of the highest cylinder pressure reading. For example, if the highest cylinder is 134 psi, the lowest should be 101. Engine should be at normal operating temperature with throttle valve in the wide open position.
The underhood specifications sticker often reflects tune-up specification changes in production. Sticker figures must be used if they disagree with those in this chart.
Hyd.—Hydraulic
① This reading measured with the vacuum hose disconnected from the fuel pressure regulator.

CAPACITIES

Year	Model	Engine ID/VIN	Engine Displacement Liters (cc)	Engine Crankcase (qts.) with Filter	Transmission (pts.) 4-Spd	Transmission (pts.) 5-Spd	Transmission (pts.) Auto.	Transfer case (pts.)	Drive Axle Front (pts.)	Drive Axle Rear (pts.)	Fuel Tank (gal.)	Cooling System (qts.)
1990	Dynasty	K	2.5 (2507)	4	—	—	18	—	—	—	16	9.0
	Dynasty	3	3.0 (2966)	4	—	—	18	—	—	—	16	9.5
	Dynasty	R	3.3 (3294)	4	—	—	18	—	—	—	16	9.5
	New Yorker Landau	3	3.0 (2966)	4	—	—	18	—	—	—	16	9.5
	New Yorker Landau	R	3.3 (3294)	4	—	—	18	—	—	—	16	9.5
	New Yorker Salon	3	3.0 (2966)	4	—	—	18	—	—	—	16	9.5
	New Yorker Salon	R	3.3 (3294)	4	—	—	18	—	—	—	16	9.5
	New Yorker 5th Avenue	R	3.3 (3294)	4	—	—	18	—	—	—	16	9.5
	Imperial	R	3.3 (3294)	4	—	—	18	—	—	—	16	9.5
1991	Dynasty	K	2.5 (2507)	4	—	—	18	—	—	—	16	9.0
	Dynasty	3	3.0 (2966)	4	—	—	18	—	—	—	16	9.5
	Dynasty	R	3.3 (3294)	4	—	—	18	—	—	—	16	9.5
	New Yorker Salon	R	3.3 (3294)	4	—	—	18	—	—	—	16	9.5
	New Yorker 5th Avenue	R	3.3 (3294)	4	—	—	18	—	—	—	16	9.5
	New Yorker 5th Avenue	L	3.8 (3786)	4	—	—	18	—	—	—	16	9.5
	Imperial	L	3.8 (3786)	4	—	—	18	—	—	—	16	9.5
1992	Dynasty	K	2.5 (2507)	4	—	—	18	—	—	—	16	9.0
	Dynasty	3	3.0 (2966)	4	—	—	18	—	—	—	16	9.5
	Dynasty	R	3.3 (3294)	4	—	—	18	—	—	—	16	9.5
	New Yorker Salon	R	3.3 (3294)	4	—	—	18	—	—	—	16	9.5
	New Yorker 5th Avenue	R	3.3 (3294)	4	—	—	18	—	—	—	16	9.5
	New Yorker 5th Avenue	L	3.8 (3786)	4	—	—	18	—	—	—	16	9.5
	Imperial	L	3.8 (3786)	4	—	—	18	—	—	—	16	9.5

CAPACITIES

Year	Model	Engine ID/VIN	Engine Displacement Liters (cc)	Engine Crankcase (qts.) with Filter	Transmission (pts.) 4-Spd	5-Spd	Auto.	Transfer case (pts.)	Drive Axle Front (pts.)	Rear (pts.)	Fuel Tank (gal.)	Cooling System (qts.)
1993	Dynasty	K	2.5 (2507)	4	—	—	18	—	—	—	16	9.0
	Dynasty	3	3.0 (2966)	4	—	—	18	—	—	—	16	9.5
	Dynasty	R	3.3 (3294)	4	—	—	18	—	—	—	16	9.5
	New Yorker Salon	R	3.3 (3294)	4	—	—	18	—	—	—	16	9.5
	New Yorker 5th Avenue	R	3.3 (3294)	4	—	—	18	—	—	—	16	9.5
	New Yorker 5th Avenue	L	3.8 (3786)	4	—	—	18	—	—	—	16	9.5
	Imperial	L	3.8 (3786)	4	—	—	18	—	—	—	16	9.5

CAMSHAFT SPECIFICATIONS

All measurements given in inches.

Year	Engine ID/VIN	Engine Displacement Liters (cc)	Journal Diameter 1	2	3	4	5	Elevation In.	Ex.	Bearing Clearance	Camshaft End Play
1990	K	2.5 (2507)	1.375–1.376	1.375–1.376	1.375–1.376	1.375–1.376	1.375–1.376	NA	NA	—	0.005–0.020
	3	3.0 (2966)	NA	NA	NA	NA	—	①	①	—	NA
	R	3.3 (3294)	1.997–1.999	1.980–1.982	1.965–1.967	1.949–1.952	—	0.400	0.400	0.001–0.005	0.005–0.012
1991	K	2.5 (2507)	1.395–1.396	1.395–1.396	1.395–1.396	1.395–1.396	1.395–1.396	NA	NA	—	0.005–0.020
	3	3.0 (2966)	NA	NA	NA	NA	—	①	①	—	NA
	R	3.3 (3294)	1.997–1.999	1.980–1.982	1.965–1.967	1.949–1.952	—	0.400	0.400	0.001–0.005	0.005–0.012
	L	3.8 (3786)	1.997–1.999	1.980–1.982	1.965–1.967	1.949–1.952	—	0.400	0.400	0.001–0.004	0.005–0.012
1992	K	2.5 (2507)	1.395–1.396	1.395–1.396	1.395–1.396	1.395–1.396	1.395–1.396	NA	NA	—	0.005–0.020
	3	3.0 (2966)	NA	NA	NA	NA	—	①	①	—	NA
	R	3.3 (3294)	1.997–1.999	1.980–1.982	1.965–1.967	1.949–1.952	—	0.400	0.400	0.001–0.005	0.005–0.012
	L	3.8 (3786)	1.997–1.999	1.980–1.982	1.965–1.967	1.949–1.952	—	0.400	0.400	0.001–0.004	0.005–0.012
1993	K	2.5 (2507)	1.395–1.396	1.395–1.396	1.395–1.396	1.395–1.396	1.395–1.396	NA	NA	—	0.005–0.020
	3	3.0 (2966)	NA	NA	NA	NA	—	①	①	—	NA
	R	3.3 (3294)	1.997–1.999	1.980–1.982	1.965–1.967	1.949–1.952	—	0.400	0.400	0.001–0.005	0.005–0.012
	L	3.8 (3786)	1.997–1.999	1.980–1.982	1.965–1.967	1.949–1.952	—	0.400	0.400	0.001–0.004	0.005–0.012

NA—Not available
① Standard Value: 1.624 in.
　Wear limit: 1.604 in.

CRANKSHAFT AND CONNECTING ROD SPECIFICATIONS

All measurements are given in inches.

Year	Engine ID/VIN	Engine Displacement Liters (cc)	Crankshaft				Connecting Rod		
			Main Brg. Journal Dia.	Main Brg. Oil Clearance	Shaft End-play	Thrust on No.	Journal Diameter	Oil Clearance	Side Clearance
1990	K	2.5 (2507)	2.362–3.363	0.0004–0.0040	0.002–0.014	3	1.968–1.969	0.0008–0.0040	0.005–0.013
	3	3.0 (2966)	2.361–2.362	0.0006–0.0020	0.002–0.010	3	1.968–1.969	0.0008–0.0028	0.004–0.010
	R	3.3 (3294)	2.519	0.0007–0.0022	0.001–0.007	2	2.283	0.0008–0.0030	0.005–0.015
1991	K	2.5 (2507)	2.362–3.363	0.0004–0.0040	0.002–0.014	3	1.968–1.969	0.0008–0.0040	0.005–0.013
	3	3.0 (2966)	2.361–2.362	0.0006–0.0020	0.002–0.010	3	1.968–1.969	0.0008–0.0028	0.004–0.010
	R	3.3 (3294)	2.519	0.0007–0.0022	0.001–0.007	2	2.283	0.0008–0.0030	0.005–0.015
	L	3.8 (3786)	2.519	0.0007–0.0022	0.003–0.009	2	2.283	0.0008–0.0030	0.005–0.015
1992	K	2.5 (2507)	2.362–3.363	0.0004–0.0040	0.002–0.014	3	1.968–1.969	0.0008–0.0040	0.005–0.013
	3	3.0 (2966)	2.361–2.362	0.0006–0.0020	0.002–0.010	3	1.968–1.969	0.0008–0.0028	0.004–0.010
	R	3.3 (3294)	2.519	0.0007–0.0022	0.001–0.007	2	2.283	0.0008–0.0030	0.005–0.015
	L	3.8 (3786)	2.519	0.0007–0.0022	0.003–0.009	2	2.283	0.0008–0.0030	0.005–0.015
1993	K	2.5 (2507)	2.362–3.363	0.0004–0.0040	0.002–0.014	3	1.968–1.969	0.0008–0.0040	0.005–0.013
	3	3.0 (2966)	2.361–2.362	0.0006–0.0020	0.002–0.010	3	1.968–1.969	0.0008–0.0028	0.004–0.010
	R	3.3 (3294)	2.519	0.0007–0.0022	0.001–0.007	2	2.283	0.0008–0.0030	0.005–0.015
	L	3.8 (3786)	2.519	0.0007–0.0022	0.003–0.009	2	2.283	0.0008–0.0030	0.005–0.015

VALVE SPECIFICATIONS

Year	Engine ID/VIN	Engine Displacement Liters (cc)	Seat Angle (deg.)	Face Angle (deg.)	Spring Test Pressure (lbs. @ in.)	Spring Installed Height (in.)	Stem-to-Guide Clearance (in.)		Stem Diameter (in.)	
							Intake	Exhaust	Intake	Exhaust
1990	K	2.5 (2507)	45.0	45.0	114 @ 1.65	1.65	0.0010–0.0030	0.0030–0.0047	0.3124	0.3103
	3	3.0 (2966)	44.5	45.5	73 @ 1.59	1.59	0.0010–0.0020	0.0020–0.0030	0.3130–0.3140	0.3120–0.3130
	R	3.3 (3294)	45.0	44.5	60 @ 1.56	1.56	0.0020–0.0160	0.0020–0.0160	0.3130–0.3140	0.3120–0.3130

VALVE SPECIFICATIONS

Year	Engine ID/VIN	Engine Displacement Liters (cc)	Seat Angle (deg.)	Face Angle (deg.)	Spring Test Pressure (lbs. @ in.)	Spring Installed Height (in.)	Stem-to-Guide Clearance (in.) Intake	Stem-to-Guide Clearance (in.) Exhaust	Stem Diameter (in.) Intake	Stem Diameter (in.) Exhaust
1991	K	2.5 (2507)	45.0	45.0	114 @ 1.65	1.65	0.0010–0.0030	0.0030–0.0047	0.3124	0.3103
	3	3.0 (2966)	44.5	45.5	73 @ 1.59	1.59	0.0010–0.0020	0.0020–0.0030	0.3130–0.3140	0.3120–0.3130
	R	3.3 (3294)	45.0	44.5	60 @ 1.56	1.56	0.0020–0.0160	0.0020–0.0160	0.3130–0.3140	0.3120–0.3130
	L	3.8 (3786)	45.0	44.5	60 @ 1.56	1.56	0.0010–0.0030	0.0020–0.0160	0.3120–0.3130	0.3110–0.3120
1992	K	2.5 (2507)	45.0	45.0	114 @ 1.65	1.65	0.0010–0.0030	0.0030–0.0047	0.3124	0.3103
	3	3.0 (2966)	44.5	45.5	73 @ 1.59	1.59	0.0010–0.0020	0.0020–0.0030	0.3130–0.3140	0.3120–0.3130
	R	3.3 (3294)	45.0	44.5	60 @ 1.56	1.56	0.0020–0.0160	0.0020–0.0160	0.3130–0.3140	0.3120–0.3130
	L	3.8 (3786)	45.0	44.5	60 @ 1.56	1.56	0.0010–0.0030	0.0020–0.0160	0.3120–0.3130	0.3110–0.3120
1993	K	2.5 (2507)	45.0	45.0	114 @ 1.65	1.65	0.0010–0.0030	0.0030–0.0047	0.3124	0.3103
	3	3.0 (2966)	44.5	45.5	73 @ 1.59	1.59	0.0010–0.0020	0.0020–0.0030	0.3130–0.3140	0.3120–0.3130
	R	3.3 (3294)	45.0	44.5	60 @ 1.56	1.56	0.0020–0.0160	0.0020–0.0160	0.3130–0.3140	0.3120–0.3130
	L	3.8 (3786)	45.0	44.5	60 @ 1.56	1.56	0.0010–0.0030	0.0020–0.0160	0.3120–0.3130	0.3110–0.3120

PISTON AND RING SPECIFICATIONS

All measurements are given in inches.

Year	Engine ID/VIN	Engine Displacement Liters (cc)	Piston Clearance	Ring Gap Top Compression	Ring Gap Bottom Compression	Ring Gap Oil Control	Ring Side Clearance Top Compression	Ring Side Clearance Bottom Compression	Ring Side Clearance Oil Control
1990	K	2.5 (2507)	0.0010–0.0027	0.0100–0.0390	0.0110–0.0390	0.015–0.074	0.0010–0.0030	0.0010–0.0030	0.0006–0.0089
	3	3.0 (2966)	0.0012–0.0020	0.0120–0.0310	0.0100–0.0300	0.012–0.039	0.0020–0.0039	0.0008–0.0039	NA
	R	3.3 (3294)	0.0009–0.0022	0.0118–0.0217	0.0118–0.0217	0.010–0.039	0.0012–0.0037	0.0012–0.0037	0.0006–0.0089
1991	K	2.5 (2507)	0.0010–0.0027	0.0100–0.0390	0.0110–0.0390	0.015–0.074	0.0010–0.0040	0.0010–0.0040	0.0006–0.0089
	3	3.0 (2966)	0.0012–0.0020	0.0120–0.0310	0.0100–0.0300	0.012–0.039	0.0020–0.0039	0.0008–0.0039	NA
	R	3.3 (3294)	0.0009–0.0022	0.0118–0.0217	0.0118–0.0217	0.010–0.039	0.0012–0.0037	0.0012–0.0037	0.0005–0.0089
	L	3.8 (3786)	0.0009–0.0022	0.0118–0.0217	0.0118–0.0217	0.010–0.039	0.0012–0.0037	0.0012–0.0037	0.0005–0.0089

PISTON AND RING SPECIFICATIONS

All measurements are given in inches.

Year	Engine ID/VIN	Engine Displacement Liters (cc)	Piston Clearance	Ring Gap			Ring Side Clearance		
				Top Compression	Bottom Compression	Oil Control	Top Compression	Bottom Compression	Oil Control
1992	K	2.5 (2507)	0.0010–0.0027	0.0100–0.0390	0.0110–0.0390	0.015–0.074	0.0010–0.0040	0.0010–0.0040	0.0006–0.0089
	3	3.0 (2966)	0.0012–0.0020	0.0120–0.0310	0.0100–0.0300	0.012–0.039	0.0020–0.0039	0.0008–0.0039	NA
	R	3.3 (3294)	0.0009–0.0022	0.0118–0.0217	0.0118–0.0217	0.010–0.039	0.0012–0.0037	0.0012–0.0037	0.0005–0.0089
	L	3.8 (3786)	0.0009–0.0022	0.0118–0.0217	0.0118–0.0217	0.010–0.039	0.0012–0.0037	0.0012–0.0037	0.0005–0.0089
1993	K	2.5 (2507)	0.0010–0.0027	0.0100–0.0390	0.0110–0.0390	0.015–0.074	0.0010–0.0040	0.0010–0.0040	0.0006–0.0089
	3	3.0 (2966)	0.0012–0.0020	0.0120–0.0310	0.0100–0.0300	0.012–0.039	0.0020–0.0039	0.0008–0.0039	NA
	R	3.3 (3294)	0.0009–0.0022	0.0118–0.0217	0.0118–0.0217	0.010–0.039	0.0012–0.0037	0.0012–0.0037	0.0005–0.0089
	L	3.8 (3786)	0.0009–0.0022	0.0118–0.0217	0.0118–0.0217	0.010–0.039	0.0012–0.0037	0.0012–0.0037	0.0005–0.0089

NA—Not available

TORQUE SPECIFICATIONS

All readings in ft. lbs.

Year	Engine ID/VIN	Engine Displacement Liters (cc)	Cylinder Head Bolts	Main Bearing Bolts	Rod Bearing Bolts	Crankshaft Damper Bolts	Flywheel Bolts	Manifold		Spark Plugs	Lug Nut
								Intake	Exhaust		
1990	K	2.5 (2507)	①	30③	40③	85	70	17	17	26	80–110
	3	3.0 (2966)	70	60	38	112	70	17	17	20	80–110
	R	3.3 (3294)	②	30③	40③	110	70	17	17	20	80–110
1991	K	2.5 (2507)	①	30③	40③	85	70	17	17	26	80–110
	3	3.0 (2966)	80	60	38	112	70	17	17	20	80–110
	R	3.3 (3294)	②	30③	40③	—	70	17	17	20	80–110
	L	3.8 (3786)	②	30③	40③	—	70	17	17	20	80–110
1992	K	2.5 (2507)	①	30③	40③	85	70	17	17	26	80–110
	3	3.0 (2966)	80	60	38	112	70	17	17	20	80–110
	R	3.3 (3294)	②	30③	40③	—	70	17	17	20	80–110
	L	3.8 (3786)	②	30③	40③	—	70	17	17	20	80–110
1993	K	2.5 (2507)	①	30③	40③	85	70	17	17	26	80–110
	3	3.0 (2966)	80	60	38	112	70	17	17	20	80–110
	R	3.3 (3294)	②	30③	40③	—	70	17	17	20	80–110
	L	3.8 (3786)	②	30③	40③	—	70	17	17	20	80–110

① Sequence: 45, 65, 65, plus ¼ turn
② Sequence: 45, 65, 65, plus ¼ turn
  Torque the small bolt in the rear of the cylinder
  head to 25 ft. lbs. (34 Nm)
③ Plus ¼ turn

TORQUE SPECIFICATIONS

Component	English	Metric
Camshaft bearing cap bolts		
2.5L engine:	18 ft. lbs.	25 Nm
3.0L engine:	15 ft. lbs.	20 Nm
Camshaft sprocket bolt		
2.5L engine:	65 ft. lbs.	88 Nm
3.0L engine:	70 ft. lbs.	95 Nm
3.3L and 3.8L engines:	40 ft. lbs.	54 Nm
Connecting rod bearing cap bolts		
2.5L, 3.3L and 3.8L engines		
Step 1:	40 ft. lbs.	54 Nm
Step 2:	+ 90 degrees turn	+ 90 degrees turn
3.0L engine:	38 ft. lbs.	52 Nm
Crankshaft damper bolt		
2.5L engine:	85 ft. lbs.	115 Nm
3.0L engine:	112 ft. lbs.	151 Nm
3.3L and 3.8L engines:	110 ft. lbs.	149 Nm
Crankshaft pulley bolt		
3.0L engine:	21 ft. lbs.	28 Nm
3.3L and 3.8L engines:	40 ft. lbs.	54 Nm
Cylinder head bolt		
2.5L engine		
Step 1:	45 ft. lbs.	61 Nm
Step 2:	65 ft. lbs.	89 Nm
Step 3:	65 ft. lbs.	89 Nm
Step 4:	+ 90 degrees turn	+ 90 degrees turn
3.0L engine		
1990:	70 ft. lbs.	95 Nm
1991–93:	80 ft. lbs.	108 Nm
3.3L and 3.8L engines		
Step 1:	45 ft. lbs.	61 Nm
Step 2:	65 ft. lbs.	89 Nm
Step 3:	65 ft. lbs.	89 Nm
Step 4:	+ 90 degrees turn[1]	+ 90 degrees turn[1]
Step 5:	25 ft. lbs.[2]	33 Nm[2]
[1] Bolt torque after ¼ turn should not exceed 90 ft. lbs. (122 Nm).		
[2] Single small head bolt		
EGR valve-to-intake manifold/plenum:	17 ft. lbs.	22 Nm
Engine-to-transmission:	70 ft. lbs.	95 Nm
Exhaust manifold:	17 ft. lbs.	23 Nm
Exhaust pipe-to-exhaust manifold nuts:	25 ft. lbs.	33 Nm
Flywheel/flexplate-to-crankshaft bolts:	70 ft. lbs.	95 Nm
Flywheel-to-converter bolts:	55 ft. lbs.	74 Nm
Fuel injection		
MPI		
Intake plenum-to-cylinder head		
3.0L engine:	11 ft. lbs.	15 Nm
3.3L and 3.8L engines:	21 ft. lbs.	28 Nm
TBI		
Throttle body-to-manifold		
2.5L engine:	15 ft. lbs.	20 Nm
3.0L engine:	19 ft. lbs.	25 Nm
Intake manifold:	17 ft. lbs.	23 Nm
Main bearing cap bolts		
2.5L, 3.3L and 3.8L engines		
Step 1:	30 ft. lbs.	41 Nm
Step 2:	+ 90 degrees turn	+ 90 degrees turn
3.0L engine:	60 ft. lbs.	80 Nm

TORQUE SPECIFICATIONS

Component	English	Metric
Oil pan		
2.5L engine		
M8 bolts:	17 ft. lbs.	23 Nm
M6 bolts:	9 ft. lbs.	12 Nm
3.0L engine:	50 inch lbs.	6 Nm
3.3L and 3.8L engines:	105 inch lbs.	12 Nm
Oil pan drain plug		
Except 3.0L engine:	20 ft. lbs.	27 Nm
3.0L engine:	30 ft. lbs.	40 Nm
Oil pump attaching bolts		
2.5L engine:	17 ft. lbs.	23 Nm
3.0L engine:	130 inch lbs.	15 Nm
3.3L and 3.8L engines:	20 ft. lbs.	27 Nm
Rocker arm shaft bolt		
3.0L engine		
Step 1:	7 ft. lbs.	10 Nm
Step 2:	15 ft. lbs.	20 Nm
3.3L and 3.8L engines:	21 ft. lbs.	28 Nm
Rocker (valve) cover		
2.5L, 3.3L and 3.8L engines:	105 inch lbs.	12 Nm
3.0L engine:	113 inch lbs.	12 Nm
Spark plug		
2.5L engine:	26 ft. lbs.	35 Nm
3.0L engine:	20 ft. lbs.	27 Nm
3.3L and 3.8L engines:	30 ft. lbs.	41 Nm
Starter-to-block bolts		
Except 3.3L and 3.8L engines:	40 ft. lbs.	54 Nm
3.3L and 3.8L engines:	50 ft. lbs.	68 Nm
Thermostat housing		
2.5L, 3.3L and 3.8L engines:	21 ft. lbs.	28 Nm
3.0L engine:	113 inch lbs.	12 Nm
Timing cover		
2.5L engine:	40 inch lbs.	4 Nm
3.0L engine:	115 inch lbs.	14 Nm
3.3L and 3.8L engines		
M8 × 1.25 bolts:	20 ft. lbs.	27 Nm
M10 × 1.5 bolts:	40 ft. lbs.	54 Nm
Water pump		
2.5L engine		
Upper bolts:	21 ft. lbs.	28 Nm
Lower bolts:	40 ft. lbs.	54 Nm
3.3L and 3.8L engines:	105 inch lbs.	12 Nm
Water pump pulley:	21 ft. lbs.	28 Nm

BRAKE SPECIFICATIONS

All measurements in inches unless noted.

Year	Model		Master Cylinder Bore	Brake Disc Original Thickness	Brake Disc Minimum Thickness	Maximum Runout	Brake Drum Diameter Original Inside Diameter	Brake Drum Diameter Max. Wear Limit	Brake Drum Diameter Maximum Machine Diameter	Minimum Lining Thickness Front	Minimum Lining Thickness Rear
1990	Dynasty	front	0.827	0.935	0.882	0.005	7.87	NA	NA	0.30	0.06
		rear	—	0.354	0.339	0.005	—	—	—	—	0.28
	New Yorker Landau	front	0.827	0.935	0.882	0.005	7.87	NA	NA	0.30	0.06
		rear	—	0.354	0.339	0.005	—	—	—	—	0.28
	New Yorker Salon	front	0.827	0.935	0.882	0.005	7.87	NA	NA	0.30	0.06
		rear	—	0.354	0.339	0.005	—	—	—	—	0.28
	New Yorker 5th Avenue	front	0.827	0.935	0.882	0.005	7.87	NA	NA	0.30	0.06
		rear	—	0.354	0.339	0.005	—	—	—	—	0.28
	Imperial	front	0.827	0.935	0.882	0.005	7.87	NA	NA	0.30	0.06
		rear	—	0.354	0.339	0.005	—	—	—	—	0.28
1991	Dynasty	front	0.827	0.935	0.882	0.005	7.87	NA	NA	0.30	0.06
		rear	—	0.354	0.339	0.005	—	—	—	—	0.28
	New Yorker Salon	front	0.827	0.935	0.882	0.005	7.87	NA	NA	0.30	0.06
		rear	—	0.354	0.339	0.005	—	—	—	—	0.28
	New Yorker 5th Avenue	front	0.827	0.935	0.882	0.005	7.87	NA	NA	0.30	0.06
		rear	—	0.354	0.339	0.005	—	—	—	—	0.28
	Imperial	front	0.827	0.935	0.882	0.005	7.87	NA	NA	0.30	0.06
		rear	—	0.354	0.339	0.005	—	—	—	—	0.28
1992	Dynasty	front	0.827	0.861	0.803	0.005	—	—	—	0.30	—
		rear	—	0.354	0.339	0.005	—	—	—	—	0.28
	New Yorker Salon	front	0.827	0.861	0.803	0.005	—	—	—	0.30	—
		rear	—	0.354	0.339	0.005	—	—	—	—	0.28
	New Yorker 5th Avenue	front	0.827	0.861	0.803	0.005	—	—	—	0.30	—
		rear	—	0.354	0.339	0.005	—	—	—	—	0.28
	Imperial	front	0.827	0.861	0.803	0.005	—	—	—	0.30	—
		rear	—	0.354	0.339	0.005	—	—	—	—	0.28
1993	Dynasty	front	0.827	0.861	0.803	0.005	—	—	—	0.30	—
		rear	—	0.354	0.339	0.005	—	—	—	—	0.28
	New Yorker Salon	front	0.827	0.861	0.803	0.005	—	—	—	0.30	—
		rear	—	0.354	0.339	0.005	—	—	—	—	0.28
	New Yorker 5th Avenue	front	0.827	0.861	0.803	0.005	—	—	—	0.30	—
		rear	—	0.354	0.339	0.005	—	—	—	—	0.28
	Imperial	front	0.827	0.861	0.803	0.005	—	—	—	0.30	—
		rear	—	0.354	0.339	0.005	—	—	—	—	0.28

WHEEL ALIGNMENT

Year	Model		Caster Range (deg.)	Caster Preferred Setting (deg.)	Camber Range (deg.)	Camber Preferred Setting (deg.)	Toe-in (in.)	Steering Axis Inclination (deg.)
1990	Dynasty	front	①	$1^3/_{16}$	$1/_4$N–$3/_4$P	$5/_{16}$P	$1/_{16}$	$13^5/_{16}$
		rear	—	—	$1^1/_4$N–$1/_4$N	$1/_2$N	0	—
	New Yorker Landau	front	①	$1^3/_{16}$	$1/_4$N–$3/_4$P	$5/_{16}$P	$1/_{16}$	$13^5/_{16}$
		rear	—	—	$1^1/_4$N–$1/_4$N	$1/_2$N	0	—
	New Yorker Salon	front	①	$1^3/_{16}$	$1/_4$N–$3/_4$P	$5/_{16}$P	$1/_{16}$	$13^5/_{16}$
		rear	—	—	$1^1/_4$N–$1/_4$N	$1/_2$N	0	—
	New Yorker 5th Avenue	front	①	$1^3/_{16}$	$1/_4$N–$3/_4$P	$5/_{16}$P	$1/_{16}$	$13^5/_{16}$
		rear	—	—	$1^1/_4$N–$1/_4$N	$1/_2$N	0	—
	Imperial	front	①	$1^3/_{16}$	$1/_4$N–$3/_4$P	$5/_{16}$P	$1/_{16}$	$13^5/_{16}$
		rear	—	—	$1^1/_4$N–$1/_4$N	$1/_2$N	0	—
1991	Dynasty	front	①	$2^3/_4$	$1/_4$N–$3/_4$P	$5/_{16}$P	$1/_{16}$	$12^1/_2$
		rear	—	—	$1^1/_4$N–$1/_4$N	$1/_2$N	0	—
	New Yorker Salon	front	①	$2^3/_4$	$1/_4$N–$3/_4$P	$5/_{16}$P	$1/_{16}$	$12^1/_2$
		rear	—	—	$1^1/_4$N–$1/_4$N	$1/_2$N	0	—
	New Yorker 5th Avenue	front	①	$2^3/_4$	$1/_4$N–$3/_4$P	$5/_{16}$P	$1/_{16}$	$12^1/_2$
		rear	—	—	$1^1/_4$N–$1/_4$N	$1/_2$N	0	—
	Imperial	front	①	3	$1/_4$N–$3/_4$P	$5/_{16}$P ②	$1/_{16}$	$12^1/_2$
		rear	—	—	$1^1/_4$N–$1/_4$N	$1/_2$N	0	—
1992	Dynasty	front	①	$2^3/_4$	$1/_4$N–$3/_4$P	$5/_{16}$P	$1/_{16}$	$12^1/_2$
		rear	—	—	$1^1/_4$N–$1/_4$N	$1/_2$N	0	—
	New Yorker Salon	front	①	$2^3/_4$	$1/_4$N–$3/_4$P	$5/_{16}$P	$1/_{16}$	$12^1/_2$
		rear	—	—	$1^1/_4$N–$1/_4$N	$1/_2$N	0	—
	New Yorker 5th Avenue	front	①	$2^3/_4$	$1/_4$N–$3/_4$P	$5/_{16}$P	$1/_{16}$	$12^1/_2$
		rear	—	—	$1^1/_4$N–$1/_4$N	$1/_2$N	0	—
	Imperial	front	①	3	$1/_4$N–$3/_4$P	$5/_{16}$P ②	$1/_{16}$	$12^1/_2$
		rear	—	—	$1^1/_4$N–$1/_4$N	$1/_2$N	0	—
1993	Dynasty	front	①	$2^3/_4$	$1/_4$N–$3/_4$P	$5/_{16}$P	$1/_{16}$	$12^1/_2$
		rear	—	—	$1^1/_4$N–$1/_4$N	$1/_2$N	0	—
	New Yorker Salon	front	①	$2^3/_4$	$1/_4$N–$3/_4$P	$5/_{16}$P	$1/_{16}$	$12^1/_2$
		rear	—	—	$1^1/_4$N–$1/_4$N	$1/_2$N	0	—
	New Yorker 5th Avenue	front	①	$2^3/_4$	$1/_4$N–$3/_4$P	$5/_{16}$P	$1/_{16}$	$12^1/_2$
		rear	—	—	$1^1/_4$N–$1/_4$N	$1/_2$N	0	—
	Imperial	front	①	3	$1/_4$N–$3/_4$P	$5/_{16}$P ②	$1/_{16}$	$12^1/_2$
		rear	—	—	$1^1/_4$N–$1/_4$N	$1/_2$N	0	—

N—Negative
P—Positive
① Not adjustable—variation between sides should not exceed $1^1/_2$°
② With air suspension—$3/_{16}$ in.

AIR CONDITIONING BELT TENSION

Year	Model	Engine Displacement Liters (cc)	Belt Type	Specifications (in.)	
				New	Used
1990	Dynasty	2.2 (2213)	Poly-V	5/16	7/16
	Dynasty	2.5 (2507)	Poly-V	5/16	7/16
	Dynasty, New Yorker, Imperial, Fifth Avenue	3.0 (2966)	Poly-V	5/16	5/16
	Dynasty, New Yorker, Imperial, Fifth Avenue	3.3 (3294)	Serpentine	②	②
1991	Dynasty	2.2 (2213)	Poly-V	5/16 ①	7/16 ①
	Dynasty	2.2 (2213) Turbo III	Serpentine	②	②
	Dynasty	2.5 (2507)	Poly-V	5/16 ①	7/16 ①
	Dynasty	2.5 (2507) Turbo	Poly-V	5/16 ①	7/16 ①
	Dynasty, New Yorker Salon, New Yorker Landau, Imperial, Fifth Avenue	3.0 (2966)	Poly-V	5/16 ①	5/16 ①
	Dynasty, New Yorker Salon, New Yorker Landau, Imperial, Fifth Avenue	3.3 (3294)	Serpentine	②	②
	Dynasty, New Yorker Salon, New Yorker Landau, Imperial, Fifth Avenue	3.8 (3786)	Serpentine	②	②
1992	Dynasty	2.2 (2213)	Poly-V	125 ③	80 ③
	Dynasty	2.2 (2213) Turbo III	Serpentine	②	②
	Dynasty	2.5 (2507)	Poly-V	125 ③	80 ③
	Dynasty	2.5 (2507) Turbo	Poly-V	125	80 ③
	Dynasty, New Yorker Salon, New Yorker Landau, Imperial, Fifth Avenue	3.0 (2966)	Poly-V	125 ③	80 ③
	New Yorker Salon, New Yorker Landau, Imperial, Fifth Avenue	3.3 (3294)	Serpentine	②	②
	New Yorker Salon, New Yorker Landau, Imperial, Fifth Avenue	3.8 (3786)	Serpentine	②	②
1993	Dynasty	2.2 (2213)	Poly-V	135 ③	80 ③
	Dynasty	2.2 (2213) Turbo III	Serpentine	②	②
	Dynasty	2.5 (2507)	Poly-V	135 ③	80 ③
	Dynasty	3.0 (2966)	Poly-V	135 ③	80 ③
	New Yorker Salon, New Yorker Landau, Imperial, Fifth Avenue	3.3 (3294)	Serpentine	②	②
	New Yorker Salon, New Yorker Landau, Imperial, Fifth Avenue	3.8 (3786)	Serpentine	②	②

① Inches of deflection at the midpoint of the belt using 10 lbs. of force
② Equipped with automatic dynamic tensioner
③ Specifications given in pounds are measured with appropriate belt tension gauge at midpoint of longest belt run

REFRIGERANT CAPACITIES

Year	Model	Refrigerant (oz.)	Oil (fl. oz.)①	Compressor Type
1990	New Yorker	38.0	11.25	Fixed Displacement C171/A590, 10PA17 or TR105
	Fifth Avenue	38.0	11.25	Fixed Displacement C171/A590, 10PA17 or TR105
	Imperial	38.0	11.25	Fixed Displacement C171/A590, 10PA17 or TR105
	Dynasty	38.0	12.75	Variable Displacement 6C17
	New Yorker	38.0	12.75	Variable Displacement 6C17
	Fifth Avenue	38.0	12.75	Variable Displacement 6C17
	Imperial	38.0	12.75	Variable Displacement 6C17
1991	New Yorker	34.0	11.25	Fixed Displacement C171/A590, 10PA17 or TR105
	Fifth Avenue	34.0	11.25	Fixed Displacement C171/A590, 10PA17 or TR105
	Imperial	34.0	11.25	Fixed Displacement C171/A590, 10PA17 or TR105
	Dynasty	34.0	12.75	Variable Displacement 6C17
	New Yorker	34.0	12.75	Variable Displacement 6C17
	Fifth Avenue	34.0	12.75	Variable Displacement 6C17
	Imperial	34.0	12.75	Variable Displacement 6C17
1992	New Yorker	32.0	11.25	Fixed Displacement 10PA17 or TR105
	Fifth Avenue	32.0	11.25	Fixed Displacement 10PA17 or TR105
	Imperial	32.0	11.25	Fixed Displacement 10PA17 or TR105
	Dynasty	32.0	12.75	Variable Displacement 6C17
	New Yorker	32.0	12.75	Variable Displacement 6C17
	Fifth Avenue	32.0	12.75	Variable Displacement 6C17
	Imperial	32.0	12.75	Variable Displacement 6C17
1993	New Yorker	32.0	11.25	Fixed Displacement 10PA17 TR105, SD709P
	Fifth Avenue	32.0	11.25	Fixed Displacement 10PA17 TR105, SD709P
	imperial	32.0	11.25	Fixed Displacement 10PA17 TR105, SD709P
	Dynasty	32.0	12.75	Variable Displacement 6C17
	New Yorker	32.0	12.75	Variable Displacement 6C17
	Fifth Avenue	32.0	12.75	Variable Displacement 6C17
	Imperial	32.0	12.75	Variable Displacement 6C17

① Note: oil figures reflect the total system capacity

MAINTENANCE INTERVALS—TYPE A: NORMAL SERVICE
Dynasty • Imperial • New Yorker Laudau • New Yorker Salon • New Yorker 5th Avenue

TO BE SERVICED	TYPE OF SERVICE	VEHICLE MILEAGE INTERVAL (X1000)							
		7.5	15	22.5	30	37.5	45	52.5	60
Oxygen Sensor	I				✔				✔
Ignition Timing	I①								
Vacuum Lines and Hoses	I				✔				✔
Ignition Wires	R								✔
Spark Plugs	R				✔				✔
Engine Oil	R	✔	✔	✔	✔	✔	✔	✔	✔
Engine Air Cleaner Element	R				✔				✔
Crankcase Emission Filter	R				✔				✔
PCV Valve	R				✔				✔
Fuel Filter	R				✔				✔
Charcoal Canister	R				✔				✔
Fuel/Vapor Return Lines	I				✔				✔
Fuel Tank Cap and Restrictor	I				✔				✔
Coolant System	R				✔				✔
Exhaust Pipe and Muffler	I				✔				✔
Engine Oil Filter	R②	✔		✔		✔		✔	
Catalytic Converter and Shield	I				✔				✔
EGR System	I				✔				✔
Automatic Transmission Fluid	R								✔
Battery Connections	I		✔		✔		✔		✔
Chassis Lubrication	L	✔		✔		✔		✔	
Timing Belt	R③								
Idle Speed System	I				✔				✔
Throttle Body Mounting Torque	I	✔							
Drive Belts	I				✔				✔
Tire Rotation	I	✔	✔	✔	✔	✔	✔	✔	✔
CV-Joints and Boots	I	✔	✔	✔	✔	✔	✔	✔	✔
Coolant Hoses and Clamps	I	✔	✔	✔	✔	✔	✔	✔	✔
Seat Belt Operation	I				✔				✔

FOR COMPLETE WARRANTY COVERAGE CONSULT INDIVIDUAL VEHICLE MANUFACTURER'S WARRANTY MAINTENANCE GUIDE.

I—Inspect
L—Lubricate
R—Replace
① Check and adjust timing as per engine emission
   label on applicable models
② Replace filter at first oil change
③ Replace timing belt if any of these
   conditions exist:
   a. Cracks on rubber back
   b. Crack or peeling of canvas
   c. Cracks on rib root
   d. Missing teeth
   e. Hardening of back rubber

MAINTENANCE INTERVALS—TYPE B: SEVERE SERVICE
Dynasty • Imperial • New Yorker Laudau • New Yorker Salon • New Yorker 5th Avenue

TO BE SERVICED	TYPE OF SERVICE	3	6	9	12	15	18	21	24	27	30
Oxygen Sensor	I										✔
Ignition Timing	I①										✔
Vacuum Lines and Hoses	I					✔					✔
Ignition Wires	I										✔
Spark Plugs	R										✔
Engine Oil	R	✔	✔	✔	✔	✔	✔	✔	✔	✔	✔
Engine Air Cleaner Element	R					✔					✔
Crankcase Emission Filter	R					✔					✔
PCV Valve	R					✔					✔
Fuel Filter	R					✔					✔
Charcoal Canister	R					✔					✔
Fuel/Vapor Return Lines	I										✔
Fuel Tank Cap and Restrictor	I										✔
Coolant System	R										✔
Exhaust Pipe and Muffler	I										✔
Engine Oil Filter	R	✔		✔		✔		✔		✔	
Catalytic Converter and Shield	I										✔
EGR System	I										✔
Automatic Transmission Fluid	R					✔					✔
Battery Connections	I		✔		✔		✔		✔		✔
Chassis Lubrication	L		✔		✔		✔		✔		✔
Timing Belt	R②										
Idle Speed System	I					✔					
Throttle Body Mounting Torque	I	✔									
Drive Belts	I					✔					✔
Tire Rotation	I		✔		✔		✔		✔		✔
CV-Joints and Boots	I	✔	✔	✔	✔	✔	✔	✔	✔	✔	✔
Coolant Hoses and Clamps	I		✔		✔		✔		✔		✔
Seat Belt Operation	I					✔					✔

FOR COMPLETE WARRANTY COVERAGE CONSULT INDIVIDUAL VEHICLE MANUFACTURER'S WARRANTY MAINTENANCE GUIDE.

I—Inspect
L—Lubricate
R—Replace
① Check and adjust timing as per engine emission label on applicable models
② Replace timing belt when any of these conditions exist:
   a. Cracks on rubber back
   b. Crack or peeling of canvas
   c. Cracks on rib root
   d. Missing teeth
   e. Hardening of back rubber

FIRING ORDERS

NOTE: To avoid confusion, always replace spark plugs and wires one at a time.

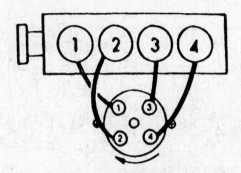

**2.2L and 2.5L Engines
Engine Firing Order: 1-3-4-2
Distributor Rotation: Clockwise**

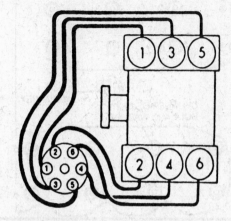

**3.0L engine
Engine Firing Order: 1–2–3–4–5–6
Distributor Rotation: Counterclockwise**

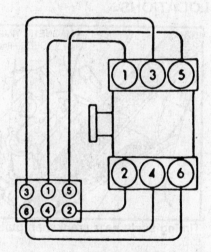

**3.3L and 3.8L Engines
Engine Firing Order: 1–2–3–4–5–6
Distributorless Ignition System**

CYLINDER HEAD TORQUE SEQUENCES

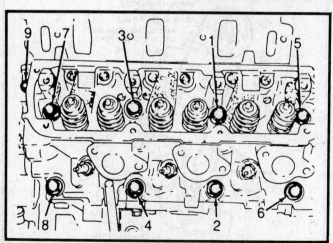

Cylinder head bolt torque sequence—3.3L and 3.8L engines

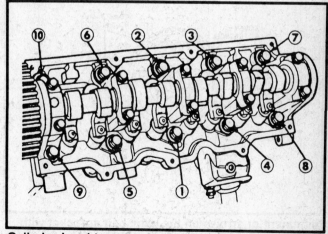

Cylinder head torque sequence—2.2L and 2.5L SOHC engines

CYLINDER HEAD TORQUE SEQUENCES

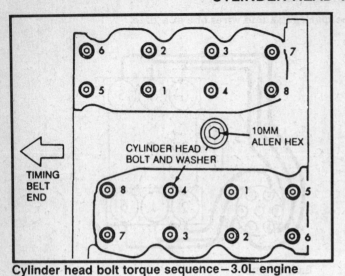

Cylinder head bolt torque sequence—3.0L engine

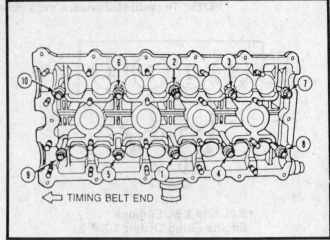

Cylinder head bolt torque sequence—2.2L DOHC engine—TC

TIMING MARK LOCATIONS

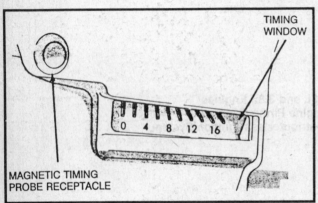

Timing scale on transaxle housing—2.2L and 2.5L engines

Timing scale near crankshaft pulley—3.0L engine

TIMING CHAIN/BELT ALIGNMENT MARKS

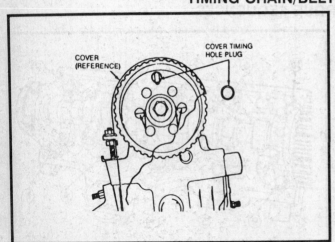

Alignment of arrows on the camshaft sprocket with the camshaft cap to cylinder head mounting line—2.5L SOHC engine

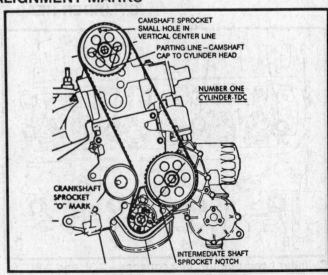

Timing belt alignment marks—2.5L engine

TIMING CHAIN/BELT ALIGNMENT MARKS

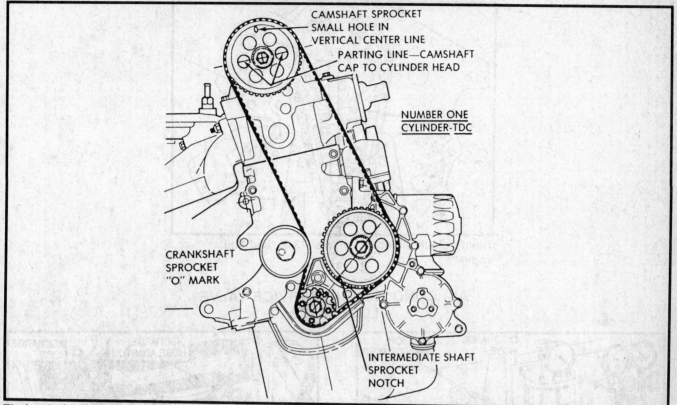

CAMSHAFT SPROCKET
SMALL HOLE IN
VERTICAL CENTER LINE
PARTING LINE—CAMSHAFT
CAP TO CYLINDER HEAD

NUMBER ONE
CYLINDER-TDC

CRANKSHAFT
SPROCKET
"O" MARK

INTERMEDIATE SHAFT
SPROCKET
NOTCH

Timing belt alignment marks—2.2L engine

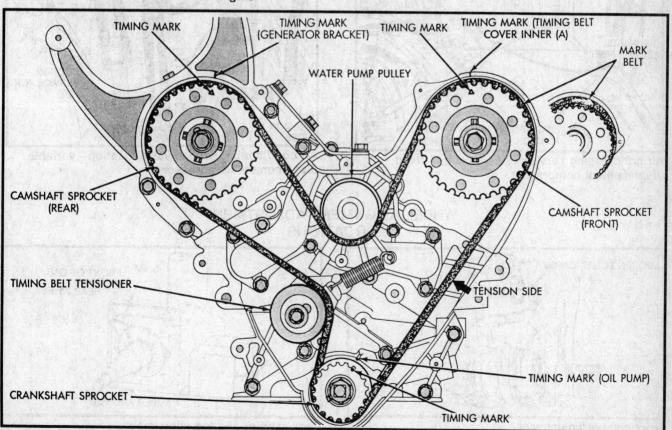

TIMING MARK
TIMING MARK (GENERATOR BRACKET)
TIMING MARK
TIMING MARK (TIMING BELT COVER INNER (A))
MARK BELT
WATER PUMP PULLEY
CAMSHAFT SPROCKET (REAR)
CAMSHAFT SPROCKET (FRONT)
TIMING BELT TENSIONER
TENSION SIDE
TIMING MARK (OIL PUMP)
CRANKSHAFT SPROCKET
TIMING MARK

Timing belt alignment marks—3.0L engine

TIMING CHAIN/BELT ALIGNMENT MARKS

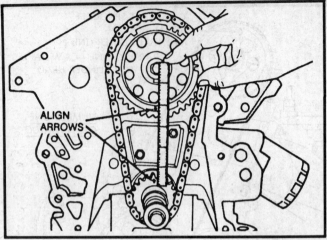

Timing chain alignment marks—3.3L and 3.8L engines

AIR CONDITIONING SERVICE VALVE LOCATIONS

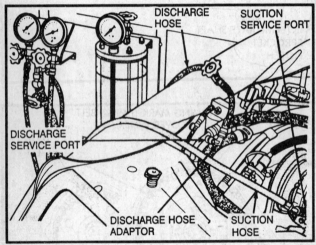

Air conditioning service valve location—fixed displacement compressor

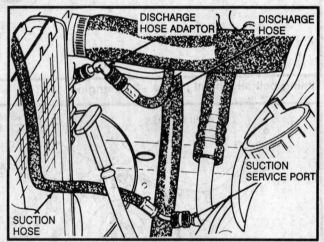

Air conditioning service valve location—variable displacement compressor

WHEEL ALIGNMENT ADJUSTMENT LOCATIONS

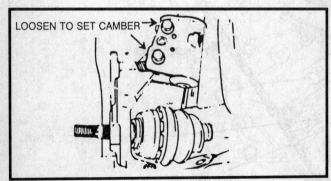

Front camber adjustment

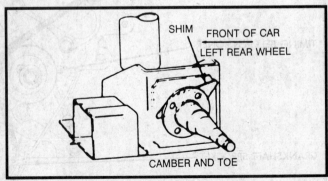

Rear camber and toe adjustment

SPECIFICATION CHARTS

VEHICLE IDENTIFICATION CHART

It is important for servicing and ordering parts to be certain of the vehicle and engine identification. The VIN (vehicle identification number) is a 17 digit number visible through the windshield on the driver's side of the dash and contains the vehicle and engine identification codes. The tenth digit indicates model year and the eighth digit indicates engine code. It can be interpreted as follows:

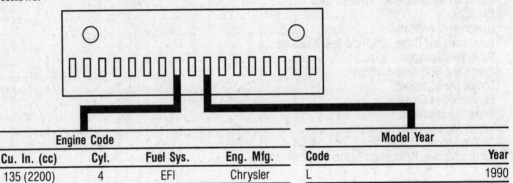

Engine Code						Model Year	
Code	Liters	Cu. In. (cc)	Cyl.	Fuel Sys.	Eng. Mfg.	Code	Year
D	2.2	135 (2200)	4	EFI	Chrysler	L	1990

EFI—Electronic Fuel Injection

ENGINE IDENTIFICATION

Year	Model	Engine Displacement Liters (cc)	Engine Series Identification (ID/VIN)	Fuel System	No. of Cylinders	Engine Type
1990	Horizon	2.2 (2200)	D	EFI	4	OHC
	Omni	2.2 (2200)	D	EFI	4	OHC

EFI—Electronic Fuel Injection
OHC—Overhead Cam

GENERAL ENGINE SPECIFICATIONS

Year	Engine ID/VIN	Engine Displacement Liters (cc)	Fuel System Type	Net Horsepower @ rpm	Net Torque @ rpm (ft. lbs.)	Bore × Stroke (in.)	Com- pression Ratio	Oil Pressure @ rpm
1990	D	2.2 (2200)	EFI	99 @ 5600	122 @ 3200	3.44 × 3.62	9.5:1	25–80 @ 3000

EFI—Electronic Fuel Injection

GASOLINE ENGINE TUNE-UP SPECIFICATIONS

Year	Engine ID/VIN	Engine Displacement Liters (cc)	Spark Plugs Gap (in.)	Ignition Timing (deg.) MT	AT	Fuel Pump (psi)	Idle Speed (rpm) MT	AT	Valve Clearance In.	Ex.
1990	D	2.2 (2200)	0.035	12B	12B	15	850	850	Hyd.	Hyd.

NOTE: The lowest cylinder pressure should be within 75% of the highest cylinder pressure reading. For example, if the highest cylinder is 134 psi, the lowest should be 101. Engine should be at normal operating temperature with throttle valve in the wide open position.
The underhood specifications sticker often reflects tune-up specification changes in production. Sticker figures must be used if they disagree with those in this chart.
Hyd.—Hydraulic

CAPACITIES

Year	Model	Engine ID/VIN	Engine Displacement Liters (cc)	Engine Crankcase (qts.) with Filter	Transmission (pts.) 4-Spd	5-Spd	Auto.	Drive Axle (pts.)	Fuel Tank (gal.)	Cooling System (qts.)
1990	Horizon	D	2.2 (2200)	4.5	—	4.8	18	—	13	9
	Omni	D	2.2 (2200)	4.5	—	4.8	18	—	13	9

CAMSHAFT SPECIFICATIONS
All measurements given in inches.

Year	Engine ID/VIN	Engine Displacement Liters (cc)	Journal Diameter 1	2	3	4	5	Elevation In.	Ex.	Bearing Clearance	Camshaft End Play
1990	D	2.2 (2200)	1.375–1.376	1.375–1.376	1.375–1.376	1.375–1.376	1.375–1.376	NA	NA	—	0.005–0.013

NA—Not available

CRANKSHAFT AND CONNECTING ROD SPECIFICATIONS
All measurements are given in inches.

Year	Engine ID/VIN	Engine Displacement Liters (cc)	Crankshaft Main Brg. Journal Dia.	Main Brg. Oil Clearance	Shaft End-play	Thrust on No.	Connecting Rod Journal Diameter	Oil Clearance	Side Clearance
1990	D	2.2 (2200)	2.362–2.363	0.0004–0.0028	0.002–0.007	3	1.968–1.969	0.0008–0.0034	0.005–0.013

VALVE SPECIFICATIONS

Year	Engine ID/VIN	Engine Displacement Liters (cc)	Seat Angle (deg.)	Face Angle (deg.)	Spring Test Pressure (lbs. @ in.)	Spring Installed Height (in.)	Stem-to-Guide Clearance (in.) Intake	Exhaust	Stem Diameter (in.) Intake	Exhaust
1990	D	2.2 (2200)	45	45	108–120 @ 165	1.65	0.009–0.026	0.0030–0.0047	0.3124	0.3103

PISTON AND RING SPECIFICATIONS
All measurements are given in inches.

Year	Engine ID/VIN	Engine Displacement Liters (cc)	Piston Clearance	Ring Gap Top Compression	Bottom Compression	Oil Control	Ring Side Clearance Top Compression	Bottom Compression	Oil Control
1990	D	2.2 (2200)	0.0005–0.0027	0.010–0.020	0.011–0.021	0.015–0.055	0.0015–0.0031	0.0015–0.0037	0.0002–0.0080

TORQUE SPECIFICATIONS

All readings in ft. lbs.

Year	Engine ID/VIN	Engine Displacement Liters (cc)	Cylinder Head Bolts	Main Bearing Bolts	Rod Bearing Bolts	Crankshaft Pulley Bolts	Flywheel Bolts	Manifold		Spark Plugs	Lug Nut
								Intake	Exhaust		
1990	D	2.2 (2200)	①	30②	40②	85	70	17	17	20	95

① Sequence:
   1st step 45 ft. lbs.
   2nd step 65 ft. lbs.
   3rd step plus ¼ turn
② Plus ¼ turn

TORQUE SPECIFICATIONS

Component	English	Metric
Balance shaft chain tensioner:	105 inch lbs.	12 Nm
Balance shaft chain sprocket:	20 ft. lbs.	28 Nm
Balance shaft carrier-to-block bolts:	40 ft. lbs.	54 Nm
Camshaft sprocket bolt:	65 ft. lbs.	88 Nm
Connecting rod bearing cap bolts		
Step 1:	40 ft. lbs.	54 Nm
Step 2:	+ 90° turn	+ 90° turn
Crankshaft sprocket bolt:	50 ft. lbs.	68 Nm
Crankshaft chain sprocket bolts:	130 inch lbs.	15 Nm
Crankshaft pulley bolt:	20 ft. lbs.	28 Nm
Cylinder head bolt		
Torque in 4 steps:	45 ft. lbs.	61 Nm
EGR valve-to-intake manifold:	20 ft. lbs.	27 Nm
Engine-to-transaxle:	70 ft. lbs.	95 Nm
Exhaust manifold:	17 ft. lbs.	23 Nm
Exhaust pipe-to-exhaust manifold nuts:	20 ft. lbs.	28 Nm
Flywheel/flexplate-to-crankshaft bolts:	70 ft. lbs.	95 Nm
Flexplate-to-converter bolts:	55 ft. lbs.	74 Nm
Intake manifold:	17 ft. lbs.	23 Nm
Main bearing cap bolts		
Step 1:	30 ft. lbs.	41 Nm
Step 2:	+ 90° turn	+ 90° turn
Oil pan		
M6 screws:	106 inch lbs	12 Nm
M8 screws:	17 ft. lbs.	23 Nm
Oil pan drain plug:	20 ft. lbs.	27 Nm
Oil pump attaching bolts:	17 ft. lbs.	23 Nmm
Rocker (valve) cover:	105 inch lbs.	12 Nm
Spark plug:	26 ft. lbs.	35 Nm
Starter-to-block bolts:	33 ft. lbs.	45 Nm
Thermostat housing:	20 ft. lbs.	28 Nm
Timing cover:	35 inch lbs.	4 Nm
Throttle body-to-intake manifold		
TBI:	35 inch lbs.	4 Nm
MPI:	13 ft. lbs.	18 Nm
Water pump		
Housing-to-pump:	105 inch lbs.	12 Nm
Housing-to-engine		
Upper:	20 ft. lbs.	28 Nm
Lower:	50 ft. lbs.	68 Nm
Water pump pulley:	105 inch lbs.	12 Nm

BRAKE SPECIFICATIONS
All measurements in inches unless noted.

| Year | Model | Master Cylinder Bore | Brake Disc | | | Brake Drum Diameter | | | Minimum Lining Thickness | |
			Original Thickness	Minimum Thickness	Maximum Runout	Original Inside Diameter	Max. Wear Limit	Maximum Machine Diameter	Front	Rear
1990	Horizon	0.827	0.490–0.505	0.431	0.005	7.87	NA	NA	0.06	0.06
	Omni	0.827	0.490–0.505	0.431	0.005	7.87	NA	NA	0.06	0.06

NA—Not available

WHEEL ALIGNMENT

| Year | Model | | Caster | | Camber | | Toe-in (in.) | Steering Axis Inclination (deg.) |
			Range (deg.)	Preferred Setting (deg.)	Range (deg.)	Preferred Setting (deg.)		
1990	Horizon	Front	①	1 9/10 P	1/4 N–3/4 P	5/16 P	1/16	13 3/8
		Rear	—	—	1 1/4 N–1/4 N	3/4 N	3/32	13 3/8
	Omni	Front	①	1 9/10 P	1/4 N–3/4 P	5/16 P	1/16	13 3/8
		Rear	—	—	1 1/4 N–1/4 N	3/4 N	3/32	13 3/8

N—Negative
P—Positive
① Variation between sides not to exceed 1 1/2

AIR CONDITIONING BELT TENSION

| Year | Model | Engine Displacement Liters (cc) | Belt Type | Specifications ① | |
				New	Used
1990	Omni	2.2 (2213)	Poly-V	5/16	7/16
		2.5 (2507)	Poly-V	5/16	7/16
	Horizon	2.2 (2213)	Poly-V	5/16	7/16
		2.5 (2507)	Poly-V	5/16	7/16

① Inches of deflection at the midpoint of the belt using 10 lbs. force

REFRIGERANT CAPACITIES

Year	Model	Refrigerant (oz.)	Oil (fl. oz.)	Compressor Type
1990	Omni	38.0	11.25	Fixed Displacement
	Horizon	38.0	11.25	Fixed Displacement

MAINTENANCE INTERVALS—TYPE A: NORMAL SERVICE
Horizon • Omni

TO BE SERVICED	TYPE OF SERVICE	VEHICLE MILEAGE INTERVAL (X1000)							
		7.5	15	22.5	30	37.5	45	52.5	60
Oxygen Sensor	I				✔				✔
Ignition Timing	I				✔				✔
Vacuum Lines and Hoses	I		✔		✔		✔		✔
Ignition Wires	R								✔
Spark Plugs	R				✔				✔
Engine Oil	R	✔	✔	✔	✔	✔	✔	✔	✔
Engine Air Cleaner Element	R				✔				✔
Crankcase Emission Filter	R				✔				✔
PCV Valve	I	✔	✔	✔	✔	✔	✔	✔	✔
Fuel Filter	R				✔				✔
Engine Oil Filter	R①	✔		✔		✔		✔	
Fuel/Vapor Return Lines	I				✔				✔
Fuel Tank Cap and Restrictor	I				✔				✔
Coolant System	R				✔				✔
Exhaust Pipe and Muffler	I				✔				✔
Coolant Hoses and Clamps	I		✔		✔		✔		✔
Catalytic Converter and Shield	I				✔				✔
EGR System	I				✔				✔
Chassis Lubrication	L	✔		✔		✔		✔	
CV-Joints and Boots	I	✔	✔	✔	✔	✔	✔	✔	✔
Tire Rotation	I	✔	✔	✔	✔	✔	✔	✔	✔
Timing Belt	R②								
Idle Speed System	I				✔				✔
Throttle Body	I				✔				✔
Drive Belts	I				✔				✔
Automatic Transaxle Fluid	R								✔
Battery Connections	I		✔		✔		✔		✔
Wheel Bearings	L				✔				✔
Brake Linings	I		✔		✔		✔		✔
Parking Brake	I		✔		✔		✔		✔
Seat Belt Operation	I		✔		✔		✔		✔

FOR COMPLETE WARRANTY COVERAGE CONSULT INDIVIDUAL VEHICLE MANUFACTURER'S WARRANTY MAINTENANCE GUIDE.

I—Inspect
L—Lubricate
R—Replace
① Replace oil filter at each oil change if accumulated mileage is less than 7,500 miles for 12 months
② Replace timing belt at 90,000 miles

MAINTENANCE INTERVALS—TYPE B: SEVERE SERVICE
Horizon • Omni

TO BE SERVICED	TYPE OF SERVICE	VEHICLE MILEAGE INTERVAL (X1000)									
		3	6	9	12	15	18	21	24	27	30
Oxygen Sensor	I										✓
Ignition Timing	I										✓
Vacuum Lines and Hoses	I					✓					✓
Ignition Wires	R①										
Spark Plugs	R										✓
Engine Oil	R	✓	✓	✓	✓	✓	✓	✓	✓	✓	✓
Engine Air Cleaner Element	R					✓					✓
Crankcase Emission Filter	R					✓					✓
PCV Valve	R					✓					✓
Fuel Filter	R					✓					✓
Engine Oil Filter	R	✓	✓	✓	✓	✓	✓	✓	✓		
Fuel/Vapor Return Lines	I										✓
Fuel Tank Cap and Restrictor	I										✓
Coolant System	R										✓
Exhaust Pipe and Muffler	I										✓
Coolant Hoses and Clamps	I					✓					✓
Catalytic Converter and Shield	I										✓
EGR System	I										✓
Chassis Lubrication	L		✓		✓		✓		✓		
CV-Joints and Boots	I	✓	✓	✓	✓	✓	✓	✓	✓	✓	✓
Tire Rotation	I		✓		✓		✓		✓		✓
Timing Belt	R②										
Idle Speed System	I					✓					✓
Throttle Body	I					✓					✓
Drive Belts	I										✓
Automatic Transaxle Fluid	R					✓					✓
Battery Connections	I					✓					✓
Wheel Bearings	L					✓					✓
Brake Linings	I					✓					✓
Parking Brake	I					✓					✓
Seat Belt Operation	I					✓					✓

FOR COMPLETE WARRANTY COVERAGE CONSULT INDIVIDUAL VEHICLE MANUFACTURER'S WARRANTY MAINTENANCE GUIDE.

I—Inspect
L—Lubricate
R—Replace
① Replace wires at 60,000 miles
② Replace timing belt at 90,000 miles

FIRING ORDERS

NOTE: To avoid confusion, always replace spark plugs and wires one at a time.

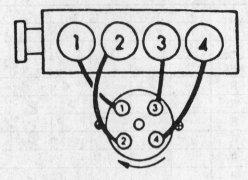

2.2L Engine
Engine Firing Order: 1–3–4–2
Distributor Rotation: Clockwise

CYLINDER HEAD TORQUE SEQUENCES

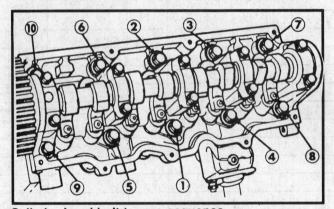

Cylinder head bolt torque sequence

TIMING MARK LOCATIONS

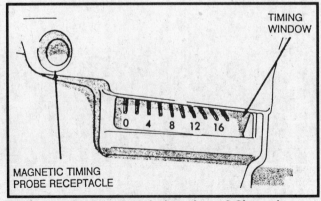

Timing scale on transaxle housing—2.2L engine

TIMING BELT ALIGNMENT MARKS

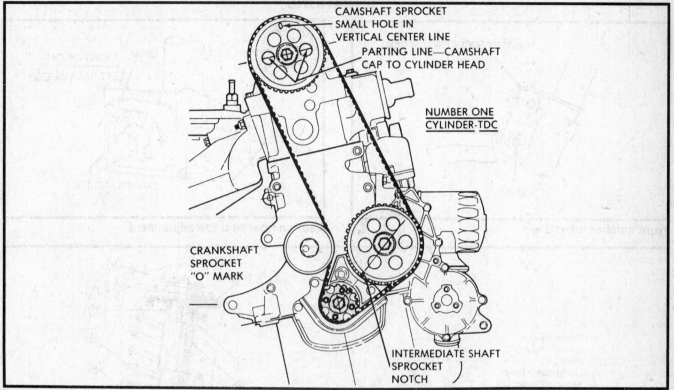

CAMSHAFT SPROCKET
SMALL HOLE IN
VERTICAL CENTER LINE
PARTING LINE—CAMSHAFT
CAP TO CYLINDER HEAD

NUMBER ONE
CYLINDER-TDC

CRANKSHAFT
SPROCKET
"O" MARK

INTERMEDIATE SHAFT
SPROCKET
NOTCH

Timing belt alignment marks—2.2L engine

AIR CONDITIONING SERVICE VALVE LOCATIONS

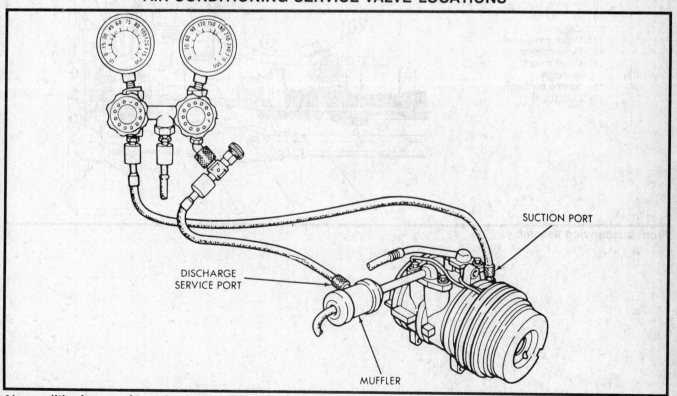

SUCTION PORT

DISCHARGE
SERVICE PORT

MUFFLER

Air conditioning service valve location

WHEEL ALIGNMENT ADJUSTMENT LOCATIONS

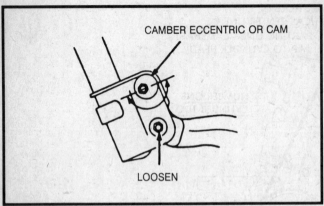

Front camber adjustment

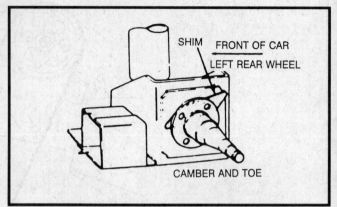

Rear camber and toe adjustment

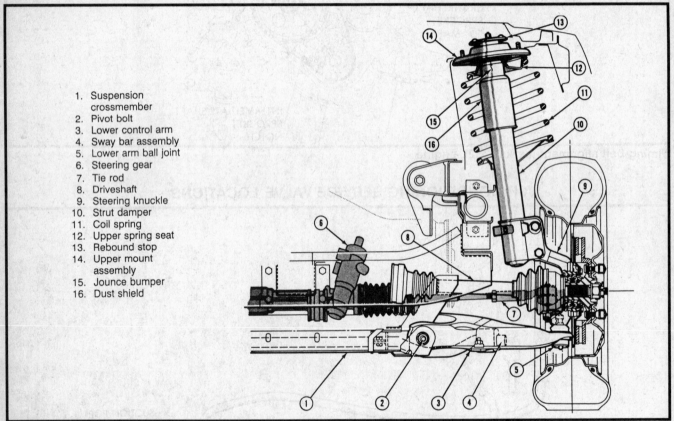

1. Suspension crossmember
2. Pivot bolt
3. Lower control arm
4. Sway bar assembly
5. Lower arm ball joint
6. Steering gear
7. Tie rod
8. Driveshaft
9. Steering knuckle
10. Strut damper
11. Coil spring
12. Upper spring seat
13. Rebound stop
14. Upper mount assembly
15. Jounce bumper
16. Dust shield

Front suspension assembly

SPECIFICATION CHARTS

VEHICLE IDENTIFICATION CHART

It is important for servicing and ordering parts to be certain of the vehicle and engine identification. The VIN (vehicle identification number) is a 17 digit number visible through the windshield on the driver's side of the dash and contains the vehicle and engine identification codes. The tenth digit indicates model year and the eighth digit indicates engine code. It can be interpreted as follows:

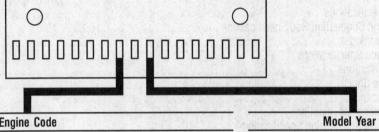

		Engine Code					Model Year	
Code	Liters	Cu. In. (cc)	Cyl.	Fuel Sys.	Eng. Mfg.		Code	Year
T	3.3	201 (3294)	6	SMPI	Chrysler		P	1993
F	3.5	215 (3518)	6	SMPI	Chrysler		R	1994

SMPI—Sequential Multi-Port Fuel Injection

ENGINE IDENTIFICATION

Year	Model	Engine Displacement Liters (cc)	Engine Series (ID/VIN)	Fuel System	No. of Cylinders	Engine Type
1993	Concorde	3.3 (3294)	T	SMPI	6	OHV
	Concorde	3.5 (3518)	F	SMPI	6	SOHC
	Vision	3.3 (3294)	T	SMPI	6	OHV
	Vision	3.5 (3518)	F	SMPI	6	SOHC
	Intrepid	3.3 (3294)	T	SMPI	6	OHV
	Intrepid	3.5 (3518)	F	SMPI	6	SOHC
1994	Concorde	3.3 (3294)	T	SMPI	6	OHV
	Concorde	3.5 (3518)	F	SMPI	6	SOHC
	Vision	3.3 (3294)	T	SMPI	6	OHV
	Vision	3.5 (3518)	F	SMPI	6	SOHC
	Intrepid	3.3 (3294)	T	SMPI	6	OHV
	Intrepid	3.5 (3518)	F	SMPI	6	SOHC
	New Yorker	3.5 (3518)	F	SMPI	6	SOHC
	LHS	3.5 (3518)	F	SMPI	6	SOHC

OHV—Overhead Valve
SMPI—Sequential Multi-Port Fuel Injection
SOHC—Single Overhead Camshaft

GENERAL ENGINE SPECIFICATIONS

Year	Engine ID/VIN	Engine Displacement Liters (cc)	Fuel System Type	Net Horsepower @ rpm	Net Torque @ rpm (ft. lbs.)	Bore × Stroke (in.)	Compression Ratio	Oil Pressure @ rpm
1993	T	3.3 (3294)	SMPI	153 @ 5300	177 @ 2800	3.661 × 3.188	8.9:1	30–80 @ 3000
	F	3.5 (3518)	SMPI	214 @ 5800	221 @ 2800	3.780 × 3.189	10.5:1	25–70 @ 3000
1994	T	3.3 (3294)	SMPI	161 @ 5300	181 @ 3200	3.661 × 3.188	8.9:1	30–80 @ 3000
	F	3.5 (3518)	SMPI	214 @ 5800	221 @ 2800	3.780 × 3.189	10.5:1	25–70 @ 3000

SMPI—Sequential Multi-Port Fuel Injection

GASOLINE ENGINE TUNE-UP SPECIFICATIONS

Year	Engine ID/VIN	Engine Displacement Liters (cc)	Spark Plugs Gap (in.)	Ignition Timing (deg.) MT	Ignition Timing (deg.) AT	Fuel Pump (psi)	Idle Speed (rpm) MT	Idle Speed (rpm) AT	Valve Clearance In.	Valve Clearance Ex.
1993	T	3.3 (3294)	0.048–0.053	—	①	46 ②	—	600–840	Hyd.	Hyd.
	F	3.5 (3518)	0.048–0.053	—	①	39 ②	—	750–1100	Hyd.	Hyd.
1994	T	3.3 (3294)	0.048–0.053	—	①	46 ②	—	600–840	Hyd.	Hyd.
	F	3.5 (3518)	0.048–0.053	—	①	39 ②	—	750–1100	Hyd.	Hyd.

NOTE: The lowest cylinder pressure should be within 75% of the highest cylinder pressure reading. For example, if the highest cylinder is 134 psi, the lowest should be 101. Engine should be at normal operating temperature with throttle valve in the wide open position.
The underhood specifications sticker often reflects tune-up specification changes in production. Sticker figures must be used if they disagree with those in this chart.
Hyd.—Hydraulic
① Basic ignition timing is not adjustable
② Pressure at idle, with vacuum applied to fuel pressure regulator.

CAPACITIES

Year	Model	Engine ID/VIN	Engine Displacement Liters (cc)	Engine Crankcase with Filter (qts.)	Transmission (pts.) 4-Spd	Transmission (pts.) 5-Spd	Transmission (pts.) Auto.	Transfer Case (pts.)	Drive Axle Front (pts.)	Drive Axle Rear (pts.)	Fuel Tank (gal.)	Cooling System (qts.)
1993	Concorde	T	3.3 (3294)	5.0	—	—	19.8①	—	—	—	18	10.17
	Concorde	F	3.5 (3518)	5.5	—	—	19.8①	—	—	—	18	11.80
	Vision	T	3.3 (3294)	5.0	—	—	19.8①	—	—	—	18	10.17
	Vision	F	3.5 (3518)	5.5	—	—	19.8①	—	—	—	18	11.80
	Intrepid	T	3.3 (3294)	5.0	—	—	19.8①	—	—	—	18	10.17
	Intrepid	F	3.5 (3518)	5.5	—	—	19.8①	—	—	—	18	11.80
1994	Concorde	T	3.3 (3294)	5.0	—	—	19.8①	—	—	—	18	10.17
	Concorde	F	3.5 (3518)	5.5	—	—	19.8①	—	—	—	18	11.80
	Vision	T	3.3 (3294)	5.0	—	—	19.8①	—	—	—	18	10.17
	Vision	F	3.5 (3518)	5.5	—	—	19.8①	—	—	—	18	11.80
	Intrepid	T	3.3 (3294)	5.0	—	—	19.8①	—	—	—	18	10.17
	Intrepid	F	3.5 (3518)	5.5	—	—	19.8①	—	—	—	18	11.80
	New Yorker	F	3.5 (3518)	5.5	—	—	19.8①	—	—	—	18	10.17
	LHS	F	3.5 (3518)	5.5	—	—	19.8①	—	—	—	18	11.80

① The differential is filled separately and will hold 2 pts.

CAMSHAFT SPECIFICATIONS

All measurements given in inches.

Year	Engine ID/VIN	Engine Displacement Liters (cc)	Journal Diameter					Elevation		Bearing Clearance	Camshaft End Play
			1	2	3	4	5	In.	Ex.		
1993	T	3.3 (3294)	1.9970–1.9990	1.9809–1.9829	1.9659–1.9679	1.9499–1.9520	—	0.400	0.400	0.001–0.003	0.005–0.012
	F	3.5 (3518)	1.6905–1.6913	1.6905–1.6913	1.6905–1.6913	1.6905–1.6913	—	0.320	0.257	0.003–0.005	0.004–0.014
1994	T	3.3 (3294)	1.9970–1.9990	1.9809–1.9829	1.9659–1.9679	1.9499–1.9520	—	0.400	0.400	0.001–0.003	0.005–0.012
	F	3.5 (3518)	1.6905–1.6913	1.6905–1.6913	1.6905–1.6913	1.6905–1.6913	—	0.320	0.257	0.003–0.005	0.004–0.014

CRANKSHAFT AND CONNECTING ROD SPECIFICATIONS

All measurements are given in inches.

Year	Engine ID/VIN	Engine Displacement Liters (cc)	Crankshaft				Connecting Rod		
			Main Brg. Journal Dia.	Main Brg. Oil Clearance	Shaft End-play	Thrust on No.	Journal Diameter	Oil Clearance	Side Clearance
1993	T	3.3 (3294)	2.5185–2.5195	0.0007–0.0040	0.004–0.017	2	2.283	0.0008–0.0030	0.005–0.015
	F	3.5 (3518)	2.5190–2.5200	0.0007–0.0028	0.004–0.017	2	2.282–2.283	0.0008–0.0034	0.005–0.015
1994	T	3.3 (3294)	2.5185–2.5195	0.0007–0.0040	0.004–0.017	2	2.283	0.0008–0.0030	0.005–0.015
	F	3.5 (3518)	2.5190–2.5200	0.0007–0.0028	0.004–0.012	2	2.282–2.283	0.0008–0.0034	0.005–0.015

VALVE SPECIFICATIONS

Year	Engine ID/VIN	Engine Displacement Liters (cc)	Seat Angle (deg.)	Face Angle (deg.)	Spring Test Pressure (lbs. @ in.)	Spring Installed Height (in.)	Stem-to-Guide Clearance (in.)		Stem Diameter (in.)	
							Intake	Exhaust	Intake	Exhaust
1993	T	3.3 (3294)	45–45.5	44.5	1.36–1.45 @ 1.14	1.539–1.598	0.0010–0.0030	0.002–0.006	0.3120–0.3130	0.3112–0.3119
	F	3.5 (3518)	45–45.5	44.5–45	①	1.496	0.0009–0.0026	0.002–0.004	0.2730–0.2737	0.2719–0.2726
1994	T	3.3 (3294)	45–45.5	44.5	②	1.622–1.681	0.0010–0.0030	0.002–0.006	0.3120–0.3130	0.3112–0.3119
	F	3.5 (3518)	45–45.5	44.5–45	①	1.496	0.0009–0.0026	0.002–0.004	0.2730–0.2737	0.2719–0.2726

① Intake: 201.7–218.3 lbs. @ 1.1752 in.
   Exhaust: 158.5–171.5 lbs. @ 1.239 in.
② 95–100 lbs. @ 1.570 in.—valve closed
   207–229 lbs. @ 1.169 in.—valve open

PISTON AND RING SPECIFICATIONS

All measurements are given in inches.

Year	Engine ID/VIN	Engine Displacement Liters (cc)	Piston Clearance	Ring Gap			Ring Side Clearance		
				Top Compression	Bottom Compression	Oil Control	Top Compression	Bottom Compression	Oil Control
1993	T	3.3 (3294)	0.0010–0.0022	0.0118–0.0217	0.0118–0.0217	0.0098–0.0394	0.0015–0.0033	0.0012–0.0037	0.0005–0.0089
	F	3.5 (3518)	0.0007–0.0020	0.0120–0.0180	0.0120–0.0220	0.0100–0.0300	0.0012–0.0031	0.0012–0.0031	0.0019–0.0077
1994	T	3.3 (3294)	0.0010–0.0022	0.0118–0.0217	0.0118–0.0217	0.0098–0.0394	0.0015–0.0033	0.0012–0.0037	0.0005–0.0089
	F	3.5 (3518)	0.0007–0.0020	0.0120–0.0180	0.0120–0.0220	0.0100–0.0300	0.0012–0.0031	0.0012–0.0031	0.0019–0.0077

TORQUE SPECIFICATIONS

All readings in ft. lbs.

Year	Engine ID/VIN	Engine Displacement Liters (cc)	Cylinder Head Bolts	Main Bearing Bolts	Rod Bearing Bolts	Crankshaft Damper Bolts	Flywheel Bolts	Manifold		Spark Plugs	Lug Nut
								Intake	Exhaust		
1993	T	3.3 (3294)	①	②	③	40	75	17	17	20	95
	F	3.5 (3518)	①	④	③	85	75	17	17	20	95
1994	T	3.3 (3294)	①	②	③	40	75	17	17	20	95
	F	3.5 (3518)	①	④	③	85	75	17	17	20	95

① Step 1: 45 ft. lbs.
Step 2: 65 ft. lbs.
Step 3: 65 ft. lbs.
Step 4: + ¼ turn
Final torque to be over 90 ft. lbs.
② 30 + ¼ turn
③ 40 + ¼ turn
④ M10 bolts—40 ft. lbs.
M11 bolts—30 ft. lbs. + ¼ turn

TORQUE SPECIFICATIONS

Component	English	Metric
Camshaft sprocket bolt		
3.3L engine:	40 ft. lbs.	54 Nm
3.5L engine:	95 ft. lbs.	127 Nm
Camshaft thrust plate		
3.3L engine:	105 inch lbs.	12 Nm
3.5L engine:	250 inch lbs.	28 Nm
Chain case cover bolt		
3.3L engine		
M8 x 1.25 bolt:	20 ft. lbs.	47 Nm
M10 x 1.5 bolt:	40 ft. lbs.	54 Nm
Connecting rod bearing cap bolts		
3.3L engine		
Step 1:	40 ft. lbs.	54 Nm
Step 2:	+ ¼ degree turn	+ ¼ degree turn
3.5L engine		
Step 1:	40 ft. lbs.	54 Nm
Step 2:	+ ¼ degree turn	+ ¼ degree turn

TORQUE SPECIFICATIONS

Component	English	Metric
Crankshaft pulley bolt		
3.3L engine:	40 ft. lbs.	54 Nm
3.5L engine:	85 ft. lbs.	115 Nm
Crankshaft main bearing bolt		
3.3L engine		
Step 1:	30 ft. lbs.	41 Nm
Step 2:	+ ¼ degree turn	+ ¼ degree turn
3.5L engine		
M10 Tie bolts:	40 ft. lbs.	54 Nm
M11 Cap bolts		
Step 1:	30 ft. lbs.	41 Nm
Step 2:	+ ¼ degree turn	+ ¼ degree turn
Cylinder head bolt		
3.3L engine		
Step 1:	45 ft. lbs.	61 Nm
Step 2:	65 ft. lbs.	88 Nm
Step 3:	65 ft. lbs.	88 Nm
Step 4:	+ ¼ degree turn	+ ¼ degree turn
3.5L engine		
Step 1:	45 ft. lbs.	61 Nm
Step 2:	65 ft. lbs.	88 Nm
Step 3:	65 ft. lbs.	88 Nm
Step 4:	+ ¼ degree turn	+ ¼ degree turn
Driveplate-to-torque converter bolts		
3.3L engine:	60 ft. lbs.	81 Nm
3.5L engine:	60 ft. lbs.	81 Nm
Engine mount bracket-to-block bolts		
3.3L engine:	45 ft. lbs.	61 Nm
3.5L engine:	65 ft. lbs.	88 Nm
EGR valve-to-intake plenum		
3.3L engine:	16 ft. lbs.	22 Nm
3.5L engine:	16 ft. lbs.	22 Nm
Exhaust manifold mounting screws		
3.3L engine		
Bolts:	20 ft. lbs.	27 Nm
Nuts:	15 ft. lbs.	20 Nm
3.5L engine:	17 ft. lbs.	23 Nm
Exhaust manifold-to-exhaust pipe		
3.3L engine:	20 ft. lbs.	27 Nm
3.5L engine:	20 ft. lbs.	27 Nm
Flywheel/flexplate-to-crankshaft bolts		
3.3L engine:	75 ft. lbs.	101 Nm
3.5L engine:	75 ft. lbs.	101 Nm
Intake manifold attaching screw		
3.3L engine		
Step 1:	10 inch lbs.	1.0 Nm
Step 2:	200 inch lbs.	22 Nm
Step 3:	200 inch lbs.	22 Nm
3.5L engine:	20 ft. lbs.	28 Nm
Oil pan mounting screws		
3.3L engine:	105 inch lbs.	12 Nm
3.5L engine:	105 inch lbs.	12 Nm
Oil pan drain plug		
3.3L engine:	20 ft. lbs.	27 Nm.
3.5L engine:	25 ft. lbs.	34 Nm.
Oil pump cover bolts		
3.3L engine:	105 inch lbs.	12 Nm.
3.5L engine:	105 inch lbs.	12 Nm.

TORQUE SPECIFICATIONS

Component	English	Metric
Oil pump pickup tube bolts		
3.3L engine:	20 ft. lbs.	28 Nm.
3.5L engine:	20 ft. lbs.	28 Nm.
Rocker shaft bracket bolt		
3.5L engine:	20 ft. lbs.	28 Nm.
Rocker (valve) cover bolts		
3.3L engine:	105 inch lbs.	12 Nm.
3.5L engine:	105 inch lbs.	12 Nm.
Spark plug tube		
3.5L engine:	30 ft. lbs.	41 Nm.
Spark plug		
3.3L engine:	20 ft. lbs.	28 Nm.
3.5L engine:	20 ft. lbs.	28 Nm.
Starter-to-block bolts		
3.3L engine:	50 ft. lbs.	68 Nm.
3.5L engine:	30 ft. lbs.	41 Nm.
TBI mounting bolts		
3.3L engine:	19 ft. lbs.	26 Nm
3.5L engine:	19 ft. lbs.	26 Nm
Thermostat housing bolt		
3.3L engine:	20 ft. lbs.	28 Nm
3.5L engine:	20 ft. lbs.	28 Nm
Timing cover bolts		
3.5L engine		
M6 bolts:	106 inch lbs.	12 Nm
M8 bolts:	20 ft. lbs.	28 Nm
M10 bolts:	40 ft. lbs.	54 Nm
Timing chain snubber bolts		
3.3L engine:	105 inch lbs.	12 Nm
Water pump mounting bolts		
3.3L engine:	105 inch lbs.	12 Nm.
3.5L engine:	105 inch lbs.	12 Nm.
Water pump pulley bolts		
3.3L engine:	20 ft. lbs.	28 Nm.

BRAKE SPECIFICATIONS

All measurements in inches unless noted.

Year	Model		Master Cylinder Bore	Brake Disc Original Thickness	Brake Disc Minimum Thickness	Brake Disc Maximum Runout	Brake Drum Diameter Original Inside Diameter	Brake Drum Diameter Max. Wear Limit	Brake Drum Diameter Maximum Machine Diameter	Minimum Lining Thickness Front [1]	Minimum Lining Thickness Rear [1]
1993	Concorde	front	0.937	0.945	0.803	0.003	—	—	—	0.31	—
		rear disc	—	0.945	0.803	0.003	—	—	—	0.31	0.28
		rear drum	—	—	—	—	8.0	NA	[1]	0.31	NA
	Vision	front	0.937	0.945	0.803	0.003	—	—	—	0.31	—
		rear disc	—	0.945	0.803	0.003	—	—	—	0.31	0.28
		rear drum	—	—	—	—	8.0	NA	[1]	0.31	NA
	Intrepid	front	0.937	0.945	0.803	0.003	—	—	—	0.31	—
		rear disc	—	0.945	0.803	0.003	—	—	—	0.31	0.28
		rear drum	—	—	—	—	8.0	NA	[1]	0.31	NA

BRAKE SPECIFICATIONS
All measurements in inches unless noted.

Year	Model		Master Cylinder Bore	Brake Disc Original Thickness	Brake Disc Minimum Thickness	Maximum Runout	Brake Drum Diameter Original Inside Diameter	Brake Drum Diameter Max. Wear Limit	Brake Drum Diameter Maximum Machine Diameter	Minimum Lining Thickness Front ①	Minimum Lining Thickness Rear ①
1994	Concorde	front	0.937	0.945	0.803	0.003	—	—	—	0.31	—
		rear disc	—	0.945	0.803	0.003	—	—	—	0.31	0.28
		rear drum	—	—	—	—	8.0	NA	①	0.31	NA
	Vision	front	0.937	0.945	0.803	0.003	—	—	—	0.31	—
		rear disc	—	0.945	0.803	0.003	—	—	—	0.31	0.28
		rear drum	—	—	—	—	8.0	NA	①	0.31	NA
	Intrepid	front	0.937	0.945	0.803	0.003	—	—	—	0.31	—
		rear disc	—	0.945	0.803	0.003	—	—	—	0.31	0.28
		rear drum	—	—	—	—	8.0	NA	①	0.31	NA
	New Yorker	front	0.937	0.945	0.803	0.003	—	—	—	0.31	—
		rear disc	—	0.945	0.803	0.003	—	—	—	0.31	0.28
	LHS	front	0.937	0.945	0.803	0.003	—	—	—	0.31	—
		rear disc	—	0.945	0.803	0.003	—	—	—	0.31	0.28

NA—Not available
① Thickness includes shoe and lining

WHEEL ALIGNMENT

Year	Model		Caster Range (deg.)	Caster Preferred Setting (deg.)	Camber Range (deg.)	Camber Preferred Setting (deg.)	Toe-in (in.)	Steering Axis Inclination (deg.)
1993	Concorde	front	2P–4P	3.0P	0.6N + 0.6P	0	0.4 in–0.0	NA
		rear	—	—	0.6N + 0.4P	0.1N	①	NA
	Vision	front	2P–4P	3.0P	0.6N + 0.6P	0	0.4 in–0.0	NA
		rear	—	—	0.6N + 0.4P	0.1N	①	NA
	Intrepid	front	2P–4P	3.0P	0.6N + 0.6P	0	0.4 in–0.0	NA
		rear	—	—	0.6N + 0.4P	0.1N	①	NA
1994	Concorde	front	2P–4P	3.0P	0.6N + 0.6P	0	0.4 in–0.0	NA
		rear	—	—	0.6N + 0.4P	0.1N	①	NA
	Vision	front	2P–4P	3.0P	0.6N + 0.6P	0	0.4 in–0.0	NA
		rear	—	—	0.6N + 0.4P	0.1N	①	NA
	Intrepid	front	2P–4P	3.0P	0.6N + 0.6P	0	0.4 in–0.0	NA
		rear	—	—	0.6N + 0.4P	0.1N	①	NA
	New Yorker	front	2P–4P	3.0P	0.6N + 0.6P	0	0.4 in–0.0	NA
		rear	—	—	0.6N + 0.4P	0.1N	①	NA
	LHS	front	2P–4P	3.0P	0.6N + 0.6P	0	0.4 in–0.0	NA
		rear	—	—	0.6N + 0.4P	0.1N	①	NA

NA—Not available
N—Negative
P—Positive
① 0.2 Out to 0.4 In

AIR CONDITIONING BELT TENSION

Year	Model	Engine Displacement Liters (cc)	Belt Type	Specifications New	Used
1993–94	Concorde	3.3 (3294)	Poly-V	①	①
	Concorde	3.5 (3518)	Poly-V	①	①
	Intrepid	3.3 (3294)	Poly-V	①	①
	Intrepid	3.5 (3518)	Poly-V	①	①
	Vision	3.3 (3294)	Poly-V	①	①
	Vision	3.5 (3518)	Poly-V	①	①

① Equipped with automatic tensioner

REFRIGERANT CAPACITIES

Year	Model	Refrigerant (oz.)	Oil (fl. oz.)	Compressor Type
1993–94	Concorde	28.0 ①	4.75 ①	10PA17-R134a ①
	Intrepid	28.0 ①	4.75 ①	10PA17-R134a ①
	Vision	28.0 ①	4.75 ①	10PA17-R134a ①

① Uses R-134a refrigerant and corresponding oil.
Do not mix any R-12 refrigerant, oil, service
equipment or components.

MAINTENANCE INTERVALS—TYPE A: NORMAL SERVICE
Concorde • Intrepid • Vision

TO BE SERVICED	TYPE OF SERVICE	7.5	15	22.5	30	37.5	45	52.5	60
Oxygen Sensor	I				✔				✔
Engine Oil Filter	R		✔		✔		✔		✔
Vacuum Lines and Hoses	I				✔				✔
Ignition Wires	R								✔
Spark Plugs	R				✔				✔
Engine Oil	R	✔	✔	✔	✔	✔	✔	✔	✔
Engine Air Cleaner Element	R				✔				✔
Crankcase Emission Filter	R				✔				✔
PCV Valve	R								✔
Fuel Filter	R				✔				✔
Charcoal Canister	R				✔				✔
Fuel/Vapor Return Lines	I				✔				✔
Fuel Tank Cap and Restrictor	I				✔				✔
Coolant System	R				✔				✔
Exhaust Pipe and Muffler	I	✔	✔	✔	✔	✔	✔	✔	✔
Manifold Heat Control Valve	I	✔	✔	✔	✔	✔	✔	✔	✔
Catalytic Converter and Shield	I	✔	✔	✔	✔	✔	✔	✔	✔
Drive Belts	I						✔		✔
Drive Belts	R								✔

MAINTENANCE INTERVALS—TYPE A: NORMAL SERVICE
Concorde • Intrepid • Vision

TO BE SERVICED	TYPE OF SERVICE	VEHICLE MILEAGE INTERVAL (X1000)							
		7.5	15	22.5	30	37.5	45	52.5	60
Automatic Transaxle Fluid	R								✔
Brake Linings Front and Rear	I								
CV-Joints and Boots	I								
Ball Joints	L		✔		✔		✔		✔
Tie Rod Ends	L		✔		✔		✔		✔
Tire Rotation	I	✔	✔	✔	✔	✔	✔	✔	✔
Battery Connections	I		✔		✔		✔		✔
Seat Belt Operation	I		✔		✔		✔		✔

FOR COMPLETE WARRANTY COVERAGE CONSULT INDIVIDUAL VEHICLE MANUFACTURER'S WARRANTY MAINTENANCE GUIDE.

I—Inspect
L—Lubricate
R—Replace

MAINTENANCE INTERVALS—TYPE B: SEVERE SERVICE
Concorde • Intrepid • Vision

TO BE SERVICED	TYPE OF SERVICE	VEHICLE MILEAGE INTERVAL (X1000)									
		3	6	9	12	15	18	21	24	27	30
Oxygen Sensor	I										✔
Engine Oil Filter	R		✔		✔		✔		✔		✔
Vacuum Lines and Hoses	I										✔
Ignition Wires	R①										
Spark Plugs	I②										
Engine Oil	R	✔	✔	✔	✔	✔	✔	✔	✔	✔	✔
Engine Air Cleaner Element	R					✔					✔
Crankcase Emission Filter	R										✔
PCV Valve	R										✔
Fuel Filter	R										✔
Charcoal Canister	R										✔
Fuel/Vapor Return Lines	I										✔
Fuel Tank Cap and Restrictor	I										✔
Coolant System	R										✔
Exhaust Pipe and Muffler	I										✔
Manifold Heat Control Valve	I										✔
Catalytic Converter and Shield	I										✔
EGR System	I										✔
Drive Belts	I					✔					✔
Drive Belts	R③										
Automatic Transaxle Fluid	R					✔					✔
Brake Linings Front and Rear	I					✔					✔
CV-Joints and Boots	I	✔	✔	✔	✔	✔	✔	✔	✔	✔	✔
Ball Joints	L					✔					✔
Tie Rod Ends	L					✔					✔
Tire Rotation	I④										

MAINTENANCE INTERVALS—TYPE B: SEVERE SERVICE
Concorde • Intrepid • Vision

TO BE SERVICED	TYPE OF SERVICE	VEHICLE MILEAGE INTERVAL (X1000)									
		3	6	9	12	15	18	21	24	27	30
Battery Connections	I					✔					✔
Seat Belt Operation	I					✔					✔

FOR COMPLETE WARRANTY COVERAGE CONSULT INDIVIDUAL VEHICLE MANUFACTURER'S WARRANTY MAINTENANCE GUIDE.

I—Inspect
L—Lubricate
R—Replace
① Replace wires at 60,000 miles
② Replace spark plugs at 60,000 miles
③ Replace at 60,000 miles
④ Rotate tires every 7,500 miles

FIRING ORDERS

NOTE: To avoid confusion, always replace spark plugs and wires one at a time.

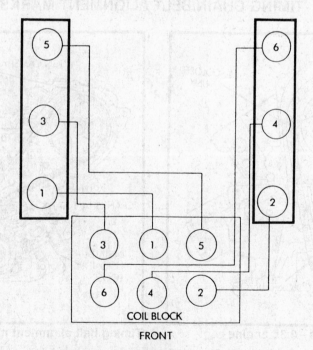

3.3L and 3.5L Engines
Engine Firing Order: 1–2–3–4–5–6
Distributorless Ignition System

CYLINDER HEAD TORQUE SEQUENCES

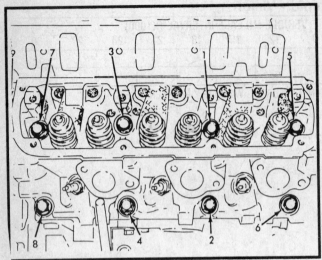

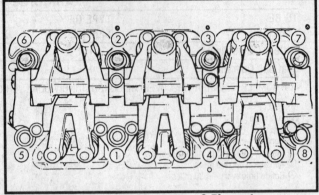

Cylinder head torque sequence—3.5L engine

Cylinder head torque sequence—3.3L engine

TIMING CHAIN/BELT ALIGNMENT MARKS

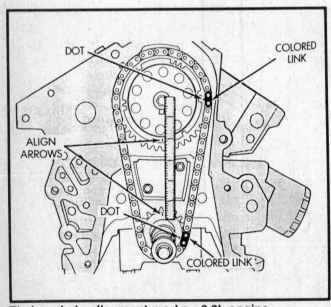

Timing chain alignment marks—3.3L engine

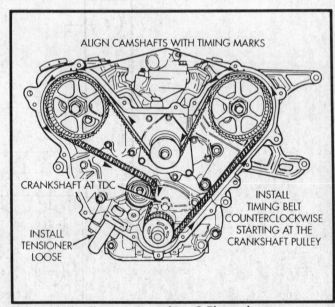

Timing belt alignment marks—3.5L engine

AIR CONDITIONING SERVICE VALVE LOCATIONS

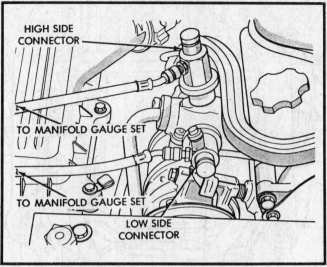

Air conditioning service valve location

WHEEL ALIGNMENT ADJUSTMENT LOCATIONS

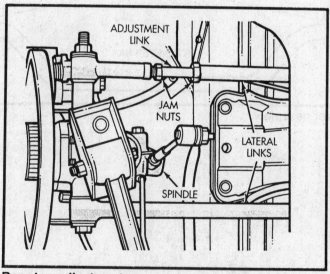

Rear toe adjustment

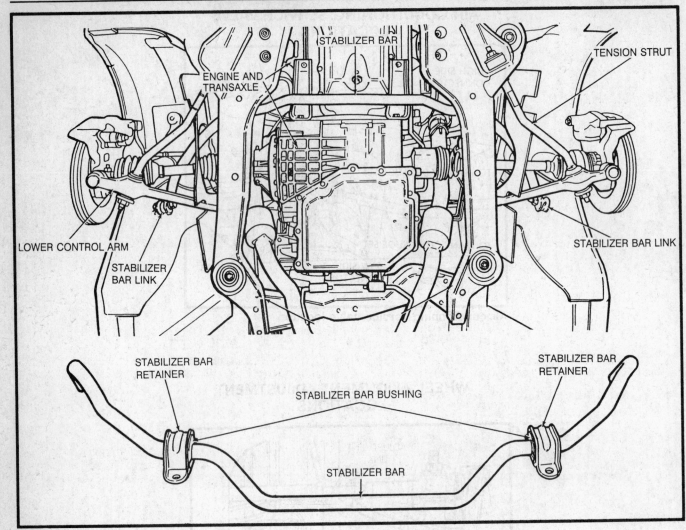

Front suspension and stabilizer assembly

SPECIFICATION CHARTS

VEHICLE IDENTIFICATION CHART

It is important for servicing and ordering parts to be certain of the vehicle and engine identification. The VIN (vehicle identification number) is a 17 digit number visible through the windshield on the driver's side of the dash and contains the vehicle and engine identification codes. The tenth digit indicates model year and the eighth digit indicates engine code. It can be interpreted as follows:

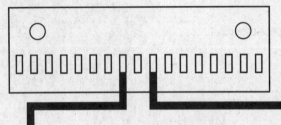

		Engine Code					Model Year	
Code	Liters	Cu. In. (cc)	Cyl.	Fuel Sys.	Eng. Mfg.	Code		Year
8	1.8	112 (1844)	4	EFI	Mazda	L		1990
9	1.9	114 (1859)	4	CFI	Ford	M		1991
J	1.9	114 (1859)	4	EFI	Ford	N		1992
X	2.3	142 (2326)	4	EFI	Ford	P		1993
S	2.3	142 (2326)	4	EFI	Ford	R		1994
U	3.0	181 (2971)	6	EFI	Ford			

CFI—Central Fuel Injection
EFI—Electronic Fuel Injection

ENGINE IDENTIFICATION

Year	Model	Engine Displacement Liters (cc)	Engine Series (ID/VIN)	Fuel System	No. of Cylinders	Engine Type
1990	Escort	1.9 (1859)	9	CFI	4	OHC
	Escort	1.9 (1859)	J	EFI	4	OHC
	Tempo	2.3 (2326)	X	EFI	4	OHV
	Tempo	2.3 (2326)	S	EFI	4	OHV
	Topaz	2.3 (2326)	X	EFI	4	OHV
	Topaz	2.3 (2326)	S	EFI	4	OHV
1991	Escort	1.8 (1844)	8	EFI	4	DOHC
	Escort	1.9 (1859)	J	EFI	4	OHC
	Tempo	2.3 (2326)	X	EFI	4	OHV
	Tempo	2.3 (2326)	S	EFI	4	OHV
	Topaz	2.3 (2326)	X	EFI	4	OHV
	Topaz	2.3 (2326)	S	EFI	4	OHV
1992	Escort	1.8 (1844)	8	EFI	4	DOHC
	Escort	1.9 (1859)	J	EFI	4	OHC
	Tempo	2.3 (2326)	X	EFI	4	OHV
	Tempo	3.0 (2971)	U	EFI	6	OHV
	Topaz	2.3 (2326)	X	EFI	4	OHV
	Topaz	3.0 (2971)	U	EFI	6	OHV

ENGINE IDENTIFICATION

Year	Model	Engine Displacement Liters (cc)	Engine Series (ID/VIN)	Fuel System	No. of Cylinders	Engine Type
1993–94	Escort	1.8 (1844)	8	EFI	4	DOHC
	Escort	1.9 (1859)	J	EFI	4	OHC
	Tempo	2.3 (2326)	X	EFI	4	OHV
	Tempo	3.0 (2971)	U	EFI	6	OHV
	Topaz	2.3 (2326)	X	EFI	4	OHV
	Topaz	3.0 (2971)	U	EFI	6	OHV

CFI—Central Fuel Injection
EFI—Electronic Fuel Injection
OHC—Overhead Cam
OHV—Overhead Valve
DOHC—Double Overhead Cam

GENERAL ENGINE SPECIFICATIONS

Year	Engine ID/VIN	Engine Displacement Liters (cc)	Fuel System Type	Net Horsepower @ rpm	Net Torque @ rpm (ft. lbs.)	Bore × Stroke (in.)	Compression Ratio	Oil Pressure @ rpm
1990	9	1.9 (1859)	CFI	90 @ 4600	106 @ 3400	3.23 × 3.46	9.0:1	35–65 @ 2000 ①
	J	1.9 (1859)	EFI	110 @ 5400	115 @ 4200	3.23 × 3.46	9.0:1	35–65 @ 2000 ①
	X	2.3 (2326)	EFI	98 @ 4400	124 @ 2200	3.70 × 3.30	9.0:1	55–70 @ 2000 ①
	S	2.3 (2326)	EFI	100 @ 4400	130 @ 2600	3.70 × 3.30	9.0:1	55–70 @ 2000 ①
1991	8	1.8 (1844)	EFI	127 @ 6500	114 @ 4500	3.27 × 3.35	9.0:1	43–57 @ 3000 ①
	J	1.9 (1859)	EFI	88 @ 4400	108 @ 3800	3.23 × 3.46	9.0:1	35–65 @ 2000 ①
	X	2.3 (2326)	EFI	98 @ 4400	124 @ 2200	3.70 × 3.30	9.0:1	55–70 @ 2000 ①
	S	2.3 (2326)	EFI	100 @ 4400	130 @ 2600	3.70 × 3.30	9.0:1	55–70 @ 2000 ①
1992	8	1.8 (1844)	EFI	127 @ 6500	114 @ 4500	3.27 × 3.35	9.0:1	43–57 @ 3000 ①
	J	1.9 (1859)	EFI	88 @ 4400	108 @ 3800	3.23 × 3.46	9.0:1	35–65 @ 2000 ①
	X	2.3 (2326)	EFI	96 @ 4400	128 @ 2600	3.70 × 3.30	9.0:1	55–70 @ 2000 ①
	U	3.0 (2971)	EFI	②	③	3.50 × 3.14	9.3:1	40–60 @ 2500 ①
1993–94	8	1.8 (1844)	EFI	127 @ 6500	114 @ 4500	3.27 × 3.35	9.0:1	43–57 @ 3000 ①
	J	1.9 (1859)	EFI	88 @ 4400	108 @ 3800	3.23 × 3.46	9.0:1	35–65 @ 2000 ①
	X	2.3 (2326)	EFI	96 @ 4200	126 @ 2600	3.70 × 3.30	9.0:1	55–70 @ 2000 ①
	U	3.0 (2971)	EFI	④	⑤	3.50 × 3.14	9.3:1	40–60 @ 2500 ①

CFI—Central Fuel Injection
EFI—Electronic Fuel Injection
① Oil at normal operating temperature
② Manual transaxle: 140 @ 4800
   Automatic transaxle: 135 @ 5500
③ Manual transaxle: 150 @ 3250
   Automatic transaxle: 150 @ 4200
④ Manual transaxle: 130 @ 4800
   Automatic transaxle: 135 @ 4800
⑤ Manual transaxle: 150 @ 3000
   Automatic transaxle: 150 @ 4250

GASOLINE ENGINE TUNE-UP SPECIFICATIONS

Year	Engine ID/VIN	Engine Displacement Liters (cc)	Spark Plugs Gap (in.)	Ignition Timing (deg.) MT	Ignition Timing (deg.) AT	Fuel Pump (psi)	Idle Speed (rpm) MT	Idle Speed (rpm) AT	Valve Clearance In.	Valve Clearance Ex.
1990	9	1.9 (1859)	0.044	10B	10B	13–17①	760–840	760–840	Hyd.	Hyd.
	J	1.9 (1859)	0.054	10B	10B	35–40①	②	②	Hyd.	Hyd.
	X	2.3 (2326)	0.054	15B	15B	50–60①	820–880	690–750	Hyd.	Hyd.
	S	2.3 (2326)	0.054	15B	15B	50–60①	810–890	680–760	Hyd.	Hyd.
1991	8	1.8 (1844)	0.041	10B	10B	64–85①	700–800	700–800	Hyd.	Hyd.
	J	1.9 (1859)	0.054	10B	10B	35–40①	②	②	Hyd.	Hyd.
	X	2.3 (2326)	0.054	15B	15B	50–60①	820–880	690–750	Hyd.	Hyd.
	S	2.3 (2326)	②	②	②	50–60①	②	②	Hyd.	Hyd.
1992	8	1.8 (1844)	0.041	10B	10B	64–85①	700–800	700–800	Hyd.	Hyd.
	J	1.9 (1859)	0.054	10B	10B	35–40①	②	②	Hyd.	Hyd.
	X	2.3 (2326)	0.054	10B	10B	50–60①	②	②	Hyd.	Hyd.
	U	3.0 (2971)	0.044	10B	10B	35–40①	②	②	Hyd.	Hyd.
1993	8	1.8 (1844)	0.041	10B	10B	64–85①	700–800	700–800	Hyd.	Hyd.
	J	1.9 (1859)	0.054	10B	10B	35–40①	②	②	Hyd.	Hyd.
	X	2.3 (2326)	0.054	10B	10B	50–60①	②	②	Hyd.	Hyd.
	U	3.0 (2971)	0.044	10B	10B	35–40①	②	②	Hyd.	Hyd.
1994	SEE UNDERHOOD SPECIFICATIONS STICKER									

NOTE: The lowest cylinder pressure should be within 75% of the highest cylinder pressure reading. For example, if the highest cylinder is 134 psi, the lowest should be 101. Engine should be at normal operating temperature with throttle valve in the wide open position.
The underhood specifications sticker often reflects tune-up specification changes in production. Sticker figures must be used if they disagree with those in this chart.
B—Before Top Dead Center
Hyd.—Hydraulic
① Key on, engine off
② Refer to vehicle emission control
   information label

CAPACITIES

Year	Model	Engine ID/VIN	Engine Displacement Liters (cc)	Engine Crankcase with Filter	Transmission (pts.) 4-Spd	Transmission (pts.) 5-Spd	Transmission (pts.) Auto.	Transfer case (pts.)	Drive Axle Front (pts.)	Drive Axle Rear (pts.)	Fuel Tank (gal.)	Cooling System (qts.)
1990	Escort	9	1.9 (1859)	4.0	6.1	6.1	16.6	—	①	—	⑥	②
	Escort	J	1.9 (1859)	4.0	—	6.1	16.6	—	①	—	⑥	②
	Tempo	X	2.3 (2326)	5.0	—	6.1	③	①	①	1.3	④	⑤
	Tempo	S	2.3 (2326)	5.0	—	6.1	③	①	①	1.3	④	⑤
	Topaz	X	2.3 (2326)	5.0	—	6.1	③	①	①	1.3	④	⑤
	Topaz	S	2.3 (2326)	5.0	—	6.1	③	①	①	1.3	④	⑤

CAPACITIES

Year	Model	Engine ID/VIN	Engine Displacement Liters (cc)	Engine Crankcase with Filter	Transmission (pts.) 4-Spd	5-Spd	Auto.	Transfer case (pts.)	Drive Axle Front (pts.)	Rear (pts.)	Fuel Tank (gal.)	Cooling System (qts.)
1991	Escort	8	1.8 (1844)	4.0	—	7.2	13.4	—	①	—	13.2	⑦
	Escort	J	1.9 (1859)	4.0	—	5.6	13.4	—	①	—	11.9	⑦
	Tempo	X	2.3 (2326)	5.0	—	6.1	③	①	①	1.3	④	⑤
	Tempo	S	2.3 (2326)	5.0	—	6.1	③	①	①	1.3	④	⑤
	Topaz	X	2.3 (2326)	5.0	—	6.1	③	①	①	1.3	④	⑤
	Topaz	S	2.3 (2326)	5.0	—	6.1	③	①	①	1.3	④	⑤
1992	Escort	8	1.8 (1844)	4.0	—	7.2	13.4	—	①	—	13.2	⑦
	Escort	J	1.9 (1859)	4.0	—	5.6	13.4	—	①	—	11.9	⑦
	Tempo	X	2.3 (2326)	5.0	—	6.1	16.6	—	①	—	15.9	⑧
	Tempo	U	3.0 (2971)	4.5	—	6.1	16.6	—	①	—	15.9	⑧
	Topaz	X	2.3 (2326)	5.0	—	6.1	16.6	—	①	—	15.9	⑧
	Topaz	U	3.0 (2971)	4.5	—	6.1	16.6	—	①	—	15.9	⑧
1993-94	Escort	8	1.8 (1844)	4.0	—	7.2	13.4	—	①	—	13.2	⑦
	Escort	J	1.9 (1859)	4.0	—	5.6	13.4	—	①	—	11.9	⑦
	Tempo	X	2.3 (2326)	5.0	—	6.1	16.6	—	①	—	15.9	⑧
	Tempo	U	3.0 (2971)	4.5	—	6.1	16.6	—	①	—	15.9	⑧
	Topaz	X	2.3 (2326)	5.0	—	6.1	16.6	—	①	—	15.9	⑧
	Topaz	U	3.0 (2971)	4.5	—	6.1	16.6	—	①	—	15.9	⑧

① Included in transaxle capacity
② Without A/C—8.3 qts.
  With A/C
  Manual transaxle—6.8 qts.
  Automatic transaxle—7.3 qts.

③ Except 4WD—16.6 pts.
  With 4WD—20.0 pts.
④ Except 4WD—15.9 gal.
  With 4WD—14.2 gal.
⑤ Manual transaxle—7.3 qts.
  Automatic transaxle—7.8 qts.

⑥ Standard—13 gal.
  Optional—11.5 gal.
⑦ Manual transaxle—5.3 qts.
  Automatic transaxle—6.3 qts.
⑧ Manual transaxle—7.8 qts.
  Automatic transaxle—8.4 qts.

CAMSHAFT SPECIFICATIONS

All measurements given in inches.

Year	Engine ID/VIN	Engine Displacement Liters (cc)	Journal Diameter 1	2	3	4	5	Elevation In.	Ex.	Bearing Clearance	Camshaft End Play
1990	9	1.9 (1859)	1.8007–1.8017	1.8007–1.8017	1.8007–1.8017	1.8007–1.8017	1.8007–1.8017	0.235–0.240	0.235–0.240	0.0013–0.0033	0.002–0.006
	J	1.9 (1859)	1.8007–1.8017	1.8007–1.8017	1.8007–1.8017	1.8007–1.8017	1.8007–1.8017	0.260–0.265	0.260–0.265	0.0013–0.0033	0.002–0.006
	X	2.3 (2326)	2.006–2.009	2.006–2.009	2.006–2.009	2.006–2.009	—	0.245–0.249	0.235–0.239	0.001–0.003	0.009
	S	2.3 (2326)	2.006–2.009	2.006–2.009	2.006–2.009	2.006–2.009	—	0.258–0.262	0.258–0.262	0.001–0.003	0.009
1991	8	1.8 (1844)	1.0213–1.0222	1.0213–1.0222	1.0213–1.0222	1.0213–1.0222	1.0213–1.0222	1.7281–① 1.7360	1.7480–① 1.7560	0.0014–0.0032	0.0028–0.0075
	J	1.9 (1859)	1.8007–1.8017	1.8007–1.8017	1.8007–1.8017	1.8007–1.8017	1.8007–1.8017	0.235–0.240	0.235–0.240	0.0013–0.0033	0.002–0.006
	X	2.3 (2326)	2.006–2.009	2.006–2.009	2.006–2.009	2.006–2.009	—	0.245–0.249	0.235–0.239	0.001–0.003	0.009
	S	2.3 (2326)	2.006–2.009	2.006–2.009	2.006–2.009	2.006–2.009	—	0.258–0.262	0.258–0.262	0.001–0.003	0.009

CAMSHAFT SPECIFICATIONS

All measurements given in inches.

Year	Engine ID/VIN	Engine Displacement Liters (cc)	Journal Diameter 1	2	3	4	5	Elevation In.	Ex.	Bearing Clearance	Camshaft End Play
1992	8	1.8 (1844)	1.0213–1.0222	1.0213–1.0222	1.0213–1.0222	1.0213–1.0222	1.0213–1.0222	1.7281–① 1.7360	1.7480–① 1.7560	0.0014–0.0032	0.0028–0.0075
	J	1.9 (1859)	1.8007–1.8017	1.8007–1.8017	1.8007–1.8017	1.8007–1.8017	1.8007–1.8017	0.240–0.245	0.240–0.245	0.0013–0.0033	0.002–0.006
	X	2.3 (2326)	2.006–2.009	2.006–2.009	2.006–2.009	2.006–2.009	—	0.245–0.249	0.235–0.239	0.001–0.003	0.009
	U	3.0 (2971)	2.0074–2.0084	2.0074–2.0084	2.0074–2.0084	2.0074–2.0084	—	0.255–0.260	0.255–0.260	0.001–0.003	0.001–0.005
1993–94	8	1.8 (1844)	1.0213–1.0222	1.0213–1.0222	1.0213–1.0222	1.0213–1.0222	1.0213–1.0222	1.7281–① 1.7360	1.7480–① 1.7560	0.0014–0.0032	0.0028–0.0075
	J	1.9 (1859)	1.8007–1.8017	1.8007–1.8017	1.8007–1.8017	1.8007–1.8017	1.8007–1.8017	0.240–0.245	0.240–0.245	0.0013–0.0033	0.002–0.006
	X	2.3 (2326)	2.006–2.009	2.006–2.009	2.006–2.009	2.006–2.009	—	0.245–0.249	0.235–0.239	0.001–0.003	0.009
	U	3.0 (2971)	2.0074–2.0084	2.0074–2.0084	2.0074–2.0084	2.0074–2.0084	—	0.255–0.260	0.255–0.260	0.001–0.003	0.001–0.005

① Specification is for cam lobe height

CRANKSHAFT AND CONNECTING ROD SPECIFICATIONS

All measurements are given in inches.

Year	Engine ID/VIN	Engine Displacement Liters (cc)	Crankshaft Main Brg. Journal Dia.	Main Brg. Oil Clearance	Shaft End-play	Thrust on No.	Connecting Rod Journal Diameter	Oil Clearance	Side Clearance
1990	9	1.9 (1859)	2.2827–2.2835	①	0.0040–0.0080	3	1.7279–1.7287	0.0008–0.0026	0.0040–0.0140
	J	1.9 (1859)	2.2827–2.2835	①	0.0040–0.0080	3	1.7279–1.7287	0.0008–0.0026	0.0040–0.0140
	X	2.3 (2326)	2.2489–2.2490	0.0008–0.0024	0.0040–0.0080	3	2.1232–2.1240	0.0008–0.0024	0.0035–0.0140
	S	2.3 (2326)	2.2489–2.2490	0.0008–0.0024	0.0040–0.0080	3	2.1232–2.1240	0.0008–0.0024	0.0035–0.0140
1991	8	1.8 (1844)	1.9661–1.9668	0.0007–0.0014	0.0031–0.0120	4	1.7692–1.7699	0.0011–0.0027	0.0043–0.0120
	J	1.9 (1859)	2.2827–2.2835	①	0.0040–0.0080	3	1.7279–1.7287	0.0008–0.0026	0.0040–0.0140
	X	2.3 (2326)	2.2489–2.2490	0.0008–0.0024	0.0040–0.0080	3	2.1232–2.1240	0.0008–0.0024	0.0035–0.0140
	S	2.3 (2326)	2.2489–2.2490	0.0008–0.0024	0.0040–0.0080	3	2.1232–2.1240	0.0008–0.0024	0.0035–0.0140
1992	8	1.8 (1844)	1.9661–1.9668	0.0007–0.0014	0.0031–0.0120	4	1.7692–1.7699	0.0011–0.0027	0.0043–0.0120
	J	1.9 (1859)	2.2827–2.2835	①	0.0040–0.0080	3	1.7279–1.7287	0.0008–0.0024	0.0040–0.0140
	X	2.3 (2326)	2.2489–2.2490	0.0008–0.0024	0.0040–0.0080	3	2.1232–2.1240	0.0008–0.0024	0.0035–0.0140
	U	3.0 (2971)	2.5190–2.5198	0.0005–0.0023	0.0040–0.0080	3	2.1253–2.1261	0.0009–0.0027	0.0060–0.0140

CRANKSHAFT AND CONNECTING ROD SPECIFICATIONS

All measurements are given in inches.

Year	Engine ID/VIN	Engine Displacement Liters (cc)	Crankshaft				Connecting Rod		
			Main Brg. Journal Dia.	Main Brg. Oil Clearance	Shaft End-play	Thrust on No.	Journal Diameter	Oil Clearance	Side Clearance
1993-94	8	1.8 (1844)	1.9661–1.9668	0.0007–0.0014	0.0031–0.0120	4	1.7692–1.7699	0.0011–0.0027	0.0043–0.0120
	J	1.9 (1859)	2.2827–2.2835	①	0.0040–0.0080	3	1.7279–1.7287	0.0008–0.0024	0.0040–0.0140
	X	2.3 (2326)	2.2489–2.2490	0.0008–0.0024	0.0040–0.0080	3	2.1232–2.1240	0.0008–0.0024	0.0035–0.0140
	U	3.0 (2971)	2.5190–2.5198	0.0005–0.0023	0.0040–0.0080	3	2.1253–2.1261	0.0009–0.0027	0.0060–0.0140

① Without cylinder head—0.0018–0.0034
With cylinder head—0.0011–0.0027

VALVE SPECIFICATIONS

Year	Engine ID/VIN	Engine Displacement Liters (cc)	Seat Angle (deg.)	Face Angle (deg.)	Spring Test Pressure (lbs. @ in.)	Spring Installed Height (in.)	Stem-to-Guide Clearance (in.)		Stem Diameter (in.)	
							Intake	Exhaust	Intake	Exhaust
1990	9	1.9 (1859)	45	45.6	200 @ 1.09	1.44–1.48	0.0008–0.0027	0.0018–0.0037	0.3159–0.3167	0.3149–0.3156
	J	1.9 (1859)	45	45.6	216 @ 1.016	1.44–1.48	0.0008–0.0027	0.0018–0.0037	0.3159–0.3167	0.3149–0.3156
	X	2.3 (2326)	44–45	44–45	174–188 @ 1.088	1.49	0.0018	0.0023	0.3415–0.3422	0.3411–0.3418
	S	2.3 (2326)	44–45	44–45	174–188 @ 1.088	1.49	0.0018	0.0023	0.3415–0.3422	0.3411–0.3418
1991	8	1.8 (1844)	45	45	NA①	NA	0.0010–0.0024	0.0012–0.0026	0.2350–0.2356	0.2348–0.2354
	J	1.9 (1859)	45	45.6	200 @ 1.09	1.44–1.48	0.0008–0.0027	0.0018–0.0037	0.3159–0.3167	0.3149–0.3156
	X	2.3 (2326)	44–45	44–45	174–188 @ 1.088	1.49	0.0018	0.0023	0.3415–0.3422	0.3411–0.3418
	S	2.3 (2326)	44–45	44–45	174–188 @ 1.088	1.49	0.0018	0.0023	0.3415–0.3422	0.3411–0.3418
1992	8	1.8 (1844)	45	45	NA①	NA	0.0010–0.0024	0.0012–0.0026	0.2350–0.2356	0.2348–0.2354
	J	1.9 (1859)	45	45.6	200 @ 1.09	1.44–1.48	0.0008–0.0027	0.0018–0.0037	0.3159–0.3167	0.3149–0.3156
	X	2.3 (2326)	44–45	44–45	179–194 @ 1.088	1.49	0.0018	0.0023	0.3415–0.3422	0.3411–0.3418
	U	3.0 (2971)	45	44	180 @ 1.16	1.58	0.0010–0.0028	0.0015–0.0033	0.3126–0.3134	0.3121–0.3129
1993-94	8	1.8 (1844)	45	45	NA①	NA	0.0010–0.0024	0.0012–0.0026	0.2350–0.2356	0.2348–0.2354
	J	1.9 (1859)	45	45.6	200 @ 1.09	1.44–1.48	0.0008–0.0027	0.0018–0.0037	0.3159–0.3167	0.3149–0.3156
	X	2.3 (2326)	44–45	44–45	179–194 @ 1.088	1.49	0.0018	0.0023	0.3415–0.3422	0.3411–0.3418

VALVE SPECIFICATIONS

Year	Engine ID/VIN	Engine Displacement Liters (cc)	Seat Angle (deg.)	Face Angle (deg.)	Spring Test Pressure (lbs. @ in.)	Spring Installed Height (in.)	Stem-to-Guide Clearance (in.) Intake	Stem-to-Guide Clearance (in.) Exhaust	Stem Diameter (in.) Intake	Stem Diameter (in.) Exhaust
1993-94	U	3.0 (2971)	45	44	180 @ 1.16	1.58	0.0010–0.0028	0.0015–0.0033	0.3126–0.3134	0.3121–0.3129

① Check valve spring free length and out-of-square
    Free length: 1.555–1.821 in.
    Out-of-square: 0.064 in. maximum

PISTON AND RING SPECIFICATIONS
All measurements are given in inches.

Year	Engine ID/VIN	Engine Displacement Liters (cc)	Piston Clearance	Ring Gap Top Compression	Ring Gap Bottom Compression	Ring Gap Oil Control	Ring Side Clearance Top Compression	Ring Side Clearance Bottom Compression	Ring Side Clearance Oil Control
1990	9	1.9 (1859)	0.0016–0.0024	0.010–0.020	0.010–0.020	0.016–0.055	0.0015–0.0032	0.0015–0.0035	Snug
	J	1.9 (1859)	0.0016–0.0024	0.010–0.020	0.010–0.020	0.016–0.055	0.0015–0.0032	0.0015–0.0035	Snug
	X	2.3 (2326)	0.0012–0.0022	0.008–0.016	0.008–0.016	0.015–0.055	0.0020–0.0040	0.0020–0.0040	Snug
	S	2.3 (2326)	0.0012–0.0022	0.008–0.016	0.008–0.016	0.015–0.055	0.0020–0.0040	0.0020–0.0040	Snug
1991	8	1.8 (1844)	0.0015–0.0020	0.006–0.012	0.006–0.012	0.008–0.028	0.0012–0.0026	0.0012–0.0028	Snug
	J	1.9 (1859)	0.0016–0.0024	0.010–0.020	0.010–0.020	0.016–0.055	0.0015–0.0032	0.0015–0.0035	Snug
	X	2.3 (2326)	0.0011–0.0022	0.008–0.016	0.008–0.016	0.015–0.055	0.0020–0.0040	0.0020–0.0040	Snug
	S	2.3 (2326)	0.0011–0.0022	0.008–0.016	0.008–0.016	0.015–0.055	0.0020–0.0040	0.0020–0.0040	Snug
1992	8	1.8 (1844)	0.0015–0.0020	0.006–0.012	0.006–0.012	0.008–0.028	0.0012–0.0028	0.0012–0.0028	Snug
	J	1.9 (1859)	0.0016–0.0024	0.010–0.020	0.010–0.020	0.016–0.055	0.0015–0.0032	0.0015–0.0032	Snug
	X	2.3 (2326)	0.0011–0.0022	0.008–0.016	0.008–0.016	0.015–0.055	0.0020–0.0040	0.0020–0.0040	Snug
	U	3.0 (2971)	0.0014–0.0022	0.010–0.020	0.010–0.020	0.010–0.049	0.0012–0.0031	0.0012–0.0031	Snug
1993-94	8	1.8 (1844)	0.0015–0.0020	0.006–0.012	0.006–0.012	0.008–0.028	0.0012–0.0028	0.0012–0.0028	Snug
	J	1.9 (1859)	0.0012–0.0028	0.010–0.030	0.010–0.030	0.016–0.066	0.0015–0.0032	0.0015–0.0032	Snug
	X	2.3 (2326)	0.0011–0.0022	0.008–0.016	0.008–0.016	0.015–0.055	0.0020–0.0040	0.0020–0.0040	Snug
	U	3.0 (2971)	0.0014–0.0022	0.010–0.020	0.010–0.020	0.010–0.049	0.0012–0.0031	0.0012–0.0031	Snug

TORQUE SPECIFICATIONS

All readings in ft. lbs.

Year	Engine ID/VIN	Engine Displacement Liters (cc)	Cylinder Head Bolts	Main Bearing Bolts	Rod Bearing Bolts	Crankshaft Damper Bolts	Flywheel Bolts	Manifold Intake	Manifold Exhaust	Spark Plugs	Lug Nut
1990	9	1.9 (1859)	①	67–80	26–30	81–96	54–64	12–15	15–20	8–15	85–105
	J	1.9 (1859)	①	67–80	26–30	81–96	54–64	12–15	15–20	8–15	85–105
	X	2.3 (2326)	②	51–66	21–26	140–170	54–64	15–22	③	6–10	85–105
	S	2.3 (2326)	②	51–66	21–26	140–170	54–64	15–22	③	6–10	85–105
1991	8	1.8 (1844)	56–60	40–43	35–37	80–87④	71–76	14–19	28–34	11–17	65–87
	J	1.9 (1859)	①	67–80	26–30	81–96	54–64	12–15	16–19	8–15	65–87
	X	2.3 (2326)	②	51–66	21–26	140–170	54–64	⑤	③	6–10	85–105
	S	2.3 (2326)	②	51–66	21–26	140–170	54–64	⑤	③	6–10	85–105
1992	8	1.8 (1844)	56–60	40–43	35–37	80–87④	71–76	14–19	28–34	11–17	65–87
	J	1.9 (1859)	①	67–80	26–30	81–96	54–64	12–15	16–19	8–15	65–87
	X	2.3 (2326)	②	51–66	21–26	140–170	54–64	⑤	③	6–10	85–105
	U	3.0 (2971)	⑥	55–63	26	93–121	59	⑦	15–22	5–11	85–105
1993–94	8	1.8 (1844)	56–60	40–43	35–37	80–87④	71–76	14–19	28–34	11–17	65–87
	J	1.9 (1859)	①	67–80	26–30	81–96	54–64	12–15	16–19	8–15	65–87
	X	2.3 (2326)	②	51–66	21–26	140–170	54–64	⑤	③	6–10	85–105
	U	3.0 (2971)	⑥	55–63	26	93–121	59	⑦	15–22	5–11	85–105

① Tighten in sequence to 44 ft. lbs.
Loosen 2 turns
Retighten in sequence to 44 ft. lbs.
Turn all bolts, in sequence, 90 degrees
Turn all bolts, in sequence, an additional
90 degrees

② Tighten, in sequence, in 2 steps:
52–59 ft. lbs.
70–76 ft. lbs.
③ Tighten in 2 steps: 5–7 ft. lbs.
20–30 ft. lbs.
④ Specification is for sprocket bolt
⑤ Tighten in 2 steps: 5–7 ft. lbs.
20–30 ft. lbs.

⑥ Tighten, in sequence, to 52–66 ft. lbs.
Loosen 1 turn
Tighten, in sequence, to 33–41 ft. lbs.
Tighten, in sequence, to 63–73 ft. lbs.
⑦ Tighten in 2 steps: 15–22 ft. lbs.
19–24 ft. lbs.

TORQUE SPECIFICATIONS

Component	English	Metric
Camshaft bearing cap bolts		
1.8L engine:	100–126 inch lbs.	11.3–14.2 Nm
Camshaft sprocket bolt		
1.8L engine:	36–45 ft. lbs.	49–61 Nm
1.9L engine:	71–84 ft. lbs.	95–115 Nm
2.3L engine:	41–56 ft. lbs.	55–75 Nm
3.0L engine:	37–51 ft. lbs.	50–70 Nm
Camshaft thrust plate		
1.8L engine:	69–95 inch lbs.	7.8–11.0 Nm
1.9L engine:	7–9 ft. lbs.	10–13 Nm
2.3L engine:	71–106 inch lbs.	8–12 Nm
3.0L engine:	7 ft. lbs.	10 Nm
Connecting rod bearing cap nuts		
1.8L engine:	35–37 ft. lbs.	47–50 Nm
1.9L engine:	26–30 ft. lbs.	35–41 Nm
2.3L engine:	21–26 ft. lbs.	28–35 Nm
3.0L engine:	26 ft. lbs.	35 Nm
Crankshaft damper bolt		
1.9L engine:	81–96 ft. lbs.	110–130 Nm
2.3L engine:	140–170 ft. lbs.	190–230 Nm
3.0L engine:	93–121 ft. lbs.	125–165 Nm
Crankshaft pulley bolt		
1.8L engine:	109–152 inch lbs.	12–17 Nm
3.0L engine:	37 ft. lbs.	50 Nm

TORQUE SPECIFICATIONS

Component	English	Metric
Crankshaft seal retainer bolts		
1.8L engine:	69–95 inch lbs.	7.8–11.0 Nm
1.9L engine:	72–96 inch lbs.	8–11 Nm
2.3L engine:	72–108 inch lbs.	8–12 Nm
Crankshaft sprocket bolt		
1.8L engine:	80–87 ft. lbs.	108–118 Nm
Cylinder head bolt		
1.8L engine:	56–60 ft. lbs.	76–81 Nm
1.9L engine *		
Step 1:	29–44 ft. lbs.	40–60 Nm
Step 2:	loosen 2 turns	loosen 2 turns
Step 3:	44 ft. lbs.	60 Nm
Step 4:	+ 90 degrees turn	+ 90 degrees turn
Step 5:	+ 90 degrees turn	+ 90 degrees turn
2.3L engine		
Step 1:	52–59 ft. lbs.	70–80 Nm
Step 2:	70–76 ft. lbs.	95–103 Nm
3.0L engine		
Step 1:	33–41 ft. lbs.	45–55 Nm
Step 2:	63–73 ft. lbs.	85–99 Nm
* NOTE: Use new bolts and oil threads		
Engine-to-transaxle		
1.8L engine		
Manual transaxle:	47–66 ft. lbs.	64–89 Nm
Automatic transaxle:	41–59 ft. lbs.	55–80 Nm
1.9L engine:	27–38 ft. lbs.	37–52 Nm
2.3L engine:	25–33 ft. lbs.	34–45 Nm
3.0L engine:	34–47 ft. lbs.	46–63 Nm
Exhaust manifold		
1.8L engine:	28–34 ft. lbs.	38–46 Nm
1.9L engine:	16–19 ft. lbs.	21–26 Nm
2.3L engine		
Step 1:	5–7 ft. lbs.	7–10 Nm
Step 2:	20–30 ft. lbs.	27–41 Nm
3.0L engine:	15–22 ft. lbs.	20–30 Nm
Exhaust flange-to-manifold nuts		
1.8L engine:	23–34 ft. lbs.	31–46 Nm
1.9L engine:	25–35 ft. lbs.	34–47 Nm
2.3L and 3.0L engines:	26–33 ft. lbs.	34–46 Nm
Flywheel/flexplate-to-crankshaft bolts		
1.8L engine:	71–76 ft. lbs.	96–103 Nm
1.9L engine:	54–67 ft. lbs.	73–91 Nm
2.3L engine:	54–64 ft. lbs.	73–87 Nm
3.0L engine:	59 ft. lbs.	80 Nm
Flywheel-to-converter bolts:	25–36 ft. lbs.	34–49 Nm
Engine/transaxle mounts		
1.8L engine		
Engine mount bolt/nuts:	49–69 ft. lbs.	67–93 Nm
Transaxle front mount nuts:	27–38 ft. lbs.	37–52 Nm
Engine mount through bolt/nut:	49–69 ft. lbs.	67–93 Nm
Engine mount-to-engine nuts:	54–76 ft. lbs.	74–103 Nm
Transaxle upper mount bolts:	32–45 ft. lbs.	43–61 Nm
Transaxle upper mount nuts:	49–69 ft. lbs.	67–93 Nm
1990 1.9L engine		
Left front No. 1 insulator		
Insulator-to-transaxle bolts:	25–37 ft. lbs.	35–50 Nm
Insulator-to-support bracket nut:	80–100 ft. lbs.	108–136 Nm
Right No. 3A insulator		
Insulator nuts:	75–100 ft. lbs.	100–135 Nm
Insulator bolts:	37–55 ft. lbs.	50–75 Nm
Insulator support-to-insulator nuts:	55–75 ft. lbs.	75–100 Nm

TORQUE SPECIFICATIONS

Component	English	Metric
Lower support bracket nut:	60–90 ft. lbs.	80–120 Nm
Insulator-to-engine bracket bolt:	60–90 ft. lbs.	80–120 Nm
Left rear No. 4 insulator		
Insulator through bolts:	30–45 ft. lbs.	41–61 Nm
Insulator-to-support bracket nuts:	80–100 ft. lbs.	108–136 Nm
Left rear support bracket bolts:	45–65 ft. lbs.	61–88 Nm
2.3L engine		
Right No. 3A intermediate bracket bolt:	55–75 ft. lbs.	75–100 Nm
Right No. 3A insulator nuts:	75–100 ft. lbs.	100–135 Nm
Left front No. 1 insulator-to-transaxle		
Bolts:	30–42 ft. lbs.	41–57 Nm
Nut:	75–100 ft. lbs.	100–135 Nm
Left rear No. 4 insulator-to-body bolts:	75–100 ft. lbs.	100–135 Nm
Left rear No. 4 insulator-to-transaxle:	35–50 ft. lbs.	50–68 Nm
No. 4 insulator bracket-to-body:	45–65 ft. lbs.	61–68 Nm
3.0L engine		
Left No. 1 and right No. 2 insulator bolts:	26–36 ft. lbs.	34–46 Nm
Left front No. 1 and right No. 2A insulator nuts:	26–36 ft. lbs.	34–46 Nm
Left rear No. 4 insulator through bolts:	30–40 ft. lbs.	41–54 Nm
Left rear No. 4 insulator-to-body nuts:	73–97 ft. lbs.	98–132 Nm
Left rear support bracket bolts:	51–67 ft. lbs.	68–92 Nm
Right insulator-to-body		
No. 3A and 4A nuts:	73–97 ft. lbs.	98–132 Nm
No. 2A and 3A bolts:	40–53 ft. lbs.	53–72 Nm
Bracket-to-insulator nuts:	51–67 ft. lbs.	68–92 Nm
Bracket-to-insulator bolts:	22–29 ft. lbs.	30–40 Nm
Bracket-to-insulator lower nut:	65–87 ft. lbs.	88–118 Nm
Insulator-to-stabilizer bar bracket		
Bolts:	40–53 ft. lbs.	53–72 Nm
Nuts:	26–36 ft. lbs.	34–46 Nm
Left rear support bracket lower nuts:	73–97 ft. lbs.	98–132 Nm
Intake manifold		
1.8L engine:	14–19 ft. lbs.	19–25 Nm
1.9L engine:	12–15 ft. lbs.	16–20 Nm
2.3L engine		
Step 1:	5–7 ft. lbs.	7–10 Nm
Step 2:	15–22 ft. lbs.	20–30 Nm
3.0L engine		
Step 1:	15–22 ft. lbs.	20–30 Nm
Step 2:	19–24 ft. lbs.	26–32 Nm
Main bearing cap bolts		
1.8L engine:	40–43 ft. lbs.	54–59 Nm
1.9L engine:	67–80 ft. lbs.	90–108 Nm
2.3L engine:	51–66 ft. lbs.	70–90 Nm
3.0L engine:	55–63 ft. lbs.	75–85 Nm
Oil pan-to-block		
1.8L engine:	69–95 inch lbs.	7.8–11.0 Nm
1.9L engine:	15–22 ft. lbs.	20–30 Nm
2.3L engine:	15–22 ft. lbs.	20–30 Nm
3.0L engine:	7–10 ft. lbs.	10–14 Nm
Oil pan-to-transaxle bolts		
1.8L engine:	27–38 ft. lbs.	37–52 Nm
1.9L engine:	30–40 ft. lbs.	40–55 Nm
2.3L engine:	30–39 ft. lbs.	40–54 Nm
Oil pan drain plug		
1.8L engine:	22–30 ft. lbs.	29–41 Nm
1.9L engine:	15–22 ft. lbs.	20–30 Nm
2.3L engine:	15–25 ft. lbs.	20–34 Nm
3.0L engine:	9–12 ft. lbs.	11–16 Nm

TORQUE SPECIFICATIONS

Component	English	Metric
Oil pump attaching bolts		
1.8L engine:	14–19 ft. lbs.	19–25 Nm
1.9L engine:	8–12 ft. lbs.	11–16 Nm
2.3L engine:	15–22 ft. lbs.	20–30 Nm
3.0L engine:	35 ft. lbs.	48 Nm
Oil pump pickup bolts		
1.8L engine:	69–95 inch lbs.	7.8–11.0 Nm
1.9L engine:	7–9 ft. lbs.	10–13 Nm
Rocker arm bolt		
1.9L engine:	17–22 ft. lbs.	23–30 Nm
2.3L engine		
Step 1:	5–7 ft. lbs.	6–10 Nm
Step 2:	20–26 ft. lbs.	26–38 Nm
3.0L engine		
Step 1:	5–11 ft. lbs.	7–15 Nm
Step 2:	20–26 ft. lbs.	26–38 Nm
Rocker arm (valve) cover		
1.8L engine:	43–78 inch lbs.	4.9–8.8 Nm
1.9L engine		
1990:	7–10 ft. lbs.	9.5–13.5 Nm
1991–93:	4–9 ft. lbs.	5–12 Nm
2.3L engine:	71–101 inch lbs.	8–11 Nm
3.0L engine:	8–10 ft. lbs.	10–14 Nm
Spark plug		
1.8L engine:	11–17 ft. lbs.	15–23 Nm
1.9L engine:	8–15 ft. lbs.	10–20 Nm
2.3L engine:	6–10 ft. lbs.	7–14 Nm
3.0L engine:	6–11 ft. lbs.	7–15 Nm
Starter-to-block bolts:	15–20 ft. lbs.	20–27 Nm
Thermostat housing		
1.8L engine:	14–19 ft. lbs.	19–25 Nm
1.9L engine:	6–9 ft. lbs.	8–11 Nm
2.3L engine:	12–18 ft. lbs.	16–24 Nm
3.0L engine:	9 ft. lbs.	12 Nm
Throttle body bolts		
1.8L engine:	14–19 ft. lbs.	19–25 Nm
1.9L engine		
1990 CFI engine		
Step 1:	5–11 ft. lbs.	7–15 Nm
Step 2:	13–19 ft. lbs.	18–26 Nm
EFI engine:	15–22 ft. lbs.	20–30 Nm
2.3L engine:	12–14 ft. lbs.	16–20 Nm
3.0L engine:	15–22 ft. lbs.	20–30 Nm
Timing cover		
1.8L engine:	69–95 inch lbs.	7.8–11.0 Nm
1.9L engine		
Nuts:	3–5 ft. lbs.	5–7 Nm
Bolts:	5–7 ft. lbs.	7–9 Nm
2.3L engine:	72–106 inch lbs.	8–12 Nm
3.0L engine:	19 ft. lbs.	25 Nm
Water pump		
1.8L engine:	14–19 ft. lbs.	19–25 Nm
1.9L engine		
1990:	6.0–8.5 ft. lbs.	8.0–11.5 Nm
1991–93:	15–22 ft. lbs.	20–30 Nm
2.3L engine:	15–22 ft. lbs.	20–30 Nm
3.0L engine:	15–22 ft. lbs.	20–30 Nm

BRAKE SPECIFICATIONS

All measurements in inches unless noted.

Year	Model	Master Cylinder Bore	Brake Disc Original Thickness	Brake Disc Minimum Thickness	Maximum Runout	Brake Drum Diameter Original Inside Diameter	Max. Wear Limit	Maximum Machine Diameter	Minimum Lining Thickness Front	Minimum Lining Thickness Rear
1990	Escort	①	0.945	0.882	0.003	②	③	NA	0.125	④
	Tempo	①	0.945	0.882	0.003	8.059	8.119	NA	0.125	④
	Topaz	①	0.945	0.882	0.003	8.059	8.119	NA	0.125	④
1991	Escort	0.875	⑤	⑥	0.004	9.000	9.040	NA	0.080	0.040
	Tempo	①	0.945	0.882	0.003	8.059	8.119	NA	0.125	④
	Topaz	①	0.945	0.882	0.003	8.059	8.119	NA	0.125	④
1992	Escort	0.875	⑤	⑥	0.004	9.000	9.040	NA	0.080	0.040
	Tempo	①	0.945	0.882	0.003	8.059	8.119	NA	0.125	④
	Topaz	①	0.945	0.882	0.003	8.059	8.119	NA	0.125	④
1993–94	Escort	0.875	⑤	⑥	0.004	7.870	7.910	NA	0.080	0.040
	Tempo	①	0.945	0.882	0.003	8.059	8.119	NA	0.125	0.062
	Topaz	①	0.945	0.882	0.003	8.059	8.119	NA	0.125	0.062

NA—Not available
① Primary bore—1.12
  Secondary bore—0.776
② Escort 2DR Hatchback without styled steel wheels—7.145 in.
  Except Escort 2DR Hatchback without styled steel wheels—8.059 in.
③ Escort 2DR Hatchback without styled steel wheels—7.205 in.
  Except Escort 2DR Hatchback without styled steel wheels—8.119 in.
④ Riveted linings—to within 0.031 in. of rivet head
  Bonded linings—0.060
⑤ Front—0.870 in.
  Rear—0.350 in.
⑥ Front—0.790 in.
  Rear—0.280 in.

WHEEL ALIGNMENT

Year	Model		Caster Range (deg.)	Caster Preferred Setting (deg.)	Camber Range (deg.)	Camber Preferred Setting (deg.)	Toe-in (in.)	Steering Axis Inclination (deg.)
1990	Escort	Front	1⁵/₈P–3¹/₈P	2³/₈P	①	②	¹/₄N–0	③
		Rear	—	—	1³/₁₆N–¹/₂P	⁵/₁₆N	0–³/₈P	—
	Tempo	Front	1¹¹/₁₆P–3³/₁₆P	2⁷/₁₆P	④	⑤	¹/₄N–0	③
		Rear	—	—	⑥	⑦	³/₁₆N–³/₁₆P	—
	Topaz	Front	1¹¹/₁₆P–3³/₁₆P	2⁷/₁₆P	④	⑤	¹/₄N–0	③
		Rear	—	—	⑥	⑦	³/₁₆N–³/₁₆P	—
1991	Escort	Front	1P–2⁷/₈P	1¹⁵/₁₆P	27/32N–11/16P	3/32N	¹/₃₂N–⁷/₃₂P	23¹³/₁₆
		Rear	—	—	13/32N–7/16P	11/32N	¹/₃₂N–⁷/₃₂P	—
	Tempo	Front	1¹¹/₁₆P–3³/₁₆P	2⁷/₁₆P	④	⑤	¹/₄N–0	③
		Rear	—	—	⑥	⑦	³/₁₆N–³/₁₆P	—
	Topaz	Front	1¹¹/₁₆P–3³/₁₆P	2⁷/₁₆P	④	⑤	¹/₄N–0	③
		Rear	—	—	⑥	⑦	³/₁₆N–³/₁₆P	—
1992	Escort	Front	1P–2⁷/₈P	1¹⁵/₁₆P	27/32N–11/16P	3/32N	¹/₃₂N–⁷/₃₂P	23¹³/₁₆
		Rear	—	—	13/32N–7/16P	11/32N	¹/₃₂N–⁷/₃₂P	—
	Tempo	Front	1¹¹/₁₆P–3³/₁₆P	2⁷/₁₆P	④	⑤	¹/₄N–0	③
		Rear	—	—	⑥	⑦	³/₁₆N–³/₁₆P	—
	Topaz	Front	1¹¹/₁₆P–3³/₁₆P	2⁷/₁₆P	④	⑤	¹/₄N–0	③
		Rear	—	—	⑥	⑦	³/₁₆N–³/₁₆P	—

WHEEL ALIGNMENT

Year	Model		Caster Range (deg.)	Caster Preferred Setting (deg.)	Camber Range (deg.)	Camber Preferred Setting (deg.)	Toe-in (in.)	Steering Axis Inclination (deg.)
1993-94	Escort	Front	1P–2⁷/₈P	1¹⁵/₁₆P	²⁷/₃₂N–1¹¹/₁₆P	³/₃₂N	¹/₃₂N–⁷/₃₂P	23¹³/₁₆
		Rear	—	—	1³/₃₂N–⁷/₁₆P	¹¹/₃₂N	¹/₃₂N–⁷/₃₂P	—
	Tempo	Front	1¹¹/₁₆P–3³/₁₆P	2⁷/₁₆P	④	⑤	¹/₄N–0	③
		Rear	—	—	⑥	⑦	³/₁₆N–³/₁₆P	—
	Topaz	Front	1¹¹/₁₆P–3³/₁₆P	2⁷/₁₆P	④	⑤	¹/₄N–0	③
		Rear	—	—	⑥	⑦	³/₁₆N–³/₁₆P	—

N—Negative
P—Positive

① Left wheel: ³/₈P–1⁷/₈P
   Right wheel: 0–1¹/₂P
② Left wheel: 1¹/₈P
   Right wheel: ³/₄P
③ Left wheel: 14²¹/₃₂
   Right wheel: 15³/₃₂

④ Left wheel: 2¹/₃₂P–2⁵/₃₂P
   Right wheel: ⁷/₃₂P–1²³/₃₂P
⑤ Left wheel: 1¹³/₃₂P
   Right wheel: 3¹/₃₂P
⑥ Front wheel drive: 2⁹/₃₂N–1⁹/₃₂P
   All wheel drive: 1³/₃₂N–1¹³/₃₂P
⑦ Front wheel drive: ⁵/₃₂N
   All wheel drive: 1¹/₃₂P

AIR CONDITIONING BELT TENSION

Year	Model	Engine Displacement Liters (cc)	Belt Type	Specifications (lbs.) New	Specifications (lbs.) Used
1990	Escort	1.9 (1859)	V-Ribbed	140–180	120–140
	Tempo	2.3 (2326)	V-Ribbed	①	①
	Topaz	2.3 (2326)	V-Ribbed	①	①
1991	Escort	1.8 (1844)	V-Ribbed	110–132	110–132
	Escort	1.9 (1859)	V-Ribbed	110–132	110–132
	Tempo	2.3 (2326)	Serpentine	①	①
	Topaz	2.3 (2326)	Serpentine	①	①
1992	Escort	1.8 (1844)	Serpentine	110–132	95–110
	Escort	1.9 (1859)	Serpentine	①	①
	Tempo	2.3 (2326)	Serpentine	①	①
	Topaz	2.3 (2326)	Serpentine	①	①
	Tempo	3.0 (2971)	Serpentine	①	①
	Topaz	3.0 (2971)	Serpentine	①	①
1993-94	Escort	1.8 (1844)	Serpentine	110–132	95–110
	Escort	1.9 (1859)	Serpentine	①	①
	Tempo	2.3 (2326)	Serpentine	①	①
	Topaz	2.3 (2326)	Serpentine	①	①
	Tempo	3.0 (2971)	Serpentine	①	①
	Topaz	3.0 (2971)	Serpentine	①	①

① Automatic tensioner
② Belt tension in lbs.

REFRIGERANT CAPACITIES

Year	Model	Refrigerant (oz.)	Oil (fl. oz.) [1]	Compressor Type
1990	Escort	35–37	10.0	10P15
	Tempo	35–37	10.0	10P15
	Topaz	35–37	10.0	10P15
1991	Escort	NA	7.75	10P13
	Tempo	35–37	12.0	10P15C
	Topaz	35–37	12.0	10P15C
1992	Tempo	35–37	10.0	FX-15 also 10P15C
	Topaz	35–37	10.0	10P15C
	Escort	35–37	10.0	10P13
1993	Tempo	35–37	10.0	10P15C
	Topaz	35–37	10.0	10P15C
	Escort	35–37	7.75	10P13

NOTE: At the time of publication, refrigerant capacity information relating to R-134a was not available from the manufacturer.
[1] These oil capacities are for compressor only

MAINTENANCE INTERVALS—TYPE A: NORMAL SERVICE
Escort • Tempo • Topaz

TO BE SERVICED	TYPE OF SERVICE	7.5	15	22.5	30	37.5	45	52.5	60
Oxygen Sensor	I				✔				✔
Ignition Timing	I [2]				✔				✔
Vacuum Lines and Hoses	I				✔				✔
Ignition Wires	I				✔				✔
Spark Plugs	R				✔				✔
Engine Oil and Filter	R	✔	✔	✔	✔	✔	✔	✔	✔
Engine Air Cleaner Element	I/R [3]		✔		✔		✔		✔
Crankcase Emission Filter	R [4]				✔				✔
PCV Valve	R				✔				✔
Fuel Filter	R				✔				✔
Charcoal Canister	I				✔				✔
Fuel/Vapor Return Lines	I				✔				✔
Fuel Tank Cap and Restrictor	I				✔				✔
Coolant System	I		✔		✔		✔		✔
Exhaust Pipe and Muffler	I		✔		✔		✔		✔
Catalytic Converter and Shield	I				✔				✔
EGR System	I				✔				✔
Timing Belt	I/R [1]								✔
Throttle Body	I		✔		✔		✔		✔
Drive Belts	I				✔				✔
Brake Pads and Linings	I				✔				✔
Brake Hoses and Lines	I				✔				✔
Ball Joints	I				✔				✔
Steering Linkage	I				✔				✔

MAINTENANCE INTERVALS—TYPE A: NORMAL SERVICE
Escort • Tempo • Topaz

TO BE SERVICED	TYPE OF SERVICE	VEHICLE MILEAGE INTERVAL (X1000)							
		7.5	15	22.5	30	37.5	45	52.5	60
Drive Axle (CV) Shaft Boots	I				✔				✔
Automatic Transaxle Fluid	I	✔	✔	✔	✔	✔	✔	✔	✔
Manual Transaxle Fluid	I		✔		✔		✔		✔
Clutch Pedal Operation	I				✔				✔
Brake Rotors and Drums	I				✔				✔
Tire Rotation	I⑤	✔		✔		✔		✔	
Hinges, Latches, etc.	L		✔		✔		✔		✔
Brake Fluid	I		✔		✔		✔		✔
Power Steering Fluid	I		✔		✔				✔
Battery Connections	I		✔		✔		✔		✔
Engine Coolant	R				✔				✔
Rear Wheel Bearings	L				✔				✔
Seat Belt Operation	I	✔			✔		✔		✔

FOR COMPLETE WARRANTY COVERAGE CONSULT INDIVIDUAL VEHICLE MANUFACTURER'S WARRANTY MAINTENANCE GUIDE.

I—Inspect
L—Lubricate
R—Replace
① Replace every 60,000 miles for 1.8L engine, inspect every 60,000 miles for 1.9L engine
② If applicable

③ Inspect every 15,000 miles, replace every 30,000 miles
④ 1.9L engine only
⑤ First at 7,500 miles, then every 15,000 miles as required

MAINTENANCE INTERVALS—TYPE B: SEVERE SERVICE
Escort • Tempo • Topaz

TO BE SERVICED	TYPE OF SERVICE	VEHICLE MILEAGE INTERVAL (X1000)									
		3	6	9	12	15	18	21	24	27	30
Oxygen Sensor	I										✔
Ignition Timing	I⑤										✔
Vacuum Lines and Hoses	I										✔
Ignition Wires	I										✔
Spark Plugs	R										✔
Engine Oil and Filter	R	✔	✔	✔	✔	✔	✔	✔	✔	✔	✔
Engine Air Cleaner Element	I/R②					✔					✔
Crankcase Emission Filter	R③										✔
PCV Valve	R										✔
Fuel Filter	R										✔
Charcoal Canister	I										✔
Fuel/Vapor Return Lines	I										✔
Fuel Tank Cap and Restrictor	I										✔
Coolant System	I					✔					✔
Exhaust Pipe and Muffler	I			✔					✔		
Catalytic Converter and Shield	I										✔
EGR System	I										✔
Timing Belt	I/R①										
Throttle Body	I					✔					✔
Drive Belts	I										✔

MAINTENANCE INTERVALS—TYPE B: SEVERE SERVICE
Escort • Tempo • Topaz

TO BE SERVICED	TYPE OF SERVICE	3	6	9	12	15	18	21	24	27	30
Brake Pads and Linings	I										✔
Brake Hoses and Lines	I										✔
Ball Joints	I										✔
Steering Linkage	I										✔
Drive Axle (CV) Shaft Boots	I										✔
Automatic Transaxle Fluid	R										✔
Manual Transaxle Fluid	I					✔					✔
Clutch Pedal Operation	I										✔
Brake Rotors and Drums	I										✔
Tire Rotation	I④		✔					✔			
Hinges, Latches, etc.	L					✔					✔
Brake Fluid	I					✔					✔
Power Steering Fluid	I					✔					✔
Battery Connections	I					✔					✔
Engine Coolant	R										✔
Rear Wheel Bearings	L										✔
Seat Belt Operation	I					✔					✔

FOR COMPLETE WARRANTY COVERAGE CONSULT INDIVIDUAL VEHICLE MANUFACTURER'S WARRANTY MAINTENANCE GUIDE.

I—Inspect
L—Lubricate
R—Replace
① Replace every 60,000 miles for 1.8L engine, inspect every 60,000 miles for 1.9L engine, not available for 2.3L and 3.0L engines

② Inspect every 15,000 miles, replace every 30,000 miles
③ 1.9L engine only
④ At 6,000 miles, then every 15,000 miles as required
⑤ If applicable

FIRING ORDERS

NOTE: To avoid confusion, always replace spark plug wires one at a time.

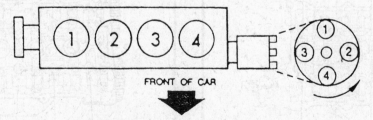

1.8L Engine
Engine Firing Order: 1–3–4–2
Distributor Rotation: Counterclockwise

FIRING ORDERS

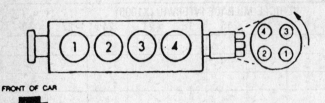

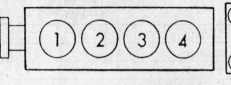

1990 1.9L Engine
Engine Firing Order: 1-3-4-2
Distributor Rotation: Counterclockwise

1991–94 1.9L Engine
Engine Firing Order: 1-3-4-2
Distributorless Ignition System

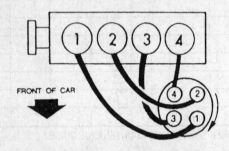

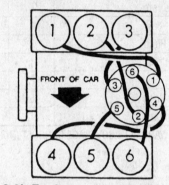

2.3L Engine
Engine Firing Order: 1–3–4–2
Distributor Rotation: Clockwise

3.0L Engine
Engine Firing Order: 1–4–2–5–3–6
Distributor Rotation: Clockwise

CYLINDER HEAD TORQUE SEQUENCES

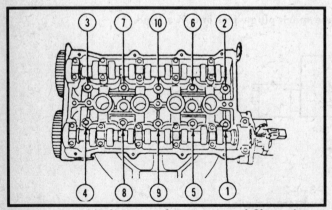

Cylinder head bolt removal sequence – 1.8L engine

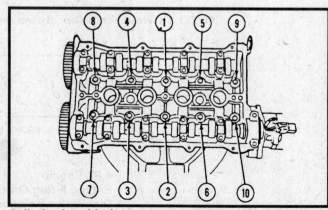

Cylinder head bolt torque sequence – 1.8L engine

CYLINDER HEAD TORQUE SEQUENCES

TIGHTENING SEQUENCE CYLINDER
HEAD ATTACHING BOLTS

9	3	1	5	7	
○	○	○	○	○	INTAKE
○	○	○	○	○	EXHAUST
8	6	2	4	10	

Cylinder head bolt torque sequence—1.9L engine

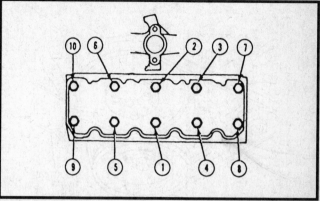

Cylinder head bolt torque sequence—2.3L engine

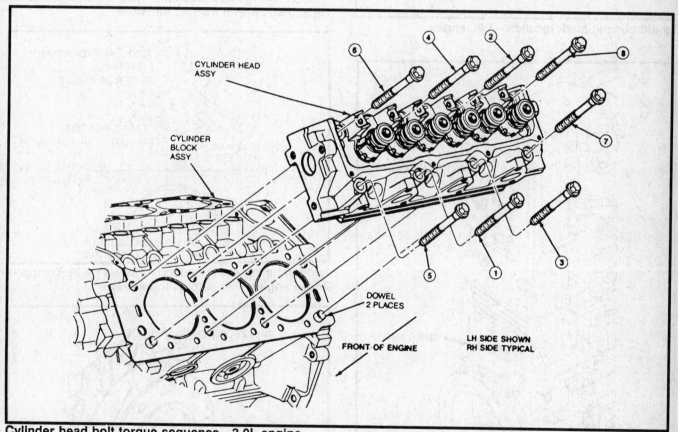

Cylinder head bolt torque sequence—3.0L engine

TIMING MARK LOCATIONS

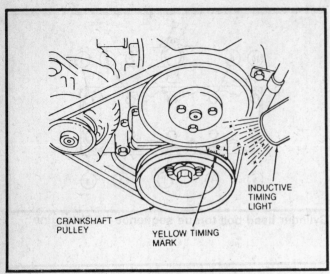

Ignition timing mark location—1.8L engine

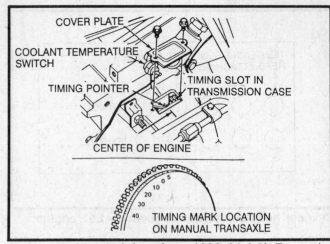

Ignition timing mark location—1990–91 2.3L Tempo/Topaz engine with manual transaxle

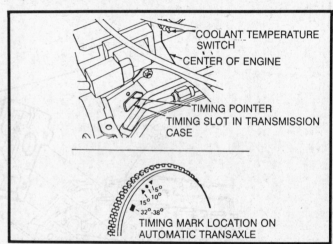

Ignition timing mark location—1990–91 2.3L Tempo/Topaz engine with automatic transaxle

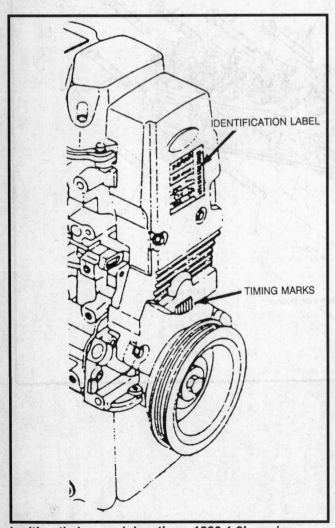

Ignition timing mark location—1990 1.9L engine

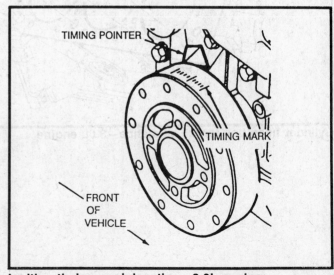

Ignition timing mark location—3.0L engine

TIMING MARK LOCATIONS

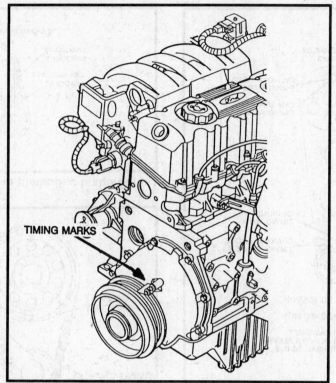

Ignition timing mark location—1992–94 2.3L Tempo/ Topaz engine

TIMING CHAIN/BELT LOCATIONS

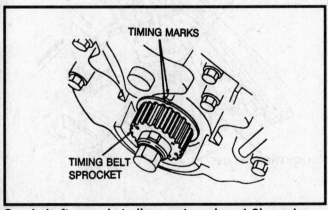

Crankshaft sprocket alignment marks—1.8L engine

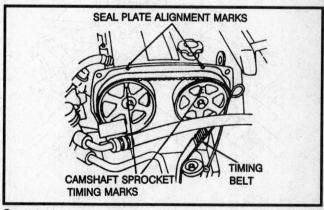

Camshaft sprocket alignment marks—1.8L engine

TIMING CHAIN/BELT LOCATIONS

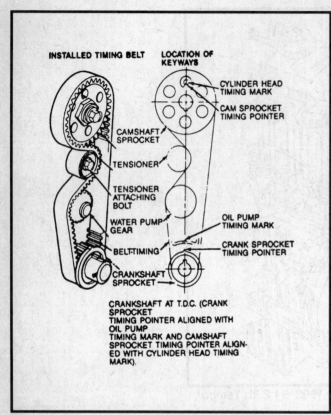

Timing belt alignment marks—1.9L engine

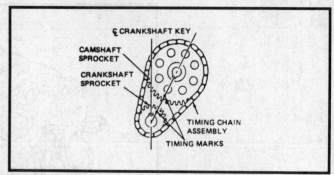

Timing chain alignment marks—2.3L engine

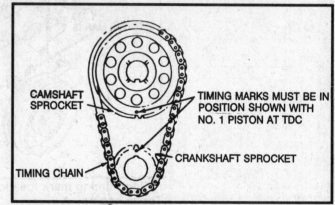

Timing chain alignment marks—3.0L engine

AIR CONDITIONING SERVICE VALVE LOCATIONS

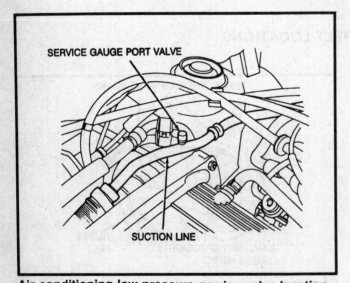

Air conditioning low pressure service valve location

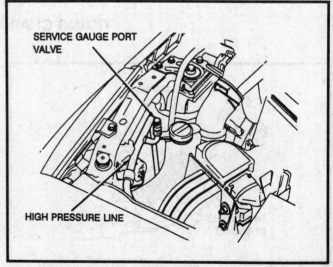

Air conditioning high pressure service valve location

WHEEL ALIGNMENT ADJUSTMENT LOCATIONS

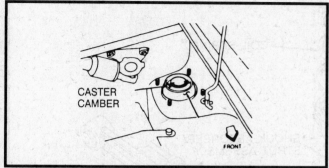

Front caster and camber adjustment—Escort

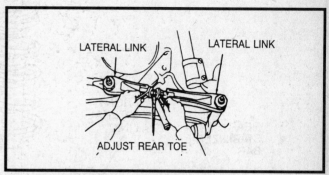

Rear toe adjustment—1991-94 Escort

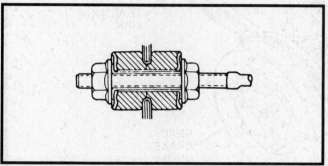

Rear toe adjustment—1990 Escort

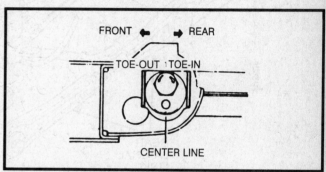

Rear toe adjustment—Tempo/Topaz

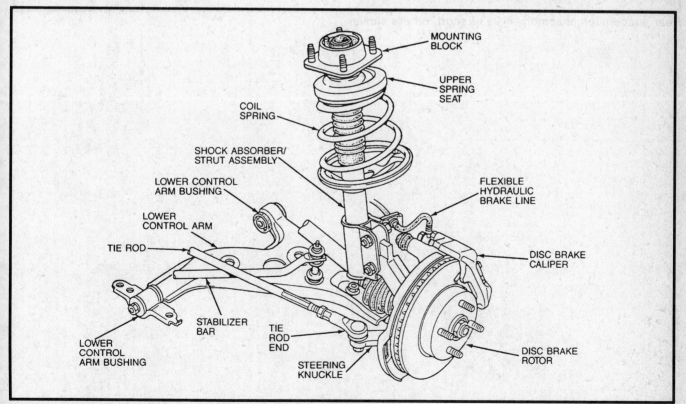

Front suspension assembly—1993 Escort, others similar

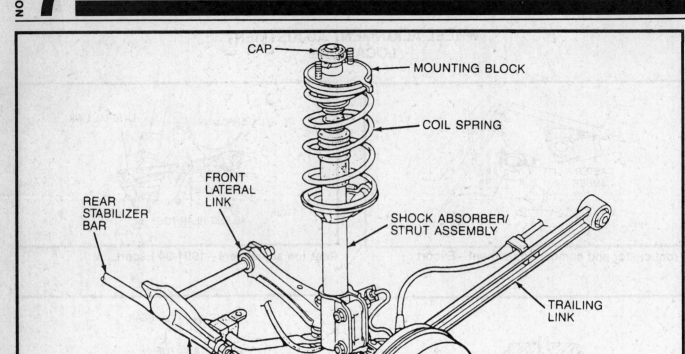

Rear suspension assembly—1993 Escort, others similar

SPECIFICATION CHARTS

VEHICLE IDENTIFICATION CHART

It is important for servicing and ordering parts to be certain of the vehicle and engine identification. The VIN (vehicle identification number) is a 20 digit number visible through the windshield on the driver's side of the dash and contains the vehicle and engine identification codes. The tenth digit indicates model year and the eighth digit indicates engine code. It can be interpreted as follows:

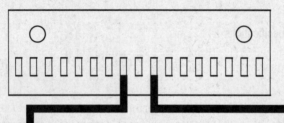

Engine Code						Model Year	
Code	Liters	Cu. In. (cc)	Cyl.	Fuel Sys.	Eng. Mfg.	Code	Year
H	1.3	81 (1319)	4	EFI	Kia Motors	L	1990
						M	1991
						N	1992
						P	1993
						R	1994

EFI—Electronic Fuel Injection

ENGINE IDENTIFICATION

Year	Model	Engine Displacement Liters (cc)	Engine Series Identification (ID/VIN)	Fuel System	No. of Cylinders	Engine Type
1990	Festiva	1.3 (1319)	H	EFI	4	SOHC
1991	Festiva	1.3 (1319)	H	EFI	4	SOHC
1992	Festiva	1.3 (1319)	H	EFI	4	SOHC
1993	Festiva	1.3 (1319)	H	EFI	4	SOHC

EFI—Electronic Fuel Injection
SOHC—Single Overhead Camshaft

GENERAL ENGINE SPECIFICATIONS

Year	Engine (ID/VIN)	Engine Displacement Liters (cc)	Fuel System Type	Net Horsepower @ rpm	Net Torque @ rpm (ft. lbs.)	Bore × Stroke (in.)	Compression Ratio	Oil Pressure @ rpm ①
1990	H	1.3 (1319)	EFI	63 @ 5000	73 @ 3000	2.79 × 3.29	9.7:1	50–64 @ 3000
1991	H	1.3 (1319)	EFI	63 @ 5000	73 @ 3000	2.79 × 3.29	9.7:1	50–64 @ 3000
1992	H	1.3 (1319)	EFI	63 @ 5000	73 @ 3000	2.79 × 3.29	9.7:1	50–64 @ 3000
1993	H	1.3 (1319)	EFI	63 @ 5000	73 @ 3000	2.79 × 3.29	9.7:1	50–64 @ 3000

EFI—Electronic Fuel Injection
① Hot

GASOLINE ENGINE TUNE-UP SPECIFICATIONS

Year	Engine (ID/VIN)	Engine Displacement Liters (cc)	Spark Plugs Gap (in.)	Ignition Timing (deg.) MT	AT	Fuel Pump (psi)	Idle Speed (rpm) MT	AT	Valve Clearance In.	Ex.
1990	H	1.3 (1319)	0.040	10B	10B	64–85 ①	680–720	830–870	Hyd.	Hyd.
1991	H	1.3 (1319)	0.040	10B	10B	64–85 ①	680–720	830–870	Hyd.	Hyd.
1992	H	1.3 (1319)	0.040	10B	10B	64–85 ①	680–720	830–870	Hyd.	Hyd.
1993	H	1.3 (1319)	0.040	10B	10B	64–85 ①	680–720	830–870	Hyd.	Hyd.
1994	SEE UNDERHOOD SPECIFICATIONS									

NOTE: The lowest cylinder pressure should be within 75% of the highest cylinder pressure reading. For example, if the highest cylinder is 134 psi, the lowest should be 101. Engine should be at normal operating temperature with throttle valve in the wide open position.
The underhood specifications sticker often reflects tune-up specification changes in production. Sticker figures must be used if they disagree with those in this chart.
Hyd.—Hydraulic
B—Before Top Dead Center
① Maximum output with key ON, engine OFF.
Regulated output with engine running 25–31 psi.

CAPACITIES

Year	Model	Engine (ID/VIN)	Engine Displacement Liters (cc)	Engine Crankcase with Filter (qts.)	Transmission (pts.) 4-Spd	5-Spd	Auto.	Drive Axle (pts.)	Fuel Tank (gal.)	Cooling System (qts.)
1990	Festiva	H	1.3 (1319)	3.6	—	5.2	11.2	—	10	5.3
1991	Festiva	H	1.3 (1319)	3.6	—	5.2	11.2	—	10	5.3
1992	Festiva	H	1.3 (1319)	3.6	—	5.2	11.2	—	10	5.3
1993	Festiva	H	1.3 (1319)	3.6	—	5.2	11.2	—	10	5.3

CAMSHAFT SPECIFICATIONS
All measurements given in inches.

Year	Engine (ID/VIN)	Engine Displacement Liters (cc)	Journal Diameter 1	2	3	4	5	Elevation ① In.	Ex.	Bearing Clearance	Camshaft End Play
1990	H	1.3 (1319)	1.7103–1.7112	1.7091–1.7100	1.7103–1.7112	—	—	1.4331–1.4371	1.4331–1.4371	②	0.002–0.007
1991	H	1.3 (1319)	1.7103–1.7112	1.7091–1.7100	1.7103–1.7112	—	—	1.4331–1.4371	1.4331–1.4371	②	0.002–0.007
1992	H	1.3 (1319)	1.7103–1.7112	1.7091–1.7100	1.7103–1.7112	—	—	1.4331–1.4371	1.4331–1.4371	②	0.002–0.007
1993	H	1.3 (1319)	1.7103–1.7112	1.7091–1.7100	1.7103–1.7112	—	—	1.4331–1.4371	1.4331–1.4371	②	0.002–0.007

① Figure shown indicates total lobe height
② Front and Rear Bearing—0.0014–0.0033 in.
Center Bearing—0.0026–0.0045

CRANKSHAFT AND CONNECTING ROD SPECIFICATIONS

All measurements are given in inches.

Year	Engine (ID/VIN)	Engine Displacement Liters (cc)	Crankshaft				Connecting Rod		
			Main Brg. Journal Dia.	Main Brg. Oil Clearance	Shaft End-play	Thrust on No.	Journal Diameter	Oil Clearance	Side Clearance
1990	H	1.3 (1319)	1.9661–1.9668	0.0009–0.0017 ①	0.0031–0.0120	4	1.5724–1.7531	0.0011–0.0027	0.0043–0.0120
1991	H	1.3 (1319)	1.9661–1.9668	0.0009–0.0017 ①	0.0031–0.0120	4	1.5724–1.5731	0.0011–0.0027	0.0043–0.0120
1992	H	1.3 (1319)	1.9661–1.9668	0.0009–0.0017 ①	0.0031–0.0120	4	1.5724–1.5731	0.0011–0.0027	0.0043–0.0120
1993	H	1.3 (1319)	1.9661–1.9668	0.0009–0.0017 ①	0.0031–0.0120	4	1.5724–1.5731	0.0011–0.0027	0.0043–0.0120

① Limit—0.0039 in.

VALVE SPECIFICATIONS

Year	Engine (ID/VIN)	Engine Displacement Liters (cc)	Seat Angle (deg.)	Face Angle (deg.)	Spring Test Pressure (lbs. @ in.)	Spring Installed Height (in.)	Stem-to-Guide Clearance (in.)		Stem Diameter (in.)	
							Intake	Exhaust	Intake	Exhaust
1990	H	1.3 (1319)	45	45	NA ①	NA ①	0.008	0.008	0.2744–0.2750	0.2742–0.2748
1991	H	1.3 (1319)	45	45	NA ①	NA ①	0.008	0.008	0.2744–0.2750	0.2742–0.2748
1992	H	1.3 (1319)	45	45	NA ①	NA ①	0.008	0.008	0.2744–0.2750	0.2742–0.2748
1993	H	1.3 (1319)	45	45	NA ①	NA ①	0.008	0.008	0.2744–0.2750	0.2742–0.2748

NA—Not available
① Check springs for free length and squareness
Free length should not be less than 1.717 in.
Maximum out-of-square is 0.059 in.

PISTON AND RING SPECIFICATIONS

All measurements are given in inches.

Year	Engine (ID/VIN)	Engine Displacement Liters (cc)	Piston Clearance	Ring Gap			Ring Side Clearance		
				Top Compression	Bottom Compression	Oil Control	Top Compression	Bottom Compression	Oil Control
1990	H	1.3 (1319)	①	0.006–0.012	0.006–0.012	0.008–0.028	0.001–0.003	0.001–0.003	snug
1991	H	1.3 (1319)	①	0.006–0.012	0.006–0.012	0.008–0.028	0.001–0.003	0.001–0.003	snug
1992	H	1.3 (1319)	①	0.006–0.012	0.006–0.012	0.008–0.028	0.001–0.003	0.001–0.003	snug
1993	H	1.3 (1319)	①	0.006–0.012	0.006–0.012	0.008–0.028	0.001–0.003	0.001–0.003	snug

① Optimum—0.0015–0.0020 in.
Limit—0.006 in.

TORQUE SPECIFICATIONS

All readings in ft. lbs.

Year	Engine (ID/VIN)	Engine Displacement Liters (cc)	Cylinder Head Bolts	Main Bearing Bolts	Rod Bearing Bolts	Crankshaft Pulley Bolts	Flywheel Bolts	Manifold Intake	Manifold Exhaust	Spark Plugs	Lug Nut
1990	H	1.3 (1319)	①	40–43	②	③	71–76	14–20	12–17	10–17	65–87
1991	H	1.3 (1319)	①	40–43	②	③	71–76	14–20	12–17	10–17	65–87
1992	H	1.3 (1319)	①	40–43	②	③	71–76	14–20	12–17	10–17	65–87
1993	H	1.3 (1319)	①	40–43	②	③	71–76	14–20	12–17	10–17	65–87

① Tighten in sequence in 2 steps:
    Step 1—35–40 ft. lbs.
    Step 2—56–60 ft. lbs.

② Tighten in 2 steps:
    Step 1—11–13 ft. lbs.
    Step 2—22–25 ft. lbs.

③ Pulley bolts—109–152 inch lbs.
    Sprocket bolt—80–87 ft. lbs.

TORQUE SPECIFICATIONS

Component	English	Metric
Air flow meter mounting nuts:	110–152 inch lbs.	13–18 Nm
Camshaft sprocket bolt:	36–45 ft. lbs.	49–61 Nm
Connecting rod bearing cap bolts		
Step 1:	11–13 ft. lbs.	15–17 Nm
Step 2:	22–25 ft. lbs.	29–34 Nm
Crankshaft pulley bolt:	109–152 inch lbs.	12–17 Nm
Cylinder head bolt		
Step 1:	35–40 ft. lbs.	50–60 Nm
Step 2:	56–60 ft. lbs.	75–81 Nm
Crankshaft rear seal retainer:	69–95 inch lbs.	8–11 Nm
Crankshaft sprocket bolt:	80–85 ft. lbs.	108–118 Nm
Engine-to-transaxle:	41–59 ft. lbs.	55–80 Nm
Exhaust manifold:	12–17 ft. lbs.	16–23 Nm
Exhaust pipe-to-exhaust manifold nuts:	23–34 ft. lbs.	31–46 Nm
Flywheel/flexplate-to-crankshaft bolts:	71–76 ft. lbs.	96–103 Nm
Flywheel-to-converter bolts:	25–36 ft. lbs.	34–49 Nm
Fuel pump-to-block:	17–22 ft. lbs.	23–29 Nm
Front engine mount nuts:	32–38 ft. lbs.	43–52 Nm
Intake manifold:	14–20 ft. lbs.	19–26 Nm
Intake manifold bracket:	22–34 ft. lbs.	31–46 Nm
Main bearing cap bolts:	40–43 ft. lbs.	54–59 Nm
Oil pan:	69–78 inch lbs.	8–9 Nm
Oil pump attaching bolts:	14–19 ft. lbs.	19–25 Nm
Oil pump inlet tube bolts:	69–95 inch lbs.	8–11 Nm
Rear engine mount nut:	21–34 ft. lbs.	28–46 Nm
Rocker arm shaft bolt:	16–21 ft. lbs.	22–28 Nm
Rocker (valve) cover:	44–80 inch lbs.	5–9 Nm
Spark plug:	10–17 ft. lbs.	14–23 Nm
Starter-to-block bolts :	23–34 ft. lbs.	31–46 Nm
Thermostat housing:	14–22 ft. lbs.	19–30 Nm
Timing belt cover:	69–95 inch lbs.	8–11 Nm
Timing belt tensioner:	14–19 ft. lbs.	19–26 Nm
Water pump:	14–19 ft. lbs.	19–26 Nm
Water pump pulley:	36–45 ft. lbs.	49–61 Nm

BRAKE SPECIFICATIONS

All measurements in inches unless noted.

| Year | Model | Master Cylinder Bore | Brake Disc | | | Brake Drum Diameter | | | Minimum Lining Thickness | |
			Original Thickness	Minimum Thickness	Maximum Runout	Original Inside Diameter	Max. Wear Limit	Maximum Machine Diameter	Front	Rear
1990	Festiva	0.75/0.59	0.050	0.43	0.003	6.69	6.75	NA	0.125	0.040
1991	Festiva	0.75/0.59	0.050	0.43	0.003	6.69	6.75	NA	0.125	0.040
1992	Festiva	0.75/0.59	0.050	0.43	0.003	6.69	6.75	NA	0.125	0.040
1993	Festiva	0.75/0.59	0.050	0.43	0.003	6.69	6.75	NA	0.125	0.040

NA—Not available

WHEEL ALIGNMENT

| Year | Model | Caster | | Camber | | Toe-in (in.) | Steering Axis Inclination (deg.) |
		Range (deg.)	Preferred Setting (deg.)	Range (deg.)	Preferred Setting (deg.)		
1990	Festiva	$1^{5}/_{16}$P–$1^{13}/_{16}$P	$1^{9}/_{16}$P	$^{1}/_{4}$N–$1^{9}/_{16}$P	$^{11}/_{16}$P	$^{1}/_{32}$–$^{1}/_{4}$	$14^{3}/_{16}$
1991	Festiva	$1^{5}/_{16}$P–$1^{13}/_{16}$P	$1^{9}/_{16}$P	$^{1}/_{4}$N–$1^{9}/_{16}$P	$^{11}/_{16}$P	$^{1}/_{32}$–$^{1}/_{4}$	$14^{3}/_{16}$
1992	Festiva	$1^{5}/_{16}$P–$1^{13}/_{16}$P	$1^{9}/_{16}$P	$^{1}/_{4}$N–$1^{9}/_{16}$P	$^{11}/_{16}$P	$^{1}/_{32}$–$^{1}/_{4}$	$14^{3}/_{16}$
1993	Festiva	$1^{5}/_{16}$P–$1^{13}/_{16}$P	$1^{9}/_{16}$P	$^{1}/_{4}$N–$1^{9}/_{16}$P	$^{11}/_{16}$P	$^{1}/_{32}$–$^{1}/_{4}$	$14^{3}/_{16}$

N—Negative
P—Positive

AIR CONDITIONING BELT TENSION

| Year | Model | Engine Displacement Liters (cc) | Belt Type | Specifications (lbs.) | |
				New	Used
1990	Festiva	1.3 (1319)	V-Ribbed	110–125	92–110
1991	Festiva	1.3 (1319)	V-Ribbed	110–125	92–110
1992	Festiva	1.3 (1319)	Serpentine	120–160	110–130
1993	Festiva	1.3 (1319)	Serpentine	120–160	110–130

REFRIGERANT CAPACITIES

Year	Model	Refrigerant (oz.)	Oil (fl. oz.)	Compressor Type
1990	Festiva	25.0	10.0	NA
1991	Festiva	25.0	10.0	NA
1992	Festiva	25.0	10.0	NA
1993	Festiva	25.0	10.0	NA

NOTE: At the time of publication, refrigerant capacity information relating to R-134a was not available from the manufacturer.

MAINTENANCE INTERVALS—TYPE A: NORMAL SERVICE
Festiva

TO BE SERVICED	TYPE OF SERVICE	VEHICLE MILEAGE INTERVAL (X1000)							
		7.5	15	22.5	30	37.5	45	52.5	60
Oxygen Sensor	I				✔				✔
Ignition Timing	I				✔				✔
Vacuum Lines and Hoses	I				✔				✔
Ignition Wires	I				✔				✔
Spark Plugs	R				✔				✔
Engine Oil	R	✔	✔	✔	✔	✔	✔	✔	✔
Engine Air Cleaner Element	R				✔				✔
PCV Valve	R				✔				✔
Fuel Filter	R				✔				✔
Charcoal Canister	I				✔				✔
Fuel/Vapor Return Lines	I				✔				✔
Fuel Tank Cap and Restrictor	I				✔				✔
Coolant System	I		✔		✔		✔		✔
Exhaust Pipe and Muffler	I				✔				✔
Catalytic Converter and Shield	I				✔				✔
EGR System	I				✔				✔
Timing Belt	R								✔
Idle Speed System	I		✔		✔		✔		✔
Throttle Body	I		✔		✔		✔		✔
Drive Belts	I								✔
Hinges, Latches, etc.	L		✔		✔		✔		✔
Power Steering Fluid	I		✔		✔		✔		✔
Brake Fluid	I		✔		✔		✔		✔
Battery Connections	I		✔		✔		✔		✔
Manual Transaxle Fluid	I		✔		✔		✔		✔
Automatic Transaxle Fluid	I	✔	✔	✔	✔	✔	✔	✔	✔
Engine Coolant	R				✔				✔
Brake Rotors and Drums	I				✔				✔
Brake Pads, Front	I				✔				✔
Brake Shoes, Rear	I				✔				✔
Clutch Pedal Operation	I				✔				✔
Brake Lines and Hoses	I				✔				✔
Ball Joints	I				✔				✔
Steering System/Rack	I				✔				✔
Wheel Bearings	L								✔
Tire Rotation	I	✔		✔		✔		✔	
Driveshaft Dust Boots	I				✔				✔
Seat Belt Operation	I		✔		✔		✔		✔

FOR COMPLETE WARRANTY COVERAGE CONSULT INDIVIDUAL VEHICLE MANUFACTURER'S WARRANTY MAINTENANCE GUIDE.

I—Inspect
L—Lubricate
R—Replace

MAINTENANCE INTERVALS—TYPE B: SEVERE SERVICE
Festiva

TO BE SERVICED	TYPE OF SERVICE	VEHICLE MILEAGE INTERVAL (X1000)									
		3	6	9	12	15	18	21	24	27	30
Oxygen Sensor	I										✔
Ignition Timing	I										✔
Vacuum Lines and Hoses	I										✔
Ignition Wires	I										✔
Spark Plugs	R										✔
Engine Oil and Filter	R	✔	✔	✔	✔	✔	✔	✔	✔	✔	✔
Engine Air Cleaner Element	R										✔
Fuel Filter	R										✔
Charcoal Canister	I										✔
Fuel/Vapor Return Lines	I										✔
Fuel Tank Cap and Restrictor	I										✔
Coolant System	I					✔					✔
Exhaust Pipe and Muffler	I										✔
Catalytic Converter and Shield	I										✔
EGR System	I										✔
Timing Belt	R①										
Idle Speed System	I					✔					✔
Throttle Body	I					✔					✔
Drive Belts	I										✔
Hinges, Latches, etc.	L					✔					✔
Power Steering Fliud	I					✔					✔
Brake Fluid	I					✔					✔
Battery Connections	I					✔					✔
Manual Transaxle Fluid	I					✔					✔
Automatic Transaxle Fluid	R										✔
Engine Coolant	R										✔
Brake Rotors and Drums	I					✔					✔
Brake Pads, Front	I					✔					✔
Brake Shoes, Rear	I					✔					✔
Clutch Pedal Operation	I					✔					✔
Brake Lines and Hoses	I										✔
Ball Joints	I										✔
Steering System/Rack	I										✔
Driveshaft Dust Boots	I										✔
Wheel Bearings	L②										
Tire Rotation	I③		✔					✔			
PCV Valve	R										✔
Seat Belt Operation	I					✔					✔

FOR COMPLETE WARRANTY COVERAGE CONSULT INDIVIDUAL VEHICLE MANUFACTURER'S WARRANTY MAINTENANCE GUIDE.

I—Inspect
L—Lubricate
R—Replace
① Replace timing belt every 60,000 miles
② Repack every 60,000 miles
③ At 6,000 miles, then every 15,000 miles, as required

FIRING ORDERS

NOTE: To avoid confusion, always replace spark plugs and wires one at a time.

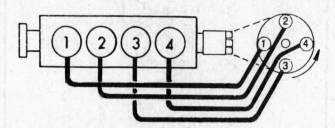

1.3L Engine
Engine Firing Order: 1–3–4–2
Distributor Rotation: Counterclockwise

CYLINDER HEAD TORQUE SEQUENCES

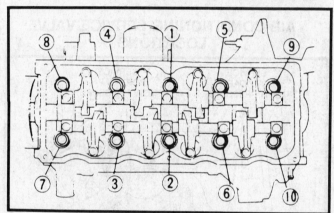

Cylinder head bolt torque sequence

TIMING MARK LOCATIONS

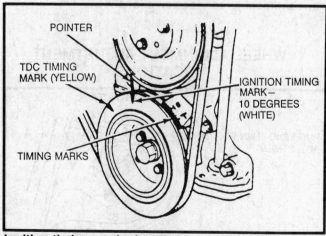

Ignition timing marks location

TIMING BELT LOCATIONS

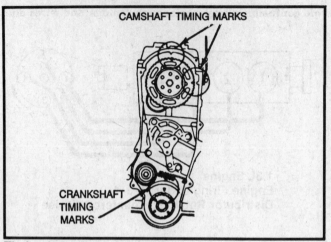

Timing belt alignment marks

AIR CONDITIONING SERVICE VALVE LOCATIONS

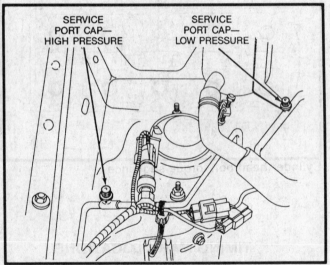

Air conditioning service valve location

WHEEL ALIGNMENT ADJUSTMENT LOCATIONS

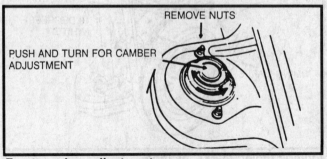

Front camber adjustment

SPECIFICATION CHARTS

VEHICLE IDENTIFICATION CHART

It is important for servicing and ordering parts to be certain of the vehicle and engine identification. The VIN (vehicle identification number) is a 17 digit number visible through the windshield on the driver's side of the dash and contains the vehicle and engine identification codes. The tenth digit indicates model year and the eighth digit indicates engine code. It can be interpreted as follows:

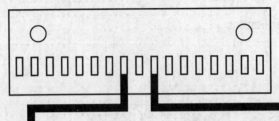

Engine Code

Code	Liters	Cu. In. (cc)	Cyl.	Fuel Sys.	Eng. Mfg.
A	2.0	122 (1993)	4	EFI	Mazda
C	2.2	133 (2189)	4	EFI	Mazda
L	2.2	133 (2189)	4	EFI ①	Mazda
B	2.5	153 (2501)	6	EFI	Mazda
U	3.0	181 (2971)	6	EFI	Ford

EFI—Electronic Fuel Injection
① Turbocharged

Model Year

Code	Year
L	1990
M	1991
N	1992
P	1993
R	1994

ENGINE IDENTIFICATION

Year	Model	Engine Displacement Liters (cc)	Engine Series (ID/VIN)	Fuel System	No. of Cylinders	Engine Type
1990	Probe GL	2.2 (2189)	C	EFI	4	OHC
	Probe LX	3.0 (2971)	U	EFI	6	OHV
	Probe GT	2.2 (2189)	L	EFI ①	4	OHC
1991	Probe GL	2.2 (2189)	C	EFI	4	OHC
	Probe LX	3.0 (2971)	U	EFI	6	OHV
	Probe GT	2.2 (2189)	L	EFI ①	4	OHC
1992	Probe GL	2.2 (2189)	C	EFI	4	OHC
	Probe LX	3.0 (2971)	U	EFI	6	OHV
	Probe GT	2.2 (2189)	L	EFI ①	4	OHC
1993	Probe	2.0 (1993)	A	EFI	4	DOHC
	Probe GT	2.5 (2501)	B	EFI	6	DOHC
1994	Probe	2.0 (1993)	A	EFI	4	DOHC
	Probe GT	2.5 (2501)	B	EFI	6	DOHC

DOHC—Double Overhead Camshaft
EFI—Electronic Fuel Injection
OHC—Overhead Camshaft
OHV—Overhead Valves
① Turbocharged

GENERAL ENGINE SPECIFICATIONS

Year	Engine ID/VIN	Engine Displacement Liters (cc)	Fuel System Type	Net Horsepower @ rpm	Net Torque @ rpm (ft. lbs.)	Bore × Stroke (in.)	Compression Ratio	Oil Pressure @ rpm
1990	C	2.2 (2189)	EFI	110 @ 4700	130 @ 3000	3.39 × 3.70	8.6:1	43–57 @ 3000
	L	2.2 (2189)	EFI①	145 @ 4300	190 @ 3500	3.39 × 3.70	7.8:1	43–57 @ 3000
	U	3.0 (2971)	EFI	140 @ 4800	160 @ 3000	3.50 × 3.14	9.3:1	40–60 @ 2500
1991	C	2.2 (2189)	EFI	110 @ 4700	130 @ 3000	3.39 × 3.70	8.6:1	43–57 @ 3000
	L	2.2 (2189)	EFI①	145 @ 4300	190 @ 3500	3.39 × 3.70	7.8:1	43–57 @ 3000
	U	3.0 (2971)	EFI	145 @ 4800	165 @ 3400	3.50 × 3.14	9.3:1	40–60 @ 2500
1992	C	2.2 (2189)	EFI	110 @ 4700	130 @ 3000	3.39 × 3.70	8.6:1	43–57 @ 3000
	L	2.2 (2189)	EFI①	145 @ 4300	190 @ 3500	3.39 × 3.70	7.8:1	43–57 @ 3000
	U	3.0 (2971)	EFI	145 @ 4800	165 @ 3400	3.50 × 3.14	9.3:1	40–60 @ 2500
1993	A	2.0 (1993)	EFI	115 @ 5500	124 @ 3500	3.27 × 3.62	9.0:1	57–71 @ 3000
	B	2.5 (2501)	EFI	164 @ 6000	156 @ 4000	3.33 × 2.92	9.2:1	49–71 @ 3000
1994	A	2.0 (1993)	EFI	115 @ 5500	124 @ 3500	3.27 × 3.62	9.0:1	57–71 @ 3000
	B	2.5 (2501)	EFI	164 @ 6000	156 @ 4000	3.33 × 2.92	9.2:1	49–71 @ 3000

EFI—Electronic Fuel Injection
① Turbocharged

GASOLINE ENGINE TUNE-UP SPECIFICATIONS

Year	Engine ID/VIN	Engine Displacement Liters (cc)	Spark Plugs Gap (in.)	Ignition Timing (deg.) MT	Ignition Timing (deg.) AT	Fuel Pump (psi)	Idle Speed (rpm) MT	Idle Speed (rpm) AT	Valve Clearance In.	Valve Clearance Ex.
1990	C	2.2 (2189)	0.040	6B	6B	64–85②	750	750	Hyd.	Hyd.
	L	2.2 (2189)	0.040	9B	9B	64–85②	750	750	Hyd.	Hyd.
	U	3.0 (2971)	0.044	10B	10B	35–40③	①	①	Hyd.	Hyd.
1991	C	2.2 (2189)	0.040	6B	6B	64–85②	750	750	Hyd.	Hyd.
	L	2.2 (2189)	0.040	9B	9B	64–85②	750	750	Hyd.	Hyd.
	U	3.0 (2971)	0.044	10B	10B	35–40③	①	①	Hyd.	Hyd.
1992	C	2.2 (2189)	0.040	6B	6B	64–85②	750	750	Hyd.	Hyd.
	L	2.2 (2189)	0.040	9B	9B	64–85②	750	750	Hyd.	Hyd.
	U	3.0 (2971)	0.044	10B	10B	35–40③	①	①	Hyd.	Hyd.
1993	A	2.0 (1993)	0.040	10B	12B	64–92②	700	700	Hyd.	Hyd.
	B	2.5 (2501)	0.040	10B	10B	72–92②	650	650	Hyd.	Hyd.
1994	A	2.0 (1993)	0.040	10B	12B	64–92②	700	700	Hyd.	Hyd.
	B	2.5 (2501)	0.040	10B	10B	72–92②	650	650	Hyd.	Hyd.

NOTE: The lowest cylinder pressure should be within 75% of the highest cylinder pressure reading. For example, if the highest cylinder is 134 psi, the lowest should be 101. Engine should be at normal operating temperature with throttle valve in the wide open position.
The underhood specifications sticker often reflects tune-up specification changes in production. Sticker figures must be used if they disagree with those in this chart.
B—Before Top Dead Center
Hyd.—Hydraulic
① Refer to Underhood Vehicle Emission Information label
② Maximum fuel pump pressure
③ Key on, engine off

CAPACITIES

Year	Model	Engine ID/VIN	Engine Displacement Liters (cc)	Engine Crankcase with Filter (qts.)	Transmission (pts.) 4-Spd	5-Spd	Auto.	Transfer Case (pts.)	Drive Axle Front (pts.)	Rear (pts.)	Fuel Tank (gal.)	Cooling System (qts.)
1990	Probe GL	C	2.2 (2189)	4.4	—	7.2	14.4	—	①	—	15.1	7.9
	Probe LX	U	3.0 (2971)	4.5	—	7.8	14.4	—	①	—	15.1	11.0
	Probe GT	L	2.2 (2189)	4.4	—	7.8	14.4	—	①	—	15.1	7.9
1991	Probe GL	C	2.2 (2189)	4.4	—	7.2	14.4	—	①	—	15.1	7.9
	Probe LX	U	3.0 (2971)	4.5	—	7.8	14.4	—	①	—	15.1	11.0
	Probe GT	L	2.2 (2189)	4.4	—	7.8	14.4	—	①	—	15.1	7.9
1992	Probe GL	C	2.2 (2189)	4.4	—	7.2	14.4	—	①	—	15.1	7.9
	Probe LX	U	3.0 (2971)	4.5	—	7.8	14.4	—	①	—	15.1	11.0
	Probe GT	L	2.2 (2189)	4.4	—	7.8	14.4	—	①	—	15.1	7.9
1993	Probe	A	2.0 (1993)	3.7	—	5.8	18.6	—	①	—	15.5	7.4
	Probe GT	B	2.5 (2501)	4.2	—	5.8	18.6	—	①	—	15.5	7.9
1994	Probe	A	2.0 (1993)	3.7	—	5.8	18.6	—	①	—	15.5	7.4
	Probe GT	B	2.5 (2501)	4.2	—	5.8	18.6	—	①	—	15.5	7.9

① Included in transaxle

CAMSHAFT SPECIFICATIONS

All measurements given in inches.

Year	Engine ID/VIN	Engine Displacement Liters (cc)	Journal Diameter 1	2	3	4	5	Elevation In.	Ex.	Bearing Clearance	Camshaft End Play
1990	C	2.2 (2189)	1.2575–1.2585	1.2563–1.2573	1.2563–1.2573	1.2563–1.2573	1.2575–1.2585	1.6200–1.6300	1.6400–1.6500	①	0.003–0.008
	L	2.2 (2189)	1.2575–1.2585	1.2563–1.2573	1.2563–1.2573	1.2563–1.2573	1.2575–1.2585	1.6200–1.6300	1.6400–1.6500	①	0.003–0.008
	U	3.0 (2971)	2.0074–2.0084	2.0074–2.0084	2.0074–2.0084	2.0074–2.0084	—	0.2550–0.2600	0.2550–0.2600	0.0010–0.0030	0.001–0.005
1991	C	2.2 (2189)	1.2575–1.2585	1.2563–1.2573	1.2563–1.2573	1.2563–1.2573	1.2575–1.2585	1.6200–1.6300	1.6400–1.6500	①	0.003–0.008
	L	2.2 (2189)	1.2575–1.2585	1.2563–1.2573	1.2563–1.2573	1.2563–1.2573	1.2575–1.2585	1.6200–1.6300	1.6400–1.6500	①	0.003–0.008
	U	3.0 (2971)	2.0074–2.0084	2.0074–2.0084	2.0074–2.0084	2.0074–2.0084	—	0.2550–0.2600	0.2550–0.2600	0.0010–0.0030	0.001–0.005
1992	C	2.2 (2189)	1.2575–1.2585	1.2563–1.2573	1.2563–1.2573	1.2563–1.2573	1.2575–1.2585	1.6200–1.6300	1.6400–1.6500	①	0.003–0.008
	L	2.2 (2189)	1.2575–1.2585	1.2563–1.2573	1.2563–1.2573	1.2563–1.2573	1.2575–1.2585	1.6200–1.6300	1.6400–1.6500	①	0.003–0.008
	U	3.0 (2971)	2.0074–2.0084	2.0074–2.0084	2.0074–2.0084	2.0074–2.0084	—	0.2550–0.2600	0.2550–0.2600	0.0010–0.0030	0.001–0.005
1993	A	2.0 (1993)	1.0213–1.0222	1.0213–1.0222	1.0213–1.0222	1.0213–1.0222	1.0213–1.0222	1.6859–1.6918	1.7003–1.7062	0.0014–0.0032	0.003–0.008
	B	2.5 (2501)	②	1.0201–1.0209	1.0201–1.0209	1.0201–1.0209	1.0213–1.0220	1.7067–1.7145	1.7067–1.7145	③	0.002–0.005

CAMSHAFT SPECIFICATIONS

All measurements given in inches.

| Year | Engine ID/VIN | Engine Displacement Liters (cc) | Journal Diameter | | | | | Elevation | | Bearing Clearance | Camshaft End Play |
			1	2	3	4	5	In.	Ex.		
1994	A	2.0 (1993)	1.0213–1.0222	1.0213–1.0222	1.0213–1.0222	1.0213–1.0222	1.0213–1.0222	1.6859–1.6918	1.7003–1.7063	0.0014–0.0032	0.003–0.008
	B	2.5 (2501)	②	1.0201–1.0209	1.0201–1.0209	1.0201–1.0209	1.0213–1.0220	1.7067–1.7145	1.7067–1.7145	③	0.002–0.005

① No. 1 & 5: 0.0014–0.0033
No. 2, 3 & 4: 0.0026–0.0045
② Right head ex., left head int.: 1.0213–1.0220
Right head int., left head ex.: 1.1801–1.1811
③ No. 1 & 5: 0.0016–0.0032
No. 2, 3 & 4: 0.0028–0.0044

CRANKSHAFT AND CONNECTING ROD SPECIFICATIONS

All measurements are given in inches.

| Year | Engine ID/VIN | Engine Displacement Liters (cc) | Crankshaft | | | | Connecting Rod | | |
			Main Brg. Journal Dia.	Main Brg. Oil Clearance	Shaft End-play	Thrust on No.	Journal Diameter	Oil Clearance	Side Clearance
1990	C	2.2 (2189)	2.3597–2.3604	①	0.0031–0.0071	3	2.0055–2.0061	0.0011–0.0026	0.004–0.012
	L	2.2 (2189)	2.3597–2.3604	①	0.0031–0.0071	3	2.0055–2.0061	0.0011–0.0026	0.004–0.012
	U	3.0 (2971)	2.5190–2.5198	0.0005–0.0023	0.0040–0.0080	3	2.1253–2.1261	0.0009–0.0027	0.006–0.014
1991	C	2.2 (2189)	2.3597–2.3604	①	0.0031–0.0071	3	2.0055–2.0061	0.0011–0.0026	0.004–0.012
	L	2.2 (2189)	2.3597–2.3604	①	0.0031–0.0071	3	2.0055–2.0061	0.0011–0.0026	0.004–0.012
	U	3.0 (2971)	2.5190–2.5198	0.0005–0.0023	0.0040–0.0080	3	2.1253–2.1261	0.0009–0.0027	0.006–0.014
1992	C	2.2 (2189)	2.3597–2.3604	①	0.0031–0.0071	3	2.0055–2.0061	0.0011–0.0026	0.004–0.012
	L	2.2 (2189)	2.3597–2.3604	①	0.0031–0.0071	3	2.0055–2.0061	0.0011–0.0026	0.004–0.012
	U	3.0 (2971)	2.5190–2.5198	0.0005–0.0023	0.0040–0.0080	3	2.1253–2.1261	0.0009–0.0027	0.006–0.014
1993	A	2.0 (1993)	2.2020–2.2029	②	0.0031–0.0118	4	1.8872–1.8880	0.0009–0.0026	0.004–0.012
	B	2.5 (2501)	2.4382–2.4392	0.0015–0.0025	0.0032–0.0125	4	2.0841–2.0848	0.0009–0.0032	0.007–0.016
1994	A	2.0 (1993)	2.2020–2.2029	②	0.0031–0.0118	4	1.8872–1.8880	0.0009–0.0029	0.004–0.012
	B	2.5 (2501)	2.4382–2.4392	0.0015–0.0025	0.0032–0.0125	4	2.0841–2.0848	0.0009–0.0032	0.007–0.016

① No. 1, 2, 4 & 5: 0.0010–0.0017
No. 3: 0.0012–0.0019
② No. 1, 2, 4 & 5: 0.0009–0.0026
No. 3: 0.0012–0.0026

VALVE SPECIFICATIONS

Year	Engine ID/VIN	Engine Displacement Liters (cc)	Seat Angle (deg.)	Face Angle (deg.)	Spring Test Pressure (lbs. @ in.)	Spring Installed Height (in.)	Stem-to-Guide Clearance (in.)		Stem Diameter (in.)	
							Intake	Exhaust	Intake	Exhaust
1990	C	2.2 (2189)	45	45	NA①	NA①	0.0080	0.0080	0.2744–0.2750	0.2742–0.2748
	L	2.2 (2189)	45	45	NA①	NA①	0.0080	0.0080	0.2744–0.2750	0.2742–0.2748
	U	3.0 (2971)	45	44	180 @ 1.16	1.58	0.0010–0.0028	0.0015–0.0033	0.3126–0.3134	0.3121–0.3129
1991	C	2.2 (2189)	45	45	NA①	NA①	0.0080	0.0080	0.2744–0.2750	0.2742–0.2748
	L	2.2 (2189)	45	45	NA①	NA①	0.0080	0.0080	0.2744–0.2750	0.2742–0.2748
	U	3.0 (2971)	45	44	180 @ 1.16	1.58	0.0010–0.0028	0.0015–0.0033	0.3126–0.3134	0.3121–0.3129
1992	C	2.2 (2189)	45	45	NA①	NA①	0.0080	0.0080	0.2744–0.2750	0.2742–0.2748
	L	2.2 (2189)	45	45	NA①	NA①	0.0080	0.0080	0.2744–0.2750	0.2742–0.2748
	U	3.0 (2971)	45	44	180 @ 1.16	1.58	0.0010–0.0028	0.0015–0.0033	0.3126–0.3134	0.3121–0.3129
1993	A	2.0 (1993)	45	45	NA①	NA①	0.0010–0.0024	0.0012–0.0026	0.2350–0.2356	0.2348–0.2354
	B	2.5 (2501)	45	45	NA①	NA①	0.0010–0.0023	0.0012–0.0026	0.2351–0.2356	0.2349–0.2354
1994	A	2.0 (1993)	45	45	NA①	NA①	0.0010–0.0024	0.0012–0.0026	0.2350–0.2356	0.2348–0.2354
	B	2.5 (2501)	45	45	NA①	NA①	0.0010–0.0023	0.0012–0.0026	0.2351–0.2356	0.2349–0.2354

NA—Not available
① Measure spring free length and out-of-square
Maximum allowable out-of-square:
 2.0L Engine—0.061
 2.2L Engine—0.067
 2.5L Engine—0.0642

Spring free length:
 2.0L Engine—1.732
 2.2L Engine
  Intake—1.902–1.949
  Exhaust—1.937–1.984

2.5L Engine
 Intake—1.729
 Exhaust—1.847

PISTON AND RING SPECIFICATIONS

All measurements are given in inches.

Year	Engine ID/VIN	Engine Displacement Liters (cc)	Piston Clearance	Ring Gap			Ring Side Clearance		
				Top Compression	Bottom Compression	Oil Control	Top Compression	Bottom Compression	Oil Control
1990	C	2.2 (2189)	0.0014–0.0030	0.008–0.014	0.006–0.012	0.012–0.035	0.0010–0.0030	0.0010–0.0030	NA
	L	2.2 (2189)	0.0014–0.0030	0.008–0.014	0.006–0.012	0.008–0.028	0.0010–0.0030	0.0010–0.0030	NA
	U	3.0 (2971)	0.0014–0.0022	0.010–0.020	0.010–0.020	0.010–0.049	0.0012–0.0031	0.0012–0.0031	NA
1991	C	2.2 (2189)	0.0014–0.0030	0.008–0.014	0.006–0.012	0.012–0.035	0.0010–0.0030	0.0010–0.0030	NA
	L	2.2 (2189)	0.0014–0.0030	0.008–0.014	0.006–0.012	0.008–0.028	0.0010–0.0030	0.0010–0.0030	NA
	U	3.0 (2971)	0.0014–0.0022	0.010–0.020	0.010–0.020	0.010–0.049	0.0012–0.0031	0.0012–0.0031	NA

PISTON AND RING SPECIFICATIONS

All measurements are given in inches.

| Year | Engine ID/VIN | Engine Displacement Liters (cc) | Piston Clearance | Ring Gap | | | Ring Side Clearance | | |
				Top Compression	Bottom Compression	Oil Control	Top Compression	Bottom Compression	Oil Control
1992	C	2.2 (2189)	0.0014–0.0030	0.008–0.014	0.006–0.012	0.012–0.035	0.0010–0.0030	0.0010–0.0030	NA
	L	2.2 (2189)	0.0014–0.0030	0.008–0.014	0.006–0.012	0.008–0.028	0.0010–0.0030	0.0010–0.0030	NA
	U	3.0 (2971)	0.0014–0.0022	0.010–0.020	0.010–0.020	0.010–0.049	0.0012–0.0031	0.0012–0.0031	NA
1993	A	2.0 (1993)	0.0015–0.0020	0.006–0.012	0.006–0.012	0.008–0.028	0.0014–0.0026	0.0014–0.0026	NA
	B	2.5 (2501)	0.0012–0.0022	0.006–0.012	0.010–0.015	0.008–0.027	0.0070–0.0130	0.0070–0.0130	NA
1994	A	2.0 (1993)	0.0015–0.0020	0.006–0.012	0.006–0.012	0.008–0.028	0.0014–0.0026	0.0014–0.0026	NA
	B	2.5 (2501)	0.0012–0.0022	0.006–0.012	0.010–0.015	0.008–0.027	0.0070–0.0130	0.0070–0.0130	NA

NA—Not available

TORQUE SPECIFICATIONS

All readings in ft. lbs.

| Year | Engine ID/VIN | Engine Displacement Liters (cc) | Cylinder Head Bolts | Main Bearing Bolts | Rod Bearing Bolts | Crankshaft Damper Bolts | Flywheel Bolts | Manifold | | Spark Plugs | Lug Nut |
								Intake	Exhaust		
1990	C	2.2 (2189)	59–64	61–65	48–51	108–116①	71–76	14–22	16–21	11–17	65–87
	L	2.2 (2189)	59–64	61–65	48–51	108–116①	71–76	14–22	16–21	11–17	65–87
	U	3.0 (2971)	②	60	25	92–122	54–64	③	15–22	7–15	65–87
1991	C	2.2 (2189)	59–64	61–65	48–51	108–116①	71–76	14–22	16–21	11–17	65–87
	L	2.2 (2189)	59–64	61–65	48–51	108–116①	71–76	14–22	16–21	11–17	65–87
	U	3.0 (2971)	④	60	25	107	54–64	③	18	7–15	65–87
1992	C	2.2 (2189)	59–64	61–65	48–51	108–116①	71–76	14–22	16–21	11–17	65–87
	L	2.2 (2189)	59–64	61–65	48–51	108–116①	71–76	14–22	16–21	11–17	65–87
	U	3.0 (2971)	④	60	25	107	54–64	③	18	7–15	65–87
1993	A	2.0 (1993)	⑤	⑥	⑥	116–123	70–75	14–19	17	11–17	65–87
	B	2.5 (2501)	⑦	⑧	⑨	116–123	45–49	14–18	14–18	11–16	65–87
1994	A	2.0 (1993)	⑤	⑥	⑥	116–123	70–75	14–19	17	11–17	65–87
	B	2.5 (2501)	⑦	⑧	⑨	116–123	45–49	14–18	14–18	11–16	65–87

① Figure given is for crankshaft sprocket bolt
② Tighten in 2 steps:
  Step 1: 33–41
  Step 2: 63–73
③ Tigthen in 2 steps:
  Step 1: 11
  Step 2: 21
④ Tighten in 4 steps:
  Step 1: 59
  Step 2: Back off all bolts 1 turn
  Step 3: 37
  Step 4: 68

⑤ Tighten in 4 steps:
  Step 1: 7–8
  Step 2: 13–16
  Step 3: Turn each bolt 90°, in sequence
  Step 4: Turn each bolt 90°, in sequence
⑥ Tighten in 2 steps:
  Step 1: 16–19
  Step 2: Turn each bolt 90°, in sequence
⑦ Tighten in 3 steps:
  Step 1: 17–19
  Step 2: Turn each bolt 90°, in sequence
  Step 3: Turn each bolt 90°, in sequence

⑧ Tighten in sequence in 3 steps:
  Step 1:
    Inner bolts: Tighten to 17–19, in 2–3 steps
    Outer bolts: Tighten to 13–15, in 2–3 steps
  Step 2:
    Inner bolts:
      Nos. 1, 2 & 3—Turn each bolt 70°
      No. 4—Turn each bolt 80°
    Outer bolts: Turn each bolt 60°
  Step 3: Repeat Step 2
⑨ Tighten in 3 steps:
  Step 1: 16–19
  Step 2: Turn each bolt 90°
  Step 3: Turn each bolt an additional 90°

TORQUE SPECIFICATIONS

Component	English	Metric
Camshaft sprocket bolt		
2.0L engine:	36–45 ft. lbs.	49–61 Nm
2.2L engine:	35–48 ft. lbs.	47–65 Nm
2.5L engine:	90–103 ft. lbs.	123–140 Nm
3.0L engine:	41–51 ft. lbs.	55–70 Nm
Camshaft thrust plate		
3.0L engine:	6–8 ft. lbs.	8–12 Nm
Connecting rod bearing cap nuts		
2.0L engine		
Step 1:	16–19 ft. lbs.	22–27 Nm
Step 2:	+ 90 degree turn	+ 90 degree turn
2.2L engine:	48–51 ft. lbs.	65–68 Nm
2.5L engine		
Step 1:	16–19 ft. lbs.	22–27 Nm
Step 2:	+ 90 degree turn	+ 90 degree turn
Step 3:	+ 90 degree turn	+ 90 degree turn
3.0L engine:	25 ft. lbs.	35 Nm
Crankshaft pulley bolt(s)		
2.0L engine:	116–123 ft. lbs.	157–167 Nm
2.2L engine:	109–152 inch lbs.	12–17 Nm
2.5L engine:	116–122 ft. lbs.	157–166 Nm
3.0L engine:	107 ft. lbs.	145 Nm
Crankshaft sprocket bolt		
2.2L engine:	108–116 ft. lbs.	147–157 Nm
Cylinder head bolt		
2.0L engine		
Step 1:	6–8 ft. lbs.	9–11 Nm
Step 2:	13–16 ft. lbs.	18–22 Nm
Step 3:	+ 90 degree turn	+ 90 degree turn
Step 4:	+ 90 degree turn	+ 90 degree turn
2.2L engine		
Step 1:	29–32 ft. lbs.	40–42 Nm
Step 2:	59–64 ft. lbs.	80–86 Nm
2.5L engine		
Step 1:	9–11 ft. lbs.	11–13 Nm
Step 2:	17–19 ft. lbs.	23–26 Nm
Step 3:	+ 90 degree turn	+ 90 degree turn
Step 4:	+ 90 degree turn	+ 90 degree turn
3.0L engine		
1990		
Step 1:	33–41 ft. lbs.	45–55 Nm
Step 2:	63–73 ft. lbs.	85–99 Nm
1991–92		
Step 1:	59 ft. lbs.	80 Nm
Step 2:	− 360 degree turn	− 360 degree turn
Step 3:	37 ft. lbs.	50 Nm
Step 4:	68 ft. lbs.	92 Nm
Cylinder head front housing bolts		
2.2L engine:	14–19 ft. lbs.	19–25 Nm
Cylinder head rear housing bolts		
2.2L engine:	14–19 ft. lbs.	19–25 Nm
Exhaust manifold		
2.0L engine		
Bolts:	12–17 ft. lbs.	16–23 Nm
Nuts:	14–21 ft. lbs.	20–28 Nm
2.2L engine:	16–21 ft. lbs.	22–28 Nm
2.5L engine:	14–18 ft. lbs.	19–25 Nm
3.0L engine:	18 ft. lbs.	25 Nm

TORQUE SPECIFICATIONS

Component	English	Metric
Exhaust pipe-to-manifold nuts		
2.0L engine:	27–38 ft. lbs.	37–52 Nm
2.2L engine:	23–34 ft. lbs.	31–46 Nm
2.5L engine:	27–38 ft. lbs.	37–52 Nm
3.0L engine:	27–37 ft. lbs.	37–50 Nm
Flywheel/flexplate-to-crankshaft bolts		
2.0L engine:	70–75 ft. lbs.	96–103 Nm
2.2L engine:	71–76 ft. lbs.	96–103 Nm
2.5L engine:	45–49 ft. lbs.	61–67 Nm
3.0L engine:	54–64 ft. lbs.	73–87 Nm
Flywheel-to-converter nuts/bolts:	32–45 ft. lbs.	44–60 Nm
Intake manifold		
2.0L engine:	14–19 ft. lbs.	19–25 Nm
2.2L engine:	14–22 ft. lbs.	19–30 Nm
2.5L engine:	14–18 ft. lbs.	19–25 Nm
3.0L engine		
Step 1:	11 ft. lbs.	15 Nm
Step 2:	21 ft. lbs.	28 Nm
Intake manifold support bracket		
2.0L engine:	28–38 ft. lbs.	38–51 Nm
2.2L engine:	14–22 ft. lbs.	19–30 Nm
Intake plenum		
2.2L engine:	14–19 ft. lbs.	19–25 Nm
Main bearing cap bolts		
2.0L engine		
Step 1:	13–16 ft. lbs.	18–22 Nm
Step 2:	+ 90 degree turn	+ 90 degree turn
2.2L engine:	61–65 ft. lbs.	82–88 Nm
2.5L engine		
Step 1:		
Inner bolts:	9–11 ft. lbs.	11–13 Nm
Outer bolts:	7–8 ft. lbs.	9–11 Nm
Step 2:		
Inner bolts:	17–19 ft. lbs.	23–25 Nm
Outer bolts:	13–15 ft. lbs.	18–21 Nm
Step 3:		
Rear inner bolts:	+ 80 degree turn	+ 80 degree turn
1–3 inner bolts:	+ 70 degree turn	+ 70 degree turn
Outer bolts:	+ 60 degree turn	+ 60 degree turn
Step 4:		
Rear inner bolts:	+ 80 degree turn	+ 80 degree turn
1–3 inner bolts:	+ 70 degree turn	+ 70 degree turn
Outer bolts:	+ 60 degree turn	+ 60 degree turn
3.0L engine:	60 ft. lbs.	80 Nm
Oil pan bolts		
2.0L engine:	14–19 ft. lbs.	19–25 Nm
2.2L engine:	69–104 inch lbs.	8–12 Nm
2.5L engine		
Short bolts:	14–18 ft. lbs.	19–25 Nm
Long bolts:	71–88 inch lbs.	8–10 Nm
3.0L engine:	9 ft. lbs.	12 Nm
Oil pump attaching bolts		
2.0L engine:	14–19 ft. lbs.	19–25 Nm
2.2L engine		
8mm bolts:	14–19 ft. lbs.	19–25 Nm
10mm bolts:	27–38 ft. lbs.	37–52 Nm
2.5L engine:	14–18 ft. lbs.	19–25 Nm
3.0L engine:	35 ft. lbs.	48 Nm

TORQUE SPECIFICATIONS

Component	English	Metric
Rocker arm/shaft bolt		
2.2L engine:	13–20 ft. lbs.	18–26 Nm
3.0L engine		
Step 1:	96 inch lbs.	11 Nm
Step 2:	24 ft. lbs.	32 Nm
Rocker arm (valve) cover bolt		
2.0L engine:	52–69 inch lbs.	6–7 Nm
2.2L engine:	52–59 inch lbs.	6–8 Nm
2.5L engine:	43–78 inch lbs.	5–8 Nm
3.0L engine:	9 ft. lbs.	12 Nm
Thermostat housing bolt		
2.0L engine:	14–18 ft. lbs.	19–25 Nm
2.2L engine:	14–22 ft. lbs.	19–30 Nm
2.5L engine:	14–18 ft. lbs.	19–25 Nm
3.0L engine:	8–10 ft. lbs.	10–14 Nm
Timing belt tensioner bolt		
2.0L engine:	27–38 ft. lbs.	37–52 Nm
2.2L engine:	27–38 ft. lbs.	37–52 Nm
2.5L engine:	14–18 ft. lbs.	19–25 Nm
Timing cover bolt		
2.0L engine:	71–88 inch lbs.	8–10 Nm
2.2L engine:	61–87 inch lbs.	7–10 Nm
2.5L engine:	71–88 inch lbs.	8–10 Nm
3.0L engine:	18 ft. lbs.	25 Nm
Water pump bolt		
2.0L engine:	14–19 ft. lbs.	19–25 Nm
2.2L engine:	14–19 ft. lbs.	19–25 Nm
2.5L engine:	14–18 ft. lbs.	19–25 Nm
3.0L engine:	15–22 ft. lbs.	20–30 Nm

BRAKE SPECIFICATIONS

All measurements in inches unless noted.

Year	Model	Master Cylinder Bore	Brake Disc Original Thickness	Brake Disc Minimum Thickness	Maximum Runout	Brake Drum Diameter Original Inside Diameter	Brake Drum Diameter Max. Wear Limit	Brake Drum Diameter Maximum Machine Diameter	Minimum Lining Thickness Front	Minimum Lining Thickness Rear
1990	Probe GL	0.875	0.940	0.860	0.004	9.0	9.060	NA	0.120	0.040
	Probe LX	0.875	①	②	0.004	—	—	—	0.120	0.040
	Probe GT	0.875	①	②	0.004	—	—	—	0.120	0.040
1991	Probe GL	0.875	0.940	0.860	0.004	9.0	9.060	NA	0.120	0.040
	Probe LX	0.875	①	②	0.004	—	—	—	0.120	0.040
	Probe GT	0.875	①	②	0.004	—	—	—	0.120	0.040
1992	Probe GL	0.875	0.940	0.860	0.004	9.0	9.060	NA	0.120	0.040
	Probe LX	0.875	①	②	0.004	—	—	—	0.120	0.040
	Probe GT	0.875	①	②	0.004	—	—	—	0.120	0.040
1993	Probe	0.937	①	③	0.004	9.0	9.060	NA	0.040	0.040
	Probe GT	0.937	①	③	0.004	—	—	—	0.040	0.040
1994	Probe	0.937	①	③	0.004	9.0	9.060	NA	0.040	0.040
	Probe GT	0.937	①	③	0.004	—	—	—	0.040	0.040

NA—Not available
① Front—0.940   Rear—0.390
② Front—0.860   Rear—0.315
③ Front—0.870   Rear—0.310

WHEEL ALIGNMENT

Year	Model		Caster Range (deg.)	Caster Preferred Setting (deg.)	Camber Range (deg.)	Camber Preferred Setting (deg.)	Toe-in (in.)	Steering Axis Inclination (deg.)
1990	Probe	Front	$11/16P–2^3/16P$	$1^7/16P$	$1N–1/2P$	$1/4N$	$1/8$	$12^{25}/32$
		Rear	—	—	$1^3/16N–^5/16P$	$^7/16N$	$1/8$	—
1991	Probe	Front	$^{15}/16P–2^7/16P$	$1^{11}/16P$	$1N–1/2P$	$1/4N$	$1/8$	$12^{25}/32$
		Rear	—	—	$1^3/16N–^5/16P$	$^7/16N$	$1/8$	—
1992	Probe	Front	$^{15}/16P–2^7/16P$	$1^{11}/16P$	$1N–1/2P$	$1/4N$	$1/8$	$12^{25}/32$
		Rear	—	—	$1^3/16N–^5/16P$	$^7/16N$	$1/8$	—
1993	Probe	Front	$2^1/4P–3^3/4P$	$3P$	①	②	$1/8$	③
		Rear	—	—	$1^1/8N–^3/8P$	$^5/8N$	$1/8$	—
1994	Probe	Front	$2^1/4P–3^3/4P$	$3P$	①	②	$1/8$	③
		Rear	—	—	$1^1/8N–^3/8P$	$^5/8N$	$1/8$	—

N—Negative
P—Positive
① 2.0L Engine: $1^7/16N–^1/16P$
   2.5L Engine: $1^{21}/32N–^5/32N$
② 2.0L Engine: $^{11}/16N$
   2.5L Engine: $^{29}/32N$
③ 2.0L Engine: $15^1/4$
   2.5L Engine: $15^3/4$

AIR CONDITIONING BELT TENSION

Year	Model	Engine Displacement Liters (cc)	Belt Type	Specifications (lbs.) New	Specifications (lbs.) Used
1990	Probe	2.2 (2189)	Serpentine	154–198	132–176
		3.0 (2971)	Serpentine	Automatic Tensioner	Automatic Tensioner
1991	Probe	2.2 (2189)	Serpentine	154–198	132–176
		3.0 (2971)	Serpentine	Automatic Tensioner	Automatic Tensioner
1992	Probe	2.2 (2189)	Serpentine	154–198	132–176
		3.0 (2971)	Serpentine	Automatic Tensioner	Automatic Tensioner
1993–94	Probe	2.0 (1993)	Serpentine	140–170	110–150
		2.5 (2501)	V-Belt	160–190	110–150

REFRIGERANT CAPACITIES

Year	Model	Refrigerant (oz.)	Oil (fl. oz.)	Compressor Type
1990	Probe	40.0	8.0	10P15A
1991	Probe	40.0	8.0	10P15A
1992	Probe	40.0	8.0	10P15A
1993	Probe	40.0	8.0	10P15A

NOTE: At the time of publication, refrigerant capacity information relating to R-134a was not available from the manufacturer.

MAINTENANCE INTERVALS—TYPE A: NORMAL SERVICE
Probe

TO BE SERVICED	TYPE OF SERVICE	VEHICLE MILEAGE INTERVAL (X1000)							
		7.5	15	22.5	30	37.5	45	52.5	60
Oxygen Sensor	I				✔				✔
Ignition Timing	I				✔				✔
Vacuum Lines and Hoses	I				✔				✔
Ignition Wires	I				✔				✔
Spark Plugs	I/R①		✔		✔		✔		✔
Engine Oil	R	✔	✔	✔	✔	✔	✔	✔	✔
Engine Air Cleaner Element	R				✔				✔
Crankcase Emission Filter	R②				✔				✔
PCV Valve	R②				✔				✔
Fuel Filter	R								✔
Charcoal Canister	I				✔				✔
Fuel/Vapor Return Lines	I				✔				✔
Fuel Tank Cap and Restrictor	I				✔				✔
Coolant System	I		✔		✔		✔		✔
Exhaust Pipe and Muffler	I				✔				✔
Catalytic Converter and Shield	I				✔				✔
EGR System	I				✔				✔
Timing Belt	R								✔
Idle Speed System	I		✔		✔		✔		✔
Throttle Body	I		✔		✔		✔		✔
Drive Belts	I				✔				✔
Brake Pads, Front	I		✔		✔		✔		✔
Brake Pads, Rear	I		✔		✔		✔		✔
Brake Shoes, Rear	I				✔				✔
Brake Drums and Rotors	I				✔				✔
Brake Hoses and Lines	I				✔				✔
Battery Connections	I		✔		✔		✔		✔
Ball Joints	I				✔				✔
Engine Coolant	R				✔				✔
Automatic Transaxle Fluid	I	✔	✔	✔	✔	✔	✔	✔	✔
Manual Transaxle Fluid	I		✔		✔		✔		✔
Clutch Pedal Operation	I				✔				✔
Tire Rotation	I	✔	✔	✔	✔	✔	✔	✔	✔
Driveshaft Dust Boots	I								✔
Steering System	I				✔				✔
Power Steering Fluid	I		✔		✔		✔		✔
Brake Fluid	I		✔		✔		✔		✔
Hinges, Latches, etc.	L		✔		✔		✔		✔
Seat Belt Operation	I		✔		✔		✔		✔

FOR COMPLETE WARRANTY COVERAGE CONSULT INDIVIDUAL VEHICLE MANUFACTURER'S WARRANTY MAINTENANCE GUIDE.

I—Inspect
L—Lubricate
R—Replace
① 2.2L Turbo engine—replace every 15,000 miles
  2.2L Non-Turbo engine—replace every 30,000 miles

3.0L engine—inspect/clean/regap every 15,000 miles—replace every 30,000 miles
3.0L engine with Platinum plugs—replace every 60,000 miles
2.5L engine—replace every 30,000 miles
② If applicable

MAINTENANCE INTERVALS—TYPE B: SEVERE SERVICE
Probe

TO BE SERVICED	TYPE OF SERVICE	VEHICLE MILEAGE INTERVAL (X1000)									
		3	6	9	12	15	18	21	24	27	30
Oxygen Sensor	I										✔
Ignition Timing	I⑤										✔
Vacuum Lines and Hoses	I										✔
Ignition Wires	I										✔
Spark Plugs	I/R①					✔					✔
Engine Oil and Filter	R	✔	✔	✔	✔	✔	✔	✔	✔	✔	✔
Engine Air Cleaner Element	I/R②					✔					✔
Crankcase Emission Filter	R⑤										✔
PCV Valve	R⑤										✔
Fuel Filter	R③										
Charcoal Canister	I										✔
Fuel/Vapor Return Lines	I										✔
Fuel Tank Cap and Restrictor	I										✔
Coolant System	I					✔					✔
Exhaust Pipe and Muffler	I										✔
Catalytic Converter and Shield	I										✔
EGR System	I										✔
Timing Belt	R④										
Idle Speed System	I					✔					✔
Throttle Body	I					✔					✔
Drive Belts	I										✔
Brake Pads, Front	I					✔					✔
Brake Pads, Rear	I					✔					✔
Brake Shoes, Rear	I										✔
Brake Drums and Rotors	I										✔
Brake Hoses and Lines	I										✔
Battery Connections	I					✔					✔
Ball Joints	I										✔
Engine Coolant	R										✔
Automatic Transaxle Fluid	R										✔
Manual Transaxle Fluid	I					✔					✔
Clutch Pedal Operation	I										✔
Tire Rotation	I⑥		✔					✔			
Driveshaft Dust Boots	I										✔
Steering System	I										✔
Power Steering Fluid	I					✔					✔
Brake Fluid	I					✔					✔
Hinges, Latches, etc.	L					✔					✔
Seat Belt Operation	I					✔					✔

FOR COMPLETE WARRANTY COVERAGE CONSULT INDIVIDUAL VEHICLE MANUFACTURER'S WARRANTY MAINTENANCE GUIDE.

I—Inspect
L—Lubricate
R—Replace
① 2.2L Turbo engine—every 15,000 miles
  2.2L Non-turbo engine—every 30,000 miles
  2.0L engine—every 30,000 miles

3.0L engine—inspect, clean and regap every 15,000 miles—replace every 30,000 miles
3.0L engine with Platinum plugs—replace every 60,000 miles
2.5L engine—replace every 30,000 miles
② Inspect and clean every 15,000 miles, replace every 30,000 miles

③ Replace every 60,000 miles
④ Replace every 60,000 miles
⑤ If applicable
⑥ First 6,000 miles, then every 15,000 miles, as required

FIRING ORDERS

NOTE: To avoid confusion, always replace spark plugs and wires one at a time.

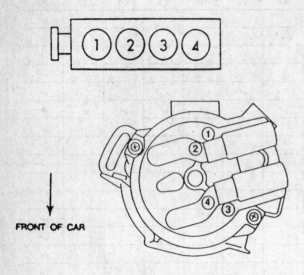

FRONT OF CAR

2.0L Engines
Engine Firing Order: 1–3–4–2
Distributor Rotation: Clockwise

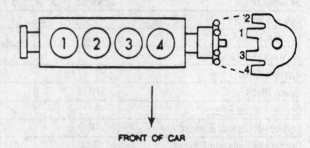

FRONT OF CAR

2.2L Engine
Engine Firing Order: 1–3–4–2
Distributor Rotation: Counterclockwise

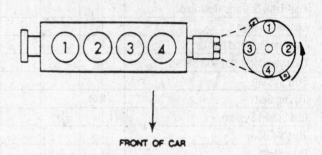

FRONT OF CAR

2.2L Turbocharged Engine
Engine Firing Order: 1–3–4–2
Distributor Rotation: Counterclockwise

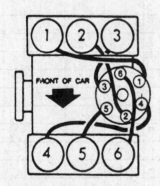

FRONT OF CAR

3.0L Engine
Engine Firing Order: 1–4–2–5–3–6
Distributor Rotation: Clockwise

No.1   No.3   No.5

RH

LH

No.2   No.4   No.6

FRONT OF CAR

2.5L Engines
Engine Firing Order: 1–2–3–4–5–6
Distributor Rotation: Counterclockwise

CYLINDER HEAD TORQUE SEQUENCES

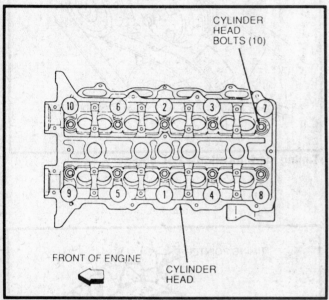

Cylinder head torque sequence—2.0L engine

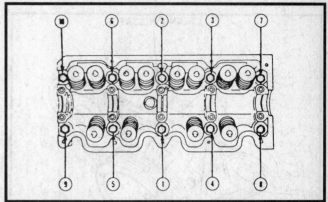

Cylinder head torque sequence—2.2L engine

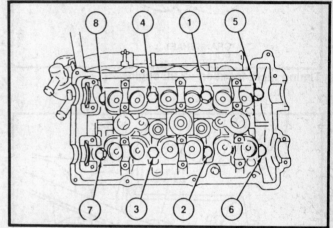

Cylinder head torque sequence—2.5L engine

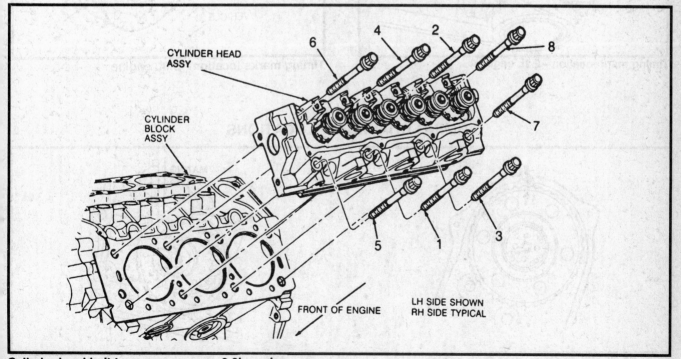

Cylinder head bolt torque sequence—3.0L engine

TIMING MARK LOCATIONS

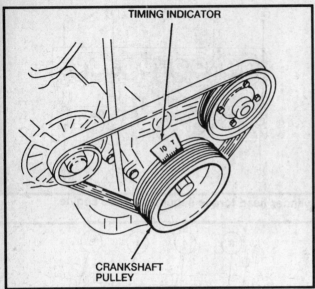

Timing mark location—2.0L engine

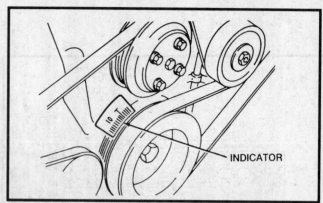

Timing mark location—2.5L engine

Timing mark location—2.2L engines

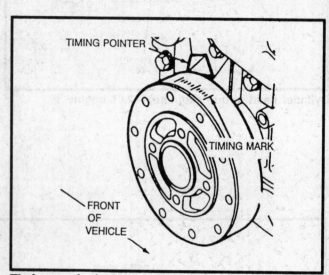

Timing marks location—3.0L engine

TIMING CHAIN/BELT LOCATIONS

Timing belt alignment marks—2.2L engine

TIMING CHAIN/BELT LOCATIONS

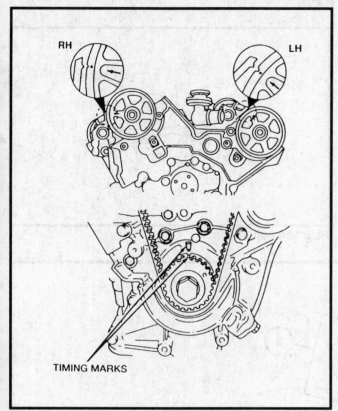

Timing belt alignment marks—2.5L engine

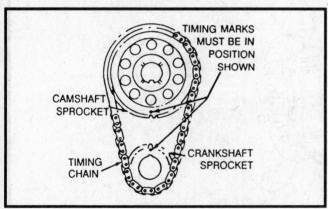

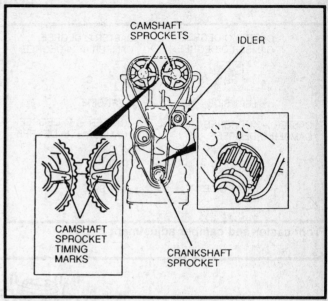

Timing belt alignment marks—2.0L engine

Timing chain alignment marks—3.0L engine

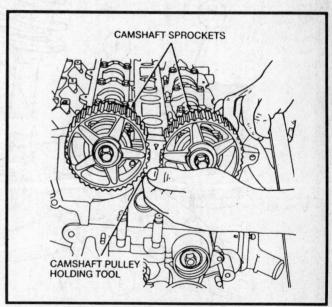

Camshaft sprocket holding tool—2.0L engine

AIR CONDITIONING SERVICE VALVE LOCATIONS

Service Gauge Valve Locations

The low pressure service valve port is located on the suction accumulator/drier. The high pressure service valve port is located on the liquid line extension in front of the fondenser.

WHEEL ALIGNMENT ADJUSTMENT LOCATIONS

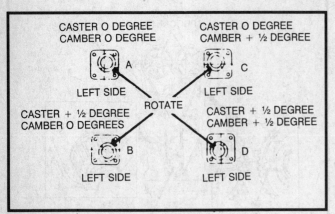

Front caster and camber adjustment

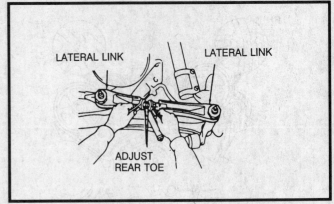

Rear toe adjustment

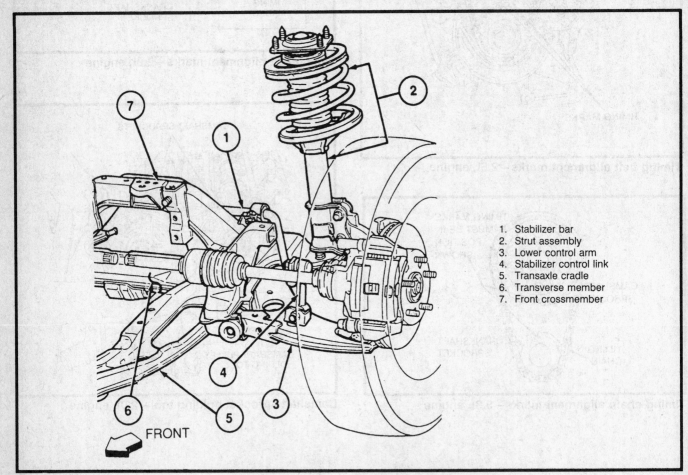

Front suspension assembly

1. Stabilizer bar
2. Strut assembly
3. Lower control arm
4. Stabilizer control link
5. Transaxle cradle
6. Transverse member
7. Front crossmember

SPECIFICATION CHARTS

VEHICLE IDENTIFICATION CHART

It is important for servicing and ordering parts to be certain of the vehicle and engine identification. The VIN (vehicle identification number) is a 17 digit number visible through the windshield on the driver's side of the dash and contains the vehicle and engine identification codes. The tenth digit indicates model year and the eighth digit indicates engine code. It can be interpreted as follows:

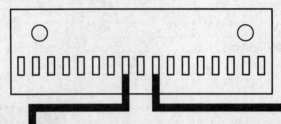

		Engine Code						Model Year	
Code	Liters	Cu. In. (cc)	Cyl.	Fuel Sys.	Eng. Mfg.		Code		Year
Z	1.6	98 (1597)	4	EFI	Mazda		M		1991
6	1.6	98 (1597)	4	EFI Turbo	Mazda		N		1992
							P		1993
							R		1994

EFI—Electronic Fuel Injection

ENGINE IDENTIFICATION

Year	Model	Engine Displacement Liters (cc)	Engine Series Identification (ID/VIN)	Fuel System	No. of Cylinders	Engine Type
1991	Capri	1.6 (1597)	Z	EFI	4	DOHC
	Capri	1.6 (1597)	6	EFI Turbo	4	DOHC
1992	Capri	1.6 (1597)	Z	EFI	4	DOHC
	Capri	1.6 (1597)	6	EFI Turbo	4	DOHC
1993–94	Capri	1.6 (1597)	Z	EFI	4	DOHC
	Capri	1.6 (1597)	6	EFI Turbo	4	DOHC

DOHC—Dual Overhead Cam Engine
EFI—Electronic Fuel Injection

GENERAL ENGINE SPECIFICATIONS

Year	Engine (ID/VIN)	Engine Displacement Liters (cc)	Fuel System Type	Net Horsepower @ rpm	Net Torque @ rpm (ft. lbs.)	Bore × Stroke (in.)	Compression Ratio	Oil Pressure @ rpm
1991	Z	1.6 (1597)	EFI	100 @ 5750	95 @ 5500	3.07 × 3.29	9.4:1	43–48 @ 3000
	6	1.6 (1597)	EFI	132 @ 6000	136 @ 3000	3.07 × 3.29	7.9:1	43–48 @ 3000
1992	Z	1.6 (1597)	EFI	100 @ 5750	95 @ 5500	3.07 × 3.29	9.4:1	43–48 @ 3000
	6	1.6 (1597)	EFI	132 @ 6000	136 @ 3000	3.07 × 3.29	7.9:1	43–48 @ 3000
1993–94	Z	1.6 (1597)	EFI	100 @ 5750	95 @ 5500	3.07 × 3.29	9.4:1	43–48 @ 3000
	6	1.6 (1597)	EFI	132 @ 6000	136 @ 3000	3.07 × 3.29	7.9:1	43–48 @ 3000

EFI—Electronic Fuel Injection

ENGINE TUNE-UP SPECIFICATIONS

Year	Engine (ID/VIN)	Engine Displacement Liters (cc)	Spark Plugs Gap (in.)	Ignition Timing (deg.) MT	AT	Fuel Pump (psi)	Idle Speed (rpm) MT	AT	Valve Clearance In.	Ex.
1991	Z	1.6 (1597)	0.040	1–3 BTDC	1–3 BTDC	①	800–900	800–900	Hyd.	Hyd.
	6	1.6 (1597)	0.040	11–13 BTDC	—	①	800–900	800–900	Hyd.	Hyd.
1992	Z	1.6 (1597)	0.040	1–3 BTDC	1–3 BTDC	①	800–900	800–900	Hyd.	Hyd.
	6	1.6 (1597)	0.040	11–13 BTDC	—	①	800–900	800–900	Hyd.	Hyd.
1993	Z	1.6 (1597)	0.040	1–3 BTDC	1–3 BTDC	①	800–900	800–900	Hyd.	Hyd.
	6	1.6 (1597)	0.040	11–13 BTDC	—	①	800–900	800–900	Hyd.	Hyd.
1994			SEE UNDERHOOD SPECIFICATIONS							

NOTE: The lowest cylinder pressure should be within 75% of the highest cylinder pressure reading. For example, if the highest cylinder is 134 psi, the lowest should be 101. Engine should be at normal operating temperature with throttle valve in the wide open position.
The underhood specifications sticker often reflects tune-up specification changes in production. Sticker figures must be used if they disagree with those in this chart.
Hyd.—Hydraulic
BTDC—Before Top Dead Center
① Key ON, engine OFF (maximum pressure):
   64–85 psi
   Engine running (regulated pressure): 28–31 psi

CAPACITIES

Year	Model	Engine (ID/VIN)	Engine Displacement Liters (cc)	Engine Crankcase with Filter (qts.)	Transmission (pts.) 4-Spd	5-Spd	Auto.	Drive Axle (pts.)	Fuel Tank (gals.)	Cooling System (qts.)
1991	Capri	Z	1.6 (1597)	3.8	—	6.8	12	—	11.1	5.3
	Capri	6	1.6 (1597)	3.8	—	6.8	—	—	11.1	6.3
1992	Capri	Z	1.6 (1597)	3.5	—	6.8	12	—	11.1	5.3
	Capri	6	1.6 (1597)	3.7	—	6.8	—	—	11.1	6.3
1993–94	Capri	Z	1.6 (1597)	3.5	—	6.8	12	—	11.1	5.3
	Capri	6	1.6 (1597)	3.7	—	6.8	—	—	11.1	6.3

CAMSHAFT SPECIFICATIONS

All measurements given in inches.

Year	Engine (ID/VIN)	Engine Displacement Liters (cc)	Journal Diameter 1	2	3	4	5	Elevation In.	Ex.	Bearing Clearance	Camshaft End Play
1991	Z	1.6 (1597)	1.0213–1.0222	1.0213–1.0222	1.0213–1.0222	1.0213–1.0222	1.0213–1.0222	1.6019–1.6098	1.6019–1.6098	0.0014–0.0032	0.0028–0.0075
	6	1.6 (1597)	1.0213–1.0222	1.0213–1.0222	1.0213–1.0222	1.0213–1.0222	1.0213–1.0222	1.6019–1.6098	1.6019–1.6098	0.0014–0.0032	0.0028–0.0075
1992	Z	1.6 (1597)	1.0213–1.0222	1.0213–1.0222	1.0213–1.0222	1.0213–1.0222	1.0213–1.0222	1.6019–1.6098	1.6019–1.6098	0.0014–0.0032	0.0028–0.0075
	6	1.6 (1597)	1.0213–1.0222	1.0213–1.0222	1.0213–1.0222	1.0213–1.0222	1.0213–1.0222	1.6019–1.6098	1.6019–1.6098	0.0014–0.0032	0.0028–0.0075

CAMSHAFT SPECIFICATIONS

All measurements given in inches.

Year	Engine (ID/VIN)	Engine Displacement Liters (cc)	Journal Diameter					Elevation		Bearing Clearance	Camshaft End Play
			1	2	3	4	5	In.	Ex.		
1993-94	Z	1.6 (1597)	1.0213–1.0222	1.0213–1.0222	1.0213–1.0222	1.0213–1.0222	1.0213–1.0222	1.6019–1.6098	1.6019–1.6098	0.0014–0.0032	0.0028–0.0075
	6	1.6 (1597)	1.0213–1.0222	1.0213–1.0222	1.0213–1.0222	1.0213–1.0222	1.0213–1.0222	1.6019–1.6098	1.6019–1.6098	0.0014–0.0032	0.0028–0.0075

CRANKSHAFT AND CONNECTING ROD SPECIFICATIONS

All measurements are given in inches.

Year	Engine (ID/VIN)	Engine Displacement Liters (cc)	Crankshaft				Connecting Rod		
			Main Brg. Journal Dia.	Main Brg. Oil Clearance	Shaft End-play	Thrust on No.	Journal Diameter	Oil Clearance	Side Clearance
1991	Z	1.6 (1597)	1.9661–1.9668	0.0010–0.0031	0.0031–0.0118	4	1.7693–1.7699	0.0011–0.0039	0.0043–0.0120
	6	1.6 (1597)	1.9661–1.9668	0.0010–0.0031	0.0031–0.0118	4	1.7693–1.7699	0.0011–0.0039	0.0043–0.0120
1992	Z	1.6 (1597)	1.9661–1.9668	0.0010–0.0031	0.0031–0.0118	4	1.7693–1.7699	0.0011–0.0039	0.0043–0.0120
	6	1.6 (1597)	1.9661–1.9668	0.0010–0.0031	0.0031–0.0118	4	1.7693–1.7699	0.0011–0.0039	0.0043–0.0120
1993-94	Z	1.6 (1597)	1.9661–1.9668	0.0010–0.0031	0.0031–0.0118	4	1.7693–1.7699	0.0011–0.0039	0.0043–0.0120
	6	1.6 (1597)	1.9661–1.9668	0.0010–0.0031	0.0031–0.0118	4	1.7693–1.7699	0.0011–0.0039	0.0043–0.0120

VALVE SPECIFICATIONS

Year	Engine (ID/VIN)	Engine Displacement Liters (cc)	Seat Angle (deg.)	Face Angle (deg.)	Spring Test Pressure (lbs. @ in.)	Spring Installed Height (in.)	Stem-to-Guide Clearance (in.)		Stem Diameter (in.)	
							Intake	Exhaust	Intake	Exhaust
1991	Z	1.6 (1597)	45	45	NA①	1.54	0.0010–0.0024	0.0012–0.0026	0.2350–0.2356	0.2348–0.2354
	6	1.6 (1597)	45	45	NA①	1.54	0.0010–0.0024	0.0012–0.0026	0.2350–0.2356	0.2348–0.2354
1992	Z	1.6 (1597)	45	45	NA①	1.54	0.0010–0.0024	0.0012–0.0026	0.2350–0.2356	0.2348–0.2354
	6	1.6 (1597)	45	45	NA①	1.54	0.0010–0.0024	0.0012–0.0026	0.2350–0.2356	0.2348–0.2354
1993-94	Z	1.6 (1597)	45	45	NA①	1.54	0.0010–0.0024	0.0012–0.0026	0.2350–0.2356	0.2348–0.2354
	6	1.6 (1597)	45	45	NA①	1.54	0.0010–0.0024	0.0012–0.0026	0.2350–0.2356	0.2348–0.2354

NA—Not available
① Check spring free length and for out-of-square
  Free length—1.803–1.858 in.
  Maximum out-of-square—0.063 in.

PISTON AND RING SPECIFICATIONS

All measurements are given in inches.

| Year | Engine (ID/VIN) | Engine Displacement Liters (cc) | Piston Clearance | Ring Gap | | | Ring Side Clearance | | |
				Top Compression	Bottom Compression	Oil Control	Top Compression	Bottom Compression	Oil Control
1991	Z	1.6 (1597)	0.0010–0.0026	0.0080–0.0157	0.0060–0.0118	0.0080–0.0280	0.0012–0.0026	0.0012–0.0026	0.0012–0.0026
	6	1.6 (1597)	0.0010–0.0026	0.0080–0.0157	0.0060–0.0118	0.0080–0.0280	0.0012–0.0026	0.0012–0.0026	0.0012–0.0026
1992	Z	1.6 (1597)	0.0010–0.0026	0.0080–0.0157	0.0060–0.0118	0.0080–0.0280	0.0012–0.0026	0.0012–0.0026	0.0012–0.0026
	6	1.6 (1597)	0.0010–0.0026	0.0080–0.0157	0.0060–0.0118	0.0080–0.0280	0.0012–0.0026	0.0012–0.0026	0.0012–0.0026
1993–94	Z	1.6 (1597)	0.0010–0.0026	0.0080–0.0157	0.0060–0.0118	0.0080–0.0280	0.0012–0.0026	0.0012–0.0026	0.0012–0.0026
	6	1.6 (1597)	0.0010–0.0026	0.0080–0.0157	0.0060–0.0118	0.0080–0.0280	0.0012–0.0026	0.0012–0.0026	0.0012–0.0026

TORQUE SPECIFICATIONS

All readings in ft. lbs.

| Year | Engine (ID/VIN) | Engine Displacement Liters (cc) | Cylinder Head Bolts | Main Bearing Bolts | Rod Bearing Bolts | Crankshaft Pulley Bolts | Flywheel Bolts | Manifold | | Spark Plugs | Lug Nut |
								Intake	Exhaust		
1991	Z	1.6 (1597)	①	40–43	35–38	80–87	71–76	14–19	29–42	11–17	67–88
	6	1.6 (1597)	①	40–43	35–38	80–87	71–76	14–19	29–42	11–17	67–88
1992	Z	1.6 (1597)	①	40–43	35–38	80–87	71–76	14–19	29–42	11–17	67–88
	6	1.6 (1597)	①	40–43	35–38	80–87	71–76	14–19	29–42	11–17	67–88
1993–94	Z	1.6 (1597)	①	40–43	35–38	80–87	71–76	14–19	29–42	11–17	67–88
	6	1.6 (1597)	①	40–43	35–38	80–87	71–76	14–19	29–42	11–17	67–88

① Tighten in sequence in 2 steps:
Step 1—14–25 ft. lbs.
Step 2—56–60 ft. lbs.

TORQUE SPECIFICATIONS

Component	English	Metric
Camshaft bearing cap bolts:	100–126 inch lbs.	11–14 Nm
Camshaft sprocket bolt:	36–45 ft. lbs.	49–61 Nm
Connecting rod bearing cap nuts:	35–38 ft. lbs.	47–52 Nm
Crankshaft sprocket bolt:	80–87 ft. lbs.	108–118 Nm
Crankshaft seal retainer bolts:	71–97 inch lbs.	8–11 Nm
Cylinder head bolt Step 1:	14–25 ft. lbs.	20–35 Nm
Step 2:	56–60 ft. lbs.	76–81 Nm
Cylinder head cover bolt:	71–97 inch lbs.	8–11 Nm
Engine-to-transaxle bolt Manual Upper:	66–86 ft. lbs.	89–117 Nm
Lower:	29–38 ft. lbs.	37–52 Nm
Automatic:	41–59 ft. lbs.	55–80 Nm
Exhaust manifold bolts:	29–42 ft. lbs.	39–57 Nm

TORQUE SPECIFICATIONS

Component	English	Metric
Exhaust flange-to-manifold nuts		
Non-turbocharged engine:	23–34 ft. lbs.	31–46 Nm
Turbocharged engine:	20–24 ft. lbs.	27–33 Nm
Flywheel/flexplate-to-crankshaft bolts:	71–76 ft. lbs.	96–103 Nm
Flywheel-to-torque converter bolts:	32 ft. lbs.	43 Nm
Engine/transaxle mounts		
Right side mount		
Small bracket-to-body bolts:	14–21 ft. lbs.	20–28 Nm
Large bracket-to-body bolt:	49–67 ft. lbs.	67–91 Nm
Mount-to-bracket nuts:	44–63 ft. lbs.	60–85 Nm
Through bolt:	33–48 ft. lbs.	45–65 Nm
Front mount		
Engine mount-to-transaxle bolts:	27–38 ft. lbs.	37–52 Nm
Engine mount-to-crossmember nuts:	47–65 ft. lbs.	64–89 Nm
Through bolt		
1991:	33–47 ft. lbs.	45–85 Nm
1992–94:	48–65 ft. lbs.	64–89 Nm
Rear mount		
Rear mount upper nut:	26–36 ft. lbs.	35–50 Nm
Rear mount lower nut:	47–66 ft. lbs.	64–89 Nm
Intake manifold bolts:	14–19 ft. lbs.	19–25 Nm
Main bearing cap bolts:	40–43 ft. lbs.	49–54 Nm
Oil pan-to-block bolts:	71–97 inch lbs.	8–11 Nm
Oil pan drain plug:	22–30 ft. lbs.	29–41 Nm
Oil pump attaching bolts:	14–19 ft. lbs.	19–25 Nm
Oil pump cover bolts:	14–19 ft. lbs.	19–25 Nm
Oil pump pickup bolts:	71–97 inch lbs.	8–11 Nm
Spark plug:	11–17 ft. lbs.	14–23 Nm
Starter-to-block bolts:	23–34 ft. lbs.	31–41 Nm
Thermostat housing bolts:	14–19 ft. lbs.	19–25 Nm
Throttle body nuts and bolt:	12–17 ft. lbs.	16–23 Nm
Timing belt tension pulley bolt:	28–38 ft. lbs.	37–52 Nm
Timing belt idler pulley bolt:	28–38 ft. lbs.	37–52 Nm
Timing cover bolts:	71–97 inch lbs.	8–11 Nm
Water pump bolts:	14–19 ft. lbs.	19–25 Nm

BRAKE SPECIFICATIONS

All measurements in inches unless noted.

Year	Model	Master Cylinder Bore	Brake Disc			Brake Drum Diameter			Minimum Lining Thickness	
			Original Thickness	Minimum Thickness	Maximum Runout	Original Inside Diameter	Max. Wear Limit	Maximum Machine Diameter	Front	Rear
1991	Capri	0.811	①	②	0.004	—	—	—	0.120	0.120
1992	Capri	0.811	①	②	0.004	—	—	—	0.120	0.120
1993–94	Capri	0.811	①	②	0.004	—	—	—	0.120	0.120

① Front—0.710 in.
  Rear—0.390 in.
② Front—0.630 in.
  Rear—0.350 in.

WHEEL ALIGNMENT

Year	Model		Caster Range (deg.)	Caster Preferred Setting (deg.)	Camber Range (deg.)	Camber Preferred Setting (deg.)	Toe-in (in.)	Steering Axis Inclination (deg.)
1991	Capri	Front	$27/32$P$-2^{11}/32$P	$1^{19}/32$P	$1/16$P$-1^9/16$P	$13/16$P	$1/32$N$-7/32$P	$12^{11}/32$
		Rear	—	—	$1^3/16$N$-^{11}/32$P	0	$0-3/16$P	—
1992	Capri	Front	$27/32$P$-2^{11}/32$P	$1^{19}/32$P	$1/16$P$-1^9/16$P	$13/16$P	$1/32$N$-7/32$P	$12^{11}/32$
		Rear	—	—	$1^3/16$N$-^{11}/32$P	0	$0-3/16$P	—
1993–94	Capri	Front	$27/32$P$-2^{11}/32$P	$1^{19}/32$P	$1/16$P$-1^9/16$P	$13/16$P	$1/32$N$-7/32$P	$12^{11}/32$
		Rear	—	—	$1^3/16$N$-^{11}/32$P	0	$0-3/16$P	—

N—Negative
P—Positive

AIR CONDITIONING BELT TENSION

Year	Model	Engine Displacement Liters (cc)	Belt Type	Specifications (lbs.) New	Specifications (lbs.) Used
1990	Capri	1.6 (1597)	V-Ribbed	110–132	110–132
1991	Capri	1.6 (1597)	V-Ribbed	110–132	110–132
1992	Capri	1.6 (1597)	Serpentine	110–132	110–132
1993–94	Capri	1.6 (1597)	Serpentine	110–132	110–132

REFRIGERANT CAPACITIES

Year	Model	Refrigerant (oz.)	Oil (fl. oz.)	Compressor Type
1990	Capri	22.4	10.0	NA
1991	Capri	22.4	10.0	NA
1992	Capri	22.4	10.0	NA
1993	Capri	22.4	10.0	NA

NOTE: At the time of publication, refrigerant capacity information relating to R-134a was not available from the manufacturer.

MAINTENANCE INTERVALS—TYPE A: NORMAL SERVICE
Capri

TO BE SERVICED	TYPE OF SERVICE	VEHICLE MILEAGE INTERVAL (X1000)							
		7.5	15	22.5	30	37.5	45	52.5	60
Oxygen Sensor	I				✔				✔
Ignition Timing	I				✔				✔
Vacuum Lines and Hoses	I				✔				✔
Ignition Wires	I				✔				✔
Spark Plugs	R①		✔		✔		✔		✔
Engine Oil and Filter	R②	✔	✔	✔	✔	✔	✔	✔	✔
Engine Air Cleaner Element	R				✔				
PCV Valve	R		✔		✔		✔		
Fuel Filter	R								✔
Charcoal Canister	I				✔				✔
Fuel/Vapor Return Lines	I				✔				✔
Fuel Tank Cap and Restrictor	I				✔				✔
Coolant System	I		✔		✔		✔		✔
Exhaust Pipe and Muffler	I				✔				✔
Catalytic Converter and Shield	I				✔				✔
EGR System	I				✔				✔
Timing Belt	R								✔
Idle Speed System	I				✔				
Throttle Body	I		✔		✔		✔		
Drive Belts	I				✔				✔
Brake Pads, Front	I		✔		✔		✔		✔
Brake Pads, Rear	I		✔		✔		✔		✔
Brake Drums and Rotors	I				✔				✔
Brake Hoses and Lines	I				✔				✔
Battery Connections	I		✔		✔		✔		
Ball Joints	I				✔				✔
Engine Coolant	R				✔				✔
Automatic Transaxle Fluid	I	✔	✔	✔	✔	✔	✔	✔	✔
Manual Transaxle Fluid	I		✔		✔		✔		✔
Clutch Pedal Operation	I				✔				✔
Tire Rotation	I	✔		✔		✔		✔	
Wheel Bearings	L				✔				✔
Driveshaft Dust Boots	I				✔				✔
Steering System	I				✔				✔
Power Steering Fluid	I		✔		✔		✔		
Brake Fluid	I		✔		✔		✔		✔
Hinges, Latches, etc.	L		✔		✔		✔		✔
Seat Belt Operation	I		✔		✔		✔		✔

FOR COMPLETE WARRANTY COVERAGE CONSULT INDIVIDUAL VEHICLE MANUFACTURER'S WARRANTY MAINTENANCE GUIDE.

I—Inspect
L—Lubricate
R—Replace
① 1.6L Turbo engine—replace spark plugs every 15,000 miles
   1.6 Non-turbo engine—replace spark plugs every 30,000 miles
② 1.6L Turbo engine—change oil every 5,000 miles

MAINTENANCE INTERVALS—TYPE B: SEVERE SERVICE
Capri

TO BE SERVICED	TYPE OF SERVICE	VEHICLE MILEAGE INTERVAL (X1000)									
		3	6	9	12	15	18	21	24	27	30
Oxygen Sensor	I										✔
Ignition Timing	I										✔
Vacuum Lines and Hoses	I										✔
Ignition Wires	I										✔
Spark Plugs	R①					✔					
Engine Oil and Filter	R	✔	✔	✔	✔	✔	✔	✔	✔	✔	✔
Engine Air Cleaner Element	I/R②					✔					✔
PCV Valve	R					✔					✔
Fuel Filter	R③										
Charcoal Canister	I										✔
Fuel/Vapor Return Lines	I										✔
Fuel Tank Cap and Restrictor	I										✔
Coolant System	I					✔					✔
Exhaust Pipe and Muffler	I										✔
Catalytic Converter and Shield	I										✔
EGR System	I										✔
Timing Belt	R④										
Idle Speed System	I										✔
Throttle Body	I					✔					✔
Drive Belts	I										✔
Brake Pads, Front	I					✔					✔
Brake Pads, Rear	I					✔					✔
Brake Drums and Rotors	I										✔
Brake Hoses and Lines	I										✔
Battery Connections	I					✔					✔
Ball Joints	I										✔
Engine Coolant	R										✔
Automatic Transaxle Fluid	R										✔
Manual Transaxle Fluid	I					✔					✔
Clutch Pedal Operation	I										✔
Tire Rotation	I⑤		✔					✔			
Wheel Bearings	L										✔
Driveshaft Dust Boots	I										✔
Steering System	I										✔
Power Steering Fluid	I					✔					✔
Brake Fluid	I					✔					✔
Hinges, Latches, Etc.	L					✔					✔
Seat Belt Operation	I					✔					✔

FOR COMPLETE WARRANTY COVERAGE CONSULT INDIVIDUAL VEHICLE MANUFACTURER'S WARRANTY MAINTENANCE GUIDE.

I—Inspect
L—Lubricate
R—Replace
① 1.6L Turbo engine—replace spark plugs every 15,000 miles
1.6 Non-turbo engine—replace spark plugs every 30,000 miles

② Inspect air cleaner element every 15,000 miles—replace every 30,000 miles
③ Replace fuel filter every 60,000 miles
④ Replace timing belt every 60,000 miles
⑤ First 6,000 miles, then every 15,000 miles, as required

FIRING ORDERS

NOTE: To avoid confusion, always replace spark plugs and wires one at a time.

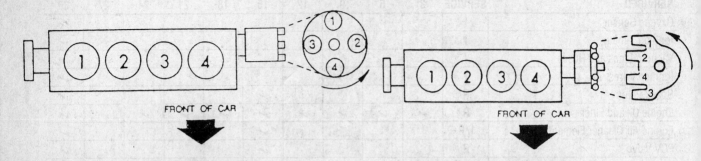

1.6L Non-turbocharged Engine
Engine Firing Order: 1-3-4-2
Distributor Rotation: Counterclockwise

1.6L Turbocharged Engine
Engine Firing Order: 1–3–4–2
Distributor Rotation: Counterclockwise

CYLINDER HEAD TORQUE SEQUENCES

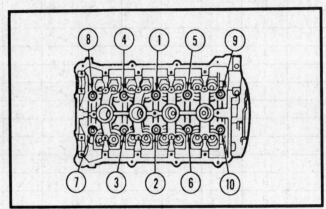

Cylinder head bolt torque sequence

TIMING MARK LOCATIONS

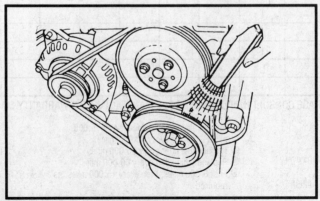

Timing mark location—1.6L engine

TIMING BELT LOCATIONS

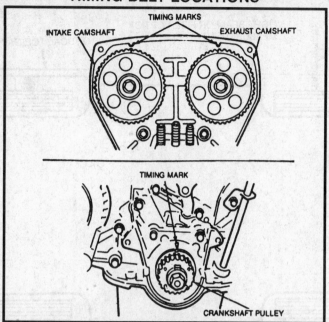

Timing belt alignment marks

AIR CONDITIONING SERVICE VALVE LOCATIONS

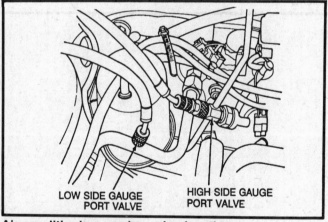

Air conditioning service valve location

WHEEL ALIGNMENT ADJUSTMENT LOCATIONS

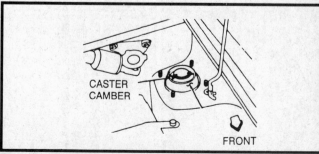

Front caster and camber adjustment

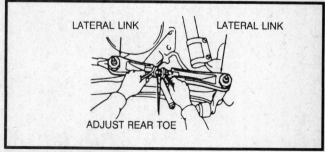

Rear toe adjustment

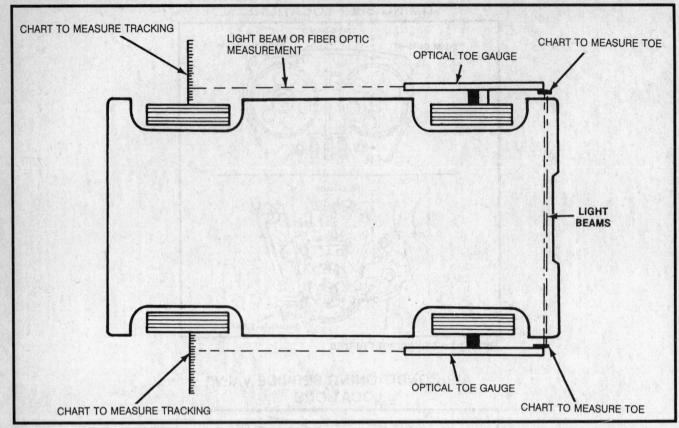

Checking vehicle tracking

SPECIFICATION CHARTS

VEHICLE IDENTIFICATION CHART

It is important for servicing and ordering parts to be certain of the vehicle and engine identification. The VIN (vehicle identification number) is a 17 digit number visible through the windshield on the driver's side of the dash and contains the vehicle and engine identification codes. The tenth digit indicates model year and the eighth digit indicates engine code. It can be interpreted as follows:

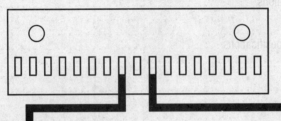

Engine Code							Model Year	
Code	Liters	Cu. In. (cc)	Cyl.	Fuel Sys.	Eng. Mfg.		Code	Year
D	2.5	154 (2524)	4	①	Ford		L	1990
U	3.0	181 (2971)	6	②	Ford		M	1991
Y	3.0	182 (2980)	6	SEFI	Yamaha		N	1992
4	3.8	232 (3801)	6	SEFI	Ford		P	1993
P	3.2	195 (3191)	6	SEFI	Yamaha		R	1994

SEFI—Sequential Electronic Fuel Injection
① 1990 Central Fuel Injection
   1991 Sequential Electronic Fuel Injection
② 1990 Electronic Fuel Injection
   1991–94 Sequential Electronic Fuel Injection

ENGINE IDENTIFICATION

Year	Model	Engine Displacement Liters (cc)	Engine Series (ID/VIN)	Fuel System	No. of Cylinders	Engine Type
1990	Taurus	2.5 (2524)	D	CFI	4	OHV
	Taurus	3.0 (2971)	U	EFI	6	OHV
	Taurus SHO	3.0 (2980)	Y	SEFI	6	DOHC
	Taurus	3.8 (3801)	4	SEFI	6	OHV
	Sable	3.0 (2971)	U	EFI	6	OHV
	Sable	3.8 (3801)	4	SEFI	6	OHV
	Continental	3.8 (3801)	4	SEFI	6	OHV
1991	Taurus	2.5 (2524)	D	SEFI	4	OHV
	Taurus	3.0 (2971)	U	SEFI	6	OHV
	Taurus SHO	3.0 (2980)	Y	SEFI	6	DOHC
	Taurus	3.8 (3801)	4	SEFI	6	OHV
	Sable	3.0 (2971)	U	SEFI	6	OHV
	Sable	3.8 (3801)	4	SEFI	6	OHV
	Continental	3.8 (3801)	4	SEFI	6	OHV
1992	Taurus	3.0 (2971)	U	SEFI	6	OHV
	Taurus SHO	3.0 (2980)	Y	SEFI	6	DOHC
	Taurus	3.8 (3801)	4	SEFI	6	OHV
	Sable	3.0 (2971)	U	SEFI	6	OHV
	Sable	3.8 (3801)	4	SEFI	6	OHV
	Continental	3.8 (3801)	4	SEFI	6	OHV

ENGINE IDENTIFICATION

Year	Model	Engine Displacement Liters (cc)	Engine Series (ID/VIN)	Fuel System	No. of Cylinders	Engine Type
1993-94	Taurus	3.0 (2971)	U	SEFI	6	OHV
	Taurus SHO	3.0 (2980)	Y	SEFI	6	DOHC
	Taurus SHO ①	3.2 (3191)	P	SEFI	6	DOHC
	Taurus	3.8 (3801)	4	SEFI	6	OHV
	Sable	3.0 (2971)	U	SEFI	6	OHV
	Sable	3.8 (3801)	4	SEFI	6	OHV
	Continental	3.8 (3801)	4	SEFI	6	OHV

CFI—Central Fuel Injection
EFI—Electronic Fuel Injection
SEFI—Sequential Electronic Fuel Injection
OHV—Overhead Valves
DOHC—Dual Overhead Cam
① Automatic Transaxle

GENERAL ENGINE SPECIFICATIONS

Year	Engine ID/VIN	Engine Displacement Liters (cc)	Fuel System Type	Net Horsepower @ rpm	Net Torque @ rpm (ft. lbs.)	Bore × Stroke (in.)	Compression Ratio	Oil Pressure @ rpm ①
1990	D	2.5 (2524)	CFI	90 @ 4400	130 @ 2600	3.68 × 3.62	9.0:1	55–70 @ 2000
	U	3.0 (2971)	EFI	140 @ 4800	160 @ 3000	3.50 × 3.14	9.3:1	40–60 @ 2500
	Y	3.0 (2980)	SEFI	220 @ 6200	200 @ 4800	3.50 × 3.15	9.8:1	12.8 @ 800
	4	3.8 (3801)	SEFI	140 @ 3800	215 @ 2200	3.81 × 3.39	9.0:1	40–60 @ 2500
1991	D	2.5 (2524)	SEFI	105 @ 4400	140 @ 2400	3.68 × 3.62	9.0:1	55–70 @ 2000
	U	3.0 (2971)	SEFI	140 @ 4800	160 @ 3000	3.50 × 3.14	9.3:1	40–60 @ 2500
	Y	3.0 (2980)	SEFI	220 @ 6200	200 @ 4800	3.50 × 3.15	9.8:1	12.8 @ 800
	4	3.8 (3801)	SEFI	②	③	3.81 × 3.39	9.0:1	40–60 @ 2500
1992	U	3.0 (2971)	SEFI	140 @ 4800	160 @ 3000	3.50 × 3.14	9.3:1	40–60 @ 2500
	Y	3.0 (2980)	SEFI	220 @ 6200	200 @ 4800	3.50 × 3.15	9.8:1	12.8 @ 800
	4	3.8 (3801)	SEFI	②	③	3.81 × 3.39	9.0:1	40–60 @ 2500
1993-94	U	3.0 (2971)	SEFI	140 @ 4800	160 @ 3000	3.50 × 3.14	9.3:1	40–60 @ 2500
	Y	3.0 (2980)	SEFI	220 @ 6200	200 @ 4800	3.50 × 3.15	9.8:1	12.8 @ 800
	P	3.2 (3191)	SEFI	220 @ 6200	215 @ 4800	3.62 × 3.15	9.8:1	12.8 @ 800
	4	3.8 (3801)	SEFI	②	③	3.81 × 3.39	9.0:1	40–60 @ 2500

CFI—Central Fuel Injection
EFI—Electronic Fuel Injection
SEFI—Sequential Electronic Fuel Injection
① Engine at normal operating temperature
② Except Continental and Taurus Police—
   140 @ 3800
  Continental and Taurus Police
    1991—155 @ 4000
    1992-94—160 @ 4400
③ Except Continental and Taurus Police—
   215 @ 2400
  Continental and Taurus Police
    1991—220 @ 2200
    1992-94—225 @ 3000

GASOLINE ENGINE TUNE-UP SPECIFICATIONS

Year	Engine ID/VIN	Engine Displacement Liters (cc)	Spark Plugs Gap (in.)	Ignition Timing (deg.)		Fuel Pump (psi)	Idle Speed (rpm)		Valve Clearance	
				MT	AT		MT	AT	In.	Ex.
1990	D	2.5 (2524)	0.044	—	10B	13–17	—	675–725	Hyd.	Hyd.
	U	3.0 (2971)	0.044	—	10B	35–40	—	①	Hyd.	Hyd.
	Y	3.0 (2980)	0.044	10B	—	30–45	①	—	0.006–0.010	0.010–0.014
	4	3.8 (3801)	0.054	—	10B	35–40	—	①	Hyd.	Hyd.
1991	D	2.5 (2524)	0.044	—	①	50–60	—	①	Hyd.	Hyd.
	U	3.0 (2971)	0.044	—	10B	35–40	—	①	Hyd.	Hyd.
	Y	3.0 (2980)	0.044	10B	—	30–45	①	—	0.006–0.010	0.010–0.014
	4	3.8 (3801)	0.054	—	10B	35–40	—	①	Hyd.	Hyd.
1992	U	3.0 (2971)	0.044	—	10B	35–40	—	①	Hyd.	Hyd.
	Y	3.0 (2980)	0.044	10B	—	30–45	①	—	0.006–0.010	0.010–0.014
	4	3.8 (3801)	0.054	—	10B	35–40	—	①	Hyd.	Hyd.
1993	U	3.0 (2971)	0.044	—	10B	35–40	—	①	Hyd.	Hyd.
	Y	3.0 (2980)	0.044	10B	—	30–45	①	—	0.006–0.010	0.010–0.014
	P	3.2 (3191)	0.044	—	10B	30–45	—	①	0.006–0.010	0.010–0.014
	4	3.8 (3801)	0.054	—	10B	35–40	—	①	Hyd.	Hyd.
1994	SEE UNDERHOOD SPECIFICATIONS STICKER									

NOTE: The lowest cylinder pressure should be within 75% of the highest cylinder pressure reading. For example, if the highest cylinder is 134 psi, the lowest should be 101. Engine should be at normal operating temperature with throttle valve in the wide open position.
The underhood specifications sticker often reflects tune-up specification changes in production. Sticker figures must be used if they disagree with those in this chart.
Hyd.—Hydraulic
B—Before Top Dead Center
① Refer to the Vehicle Emission Control information label

CAPACITIES

Year	Model	Engine ID/VIN	Engine Displacement Liters (cc)	Engine Crankcase with Filter	Transmission (pts.)			Drive Axle Front (pts.)	Fuel Tank (gal.)	Cooling System (qts.)
					4-Spd	5-Spd	Auto.			
1990	Taurus	D	2.5 (2524)	5.0	—	—	16.8	①	②	8.3
	Taurus	U	3.0 (2971)	4.5	—	—	25.6	①	②	③
	Taurus	Y	3.0 (2980)	5.0	—	6.2	—	①	18.6	11.6
	Taurus	4	3.8 (3801)	4.5	—	—	25.6	①	②	12.1
	Sable	U	3.0 (2971)	4.5	—	—	25.6	①	②	③
	Sable	4	3.8 (3801)	4.5	—	—	25.6	①	②	12.1
	Continental	4	3.8 (3801)	4.5	—	—	25.6	①	18.6	11.1

CAPACITIES

Year	Model	Engine ID/VIN	Engine Displacement Liters (cc)	Engine Crankcase with Filter	Transmission (pts.)			Drive Axle Front (pts.)	Fuel Tank (gal.)	Cooling System (qts.)
					4-Spd	5-Spd	Auto.			
1991	Taurus	D	2.5 (2524)	5.0	—	—	25.6	①	②	8.3
	Taurus	U	3.0 (2971)	4.5	—	—	25.6	①	②	③
	Taurus	Y	3.0 (2980)	5.0	—	6.2	—	①	18.6	11.6
	Taurus	4	3.8 (3801)	4.5	—	—	25.6	①	②	12.1
	Sable	U	3.0 (2971)	4.5	—	—	25.6	①	②	③
	Sable	4	3.8 (3801)	4.5	—	—	25.6	①	②	12.1
	Continental	4	3.8 (3801)	4.5	—	—	25.6	①	18.6	11.1
1992	Taurus	U	3.0 (2971)	4.5	—	—	25.6	①	②	③
	Taurus	Y	3.0 (2980)	5.0	—	6.2	—	①	18.6	11.6
	Taurus	4	3.8 (3801)	4.5	—	—	25.6	①	②	12.1
	Sable	U	3.0 (2971)	4.5	—	—	25.6	①	②	③
	Sable	4	3.8 (3801)	4.5	—	—	25.6	①	②	12.1
	Continental	4	3.8 (3801)	4.5	—	—	25.6	①	18.4	11.1
1993–94	Taurus	U	3.0 (2971)	4.5	—	—	25.6	①	②	③
	Taurus	Y	3.0 (2980)	5.0	—	6.2	—	①	18.6	11.6
	Taurus	P	3.2 (3191)	5.0	—	—	25.6	①	18.6	11.4
	Taurus	4	3.8 (3801)	4.5	—	—	25.6	①	②	12.1
	Sable	U	3.0 (2971)	4.5	—	—	25.6	①	②	③
	Sable	4	3.8 (3801)	4.5	—	—	25.6	①	②	12.1
	Continental	4	3.8 (3801)	4.5	—	—	25.6	①	18.4	11.1

① Included in transaxle capacity
② Standard—16.0 gals.
   Optional extended range—18.6 gals.
③ Sedan—11.0 qts.
   Wagon—11.8 qts.

CAMSHAFT SPECIFICATIONS

All measurements given in inches.

Year	Engine ID/VIN	Engine Displacement Liters (cc)	Journal Diameter					Elevation		Bearing Clearance	Camshaft End Play
			1	2	3	4	5	In.	Ex.		
1990	D	2.5 (2524)	2.0060–2.0090	2.0060–2.0090	2.0060–2.0090	2.0060–2.0090	2.0060–2.0090	0.244–0.249	0.234–0.239	0.0010–0.0030	0.009
	U	3.0 (2971)	2.0074–2.0084	2.0074–2.0084	2.0074–2.0084	2.0074–2.0084	—	0.255–0.260	0.255–0.260	0.0010–0.0030	0.001–0.005
	Y	3.0 (2980)	1.2189–1.2195	1.2189–1.2195	1.2189–1.2195	1.2189–1.2195	1.2189–1.2195	0.335	0.315	0.0010–0.0026	0.012
	4	3.8 (3801)	2.0505–2.0515	2.0505–2.0515	2.0505–2.0515	2.0505–2.0515	—	0.240–0.245	0.254–0.259	0.0010–0.0030	①
1991	D	2.5 (2524)	2.0060–2.0090	2.0060–2.0090	2.0060–2.0090	2.0060–2.0090	2.0060–2.0090	0.244–0.249	0.234–0.239	0.0010–0.0030	0.009
	U	3.0 (2971)	2.0074–2.0084	2.0074–2.0084	2.0074–2.0084	2.0074–2.0084	—	0.255–0.260	0.255–0.260	0.0010–0.0030	0.001–0.005
	Y	3.0 (2980)	1.2189–1.2195	1.2189–1.2195	1.2189–1.2195	1.2189–1.2195	1.2189–1.2195	0.335	0.315	0.0010–0.0026	0.012
	4	3.8 (3801)	2.0505–2.0515	2.0505–2.0515	2.0505–2.0515	2.0505–2.0515	—	0.240–0.245	0.254–0.259	0.0010–0.0030	0.001–0.006

CAMSHAFT SPECIFICATIONS

All measurements given in inches.

Year	Engine ID/VIN	Engine Displacement Liters (cc)	Journal Diameter 1	2	3	4	5	Elevation In.	Ex.	Bearing Clearance	Camshaft End Play
1992	U	3.0 (2971)	2.0074–2.0084	2.0074–2.0084	2.0074–2.0084	2.0074–2.0084	—	0.255–0.260	0.255–0.260	0.0010–0.0030	0.001–0.005
	Y	3.0 (2980)	1.2189–1.2195	1.2189–1.2195	1.2189–1.2195	1.2189–1.2195	1.2189–1.2195	0.335	0.315	0.0010–0.0026	0.012
	4	3.8 (3801)	2.0505–2.0515	2.0505–2.0515	2.0505–2.0515	2.0505–2.0515	—	0.240–0.245	0.254–0.259	0.0010–0.0030	0.001–0.006
1993–94	U	3.0 (2971)	2.0074–2.0084	2.0074–2.0084	2.0074–2.0084	2.0074–2.0084	—	0.255–0.260	0.255–0.260	0.0010–0.0030	0.001–0.005
	Y	3.0 (2980)	1.2189–1.2195	1.2189–1.2195	1.2189–1.2195	1.2189–1.2195	1.2189–1.2195	0.335	0.315	0.0010–0.0026	0.012
	P	3.2 (3191)	1.2189–1.2195	1.2189–1.2195	1.2189–1.2195	1.2189–1.2195	1.2189–1.2195	0.315	0.315	0.0010–0.0026	0.012
	4	3.8 (3801)	2.0505–2.0515	2.0505–2.0515	2.0505–2.0515	2.0505–2.0515	—	0.240–0.245	0.254–0.259	0.0010–0.0030	0.001–0.006

① The camshaft is restrained by a spring; there is no endplay.

CRANKSHAFT AND CONNECTING ROD SPECIFICATIONS

All measurements are given in inches.

Year	Engine ID/VIN	Engine Displacement Liters (cc)	Crankshaft Main Brg. Journal Dia.	Main Brg. Oil Clearance	Shaft End-play	Thrust on No.	Connecting Rod Journal Diameter	Oil Clearance	Side Clearance
1990	D	2.5 (2524)	2.2489–2.2490	0.0008–0.0024	0.004–0.008	3	2.1232–2.1240	0.0008–0.0024	0.0035–0.0140
	U	3.0 (2971)	2.5190–2.5198	0.0005–0.0023	0.004–0.008	3	2.1253–2.1261	0.0009–0.0027	0.0060–0.0140
	Y	3.0 (2980)	2.5187–2.5197	0.0011–0.0031	0.001–0.008	3	2.0463–2.0472	0.0009–0.0031	0.0063–0.0138
	4	3.8 (3801)	2.5190–2.5198	0.0005–0.0023	0.004–0.008	3	2.3103–2.3111	0.0009–0.0027	0.0047–0.0140
1991	D	2.5 (2524)	2.2489–2.2490	0.0008–0.0024	0.004–0.008	3	2.1232–2.1240	0.0008–0.0024	0.0035–0.0140
	U	3.0 (2971)	2.5190–2.5198	0.0005–0.0023	0.004–0.008	3	2.1253–2.1261	0.0009–0.0027	0.0060–0.0140
	Y	3.0 (2980)	2.5187–2.5197	0.0011–0.0031	0.001–0.008	3	2.0463–2.0472	0.0009–0.0031	0.0063–0.0138
	4	3.8 (3801)	2.5190–2.5198	0.0005–0.0023	0.004–0.008	3	2.3103–2.3111	0.0009–0.0027	0.0047–0.0140
1992	U	3.0 (2971)	2.5190–2.5198	0.0005–0.0023	0.004–0.008	3	2.1253–2.1261	0.0009–0.0027	0.0060–0.0140
	Y	3.0 (2980)	2.5187–2.5197	0.0011–0.0031	0.001–0.008	3	2.0463–2.0472	0.0009–0.0031	0.0063–0.0138
	4	3.8 (3801)	2.5190–2.5198	0.0005–0.0023	0.004–0.008	3	2.3103–2.3111	0.0009–0.0027	0.0047–0.0140

CRANKSHAFT AND CONNECTING ROD SPECIFICATIONS

All measurements are given in inches.

Year	Engine ID/VIN	Engine Displacement Liters (cc)	Crankshaft Main Brg. Journal Dia.	Crankshaft Main Brg. Oil Clearance	Crankshaft Shaft End-play	Crankshaft Thrust on No.	Connecting Rod Journal Diameter	Connecting Rod Oil Clearance	Connecting Rod Side Clearance
1993–94	U	3.0 (2971)	2.5190–2.5198	0.0005–0.0023	0.004–0.008	3	2.1253–2.1261	0.0009–0.0027	0.0060–0.0140
	Y	3.0 (2980)	2.5187–2.5197	0.0011–0.0031	0.001–0.008	3	2.0463–2.0472	0.0009–0.0031	0.0063–0.0138
	P	3.2 (3191)	2.5187–2.5197	0.0011–0.0031	0.001–0.008	3	2.0463–2.0472	0.0009–0.0031	0.0063–0.0138
	4	3.8 (3801)	2.5190–2.5198	0.0005–0.0023	0.004–0.008	3	2.3103–2.3111	0.0009–0.0027	0.0047–0.0140

VALVE SPECIFICATIONS

Year	Engine ID/VIN	Engine Displacement Liters (cc)	Seat Angle (deg.)	Face Angle (deg.)	Spring Test Pressure (lbs. @ in.)	Spring Installed Height (in.)	Stem-to-Guide Clearance (in.) Intake	Stem-to-Guide Clearance (in.) Exhaust	Stem Diameter (in.) Intake	Stem Diameter (in.) Exhaust
1990	D	2.5 (2524)	44–45	44–45	174–190 @ 1.11	1.49	0.0018	0.0023	0.3415–0.3422	0.3411–0.3418
	U	3.0 (2971)	45	44	180 @ 1.16	1.58	0.0010–0.0028	0.0015–0.0033	0.3126–0.3134	0.3121–0.3129
	Y	3.0 (2980)	45	45.5	120.8 @ 1.19	1.52	0.0010–0.0023	0.0012–0.0025	0.2346–0.2352	0.2344–0.2350
	4	3.8 (3801)	44.5	45.8	220 @ 1.18	1.65	0.0010–0.0028	0.0015–0.0033	0.3415–0.3423	0.3410–0.3418
1991	D	2.5 (2524)	44–45	44–45	174–190 @ 1.11	1.49	0.0018	0.0023	0.3415–0.3422	0.3411–0.3418
	U	3.0 (2971)	45	44	180 @ 1.16	1.58	0.0010–0.0028	0.0015–0.0033	0.3126–0.3134	0.3121–0.3129
	Y	3.0 (2980)	45	45.5	120.8 @ 1.19	1.52	0.0010–0.0023	0.0012–0.0025	0.2346–0.2352	0.2344–0.2350
	4	3.8 (3801)	44.5	45.8	220 @ 1.18	1.65	0.0010–0.0028	0.0015–0.0033	0.3415–0.3423	0.3410–0.3418
1992	U	3.0 (2971)	45	44	180 @ 1.16	1.58	0.0010–0.0028	0.0015–0.0033	0.3126–0.3134	0.3121–0.3129
	Y	3.0 (2980)	45	45.5	120.8 @ 1.19	1.52	0.0010–0.0023	0.0012–0.0025	0.2346–0.2352	0.2344–0.2350
	4	3.8 (3801)	44.5	45.8	220 @ 1.18	1.65	0.0010–0.0028	0.0015–0.0033	0.3415–0.3423	0.3410–0.3418
1993–94	U	3.0 (2971)	45	44	180 @ 1.16	1.58	0.0010–0.0028	0.0015–0.0033	0.3126–0.3134	0.3121–0.3129
	Y	3.0 (2980)	45	45.5	120.8 @ 1.19	1.52	0.0010–0.0023	0.0012–0.0025	0.2346–0.2352	0.2344–0.2350
	P	3.2 (3191)	45	45.5	120.8 @ 1.19	1.52	0.0010–0.0023	0.0012–0.0025	0.2346–0.2352	0.2344–0.2350
	4	3.8 (3801)	44.5	45.8	220 @ 1.18	1.65	0.0010–0.0028	0.0015–0.0033	0.3415–0.3423	0.3410–0.3418

PISTON AND RING SPECIFICATIONS

All measurements are given in inches.

| Year | Engine ID/VIN | Engine Displacement Liters (cc) | Piston Clearance | Ring Gap | | | Ring Side Clearance | | |
				Top Compression	Bottom Compression	Oil Control	Top Compression	Bottom Compression	Oil Control
1990	D	2.5 (2524)	0.0012–0.0022	0.008–0.016	0.008–0.016	0.015–0.055	0.0020–0.0040	0.0020–0.0040	Snug
	U	3.0 (2971)	0.0014–0.0022	0.010–0.020	0.010–0.020	0.010–0.049	0.0012–0.0031	0.0012–0.0031	Snug
	Y	3.0 (2980)	0.0012–0.0020	0.012–0.018	0.012–0.018	0.008–0.020	0.0008–0.0024	0.0006–0.0022	0.0024–0.0059
	4	3.8 (3801)	0.0014–0.0032	0.011–0.022	0.010–0.020	0.015–0.058	0.0016–0.0034	0.0016–0.0034	Snug
1991	D	2.5 (2524)	0.0011–0.0022	0.008–0.016	0.008–0.016	0.015–0.055	0.0020–0.0040	0.0020–0.0040	Snug
	U	3.0 (2971)	0.0014–0.0022	0.010–0.020	0.010–0.020	0.010–0.049	0.0012–0.0031	0.0012–0.0031	Snug
	Y	3.0 (2980)	0.0012–0.0020	0.012–0.018	0.012–0.018	0.008–0.020	0.0008–0.0024	0.0006–0.0022	0.0024–0.0059
	4	3.8 (3801)	0.0014–0.0032	0.011–0.022	0.010–0.020	0.015–0.058	0.0016–0.0034	0.0016–0.0034	Snug
1992	U	3.0 (2971)	0.0014–0.0022	0.010–0.020	0.010–0.020	0.010–0.049	0.0012–0.0031	0.0012–0.0031	Snug
	Y	3.0 (2980)	0.0012–0.0020	0.012–0.018	0.012–0.018	0.008–0.020	0.0008–0.0024	0.0006–0.0022	0.0024–0.0059
	4	3.8 (3801)	0.0014–0.0032	0.011–0.022	0.010–0.020	0.015–0.058	0.0016–0.0034	0.0016–0.0034	Snug
1993–94	U	3.0 (2971)	0.0014–0.0022	0.010–0.020	0.010–0.020	0.010–0.049	0.0012–0.0031	0.0012–0.0031	Snug
	Y	3.0 (2980)	0.0012–0.0020	0.012–0.018	0.012–0.018	0.008–0.020	0.0008–0.0024	0.0006–0.0022	0.0024–0.0059
	P	3.2 (3191)	0.0012–0.0020	0.012–0.018	0.018–0.024	0.008–0.020	0.0016–0.0031	0.0008–0.0024	0.0024–0.0059
	4	3.8 (3801)	0.0014–0.0032	0.011–0.022	0.010–0.020	0.015–0.058	0.0016–0.0034	0.0016–0.0034	Snug

TORQUE SPECIFICATIONS

All readings in ft. lbs.

| Year | Engine ID/VIN | Engine Displacement Liters (cc) | Cylinder Head Bolts | Main Bearing Bolts | Rod Bearing Bolts | Crankshaft Damper Bolts | Flywheel Bolts | Manifold | | Spark Plugs | Lug Nut |
								Intake	Exhaust		
1990	D	2.5 (2524)	①	52–66	21–26	140–170	54–64	15–23	②	6–10	85–105
	U	3.0 (2971)	③	63–69	26	107	59	⑪	19	5–11	85–105
	Y	3.0 (2980)	⑤	⑥	⑦	113–126	⑧	11–17	26–38	17–19	85–105
	4	3.8 (3801)	⑨	65–81	31–36	103–132	54–64	⑩	15–22	5–11	85–105
1991	D	2.5 (2524)	①	52–66	21–26	140–170	54–64	15–22	②	6–10	85–105
	U	3.0 (2971)	③	55–63	26	107	59	⑪	19	5–11	85–105
	Y	3.0 (2980)	⑤	⑥	⑦	113–126	⑧	11–17	26–38	17–19	85–105
	4	3.8 (3801)	⑫	65–81	31–36	103–132	54–64	⑩	15–22	5–11	85–105

TORQUE SPECIFICATIONS
All readings in ft. lbs.

Year	Engine ID/VIN	Engine Displacement Liters (cc)	Cylinder Head Bolts	Main Bearing Bolts	Rod Bearing Bolts	Crankshaft Damper Bolts	Flywheel Bolts	Manifold Intake	Manifold Exhaust	Spark Plugs	Lug Nut
1992	U	3.0 (2971)	③	58–63	26	93–121	59	15–22	15–22	5–11	85–105
	Y	3.0 (2980)	⑤	⑥	⑦	113–126	⑧	11–16	26–38	17–19	85–105
	4	3.8 (3801)	⑫	65–81	31–36	103–132	54–64	④	15–22	5–11	85–105
1993–94	U	3.0 (2971)	③	58–63	26	93–121	59	15–22	15–22	5–11	85–105
	Y	3.0 (2980)	⑤	⑥	⑦	113–126	⑧	11–16	26–38	17–19	85–105
	P	3.2 (3191)	⑤	⑥	⑦	112–127	⑧	11–17	26–38	16–20	85–105
	4	3.8 (3801)	⑫	65–81	31–36	103–132	54–64	④	15–22	5–11	85–105

① Tighten in 2 steps:
Step 1: 52–59 ft. lbs.
Step 2: 70–76 ft. lbs.
② Tighten in 2 steps:
Step 1: 5–7 ft. lbs.
Step 2: 20–30 ft. lbs.
③ Tighten in 2 steps:
Step 1: 37 ft. lbs.
Step 2: 68 ft. lbs.
④ Tighten in 2 steps:
Step 1: 8 ft. lbs.
Step 2: 11 ft. lbs.
⑤ Tighten in 2 steps:
Step 1: 37–50 ft. lbs.
Step 2: 62–68 ft. lbs.
⑥ Tighten in 2 steps:
Step 1: 37–50 ft. lbs.
Step 2: 58–64 ft. lbs.

⑦ Tighten in 2 steps:
Step 1: 22–26 ft. lbs.
Step 2: 33–36 ft. lbs.
⑧ Tighten in 2 steps:
Step 1: 29–43 ft. lbs.
Step 2: 51–58 ft. lbs.
⑨ Tighten in 6 steps:
Step 1: 37 ft. lbs.
Step 2: 45 ft. lbs.
Step 3: 52 ft. lbs.
Step 4: 59 ft. lbs.
Step 5: Back off all bolts 2–3 turns
Step 6: Repeat steps 1–4
⑩ Tighten in 3 steps:
Step 1: 7 ft. lbs.
Step 2: 15 ft. lbs.
Step 3: 24 ft. lbs.

⑪ Tighten in 2 steps:
Step 1: 11 ft. lbs.
Step 2: 21 ft. lbs.
⑫ Tighten in 7 steps:
Step 1: 37 ft. lbs.
Step 2: 45 ft. lbs.
Step 3: 52 ft. lbs.
Step 4: 59 ft. lbs.
Step 5: In sequence, loosen all bolts 2–3 turns
Step 6: Tighten long bolts to 11–18 ft. lbs., then an additional 85–105 degrees
Step 7: Tighten short bolts to 11–18 ft. lbs., then an additional 65–85 degrees

TORQUE SPECIFICATIONS

Component	English	Metric
Balance shaft thrust plate 3.8L engine:	72–120 inch lbs.	8–14 Nm
Camshaft bearing cap bolt 3.0L SHO engine		
Step 1:	71–106 inch lbs.	8–12 Nm
Step 2:	12–16 ft. lbs.	16–22 Nm
Camshaft sprocket bolt		
2.5L engine:	41–56 ft. lbs.	55–75 Nm
3.0L engine:	46 ft. lbs.	63 Nm
3.0L SHO engine		
Chain sprocket:	10–13 ft. lbs.	14–18 Nm
Belt sprocket:	15–18 ft. lbs.	21–25 Nm
3.8L engine:	30–37 ft. lbs.	40–50 Nm
Camshaft thrust plate bolt		
2.5L engine:	6–9 ft. lbs.	8–12 Nm
3.0L engine:	7 ft. lbs.	10 Nm
3.8L engine:	6–10 ft. lbs.	8–14 Nm
Connecting rod bearing cap nuts		
2.5L engine:	21–26 ft. lbs.	28–35 Nm
3.0L engine:	26 ft. lbs.	35 Nm
3.0L SHO engine		
Step 1:	22–26 ft. lbs.	30–35 Nm
Step 2:	33–36 ft. lbs.	45–50 Nm
3.8L engine:	31–36 ft. lbs.	41–49 Nm

TORQUE SPECIFICATIONS

Component	English	Metric
Crankshaft damper bolt		
2.5L engine:	140–170 ft. lbs.	190–230 Nm
3.0L engine		
1989:	141–169 ft. lbs.	190–230 Nm
1990–94:	93–121 ft. lbs.	125–165 Nm
3.0L SHO engine:	113–126 ft. lbs.	152–172 Nm
3.8L engine		
1989:	93–121 ft. lbs.	125–165 Nm
1990–94:	103–132 ft. lbs.	140–180 Nm
Crankshaft seal retainer bolts		
2.5L engine:	6–9 ft. lbs.	8–12 Nm
3.0L SHO engine:	55–82 inch lbs.	6.3–9.4 Nm
Cylinder head bolt		
2.5L engine		
Step 1:	52–59 ft. lbs.	70–80 Nm
Step 2:	70–76 ft. lbs.	95–103 Nm
3.0L engine		
Step 1:	37 ft. lbs.	50 Nm
Step 2:	68 ft. lbs.	68 Nm
3.0L SHO engine		
Step 1:	37–50 ft. lbs.	49–69 Nm
Step 2:	62–68 ft. lbs.	83–93 Nm
3.8L engine		
Step 1:	37 ft. lbs.	50 Nm
Step 2:	45 ft. lbs.	60 Nm
Step 3:	52 ft. lbs.	70 Nm
Step 4:	59 ft. lbs.	80 Nm
Step 5:	loosen 2–3 turns	loosen 2–3 turns
Step 6:	11–18 ft. lbs.	15–25 Nm
Long bolts:	+ 85–105 degree turn	+ 85–105 degree turn
Short bolts:	+ 65–85 degree turn	+ 65–85 degree turn
Engine-to-transaxle		
2.5L engine:	26–34 ft. lbs.	34–47 Nm
3.0L engine:	41–50 ft. lbs.	55–68 Nm
3.0L (SHO) engine:	28–31 ft. lbs.	38–42 Nm
3.8L engine:	41–50 ft. lbs.	55–68 Nm
Engine/transaxle mounts		
2.5L and 3.0L engines		
Right rear engine insulator		
Insulator-to-engine bracket:	40–55 ft. lbs.	54–75 Nm
Insulator-to-frame nuts:	55–75 ft. lbs.	75–102 Nm
Left engine insulator/support		
Support retaining bolts:	40–55 ft. lbs.	54–75 Nm
Insulator-to-frame bolts:	60–86 ft. lbs.	81–116 Nm
Insulator-to-support nuts:	55–75 ft. lbs.	74–102 Nm
Right front engine insulator		
Insulator-to-engine bracket bolts		
2.5L engine:	40–55 ft. lbs.	54–75 Nm
3.0L engine:	71–95 ft. lbs.	90–130 Nm
Insulator-to-frame nuts:	55–75 ft. lbs.	74–102 Nm
3.0L SHO engine		
Right front and right rear insulators		
Insulator-to-engine bracket bolts:	40–55 ft. lbs.	54–75 Nm
Insulator-to-frame nuts:	50–70 ft. lbs.	68–95 Nm
Roll damper retaining nuts:	40–55 ft. lbs.	54–75 Nm
Engine damper-to-engine bolt:	40–55 ft. lbs.	54–75 Nm
Left engine insulator/support		
Damper bracket-to-insulator nuts:	40–55 ft. lbs.	54–75 Nm
Insulator-to-transaxle bolts:	70–95 ft. lbs.	95–130 Nm
Insulator-to-frame bolts:	60–85 ft. lbs.	81–116 Nm
Damper-to-damper bracket bolt:	40–55 ft. lbs.	54–75 Nm

TORQUE SPECIFICATIONS

Component	English	Metric
3.8L engine		
Right front engine insulator		
Upper insulator nut:	40–55 ft. lbs.	54–75 Nm
Lower insulator nut:	50–70 ft. lbs.	68–95 Nm
Right rear engine insulator		
Top insulator retaining nut:	40–55 ft. lbs.	54–75 Nm
Engine mount retaining nuts:	50–70 ft. lbs.	68–95 Nm
Left engine mount/support		
Support-to-transaxle bolts		
1989–91:	35 ft. lbs.	48 Nm
1992–94:	40–55 ft. lbs.	54–75 Nm
Mount-to-frame bolts:	60–86 ft. lbs.	81–116 Nm
Transaxle mount-to-support nut:	55–75 ft. lbs.	74–102 Nm
Vertical restrictor assembly bolts:	40–55 ft. lbs.	54–75 Nm
Exhaust manifold		
2.5L engine		
Step 1:	5–7 ft. lbs.	7–10 Nm
Step 2:	20–30 ft. lbs.	27–41 Nm
3.0L engine:	19 ft. lbs.	25 Nm
3.0L SHO engine:	26–38 ft. lbs.	35–52 Nm
3.8L engine:	15–22 ft. lbs.	20–30 Nm
Exhaust pipe-to-manifold nuts		
2.5L engine:	25–34 ft. lbs.	34–47 Nm
3.0L engine:	25–34 ft. lbs.	34–47 Nm
3.0L SHO engine:	16–24 ft. lbs.	21–32 Nm
3.8L engine:	25–34 ft. lbs.	34–47 Nm
Flywheel/flexplate-to-crankshaft bolts		
2.5L engine:	54–64 ft. lbs.	73–87 Nm
3.0L engine:	54–64 ft. lbs.	73–87 Nm
3.0L SHO engine		
Step 1:	29–43 ft. lbs.	39–50 Nm
Step 2:	51–58 ft. lbs.	69–78 Nm
3.8L engine:	54–64 ft. lbs.	73–87 Nm
Flywheel-to-torque converter bolts:	23–39 ft. lbs.	31–53 Nm
Intake manifold		
2.5L engine:	15–22 ft. lbs.	20–30 Nm
3.0L engine		
1989		
Step 1:	11 ft. lbs.	15 Nm
Step 2:	18 ft. lbs.	25 Nm
Step 3:	24 ft. lbs.	33 Nm
1990–94		
Step 1:	11 ft. lbs.	15 Nm
Step 2:	21 ft. lbs.	28 Nm
3.0L SHO engine:	11–17 ft. lbs.	15–23 Nm
3.8L engine		
1989–91		
Step 1:	8 ft. lbs.	11 Nm
Step 2:	15 ft. lbs.	20 Nm
Step 3:	24 ft. lbs.	32 Nm
1992–94		
Step 1:	8 ft. lbs.	11 Nm
Step 2:	11 ft. lbs.	15 Nm
Main bearing cap bolts		
2.5L engine:	52–66 ft. lbs.	70–90 Nm
3.0L engine		
1989–90:	63–69 ft. lbs.	86–94 Nm
1991–94:	55–63 ft. lbs.	75–85 Nm
3.0L SHO engine		
Step 1:	37–50 ft. lbs.	46–69 Nm
Step 2:	58–64 ft. lbs.	78–88 Nm
3.8L engine:	65–81 ft. lbs.	88–110 Nm

TORQUE SPECIFICATIONS

Component	English	Metric
Main bearing cap support		
3.0L SHO engine:	16–23 ft. lbs.	21–32 Nm
Oil pan-to-block bolts		
2.5L engine:	6–9 ft. lbs.	8–12 Nm
3.0L engine:	8–10 ft. lbs.	10–14 Nm
3.0L SHO engine:	11–16 ft. lbs.	15–23 Nm
3.8L engine:	7–9 ft. lbs.	9–12 Nm
Oil pan–to–transaxle bolts		
2.5L engine:	30–39 ft. lbs.	40–50 Nm
Oil pan drain plug		
2.5L engine:	15–25 ft. lbs.	20–34 Nm
3.0L engine:	9–12 ft. lbs.	11–16 Nm
3.0L SHO engine:	15–24 ft. lbs.	20–33 Nm
3.8L engine:	15–25 ft. lbs.	20–34 Nm
Oil pump attaching bolts		
2.5L engine:	15–22 ft. lbs.	20–30 Nm
3.0L engine:	35 ft. lbs.	48 Nm
3.0L SHO engine:	11–17 ft. lbs.	15–23 Nm
Oil pump cover bolts		
3.8L engine:	18–22 ft. lbs.	25–30 Nm
Rocker arm bolt		
2.5L engine		
Step 1:	6–8 ft. lbs.	8–12 Nm
Step 2:	20–26 ft. lbs.	28–35 Nm
3.0L engine		
Step 1:	8 ft. lbs.	11 Nm
Step 2:	24 ft. lbs.	32 Nm
3.8L engine		
Step 1:	44 inch lbs.	5 Nm
Step 2:	19–25 ft. lbs.	25–35 Nm
Rocker arm (valve) cover		
2.5L engine:	6–8 ft. lbs.	8–12 Nm
3.0L engine:	9 ft. lbs.	12 Nm
3.0L SHO engine:	8–11 ft. lbs.	10–16 Nm
3.8L engine:	80–106 inch lbs.	9–12 Nm
Spark plug		
2.5L engine:	6–10 ft. lbs.	7–14 Nm
3.0L engine:	5–11 ft. lbs.	7–15 Nm
3.0L SHO engine:	17–19 ft. lbs.	22–27 Nm
3.8L engine:	60–132 inch lbs.	7–17 Nm
Thermostat housing		
2.5L engine:	12–18 ft. lbs.	16–24 Nm
3.0L engine:	9 ft. lbs.	12 Nm
3.0L SHO engine:	5–8 ft. lbs.	7–11 Nm
3.8L engine:	15–22 ft. lbs.	20–30 Nm
Throttle body bolts		
2.5L engine		
CFI system:	15–25 ft. lbs.	20–34 Nm
SEFI system:	6.0–8.5 ft. lbs.	8.0–11.5 Nm
3.0L engine:*	19 ft. lbs.	25 Nm
3.0L SHO engine:	11–17 ft. lbs.	15–23 Nm
3.8L engine:	19 ft. lbs.	25 Nm

* NOTE: oil the bolt threads

TORQUE SPECIFICATIONS

Component	English	Metric
Timing cover		
2.5L engine:	6–9 ft. lbs.	10–12 Nm
3.0L engine		
8mm bolts:	19 ft. lbs.	25 Nm
6mm bolts:	7 ft. lbs.	10 Nm
3.0L SHO engine:	60–90 inch lbs.	7–11 Nm
3.8L engine:	15–22 ft. lbs.	20–30 Nm
Water pump		
2.5L engine:	15–23 ft. lbs.	20–30 Nm
3.0L engine		
8mm bolts:	15–22 ft. lbs.	20–30 Nm
6mm bolts:	71–106 inch lbs.	8–12 Nm
3.0L SHO engine:	12–16 ft. lbs.	15–23 Nm
3.8L engine:	15–22 ft. lbs.	20–30 Nm

BRAKE SPECIFICATIONS

All measurements in inches unless noted.

Year	Model	Master Cylinder Bore	Brake Disc Original Thickness	Brake Disc Minimum Thickness	Brake Disc Maximum Runout	Brake Drum Diameter Original Inside Diameter	Brake Drum Diameter Max. Wear Limit	Brake Drum Diameter Maximum Machine Diameter	Minimum Lining Thickness Front	Minimum Lining Thickness Rear
1990	Taurus	0.940	④	⑤	③	①	NA	②	0.125	⑥
	Taurus SHO	1.000	④	⑤	③	—	—	—	0.125	0.123
	Sable	0.940	④	⑤	③	①	NA	②	0.125	⑥
	Continental	1.000	1.020	0.970	0.002	—	—	—	0.125	0.123
1991	Taurus	0.940	④	⑤	③	①	NA	②	0.125	⑥
	Taurus SHO	1.000	④	⑤	③	—	—	—	0.125	0.123
	Sable	0.940	④	⑤	③	①	NA	②	0.125	⑥
	Continental	1.000	④	⑤	⑦	—	—	—	0.125	0.123
1992	Taurus	1.000	④	⑤	③	①	NA	②	0.125	⑥
	Taurus SHO	1.000	④	⑤	③	—	—	—	0.125	0.123
	Sable	1.000	④	⑤	③	①	NA	②	0.125	⑥
	Continental	1.000	④	⑤	0.003	—	—	—	0.125	0.123
1993–94	Taurus	1.000	④	⑤	③	①	NA	②	0.125	⑥
	Taurus SHO	1.000	④	⑤	③	—	—	—	0.125	0.123
	Sable	1.000	④	⑤	③	①	NA	②	0.125	⑥
	Continental	1.000	④	⑤	⑧	—	—	—	0.125	0.123

NA—Not available
① Sedan—8.85 in.
 Wagon—9.84 in.
② Sedan—8.91 in.
 Wagon—9.90 in.
③ Front—0.003
 Rear—0.002
④ Front—1.024
 Rear—0.940
⑤ Front—0.974
 Rear—0.900
⑥ With disc brakes—0.123
 With drum brakes—0.030
⑦ Front—0.002
 Rear—0.003
⑧ Front—0.003
 Rear—0.0014

WHEEL ALIGNMENT

Year	Model		Caster Range (deg.)	Caster Preferred Setting (deg.)	Camber Range (deg.)	Camber Preferred Setting (deg.)	Toe (in.)	Steering Axis Inclination (deg.)
1990	Taurus	Front	⑤	⑥	⑦	⑧	7/32N-1/32P	15½
		Rear	—	—	1⅝N-7/32N	15/16N	1/16N-3/16P	—
	Sable	Front	⑨	⑩	⑪	⑫	7/32N-1/32P	15½
		Rear	—	—	1⅝N-7/32N	15/16N	1/16N-3/16P	—
	Continental	Front	3⅝P-5⅛P	4⅜P	1 11/16N-½N	1⅛N	7/32N-1/32P	15½
		Rear	—	—	2N-⅝N	15/16N	1/32N-7/32P	—
1991	Taurus	Front	①	②	⑦	⑧	7/32N-1/32P	15½
		Rear	—	—	1⅝N-7/32N	15/16N	1/16N-3/16P	—
	Sable	Front	③	④	⑪	⑫	7/32N-1/32P	15½
		Rear	—	—	1⅝N-7/32N	15/16N	1/16N-3/16P	—
	Continental	Front	3⅝P-5⅛P	4⅜P	1 11/16N-½N	1⅛N	7/32N-1/32P	15½
		Rear	—	—	2N-⅝N	15/16N	1/32N-7/32P	—
1992	Taurus	Front	①	②	⑦	⑧	7/32N-1/32P	15½
		Rear	—	—	1⅝N-7/32N	15/16N	1/16N-3/16P	—
	Sable	Front	③	④	⑪	⑫	7/32N-1/32P	15½
		Rear	—	—	1⅝N-7/32N	15/16N	1/16N-3/16P	—
	Continental	Front	3⅝P-5⅛P	4⅜P	1 11/16N-½N	1⅛N	7/32N-1/32P	15½
		Rear	—	—	2N-⅝N	15/16N	1/32N-7/32P	—
1993-94	Taurus	Front	①	②	⑦	⑧	7/32N-1/32P	15½
		Rear	—	—	1⅝N-7/32N	15/16N	1/16N-3/16P	—
	Sable	Front	③	④	⑪	⑫	7/32N-1/32P	15½
		Rear	—	—	1⅝N-7/32N	15/16N	1/16N-3/16P	—
	Continental	Front	3⅝P-5⅛P	4⅜P	1 11/16N-½N	1⅛N	7/32N-1/32P	15½
		Rear	—	—	2N-⅝N	15/16N	1/32N-7/32P	—

N—Negative
P—Positive

① Sedan—2 13/16P-4 13/16P
   Wagon—2⅝P-4⅝P
② Sedan—3 13/16P
   Wagon—3⅝P
③ Sedan—2 11/16P-4 11/16P
   Wagon—2⅝P-4⅝P

④ Sedan—3 11/16P
   Wagon—3⅝P
⑤ Sedan—2 13/16P-5 13/16P
   Wagon—2⅝P-5⅝P
⑥ Sedan—3 13/16P
   Wagon—3⅝P
⑦ Sedan—1⅛N-⅛P
   Wagon—1 1/16N-3/16P

⑧ Sedan—½N
   Wagon—7/16N
⑨ Sedan—2 11/16P-5 11/16P
   Wagon—2⅝P-5⅝P
⑩ Sedan—3 11/16P
   Wagon—3⅝P

⑪ Sedan—1⅛N-⅛P
   Wagon—1 1/16N-3/16P
⑫ Sedan—½N
   Wagon—7/16N

AIR CONDITIONING BELT TENSION

Year	Model	Engine Displacement Liters (cc)	Belt Type	Specification New (lbs.)	Specification Used (lbs.)
1990	Taurus	2.5 (2524)	V-Ribbed	①	①
	Taurus	3.0 (2971)	V-Ribbed	①	①
	Sable	3.0 (2971)	V-Ribbed	①	①
	Continental	3.8 (3801)	V-Ribbed	①	①

AIR CONDITIONING BELT TENSION

Year	Model	Engine Displacement Liters (cc)	Belt Type	Specification	
				New (lbs.)	Used (lbs.)
1991	Taurus	2.5 (2524)	V-Ribbed	① ②	① ②
	Sable	2.5 (2524)	V-Ribbed	①	①
	Taurus	3.0 (2980)	V-Ribbed	① ②	① ②
	Sable	3.0 (2980)	V-Ribbed	①	①
	Taurus	3.8 (3801)	V-Ribbed	① ②	① ②
	Sable	3.8 (3801)	V-Ribbed	①	①
	Continental	3.8 (3801)	V-Ribbed	①	①
1992	Taurus	3.0 (2971)	V-Ribbed	① ②	① ②
	Sable	3.0 (2971)	V-Ribbed	①	①
	Taurus	3.8 (3801)	V-Ribbed	① ②	① ②
	Sable	3.8 (3801)	V-Ribbed	①	①
	Continental	3.8 (3801)	V-Ribbed	①	①
1993–94	Taurus	3.0 (2890)	V-Ribbed	① ②	① ②
	Sable	3.0 (2890)	V-Ribbed	①	①
	Taurus	3.2 (3196)	V-Ribbed	① ②	① ②
	Sable	3.2 (3196)	V-Ribbed	①	①
	Taurus	3.8 (3801)	V-Ribbed	① ②	① ②
	Sable	3.8 (3801)	V-Ribbed	①	①
	Continental	3.8 (3801)	V-Ribbed	①	①

① Automatic tensioner, no adjustment required
② 3.0L SHO: 220–265 lbs. new; 148–192 lbs. used.

REFRIGERANT CAPACITIES

Year	Model	Refrigerant (oz.)	Oil (fl. oz.)	Compressor Type
1990	Taurus	①	②	③
	Sable	①	②	③
	Continental	38–42	8	10P15C
1991	Taurus w/2.5L	42–46	10	FS-6
	Sable w/2.5L	42–46	10	FS-6
	Taurus w/3.0L	42–46	7	FX-15
	Sable w/3.0L	42–46	7	FX-15
	Taurus w/3.8L	38–42	7	FX-15
	Sable w/3.8L	38–42	7	FX-15
	Continental	38–42	8	FX-15
1992	Taurus	39–41 ④	7	FX-15
	Sable	39–41 ④	7	FX-15
	Taurus 3.0L SHO	39–41	8	10P15F
	Continental	39–41	7	FX-15

REFRIGERANT CAPACITIES

Year	Model	Refrigerant (oz.)	Oil (fl. oz.)	Compressor Type
1993–94	Taurus	31–33	7	FX-15
	Sable	31–33	7	FX-15
	Taurus SHO	31–33	8	10P15F
	Continental	39–41	7⑤	FX-15

① 2.5L and 3.0L engines: 42–46 oz.
② 2.5L engine: 10 oz., 3.0L engine: 7 oz.,
  3.0L SHO and 3.8L engines: 8 oz.
③ 2.5L engine: FS-6, 3.0L engine: FX-15, 3.0L
  SHO engine: 10P15F, 3.8L engine: 10P15C
④ Some Taurus 3.0L use R134a refrigerant
  system
⑤ 10 oz. with auxiliary system

MAINTENANCE INTERVALS—TYPE A: NORMAL SERVICE
Continental • Sable • Taurus

TO BE SERVICED	TYPE OF SERVICE	VEHICLE MILEAGE INTERVAL (X1000)							
		7.5	15	22.5	30	37.5	45	52.5	60
Oxygen Sensor	I				✔				✔
Ignition Timing	I①				✔				✔
Vacuum Lines and Hoses	I				✔				✔
Ignition Wires	I				✔				✔
Spark Plugs	R②				✔				✔
Engine Oil and Filter	R	✔	✔	✔	✔	✔	✔	✔	✔
Engine Air Cleaner Element	R				✔				✔
Crankcase Emission Filter	R③				✔				✔
PCV Valve	R				✔				✔
Fuel Filter	R								✔
Charcoal Canister	I				✔				✔
Fuel/Vapor Return Lines	I				✔				✔
Fuel Tank Cap and Restrictor	I				✔				✔
Coolant System	I		✔		✔		✔		✔
Exhaust Pipe and Muffler	I				✔				✔
Catalytic Converter and Shield	I				✔				✔
EGR System	I				✔				✔
Valve Clearance	I④								✔
Timing Belt	R④								✔
Throttle Body	I		✔		✔		✔		✔
Drive Belts	I				✔				✔
Brake Pads, Front	I				✔				✔
Brake Pads, Rear	I				✔				✔
Brake Shoes, Rear	I				✔				✔
Brake Drums and Rotors	I				✔				✔
Brake Hoses and Lines	I				✔				✔
Battery Connections	I		✔		✔		✔		✔
Ball Joints	I				✔				✔
Engine Coolant	R								

MAINTENANCE INTERVALS—TYPE A: NORMAL SERVICE
Continental • Sable • Taurus

TO BE SERVICED	TYPE OF SERVICE	VEHICLE MILEAGE INTERVAL (X1000)							
		7.5	15	22.5	30	37.5	45	52.5	60
Automatic Transaxle Fluid	I	✔	✔	✔	✔	✔	✔	✔	✔
Manual Transaxle Fluid	I		✔		✔		✔		✔
Clutch Pedal Operation	I				✔				
Tire Rotation	I	✔		✔		✔		✔	
Driveshaft Dust Boots	I				✔				
Steering System	I				✔				
Power Steering Fluid	I		✔		✔		✔		✔
Brake Fluid	I		✔		✔		✔		✔
Hinges, Latches, etc.	I		✔		✔		✔		✔
Battery Fluid Level	I⑤		✔		✔		✔		✔
Seat Belt Operation	I		✔		✔		✔		✔

FOR COMPLETE WARRANTY COVERAGE CONSULT INDIVIDUAL VEHICLE MANUFACTURER'S WARRANTY MAINTENANCE GUIDE.

I—Inspect
L—Lubricate
R—Replace
① If applicable
② 3.0L OHV engines—if equipped with Platinum spark plugs, first change interval is 60,000 miles

3.0L and 3.2L SHO engines—first change interval is 60,000 miles (all are equipped with Platinum spark plugs)
③ 2.5L engine only
④ 3.0L and 3.2L SHO engines only
⑤ Taurus SHO only

MAINTENANCE INTERVALS—TYPE B: SEVERE SERVICE
Continental • Sable • Taurus

TO BE SERVICED	TYPE OF SERVICE	VEHICLE MILEAGE INTERVAL (X1000)									
		3	6	9	12	15	18	21	24	27	30
Oxygen Sensor	I										✔
Ignition Timing	I①										✔
Vacuum Lines and Hoses	I										✔
Ignition Wires	I										✔
Spark Plugs	R②										✔
Engine Oil and Filter	R	✔	✔	✔	✔	✔	✔	✔	✔	✔	
Engine Air Cleaner Element	R										✔
Crankcase Emission Filter	R③										✔
PCV Valve	R										✔
Fuel Filter	R④										
Charcoal Canister	I										✔
Fuel/Vapor Return Lines	I										✔
Fuel Tank Cap and Restrictor	I										✔
Coolant System	R					✔					✔
Exhaust Pipe and Muffler	I										✔
Catalytic Converter and Shield	I										✔
EGR System	I										✔
Valve Clearance	I⑤										
Timing Belt	R⑤										
Throttle Body	I					✔					
Drive Belts	I										✔
Brake Pads, Front	I										✔

MAINTENANCE INTERVALS—TYPE B: SEVERE SERVICE
Continental • Sable • Taurus

TO BE SERVICED	TYPE OF SERVICE	VEHICLE MILEAGE INTERVAL (X1000)									
		3	6	9	12	15	18	21	24	27	30
Brake Pads, Rear	I										✔
Brake Shoes, Rear	I										✔
Brake Drums and Rotors	I										✔
Brake Hoses and Lines	I										✔
Battery Connections	I					✔					✔
Ball Joints	I										✔
Engine Coolant	R										✔
Automatic Transaxle Fluid	R										✔
Manual Transaxle Fluid	I					✔					✔
Clutch Pedal Operation	I										✔
Tire Rotation	I⑥		✔				✔				
Driveshaft Dust Boots	I										✔
Steering System	I										✔
Power Steering Fluid	I					✔					✔
Brake Fluid	I					✔					✔
Hinges, Latches, etc.	L					✔					✔
Battery Fluid Level	I⑦					✔				\	✔
Seat Belt Operation	I					✔					✔

FOR COMPLETE WARRANTY COVERAGE CONSULT INDIVIDUAL VEHICLE MANUFACTURER'S WARRANTY MAINTENANCE GUIDE.

I—Inspect
L—Lubricate
R—Replace
① If applicable
② 3.0L OHV engines—if equipped with platinum spark plugs, replace every 60,000 miles
3.0L and 3.2L SHO engines—replace every 60,000 miles (all are equipped with platinum spark plugs)

③ 2.5L engine only
④ Replace fuel filter every 60,000 miles
⑤ 3.0L and 3.2L SHO engines only—replace timing belt and adjust valve lash every 60,000 miles
⑥ First 6,000 miles, then every 15,000 miles as required
⑦ Taurus SHO only

FIRING ORDERS

NOTE: To avoid confusion, always replace spark plugs and wires one at a time.

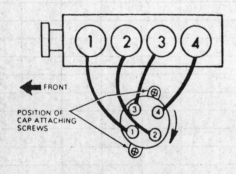

2.5L Engine
Engine Firing Order: 1–3–4–2
Distributor Rotation: Clockwise

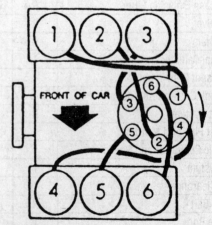

3.0L Engine
Engine Firing Order: 1–4–2–5–3–6
Distributor Rotation: Clockwise

FIRING ORDERS

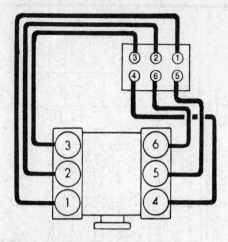

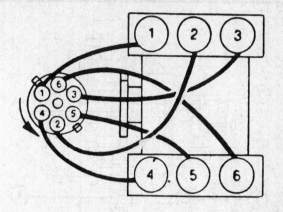

3.0L and 3.2L SHO Engines
Engine Firing Order: 1–4–2–5–3–6
Distributorless Ignition System

3.8L Engine
Engine Firing Order: 1–4–2–5–3–6
Distributor Rotation: Counterclockwise

CYLINDER HEAD TORQUE SEQUENCES

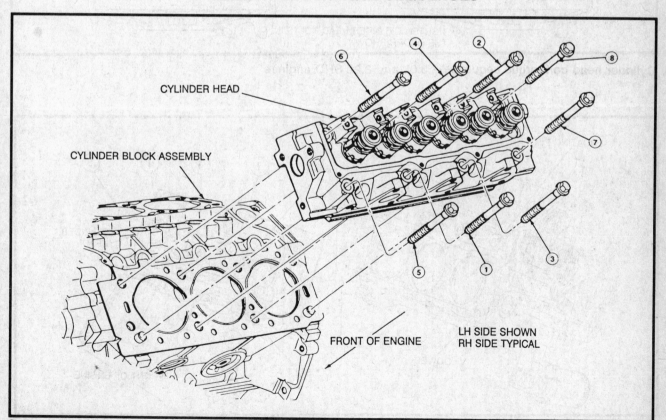

Cylinder head bolt torque sequence—3.0L engine

CYLINDER HEAD TORQUE SEQUENCES

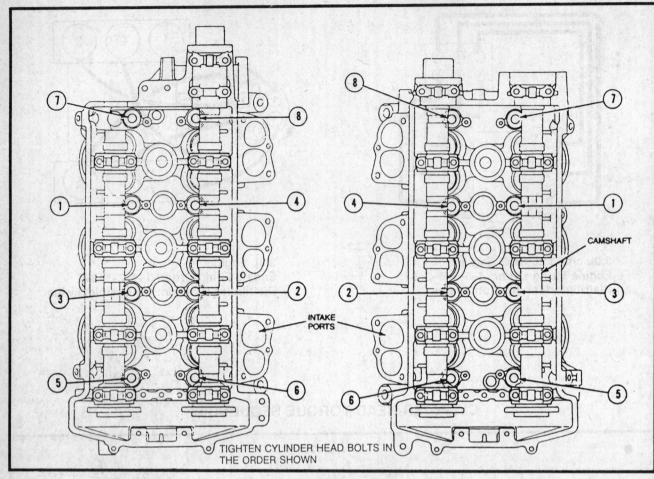

Cylinder head bolt torque sequence— 3.0L and 3.2L SHO engines

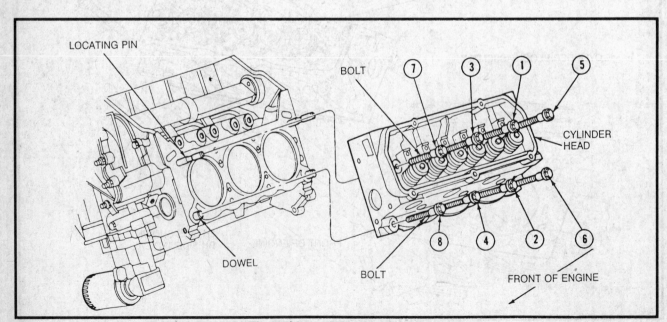

Cylinder head bolt torque sequence—3.8L engine

CYLINDER HEAD TORQUE SEQUENCES

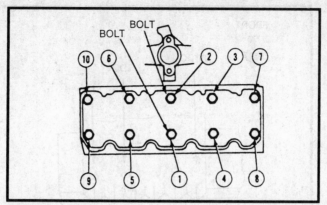

Cylinder head bolt torque sequence—2.5L engine

TIMING MARK LOCATIONS

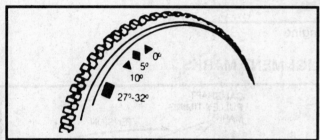

Timing mark location—2.5L engine with automatic transaxle

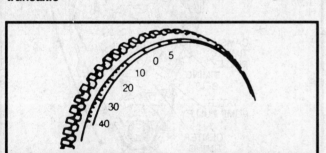

Timing mark location—2.5L engine with manual transaxle

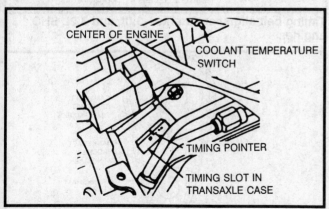

Timing mark location—2.5L engine with automatic transaxle

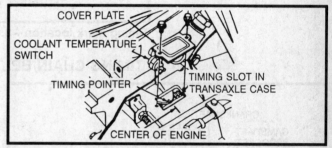

Timing mark location—2.5L engine with manual transaxle

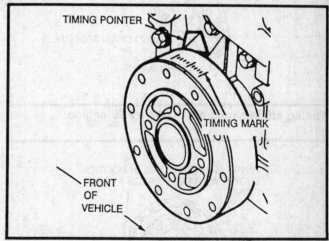

Timing marks location—3.0L engine

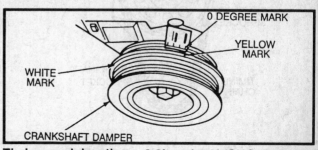

Timing mark location— 3.0L and 3.2L SHO engines

TIMING MARK LOCATIONS

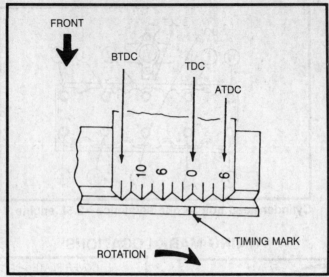

Timing mark location—3.8L engine

TIMING CHAIN/BELT ALIGNMENT MARKS

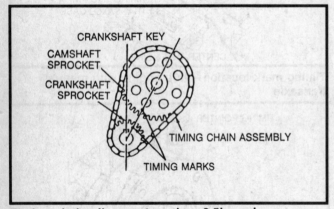

Timing chain alignment marks—2.5L engine

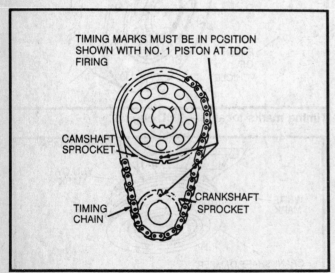

Timing chain alignment marks—3.0L SOHC engine

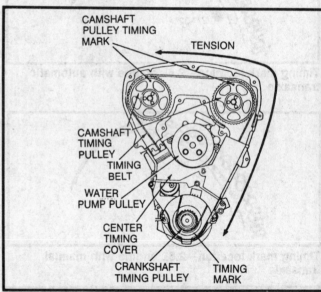

Timing belt alignment marks—3.0L and 3.2L SHO engines

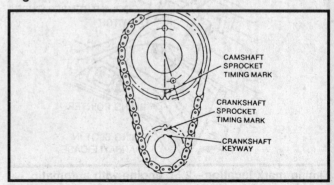

Timing chain alignment marks—3.8L engine

AIR CONDITIONING SERVICE VALVE LOCATIONS

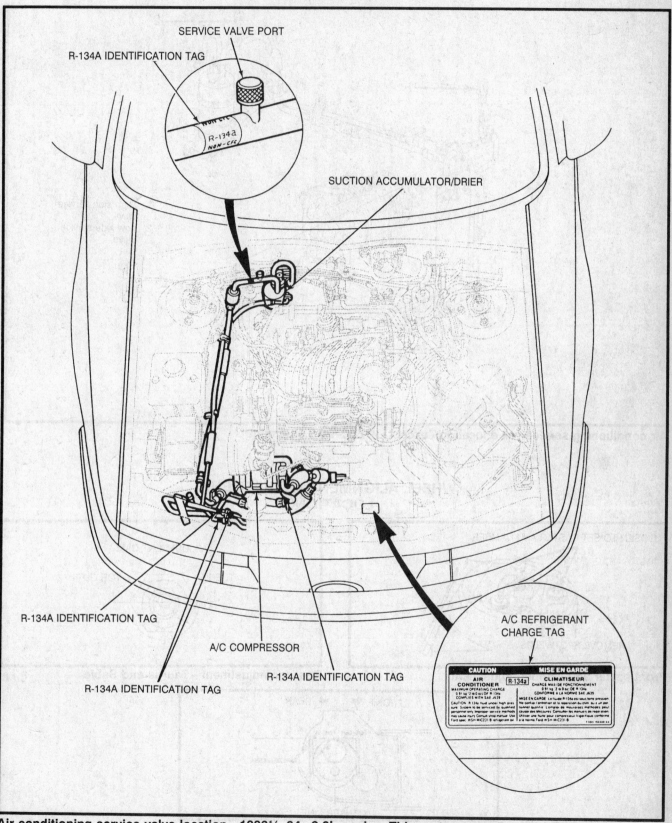

Air conditioning service valve location – 1992½–94 3.0L engine. This system uses R-134a refrigerant

AIR CONDITIONING SERVICE VALVE LOCATIONS

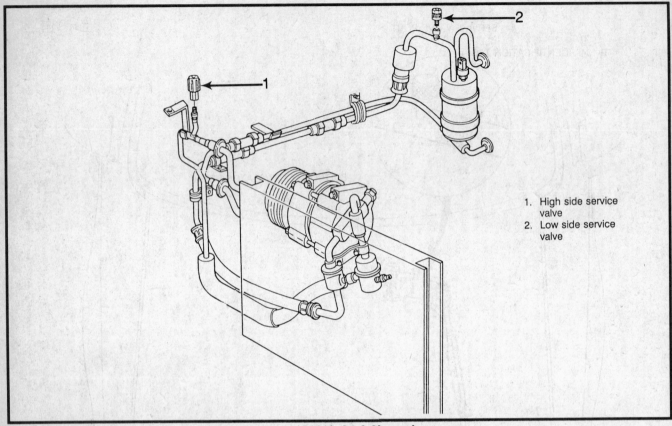

1. High side service valve
2. Low side service valve

Air conditioning service valve location—except 1992½–94 3.0L engine

WHEEL ALIGNMENT ADJUSTMENT LOCATIONS

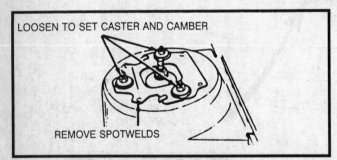

LOOSEN TO SET CASTER AND CAMBER

REMOVE SPOTWELDS

Front caster and camber adjustment

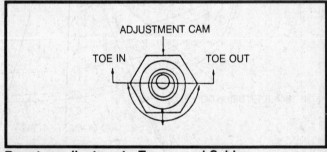

ADJUSTMENT CAM

TOE IN   TOE OUT

Rear toe adjustment—Taurus and Sable

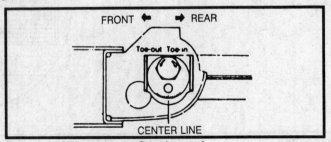

FRONT ← → REAR

Toe-out Toe-in

CENTER LINE

Rear toe adjustment—Continental

SPECIFICATION CHARTS

VEHICLE IDENTIFICATION CHART

It is important for servicing and ordering parts to be certain of the vehicle and engine identification. The VIN (vehicle identification number) is a 17 digit number visible through the windshield on the driver's side of the dash and contains the vehicle and engine identification codes. The tenth digit indicates model year and the eighth digit indicates engine code. It can be interpreted as follows:

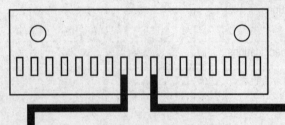

Engine Code						Model Year	
Code	Liters	Cu. In. (cc)	Cyl.	Fuel Sys.	Eng. Mfg.	Code	Year
5	1.6	98 (1597)	4	EFI	Ford	L	1990
8	1.8	112 (1839)	4	EFI	Mazda	M	1991
J	1.9	114 (1859)	4	SFI	Ford	N	1992
						P	1993
						R	1994

EFI—Electronic Fuel Injection
SFI—Sequential Multi-Port Fuel Injection

ENGINE IDENTIFICATION

Year	Model	Engine Displacement Liters (cc)	Engine Series (ID/VIN)	Fuel System	No. of Cylinders	Engine Type
1990	Tracer	1.6 (1597)	5	EFI	4	OHC
1991	Tracer	1.8 (1839)	8	EFI	4	DOHC
	Tracer	1.9 (1859)	J	SFI	4	OHC
1992	Tracer	1.8 (1839)	8	EFI	4	DOHC
	Tracer	1.9 (1859)	J	SFI	4	OHC
1993–94	Tracer	1.8 (1839)	8	EFI	4	DOHC
	Tracer	1.9 (1859)	J	SFI	4	OHC

EFI—Electronic Fuel Injection
OHC—Overhead Camshaft
DOHC—Double Overhead Camshaft
SFI—Sequential Multi-Port Fuel Injection

GENERAL ENGINE SPECIFICATIONS

Year	Engine ID/VIN	Engine Displacement Liters (cc)	Fuel System Type	Net Horsepower @ rpm	Net Torque @ rpm (ft. lbs.)	Bore × Stroke (in.)	Compression Ratio	Oil Pressure @ rpm
1990	5	1.6 (1597)	EFI	82 @ 5000	92 @ 2500	3.07 × 3.29	9.3:1	50–64 @ 3000 ①
1991	8	1.8 (1839)	EFI	127 @ 6500	114 @ 4500	3.27 × 3.35	9.0:1	43–57 @ 3000 ①
	J	1.9 (1859)	SFI	88 @ 4400	108 @ 3800	3.23 × 3.46	9.0:1	35–65 @ 2000 ①
1992	8	1.8 (1839)	EFI	127 @ 6500	114 @ 4500	3.27 × 3.35	9.0:1	43–57 @ 3000 ①
	J	1.9 (1859)	SFI	88 @ 4400	108 @ 3800	3.23 × 3.46	9.0:1	35–65 @ 2000 ①
1993–94	8	1.8 (1839)	EFI	127 @ 6500	114 @ 4500	3.27 × 3.35	9.0:1	43–57 @ 3000 ①
	J	1.9 (1859)	SFI	88 @ 4400	108 @ 3800	3.23 × 3.46	9.0:1	35–65 @ 2000 ①

EFI—Electronic Fuel Injection
SFI—Sequential Multi-Port Fuel Injection
① Oil at normal operating temperature

GASOLINE ENGINE TUNE-UP SPECIFICATIONS

Year	Engine ID/VIN	Engine Displacement Liters (cc)	Spark Plugs Gap (in.)	Ignition Timing (deg.) MT	Ignition Timing (deg.) AT	Fuel Pump (psi)	Idle Speed (rpm) MT	Idle Speed (rpm) AT	Valve Clearance In.	Valve Clearance Ex.
1990	5	1.6 (1597)	0.041	2B①	2B①	64–85②	800–900	800–900	0.012④	0.012④
1991	8	1.8 (1839)	0.041	10B	10B	64–85②	700–800	700–800	Hyd.	Hyd.
	J	1.9 (1859)	③	10B	10B	35–40②	③	③	Hyd.	Hyd.
1992	8	1.8 (1839)	0.041	10B	10B	64–85②	700–800	700–800	Hyd.	Hyd.
	J	1.9 (1859)	③	10B	10B	35–40②	③	③	Hyd.	Hyd.
1993–94	8	1.8 (1839)	0.041	10B	10B	64–85②	700–800	700–800	Hyd.	Hyd.
	J	1.9 (1859)	③	10B	10B	35–40②	③	③	Hyd.	Hyd.

NOTE: The lowest cylinder pressure should be within 75% of the highest cylinder pressure reading. For example, if the highest cylinder is 134 psi, the lowest should be 101. Engine should be at normal operating temperature with throttle valve in the wide open position.
The underhood specifications sticker often reflects tune-up specification changes in production. Sticker figures must be used if they disagree with those in this chart.
B—Before Top Dead Center
Hyd.—Hydraulic
① Vacuum hoses disconnected and plugged
② Key on, engine off
③ Refer to Vehicle Emission Control information label
④ Engine warm

CAPACITIES

Year	Model	Engine ID/VIN	Engine Displacement Liters (cc)	Engine Crankcase with Filter (qts.)	Transmission (pts.) 4-Spd	Transmission (pts.) 5-Spd	Transmission (pts.) Auto.	Transfer case (pts.)	Drive Axle Front (pts.)	Drive Axle Rear (pts.)	Fuel Tank (gal.)	Cooling System (qts.)
1990	Tracer	5	1.6 (1597)	3.6	—	6.8	12	—	①	—	12.7	②
1991	Tracer	8	1.8 (1839)	4.0	—	7.2	12.2	—	①	—	13.2	②
	Tracer	J	1.9 (1859)	4.0	—	5.6	12.2	—	①	—	11.9	②
1992	Tracer	8	1.8 (1839)	4.0	—	7.2	12.2	—	①	—	13.2	②
	Tracer	J	1.9 (1859)	4.0	—	5.6	12.2	—	①	—	11.9	②
1993–94	Tracer	8	1.8 (1839)	4.0	—	7.2	12.2	—	①	—	13.2	②
	Tracer	J	1.9 (1859)	4.0	—	5.6	12.2	—	①	—	11.9	②

① Included in transaxle capacity
② Manual transaxle—5.3 qts.
   Automatic transaxle—6.3 qts.

CAMSHAFT SPECIFICATIONS

All measurements given in inches.

Year	Engine ID/VIN	Engine Displacement Liters (cc)	Journal Diameter 1	2	3	4	5	Elevation In.	Elevation Ex.	Bearing Clearance	Camshaft End Play
1990	5	1.6 (1597)	1.7103–1.7112	1.6870–1.7091	1.7103–1.7112	—	—	1.4329–1.4437①	1.4329–1.4437①	②	0.002–0.008
1991	8	1.8 (1839)	1.0213–1.0222	1.0213–1.0222	1.0213–1.0222	1.0213–1.0222	1.0213–1.0222	1.7281–1.7360①	1.7480–1.7560①	0.0014–0.0032	0.003–0.007
	J	1.9 (1859)	1.8007–1.8017	1.8007–1.8017	1.8007–1.8017	1.8007–1.8017	1.8007–1.8017	0.2350–0.2400	0.2350–0.2400	0.0013–0.0033	0.002–0.006

CAMSHAFT SPECIFICATIONS

All measurements given in inches.

Year	Engine ID/VIN	Engine Displacement Liters (cc)	Journal Diameter 1	2	3	4	5	Elevation In.	Ex.	Bearing Clearance	Camshaft End Play
1992	8	1.8 (1839)	1.0213–1.0222	1.0213–1.0222	1.0213–1.0222	1.0213–1.0222	1.0213–1.0222	1.7281–1.7360①	1.7480–1.7560①	0.0014–0.0032	0.003–0.007
	J	1.9 (1859)	1.8007–1.8017	1.8007–1.8017	1.8007–1.8017	1.8007–1.8017	1.8007–1.8017	0.2400–0.2450	0.2400–0.2450	0.0013–0.0033	0.002–0.006
1993–94	8	1.8 (1839)	1.0213–1.0222	1.0213–1.0222	1.0213–1.0222	1.0213–1.0222	1.0213–1.0222	1.7281–1.7360①	1.7480–1.7560①	0.0014–0.0032	0.003–0.007
	J	1.9 (1859)	1.8007–1.8017	1.8007–1.8017	1.8007–1.8017	1.8007–1.8017	1.8007–1.8017	0.2400–0.2450	0.2400–0.2450	0.0013–0.0033	0.002–0.006

① Specification is for total lobe height
② No. 1 and No. 3—0.0014–0.0059
No. 2—0.0026–0.0059

CRANKSHAFT AND CONNECTING ROD SPECIFICATIONS

All measurements are given in inches.

Year	Engine ID/VIN	Engine Displacement Liters (cc)	Crankshaft Main Brg. Journal Dia.	Main Brg. Oil Clearance	Shaft End-play	Thrust on No.	Connecting Rod Journal Diameter	Oil Clearance	Side Clearance
1990	5	1.6 (1597)	1.9661–1.9668	0.0011–0.0039	0.003–0.012	4	1.7693–1.7699	0.0009–0.0039	0.012
1991	8	1.8 (1839)	1.9661–1.9668	0.0007–0.0014	0.003–0.012	4	1.7692–1.7699	0.0011–0.0027	0.004–0.012
	J	1.9 (1859)	2.2827–2.2835	①	0.004–0.008	3	1.7279–1.7287	0.0008–0.0026	0.004–0.014
1992	8	1.8 (1839)	1.9661–1.9668	0.0007–0.0014	0.003–0.012	4	1.7692–1.7699	0.0011–0.0027	0.004–0.012
	J	1.9 (1859)	2.2827–2.2835	①	0.004–0.008	3	1.7279–1.7287	0.0008–0.0026	0.004–0.014
1993–94	8	1.8 (1839)	1.9661–1.9668	0.0007–0.0014	0.003–0.012	4	1.7692–1.7699	0.0011–0.0027	0.004–0.012
	J	1.9 (1859)	2.2827–2.2835	①	0.004–0.008	3	1.7279–1.7287	0.0008–0.0026	0.004–0.014

① Without cylinder head—0.0018–0.0034
With cylinder head—0.0011–0.0027

VALVE SPECIFICATIONS

Year	Engine ID/VIN	Engine Displacement Liters (cc)	Seat Angle (deg.)	Face Angle (deg.)	Spring Test Pressure (lbs. @ in.)	Spring Installed Height (in.)	Stem-to-Guide Clearance (in.) Intake	Exhaust	Stem Diameter (in.) Intake	Exhaust
1990	5	1.6 (1597)	45	45	NA①	NA①	0.0080②	0.0080②	0.2744–0.2750	0.2742–0.2748
1991	8	1.8 (1839)	45	45	NA③	NA③	0.0010–0.0024	0.0012–0.0026	0.2350–0.2356	0.2348–0.2354
	J	1.9 (1859)	45	45.6	200 @ 1.09	1.44–1.48	0.0008–0.0027	0.0018–0.0037	0.3159–0.3167	0.3149–0.3156

VALVE SPECIFICATIONS

Year	Engine ID/VIN	Engine Displacement Liters (cc)	Seat Angle (deg.)	Face Angle (deg.)	Spring Test Pressure (lbs. @ in.)	Spring Installed Height (in.)	Stem-to-Guide Clearance (in.)		Stem Diameter (in.)	
							Intake	Exhaust	Intake	Exhaust
1992	8	1.8 (1839)	45	45	NA③	NA③	0.0010–0.0024	0.0012–0.0026	0.2350–0.2356	0.2348–0.2354
	J	1.9 (1859)	45	45.6	200 @ 1.09	1.44–1.48	0.0008–0.0027	0.0018–0.0037	0.3159–0.3167	0.3149–0.3156
1993-94	8	1.8 (1839)	45	45	NA③	NA③	0.0010–0.0024	0.0012–0.0026	0.2350–0.2356	0.2348–0.2354
	J	1.9 (1859)	45	45.6	200 @ 1.09	1.44–1.48	0.0008–0.0027	0.0018–0.0037	0.3159–0.3167	0.3149–0.3156

NA—Not available
① Check spring free length and out of square.
    Free length: 1.665–1.720 inch
    Maximum allowable out of square: 0.059 inch
② Service limit
③ Check spring free length and out of square.
    Free length: 1.555–1.821 inch
    Maximum allowable out of square: 0.059 inch

PISTON AND RING SPECIFICATIONS

All measurements are given in inches.

Year	Engine ID/VIN	Engine Displacement liter (cc)	Piston Clearance	Ring Gap			Ring Side Clearance		
				Top Compression	Bottom Compression	Oil Control	Top Compression	Bottom Compression	Oil Control
1990	5	1.6 (1597)	0.0060①	0.006–0.012	0.006–0.012	0.008–0.028	0.0010–0.0030	0.0010–0.0030	SNUG
1991	8	1.8 (1839)	0.0015–0.0020	0.006–0.012	0.006–0.012	0.008–0.028	0.0012–0.0026	0.0012–0.0028	SNUG
	J	1.9 (1859)	0.0012–0.0020	0.010–0.030	0.010–0.030	0.016–0.066	0.0015–0.0032	0.0015–0.0035	SNUG
1992	8	1.8 (1839)	0.0015–0.0020	0.006–0.012	0.006–0.012	0.008–0.028	0.0012–0.0026	0.0012–0.0028	SNUG
	J	1.9 (1859)	0.0012–0.0020	0.010–0.030	0.010–0.030	0.016–0.066	0.0015–0.0032	0.0015–0.0035	SNUG
1993-94	8	1.8 (1839)	0.0015–0.0020	0.006–0.012	0.006–0.012	0.008–0.028	0.0012–0.0026	0.0012–0.0028	SNUG
	J	1.9 (1859)	0.0012–0.0020	0.010–0.030	0.010–0.030	0.016–0.066	0.0015–0.0032	0.0015–0.0035	SNUG

① Maximum allowable

TORQUE SPECIFICATIONS

All readings in ft. lbs.

Year	Engine ID/VIN	Engine Displacement Liter (cc)	Cylinder Head Bolts	Main Bearing Bolts	Rod Bearing Bolts	Crankshaft Damper Bolts	Flywheel Bolts	Manifold		Spark Plugs	Lug Nut
								Intake	Exhaust		
1990	5	1.6 (1597)	56–60	40–43	37–41	①	71–76	14–19	12–17	11–17	65–87
1991	8	1.8 (1839)	56–60	40–43	35–37	②	71–76	14–19	28–34	11–17	65–87
	J	1.9 (1859)	③	67–80	26–30	81–96	54–67	12–15	16–19	7–15	65–87
1992	8	1.8 (1839)	56–60	40–43	35–37	②	71–76	14–19	28–34	11–17	65–87
	J	1.9 (1859)	③	67–80	26–30	81–96	54–67	12–15	16–19	7–15	65–87

TORQUE SPECIFICATIONS

All readings in ft. lbs.

Year	Engine ID/VIN	Engine Displacement Liter (cc)	Cylinder Head Bolts	Main Bearing Bolts	Rod Bearing Bolts	Crankshaft Damper Bolts	Flywheel Bolts	Manifold Intake	Manifold Exhaust	Spark Plugs	Lug Nut
1993-94	8	1.8 (1839)	56-60	40-43	35-37	②	71-76	14-19	28-34	11-17	65-87
	J	1.9 (1859)	③	67-80	26-30	81-96	54-67	12-15	16-19	7-15	65-87

① Pulley bolts 36–45 ft. lbs.
   Sprocket bolt 80–94 ft. lbs.
② Pulley bolts 109–152 inch lbs.
   Sprocket bolt 80–87 ft. lbs.
③ Tighten in sequence to 44 ft. lbs.
   Loosen 2 turns
   Retighten in sequence to 44 ft. lbs.
   Turn all bolts, in sequence, 90 degrees
   Turn all bolts, in sequence, an additional
   90 degrees

TORQUE SPECIFICATIONS

Component	English	Metric
Camshaft bearing cap bolts		
1.8L engine:	100–126 inch lbs.	11.3–14.2 Nm
Camshaft sprocket bolt		
1.6L engine:	36–45 ft. lbs.	49–61 Nm
1.8L engine:	36–45 ft. lbs.	49–61 Nm
1.9L engine:	71–84 ft. lbs.	95–115 Nm
Camshaft thrust plate		
1.6L engine:	6–9 ft. lbs.	8–12 Nm
1.8L engine:	69–95 inch lbs.	7.8–11.0 Nm
1.9L engine:	6–9 ft. lbs.	8–13 Nm
Connecting rod bearing cap nuts		
1.6L engine		
Step 1:	25–30 ft. lbs.	34–41 Nm
Step 2:	37–41 ft. lbs.	50–55 Nm
1.8L engine:	35–37 ft. lbs.	47–50 Nm
1.9L engine:	26–30 ft. lbs.	35–41 Nm
Crankshaft damper bolt		
1.9L engine:	81–96 ft. lbs.	110–130 Nm
Crankshaft pulley bolt		
1.6L engine:	36–45 ft. lbs.	49–61 Nm
1.8L engine:	109–152 inch lbs.	12–17 Nm
Crankshaft seal retainer bolts		
1.6L engine:	69–95 inch lbs.	7.8–11.0 Nm
1.8L engine:	69–95 inch lbs.	7.8–11.0 Nm
1.9L engine:	72–96 inch lbs.	8–11 Nm
Crankshaft sprocket bolt		
1.6L engine:	80–94 ft. lbs.	108–128 Nm
1.8L engine:	80–87 ft. lbs.	108–118 Nm
Cylinder head bolt		
1.6L engine:	56–60 ft. lbs.	76–81 Nm
1.8L engine:	56–60 ft. lbs.	76–81 Nm
1.9L engine *		
Step 1:	29–44 ft. lbs.	40–60 Nm
Step 2:	loosen 2 turns	loosen 2 turns
Step 3:	44 ft. lbs.	60 Nm
Step 4:	+ 90 degrees turn	+ 90 degrees turn
Step 5:	+ 90 degrees turn	+ 90 degrees turn

* NOTE: Use new bolts and oil the
threads

TORQUE SPECIFICATIONS

Component	English	Metric
Engine-to-transaxle		
1.6L engine:	47–66 ft. lbs.	64–89 Nm
1.8L engine		
Manual transaxle:	47–66 ft. lbs.	64–89 Nm
Automatic transaxle:	41–59 ft. lbs.	55–80 Nm
1.9L engine:	27–38 ft. lbs.	37–52 Nm
Engine/transaxle mounts		
1.8L engine		
Engine mount bolt/nuts:	49–69 ft. lbs.	67–93 Nm
Transaxle front mount nuts:	27–38 ft. lbs.	37–52 Nm
Engine mount through bolt/nut:	49–69 ft. lbs.	67–93 Nm
Engine mount-to-engine nuts:	54–76 ft. lbs.	74–103 Nm
Transaxle upper mount bolts:	32–45 ft. lbs.	43–61 Nm
Transaxle upper mount nuts:	49–69 ft. lbs.	67–93 Nm
Exhaust manifold		
1.6L engine:	23–34 ft. lbs.	31–46 Nm
1.8L engine:	28–34 ft. lbs.	38–46 Nm
1.9L engine:	16–19 ft. lbs.	21–26 Nm
Exhaust flange-to-manifold nuts		
1.8L engine:	23–34 ft. lbs.	31–46 Nm
1.9L engine:	25–35 ft. lbs.	34–47 Nm
Flywheel-to-crankshaft bolts		
1.6L engine:	71–76 ft. lbs.	96–103 Nm
1.8L engine:	71–76 ft. lbs.	96–103 Nm
1.9L engine:	54–67 ft. lbs.	73–91 Nm
Flywheel-to-torque converter bolts:	25–36 ft. lbs.	34–49 Nm
Intake manifold		
1.6L engine:	14–19 ft. lbs.	19–26 Nm
1.8L engine:	14–19 ft. lbs.	19–26 Nm
1.9L engine:	12–15 ft. lbs.	16–20 Nm
Main bearing cap bolts		
1.6L engine		
Step 1:	22–27 ft. lbs.	36–43 Nm
Step 2:	40–43 ft. lbs.	54–59 Nm
1.8L engine:	40–43 ft. lbs.	54–59 Nm
1.9L engine:	67–80 ft. lbs.	90–108 Nm
Oil pan-to-block		
1.6L engine:	69–78 inch lbs.	8–9 Nm
1.8L engine:	69–95 inch lbs.	7.8–11 Nm
1.9L engine:	15–22 ft. lbs.	20–30 Nm
Oil pan-to-transaxle bolts		
1.8L engine:	27–38 ft. lbs.	37–52 Nm
1.9L engine:	30–40 ft. lbs.	40–55 Nm
Oil pan drain plug		
1.6L engine:	22–30 ft. lbs.	29–41 Nm
1.8L engine:	22–30 ft. lbs.	29–41 Nm
1.9L engine:	15–22 ft. lbs.	20–30 Nm
Oil pump attaching bolts		
1.6L engine:	14–19 ft. lbs.	19–25 Nm
1.8L engine:	14–19 ft. lbs.	19–25 Nm
1.9L engine:	8–12 ft. lbs.	11–16 Nm
Oil pump pickup bolts		
1.6L engine:	69–95 inch lbs.	8–11 Nm
1.8L engine:	69–95 inch lbs.	7.8–11.0 Nm
1.9L engine:	7–9 ft. lbs.	10–13 Nm
Rocker arm/shaft bolt		
1.6L engine:	16–21 ft. lbs.	22–28 Nm
1.9L engine:	17–22 ft. lbs.	23–30 Nm

TORQUE SPECIFICATIONS

Component	English	Metric
Rocker arm (valve) cover		
1.6L engine:	43–78 inch lbs.	5–9 Nm
1.8L engine:	43–78 inch lbs.	5–9 Nm
1.9L engine:	4–9 ft. lbs.	5–12 Nm
Spark plug		
1.6L engine:	11–17 ft. lbs.	15–23 Nm
1.8L engine:	11–17 ft. lbs.	15–23 Nm
1.9L engine:	8–15 ft. lbs.	10–20 Nm
Starter-to-block bolts		
1.6L engine:	23–30 ft. lbs.	31–41 Nm
1.8L engine:	15–20 ft. lbs.	20–27 Nm
1.9L engine:	15–20 ft. lbs.	20–27 Nm
Thermostat housing		
1.6L engine:	14–22 ft. lbs.	19–30 Nm
1.8L engine:	14–19 ft. lbs.	19–25 Nm
1.9L engine:	6–9 ft. lbs.	8–11 Nm
Throttle body bolts		
1.8L engine:	14–19 ft. lbs.	19–25 Nm
1.9L engine:	15–22 ft. lbs.	20–30 Nm
Timing cover		
1.6L engine:	69–95 inch lbs.	8–11 Nm
1.8L engine:	69–95 inch lbs.	8–11 Nm
1.9L engine		
Nuts:	3–5 ft. lbs.	5–7 Nm
Bolts:	5–7 ft. lbs.	7–9 Nm
Water pump		
1.6L engine:	14–19 ft. lbs.	19–25 Nm
1.8L engine:	14–19 ft. lbs.	19–25 Nm
1.9L engine:	15–22 ft. lbs.	20–30 Nm

BRAKE SPECIFICATIONS

All measurements in inches unless noted.

Year	Model	Master Cylinder Bore	Brake Disc Original Thickness	Brake Disc Minimum Thickness	Maximum Runout	Brake Drum Diameter Original Inside Diameter	Brake Drum Diameter Max. Wear Limit	Brake Drum Diameter Maximum Machine Diameter	Minimum Lining Thickness Front	Minimum Lining Thickness Rear
1990	Tracer	0.875	①	②	0.003	7.870	7.910	NA	0.120	0.040
1991	Tracer	0.875	③	④	0.004	9.000	9.040	NA	0.080	0.040
1992	Tracer	0.875	③	④	0.004	9.000	9.040	NA	0.080	0.040
1993-94	Tracer	0.875	③	④	0.004	7.870	7.910	NA	0.080	0.040

NA—Not available
① Front 0.710
  Rear 0.390
② Front 0.630
  Rear 0.350
③ Front 0.870
  Rear 0.350
④ Front 0.790
  Rear 0.280

WHEEL ALIGNMENT

Year	Model		Caster Range (deg.)	Caster Preferred Setting (deg.)	Camber Range (deg.)	Camber Preferred Setting (deg.)	Toe-in (in.)	Steering Axis Inclination (deg.)
1990	Tracer	Front	$27/32P$–$2\,11/32P$	$1\,19/32P$	$1/16P$–$1\,9/16P$	$13/16P$	$5/64$	$12\,11/32$
		Rear	—	—	$3/4N$–$3/4P$	0	$5/64$	—
1991	Tracer	Front	$1P$–$2\,7/8P$	$1\,15/16P$	$27/32N$–$11/16P$	$3/32N$	$3/32$	$23\,13/16$
		Rear	—	—	$1\,3/32N$–$7/16P$	$11/32N$	$3/32$	—
1992	Tracer	Front	$1P$–$2\,7/8P$	$1\,15/16P$	$27/32N$–$11/16P$	$3/32N$	$3/32$	$23\,13/16$
		Rear	—	—	$1\,3/32N$–$7/16P$	$11/32N$	$3/32$	—
1993–94	Tracer	Front	$1P$–$2\,7/8P$	$1\,15/16P$	$27/32N$–$11/16P$	$3/32N$	$3/32$	$23\,13/16$
		Rear	—	—	$1\,3/32N$–$7/16P$	$11/32N$	$3/32$	—

N—Negative
P—Positive

AIR CONDITIONING BELT TENSION

Year	Model	Engine Displacement Liters (cc)	Belt Type	Specifications (lbs.) New	Used
1990	Tracer	1.6 (1597)	Poly-V	110–132	95–110
1991	Tracer	1.8 (1844)	Serpentine	110–132	95–110
1992	Tracer	1.8 (1844)	Serpentine	110–132	95–110
1993	Tracer	1.8 (1844)	Serpentine	110–132	95–110

REFRIGERANT CAPACITIES

Year	Model	Refrigerant (oz.)	Oil (fl. oz.)	Compressor Type
1990	Tracer	24.8	10.0	NA
1991	Tracer	NA	7.75	10P13
1992	Tracer	NA	7.75	10P13
1993	Tracer	NA	7.75	10P13

NOTE: At the time of publication, refrigerant capacity information relating to R-134a was not available from the manufacturer.

MAINTENANCE INTERVALS—TYPE A: NORMAL SERVICE
Tracer

TO BE SERVICED	TYPE OF SERVICE	7.5	15	22.5	30	37.5	45	52.5	60
Oxygen Sensor	I				✔				✔
Ignition Timing	I				✔				✔
Vacuum Lines and Hoses	I				✔				✔
Ignition Wires	I				✔				✔
Spark Plugs	R				✔				✔

MAINTENANCE INTERVALS—TYPE A: NORMAL SERVICE
Tracer

TO BE SERVICED	TYPE OF SERVICE	VEHICLE MILEAGE INTERVAL (X1000)							
		7.5	15	22.5	30	37.5	45	52.5	60
Engine Oil and Filter	R	✔	✔	✔	✔	✔	✔	✔	✔
Engine Air Cleaner Element	R				✔				✔
Crankcase Emission Filter	R④				✔				✔
PCV Valve	R⑤				✔				✔
Fuel Filter	R				✔				✔
Charcoal Canister	I				✔				✔
Fuel/Vapor Return Lines	I				✔				✔
Fuel Tank Cap and Restrictor	I				✔				✔
Coolant System	I		✔		✔		✔		✔
Exhaust Pipe and Muffler	I				✔				✔
Catalytic Converter and Shield	I				✔				✔
EGR System	I				✔				✔
Valve Clearance	I①		✔		✔		✔		✔
Timing Belt	I/R②								✔
Idle Speed System	I				✔				✔
Throttle Body	I		✔		✔		✔		✔
Drive Belts	I				✔				✔
Brake Pads, Front	I		✔		✔		✔		✔
Brake Pads, Rear	I		✔		✔		✔		✔
Brake Shoes, Rear	I				✔				✔
Brake Drums and Rotors	I				✔				✔
Brake Hoses and Lines	I				✔				✔
Battery Connections	I		✔		✔		✔		✔
Ball Joints	I				✔				✔
Engine Coolant	R				✔				✔
Automatic Transaxle Fluid	I	✔	✔	✔	✔	✔	✔	✔	✔
Manual Transaxle Fluid	I		✔		✔		✔		✔
Clutch Pedal Operation	I⑤		✔		✔		✔		✔
Tire Rotation	I	✔		✔		✔		✔	
Wheel Bearings	L③								✔
Driveshaft Dust Boots	I				✔				✔
Steering System	I				✔				✔
Power Steering Fluid	I		✔		✔		✔		✔
Brake Fluid	I		✔		✔		✔		✔
Hinges, Latches, etc.	L		✔		✔		✔		✔
Seat Belt Operation	I		✔		✔		✔		✔

FOR COMPLETE WARRANTY COVERAGE CONSULT INDIVIDUAL VEHICLE MANUFACTURER'S WARRANTY MAINTENANCE GUIDE.

I—Inspect
L—Lubricate
R—Replace
① Adjust every 15,000 miles, 1.6L engine only—all others have hydraulic lifters
② Replace every 60,000 miles—1.6L and 1.8L engines; inspect every 60,000 miles for 1.9L engine
③ Repack every 60,000 miles for 1990 only; all others have sealed bearings
④ 1.9L engine only
⑤ If applicable

MAINTENANCE INTERVALS—TYPE B: SEVERE SERVICE
Tracer

TO BE SERVICED	TYPE OF SERVICE	VEHICLE MILEAGE INTERVAL (X1000)									
		3	6	9	12	15	18	21	24	27	30
Oxygen Sensor	I										✔
Ignition Timing	I										✔
Vacuum Lines and Hoses	I										✔
Ignition Wires	I										✔
Spark Plugs	I/R①					✔					✔
Engine Oil and Filter	R	✔	✔	✔	✔	✔	✔	✔	✔	✔	✔
Engine Air Cleaner Element	I/R②					✔					✔
Crankcase Emission Filter	R③										✔
PCV Valve	R⑧										✔
Fuel Filter	R④										✔
Charcoal Canister	I										✔
Fuel/Vapor Return Lines	I										✔
Fuel Tank Cap and Restrictor	I										✔
Coolant System	I					✔					✔
Exhaust Pipe and Muffler	I										✔
Catalytic Converter and Shield	I										✔
EGR System	I										✔
Valve Clearance	I⑤					✔					✔
Timing Belt	I/R⑥										
Idle Speed System	I										✔
Throttle Body	I					✔					✔
Drive Belts	I										✔
Brake Pads, Front	I					✔					✔
Brake Pads, Rear	I					✔					✔
Brake Shoes, Rear	I										✔
Brake Drums and Rotors	I										✔
Brake Hoses and Lines	I										✔
Battery Connections	I					✔					✔
Ball Joints	I										✔
Engine Coolant	R										✔
Automatic Transaxle Fluid	R										✔
Manual Transaxle Fluid	I					✔					✔
Clutch Pedal Operation	I⑧					✔					✔
Tire Rotation	I⑨		✔					✔			
Wheel Bearings	L⑦										
Driveshaft Dust Boots	I										✔
Steering System	I										✔
Power Steering Fluid	I					✔					✔
Brake Fluid	I					✔					✔

MAINTENANCE INTERVALS—TYPE B: SEVERE SERVICE
Tracer

TO BE SERVICED	TYPE OF SERVICE	VEHICLE MILEAGE INTERVAL (X1000)									
		3	6	9	12	15	18	21	24	27	30
Hinges, Latches, etc.	L					✔					✔
Seat Belt Operation	I					✔					✔

FOR COMPLETE WARRANTY COVERAGE CONSULT INDIVIDUAL VEHICLE MANUFACTURER'S WARRANTY MAINTENANCE GUIDE.

I—Inspect
L—Lubricate
R—Replace
① Inspect/clean every 15,000 miles; replace every 30,000 miles
② Inspect every 15,000 miles (1.8L engine only); replace every 30,000 miles—all engines
③ 1.9L engine only
④ Replace every 60,000 miles

⑤ Adjust every 15,000 miles, 1.6L engine only; all others use hydraulic lifters
⑥ Replace every 60,000 miles for 1.6 and 1.8L engines; inspect every 60,000 for 1.9L engine
⑦ Repack every 60,000 miles for 1990 only; all others sealed bearings
⑧ If applicable
⑨ First 6,000 miles, then every 15,000 miles, or as required

FIRING ORDERS

NOTE: To avoid confusion, always replace spark plug wires one at a time.

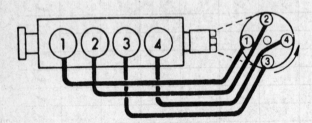

1.6L Engine
Engine Firing Order: 1–3–4–2
Distributor Rotation: Counterclockwise

FRONT OF CAR

1.9L Engine
Engine Firing Order: 1–3–4–2
Distributorless Ignition System

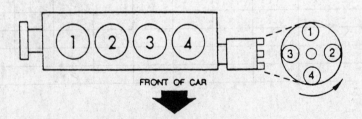

FRONT OF CAR

1.8L Engine
Engine Firing Order: 1–3–4–2
Distributor Rotation: Counterclockwise

CYLINDER HEAD TORQUE SEQUENCES

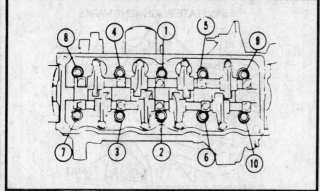

Cylinder head bolt torque sequence—1.6L engine

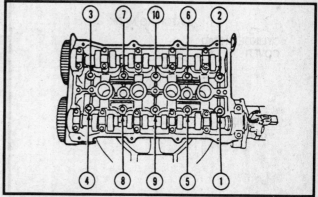

Cylinder head bolt removal sequence—1.8L engine

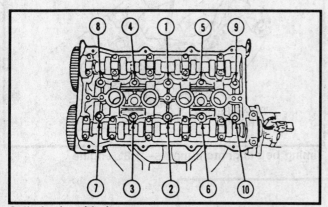

Cylinder head bolt torque sequence—1.8L engine

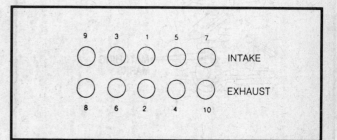

Cylinder head bolt torque sequence—1.9L engine

TIMING MARK LOCATIONS

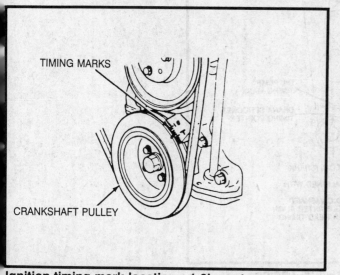

Ignition timing mark location—1.6L engine

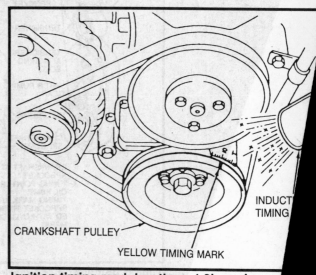

Ignition timing mark location—1.8L engine

TIMING BELT ALIGNMENT MARKS

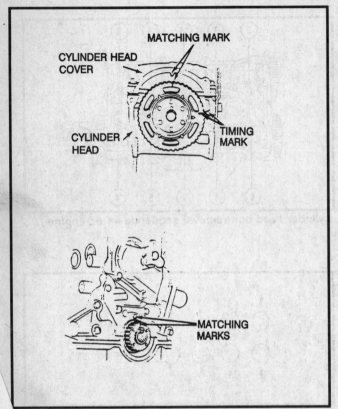

Timing belt alignment marks—1.6L engine

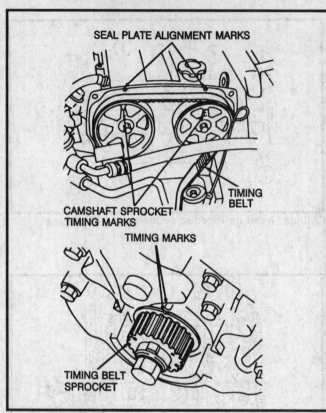

Timing belt alignment marks—1.8L engine

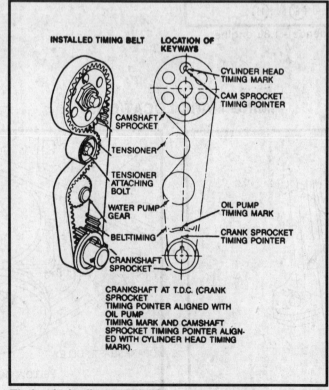

Timing belt alignment marks—1.9L engine

AIR CONDITIONING SERVICE VALVE
LOCATIONS

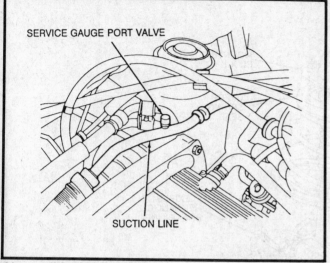

Air conditioning low side service valve location

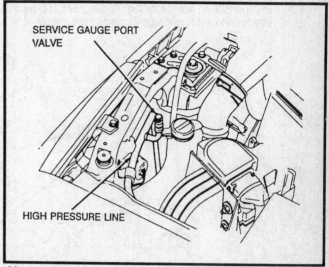

Air conditioning high side service valve location

WHEEL ALIGNMENT ADJUSTMENT
LOCATIONS

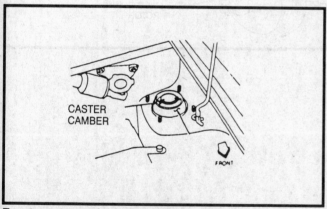

Front caster and camber adjustment

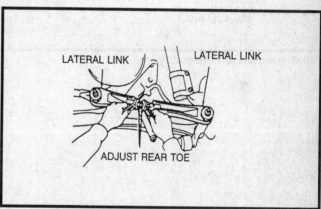

Rear toe adjustment

The front suspension is a MacPherson strut design with cast steering knuckles. The shock absorber strut assembly includes a mounting block, a thrust bearing, an upper spring seat, a rubber spring seat, a bound stopper and a coil spring mounted to the shock strut.

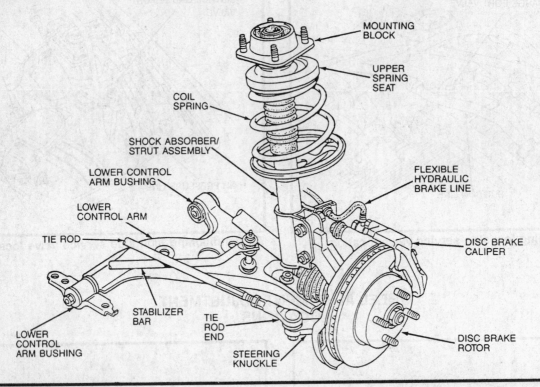

MOUNTING BLOCK

UPPER SPRING SEAT

COIL SPRING

SHOCK ABSORBER/ STRUT ASSEMBLY

LOWER CONTROL ARM BUSHING

LOWER CONTROL ARM

TIE ROD

STABILIZER BAR

TIE ROD END

LOWER CONTROL ARM BUSHING

STEERING KNUCKLE

FLEXIBLE HYDRAULIC BRAKE LINE

DISC BRAKE CALIPER

DISC BRAKE ROTOR

Front suspension assembly

SPECIFICATION CHARTS

VEHICLE IDENTIFICATION CHART

It is important for servicing and ordering parts to be certain of the vehicle and engine identification. The VIN (vehicle identification number) is a 17 digit number visible through the windshield on the driver's side of the dash and contains the vehicle and engine identification codes. The tenth digit indicates model year and the eighth digit indicates engine code. It can be interpreted as follows:

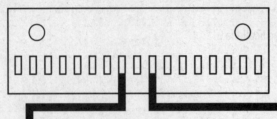

Engine Code

Code	Liters	Cu. In. (cc)	Cyl.	Fuel Sys.	Eng. Mfg.
A	2.3	140 (2295)	4	EFI	Ford
M	2.3	140 (2295)	4	EFI	Ford
4	3.8	232 (3801)	6	SEFI	Ford
R	3.8	232 (3801)	6	SEFI	Ford
C②	3.8	232 (3801)	6	SEFI	Ford
E	5.0	302 (4943)	8	SEFI	Ford
T	5.0	302 (4943)	8	SEFI	Ford
V	4.6	281 (4601)	8	SEFI	Ford
E①	5.0	302 (4943)	8	SEFI	Ford

Model Year

Code	Year
L	1990
M	1991
N	1992
P	1993
R	1994

EFI—Electronic Fuel Injection
SEFI—Sequential Electronic Fuel Injection
① Cobra
② Early production vehicles may be "C"

ENGINE IDENTIFICATION

Year	Model	Engine Displacement Liters (cc)	Engine Series (ID/VIN)	Fuel System	No. of Cylinders	Engine Type
1990	Mustang	2.3 (2295)	A	EFI	4	OHC
	Mustang	5.0 (4943)	E	SEFI	8	OHV
	Thunderbird	3.8 (3801)	4	SEFI	6	OHV
	Thunderbird SC	3.8 (3801)	R①	SEFI	6	OHV
	Cougar	3.8 (3801)	4	SEFI	6	OHV
	Cougar XR7	3.8 (3801)	R①	SEFI	6	OHV
	Mark VII	5.0 (4943)	E	SEFI	8	OHV
1991	Mustang	2.3 (2295)	M	EFI	4	OHC
	Mustang	5.0 (4943)	E	SEFI	8	OHV
	Thunderbird	3.8 (3801)	4	SEFI	6	OHV
	Thunderbird SC	3.8 (3801)	R	SEFI	6	OHV
	Thunderbird	5.0 (4943)	T	SEFI	8	OHV
	Cougar	3.8 (3801)	4	SEFI	6	OHV
	Cougar	5.0 (4943)	T	SEFI	8	OHV
	Mark VII	5.0 (4943)	E	SEFI	8	OHV

ENGINE IDENTIFICATION

Year	Model	Engine Displacement Liters (cc)	Engine Series (ID/VIN)	Fuel System	No. of Cylinders	Engine Type
1992	Mustang	2.3 (2295)	M	EFI	4	OHC
	Mustang	5.0 (4943)	E	SEFI	8	OHV
	Thunderbird	3.8 (3801)	4	SEFI	6	OHV
	Thunderbird SC	3.8 (3801)	R	SEFI	6	OHV
	Thunderbird	5.0 (4943)	T	SEFI	8	OHV
	Cougar	3.8 (3801)	4	SEFI	6	OHV
	Cougar	5.0 (4943)	T	SEFI	8	OHV
	Mark VII	5.0 (4943)	E	SEFI	8	OHV
1993-94	Mustang	5.0 (4943)	E	SEFI②	8	OHV
	Mustang	2.3 (2295)	M	EFI	4	OHC
	Mustang	5.0 (4943)	E	SEFI	8	OHV
	Thunderbird	3.8 (3801)	4	SEFI	6	OHV
	Thunderbird SC	3.8 (3801)	R	SEFI	6	OHV
	Thunderbird	5.0 (4943)	T	SEFI	8	OHV
	Cougar	3.8 (3801)	4	SEFI	6	OHV
	Cougar	5.0 (4943)	T	SEFI	8	OHV
	Mark VIII	4.6 (4601)	V	SEFI	8	DOHC

EFI—Electronic Fuel Injection
SEFI—Sequential Electronic Fuel Injection
OHC—Overhead Cam
OHV—Overhead Valve
DOHC—Dual Overhead Cam
① Early production vehicles may be ''C''.
② Cobra

GENERAL ENGINE SPECIFICATIONS

Year	Engine ID/VIN	Engine Displacement Liters (cc)	Fuel System Type	Net Horsepower @ rpm	Net Torque @ rpm (ft. lbs.)	Bore × Stroke (in.)	Compression Ratio	Oil Pressure @ rpm
1990	A	2.3 (2295)	EFI	88 @ 4000	132 @ 2600	3.78 × 3.12	9.5:1	40–60 @ 2000①
	4	3.8 (3801)	SEFI	140 @ 3800	215 @ 2400	3.81 × 3.39	9.0:1	40–60 @ 2500①
	R	3.8 (3801)	SEFI	210 @ 4000	315 @ 2600	3.81 × 3.39	8.2:1	40–60 @ 2500①
	E	5.0 (4943)	SEFI	225 @ 4200	300 @ 3200	4.00 × 3.00	9.0:1	40–60 @ 2000①
1991	M	2.3 (2295)	EFI	105 @ 4600	135 @ 2600	3.78 × 3.12	9.5:1	40–60 @ 2000①
	4	3.8 (3801)	SEFI	140 @ 3800	215 @ 2400	3.81 × 3.39	9.0:1	40–60 @ 2500①
	R	3.8 (3801)	SEFI	210 @ 4000	315 @ 2600	3.81 × 3.39	8.2:1	40–60 @ 2500①
	E	5.0 (4943)	SEFI	225 @ 4200	300 @ 3200	4.00 × 3.39	9.0:1	40–60 @ 2000①
	T	5.0 (4943)	SEFI	200 @ 4000	275 @ 3000	4.00 × 3.39	9.0:1	40–60 @ 2000①
1992	M	2.3 (2295)	EFI	105 @ 4600	135 @ 2600	3.78 × 3.12	9.5:1	40–60 @ 2000①
	4	3.8 (3801)	SEFI	140 @ 3800	215 @ 2400	3.81 × 3.39	9.0:1	40–60 @ 2500①
	R	3.8 (3801)	SEFI	210 @ 4000	315 @ 2600	3.81 × 3.39	8.2:1	40–60 @ 2500①
	E	5.0 (4943)	SEFI	225 @ 4200	300 @ 3200	4.00 × 3.00	9.0:1	40–60 @ 2000①
	T	5.0 (4943)	SEFI	200 @ 4000	275 @ 3000	4.00 × 3.39	9.0:1	40–60 @ 2000①

GENERAL ENGINE SPECIFICATIONS

Year	Engine ID/VIN	Engine Displacement Liters (cc)	Fuel System Type	Net Horsepower @ rpm	Net Torque @ rpm (ft. lbs.)	Bore × Stroke (in.)	Compression Ratio	Oil Pressure @ rpm
1993–94	M	2.3 (2295)	EFI	105 @ 4600	135 @ 2600	3.78 × 3.12	9.5:1	40–60 @ 2000 ①
	4	3.8 (3801)	SEFI	140 @ 3800	215 @ 2400	3.81 × 3.39	9.0:1	40–60 @ 2500 ①
	R	3.8 (3801)	SEFI	210 @ 4000	315 @ 2600	3.81 × 3.39	8.2:1	40–60 @ 2500 ①
	E	5.0 (4943)	SEFI	225 @ 4200	300 @ 3200	4.00 × 3.00	9.0:1	40–60 @ 2000 ①
	T	5.0 (4943)	SEFI	200 @ 4000	275 @ 3000	4.00 × 3.39	9.0:1	40–60 @ 2000 ①
	V	4.6 (4601)	SEFI	280 @ 5500	285 @ 4500	3.55 × 3.54	9.8:1	20–45 @ 1500 ①
	E	5.0 (4943)	SEFI ②	235 @ 4600	280 @ 4000	4.00 × 3.00	9.0:1	40–60 @ 2000 ①

EFI—Electronic Fuel Injection
SEFI—Sequential Electronic Fuel Injection
① With engine at normal operating temperature
② Cobra

GASOLINE ENGINE TUNE-UP SPECIFICATIONS

Year	Engine ID/VIN	Engine Displacement Liters (cc)	Spark Plugs Gap (in.)	Ignition Timing (deg.) MT	Ignition Timing (deg.) AT	Fuel Pump (psi) ②	Idle Speed (rpm) MT	Idle Speed (rpm) AT	Valve Clearance In.	Valve Clearance Ex.
1990	A	2.3 (2295)	0.044	10B	10B	35–40	①	①	Hyd.	Hyd.
	4	3.8 (3801)	0.054	—	10B	35–40	—	①	Hyd.	Hyd.
	R	3.8 (3801)	0.054	10B	10B	35–40	700–800	550–650	Hyd.	Hyd.
	E	5.0 (4943)	0.054	10B	10B	35–40	①	①	Hyd.	Hyd.
1991	M	2.3 (2295)	0.044	10B	10B	35–40	①	①	Hyd.	Hyd.
	4	3.8 (3801)	0.054	—	10B	35–40	—	①	Hyd.	Hyd.
	R	3.8 (3801)	0.054	10B	10B	35–40	750	550	Hyd.	Hyd.
	E	5.0 (4943)	0.054	10B	10B	35–40	①	①	Hyd.	Hyd.
	T	5.0 (4943)	0.054	—	10B	35–40	—	①	Hyd.	Hyd.
1992	M	2.3 (2295)	0.044	10B	10B	35–40	①	①	Hyd.	Hyd.
	4	3.8 (3801)	0.054	—	10B	35–40	①	①	Hyd.	Hyd.
	R	3.8 (3801)	0.054	10B	10B	35–40	①	①	Hyd.	Hyd.
	E	5.0 (4943)	0.054	10B	10B	35–40	①	①	Hyd.	Hyd.
	T	5.0 (4943)	0.054	—	10B	35–40	①	①	Hyd.	Hyd.
1993	M	2.3 (2295)	0.044	10B	10B	35–40	①	①	Hyd.	Hyd.
	4	3.8 (3801)	0.054	—	10B	35–40	①	①	Hyd.	Hyd.
	R	3.8 (3801)	0.054	10B	10B	35–40	①	①	Hyd.	Hyd.
	E	5.0 (4943)	0.054	10B	10B	35–40	①	①	Hyd.	Hyd.
	T	5.0 (4943)	0.054	—	10B	35–40	①	①	Hyd.	Hyd.
	V	4.6 (4601)	①	—	10B	35–40	①	①	Hyd.	Hyd.
1994	REFER TO UNDERHOOD SPECIFICATIONS STICKER									

NOTE: The lowest cylinder pressure should be within 75% of the highest cylinder pressure reading. For example, if the highest cylinder is 134 psi, the lowest should be 101. Engine should be at normal operating temperature with throttle valve in the wide open position.
The underhood specifications sticker often reflects tune-up specification changes in production. Sticker figures must be used if they disagree with those in this chart.
B—Before Top Dead Center
Hyd.—Hydraulic
① Refer to Vehicle Emission Information Label
② Key on, engine off

CAPACITIES

Year	Model	Engine ID/VIN	Engine Displacement Liters (cc)	Engine Crankcase with Filter (qts.)	Transmission (pts.)			Transfer case (pts.)	Drive Axle		Fuel Tank (gal.)	Cooling System (qts.)
					4-Spd	5-Spd	Auto.		Front (pts.)	Rear (pts.)		
1990	Mustang	A	2.3 (2295)	5	—	5.6	19.4	—	—	①	15.4	②
	Mustang	E	5.0 (4943)	5	—	5.6	24.6	—	—	①	15.4	14.1
	Thunderbird	4	3.8 (3801)	5	—	—	24.6	—	—	③	18.8	11.8
	Thunderbird SC	R	3.8 (3801)	5	—	6.3	24.6	—	—	③	18.8	11.9
	Cougar	4	3.8 (3801)	5	—	—	24.6	—	—	③	18.8	11.8
	Cougar XR7	R	3.8 (3801)	5	—	6.3	24.6	—	—	③	18.8	11.9
	Mark VII	E	5.0 (4943)	5	—	—	24.6	—	—	3.75	22.1	14.1
1991	Mustang	M	2.3 (2295)	5	—	5.6	19.4	—	—	①	15.4	②
	Mustang	E	5.0 (4943)	5	—	5.6	24.6	—	—	①	15.4	14.1
	Thunderbird	4	3.8 (3801)	5	—	—	24.6	—	—	③	19.0	11.8
	Thunderbird SC	R	3.8 (3801)	5	—	6.3	24.6	—	—	③	19.0	11.9
	Thunderbird	T	5.0 (4943)	5	—	—	24.6	—	—	③	19.0	14.1
	Cougar	4	3.8 (3801)	5	—	—	24.6	—	—	③	19.0	11.8
	Cougar	T	5.0 (4943)	5	—	—	24.6	—	—	③	19.0	14.1
	Mark VII	E	5.0 (4943)	5	—	—	24.6	—	—	3.75	22.1	14.1
1992	Mustang	M	2.3 (2295)	5	—	5.6	19.4	—	—	①	15.4	②
	Mustang	E	5.0 (4943)	5	—	5.6	24.6	—	—	①	15.4	14.1
	Thunderbird	4	3.8 (3801)	5	—	—	24.6	—	—	③	19.0	11.8
	Thunderbird SC	R	3.8 (3801)	5	—	6.3	24.6	—	—	③	19.0	11.9
	Thunderbird	T	5.0 (4943)	5	—	—	24.6	—	—	③	19.0	14.1
	Cougar	4	3.8 (3801)	5	—	—	24.6	—	—	③	19.0	11.8
	Cougar	T	5.0 (4943)	5	—	—	24.6	—	—	③	19.0	14.1
	Mark VII	E	5.0 (4943)	5	—	—	24.6	—	—	3.75	22.1	14.1
1993-94	Mustang	M	2.3 (2295)	5	—	5.6	19.4	—	—	①	15.4	②
	Mustang	E	5.0 (4943)	5	—	5.6	24.6	—	—	①	15.4	14.1
	Thunderbird	4	3.8 (3801)	5	—	—	24.6	—	—	③	18.0	11.8
	Thunderbird SC	R	3.8 (3801)	5	—	6.3	24.6	—	—	③	18.0	11.9
	Thunderbird	T	5.0 (4943)	5	—	—	24.6	—	—	③	18.0	14.1
	Cougar	4	3.8 (3801)	5	—	—	24.6	—	—	③	19.0	11.8
	Cougar	T	5.0 (4943)	5	—	—	24.6	—	—	③	19.0	14.1
	Mark VIII	V	4.6 (4601)	6	—	—	25.0	—	—	3.0	18.0	16.0

① With 7.5 in. axle—3.5 pts.
With 7.5 in. limited slip, 8.8 in. standard and limited slip axles—3.75 pts.
② With manual transmission and A/C—9.7 qts.
Except with manual transmission and A/C—10 qts.
③ With 7.5 in. axle—3 pts.
With 7.5 in. limited slip axle—2.75 pts.
With 8.8 in. standard and limited slip axles—3.25 pts.

CAMSHAFT SPECIFICATIONS
All measurements given in inches.

Year	Engine ID/VIN	Engine Displacement Liters (cc)	Journal Diameter 1	2	3	4	5	Elevation In.	Ex.	Bearing Clearance	Camshaft End Play
1990	A	2.3 (2295)	1.7713–1.7720	1.7713–1.7720	1.7713–1.7720	1.7713–1.7720	—	0.4000	0.4000	0.001–0.006	0.0010–0.0090
	4	3.8 (3801)	2.0505–2.0515	2.0505–2.0515	2.0505–2.0515	2.0505–2.0515	—	0.2400–0.2450	0.2540–0.2590	0.001–0.003	①
	R	3.8 (3801)	2.0505–2.0515	2.0505–2.0515	2.0505–2.0515	2.0505–2.0515	—	0.2400–0.2450	0.2540–0.2590	0.001–0.003	①
	E	5.0 (4943)	2.0805–2.0815	2.0655–2.0665	2.0505–2.0515	2.0355–2.0365	2.0205–2.0215	0.2780	0.2780	0.001–0.006	0.0050–0.0090
1991	M	2.3 (2295)	1.7713–1.7720	1.7713–1.7720	1.7713–1.7720	1.7713–1.7720	—	0.2381	0.2381	0.001–0.006	0.0010–0.0090
	4	3.8 (3801)	2.0505–2.0515	2.0505–2.0515	2.0505–2.0515	2.0505–2.0515	—	0.2400–0.2450	0.2540–0.2590	0.001–0.003	0.0010–0.0060
	R	3.8 (3801)	2.0505–2.0515	2.0505–2.0515	2.0505–2.0515	2.0505–2.0515	—	0.2400–0.2450	0.2540–0.2590	0.001–0.003	0.0010–0.0060
	E	5.0 (4943)	2.0805–2.0815	2.0655–2.0665	2.0505–2.0515	2.0355–2.0365	2.0205–2.0215	0.2780	0.2780	0.001–0.006	0.0050–0.0090
	T	5.0 (4943)	2.0805–2.0815	2.0655–2.0665	2.0505–2.0515	2.0355–2.0365	2.0205–2.0215	0.2780	0.2780	0.001–0.006	0.0050–0.0090
1992	M	2.3 (2295)	1.7713–1.7720	1.7713–1.7720	1.7713–1.7720	1.7713–1.7720	—	0.2381	0.2381	0.001–0.006	0.0010–0.0090
	4	3.8 (3801)	2.0505–2.0515	2.0505–2.0515	2.0505–2.0515	2.0505–2.0515	—	0.2400–0.2450	0.2540–0.2590	0.001–0.003	0.0010–0.0060
	R	3.8 (3801)	2.0505–2.0515	2.0505–2.0515	2.0505–2.0515	2.0505–2.0515	—	0.2400–0.2450	0.2540–0.2590	0.001–0.003	0.0010–0.0060
	E	5.0 (4943)	2.0805–2.0815	2.0655–2.0665	2.0505–2.0515	2.0355–2.0365	2.0205–2.0215	0.2780	0.2780	0.001–0.006	0.0050–0.0090
	T	5.0 (4943)	2.0805–2.0815	2.0655–2.0665	2.0505–2.0515	2.0355–2.0365	2.0205–2.0215	0.2780	0.2780	0.001–0.006	0.0050–0.0090
1993–94	M	2.3 (2295)	1.7713–1.7720	1.7713–1.7720	1.7713–1.7720	1.7713–1.7720	—	0.2381	0.2381	0.001–0.006	0.0010–0.0090
	4	3.8 (3801)	2.0505–2.0515	2.0505–2.0515	2.0505–2.0515	2.0505–2.0515	—	0.2400–0.2450	0.2540–0.2590	0.001–0.003	0.0010–0.0060
	R	3.8 (3801)	2.0505–2.0515	2.0505–2.0515	2.0505–2.0515	2.0505–2.0515	—	0.2400–0.2450	0.2540–0.2590	0.001–0.003	0.0010–0.0060
	E	5.0 (4943)	2.0805–2.0815	2.0655–2.0665	2.0505–2.0515	2.0355–2.0365	2.0205–2.0215	0.2780	0.2780	0.001–0.006	0.0050–0.0090
	T	5.0 (4943)	2.0805–2.0815	2.0655–2.0665	2.0505–2.0515	2.0355–2.0365	2.0205–2.0215	0.2780	0.2780	0.001–0.006	0.0050–0.0090
	V	4.6 (4601)	1.0605–1.0615	1.0605–1.0615	1.0605–1.0615	1.0605–1.0615	1.0605–1.0615	②	0.2186	0.001–0.005	0.0010–0.0090
	E③	5.0 (4943)	2.8050–2.8150	2.8050–2.8150	2.8050–2.8150	2.8050–2.8150	2.8050–2.8150	0.2822	0.2822	0.001–0.006	0.0050–0.0090

① The endplay is controlled by the button and
spring on the camshaft end.
② Primary: 0.2195
Secondary: 0.2188
③ Cobra

CRANKSHAFT AND CONNECTING ROD SPECIFICATIONS

All measurements are given in inches.

Year	Engine ID/VIN	Engine Displacement Liters (cc)	Crankshaft Main Brg. Journal Dia.	Crankshaft Main Brg. Oil Clearance	Crankshaft Shaft End-play	Crankshaft Thrust on No.	Connecting Rod Journal Diameter	Connecting Rod Oil Clearance	Connecting Rod Side Clearance
1990	A	2.3 (2295)	2.3982–2.3990	0.0008–0.0026	0.004–0.012	3	2.0465–2.0472	0.0008–0.0026	0.0035–0.0140
	4	3.8 (3801)	2.5190–2.5198	0.0005–0.0023	0.004–0.008	3	2.3103–2.3111	0.0009–0.0027	0.0047–0.0140
	R	3.8 (3801)	①	②	0.004–0.008	3	2.3103–2.3111	0.0009–0.0027	0.0047–0.0140
	E	5.0 (4943)	2.2482–2.2490	0.0004–0.0021	0.004–0.012	3	2.1228–2.1236	0.0008–0.0024	0.0100–0.0230
1991	M	2.3 (2295)	2.2051–2.2059	0.0008–0.0026	0.003–0.012	3	2.0462–2.0472	0.0008–0.0026	0.0035–0.0140
	4	3.8 (3801)	2.5190–2.5198	0.0005–0.0023	0.004–0.008	3	2.3103–2.3111	0.0009–0.0027	0.0047–0.0140
	R	3.8 (3801)	①	②	0.004–0.008	3	2.3103–2.3111	0.0009–0.0027	0.0047–0.0140
	E	5.0 (4943)	2.2482–2.2490	0.0004–0.0021	0.004–0.012	3	2.1228–2.1236	0.0008–0.0024	0.0100–0.0230
	T	5.0 (4943)	2.2482–2.2490	0.0004–0.0021	0.004–0.012	3	2.1228–2.1236	0.0008–0.0024	0.0100–0.0230
1992	M	2.3 (2295)	2.2051–2.2059	0.0008–0.0026	0.003–0.012	3	2.0462–2.0472	0.0008–0.0026	0.0035–0.0140
	4	3.8 (3801)	2.5190–2.5198	0.0005–0.0023	0.004–0.008	3	2.3103–2.3111	0.0009–0.0027	0.0047–0.0140
	R	3.8 (3801)	①	②	0.004–0.008	3	2.3103–2.3111	0.0009–0.0027	0.0047–0.0140
	E	5.0 (4943)	2.2482–2.2490	0.0004–0.0021	0.004–0.012	3	2.1228–2.1236	0.0008–0.0024	0.0100–0.0230
	T	5.0 (4943)	2.2482–2.2490	0.0004–0.0021	0.004–0.012	3	2.1228–2.1236	0.0008–0.0024	0.0100–0.0230
1993–94	M	2.3 (2295)	2.2051–2.2059	0.0008–0.0026	0.003–0.012	3	2.0462–2.0472	0.0008–0.0026	0.0035–0.0140
	4	3.8 (3801)	2.5190–2.5198	0.0005–0.0023	0.004–0.008	3	2.3103–2.3111	0.0009–0.0027	0.0047–0.0140
	R	3.8 (3801)	①	②	0.004–0.008	3	2.3103–2.3111	0.0009–0.0027	0.0047–0.0140
	E	5.0 (4943)	2.2482–2.2490	0.0004–0.0021	0.004–0.012	3	2.1228–2.1236	0.0008–0.0024	0.0100–0.0230
	T	5.0 (4943)	2.2482–2.2490	0.0004–0.0021	0.004–0.012	3	2.1228–2.1236	0.0008–0.0024	0.0100–0.0230
	V	4.6 (4601)	2.8505–2.8513	0.0010–0.0020	0.005–0.012	3	2.0874–2.0891	0.0011–0.0027	0.0059–0.0197

① No. 1, 2 & 3—2.5190–2.5198
No. 4—2.5096–2.5104
② No. 1, 2 & 3—0.0005–0.0023
No. 4—0.0010–0.0028

VALVE SPECIFICATIONS

Year	Engine ID/VIN	Engine Displacement Liters (cc)	Seat Angle (deg.)	Face Angle (deg.)	Spring Test Pressure (lbs. @ in.)	Spring Installed Height (in.)	Stem-to-Guide Clearance (in.)		Stem Diameter (in.)	
							Intake	Exhaust	Intake	Exhaust
1990	A	2.3 (2295)	45	44	128.1–141.6 @ 1.12	1.52	0.0010–0.0027	0.0015–0.0032	0.3416–0.3423	0.3411–0.3418
	4	3.8 (3801)	44.5	45.8	220 @ 1.18	1.65	0.0010–0.0028	0.0015–0.0033	0.3415–0.3423	0.3410–0.3418
	R	3.8 (3801)	44.5	45.8	220 @ 1.18	1.65	0.0010–0.0028	0.0015–0.0033	0.3415–0.3423	0.3410–0.3418
	E	5.0 (4943)	45	44	①	②	0.0010–0.0027	0.0015–0.0032	0.3416–0.3423	0.3411–0.3418
1991	M	2.3 (2295)	45	44	128–142 @ 1.12	1.52	0.0010–0.0027	0.0015–0.0032	0.3416–0.3423	0.3411–0.3418
	4	3.8 (3801)	44.5	45.8	220 @ 1.18	1.65	0.0010–0.0028	0.0015–0.0033	0.3415–0.3423	0.3410–0.3418
	R	3.8 (3801)	44.5	45.8	220 @ 1.18	1.65	0.0010–0.0028	0.0015–0.0033	0.3415–0.3423	0.3410–0.3418
	E	5.0 (4943)	45	44	①	②	0.0010–0.0027	0.0015–0.0032	0.3416–0.3423	0.3411–0.3418
	T	5.0 (4943)	45	44	①	②	0.0010–0.0027	0.0015–0.0032	0.3416–0.3423	0.3411–0.3418
1992	M	2.3 (2295)	45	44	128–142 @ 1.12	1.52	0.0010–0.0027	0.0015–0.0032	0.3416–0.3423	0.3411–0.3418
	4	3.8 (3801)	44.5	45.8	220 @ 1.18	1.65	0.0010–0.0028	0.0015–0.0033	0.3415–0.3423	0.3410–0.3418
	R	3.8 (3801)	44.5	45.8	220 @ 1.18	1.65	0.0010–0.0028	0.0015–0.0033	0.3415–0.3423	0.3410–0.3418
	E	5.0 (4943)	45	44	①	②	0.0010–0.0027	0.0015–0.0032	0.3416–0.3423	0.3411–0.3418
	T	5.0 (4943)	45	44	①	②	0.0010–0.0027	0.0015–0.0032	0.3416–0.3423	0.3411–0.3418
1993–94	M	2.3 (2295)	45	44	128–142 @ 1.12	1.52	0.0010–0.0027	0.0015–0.0032	0.3416–0.3423	0.3411–0.3418
	4	3.8 (3801)	44.5	45.8	220 @ 1.18	1.65	0.0010–0.0028	0.0015–0.0033	0.3415–0.3423	0.3410–0.3418
	R	3.8 (3801)	44.5	45.8	220 @ 1.18	1.65	0.0010–0.0028	0.0015–0.0033	0.3415–0.3423	0.3410–0.3418
	E	5.0 (4943)	45	44	①	②	0.0010–0.0027	0.0015–0.0032	0.3416–0.3423	0.3411–0.3418
	T	5.0 (4943)	45	44	①	②	0.0010–0.0027	0.0015–0.0032	0.3416–0.3423	0.3411–0.3418
	V	4.6 (4601)	45	45.5	180 @ 1.43	1.31	0.0008–0.0027	0.0018–0.0037	0.2746–0.2754	0.2736–0.2744
	E③	5.0 (4943)	45	44	④	⑤	0.0015–0.0027	0.0015–0.0032	0.3416–0.3423	0.3411–0.3418

① Intake: 211–230 @ 1.33
 Exhaust: 200–226 @ 1.15
② Intake: 1.75–1.80 in.
 Exhaust: 1.58–1.64 in.
③ Cobra
④ Intake: 280 @ 1.30
 Exhaust: 264 @ 1.12
⑤ Intake: 1.80
 Exhaust: 1.62

PISTON AND RING SPECIFICATIONS

All measurements are given in inches.

Year	Engine ID/VIN	Engine Displacement Liters (cc)	Piston Clearance	Ring Gap			Ring Side Clearance		
				Top Compression	Bottom Compression	Oil Control	Top Compression	Bottom Compression	Oil Control
1990	A	2.3 (2295)	0.0030–0.0038	0.010–0.020	0.010–0.020	0.010–0.049	0.0020–0.0040	0.0020–0.0040	Snug
	4	3.8 (3801)	0.0014–0.0032	0.011–0.012	0.009–0.020	0.015–0.058	0.0016–0.0034	0.0016–0.0034	Snug
	R	3.8 (3801)	0.0040–0.0045	0.011–0.012	0.009–0.020	0.015–0.058	0.0016–0.0034	0.0016–0.0034	Snug
	E	5.0 (4943)	0.0030–0.0038	0.010–0.020	0.010–0.020	0.015–0.055	0.0020–0.0040	0.0020–0.0040	Snug
1991	M	2.3 (2295)	0.0024–0.0033	0.010–0.020	0.010–0.020	0.015–0.049	0.0016–0.0033	0.0016–0.0033	Snug
	4	3.8 (3801)	0.0014–0.0032	0.011–0.012	0.009–0.020	0.015–0.058	0.0016–0.0034	0.0016–0.0034	Snug
	R	3.8 (3801)	0.0040–0.0045	0.011–0.012	0.009–0.020	0.015–0.058	0.0016–0.0034	0.0016–0.0034	Snug
	E	5.0 (4943)	0.0030–0.0038	0.010–0.020	0.010–0.020	0.015–0.055	0.0020–0.0040	0.0020–0.0040	Snug
	T	5.0 (4943)	0.0030–0.0038	0.010–0.020	0.010–0.020	0.015–0.055	0.0020–0.0040	0.0020–0.0040	Snug
1992	M	2.3 (2295)	0.0019–0.0029	0.010–0.020	0.015–0.025	0.010–0.040	0.0016–0.0033	0.0016–0.0033	Snug
	4	3.8 (3801)	0.0014–0.0032	0.011–0.012	0.009–0.020	0.015–0.058	0.0016–0.0034	0.0016–0.0034	Snug
	R	3.8 (3801)	0.0015–0.0025	0.011–0.012	0.009–0.020	0.015–0.058	0.0016–0.0034	0.0016–0.0034	Snug
	E	5.0 (4943)	0.0030–0.0038	0.010–0.020	0.010–0.020	0.015–0.055	0.0020–0.0040	0.0020–0.0040	Snug
	T	5.0 (4943)	0.0030–0.0038	0.010–0.020	0.010–0.020	0.015–0.055	0.0020–0.0040	0.0020–0.0040	Snug
1993–94	M	2.3 (2295)	0.0019–0.0029	0.010–0.020	0.015–0.025	0.010–0.040	0.0016–0.0033	0.0016–0.0033	Snug
	4	3.8 (3801)	0.0014–0.0032	0.011–0.012	0.009–0.020	0.015–0.058	0.0016–0.0034	0.0016–0.0034	Snug
	R	3.8 (3801)	0.0015–0.0025	0.011–0.012	0.009–0.020	0.015–0.058	0.0016–0.0034	0.0016–0.0034	Snug
	E	5.0 (4943)	0.0012–0.0020	0.010–0.020	0.018–0.028	0.010–0.040	0.0020–0.0040	0.0020–0.0040	Snug
	T	5.0 (4943)	0.0012–0.0020	0.010–0.020	0.018–0.028	0.010–0.040	0.0020–0.0040	0.0020–0.0040	Snug
	V	4.6 (4601)	0.0007–0.0018	0.010–0.020	0.009–0.020	0.006–0.026	0.0016–0.0035	0.0012–0.0032	Snug

TORQUE SPECIFICATIONS
All readings in ft. lbs.

Year	Engine ID/VIN	Engine Displacement Liters (cc)	Cylinder Head Bolts	Main Bearing Bolts	Rod Bearing Bolts	Crankshaft Damper Bolts	Flywheel Bolts	Manifold Intake	Manifold Exhaust	Spark Plugs	Lug Nut
1990	A	2.3 (2295)	①	②	③	103–133	56–64	20–29	④	5–10	85–105
	4	3.8 (3801)	⑩	65–81	31–36	103–132	54–64	⑥	15–22	5–11	85–105
	R	3.8 (3801)	⑪	65–81	31–36	103–132	54–64	⑦	15–22	5–11	85–105
	E	5.0 (4943)	⑧	60–70	19–24	70–90	75–85	⑨	18–24	5–10	85–105
1991	M	2.3 (2295)	①	②	③	114–151	56–64	19–28	④	5–10	85–105
	4	3.8 (3801)	⑩	65–81	31–36	103–132	54–64	⑥	15–22	5–11	85–105
	R	3.8 (3801)	⑪	65–81	31–36	103–132	54–64	⑦	15–22	5–11	85–105
	E	5.0 (4943)	⑧	60–70	19–24	70–90	75–85	⑨	18–24	5–10	85–105
	T	5.0 (4943)	⑧	60–70	19–24	70–90	75–85	⑨	18–24	5–10	85–105
1992	M	2.3 (2295)	①	②	③	114–151	56–64	19–28	④	5–10	85–105
	4	3.8 (3801)	⑩	65–81	31–36	103–132	54–64	⑦	15–22	5–11	85–105
	R	3.8 (3801)	⑪	65–81	31–36	103–132	54–64	⑦	15–22	5–11	85–105
	E	5.0 (4943)	⑧	60–70	19–24	70–90	75–85	⑫	18–24	5–10	85–105
	T	5.0 (4943)	⑧	60–70	19–24	70–90	75–85	⑫	18–24	5–10	85–105
1993–94	M	2.3 (2295)	①	②	③	114–151	56–64	19–28	④	5–10	85–105
	4	3.8 (3801)	⑩	66–81	31–36	103–132	54–64	⑦	15–22	5–11	85–105
	R	3.8 (3801)	⑪	66–81	31–36	103–132	54–64	⑦	15–22	5–11	85–105
	E	5.0 (4943)	⑤	60–70	19–24	70–90	75–85	⑫	26–32	5–10	85–105
	T	5.0 (4943)	⑤	60–70	19–24	70–90	75–85	⑫	26–32	5–10	85–105
	V	4.6 (4601)	⑬	⑭	⑮	114–121	54–64	⑯	15–22	7	85–105

① Tighten in 2 steps:
Step 1: 50–60 ft. lbs.
Step 2: 80–90 ft. lbs.

② Tighten in 2 steps:
Step 1: 50–60 ft. lbs.
Step 2: 75–85 ft. lbs.

③ Tighten in 2 steps:
Step 1: 25–30 ft. lbs.
Step 2: 30–36 ft. lbs.

④ Tighten in 2 steps:
Step 1: 178–204 inch lbs.
Step 2: 20–30 ft. lbs.

⑤ Standard hex head bolts
Tighten in 2 steps:
Step 1: 55–65 ft. lbs.
Step 2: 65–72 ft. lbs.
Flanged hex head bolts
Tighten in 3 steps:
Step 1: 25–35 ft. lbs.
Step 2: 45–55 ft. lbs.
Step 3: Rotate 85–95 degrees

⑥ Tighten in 3 steps:
Step 1: 7.5 ft. lbs.
Step 2: 15 ft. lbs.
Step 3: 24 ft. lbs.

⑦ Tighten in 2 steps:
Step 1: 7.5 ft. lbs.
Step 2: 11 ft. lbs.

⑧ Tighten in 2 steps:
Step 1: 55–65 ft. lbs.
Step 2: 65–72 ft. lbs.

⑨ Tighten in 3 steps:
Step 1: 15–20 ft. lbs.
Step 2: 23–25 ft. lbs.
Step 3: Retorque with engine hot

⑩ Tighten in 6 steps:
Step 1: 37 ft. lbs.
Step 2: 45 ft. lbs.
Step 3: 52 ft. lbs.
Step 4: 59 ft. lbs.
Step 5: Back off all bolts 2–3 turns
Step 6: Tighten to 11–18 ft. lbs., rotate long bolts an additional 85–105 degrees, short bolts 65–85 degrees, go to next bolt in sequence.

⑪ Tighten in 6 steps:
Step 1: 37 ft. lbs.
Step 2: 45 ft. lbs.
Step 3: 52 ft. lbs.
Step 4: 59 ft. lbs.
Step 5: Back off all bolts 2–3 turns
Step 6: Tighten to 48–55 ft. lbs., rotate bolts an additional 90–110 degrees, go to next bolt in sequence.

⑫ Tighten in 2 steps:
Step 1: 15–20 ft. lbs.
Step 2: 23–25 ft. lbs.

⑬ Tighten in 3 steps:
Step 1: 27–32 ft. lbs.
Step 2: Rotate 85–95 degrees
Step 3: Rotate 85–95 degrees

⑭ Tighten in 4 steps:
Step 1: Tighten #1-20 to 6–8.8 ft. lbs.
Step 2: Tighten #1-10 to 16–21 ft. lbs.
Step 3: Tighten #1-20 to 27–32 ft. lbs.
Step 4: Rotate 85–95 degrees

⑮ Tighten in 2 steps:
Step 1: 22–25 ft. lbs.
Step 2: Rotate 85–95 degrees

⑯ Tighten in 3 steps:
Step 1: #5, 7, 9 and 11 to 9–11 ft. lbs.
Step 2: All others 7–13 ft. lbs.
Step 3: Rotate 85–95 degrees

TORQUE SPECIFICATIONS

Component	English	Metric
Auxiliary shaft sprocket bolt		
2.3L engine:	30–41 ft. lbs.	40–55 Nm
Auxiliary shaft thrust plate bolt		
2.3L engine:	6–9 ft. lbs.	8–12 Nm
Camshaft sprocket bolt		
2.3L engine:	52–70 ft. lbs.	70–95 Nm
3.8L engine:	30–37 ft. lbs.	40–45 Nm
4.6L engine:	81–95 ft. lbs.	110–130 Nm
5.0L engine:	40–45 ft. lbs.	54–61 Nm
Camshaft thrust plate		
2.3L engine:	6–9 ft. lbs.	8–12 Nm
3.8L engine:	6–10 ft. lbs.	8–14 Nm
5.0L engine:	9–12 ft. lbs.	12–16 Nm
Connecting rod bearing cap nuts		
2.3L engine		
Step 1:	25–30 ft. lbs.	34–41 Nm
Step 2:	30–36 ft. lbs.	41–48 Nm
3.8L engine:	31–36 ft. lbs.	41–49 Nm
4.6L engine		
Step 1:	22–25 ft. lbs.	30–35 Nm
Step 2:	+ 85–95 degree turn	+ 85–95 degree turn
5.0L engine:	19–24 ft. lbs.	25–33 Nm
Crankshaft damper bolt		
2.3L engine		
1990:	103–133 ft. lbs.	137–180 Nm
1991–93:	114–151 ft. lbs.	155–205 Nm
3.8L engine:	103–132 ft. lbs.	140–180 Nm
4.6L engine:	114–121 ft. lbs.	155–165 Nm
5.0L engine:	70–90 ft. lbs.	95–122 Nm
Cylinder head bolt		
2.3L engine		
Step 1:	50–60 ft. lbs.	55–81 Nm
Step 2:	80–90 ft. lbs.	108–122 Nm
3.8L engine		
EFI engine *		
Step 1:	37 ft. lbs.	50 Nm
Step 2:	45 ft. lbs.	61 Nm
Step 3:	52 ft. lbs.	71 Nm
Step 4:	59 ft. lbs.	80 Nm
Step 5:	loosen bolts 2–3 turns	loosen bolts 2–3 turns
Step 6:	11–18 ft. lbs.	15–25 Nm
Step 7:		
Long bolts:	+ 85–95 degree turn	+ 85–95 degree turn
Short bolts:	+ 85–95 degree turn	+ 85–95 degree turn
SC engine *		
Step 1:	37 ft. lbs.	50 Nm
Step 2:	45 ft. lbs.	61 Nm
Step 3:	52 ft. lbs.	71 Nm
Step 4:	59 ft. lbs.	80 Nm
Step 5:	loosen bolts 2–3 turns	loosen bolts 2–3 turns
Step 6:	48–55 ft. lbs.	65–75 Nm
Step 7:	+ 90–110 degree turn	+ 90–110 degree turn
4.6L engine		
Step 1:	27–32 ft. lbs.	37–43 Nm
Step 2:	+ 85–95 degree turn	+ 85–95 degree turn
Step 3:	+ 85–95 degree turn	+ 85–95 degree turn
5.0L engine		
Standard hex head bolts		
Step 1:	55–65 ft. lbs.	75–88 Nm
Step 2:	65–72 ft. lbs.	88–98 Nm

TORQUE SPECIFICATIONS

Component	English	Metric
Flanged hex head bolts		
Step 1:	25–35 ft. lbs.	34–47 Nm
Step 2:	44–55 ft. lbs.	61–75 Nm
Step 3:	+ 85–95 degree turn	+ 85–95 degree turn
* NOTE: Use new bolts and oil the threads		
EGR valve		
2.3L engine:	15–22 ft. lbs.	20–30 Nm
3.8L engine:	15–22 ft. lbs.	20–30 Nm
4.6L engine:	26–33 ft. lbs.	35–45 Nm
5.0L engine:	12–18 ft. lbs.	16–24 Nm
Engine-to-transmission		
2.3L engine:	28–38 ft. lbs.	38–51 Nm
3.8L engine:	40–50 ft. lbs.	55–68 Nm
4.6L engine:	30–44 ft. lbs.	40–60 Nm
5.0L engine:	40–50 ft. lbs.	55–68 Nm
Engine/transmission mounts		
2.3L engine		
Front		
Mount-to-engine bolts:	35–46 ft. lbs.	47–63 Nm
Mount through bolts:	35–46 ft. lbs.	47–63 Nm
Flange nut (convertible):	73–106 ft. lbs.	98–144 Nm
Rear		
Mount-to-transmission bolts		
Manual transmission:	51–70 ft. lbs.	68–95 Nm
Automatic transmission:	35–50 ft. lbs.	47–68 Nm
Crossmember-to-body bolts:	35–50 ft. lbs.	47–68 Nm
Mount-to-crossmember nut(s)		
Manual transmission:	26–35 ft. lbs.	34–48 Nm
Automatic transmission:	65–87 ft. lbs.	88–119 Nm
3.8L engine		
Front		
Mount-to-engine bolts:	26–34 ft. lbs.	34–47 Nm
Mount through bolts:	35–50 ft. lbs.	47–68 Nm
Retaining strap bolt (SC engine)		
1990–92:	34–44 ft. lbs.	45–61 Nm
1993–94:	25–35 ft. lbs.	34–47 Nm
Rear		
Mount-to-transmission bolts:	35–50 ft. lbs.	47–68 Nm
Crossmember-to-body bolts:	34–47 ft. lbs.	45–65 Nm
Mount-to-crossmember nut:	65–84 ft. lbs.	88–115 Nm
5.0L engine		
Front		
Mount-to-engine bolts:	45–59 ft. lbs.	61–81 Nm
Transmission brace-to-mount nut:	45–59 ft. lbs.	61–81 Nm
Mount-to-crossmember nuts:	73–106 ft. lbs.	98–144 Nm
Mount through bolts:	35–45 ft. lbs.	45–61 Nm
Rear		
Mustang		
Mount-to-transmission bolts:	51–70 ft. lbs.	68–95 Nm
Crossmember-to-body nuts:	35–50 ft. lbs.	47–68 Nm
Mount-to-crossmember nuts:	26–35 ft. lbs.	34–48 Nm
Thunderbird and Cougar		
Mount-to-transmission bolts:	35–50 ft. lbs.	47–68 Nm
Crossmember-to-body bolts:	34–47 ft. lbs.	45–65 Nm
Mount-to-crossmember nut:	65–85 ft. lbs.	88–115 Nm
Mark VII		
Crossmember-to-body bolts:	45–70 ft. lbs.	60–95 Nm
Crossmember-to-transmission		
bolts:	35–50 ft. lbs.	47–68 Nm

TORQUE SPECIFICATIONS

Component	English	Metric
Exhaust pipe-to-manifold nuts		
1990–92:	17–23 ft. lbs.	22–32 Nm
1993–94		
2.3L engine:	25–34 ft. lbs.	36–46 Nm
3.8L engine:	17–23 ft. lbs.	22–41 Nm
4.6L engine:	20–30 ft. lbs.	27–41 Nm
5.0L engine:	16–30 ft. lbs.	22–41 Nm
Exhaust manifold		
2.3L engine		
Step 1:	15–17 ft. lbs.	20–23 Nm
Step 2:	20–30 ft. lbs.	27–41 Nm
3.8L engine:	15–22 ft. lbs.	20–30 Nm
4.6L engine:	15–22 ft. lbs.	20–30 Nm
5.0L engine		
1990–92	18–24 ft. lbs.	25–33 Nm
1993–94:	26–32 ft. lbs.	32–43 Nm
Flywheel/flexplate-to-crankshaft bolts		
2.3L engine:	56–64 ft. lbs.	76–87 Nm
3.8L engine:	54–64 ft. lbs.	75–87 Nm
4.6L engine:	54–64 ft. lbs.	73–87 Nm
5.0L engine:	75–85 ft. lbs.	102–116 Nm
Flywheel-to-converter bolts		
Except 4.6L engine:	20–34 ft. lbs.	27–46 Nm
4.6L engine:	22–25 ft. lbs.	30–35 Nm
Fuel rail-to-intake manifold bolts		
2.3L engine:	15–22 ft. lbs.	20–30 Nm
3.8L engine:	87 inch lbs.	10 Nm
4.6L engine:	71–106 ft. lbs.	8–12 Nm
5.0L engine:	71–106 ft. lbs.	8–12 Nm
Intake manifold		
2.3L engine		
1990:	20–29 ft. lbs.	27–41 Nm
1991–93:	19–28 ft. lbs.	26–40 Nm
3.8L engine		
1990–91 EFI engine		
Step 1:	8 ft. lbs.	11 Nm
Step 2:	15 ft. lbs.	20 Nm
Step 3:	24 ft. lbs.	33 Nm
SC and 1992–94 EFI engines		
Step 1:	8 ft. lbs.	11 Nm
Step 2:	11 ft. lbs.	15 Nm
4.6L engine		
Step 1		
No. 5, 7, 9 and 11:	9–11 ft. lbs.	12–15 Nm
All others:	7–13 ft. lbs.	10–18 Nm
Step 2:	+ 85–95 degree turn	+ 85–95 degree turn
5.0L engine		
1990–91		
Step 1:	15–20 ft. lbs.	20–27 Nm
Step 2:	23–25 ft. lbs.	31–34 Nm
Step 3:	retorque–engine hot	retorque–engine hot
1992–94		
Step 1:	15–20 ft. lbs.	20–27 Nm
Step 2:	23–25 ft. lbs. engine hot	31–34 Nm engine hot
Intake plenum-to-lower manifold		
2.3L engine:	15–22 ft. lbs.	20–30 Nm
3.8L engine:	24 ft. lbs.	32 Nm
5.0L engine:	12–17 ft. lbs.	16–24 Nm

TORQUE SPECIFICATIONS

Component	English	Metric
Main bearing cap bolts		
2.3L engine		
Step 1:	50–60 ft. lbs.	68–81 Nm
Step 2:	75–85 ft. lbs.	102–116 Nm
3.8L engine:	65–81 ft. lbs.	88–110 Nm
4.6L engine		
Step 1 (No. 1–20):	6–9 ft. lbs.	8–12 Nm
Step 2 (No. 1–10):	15–22 ft. lbs.	22–28 Nm
Step 3 (No. 1–20):	18–31 ft. lbs.	23–43 Nm
Step 4:	+ 85–95 degree turn	+ 85–95 degree turn
5.0L engine:	60–70 ft. lbs.	81–95 Nm
Oil pan-to-block		
2.3L engine		
1990:	71–106 inch lbs.	8–12 Nm
1991–93:	90–120 inch lbs.	10–13 Nm
3.8L engine:	80–106 inch lbs.	9–12 Nm
4.6L engine:	15–22 ft. lbs.	20–30 Nm
5.0L engine:	9 ft. lbs.	12 Nm
Oil pan drain plug:	15–25 ft. lbs.	20–34 Nm
Oil level low sensor:	20–30 ft. lbs.	27–41 Nm
Oil pump attaching bolts		
2.3L engine:	14–22 ft. lbs.	20–30 Nm
3.8L engine:	18–22 ft. lbs.	25–30 Nm
4.6L engine:	7–8 ft. lbs.	8–12 Nm
5.0L engine:	22–32 ft. lbs.	30–43 Nm
Rocker arm bolt		
3.8L engine		
Step 1:	5–11 ft. lbs.	7–15 Nm
Step 2:	19–25 ft. lbs.	25–35 Nm
5.0L engine:	18–25 ft. lbs.	24–34 Nm
Rocker arm (valve) cover		
2.3L engine:	62–97 inch lbs.	7–11 Nm
3.8L engine:	80–106 inch lbs.	9–12 Nm
4.6L engine:	7–8 ft. lbs.	8–12 Nm
5.0L engine		
1990–92:	10–13 ft. lbs.	14–18 Nm
1993–94:	12–15 ft. lbs.	16–20 Nm
Spark plug (except 4.6L engine):	5–11 ft. lbs.	7–15 Nm
4.6L engine:	7–8 ft. lbs.	9–20 Nm
Starter-to-block bolts:	15–20 ft. lbs.	20–27 Nm
Thermostat housing		
2.3L engine:	14–21 ft. lbs.	19–29 Nm
3.8L engine:	15–22 ft. lbs.	20–30 Nm
4.6L engine:	15–22 ft. lbs.	20–30 Nm
5.0L engine:	12–18 ft. lbs.	16–24 Nm
Throttle body nuts		
2.3L engine:	15–22 ft. lbs.	20–30 Nm
3.8L engine:	15–22 ft. lbs.	20–30 Nm
4.6L engine:	6–9 ft. lbs.	8–12 Nm
5.0L engine:	12–17 ft. lbs.	16–24 Nm
Timing belt/chain tensioner adjustment bolt		
2.3L engine:	29–40 ft. lbs.	40–55 Nm
4.6L engine:	15–22 ft. lbs.	20–30 Nm
Timing belt tensioner pivot bolt		
2.3L engine:	14–22 ft. lbs.	20–30 Nm

TORQUE SPECIFICATIONS

Component	English	Metric
Timing cover		
2.3L engine:	71–106 inch lbs.	8–12 Nm
3.8L engine:	15–22 ft. lbs.	20–30 Nm
4.6L engine:	15–22 ft. lbs.	20–30 Nm
5.0L engine:	12–18 ft. lbs.	16–24 Nm
Water pump		
2.3L engine:	14–21 ft. lbs.	19–29 Nm
3.8L engine:	15–22 ft. lbs.	20–30 Nm
4.6L engine:	15–22 ft. lbs.	20–30 Nm
5.0L engine:	12–18 ft. lbs.	16–24 Nm

BRAKE SPECIFICATIONS

All measurements in inches unless noted.

Year	Model	Master Cylinder Bore	Brake Disc Original Thickness	Brake Disc Minimum Thickness	Maximum Runout	Brake Drum Diameter Original Inside Diameter	Max. Wear Limit	Maximum Machine Diameter	Minimum Lining Thickness Front	Rear
1990	Mustang	0.872	①	②	0.003	9.000	9.060	NA	0.125	0.031
	Thunderbird	0.938③	④	⑤	0.003	9.843	9.904	NA	0.125	⑥
	Cougar	0.938③	④	⑤	0.003	9.843	9.904	NA	0.125	⑥
	Mark VII	1.125	⑦	⑧	⑨	—	—	—	0.125	0.125
1991	Mustang	0.872	①	②	0.003	9.000	9.060	NA	0.125	0.031
	Thunderbird	0.938③	④	⑤	0.003	9.843	9.904	NA	0.125	⑥
	Cougar	0.938③	④	⑤	0.003	9.843	9.904	NA	0.125	⑥
	Mark VII	1.125	⑦	⑧	⑩	—	—	—	0.125	0.123
1992	Mustang	0.872	①	②	0.003	9.000	9.060	NA	0.125	0.031
	Thunderbird	0.938③	④	⑪	0.003	9.843	9.904	NA	0.125	⑥
	Cougar	0.938③	④	⑪	0.003	9.843	9.904	NA	0.125	⑥
	Mark VII	1.125	⑦	⑧	⑨	—	—	—	0.125	0.123
1993–94	Mustang	⑭	①	②	0.003	9.000	9.060	NA	0.125	⑥
	Thunderbird	0.938③	⑫	⑬	0.003	9.843	9.904	NA	0.125	⑥
	Cougar	0.938③	⑫	⑬	0.003	9.843	9.904	NA	0.125	⑥
	Mark VIII	1.000	⑫	⑬	⑨	—	—	—	0.040	0.123

NA—Not available
① 2.3L Engine—0.870 in.
  5.0L Engine—1.03 in.
② 2.3L Engine—0.810 in.
  5.0L Engine—0.972 in.
③ Except ABS equipped
④ Front—1.024 in.
  Rear—0.945 in.
⑤ Front—0.935 in.
  Rear—0.896 in.
⑥ With drum brakes—0.031 in.
  With disc brakes—0.123 in.
⑦ Front—1.03 in.
  Rear—0.945 in.

⑧ Front—0.972 in.
  Rear—0.895 in.
⑨ Front—0.003 in.
  Rear—0.004 in.
⑩ Front—0.003 in.
  Rear—0.002 in.
⑪ Front—0.974 in.
  Rear—0.896 in.
⑫ Front—1.025 in.
  Rear—0.710 in.
⑬ Front—0.974 in.
  Rear—0.657 in.
⑭ 2.3L Engine—0.827
  5.0L Engine—1.125

WHEEL ALIGNMENT

Year	Model		Caster Range (deg.)	Caster Preferred Setting (deg.)	Camber Range (deg.)	Camber Preferred Setting (deg.)	Toe-in (in.)	Steering Axis Inclination (deg.)
1990	Mustang	Exc. 5.0L GT	$1^{5}/_{32}$P–$2^{5}/_{8}$P	$1^{29}/_{32}$P	$1^{1}/_{4}$N–$^{1}/_{4}$P	$^{1}/_{2}$N	$^{1}/_{8}$ ①	$15^{23}/_{32}$
		5.0L GT	$1^{5}/_{32}$P–$2^{5}/_{8}$P	$1^{29}/_{32}$P	$1^{3}/_{8}$N–$^{1}/_{8}$P	$^{5}/_{8}$N	$^{1}/_{8}$ ①	$15^{23}/_{32}$
	Thunderbird	Front	$4^{3}/_{4}$P–$6^{1}/_{4}$P	$5^{1}/_{2}$P	$1^{1}/_{4}$N–$^{1}/_{4}$P	$^{1}/_{2}$N	$^{1}/_{8}$	$15^{23}/_{32}$
		Rear	—	—	1N–0	$^{1}/_{2}$N	$^{1}/_{16}$	—
	Cougar	Front	$4^{3}/_{4}$P–$6^{1}/_{4}$P	$5^{1}/_{2}$P	$1^{1}/_{4}$N–$^{1}/_{4}$P	$^{1}/_{2}$N	$^{1}/_{8}$	$15^{23}/_{32}$
		Rear	—	—	1N–0	$^{1}/_{2}$N	$^{1}/_{16}$	—
	Mark VII	—	$^{5}/_{8}$P–$2^{3}/_{4}$P	$1^{1}/_{2}$P	$^{3}/_{4}$N–$^{3}/_{4}$P	0	$^{1}/_{8}$	11
1991	Mustang	Exc. 5.0L GT	$1^{5}/_{32}$P–$2^{5}/_{8}$P	$1^{29}/_{32}$P	$1^{1}/_{4}$N–$^{1}/_{4}$P	$^{1}/_{2}$N	$^{1}/_{8}$ ①	$15^{23}/_{32}$
		5.0L GT	$1^{5}/_{32}$P–$2^{5}/_{8}$P	$1^{29}/_{32}$P	$1^{3}/_{8}$N–$^{1}/_{8}$P	$^{5}/_{8}$N	$^{1}/_{8}$ ①	$15^{23}/_{32}$
	Thunderbird	Front	$4^{3}/_{4}$P–$6^{1}/_{4}$P	$5^{1}/_{2}$P	$1^{1}/_{4}$N–$^{1}/_{4}$P	$^{1}/_{2}$N	$^{1}/_{8}$	$15^{23}/_{32}$
		Rear	—	—	1N–0	$^{1}/_{2}$N	$^{1}/_{16}$	—
	Cougar	Front	$4^{3}/_{4}$P–$6^{1}/_{4}$P	$5^{1}/_{2}$P	$1^{1}/_{4}$N–$^{1}/_{4}$P	$^{1}/_{2}$N	$^{1}/_{8}$	$15^{23}/_{32}$
		Rear	—	—	1N–0	$^{1}/_{2}$N	$^{1}/_{16}$	—
	Mark VII	—	$^{5}/_{8}$P–$2^{3}/_{4}$P	$1^{1}/_{2}$P	$^{3}/_{4}$N–$^{3}/_{4}$P	0	$^{1}/_{8}$	11
1992	Mustang	Exc. 5.0L GT	$1^{5}/_{32}$P–$2^{5}/_{8}$P	$1^{29}/_{32}$P	$1^{1}/_{4}$N–$^{1}/_{4}$P	$^{1}/_{2}$N	$^{1}/_{8}$ ①	$15^{23}/_{32}$
		5.0L GT	$1^{5}/_{32}$P–$2^{5}/_{8}$P	$1^{29}/_{32}$P	$1^{3}/_{8}$N–$^{1}/_{8}$P	$^{5}/_{8}$N	$^{1}/_{8}$ ①	$15^{23}/_{32}$
	Thunderbird	Front	$4^{3}/_{4}$P–$6^{1}/_{4}$P	$5^{1}/_{2}$P	$1^{1}/_{4}$N–$^{1}/_{4}$P	$^{1}/_{2}$N	$^{1}/_{8}$	$15^{23}/_{32}$
		Rear	—	—	1N–0	$^{1}/_{2}$N	$^{1}/_{16}$	—
	Cougar	Front	$4^{3}/_{4}$P–$6^{1}/_{4}$P	$5^{1}/_{2}$P	$1^{1}/_{4}$N–$^{1}/_{4}$P	$^{1}/_{2}$N	$^{1}/_{8}$	$15^{23}/_{32}$
		Rear	—	—	1N–0	$^{1}/_{2}$N	$^{1}/_{16}$	—
	Mark VII	—	$^{5}/_{8}$P–$2^{3}/_{4}$P	$1^{1}/_{2}$P	$^{3}/_{4}$N–$^{3}/_{4}$P	0	$^{1}/_{8}$	11
1993–94	Mustang	Cobra	$1^{5}/_{32}$P–$2^{21}/_{32}$P	$1^{29}/_{32}$P	$1^{3}/_{8}$N–$^{1}/_{8}$P	$^{5}/_{8}$N	0	$15^{23}/_{32}$
	Mustang	Exc. 5.0L GT	$1^{5}/_{32}$P–$2^{5}/_{8}$P	$1^{29}/_{32}$P	$1^{1}/_{4}$N–$^{1}/_{4}$P	$^{1}/_{2}$N	$^{1}/_{8}$ ①	$15^{23}/_{32}$
		5.0L GT	$1^{5}/_{32}$P–$2^{5}/_{8}$P	$1^{29}/_{32}$P	$1^{3}/_{8}$N–$^{1}/_{8}$P	$^{5}/_{8}$N	$^{1}/_{8}$ ①	$15^{23}/_{32}$
	Thunderbird	Front	$4^{3}/_{4}$P–$6^{1}/_{4}$P	$5^{1}/_{2}$P	$1^{1}/_{4}$N–$^{1}/_{4}$P	$^{1}/_{2}$N	$^{5}/_{64}$	$15^{23}/_{32}$
		Rear	—	—	1N–0	$^{1}/_{2}$N	$^{1}/_{16}$	—
	Cougar	Front	$4^{3}/_{4}$P–$6^{1}/_{4}$P	$5^{1}/_{2}$P	$1^{1}/_{4}$N–$^{1}/_{4}$P	$^{1}/_{2}$N	$^{5}/_{64}$	$15^{23}/_{32}$
		Rear	—	—	1N–0	$^{1}/_{2}$N	$^{1}/_{16}$	—
	Mark VIII	Front	$4^{3}/_{4}$P–$6^{1}/_{4}$P	$5^{1}/_{2}$P	$1^{1}/_{4}$N–$^{1}/_{4}$P	$^{1}/_{2}$N	$^{1}/_{8}$	NA
		Rear	—	—	1N–0	$^{1}/_{2}$N	$^{1}/_{16}$	—

N—Negative
P—Positive
NA—Not available
① Toe-out

AIR CONDITIONING BELT TENSION

Year	Model	Engine Displacement Liters (cc)	Belt Type	Specifications New ①	Specifications Used ①
1990	Mustang	2.3 (2295)	Serpentine	②	②
	Mustang	5.0 (4943)	Serpentine	②	②
	Thunderbird	3.8 (3801)	Serpentine	②	②
	Cougar	3.8 (3801)	Serpentine	②	②
	Mark VII	5.0 (4943)	Serpentine	②	②

AIR CONDITIONING BELT TENSION

Year	Model	Engine Displacement Liters (cc)	Belt Type	Specifications New ①	Used ①
1991	Mustang	2.3 (2295)	Poly-V	②	②
	Mustang	5.0 (4943) HO	Serpentine	②	②
	Thunderbird	3.8 (3801)	Serpentine	②	②
	Cougar	3.8 (3801)	Serpentine	②	②
	Thunderbird	3.8 (3801) SC	Serpentine	②	②
	Thunderbird	5.0 (4943) HO	Serpentine	②	②
	Cougar	5.0 (4943) HO	Serpentine	②	②
	Mark VII	5.0 (4943) HO	Serpentine	②	②
1992	Mustang	2.3 (2295)	Poly-V	②	②
	Mustang	5.0 (4943) HO	Serpentine	②	②
	Thunderbird	3.8 (3801)	Serpentine	②	②
	Cougar	3.8 (3801)	Serpentine	②	②
	Thunderbird	3.8 (3801) SC	Serpentine	②	②
	Thunderbird	5.0 (4943) HO	Serpentine	②	②
	Cougar	5.0 (4943) HO	Serpentine	②	②
	Mark VII	5.0 (4943) HO	Serpentine	②	②
1993–94	Mustang	2.3 (2295)	Poly-V	②	②
	Mustang	5.0 (4943) HO	Serpentine	②	②
	Thunderbird	3.8 (3801)	Serpentine	②	②
	Cougar	3.8 (3801)	Serpentine	②	②
	Thunderbird	3.8 (3801) SC	Serpentine	②	②
	Thunderbird	5.0 (4943) HO	Serpentine	②	②
	Cougar	5.0 (4943) HO	Serpentine	②	②
	Mark VIII	4.6 (4593)	Serpentine	②	②

① Lbs. using a belt tension gauge
② Automatic belt tensioner

REFRIGERANT CAPACITIES

Year	Model	Refrigerant (oz.)	Oil (fl. oz.)	Compressor Type
1990	Mustang	38–42	①	②
	Thunderbird	38–42	7	FX-15
	Cougar	38–42	7	FX-15
	Mark VII	38–42	8	10PA17
1991	Mustang (2.3)	38–42	8	10P15C
	Mustang (5.0)	38–40	10	6P148
	Thunderbird	38–40	7	FX-15
	Cougar	38–40	7	FX-15
	Mark VII	38–40	8	10PA17
1992	Mustang (2.3)	38–42	8	10P15C
	Mustang (5.0)	38–42	10	6P148
	Thunderbird	38–40	7	FX-15
	Cougar	38–40	7	FX-15
	Mark VII	38–40	8	10PA17A

REFRIGERANT CAPACITIES

Year	Model	Refrigerant (oz.)	Oil (fl. oz.)	Compressor Type
1993	Mustang (2.3)	38–42	8	10P15C
	Mustang (5.0)	38–42	10	6P148
	Thunderbird	38–42	7	FX-15
	Cougar	38–42	7	FX-15
	Mark VIII	33–35	7 ③	FX-15

NOTE: At the time of publication, refrigerant capacity information relating to R-134a was not available from the manufacturer.

① 2.3L Engine—8
  5.0L Engine—10
② 2.3L Engine—10P15
  5.0L Engine—6P148
③ 10 oz. with auxiliary A/C

MAINTENANCE INTERVALS—TYPE A: NORMAL SERVICE
Mark VII • Mark VIII • Mustang

TO BE SERVICED	TYPE OF SERVICE	7.5	15	22.5	30	37.5	45	52.5	60
Oxygen Sensor	I				✔				✔
Ignition Timing	I①				✔				✔
Vacuum Lines and Hoses	I				✔				✔
Ignition Wires	I				✔				✔
Spark Plugs	R				✔				✔
Engine Oil and Filter	R④	✔	✔	✔	✔	✔	✔	✔	✔
Engine Air Cleaner Element	R				✔				✔
Crankcase Emission Filter	R②				✔				✔
PCV Valve	R				✔				✔
Fuel Filter	R								✔
Charcoal Canister	I				✔				✔
Fuel/Vapor Return Lines	I				✔				✔
Fuel Tank Cap and Restrictor	I				✔				✔
Coolant System	I		✔		✔		✔		✔
Exhaust Pipe and Muffler	I				✔				✔
Catalytic Converter and Shield	I				✔				✔
EGR System	I				✔				✔
Air Pump and Connections	I②				✔				✔
Timing Belt	I③								✔
Tie Rod Ends	I/L				✔				✔
Throttle Body	I		✔		✔		✔		✔
Drive Belts	I				✔				✔
Maintenance Indicator	I⑤								
Brake Pads, Front	I				✔				✔
Brake Pads, Rear	I				✔				✔
Brake Shoes, Rear	I				✔				✔
Brake Drums and Rotors	I				✔				✔
Brake Hoses and Lines	I				✔				✔
Battery Connections	I		✔		✔		✔		✔

MAINTENANCE INTERVALS—TYPE A: NORMAL SERVICE
Mark VII • Mark VIII • Mustang

TO BE SERVICED	TYPE OF SERVICE	VEHICLE MILEAGE INTERVAL (X1000)							
		7.5	15	22.5	30	37.5	45	52.5	60
Ball Joints	I/L				✔				✔
Engine Coolant	R				✔				✔
Automatic Transmission Fluid	I	✔	✔	✔	✔	✔	✔	✔	✔
Manual Transmission Fluid	I		✔		✔		✔		✔
Clutch Pedal Operation	I⑥	✔	✔	✔	✔	✔	✔	✔	✔
Tire Rotation	I	✔		✔		✔		✔	
Front Wheel Bearings	L				✔				✔
Rear Axle Halfshaft Dust Boots	I⑦				✔				✔
Steering System	I				✔				✔
Power Steering Fluid	I		✔		✔		✔		✔
Brake Fluid	I		✔		✔		✔		✔
Hinges, Latches, etc.	L		✔		✔		✔		✔
Seat Belt Operation	I		✔		✔		✔		✔

FOR COMPLETE WARRANTY COVERAGE CONSULT INDIVIDUAL VEHICLE MANUFACTURER'S WARRANTY MAINTENANCE GUIDE.

I—Inspect
L—Lubricate
R—Replace
① If applicable
② 5.0L engine only
③ 2.3L engine only
④ If equipped with vehicle maintenance monitor, change oil and filter when indicated, but do not go beyond 7,500 miles or 6 months, whichever occurs first.
⑤ Reset after indicated services are performed.
⑥ Adjust clutch by lifting pedal every 7,500 miles, Mustang only.
⑦ 1993–94 Mark VIII only

MAINTENANCE INTERVALS—TYPE B: SEVERE SERVICE
Mark VII • Mark VIII • Mustang

TO BE SERVICED	TYPE OF SERVICE	VEHICLE MILEAGE INTERVAL (X1000)									
		3	6	9	12	15	18	21	24	27	30
Oxygen Sensor	I										✔
Ignition Timing	I①										✔
Vacuum Lines and Hoses	I										✔
Ignition Wires	I										✔
Spark Plugs	R										✔
Engine Oil and Filter	R	✔	✔	✔	✔	✔	✔	✔	✔	✔	✔
Engine Air Cleaner Element	R										✔
Crankcase Emission Filter	R②										✔
PCV Valve	R										✔
Fuel Filter	R③										
Charcoal Canister	I										✔
Fuel/Vapor Return Lines	I										✔
Fuel Tank Cap and Restrictor	I										✔
Coolant System	I										✔
Exhaust Pipe and Muffler	I										✔
Catalytic Converter and Shield	I										✔
EGR System	I										✔
Air Pump and Connections	I②										✔
Timing Belt	I④										

MAINTENANCE INTERVALS—TYPE B: SEVERE SERVICE
Mark VII • Mark VIII • Mustang

TO BE SERVICED	TYPE OF SERVICE	VEHICLE MILEAGE INTERVAL (X1000)									
		3	6	9	12	15	18	21	24	27	30
Tie Rod Ends	I/L										✔
Throttle Body	I					✔					✔
Drive Belts	I										✔
Maintenance Indicator	I⑦										
Brake Pads, Front	I										✔
Brake Pads, Rear	I										✔
Brake Shoes, Rear	I										✔
Brake Drums and Rotors	I										✔
Brake Hoses and Lines	I										✔
Battery Connections	I					✔					✔
Ball Joints	I/L										✔
Engine Coolant	R										✔
Automatic Transmission Fluid	R										✔
Manual Transmission Fluid	I					✔					✔
Clutch Pedal Operation	I⑤		✔		✔		✔		✔		✔
Tire Rotation	I		✔					✔			
Front Wheel Bearings	L										✔
Rear Axle Halfshaft Dust Boots	I⑥										✔
Steering System	I										✔
Power Steering Fluid	I					✔					✔
Brake Fluid	I					✔					✔
Hinges, Latches, etc.	L					✔					✔
Seat Belt Operation	I					✔					✔

FOR COMPLETE WARRANTY COVERAGE CONSULT INDIVIDUAL VEHICLE MANUFACTURER'S WARRANTY MAINTENANCE GUIDE.

I—Inspect
L—Lubricate
R—Replace
① If applicable
② 5.0L engine only
③ Replace fuel filter every 60,000 miles

④ Inspect timing belt every 60,000 miles, 2.3L engine only
⑤ Adjust clutch by lifting pedal every 6,000 miles, Mustang only
⑥ 1993–94 Mark VIII only
⑦ Reset after indicated services are performed

MAINTENANCE INTERVALS—TYPE A: NORMAL SERVICE
Cougar • Thunderbird

TO BE SERVICED	TYPE OF SERVICE	VEHICLE MILEAGE INTERVAL (X1000)							
		7.5	15	22.5	30	37.5	45	52.5	60
Oxygen Sensor	I				✔				✔
Ignition Timing	I①				✔				✔
Vacuum Lines and Hoses	I				✔				✔
Ignition Wires	I				✔				✔
Spark Plugs	I②				✔				✔
Engine Oil and Filter	R③	✔	✔	✔	✔	✔	✔	✔	✔
Engine Air Cleaner Element	R				✔				✔
Crankcase Emission Filter	R④				✔				✔
PCV Valve	R				✔				✔

MAINTENANCE INTERVALS—TYPE A: NORMAL SERVICE
Cougar • Thunderbird

TO BE SERVICED	TYPE OF SERVICE	VEHICLE MILEAGE INTERVAL (X1000)							
		7.5	15	22.5	30	37.5	45	52.5	60
Fuel Filter	R								✔
Charcoal Canister	I				✔				✔
Fuel/Vapor Return Lines	I				✔				✔
Fuel Tank Cap and Restrictor	I				✔				✔
Coolant System	I		✔		✔		✔		✔
Exhaust Pipe and Muffler	I				✔				✔
Clutch Hydraulic Fluid	I				✔				✔
Catalytic Converter and Shield	I				✔				✔
EGR System	I				✔				✔
Air Pump and Connections	I④				✔				✔
Supercharger Lubricant	I⑤				✔				✔
Tie Rod Ends	I/L				✔				✔
Throttle Body	I		✔		✔		✔		✔
Drive Belts	I				✔				✔
Maintenance Indicator	I⑥								
Brake Pads, Front	I				✔				✔
Brake Pads, Rear	I				✔				✔
Brake Shoes, Rear	I				✔				✔
Brake Drums and Rotors	I				✔				✔
Brake Hoses and Lines	I				✔				✔
Battery Connections	I		✔		✔		✔		✔
Ball Joints	I/L				✔				✔
Engine Coolant	R				✔				✔
Automatic Transmission Fluid	I	✔	✔	✔	✔	✔	✔	✔	✔
Manual Transmission Fluid	I		✔		✔		✔		✔
Clutch Pedal Operation	I				✔				✔
Tire Rotation	I	✔		✔		✔		✔	
Rear Axle Halfshaft Dust Boots	I				✔				✔
Steering System	I				✔				✔
Power Steering Fluid	I		✔		✔		✔		✔
Brake Fluid	I		✔		✔		✔		✔
Hinges, Latches, etc.	L		✔		✔		✔		✔
Seat Belt Operation	I		✔		✔		✔		✔

FOR COMPLETE WARRANTY COVERAGE CONSULT INDIVIDUAL VEHICLE MANUFACTURER'S WARRANTY MAINTENANCE GUIDE.

I—Inspect
L—Lubricate
R—Replace
① If applicable
② 3.8L and 5.0L engines—replace spark plugs every 30,000 miles
3.8L Supercharged engine—replace Platinum spark plugs every 60,000 miles
③ If equipped with vehicle maintenance monitor, change oil and filter when indicated, but do not go beyond 7,500 miles or 6 months, whichever occurs first. Supercharged engines—change oil and filter every 5,000 miles, or sooner if indicated by vehicle maintenance monitor, if equipped.
④ 5.0L engine only
⑤ 3.8L Supercharged engine only
⑥ Reset after indicated services are performed

MAINTENANCE INTERVALS—TYPE B: SEVERE SERVICE
Cougar • Thunderbird

TO BE SERVICED	TYPE OF SERVICE	VEHICLE MILEAGE INTERVAL (X1000)									
		3	6	9	12	15	18	21	24	27	30
Oxygen Sensor	I										✔
Ignition Timing	I ①										✔
Vacuum Lines and Hose	I										✔
Ignition Wires	I										✔
Spark Plugs	R ②										✔
Engine Oil and Filter	R	✔	✔	✔	✔	✔	✔	✔	✔	✔	✔
Engine Air Cleaner Element	R										✔
Crankcase Emission Filter	R ③										✔
PCV Valve	R										✔
Fuel Filter	R ④										✔
Charcoal Canister	I										✔
Fuel/Vapor Return Lines	I										✔
Fuel Tank Cap and Restrictor	I										✔
Coolant System	I					✔					✔
Exhaust Pipe and Muffler	I										✔
Clutch Hydraulic Fluid	I										✔
Catalytic Converter and Shield	I										✔
EGR System	I										✔
Air Pump and Connections	I ③										✔
Supercharger Lubricant	I ⑤										✔
Tie Rod Ends	I/L										
Throttle Body	I					✔					✔
Drive Belts	I										✔
Miantenance Indicator	I ⑥										
Brake Pads, Front	I										✔
Brake Pads, Rear	I										✔
Brake Shoes, Rear	I										✔
Brake Drums and Rotors	I										✔
Brake Hoses and Lines	I										✔
Battery Connections	I					✔					✔
Ball Joints	I/L										✔
Engine Coolant	R										✔
Automatic Transmission Fluid	R										✔
Manual Transmission Fluid	I					✔					✔
Clutch Pedal Operation	I										✔
Tire Rotation	I		✔					✔			
Rear Axle Halfshaft Dust Boots	I										✔
Steering System	I										✔
Power Steering Fluid	I					✔					✔
Brake Fluid	I					✔					✔

MAINTENANCE INTERVALS—TYPE B: SEVERE SERVICE
Cougar • Thunderbird

TO BE SERVICED	TYPE OF SERVICE	VEHICLE MILEAGE INTERVAL (X1000)									
		3	6	9	12	15	18	21	24	27	30
Hinges, Latches, etc.	L					✔					✔
Seat Belt Operation	I					✔					✔

FOR COMPLETE WARRANTY COVERAGE CONSULT INDIVIDUAL VEHICLE MANUFACTURER'S WARRANTY MAINTENANCE GUIDE.

I—Inspect
L—Lubricate
R—Replace
① If applicable
② 3.8L and 5.0L engines—replace spark plugs every 30,000 miles
3.8L Supercharged engine—replace Platinum spark plugs every 60,000 miles

③ 5.0L engine only
④ Replace fuel filter every 60,000 miles
⑤ 3.8L Supercharged engine only
⑥ Reset after indicated services are performed

FIRING ORDERS

NOTE: To avoid confusion, always replace spark plugs and wires one at a time.

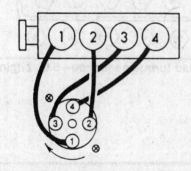

1990 2.3L Engine
Engine Firing Order: 1-3-4-2
Distributor Rotation: Clockwise

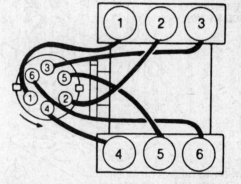

3.8L (except SC) Engine
Engine Firing Order: 1–4–2–5–3–6
Distributor Rotation: Counterclockwise

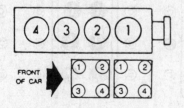

1991–94 2.3L Engine
Engine Firing Order: 1-3-4-2
Distributorless Ignition System

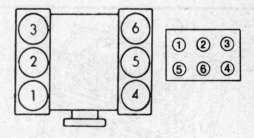

3.8L SC Engine
Engine Firing Order: 1-4-2-5-3-6
Distributorless Ignition System

FIRING ORDERS

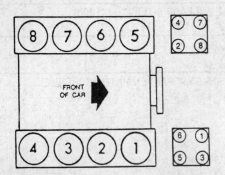

4.6L Engine
Engine Firing Order: 1–3–7–2–6–5–4–8
Distributorless Ignition System

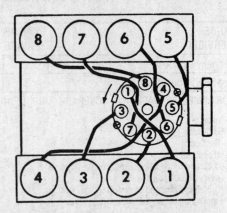

5.0L Engine
Engine Firing Order: 1–3–7–2–6–5–4–8
Distributor Rotation: Counterclockwise

CYLINDER HEAD TORQUE SEQUENCES

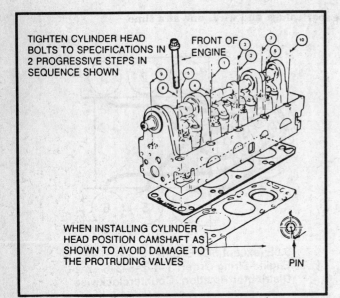

TIGHTEN CYLINDER HEAD BOLTS TO SPECIFICATIONS IN 2 PROGRESSIVE STEPS IN SEQUENCE SHOWN

FRONT OF ENGINE

WHEN INSTALLING CYLINDER HEAD POSITION CAMSHAFT AS SHOWN TO AVOID DAMAGE TO THE PROTRUDING VALVES

PIN

Cylinder head bolt torque sequence—2.3L engine

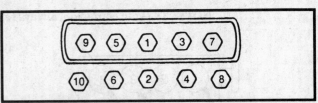

Cylinder head torque sequence—5.0L engine

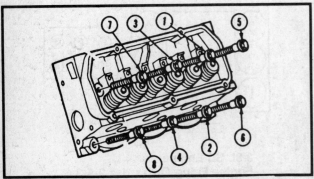

Cylinder head bolt torque sequence—3.8L engine

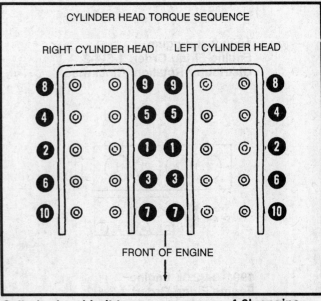

CYLINDER HEAD TORQUE SEQUENCE

RIGHT CYLINDER HEAD   LEFT CYLINDER HEAD

FRONT OF ENGINE

Cylinder head bolt torque sequence—4.6L engine

TIMING MARK LOCATIONS

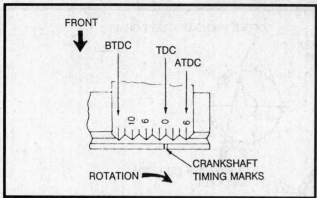

Timing mark location—3.8L engine

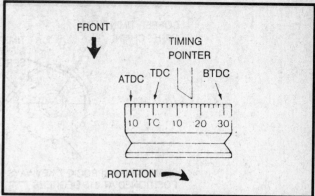

Timing mark location—2.3L engine

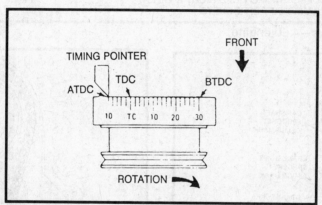

Timing mark location—5.0L engine

TIMING CHAIN/BELT ALIGNMENT MARKS

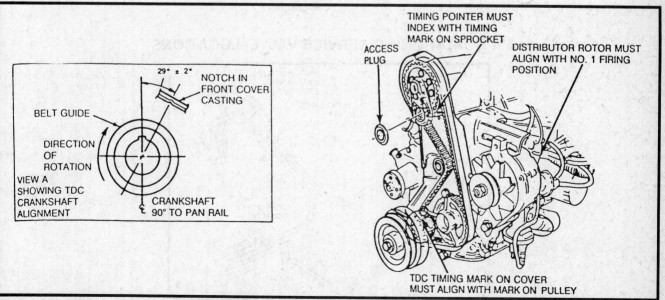

Timing belt alignment marks—2.3L engine

TIMING CHAIN/BELT ALIGNMENT MARKS

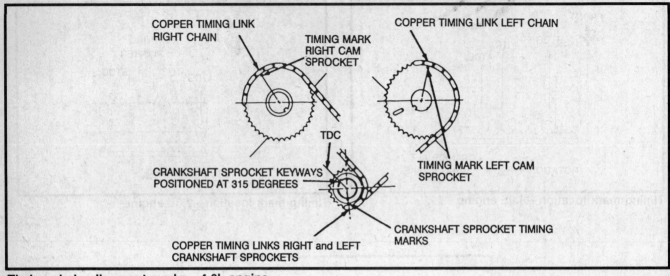

Timing chain alignment marks—4.6L engine

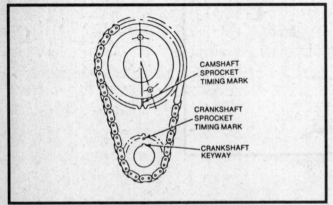

Timing chain alignment marks—V6 engine

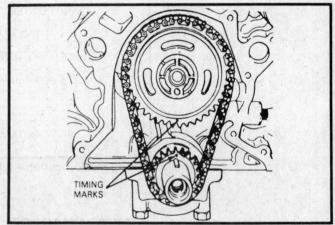

Timing chain alignment marks—5.0L and 5.8L engines

AIR CONDITIONING SERVICE VALVE LOCATIONS

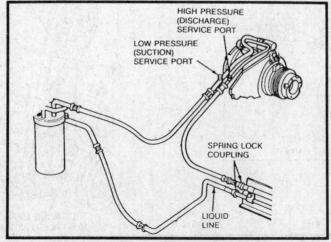

Air conditioning service valve location

WHEEL ALIGNMENT ADJUSTMENT
LOCATIONS

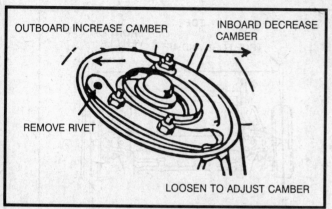

Front camber adjustment—Mustang and Mark VII

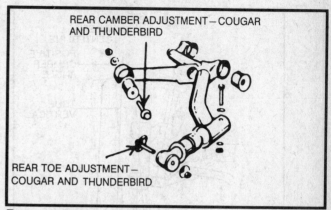

Rear camber and toe adjustment

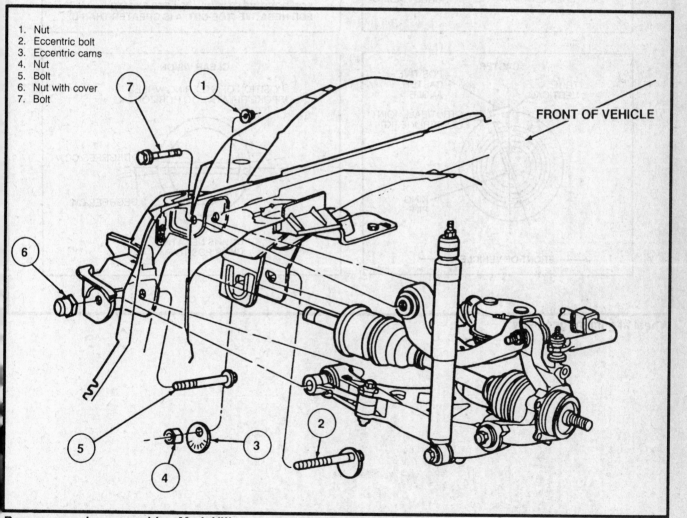

1. Nut
2. Eccentric bolt
3. Eccentric cams
4. Nut
5. Bolt
6. Nut with cover
7. Bolt

Rear suspension assembly—Mark VIII

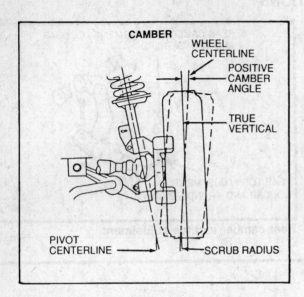

CAMBER

WHEEL CENTERLINE

POSITIVE CAMBER ANGLE

TRUE VERTICAL

PIVOT CENTERLINE

SCRUB RADIUS

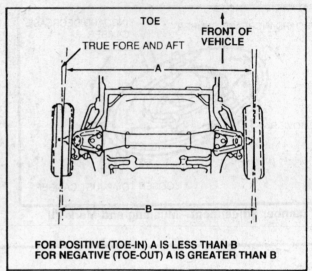

TOE

FRONT OF VEHICLE

TRUE FORE AND AFT

A

B

FOR POSITIVE (TOE-IN) A IS LESS THAN B
FOR NEGATIVE (TOE-OUT) A IS GREATER THAN B

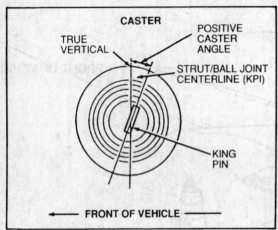

CASTER

TRUE VERTICAL

POSITIVE CASTER ANGLE

STRUT/BALL JOINT CENTERLINE (KPI)

KING PIN

← FRONT OF VEHICLE →

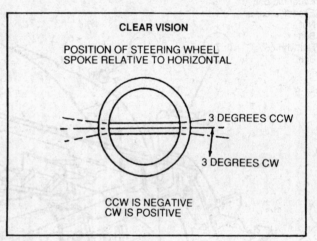

CLEAR VISION

POSITION OF STEERING WHEEL SPOKE RELATIVE TO HORIZONTAL

3 DEGREES CCW

3 DEGREES CW

CCW IS NEGATIVE
CW IS POSITIVE

Wheel alignment geometry

SPECIFICATION CHARTS

VEHICLE IDENTIFICATION CHART

It is important for servicing and ordering parts to be certain of the vehicle and engine identification. The VIN (vehicle identification number) is a 17 digit number visible through the windshield on the driver's side of the dash and contains the vehicle and engine identification codes. The tenth digit indicates model year and the eighth digit indicates engine code. It can be interpreted as follows:

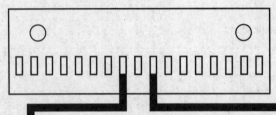

		Engine Code					Model Year	
Code	Liters	Cu. In. (cc)	Cyl.	Fuel Sys.	Eng. Mfg.		Code	Year
W	4.6	280 (4593)	8	SEFI	Ford		L	1990
F	5.0	302 (4943)	8	SEFI	Ford		M	1991
G	5.8	351 (5767)	8	VV	Ford		N	1992
							P	1993
							R	1994

SEFI—Sequential Electronic Fuel Injection
VV—Variable Venturi Carburetor

ENGINE IDENTIFICATION

Year	Model	Engine Displacement Liters (cc)	Engine Series (ID/VIN)	Fuel System	No. of Cylinders	Engine Type
1990	Crown Victoria	5.0 (4943)	F	SEFI	8	OHV
	Crown Victoria	5.8 (5767)	G	VV	8	OHV
	Grand Marquis	5.0 (4943)	F	SEFI	8	OHV
	Grand Marquis	5.8 (5767)	G	VV	8	OHV
	Town Car	5.0 (4943)	F	SEFI	8	OHV
1991	Crown Victoria	5.0 (4943)	F	SEFI	8	OHV
	Crown Victoria	5.8 (5767)	G	VV	8	OHV
	Grand Marquis	5.0 (4943)	F	SEFI	8	OHV
	Grand Marquis	5.8 (5767)	G	VV	8	OHV
	Town Car	4.6 (4593)	W	SEFI	8	OHC
1992	Crown Victoria	4.6 (4593)	W	SEFI	8	OHC
	Grand Marquis	4.6 (4593)	W	SEFI	8	OHC
	Town Car	4.6 (4593)	W	SEFI	8	OHC
1993-94	Crown Victoria	4.6 (4593)	W	SEFI	8	OHC
	Grand Marquis	4.6 (4593)	W	SEFI	8	OHC
	Town Car	4.6 (4593)	W	SEFI	8	OHC

SEFI—Sequential Electronic Fuel Injection
VV—Variable Venturi Carburetor
OHV—Overhead Valve
OHC—Overhead Camshaft

GENERAL ENGINE SPECIFICATIONS

Year	Engine ID/VIN	Engine Displacement Liters (cc)	Fuel System Type	Net Horsepower @ rpm	Net Torque @ rpm (ft. lbs.)	Bore × Stroke (in.)	Compression Ratio	Oil Pressure @ rpm ③
1990	F	5.0 (4943)	SEFI	①	②	4.00 × 3.00	8.9:1	40–60 @ 2000
	G	5.8 (5767)	VV	180 @ 3600	285 @ 2400	4.00 × 3.50	8.3:1	40–60 @ 2000
1991	W	4.6 (4593)	SEFI	④	⑤	3.55 × 3.54	9.0:1	20–45 @ 1500
	F	5.0 (4943)	SEFI	①	②	4.00 × 3.00	8.9:1	40–60 @ 2000
	G	5.8 (5767)	VV	180 @ 3600	285 @ 2400	4.00 × 3.50	8.3:1	40–60 @ 2000
1992	W	4.6 (4593)	SEFI	④	⑤	3.55 × 3.54	9.0:1	20–45 @ 1500
1993–94	W	4.6 (4593)	SEFI	④	⑤	3.55 × 3.54	9.0:1	20–45 @ 1500

SEFI—Sequential Electronic Fuel Injection
VV—Variable Venturi Carburetor
① Single exhaust: 150 @ 3200
   Dual exhaust: 160 @ 3400
② Single exhaust: 270 @ 2000
   Dual exhaust: 280 @ 2200

③ Engine at normal operating temperature
④ Single exhaust: 190 @ 4200
   Dual exhaust: 210 @ 4600
⑤ Single exhaust: 260 @ 3200
   Dual exhaust: 270 @ 3400

GASOLINE ENGINE TUNE-UP SPECIFICATIONS

Year	Engine ID/VIN	Engine Displacement Liters (cc)	Spark Plugs Gap (in.)	Ignition Timing (deg.) MT	AT	Fuel Pump (psi)	Idle Speed (rpm) MT	AT	Valve Clearance In.	Ex.
1990	F	5.0 (4943)	0.050	—	10B	35–40 ③	—	①	Hyd.	Hyd.
	G	5.8 (5767)	0.044	—	14B	6–8	—	①	Hyd.	Hyd.
1991	W	4.6 (4593)	0.054	—	10B	35–40	560 ②		Hyd.	Hyd.
	F	5.0 (4943)	0.050	—	10B	35–40 ③	—	①	Hyd.	Hyd.
	G	5.8 (5767)	0.044	—	14B	6–8	—	①	Hyd.	Hyd.
1992	W	4.6 (4593)	0.054	—	10B	35–40	—	560 ②	Hyd.	Hyd.
1993	W	4.6 (4593)	0.054	—	10B	35–40	—	560 ②	Hyd.	Hyd.
1994			SEE UNDERHOOD SPECIFICATIONS STICKER							

NOTE: The lowest cylinder pressure should be within 75% of the highest cylinder pressure reading. For example, if the highest cylinder is 134 psi, the lowest should be 101. Engine should be at normal operating temperature with throttle valve in the wide open position.
The underhood specifications sticker often reflects tune-up specification changes in production. Sticker figures must be used if they disagree with those in this chart.
Hyd.—Hydraulic
B—Before Top Dead Center
① Refer to the underhood specifications sticker
② Transmission in drive
③ Key on, engine off

CAPACITIES

Year	Model	Engine ID/VIN	Engine Displacement Liters (cc)	Engine Crankcase with Filter (qts.)	Transmission (pts.) 4-Spd	5-Spd	Auto.	Transfer case (pts.)	Drive Axle Front (pts.)	Rear (pts.)	Fuel Tank (gal.)	Cooling System (qts.)
1990	Crown Victoria	F	5.0 (4943)	5	—	—	24.6	—	—	4.0	18.0	14.1
	Crown Victoria	G	5.8 (5767)	5	—	—	24.6	—	—	4.0	20.0	14.1
	Grand Marquis	F	5.0 (4943)	5	—	—	24.6	—	—	4.0	18.0	14.1
	Grand Marquis	G	5.8 (5767)	5	—	—	24.6	—	—	4.0	20.0	14.1
	Town Car	F	5.0 (4943)	5	—	—	24.6	—	—	4.0	18.0	14.1

CAPACITIES

Year	Model	Engine ID/VIN	Engine Displacement Liters (cc)	Engine Crankcase with Filter (qts.)	Transmission (pts.) 4-Spd	5-Spd	Auto.	Transfer case (pts.)	Drive Axle Front (pts.)	Rear (pts.)	Fuel Tank (gal.)	Cooling System (qts.)
1991	Crown Victoria	F	5.0 (4943)	5	—	—	24.6	—	—	4.0	18.0	14.1
	Crown Victoria	G	5.8 (5767)	5	—	—	24.6	—	—	4.0	20.0	14.1
	Grand Marquis	F	5.0 (4943)	5	—	—	24.6	—	—	4.0	18.0	14.1
	Grand Marquis	G	5.8 (5767)	5	—	—	24.6	—	—	4.0	20.0	14.1
	Town Car	W	4.6 (4593)	5	—	—	24.6	—	—	4.0	20.0	14.1
1992	Crown Victoria	W	4.6 (4593)	5	—	—	24.6	—	—	4.0	20.0	14.1
	Grand Marquis	W	4.6 (4593)	5	—	—	24.6	—	—	4.0	20.0	14.1
	Town Car	W	4.6 (4593)	5	—	—	24.6	—	—	4.0	20.0	14.1
1993-94	Crown Victoria	W	4.6 (4593)	5	—	—	27.0	—	—	4.0	20.0	14.1
	Grand Marquis	W	4.6 (4593)	5	—	—	27.0	—	—	4.0	20.0	14.1
	Town Car	W	4.6 (4593)	5	—	—	28.0	—	—	4.0	20.0	14.1

CAMSHAFT SPECIFICATIONS

All measurements given in inches.

Year	Engine ID/VIN	Engine Displacement Liters (cc)	Journal Diameter 1	2	3	4	5	Elevation In.	Ex.	Bearing Clearance	Camshaft End Play
1990	F	5.0 (4943)	2.0805–2.0815	2.0655–2.0665	2.0505–2.0515	2.0355–2.0365	2.0205–2.0215	0.2325–0.2375	0.2424–0.2474	0.0010–0.0060	0.0005–0.0090
	G	5.8 (5767)	2.0805–2.0815	2.0655–2.0665	2.0505–2.0515	2.0355–2.0365	2.0205–2.0215	0.2730–0.2780	0.2780–0.2830	0.0010–0.0060	0.0010–0.0090
1991	W	4.6 (4593)	1.0605–1.0615	1.0605–1.0615	1.0605–1.0615	1.0605–1.0615	1.0605–1.0615	0.2590	0.2590	0.0010–0.0060	0.0010–0.0070
	F	5.0 (4943)	2.0805–2.0815	2.0655–2.0665	2.0505–2.0515	2.0355–2.0365	2.0205–2.0215	0.2325–0.2375	0.2424–0.2474	0.0010–0.0060	0.0005–0.0090
	G	5.8 (5767)	2.0805–2.0815	2.0655–2.0665	2.0505–2.0515	2.0355–2.0365	2.0205–2.0215	0.2730–0.2780	0.2780–0.2830	0.0010–0.0060	0.0005–0.0090
1992	W	4.6 (4593)	1.0605–1.0615	1.0605–1.0615	1.0605–1.0615	1.0605–1.0615	1.0605–1.0615	0.2590	0.2590	0.0010–0.0060	0.0010–0.0070
1993-94	W	4.6 (4593)	1.0605–1.0615	1.0605–1.0615	1.0605–1.0615	1.0605–1.0615	1.0605–1.0615	0.2590	0.2590	0.0010–0.0060	0.0005–0.0070

CRANKSHAFT AND CONNECTING ROD SPECIFICATIONS

All measurements are given in inches.

Year	Engine ID/VIN	Engine Displacement Liters (cc)	Crankshaft Main Brg. Journal Dia.	Main Brg. Oil Clearance	Shaft End-play	Thrust on No.	Connecting Rod Journal Diameter	Oil Clearance	Side Clearance
1990	F	5.0 (4943)	2.2482–2.2490	0.0004–0.0021	0.004–0.012	3	2.1228–2.1236	0.0008–0.0024	0.010–0.023
	G	5.8 (5767)	2.9994–3.0002	0.0008–0.0026	0.004–0.012	3	2.3103–2.3111	0.0007–0.0025	0.010–0.023

CRANKSHAFT AND CONNECTING ROD SPECIFICATIONS

All measurements are given in inches.

Year	Engine ID/VIN	Engine Displacement Liters (cc)	Crankshaft				Connecting Rod		
			Main Brg. Journal Dia.	Main Brg. Oil Clearance	Shaft End-play	Thrust on No.	Journal Diameter	Oil Clearance	Side Clearance
1991	W	4.6 (4593)	2.6575	0.0011–0.0025	0.005–0.010	5	2.0866	0.0011–0.0027	0.006–0.019
	F	5.0 (4943)	2.2482–2.2490	0.0004–0.0024	0.004–0.012	3	2.1228–2.1236	0.0008–0.0026	0.010–0.023
	G	5.8 (5767)	2.9994–3.0002	0.0008–0.0025	0.004–0.012	3	2.3103–2.3111	0.0007–0.0025	0.010–0.023
1992	W	4.6 (4593)	2.6578–2.6598	0.0011–0.0025	0.005–0.010	5	2.0866	0.0011–0.0027	0.006–0.019
1993–94	W	4.6 (4593)	2.6578–2.6598	0.0011–0.0025	0.005–0.010	5	2.0866	0.0011–0.0027	0.006–0.019

VALVE SPECIFICATIONS

Year	Engine ID/VIN	Engine Displacement Liters (cc)	Seat Angle (deg.)	Face Angle (deg.)	Spring Test Pressure (lbs. @ in.)	Spring Installed Height (in.)	Stem-to-Guide Clearance (in.)		Stem Diameter (in.)	
							Intake	Exhaust	Intake	Exhaust
1990	F	5.0 (4943)	45	44	①	②	0.0010–0.0027	0.0015–0.0032	0.3416–0.3423	0.3411–0.3418
	G	5.8 (5767)	45	44	195–215 @ 1.05	②	0.0010–0.0027	0.0015–0.0032	0.3416–0.3423	0.3411–0.3418
1991	W	4.6 (4593)	45	45.5	132 @ 1.10	1.57	0.0008–0.0027	0.0018–0.0037	0.2746–0.2754	0.2736–0.2744
	F	5.0 (4943)	45	44	①	②	0.0010–0.0027	0.0015–0.0032	0.3416–0.3423	0.3411–0.3418
	G	5.8 (5767)	45	44	195–215 @ 1.05	②	0.0010–0.0027	0.0015–0.0032	0.3416–0.3423	0.3411–0.3418
1992	W	4.6 (4593)	45	45.5	132 @ 1.10	1.57	0.0008–0.0027	0.0018–0.0037	0.2746–0.2754	0.2736–0.2744
1993–94	W	4.6 (4593)	45	45.5	132 @ 1.10	1.57	0.0008–0.0027	0.0018–0.0037	0.2746–0.2754	0.2736–0.2744

① Intake: 194–214 @ 1.36
   Exhaust: 190–210 @ 1.20
② Intake: 1.75–1.80
   Exhaust: 1.58–1.64

PISTON AND RING SPECIFICATIONS

All measurements are given in inches.

Year	Engine ID/VIN	Engine Displacement Liters (cc)	Piston Clearance	Ring Gap			Ring Side Clearance		
				Top Compression	Bottom Compression	Oil Control	Top Compression	Bottom Compression	Oil Control
1990	F	5.0 (4943)	0.0014–0.0022	0.010–0.020	0.010–0.020	0.015–0.055	0.0020–0.0040	0.0020–0.0040	Snug
	G	5.8 (5767)	0.0018–0.0026	0.010–0.020	0.010–0.020	0.015–0.055	0.0020–0.0040	0.0020–0.0040	Snug

PISTON AND RING SPECIFICATIONS

All measurements are given in inches.

Year	Engine ID/VIN	Engine Displacement Liters (cc)	Piston Clearance	Ring Gap			Ring Side Clearance		
				Top Compression	Bottom Compression	Oil Control	Top Compression	Bottom Compression	Oil Control
1991	W	4.6 (4593)	0.0008–0.0018	0.009–0.019	0.009–0.019	0.010–0.030	0.0016–0.0035	0.0012–0.0031	Snug
	F	5.0 (4943)	0.0014–0.0022	0.010–0.020	0.010–0.020	0.015–0.055	0.0020–0.0040	0.0020–0.0040	Snug
	G	5.8 (5767)	0.0018–0.0026	0.010–0.020	0.010–0.020	0.015–0.055	0.0020–0.0040	0.0020–0.0040	Snug
1992	W	4.6 (4593)	0.0008–0.0016	0.009–0.019	0.009–0.019	0.010–0.030	0.0016–0.0035	0.0012–0.0031	Snug
1993–94	W	4.6 (4593)	0.0008–0.0016	0.009–0.019	0.009–0.019	0.010–0.030	0.0016–0.0035	0.0012–0.0031	Snug

TORQUE SPECIFICATIONS

All readings in ft. lbs.

Year	Engine ID/VIN	Engine Displacement Liters (cc)	Cylinder Head Bolts	Main Bearing Bolts	Rod Bearing Bolts	Crankshaft Damper Bolts	Flywheel Bolts	Manifold		Spark Plugs	Lug Nut
								Intake	Exhaust		
1990	F	5.0 (4943)	①	60–70	19–24	70–90	75–85	23–25②	18–24	5–10	85–105
	G	5.8 (5767)	③	90–105	40–45	70–90	75–85	23–25②	18–24	10–15	85–105
1991	W	4.6 (4593)	④	⑤	⑥	114–121	54–64	15–22②	15–22	7	85–105
	F	5.0 (4943)	①	60–70	19–24	70–90	75–85	23–25②	18–24	5–10	85–105
	G	5.8 (5767)	③	95–105	40–45	70–90	75–85	23–25②	18–24	10–15	85–105
1992	W	4.6 (4593)	④	⑤	⑥	114–121	54–64	15–22②	15–22	7	85–105
1993–94	W	4.6 (4593)	⑦	⑤	⑧	114–121	54–64	15–22②	15–22②	7	85–105

① Tighten in 2 steps:
Step 1: 55–65 ft. lbs.
Step 2: 65–72 ft. lbs.
② Retorque with engine hot
③ Tighten in 3 steps:
Step 1: 85 ft. lbs.
Step 2: 95 ft. lbs.
Step 3: 105–112 ft. lbs.

④ Tighten in 3 steps:
Step 1: 15–22 ft. lbs.
Step 2: Turn each bolt 85–95 degrees, in sequence
Step 3: Turn each bolt 85–95 degrees, in sequence
⑤ Tighten in 2 steps:
Step 1: 22–25 ft. lbs.
Step 2: Turn each bolt 85–95 degrees

⑥ Tighten in 2 steps:
Step 1: 18–25 ft. lbs.
Step 2: Turn each bolt 85–95 degrees
⑦ Tighten in 3 steps:
Step 1: 25–30 ft. lbs.
Step 2: Rotate 85–95 degrees
Step 3: Rotate 85–95 degrees
⑧ Tighten in 2 steps:
Step 1: 12 ft. lbs.
Step 2: Rotate 85–95 degrees

TORQUE SPECIFICATIONS

Component	English	Metric
Camshaft cap bolts		
4.6L engine		
Step 1:	6.0–8.8 ft. lbs.	8–12 Nm
Step 2:	loosen bolts 2–3 turns	loosen bolts 2–3 turns
Step 3:	6.0–8.8 ft. lbs.	8–12 Nm
Camshaft sprocket bolt		
4.6L engine:	81–95 ft. lbs.	110–130 Nm
5.0L engine:	40–45 ft. lbs.	54–61 Nm
5.8L engine:	40–45 ft. lbs.	54–61 Nm
Camshaft thrust plate		
5.0L engine:	9–12 ft. lbs.	12–16 Nm
5.8L engine:	9–12 ft. lbs.	12–16 Nm

TORQUE SPECIFICATIONS

Component	English	Metric
Carburetor-to-intake manifold		
5.8L engine:	12–15 ft. lbs.	16–20 Nm
Connecting rod bearing cap nuts/bolts		
4.6L engine		
Step 1:	18–25 ft. lbs.	25–34 Nm
Step 2:	+ 85–95 degrees turn	+ 85–95 degrees turn
5.0L engine:	19–24 ft. lbs.	25–33 Nm
5.8L engine:	40–45 ft. lbs.	54–61 Nm
Crankshaft damper bolt		
4.6L engine:	114–121 ft. lbs.	155–165 Nm
5.0L engine:	70–90 ft. lbs.	95–122 Nm
5.8L engine:	70–90 ft. lbs.	95–122 Nm
Cylinder head bolt		
4.6L engine *		
Step 1:	15–22 ft. lbs.	20–30 Nm
Step 2:	+ 85–95 degrees turn	+ 85–95 degrees turn
Step 3:	+ 85–95 degrees turn	+ 85–95 degrees turn
5.0L engine		
Step 1:	55–65 ft. lbs.	75–88 Nm
Step 2:	65–72 ft. lbs.	88–98 Nm
5.8L engine		
Step 1:	85 ft. lbs.	116 Nm
Step 2:	95 ft. lbs.	129 Nm
Step 3:	105–112 ft. lbs.	143–152 Nm
* NOTE: Use new bolts and oil the threads		
Distributor hold-down:	18–26 ft. lbs.	24–35 Nm
EGR valve		
4.6L engine:	15–22 ft. lbs.	20–30 Nm
5.0L and 5.8L engines:	15–22 ft. lbs.	20–30 Nm
EGR valve-to-spacer plate		
5.0L engine:	12–18 ft. lbs.	16–24 Nm
5.8L engine:	12–18 ft. lbs.	16–24 Nm
EGR supply tube		
4.6L engine:	33–48 ft. lbs.	45–65 Nm
Engine-to-transmission:	40 ft. lbs.	55 Nm
Engine/transmission mounts		
4.6L engine		
Front		
Mount-to-engine block:	45–60 ft. lbs.	60–81 Nm
Mount through bolts:	15–22 ft. lbs.	20–30 Nm
Rear		
Mount-to-transmission:	50–70 ft. lbs.	68–95 Nm
Mount-to-crossmember:	35–50 ft. lbs.	48–68 Nm
5.0L and 5.8L engines		
Front		
Mount-to-frame:	26–38 ft. lbs.	35–52 Nm
Mount through bolts:	45–65 ft. lbs.	61–88 Nm
Rear		
Mount-to-transmission:	50–70 ft. lbs.	68–95 Nm
Mount-to-crossmember:	35–50 ft. lbs.	48–68 Nm
Exhaust flange-to-manifold nuts:	20–30 ft. lbs.	27–41 Nm
Exhaust manifold		
4.6L engine:	15–22 ft. lbs.	20–30 Nm
5.0L engine:	18–24 ft. lbs.	25–33 Nm
5.8L engine:	18–24 ft. lbs.	25–33 Nm
Flywheel/flexplate-to-crankshaft bolts		
4.6L engine:	54–64 ft. lbs.	75–87 Nm
5.0L engine:	75–85 ft. lbs.	102–116 Nm
5.8L engine:	75–85 ft. lbs.	102–116 Nm

TORQUE SPECIFICATIONS

Component	English	Metric
Flywheel-to-converter bolts:	20–34 ft. lbs.	27–46 Nm
Fuel pump-to-block		
5.8L engine:	19–27 ft. lbs.	26–37 Nm
Fuel rail-to-intake manifold bolts:	70–105 ft. lbs.	8–12 Nm
Generator brace-to-intake manidold:	6–8.8 ft. lbs.	8–12 Nm
Intake manifold		
4.6L engine		
Step 1:	15–22 ft. lbs.	20–30 Nm
Step 2:	retorque when hot	retorque when hot
5.0L and 5.8L engines		
Step 1:	23–25 ft. lbs.	31–34 Nm
Step 2:	retorque when hot	retorque when hot
Intake plenum-to-lower manifold		
5.0L engine:	12–18 ft. lbs.	16–24 Nm
Main bearing cap bolts		
4.6L engine		
Step 1:	22–25 ft. lbs.	30–35 Nm
Step 2:	+ 85–95 degrees turn	+ 85–95 degrees turn
5.0L engine:	60–70 ft. lbs.	81–95 Nm
5.8L engine:	95–105 ft. lbs.	129–143 Nm
Main bearing cap jack screws/side bolts		
4.6L engine		
Screws		
Step 1:	44 inch lbs.	5 Nm
Step 2:	80–97 inch lbs.	9–11 Nm
Side bolts		
Step 1:	88 inch lbs.	10 Nm
Step 2:	14–17 ft. lbs.	19–23 Nm
Oil pan-to-block		
4.6L engine:	15–22 ft. lbs.	20–30 Nm
5.0L and 5.8L engines:	10 ft. lbs.	14 Nm
Oil pan drain plug		
4.6L engine:	8–12 ft. lbs.	11–16 Nm
5.0L and 5.8L engines:	15–25 ft. lbs.	20–34 Nm
Oil pump attaching bolts		
4.6L engine:	6.0–8.8 ft. lbs.	8–12 Nm
5.0L engine:	22–32 ft. lbs.	30–43 Nm
5.8L engine:	22–32 ft. lbs.	30–43 Nm
Rocker arm bolt		
5.0L engine:	18–25 ft. lbs.	24–34 Nm
5.8L engine:	18–25 ft. lbs.	24–34 Nm
Rear main oil seal retainer:	6–8.8 ft. lbs.	8–12 Nm
Rocker arm (valve) cover		
4.6L engine:	6.0–8.8 ft. lbs.	8–12 Nm
5.0L engine:	10–13 ft. lbs.	14–18 Nm
5.8L engine		
1990	3–5 ft. lbs.	4–7 Nm
1991:	10–13 ft. lbs.	14–18 Nm
Spark plug		
4.6L engine:	7 ft. lbs.	10 Nm
5.0L engine:	5–10 ft. lbs.	7–14 Nm
5.8L engine:	10–15 ft. lbs.	14–20 Nm
Starter-to-block bolts:	15–20 ft. lbs.	20–27 Nm
Thermostat housing		
4.6L engine:	15–22 ft. lbs.	20–30 Nm
5.0L and 5.8L engines:	12–18 ft. lbs.	16–24 Nm
Throttle body nuts/bolts		
4.6L engine:	6.0–8.5 ft. lbs.	8.0–11.5 Nm
5.0L engine:	12–18 ft. lbs.	16–24 Nm

TORQUE SPECIFICATIONS

Component	English	Metric
Timing chain tensioner bolt		
4.6L engine:	15–22 ft. lbs.	20–30 Nm
Timing cover		
4.6L engine:	15–22 ft. lbs.	20–30 Nm
5.0L engine:	15–18 ft. lbs.	20–24 Nm
5.8L engine:	15–18 ft. lbs.	20–24 Nm
Water pump:		
4.6L engine:	15–22 ft. lbs.	20–30 Nm
5.0L engine:	12–18 ft. lbs.	16–24 Nm
5.8L engine:	12–18 ft. lbs.	16–24 Nm

BRAKE SPECIFICATIONS

All measurements in inches unless noted.

Year	Model	Master Cylinder Bore	Brake Disc Original Thickness	Brake Disc Minimum Thickness	Brake Disc Maximum Runout	Brake Drum Diameter Original Inside Diameter	Brake Drum Diameter Max. Wear Limit	Brake Drum Diameter Maximum Machine Diameter	Minimum Lining Thickness Front	Minimum Lining Thickness Rear
1990	Crown Victoria	1.00	1.03	0.972	0.003	①	NA	②	0.125	0.031
	Grand Marquis	1.00	1.03	0.972	0.003	①	NA	②	0.125	0.031
	Town Car	1.00	1.03	0.972	0.003	10.000	NA	10.060	0.125	0.031
1991	Crown Victoria	1.00	1.03	0.972	0.003	①	NA	②	0.125	0.031
	Grand Marquis	1.00	1.03	0.972	0.003	①	NA	②	0.125	0.031
	Town Car	1.00	③	④	0.003	—	—	—	0.125	0.123
1992	Crown Victoria	1.00	③	④	⑤	—	—	—	0.125	0.123
	Grand Marquis	1.00	③	④	⑤	—	—	—	0.125	0.123
	Town Car	1.00	③	④	⑤	—	—	—	0.125	0.123
1993–94	Crown Victoria	1.00	③	④	⑤	—	—	—	0.125	0.123
	Grand Marquis	1.00	③	④	⑤	—	—	—	0.125	0.123
	Town Car	1.00	③	④	⑤	—	—	—	0.125	0.123

NA—Not available
① Sedan except Police, Taxi and trailer tow:
10.000
Station Wagon, Police, Taxi and trailer tow:
11.030

② Sedan except Police, Taxi and trailer tow:
10.060
Station Wagon, Police, Taxi and trailer tow:
11.090
③ Front: 1.03
Rear: 0.50

④ Front: 0.974
Rear: 0.44
⑤ Front: 0.003
Rear: 0.003

WHEEL ALIGNMENT

Year	Model	Caster Range (deg.)	Caster Preferred Setting (deg.)	Camber Range (deg.)	Camber Preferred Setting (deg.)	Toe-in (in.)	Steering Axis Inclination (deg.)
1990	Crown Victoria	2½P–4½P	3½P	1¼N–¼P	½N	1/16	11
	Grand Marquis	2½P–4½P	3½P	1¼N–¼P	½N	1/16	11
	Town Car	2½P–4½P	3½P	1¼N–¼P	½N	1/16	11
1991	Crown Victoria	2½P–4½P	3½P	1¼N–¼P	½N	1/16	11
	Grand Marquis	2½P–4½P	3½P	1¼N–¼P	½N	1/16	11
	Town Car	4¾P–6¼P	5½P	1¼N–¼P	½N	1/16	11

WHEEL ALIGNMENT

Year	Model	Caster Range (deg.)	Caster Preferred Setting (deg.)	Camber Range (deg.)	Camber Preferred Setting (deg.)	Toe-in (in.)	Steering Axis Inclination (deg.)
1992	Crown Victoria	4³⁄₄P–6¹⁄₄P	5¹⁄₂P	1¹⁄₄N–¹⁄₄P	¹⁄₂N	¹⁄₁₆	11
	Grand Marquis	4³⁄₄P–6¹⁄₄P	5¹⁄₂P	1¹⁄₄N–¹⁄₄P	¹⁄₂N	¹⁄₁₆	11
	Town Car	5¹⁄₄P–6³⁄₄P	6P	1¹⁄₄N–¹⁄₄P	¹⁄₂N	¹⁄₁₆	11
1993–94	Crown Victoria	4³⁄₄P–6¹⁄₄P	5¹⁄₂P	1¹⁄₄N–¹⁄₄P	¹⁄₂N	¹⁄₁₆	11
	Grand Marquis	4³⁄₄P–6¹⁄₄P	5¹⁄₂P	1¹⁄₄N–¹⁄₄P	¹⁄₂N	¹⁄₁₆	11
	Town Car	5¹⁄₄P–6³⁄₄P	6P	1¹⁄₄N–¹⁄₄P	¹⁄₂N	¹⁄₁₆	11

N—Negative
P—Positive

AIR CONDITIONING BELT TENSION

Year	Model	Engine Displacement Liters (cc)	Belt Type	Specifications New ①	Specifications Used ①
1990	Crown Victoria	5.0 (4943)	V-Ribbed	170	140
	Grand Marquis	5.0 (4943)	V-Ribbed	170	140
	Town Car	5.0 (4943)	V-Ribbed	170	140
1991	Crown Victoria	5.0 (4943)	Poly-V	170	150
	Grand Marquis	5.0 (4943)	Poly-V	170	150
	Crown Victoria	5.8 (5767)	Poly-V	170	150
	Grand Marquis	5.8 (5767)	Poly-V	170	150
	Town Car	4.6 (4593)	Serpentine	②	②
1992	Crown Victoria	4.6 (4593)	Serpentine	②	②
	Grand Marquis	4.6 (4593)	Serpentine	②	②
	Town Car	4.6 (4593)	Serpentine	②	②
1993–94	Crown Victoria	4.6 (4593)	Serpentine	②	②
	Grand Marquis	4.6 (4593)	Serpentine	②	②
	Town Car	4.6 (4593)	Serpentine	②	②

① Lbs. using a belt tension gauge
② Automatic belt tensioner

REFRIGERANT CAPACITIES

Year	Model	Refrigerant (oz.)	Oil (fl. oz.)	Compressor Type
1990	Crown Victoria	48–52 ①	8.0	10PA17
	Grand Marquis	48–52 ①	8.0	10PA17
	Town Car	48–52 ①	8.0	10PA17
1991	Crown Victoria	48–52	7.0	FX-15
	Grand Marquis	48–52	7.0	FX-15
	Town Car	39–41	7.0	FX-15
1992	Crown Victoria	48–52	7.0	FX-15
	Grand Marquis	48–52	7.0	FX-15
	Town Car	39–41	7.0	FX-15

REFRIGERANT CAPACITIES

Year	Model	Refrigerant (oz.)	Oil (fl. oz.)	Compressor Type
1993	Crown Victoria	38–39	7.0①	FX-15
	Grand Marquis	38–39	7.0①	FX-15
	Town Car	36–37	7.0①	FX-15

NOTE: At the time of publication, refrigerant capacity information relating to R-134a was not available from the manufacturer.
① 48 oz. is preferred
② 10 oz. with auxiliary A/C

MAINTENANCE INTERVALS—TYPE A: NORMAL SERVICE
Crown Victoria • Grand Marquis • Town Car

TO BE SERVICED	TYPE OF SERVICE	VEHICLE MILEAGE INTERVAL (X1000)							
		7.5	15	22.5	30	37.5	45	52.5	60
Oxygen Sensor(s)	I				✓				✓
Ignition Timing	I①				✓				✓
Vacuum Lines and Hoses	I				✓				✓
Ignition Wires	I				✓				✓
Spark Plugs	R				✓				✓
Engine Oil and Filter	R④	✓	✓	✓	✓	✓	✓	✓	✓
Engine Air Cleaner Element	R				✓				✓
Crankcase Emission Filter	R②				✓				✓
PCV Valve	R				✓				✓
Fuel Filter	R				✓				✓
Charcoal Canister	I				✓				✓
Fuel/Vapor Return Lines	I				✓				✓
Fuel Tank Cap and Restrictor	I				✓				✓
Coolant System	I		✓		✓		✓		✓
Exhaust Pipe and Muffler	I				✓				✓
Choke Linkage	I③				✓				✓
Catalytic Converter and Shield	I				✓				✓
EGR System	I				✓				✓
Air Pump and Connections	I①				✓				✓
Throttle Body	I④		✓		✓		✓		✓
Drive Belts	I				✓				✓
Brake Pads, Front	I				✓				✓
Brake Pads, Rear	I				✓				✓
Brake Shoes, Rear	I				✓				✓
Brake Drums and Rotors	I				✓				✓
Brake Hoses and Lines	I				✓				✓
Battery Connections	I		✓		✓		✓		✓
Suspension/Ball Joints, etc.	I/L		✓		✓		✓		✓
Engine Coolant	R				✓				✓
Automatic Transmission Fluid	I	✓	✓	✓	✓	✓	✓	✓	✓
Steering Linkage	I/L		✓		✓		✓		✓
Tire Rotation	I	✓		✓		✓		✓	
Front Wheel Bearings	L⑤				✓				✓

MAINTENANCE INTERVALS—TYPE A: NORMAL SERVICE
Crown Victoria • Grand Marquis • Town Car

TO BE SERVICED	TYPE OF SERVICE	VEHICLE MILEAGE INTERVAL (X1000)							
		7.5	15	22.5	30	37.5	45	52.5	60
Steering System	I				✔				✔
Power Steering Fulid	I		✔		✔		✔		✔
Brake Fluid	I		✔		✔		✔		✔
Hinges, Latches, etc.	L		✔		✔		✔		✔
Seat Belt Operation	I		✔		✔		✔		✔

FOR COMPLETE WARRANTY COVERAGE CONSULT INDIVIDUAL VEHICLE MANUFACTURER'S WARRANTY MAINTENANCE GUIDE.

I—Inspect
L—Lubricate
R—Replace
① If applicable
② All except 4.6L engine

③ 5.8L engine only
④ All except 5.8L engine
⑤ 1990–91 Crown Victoria, Grand Marquis and 1990 Town Car only. Subsequent models have sealed front wheel bearing assemblies.

MAINTENANCE INTERVALS—TYPE B: SEVERE SERVICE
Crown Victoria • Grand Marquis • Town Car

TO BE SERVICED	TYPE OF SERVICE	VEHICLE MILEAGE INTERVAL (X1000)									
		3	6	9	12	15	18	21	24	27	30
Oxygen Sensor(s)	I										✔
Ignition Timing	I①										✔
Vacuum Lines and Hoses	I										✔
Ignition Wires	I										✔
Spark Plugs	R										✔
Engine Oil and Filter	R	✔	✔	✔	✔	✔	✔	✔	✔	✔	✔
Engine Air Cleaner Element	R										✔
Crankcase Emission Filter	R②										✔
PCV Valve	R										✔
Fuel Filter	R③										✔
Charcoal Canister	I										✔
Fuel/Vapor Return Lines	I										✔
Fuel Tank Cap and Restrictor	I										✔
Coolant System	I					✔					✔
Exhaust Pipe and Muffler	I										✔
Choke Linkage	I④										✔
Catalytic Converter and Shield	I										✔
EGR System	I										✔
Air Pump and Connections	I①										✔
Throttle Body	I⑤					✔					
Drive Belts	I										✔
Brake Pads, Front	I										✔
Brake Pads, Rear	I										✔
Brake Shoes, Rear	I										✔
Brake Drums and Rotors	I										✔
Brake Hoses and Lines	I										✔
Battery Connections	I					✔					✔
Suspension/Ball Joints, etc.	I/L					✔					✔
Engine Coolant	R										✔

MAINTENANCE INTERVALS—TYPE B: SEVERE SERVICE
Crown Victoria • Grand Marquis • Town Car

TO BE SERVICED	TYPE OF SERVICE	VEHICLE MILEAGE INTERVAL (X1000)									
		3	6	9	12	15	18	21	24	27	30
Automatic Transmission Fluid	R										✔
Steering Linkage	I/L					✔					✔
Tire Rotation	I		✔					✔			
Front Wheel Bearings	L⑥										✔
Steering System	I										✔
Power Steering Fluid	I					✔					✔
Brake Fluid	I					✔					✔
Hinges, Latches, etc.	L					✔					✔
Seat Belt Operation	I					✔					✔

FOR COMPLETE WARRANTY COVERAGE CONSULT INDIVIDUAL VEHICLE MANUFACTURER'S WARRANTY MAINTENANCE GUIDE.

I—Inspect
L—Lubricate
R—Replace
① If applicable
② All except 4.6L engine
③ Replace fuel filter at 60,000 miles

④ 5.8L engine only
⑤ All except 5.8L engine
⑥ 1990–91 Crown Victoria, Grand Marquis and 1990 Town Car only. Subsequent models have sealed front wheel bearing assemblies

FIRING ORDERS

NOTE: To avoid confusion, always replace spark plugs and wires one at a time.

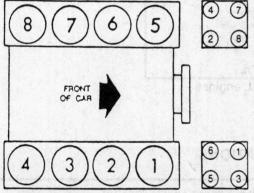

4.6L Engine
Engine Firing Order: 1–3–7–2–6–5–4–8
Distributorless Ignition System

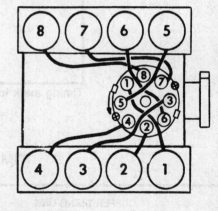

5.0L Engines
Engine Firing Order: 1–5–4–2–6–3–7–8
Distributor Rotation: Counterclockwise

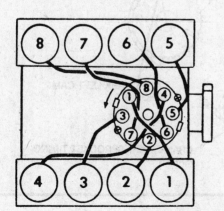

5.8L Engines
Engine Firing Order: 1–3–7–2–6–5–4–8
Distributor Rotation: Counterclockwise

CYLINDER HEAD TORQUE SEQUENCES

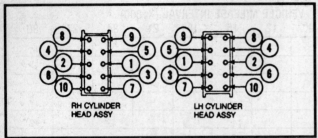

Cylinder head bolt torque sequence—4.6L engine

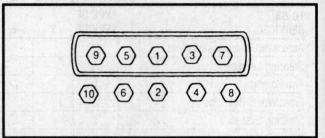

Cylinder head bolt torque sequence—5.0L and 5.8L engines

TIMING MARK LOCATIONS

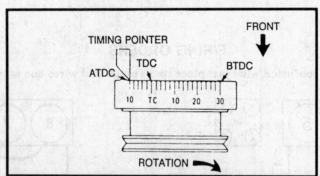

Timing mark location—5.0L and 5.8L engines

TIMING CHAIN LOCATIONS

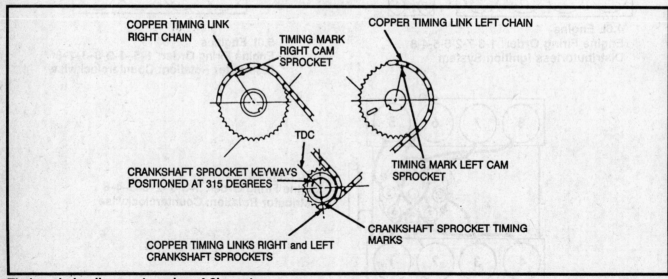

Timing chain alignment marks—4.6L engine

TIMING CHAIN LOCATIONS

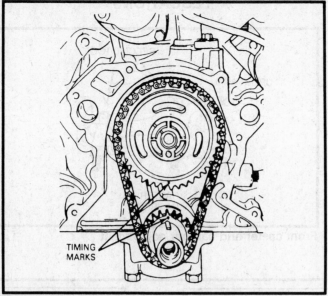

Timing chain alignment marks—5.0L and 5.8L engines

AIR CONDITIONING SERVICE VALVE LOCATIONS

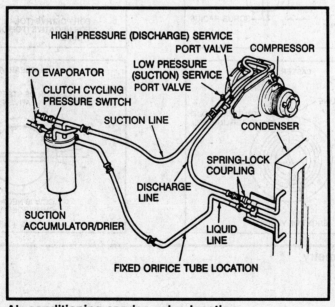

Air conditioning service valve location

WHEEL ALIGNMENT ADJUSTMENT LOCATIONS

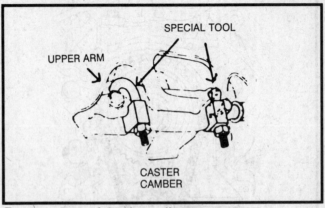

Front caster and camber adjustment

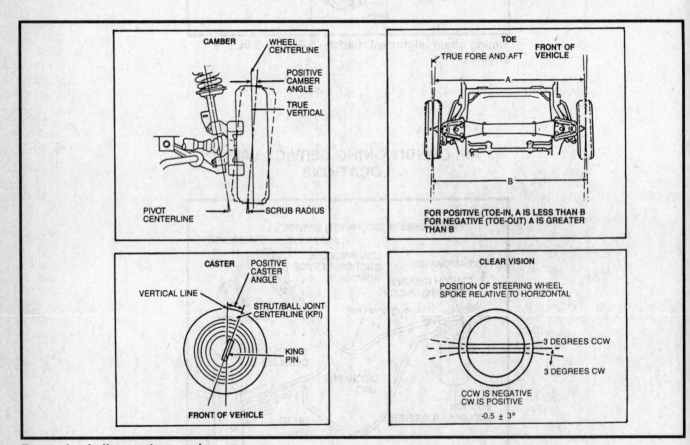

Front wheel alignment geometry

SPECIFICATION CHARTS

VEHICLE IDENTIFICATION CHART

It is important for servicing and ordering parts to be certain of the vehicle and engine identification. The VIN (vehicle identification number) is a 17 digit number visible through the windshield on the driver's side of the dash and contains the vehicle and engine identification codes. The tenth digit indicates model year and the eighth digit indicates engine code. It can be interpreted as follows:

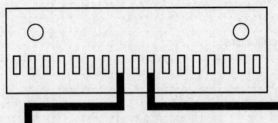

Engine Code							Model Year	
Code	Liters	Cu. In. (cc)	Cyl.	Fuel Sys.	Eng. Mfg.		Code	Year
4	2.2	133 (2180)	4	PFI	BOC		L	1990
R	2.5	151 (2475)	4	TBI	CPC		M	1991
T	3.1	192 (3147)	6	PFI	CPC		N	1992
M	3.1	191 (3130)	6	PFI	BOC		P	1993
N	3.3	204 (3344)	6	PFI	BOC		R	1994

TBI—Throttle Body Injection
PFI—Port Fuel Injection
CPC—Chevrolet Pontiac Canada
BOC—Buick Oldsmobile Cadillac

ENGINE IDENTIFICATION

Year	Model	Engine Displacement Liters (cc)	Engine Series (ID/VIN)	Fuel System	No. of Cylinders	Engine Type
1990	Celebrity	2.5 (2475)	R	TBI	4	OHV
	Celebrity	3.1 (3147)	T	PFI	6	OHV
	Century	2.5 (2475)	R	TBI	4	OHV
	Century	3.3 (3344)	N	PFI	6	OHV
	Cutlass ①	2.5 (2475)	R	TBI	4	OHV
	Cutlass ①	3.3 (3344)	N	PFI	6	OHV
	6000	2.5 (2475)	R	TBI	4	OHV
	6000	3.1 (3147)	T	PFI	6	OHV
1991	Century	2.5 (2475)	R	TBI	4	OHV
	Century	3.3 (3344)	N	PFI	6	OHV
	Cutlass ①	2.5 (2475)	R	TBI	4	OHV
	Cutlass ①	3.3 (3344)	N	PFI	6	OHV
	6000	2.5 (2475)	R	TBI	4	OHV
	6000	3.1 (3147)	T	PFI	6	OHV
1992	Century	2.5 (2475)	R	TBI	4	OHV
	Century	3.3 (3344)	N	PFI	6	OHV
	Cutlass ①	2.5 (2475)	R	TBI	4	OHV
	Cutlass ①	3.3 (3344)	N	PFI	6	OHV

ENGINE IDENTIFICATION

Year	Model	Engine Displacement Liters (cc)	Engine Series (ID/VIN)	Fuel System	No. of Cylinders	Engine Type
1993-94	Century	2.2 (2180)	4	PFI	4	OHV
	Century	3.1 (3130)	M	PFI	6	OHV
	Century	3.3 (3344)	N	PFI	6	OHV
	Cutlass ①	2.2 (2180)	4	PFI	4	OHV
	Cutlass ①	3.1 (3130)	M	PFI	6	OHV
	Cutlass ①	3.3 (3344)	N	PFI	6	OHV

TBI—Throttle Body Injection
PFI—Port Fuel Injection
OHV—Overhead Valves
① Ciera and Cruiser

GENERAL ENGINE SPECIFICATIONS

Year	Engine ID/VIN	Engine Displacement Liters (cc)	Fuel System Type	Net Horsepower @ rpm	Net Torque @ rpm (ft. lbs.)	Bore × Stroke (in.)	Compression Ratio	Oil Pressure @ rpm
1990	R	2.5 (2475)	TBI	92 @ 4400	134 @ 2800	4.000 × 3.000	8.3:1	37.5 @ 2000
	T	3.1 (3147)	PFI	120 @ 4200	175 @ 2200	3.503 × 3.312	8.8:1	50–65 @ 2400
	N	3.3 (3344)	PFI	160 @ 5200	185 @ 2000	3.700 × 3.160	9.0:1	45 @ 2000
1991	R	2.5 (2475)	TBI	110 @ 5200	135 @ 3200	4.000 × 3.000	8.3:1	26 @ 800
	T	3.1 (3147)	PFI	140 @ 4400	185 @ 3200	3.503 × 3.312	8.8:1	15 @ 1100
	N	3.3 (3344)	PFI	160 @ 5200	185 @ 2000	3.700 × 3.160	9.0:1	60 @ 1850
1992	R	2.5 (2475)	TBI	110 @ 5200	135 @ 3200	4.000 × 3.000	8.3:1	26 @ 800
	N	3.3 (3344)	PFI	160 @ 5200	185 @ 2000	3.700 × 3.160	9.0:1	60 @ 1850
1993-94	4	2.2 (2180)	PFI	120 @ 5200	130 @ 4000	3.500 × 3.460	9.0:1	56 @ 3000
	M	3.1 (3130)	PFI	160 @ 5200	185 @ 4000	3.500 × 3.300	9.5:1	NA
	N	3.3 (3344)	PFI	160 @ 5200	185 @ 2000	3.700 × 3.160	9.0:1	60 @ 1850

NA—Not Available
TBI—Throttle Body Injection
PFI—Port Fuel Injection

GASOLINE ENGINE TUNE-UP SPECIFICATIONS

Year	Engine ID/VIN	Engine Displacement Liters (cc)	Spark Plugs Gap (in.)	Ignition Timing (deg.) MT	Ignition Timing (deg.) AT	Fuel Pump (psi)	Idle Speed (rpm) MT	Idle Speed (rpm) AT	Valve Clearance In.	Valve Clearance Ex.
1990	R	2.5 (2475)	0.060	①	①	6.0–7.0	①	①	Hyd.	Hyd.
	T	3.1 (3147)	0.045	①	①	34.0–47.0	①	①	Hyd.	Hyd.
	N	3.3 (3344)	0.060	①	①	37.0–43.0	①	①	Hyd.	Hyd.
1991	R	2.5 (2475)	0.060	①	①	9.0–13.0	①	①	Hyd.	Hyd.
	T	3.1 (3147)	0.045	①	①	40.5–47.0	①	①	Hyd.	Hyd.
	N	3.3 (3344)	0.060	①	①	41.0–47.0	①	①	Hyd.	Hyd.
1992	R	2.5 (2475)	0.060	①	①	9.0–13.0	①	①	Hyd.	Hyd.
	N	3.3 (3344)	0.060	①	①	41.0–47.0	①	①	Hyd.	Hyd.

GASOLINE ENGINE TUNE-UP SPECIFICATIONS

Year	Engine ID/VIN	Engine Displacement Liters (cc)	Spark Plugs Gap (in.)	Ignition Timing (deg.) MT	AT	Fuel Pump (psi)	Idle Speed (rpm) MT	AT	Valve Clearance In.	Ex.
1993	4	2.2 (2180)	0.045	①	①	9.0–13.0	①	①	Hyd.	Hyd.
	N	3.3 (3344)	0.060	①	①	41.0–47.0	①	①	Hyd.	Hyd.
1994			SEE UNDERHOOD SPECIFICATIONS STICKER							

NOTE: The lowest cylinder pressure should be within 75% of the highest cylinder pressure reading. For example, if the highest cylinder is 134 psi, the lowest should be 101. Engine should be at normal operating temperature with throttle valve in the wide open position.
The underhood specifications sticker often reflects tune-up specification changes in production. Sticker figures must be used if they disagree with those in this chart.
Hyd.—Hydraulic
① Refer to underhood specifications sticker

CAPACITIES

Year	Model	Engine ID/VIN	Engine Displacement Liters (cc)	Engine Crankcase with Filter	Transmission (pts.) 4-Spd	5-Spd	Auto.	Transfer case (pts.)	Drive Axle Front (pts.)	Rear (pts.)	Fuel Tank (gal.)	Cooling System (qts.)
1990	Celebrity	R	2.5 (2475)	4.0	—	—	①	—	—	—	15.7	9.7②
	Celebrity	T	3.1 (3147)	4.0	—	—	①	—	—	—	15.7	12.8
	Century	R	2.5 (2475)	4.0	—	—	①	—	—	—	15.7	9.7②
	Century	N	3.3 (3344)	4.0	—	—	①	—	—	—	15.7	12.0③
	Cutlass⑤	R	2.5 (2475)	4.0	—	—	①	—	—	—	15.7	9.7②
	Cutlass⑤	N	3.3 (3344)	4.0	—	—	①	—	—	—	15.7	12.9④
	6000	R	2.5 (2475)	4.0	—	—	①	—	—	—	15.7	9.7②
	6000	T	3.1 (3147)	4.0	—	—	①	—	—	—	15.7	12.6
1991	Century	R	2.5 (2475)	4.0	—	—	①	—	—	—	15.7	9.7②
	Century	N	3.3 (3344)	4.0	—	—	①	—	—	—	15.7	12.9④
	Cutlass⑤	R	2.5 (2475)	4.0	—	—	①	—	—	—	15.7	9.7②
	Cutlass⑤	N	3.3 (3344)	4.0	—	—	①	—	—	—	15.7	12.9④
	6000	R	2.5 (2475)	4.0	—	—	①	—	—	—	15.7	9.7②
	6000	T	3.1 (3147)	4.0	—	—	①	—	—	—	15.7	12.6
1992	Century	R	2.5 (2475)	4.0	—	—	①	—	—	—	15.7	9.7②
	Century	N	3.3 (3344)	4.0	—	—	①	—	—	—	15.7	12.9④
	Cutlass⑤	R	2.5 (2475)	4.0	—	—	①	—	—	—	15.7	9.7②
	Cutlass⑤	N	3.3 (3344)	4.0	—	—	①	—	—	—	15.7	12.9④
1993-94	Century	4	2.2 (2180)	5.0	—	—	⑥	—	—	—	16.5	7.6
	Century	M	3.1 (3130)	5.0	—	—	⑥	—	—	—	16.5	NA
	Century	N	3.3 (3344)	4.0	—	—	①	—	—	—	16.5	13.2⑦
	Cutlass⑤	4	2.2 (2180)	5.0	—	—	⑥	—	—	—	16.5	7.6
	Cutlass⑤	M	3.1 (3130)	5.0	—	—	⑥	—	—	—	16.5	NA
	Cutlass⑤	N	3.3 (3344)	4.0	—	—	①	—	—	—	16.5	13.2⑦

NA—Not available
① 125C—8 pts.
  Overhaul—12 pts.
  440.T4—13 pts.
  Overhaul—20 pts.
② Air Cond.—9.9 pts.
③ Air Cond.—12.7 pts.
④ Air Cond. & Heavy Duty Radiator—13.2 qts.
⑤ Ciera and Cruiser
⑥ 3 speed-overhaul—17.9 pts.
  4 speed overhaul—26.8 pts.
⑦ Heavy duty cooling system—13.5

CAMSHAFT SPECIFICATIONS

All measurements given in inches.

Year	Engine ID/VIN	Engine Displacement Liters (cc)	Journal Diameter					Elevation		Bearing Clearance	Camshaft End Play
			1	2	3	4	5	In.	Ex.		
1990	R	2.5 (2475)	1.8690	1.8690	1.8690	—	—	0.248	0.248	0.0007–0.0027	0.0015–0.0050
	T	3.1 (3147)	1.8678–1.8815	1.8678–1.8815	1.8678–1.8815	1.8678–1.8815	—	0.263	0.273	0.0010–0.0040	NA
	N	3.3 (3344)	1.7850–1.7860	1.7850–1.7860	1.7850–1.7860	1.7850–1.7860	—	0.250	0.255	0.0005–0.0035	NA
1991	R	2.5 (2475)	1.8690	1.8690	1.8690	—	—	0.248	0.248	0.0007–0.0027	0.0015–0.0050
	T	3.1 (3147)	1.8677–1.8815	1.8677–1.8815	1.8677–1.8815	1.8677–1.8815	—	0.263	0.273	0.0010–0.0040	NA
	N	3.3 (3344)	1.7850–1.7860	1.7850–1.7860	1.7850–1.7860	1.7850–1.7860	—	0.250	0.255	0.0005–0.0035	NA
1992	R	2.5 (2475)	1.8690	1.8690	1.8690	—	—	0.248	0.248	0.0007–0.0027	0.0015–0.0050
	N	3.3 (3344)	1.7848–1.7862	1.7848–1.7862	1.7848–1.7862	1.7848–1.7862	—	0.250	0.255	0.0005–0.0035	NA
1993–94	4	2.2 (2180)	1.8670–1.8690	1.8670–1.8690	1.8670–1.8690	1.8670–1.8690	—	0.259	0.259	0.0010–0.0039	NA
	N	3.3 (3344)	1.7848–1.7862	1.7848–1.7862	1.7848–1.7862	1.7848–1.7862	—	0.250	0.255	0.0005–0.0035	NA

NA—Not available

CRANKSHAFT AND CONNECTING ROD SPECIFICATIONS

All measurements are given in inches.

Year	Engine ID/VIN	Engine Displacement Liters (cc)	Crankshaft				Connecting Rod		
			Main Brg. Journal Dia.	Main Brg. Oil Clearance	Shaft End-play	Thrust on No.	Journal Diameter	Oil Clearance	Side Clearance
1990	R	2.5 (2475)	2.3000	0.0005–0.0022	0.003–0.008	5	1.9995–2.0005	0.0005–0.0026	0.006–0.022
	T	3.1 (3147)	2.6473–2.6483	0.0012–0.0027	0.002–0.008	3	1.9983–1.9994	0.0013–0.0031	0.014–0.027
	N	3.3 (3344)	2.4988–2.4998	0.0003–0.0018	0.003–0.011	3	2.2487–2.2499	0.0003–0.0026	0.003–0.015
1991	R	2.5 (2475)	2.3000	0.0005–0.0022	0.005–0.010	5	2.0000	0.0005–0.0030	0.006–0.024
	T	3.1 (3147)	2.6473–2.6483	0.0012–0.0030	0.002–0.008	3	1.9983–1.9994	0.0011–0.0034	0.014–0.027
	N	3.3 (3344)	2.4988–2.4998	0.0003–0.0018	0.003–0.011	3	2.2487–2.2499	0.0003–0.0026	0.003–0.015
1992	R	2.5 (2475)	2.3000	0.0005–0.0022	0.005–0.010	5	2.0000	0.0005–0.0030	0.006–0.024
	N	3.3 (3344)	2.4988–2.4998	0.0008–0.0022	0.003–0.011	3	2.2487–2.2499	0.0008–0.0022	0.003–0.015
1993–94	4	2.2 (2180)	2.4945–2.4954	0.0006–0.0019	0.002–0.007	4	1.9983–1.9994	0.0010–0.0031	0.004–0.015
	N	3.3 (3344)	2.4988–2.4998	0.0008–0.0022	0.003–0.011	3	2.2487–2.2499	0.0008–0.0022	0.003–0.015

VALVE SPECIFICATIONS

Year	Engine ID/VIN	Engine Displacement Liters (cc)	Seat Angle (deg.)	Face Angle (deg.)	Spring Test Pressure (lbs. @ in.)	Spring Installed Height (in.)	Stem-to-Guide Clearance (in.)		Stem Diameter (in.)	
							Intake	Exhaust	Intake	Exhaust
1990	R	2.5 (2475)	46	46	176 @ 1.254	1.440	0.0010–0.0028	0.0013–0.0041	NA	NA
	T	3.1 (3147)	46	45	215 @ 1.291	1.575	0.0010–0.0027	0.0010–0.0027	NA	NA
	N	3.3 (3344)	45	45	215 @ 1.291	1.701	0.0010–0.0027	0.0010–0.0027	NA	NA
1991	R	2.5 (2475)	46	45	173 @ 1.240	1.680	0.0010–0.0028	0.0013–0.0041	NA	NA
	T	3.1 (3147)	46	45	215 @ 1.291	1.575	0.0010–0.0027	0.0010–0.0027	NA	NA
	N	3.3 (3344)	45	45	210 @ 1.315	1.690–1.720	0.0015–0.0035	0.0015–0.0032	NA	NA
1992	R	2.5 (2475)	46	45	173 @ 1.240	1.680	0.0010–0.0028	0.0013–0.0041	NA	NA
	N	3.3 (3344)	45	45	210 @ 1.315	1.690–1.720	0.0015–0.0035	0.0015–0.0035	NA	NA
1993–94	4	2.2 (2180)	46	45	225–233 ① 1.25 ①	1.64 ②	0.0011–0.0026	0.0014–0.0031	NA	NA
	N	3.3 (3344)	45	45	210 @ 1.315	1.690–1.770	0.0015–0.0035	0.0015–0.0035	NA	NA

① With valve open
② With valve closed

PISTON AND RING SPECIFICATIONS
All measurements are given in inches.

Year	Engine ID/VIN	Engine Displacement Liters (cc)	Piston Clearance	Ring Gap			Ring Side Clearance		
				Top Compression	Bottom Compression	Oil Control	Top Compression	Bottom Compression	Oil Control
1990	R	2.5 (2475)	0.0014–0.0022 ①	0.010–0.020	0.010–0.020	0.020–0.060	0.0020–0.0030	0.0010–0.0030	0.0150–0.0550
	T	2.8 (2835)	0.0022–0.0028	0.010–0.020	0.010–0.020	0.010–0.050	0.0020–0.0040	0.0020–0.0040	0.0080 ②
	N	3.3 (3344)	0.0004–0.0022 ③	0.010–0.025	0.010–0.025	0.010–0.040	0.0010–0.0030	0.0010–0.0030	0.0010–0.0080
1991	R	2.5 (2475)	0.0014–0.0022 ①	0.010–0.020	0.010–0.020	0.020–0.060	0.0020–0.0030	0.0010–0.0030	0.0150–0.0550
	T	2.8 (2835)	0.0009–0.0022	0.010–0.020	0.010–0.020	0.010–0.028	0.0020–0.0035	0.0020–0.0035	0.0080 ②
	N	3.3 (3344)	0.0004–0.0022 ③	0.010–0.025	0.010–0.025	0.010–0.040	0.0013–0.0031	0.0013–0.0031	0.0011–0.0081
1992	R	2.5 (2475)	0.0014–0.0022 ①	0.010–0.020	0.010–0.020	0.020–0.060	0.0020–0.0030	0.0010–0.0030	0.0150–0.0550
	N	3.3 (3344)	0.0004–0.0022 ③	0.010–0.025	0.010–0.025	0.015–0.055	0.0013–0.0031	0.0013–0.0031	0.0011–0.0081
1993–94	4	2.2 (2180)	0.0007–0.0017	0.010–0.020	0.010–0.020	0.010–0.050	0.0020–0.0030	0.0020–0.0030	0.0020–0.0082
	N	3.3 (3344)	0.0004–0.0022 ③	0.010–0.025	0.010–0.025	0.015–0.055	0.0013–0.0031	0.0013–0.0031	0.0011–0.0081

① Measured ⅛ in. down from piston top.   ② Maximum clearance   ③ 44 mm from top of piston

TORQUE SPECIFICATIONS

All readings in ft. lbs.

Year	Engine ID/VIN	Engine Displacement Liters (cc)	Cylinder Head Bolts	Main Bearing Bolts	Rod Bearing Bolts	Crankshaft Damper Bolts	Flywheel Bolts	Manifold Intake	Manifold Exhaust	Spark Plugs	Lug Nut
1990	R	2.5 (2475)	①	65	29	162	55	25	③	15	100
	T	3.1 (3147)	②	73	39	76	52	⑨	19	10–25	100
	N	3.3 (3344)	⑥	⑦	⑧	219	④	88⑤	41	20	100
1991	R	2.5 (2475)	①	65	29	162	55	25	③	20	100
	T	3.1 (3147)	②	73	39	76	52	⑨	19	18	100
	N	3.3 (3344)	⑥	⑦	⑧	219	④	89⑤	41	20	100
1992	R	2.5 (2475)	①	65	29	162	55	25	③	20	103
	N	3.3 (3344)	⑥	⑦	⑧	219	④	89⑤	41	20	103
1993–94	4	2.2 (2180)	⑩	70	38	77⑪	52⑫	22	⑬	11	100
	N	3.3 (3344)	⑥	⑦	⑧	219	④	89⑤	41	20	100

① Step 1: All bolts to 18 ft. lbs.
 Step 2: Except position "1 or 9" to 26 ft. lbs.
 Step 3: Retorque position "1 or 9" to 18 ft. lbs.
 Step 4: All bolts +90° turn
② Step 1: 33 ft. lbs.
 Step 2: +90° turn
③ Inner bolts: 37 ft. lbs.
 Outer bolts: 28 ft. lbs.
④ Step 1: 89 inch lbs.
 Step 2: +90° turn
⑤ Inch lbs.
⑥ Step 1: 35 ft. lbs.
 Step 2: +130° turn
 Step 3: +30° turn on 4 center bolts only
⑦ Step 1: 26 ft. lbs.
 Step 2: +45° turn

⑧ Step 1: 20 ft. lbs.
 Step 2: +50° turn
⑨ Manifold-to-cylinder head: 24 ft. lbs.
 Manifold-to-plenum: 16 ft. lbs.
⑩ Tighten all bolts in sequence to: long bolts (8, 4, 1, 5 and 9) to 46 ft. lbs. and the short bolts (7, 3, 2, 6 and 10) to 43 ft. lbs. Then tighten all bolts an additional 90° in sequence.
⑪ Specification is for crankshaft center bolt. Torque the pulley to hub bolts to 37 ft. lbs.
⑫ Specification is for the automatic transaxle. Torque the manual transaxle bolts to 55 ft. lbs.
⑬ Nuts—115 inch lbs.
 Bolts—89 inch lbs.

TORQUE SPECIFICATIONS

Component	English	Metric
Camshaft sprocket bolt		
2.2L engine:	77 ft. lbs.	105 Nm
2.5L engine:	43 ft. lbs.	58 Nm
3.1L (VIN T) engine:	21 ft. lbs.	28 Nm
3.3L engine		
Step 1:	52 ft. lbs.	70 Nm
Step 2:	+ 110 degrees turn	+ 110 degrees turn
Connecting rod bearing cap bolts/nuts		
2.2L engine:	38 ft. lbs.	52 Nm
2.5L engine:	29 ft. lbs.	40 Nm
3.1L (VIN T) engine:	39 ft. lbs.	53 Nm
3.3L engine		
Step 1:	20 ft. lbs.	27 Nm
Step 2:	+ 50 degrees turn	+ 50 degrees turn
Crankshaft damper bolt		
2.5L engine:	162 ft. lbs.	220 Nm
3.1L (VIN T) engine:	76 ft. lbs.	103 Nm
3.3L engine:	219 ft. lbs.	297 Nm

TORQUE SPECIFICATIONS

Component	English	Metric
Cylinder head bolt		
2.2L engine		
Step 1 (long bolts):	46 ft. lbs.	63 Nm
Step 2 (short bolts):	43 ft. lbs.	58 Nm
Step 3 (all bolts):	+ 90 degrees turn	+ 90 degrees turn
2.5L engine		
Step 1 (all bolts):	18 ft. lbs.	25 Nm
Step 2 (except position "9 or i" (R/F):	26 ft. lbs.	35 Nm
Step 3 (retorque position "9 or i" (R/F):	18 ft. lbs.	25 Nm
Step 4 (all bolts):	+ 90 degrees turn	+ 90 degrees turn
3.1L (VIN T) engine		
Step 1:	33 ft. lbs.	45 Nm
Step 2:	+ 90 degrees turn	+ 90 degrees turn
3.3L engine		
Step 1:	35 ft. lbs.	47 Nm
Step 2:	+ 130 degrees turn	+ 130 degrees turn
Step 3: (4) center bolts	+ 30 degrees turn	+ 30 degrees turn
EGR valve-to-intake plenum		
2.5L engine:	16 ft. lbs.	22 Nm
3.1L (VIN T) engine:	22 ft. lbs.	30 Nm
Engine-to-transmission:	55 ft. lbs.	75 Nm
Exhaust manifold		
2.2L engine:	22 ft. lbs.	30 Nm
2.5L engine		
Inner bolt:	37 ft. lbs.	50 Nm
Outer bolt:	28 ft. lbs.	38 Nm
3.1L (VIN T) engine:	19 ft. lbs.	25 Nm
3.3L engine:	38 ft. lbs.	52 Nm
Exhaust system		
Crossover pipe-to-exhaust manifold:	19 ft. lbs.	26 Nm
Exhaust pipe-to-manifold:	22 ft. lbs.	30 Nm
Flywheel/flexplate-to-crankshaft bolts		
2.2L engine:	54 ft. lbs.	73 Nm
2.5L engine:	55 ft. lbs.	75 Nm
3.1L (VIN T) engine:	52 ft. lbs.	70 Nm
3.3L engine		
Step 1:	11 ft. lbs.	15 Nm
Step 2:	+ 50 degrees turn	+ 50 degrees turn
Flywheel-to-converter bolt:	46 ft. lbs.	62 Nm
Intake manifold		
2.2L engine:	24 ft. lbs.	33 Nm
2.5L engine:	25 ft. lbs.	34 Nm
3.1L (VIN T) engine:	24 ft. lbs.	33 Nm
3.3L engine:	89 inch lbs.	10 Nm
Main bearing cap bolts		
2.2L engine:	66 ft. lbs.	90 Nm
2.5L engine:	65 ft. lbs.	88 Nm
3.1L (VIN T) engine:	73 ft. lbs.	99 Nm
3.3L engine		
Step 1:	26 ft. lbs.	35 Nm
Step 2:	+ 45 degrees turn	+ 45 degrees turn

TORQUE SPECIFICATIONS

Component	English	Metric
Oil pan		
2.2L engine:	89 inch lbs.	10 Nm
2.5L engine:	89 inch lbs.	10 Nm
3.1L (VIN T) engine (1990)		
Rear bolts (2):	18 ft. lbs.	25 Nm
Studs and nuts (4):	13 ft. lbs.	17 Nm
All other bolts:	89 inch lbs.	10 Nm
3.1L (VIN T) engine (1991–94)		
Rear bolts (2):	18 ft. lbs.	25 Nm
All other bolts:	71 inch lbs.	8 Nm
3.3L engine		
Oil pan to cylinder block bolts:	12 ft. lbs.	16 Nm
Oil pan to front cover bolts:	124 inch lbs.	14 Nm
Oil pan drain plug		
Except 3.3L engine:	25 ft. lbs.	34 Nm
3.3L engine:	30 ft. lbs.	40 Nm
Oil pump attaching bolts		
2.2L engine:	32 ft. lbs.	44 Nm
3.1L (VIN T) engine:	30 ft. lbs.	41 Nm
3.3L engine:	97 inch lbs.	11 Nm
Rocker arm pivot bolt		
2.2L engine:	22 ft. lbs.	34 Nm
2.5L engine:	20 ft. lbs.	27 Nm
1990 3.1L (VIN T) engine:	20 ft. lbs.	27 Nm
1991–94 3.1L (VIN T) engines:	18 ft. lbs.	24 Nm
3.3L engine:	28 ft. lbs.	38 Nm
Rocker (valve) cover		
Except 2.5L engine:	89 ft. lbs.	10 Nm
2.5L engine		
1990–93:	80 inch lbs.	9 Nm
Spark plug		
2.2L, 2.5L and 3.3L engines:	11 ft. lbs.	15 Nm
3.1L (VIN T) engine:	18 ft. lbs.	24 Nm
Starter-to-block bolts		
All engines except 2.2L:	32 ft. lbs.	43 Nm
2.2L engine		
Bracket to engine bolt:	26 ft. lbs.	32 Nm
Bracket to starter nuts:	80 inch lbs.	9 Nm
Thermostat housing		
2.2L engine:	89 inch lbs.	10 Nm
2.5L engine:	17 ft. lbs.	23 Nm
3.1L (VIN T) engine:	18 ft. lbs.	25 Nm
3.3L engine:	21 ft. lbs.	28 Nm
TBI-to-fuel meter body screws:	31 inch lbs.	3.5 Nm
TBI fuel feed/return line:	30 ft. lbs.	41 Nm
TBI mounting bolts/nuts:	18 ft. lbs.	25 Nm
Timing cover		
2.2L engine:	98 inch lbs.	11 Nm
2.5L engine:	89 inch lbs.	10 Nm
3.3L engine:	22 ft. lbs.	30 Nm
Water pump		
2.2L engine:	18 ft. lbs.	25 Nm
2.5L engine:	24 ft. lbs.	33 Nm
3.1L (VIN T) engine:	89 inch lbs.	10 Nm
3.3L engine		
Short bolts:	97 inch lbs.	11 Nm
Long bolts:	29 ft. lbs.	39 Nm

BRAKE SPECIFICATIONS
All measurements in inches unless noted.

Year	Model	Master Cylinder Bore	Brake Disc Original Thickness	Brake Disc Minimum Thickness	Maximum Runout	Brake Drum Diameter Original Inside Diameter	Brake Drum Diameter Max. Wear Limit	Brake Drum Diameter Maximum Machine Diameter	Minimum Lining Thickness Front	Minimum Lining Thickness Rear
1990	Celebrity	0.874②	0.885①	0.830③④	0.004⑤	8.863	0.057	8.920⑦	0.030	0.030
	Century	0.874②	0.885①	0.830③	0.004	8.863	0.057	8.920⑦	0.030	0.030
	Cutlass⑥	0.874②	0.885①	0.830③	0.004	8.863	0.057	8.920⑦	0.030	0.030
	6000	0.874②	0.885①	0.830③④	0.004⑤	8.863	0.057	8.920⑦	0.030	0.030
1991	Century	0.874②	0.885①	0.830③④	0.004	8.863	0.057	8.920⑦	0.030	0.030
	Cutlass⑥	0.874②	0.885①	0.830③	0.004	8.863	0.057	8.920⑦	0.030	0.030
	6000	0.874②	0.885①	0.830③	0.004⑤	8.863	0.057	8.920⑦	0.030	0.030
1992	Century	0.874②	0.885①	0.830③	0.004	8.863	0.057	8.920⑦	0.030	0.030
	Cutlass⑥	0.874②	0.885①	0.830③	0.004	8.863	0.057	8.920⑦	0.030	0.030
1993-94	Century	0.874②	0.885①	0.830③	0.004	8.863	0.057	8.920⑦	0.030	0.030
	Cutlass⑥	0.874②	0.885①	0.830③	0.004	8.863	0.057	8.920⑦	0.030	0.030

① Medium & heavy duty—1.043
② Medium and heavy duty—0.944
③ Medium & heavy duty—0.972
④ Rear disc—0.756
⑤ Rear disc—0.003
⑥ Ciera and Cutlass
⑦ Wagon—8.877
⑧ Medium & heavy duty—1.043

WHEEL ALIGNMENT

Year	Model	Caster Range (deg.)	Caster Preferred Setting (deg.)	Camber Range (deg.)	Camber Preferred Setting (deg.)	Toe-in (in.)	Steering Axis Inclination (deg.)
1990	Celebrity	11/16P–2 11/16	1 11/16P	1/2N–1/2P	0	3/32N–3/32P	NA
	Century	3/4P–2 3/4P	1 3/4P	1/2N–1/2P	0	3/32N–3/32P	NA
	Cutlass①	1 1/2P–2 1/2P	2P	3/16P–1 3/16P	11/16P	3/32N–3/32P	NA
	6000	11/16P–2 11/16P	1 11/16P	1/2N–1/2P	0	3/32N–3/32P	NA
1991	Century	3/4P–2 3/4P	1 3/4P	1/2N–1/2P	0	3/32N–3/32P	NA
	Cutlass①	1 1/2P–2 1/2P	2P	3/16P–1 3/16P	11/16P	3/32N–3/32P	NA
	6000	11/16P–2 11/16P	1 11/16P	1/2N–1/2P	0	3/32N–3/32P	NA
1992	Century	7/10P–1 7/10P	1 1/5P	1/2N–1/2P	0	1/5N–1/5P	NA
	Cutlass①	7/10P–1 7/10P	1 3/4P	1/2N–1/2P	0	1/5N–1/5P	NA
1993-94	Century	7/10P–1 7/10P	1 1/5P	1/2N–1/2P	0	1/5N–1/5P	NA
	Cutlass①	7/10P–1 7/10P	1 3/4P	1/2N–1/2P	0	1/5N–1/5P	NA

NA—Not available
N—Negative
P—Positive
① Ciera and Cruiser

AIR CONDITIONING BELT TENSION

Year	Engine VIN	Engine Displacement Liters (cc)	Belt Type	Specifications (lbs.) New	Used
1990	R	2.5 (2476)	Serpentine	50–70 ①	50–70 ①
	N	3.3 (3346)	Serpentine	67 ①	67 ①
	T	3.1 (3149)	Serpentine	50–70 ①	50–70 ①
1991	R	2.5 (2476)	Serpentine	50–70 ①	50–70 ①
	N	3.3 (3346)	Serpentine	67 ①	67 ①
	T	3.1 (3149)	Serpentine	50–70 ①	50–70 ①
1992	R	2.5 (2476)	Serpentine	50–70 ①	50–70 ①
	N	3.3 (3346)	Serpentine	67 ①	67 ①
1993–94	4	2.2 (2198)	Serpentine	50–70 ①	50–70 ①
	N	3.3 (3346)	Serpentine	67 ①	67 ①

① Equipped with automatic tensioner; however, the specification given (in pounds) is for testing whether the tensioner is maintaining its proper tension (specification given is the average of 3 readings back-to-back).

REFRIGERANT CAPACITIES

Year	Model	Refrigerant (oz.)	Oil (fl. oz.)	Compressor Type
1990	Century, Celebrity, Cutlass Ciera, Pontiac 6000	44.0	8.0	V5, HR6
1991	Century, Cutlass Ciera, Pontiac 6000	44.0	8.0	V5, HR6-HE
1992	Century, Cutlass Ciera	38.0	9.0	V5, HR6, HR6-HE
1993	Century, Cutlass Ciera	38.0	9.0	V5, HR6-HE

NOTE: At the time of publication, refrigerant capacity information relating to R-134a was not available from the manufacturer.

MAINTENANCE INTERVALS—TYPE A: NORMAL SERVICE
Celebrity • Century • Cutlass Ciera • Cutlass Cruiser • 6000

TO BE SERVICED	TYPE OF SERVICE	VEHICLE MILEAGE INTERVAL (X1000) 7.5	15	22.5	30	37.5	45	52.5	60
Oxygen Sensor	I				✔				✔
Ignition Timing	I ①				✔				✔
Vacuum Lines and Hoses	I				✔				✔
Ignition Wires	I				✔				✔
Spark Plugs	R				✔				✔
Engine Oil	R	✔	✔	✔	✔	✔	✔	✔	✔
Engine Air Cleaner Element	R				✔				✔
Crankcase Emission Filter	R				✔				✔
PCV Valve	R				✔				✔
Fuel Filter	R				✔				✔
Engine Oil Filter	R ②	✔		✔		✔		✔	
Fuel/Vapor Return Lines	I				✔				✔
Fuel Tank Cap and Restrictor	I				✔				✔

MAINTENANCE INTERVALS—TYPE A: NORMAL SERVICE
Celebrity • Century • Cutlass Ciera • Cutlass Cruiser • 6000

TO BE SERVICED	TYPE OF SERVICE	VEHICLE MILEAGE INTERVAL (X1000)							
		7.5	15	22.5	30	37.5	45	52.5	60
Coolant System	R				✔				✔
Exhaust Pipe and Muffler	I				✔				✔
Catalytic Converter and Shield	I				✔				✔
EGR System	I				✔				✔
Chassis Lubrication	L	✔	✔	✔	✔	✔	✔	✔	✔
Battery Connections	I				✔				✔
Automatic Transaxle Fluid	R③								
Tire Rotation	I④	✔		✔		✔		✔	
Coolant Hoses and Belts	I				✔				✔
Drive Belts	I				✔				✔
CV-Joints and Boots	I	✔	✔	✔	✔	✔	✔	✔	✔
Brake Linings	I		✔		✔		✔		✔
Parking Brake	I		✔		✔		✔		✔
Seat Belt Operation	I		✔		✔		✔		✔

FOR COMPLETE WARRANTY COVERAGE CONSULT INDIVIDUAL VEHICLE MANUFACTURER'S WARRANTY MAINTENANCE GUIDE.

I—Inspect
L—Lubricate
R—Replace
① Check and adjust timing as per engine emission label on applicable vehicles
② Replace oil filter every other oil change
③ Replace transmission fluid and filter at 100,000 miles
④ Rotate tires at 7,500 miles and then every 15,000 miles

MAINTENANCE INTERVALS—TYPE B: SEVERE SERVICE
Celebrity • Century • Cutlass Ciera • Cutlass Cruiser • 6000

TO BE SERVICED	TYPE OF SERVICE	VEHICLE MILEAGE INTERVAL (X1000)									
		3	6	9	12	15	18	21	24	27	30
Oxygen Sensor	I										✔
Ignition Timing	I①										✔
Vacuum Lines and Hoses	I					✔					✔
Ignition Wires	I										✔
Spark Plugs	R										✔
Engine Oil and Filter	R	✔	✔	✔	✔	✔	✔	✔	✔	✔	✔
Engine Air Cleaner Element	R					✔					✔
Crankcase Emission Filter	R					✔					✔
PCV Valve	R					✔					✔
Fuel Filter	R					✔					✔
Coolant Hoses and Clamps	I					✔					✔
Fuel/Vapor Return Lines	I										✔
Fuel Tank Cap and Restrictor	I										✔
Coolant System	R										✔
Exhaust Pipe and Muffler	I										✔

MAINTENANCE INTERVALS—TYPE B: SEVERE SERVICE
Celebrity • Century • Cutlass Ciera • Cutlass Cruiser • 6000

TO BE SERVICED	TYPE OF SERVICE	VEHICLE MILEAGE INTERVAL (X1000)									
		3	6	9	12	15	18	21	24	27	30
Catalytic Converter and Shield	I										✔
EGR System	I										✔
Chassis Lubrication	L	✔		✔		✔		✔		✔	
Battery Connections	I					✔					✔
Automatic Transaxle Fluid	R					✔					✔
Tire Rotation	I		✔								
Throttle Body Mounting Torque	I		✔								
Drive Belts	I										✔
CV-Joints and Boots	I	✔	✔	✔	✔	✔	✔	✔	✔	✔	✔
Brake Linings	I					✔					✔
Parking Brake	I					✔					✔
Seat Belt Operation	I					✔					✔

FOR COMPLETE WARRANTY COVERAGE CONSULT INDIVIDUAL VEHICLE MANUFACTURER'S WARRANTY MAINTENANCE GUIDE.

I—Inspect
L—Lubricate
R—Replace
① Check and adjust timing as per engine emission label on applicable vehicles

FIRING ORDERS

NOTE: To avoid confusion, always replace spark plugs and wires one at a time.

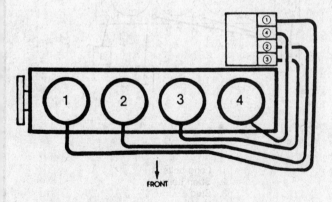

**2.2L (VIN 4) and 2.5L (VIN R) Engines
Engine Firing Order: 1-3-4-2
Distributorless Ignition System**

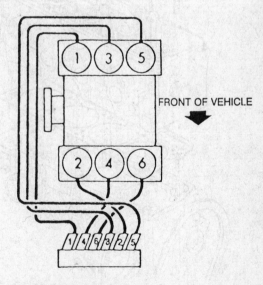

**3.1L Engines
Engine Firing Order: 1-2-3-4-5-6
Distributorless Ignition System**

FIRING ORDERS

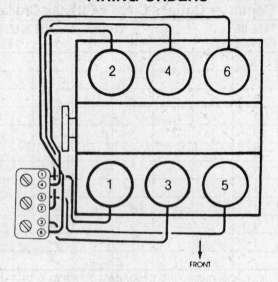

3.3L Engine
Engine Firing Order: 1–6–5–4–3–2
Distributorless Ignition System

CYLINDER HEAD TORQUE SEQUENCES

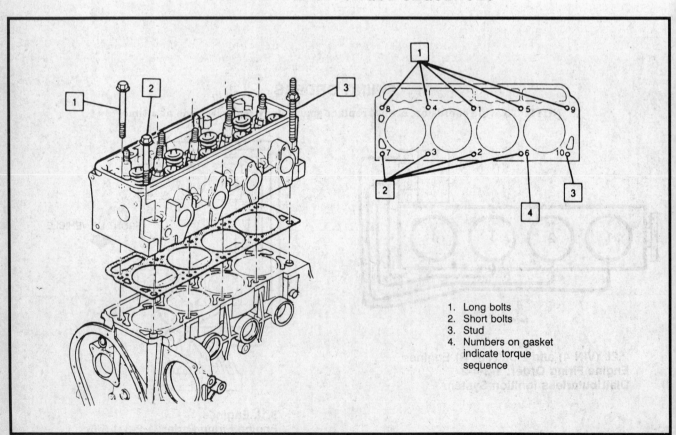

1. Long bolts
2. Short bolts
3. Stud
4. Numbers on gasket indicate torque sequence

Cylinder head bolt torque sequence—2.2L engine

CYLINDER HEAD TORQUE SEQUENCES

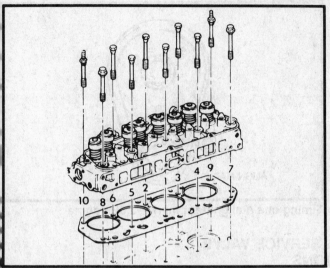

Cylinder head torque sequence—2.5L engine

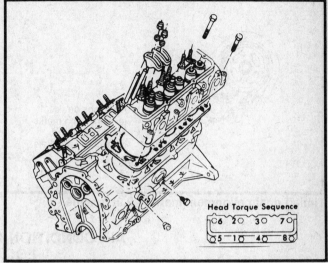

Cylinder head bolt torque sequence—3.1L engine

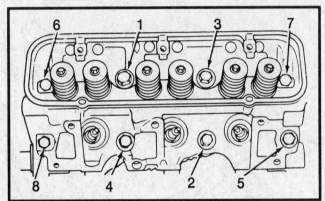

Cylinder head torque sequence—3.3L engine

TIMING CHAIN ALIGNMENT MARKS

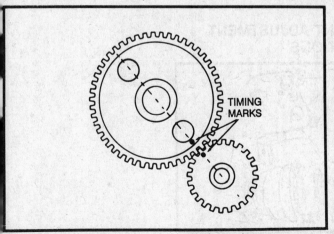

Timing chain alignment mark—2.5L engine

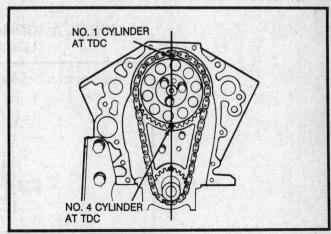

Timing chain alignment mark—3.1L engine

TIMING CHAIN ALIGNMENT MARKS

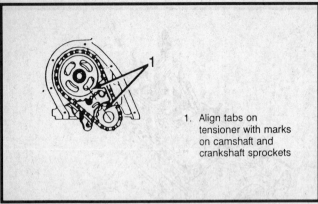

1. Align tabs on tensioner with marks on camshaft and crankshaft sprockets

Timing chain alignment marks—2.2L engine

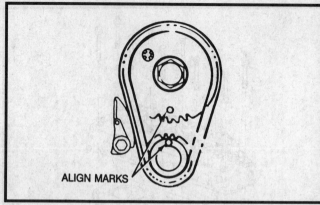

ALIGN MARKS

Timing chain alignment mark—3.3L engine

AIR CONDITIONING SERVICE VALVE LOCATIONS

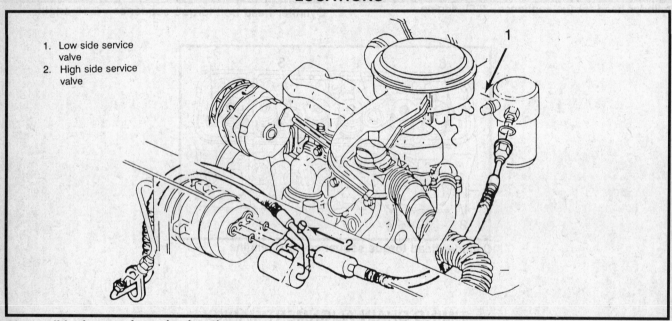

1. Low side service valve
2. High side service valve

Air conditioning service valve location

WHEEL ALIGNMENT ADJUSTMENT LOCATIONS

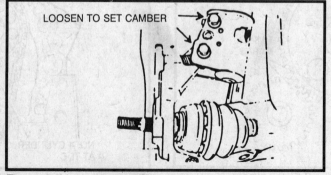

LOOSEN TO SET CAMBER

Front camber adjustment

16 General Motors—"C" and "H" Body 16

BONNEVILLE • DELTA 88 • DEVILLE • ELECTRA • FLEETWOOD • LESABRE •
PARK AVENUE • PARK AVENUE ULTRA • NINETY-EIGHT • 88 ROYALE

SPECIFICATION CHARTS

VEHICLE IDENTIFICATION CHART

It is important for servicing and ordering parts to be certain of the vehicle and engine identification. The VIN (vehicle identification number) is a 17 digit number visible through the windshield on the driver's side of the dash and contains the vehicle and engine identification codes. The tenth digit indicates model year and the eighth digit indicates engine code. It can be interpreted as follows:

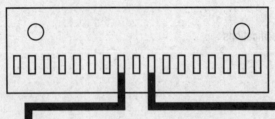

Engine Code						Model Year	
Code	Liters	Cu. In. (cc)	Cyl.	Fuel Sys.	Eng. Mfg.	Code	Year
C	3.8	231 (3786)	6	SFI	Buick	L	1990
L	3.8	231 (3786)	6	PFI	Buick	M	1991
3	4.5	273 (4474)	8	PFI	Cadillac	N	1992
B	4.9	300 (4894)	8	PFI	Cadillac	P	1993
1	3.8	231 (3786)	6	PFI	Buick	R	1994
9	4.6	279 (4573)	8	PFI	Cadillac		

PFI—Port Fuel Injection
SFI—Sequential Fuel Injection
TBI—Throttle Body Injection

ENGINE IDENTIFICATION

Year	Model	Engine Displacement Liters (cc)	Engine Series (ID/VIN)	Fuel System	No. of Cylinders	Engine Type
1990	DeVille	4.5 (4474)	3	PFI	8	OHV
	Fleetwood	4.5 (4474)	3	PFI	8	OHV
	Electra	3.8 (3786)	C	SFI	6	OHV
	Park Avenue	3.8 (3786)	C	SFI	6	OHV
	LeSabre	3.8 (3786)	C	SFI	6	OHV
	Ninety Eight	3.8 (3786)	C	SFI	6	OHV
	Delta 88	3.8 (3786)	C	SFI	6	OHV
	Bonneville	3.8 (3786)	C	SFI	6	OHV
1991	DeVille	4.9 (4894)	B	PFI	8	OHV
	Fleetwood	4.9 (4894)	B	PFI	8	OHV
	Park Avenue	3.8 (3786)	L	PFI	6	OHV
	LeSabre	3.8 (3786)	C	SFI	6	OHV
	Ninety Eight	3.8 (3786)	L	PFI	6	OHV
	88 Royale	3.8 (3786)	L	PFI	6	OHV
	Bonneville	3.8 (3786)	C	SFI	6	OHV

ENGINE IDENTIFICATION

Year	Model	Engine Displacement Liters (cc)	Engine Series (ID/VIN)	Fuel System	No. of Cylinders	Engine Type
1992	DeVille	4.9 (4894)	B	PFI	8	OHV
	Fleetwood	4.9 (4894)	B	PFI	8	OHV
	Park Avenue	3.8 (3786)	L	PFI	6	OHV
	LeSabre	3.8 (3786)	L	SFI	6	OHV
	Ninety Eight	3.8 (3786)	L	PFI	6	OHV
	Ninety Eight	3.8 (3786)	1	PFI	6	OHV
	88 Royale	3.8 (3786)	L	PFI	6	OHV
	Bonneville	3.8 (3786)	L	PFI	6	OHV
	Bonneville	3.8 (3786)	1	PFI	6	OHV
1993–94	DeVille	4.9 (4894)	B	PFI	8	OHV
	Deville	4.6 (4573)	9	PFI	8	OHV
	Park Avenue	3.8 (3786)	L	PFI	6	OHV
	Park Avenue	3.8 (3786)	1	PFI	6	OHV
	LeSabre	3.8 (3786)	L	PFI	6	OHV
	Ninety Eight	3.8 (3786)	L	PFI	6	OHV
	Ninety Eight	3.8 (3786)	1	PFI	6	OHV
	88 Royale	3.8 (3786)	L	PFI	6	OHV
	Bonneville	3.8 (3786)	L	PFI	6	OHV
	Bonneville	3.8 (3786)	1	PFI	6	OHV

PFI—Port Fuel Injection
SFI—Sequential Fuel Injection
OHV—Overhead Valves

GENERAL ENGINE SPECIFICATIONS

Year	Engine ID/VIN	Engine Displacement Liters (cc)	Fuel System Type	Net Horsepower @ rpm	Net Torque @ rpm (ft. lbs.)	Bore × Stroke (in.)	Compression Ratio	Oil Pressure @ rpm
1990	3	4.5 (4474)	PFI	180 @ 4300	245 @ 3000	3.622 × 3.307	9.5:1	37 @ 1500
	C	3.8 (3786)	SFI	165 @ 5200	210 @ 2000	3.800 × 3.400	8.5:1	40 @ 1850
1991	C	3.8 (3786)	SFI	165 @ 5200	210 @ 2000	3.800 × 3.400	8.5:1	60 @ 1850
	L	3.8 (3786)	PFI	170 @ 4800	220 @ 3200	3.800 × 3.400	8.5:1	60 @ 1850
	B	4.9 (4894)	PFI	200 @ 4100	275 @ 3000	3.623 × 3.623	9.5:1	53 @ 2000
1992	B	4.9 (4894)	PFI	200 @ 4100	275 @ 3000	3.623 × 3.623	9.5:1	53 @ 2000
	L	3.8 (3786)	PFI	170 @ 4800	220 @ 3200	3.800 × 3.400	8.5:1	60 @ 1850
	1	3.8 (3786)	PFI	205 @ 4400	260 @ 2600	3.800 × 3.400	8.5:1	60 @ 1850
1993–94	B	4.9 (4894)	PFI	200 @ 4100	275 @ 3000	3.623 × 3.623	9.5:1	53 @ 2000
	L	3.8 (3786)	PFI	170 @ 4800	225 @ 3200	3.800 × 3.400	9.0:1	60 @ 1850
	1	3.8 (3786)	PFI	205 @ 4400	260 @ 2600	3.800 × 3.400	9.0:1	60 @ 1850
	9	4.6 (4573)	PFI	290 @ 5600	300 @ 4000	3.660 × 3.310	10.3:1	NA

NA—Not available
PFI—Port Fuel Injection
SFI—Sequential Fuel Injection

GASOLINE ENGINE TUNE-UP SPECIFICATIONS

Year	Engine ID/VIN	Engine Displacement Liters (cc)	Spark Plugs Gap (in.)	Ignition Timing (deg.) MT	AT	Fuel Pump (psi)	Idle Speed (rpm) MT	AT	Valve Clearance In.	Ex.
1990	3	4.5 (4474)	0.060	—	①	40–47	—	①	Hyd.	Hyd.
	C	3.8 (3786)	0.060	—	①	40–47	—	①	Hyd.	Hyd.
1991	C	3.8 (3786)	0.060	—	①	40–47	—	①	Hyd.	Hyd.
	L	3.8 (3786)	0.060	—	①	40–47	—	①	Hyd.	Hyd.
	B	4.9 (4894)	0.060	—	①	40–50	—	①	Hyd.	Hyd.
1992	1	3.8 (3786)	0.060	—	①	40–47	—	①	Hyd.	Hyd.
	L	3.8 (3786)	0.060	—	①	40–47	—	①	Hyd.	Hyd.
	B	4.9 (4894)	0.060	—	①	40–50	—	①	Hyd.	Hyd.
1993	1	3.8 (3786)	0.060	—	①	40–47	—	①	Hyd.	Hyd.
	L	3.8 (3786)	0.060	—	①	40–47	—	①	Hyd.	Hyd.
	B	4.9 (4894)	0.060	—	①	40–50	—	①	Hyd.	Hyd.
1994	REFER TO UNDERHOOD SPECIFICATIONS STICKER									

NOTE: The lowest cylinder pressure should be within 75% of the highest cylinder pressure reading. For example, if the highest cylinder is 134 psi, the lowest should be 101. Engine should be at normal operating temperature with throttle valve in the wide open position.
The underhood specifications sticker often reflects tune-up specification changes in production. Sticker figures must be used if they disagree with those in this chart.

① These vehicles are equipped with computerized emissions systems which have no distributor vacuum advance unit. The idle speed and ignition timing are controlled by the ECM/PCM.
Hyd.—Hydraulic

CAPACITIES

Year	Model	Engine ID/VIN	Engine Displacement Liters (cc)	Engine Crankcase with Filter (qts.)	Transmission (pts.) 4-Spd	5-Spd	Auto.	Drive Axle Front (pts.)	Rear (pts.)	Fuel Tank (gal.)	Cooling System (qts.)
1990	DeVille	3	4.5 (4474)	5.5	—	—	22③	—	—	18	13.2
	Fleetwood	3	4.5 (4474)	5.5	—	—	22③	—	—	18	13.2
	Electra	C	3.8 (3786)	4.0①	—	—	22③	—	—	18	13.0
	Park Avenue	C	3.8 (3786)	4.0①	—	—	22③	—	—	18	13.0
	LeSabre	C	3.8 (3786)	4.0①	—	—	22③	—	—	18	13.0
	Ninety Eight	C	3.8 (3786)	4.0①	—	—	22③	—	—	18	13.0
	Delta 88	C	3.8 (3786)	4.0①	—	—	22③	—	—	18	13.0
	Bonneville	C	3.8 (3786)	4.0① ②	—	—	22③	—	—	18	13.0
1991	DeVille	B	4.9 (4894)	5.5	—	—	22③	—	—	18	13.2
	Fleetwood	B	4.9 (4894)	5.5	—	—	22③	—	—	18	13.2
	Park Avenue	L	3.8 (3786)	4.0①	—	—	22③	—	—	18	13.0
	LeSabre	C	3.8 (3786)	4.0①	—	—	22③	—	—	18	13.0
	Ninety Eight	L	3.8 (3786)	4.0①	—	—	22③	—	—	18	13.0
	88 Royale	L	3.8 (3786)	4.0①	—	—	22③	—	—	18	13.0
	Bonneville	C	3.8 (3786)	4.0① ②	—	—	22③	—	—	18	13.0

CAPACITIES

Year	Model	Engine ID/VIN	Engine Displacement Liters (cc)	Engine Crankcase with Filter (qts.)	Transmission (pts.) 4-Spd	5-Spd	Auto.	Drive Axle Front (pts.)	Rear (pts.)	Fuel Tank (gal.)	Cooling System (qts.)
1992	DeVille	B	4.9 (4894)	5.5	—	—	22③	—	—	18	13.2
	Fleetwood	B	4.9 (4894)	5.5	—	—	22③	—	—	18	13.2
	Park Avenue	L	3.8 (3786)	5.0	—	—	22③	—	—	18	13.0
	Park Avenue	1	3.8 (3786)	5.0	—	—	22③	—	—	18	13.0
	LeSabre	L	3.8 (3786)	5.0	—	—	22③	—	—	18	13.0
	Ninety Eight	1	3.8 (3786)	5.0	—	—	22③	—	—	18	13.0
	Ninety Eight	L	3.8 (3786)	5.0	—	—	22③	—	—	18	13.0
	88 Royale	L	3.8 (3786)	5.0	—	—	22③	—	—	18	13.0
	Bonneville	L	3.8 (3786)	5.0②	—	—	22③	—	—	18	13.0
	Bonneville	1	3.8 (3786)	5.0	—	—	22③	—	—	18	13.0
1993–94	DeVille	B	4.9 (4894)	5.5	—	—	22③	—	—	18	12.1
	Deville	9	4.6 (4573)	7.0	—	—	NA	—	—	NA	12.3
	Park Avenue	L	3.8 (3786)	5.0	—	—	22③	—	—	18	13.0
	Park Avenue	1	3.8 (3786)	5.0	—	—	22③	—	—	18	13.0
	LeSabre	L	3.8 (3786)	5.0	—	—	22③	—	—	18	13.0
	Ninety Eight	L	3.8 (3786)	5.0	—	—	22③	—	—	18	13.0
	Ninety Eight	1	3.8 (3786)	5.0	—	—	22③	—	—	18	13.0
	88 Royale	L	3.8 (3786)	5.0	—	—	22③	—	—	18	13.0
	Bonneville	L	3.8 (3786)	5.0②	—	—	22③	—	—	18	13.0
	Bonneville	1	3.8 (3786)	5.0	—	—	22③	—	—	18	13.0

NA—Not available
① Additional oil may be necessary to bring level to full
② SSE—5.5 qts.
③ Specification for transaxle overhaul. 12 pts for fluid and filter change.

CAMSHAFT SPECIFICATIONS

All measurements given in inches.

Year	Engine ID/VIN	Engine Displacement Liters (cc)	Journal Diameter 1	2	3	4	5	Elevation In.	Ex.	Bearing Clearance	Camshaft End Play
1990	C	3.8 (3786)	1.7850–1.7860	1.7850–1.7860	1.7850–1.7860	1.7850–1.7860	—	0.250	0.255	0.0005–0.0035	NA
	3	4.5 (4474)	2.6350–2.6360	2.6350–2.6360	2.6350–2.6360	2.6350–2.6360	2.6350–2.6360	0.384	0.396	0.0018–0.0037	NA
1991	B	4.9 (4894)	2.6350–2.6360	2.6350–2.6360	2.6350–2.6360	2.6350–2.6360	2.6350–2.6360	0.384	0.396	0.0018–0.0037	NA
	L	3.8 (3786)	1.7850–1.7860	1.7850–1.7860	1.7850–1.7860	1.7850–1.7860	—	0.250	0.255	0.0005–0.0035	NA
	C	3.8 (3786)	1.7850–1.7860	1.7850–1.7860	1.7850–1.7860	1.7850–1.7860	—	0.250	0.255	0.0005–0.0035	NA

CAMSHAFT SPECIFICATIONS

All measurements given in inches.

| Year | Engine ID/VIN | Engine Displacement Liters (cc) | Journal Diameter | | | | | Elevation | | Bearing Clearance | Camshaft End Play |
			1	2	3	4	5	In.	Ex.		
1992	B	4.9 (4894)	2.6350–2.6360	2.6350–2.6360	2.6350–2.6360	2.6350–2.6360	2.6350–2.6360	0.384	0.396	0.0018–0.0037	NA
	L	3.8 (3786)	1.7850–1.7860	1.7850–1.7860	1.7850–1.7860	1.7850–1.7860	—	0.250	0.255	0.0005–0.0035	NA
	1	3.8 (3786)	1.7850–1.7860	1.7850–1.7860	1.7850–1.7860	1.7850–1.7860	—	0.250	0.255	0.0005–0.0035	NA
1993–94	B	4.9 (4894)	2.6350–2.6360	2.6350–2.6360	2.6350–2.6360	2.6350–2.6360	2.6350–2.6360	0.384	0.396	0.0018–0.0037	NA
	9	4.6 (4573)	1.0610–1.0620	1.0610–1.0620	1.0610–1.0620	1.0610–1.0620	1.0610–1.0620	0.370	0.339	0.0020–0.0060	NA
	L	3.8 (3786)	1.7850–1.7860	1.7850–1.7860	1.7850–1.7860	1.7850–1.7860	—	0.250	0.255	0.0005–0.0035	NA
	1	3.8 (3786)	1.7850–1.7860	1.7850–1.7860	1.7850–1.7860	1.7850–1.7860	—	0.250	0.255	0.0005–0.0035	NA

NA—Not available

CRANKSHAFT AND CONNECTING ROD SPECIFICATIONS

All measurements are given in inches.

| Year | Engine ID/VIN | Engine Displacement Liters (cc) | Crankshaft | | | | Connecting Rod | | |
			Main Brg. Journal Dia.	Main Brg. Oil Clearance	Shaft End-play	Thrust on No.	Journal Diameter	Oil Clearance	Side Clearance
1990	C	3.8 (3786)	2.4988–2.4998	0.0003–0.0018	0.003–0.011	2	2.2487–2.2499	0.0003–0.0026	0.003–0.015
	3	4.5 (4474)	2.6354–2.6364	①	0.001–0.007	3	2.0520–2.0540	0.0005–0.0028	0.008–0.020
1991	C	3.8 (3786)	2.4988–2.4998	0.0003–0.0018	0.003–0.011	2	2.2487–2.2499	0.0003–0.0026	0.003–0.015
	L	3.8 (3786)	2.4988–2.4998	0.0003–0.0018	0.003–0.011	2	2.2487–2.2499	0.0003–0.0026	0.003–0.015
	B	4.9 (4894)	2.6354–2.6364	①	0.001–0.008	3	2.0520–2.0530	0.0005–0.0028	0.008–0.020
1992	1	3.8 (3786)	2.4988–2.4998	0.0003–0.0018	0.003–0.011	2	2.2487–2.2499	0.0003–0.0026	0.003–0.015
	L	3.8 (3786)	2.4988–2.4998	0.0003–0.0018	0.003–0.011	2	2.2487–2.2499	0.0003–0.0026	0.003–0.015
	B	4.9 (4894)	2.6354–2.6364	①	0.001–0.008	3	2.0520–2.0530	0.0005–0.0028	0.008–0.020
1993–94	B	4.9 (4894)	2.6354–2.6364	①	0.001–0.008	3	2.0520–2.0530	0.0005–0.0028	0.008–0.020
	9	4.6 (4573)	2.5200–2.5205	0.0005–0.0020	0.002–0.019	3	NA	0.001–0.003	NA
	L	3.8 (3786)	2.4988–2.4998	0.0008–0.0022	0.003–0.011	2	2.2487–2.2499	0.0008–0.0022	0.003–0.015
	1	3.8 (3786)	2.4988–2.4998	0.0008–0.0022	0.003–0.011	2	2.2487–2.2499	0.0008–0.0022	0.003–0.015

NA—Not available
① No. 1 bearing—0.0008–0.0031
No. 2–5 bearing—0.0016–0.0039

VALVE SPECIFICATIONS

Year	Engine ID/VIN	Engine Displacement Liters (cc)	Seat Angle (deg.)	Face Angle (deg.)	Spring Test Pressure (lbs. @ in.)	Spring Installed Height (in.)	Stem-to-Guide Clearance (in.) Intake	Stem-to-Guide Clearance (in.) Exhaust	Stem Diameter (in.) Intake	Stem Diameter (in.) Exhaust
1990	C	3.8 (3786)	45	45	200–220 @ 1.315 in.	1.690–1.750	0.0015–0.0035	0.0015–0.0032	0.3401–0.3412	0.3405–0.3412
	3	4.5 (4474)	45	44	214–232 @ 1.35 in.	NA	0.0010–0.0030	0.0020–0.0040	0.3413–0.3420	0.3401–0.3408
1991	C	3.8 (3786)	45	45	210 @ 1.315 in.	1.690–1.720	0.0015–0.0035	0.0015–0.0035	NA	NA
	L	3.8 (3786)	45	45	210 @ 1.315 in.	1.690–1.720	0.0015–0.0035	0.0015–0.0035	NA	NA
	B	4.9 (4894)	45	45	214–232 @ 1.35 in.	NA	0.0010–0.0030	0.0020–0.0040	0.3413–0.3420	0.3401–0.3408
1992	B	4.9 (4894)	45	45	214–232 @ 1.35 in.	NA	0.0010–0.0030	0.0020–0.0040	0.3413–0.3420	0.3401–0.3408
	L	3.8 (3786)	45	45	210 @ 1.315 in.	1.690–1.720	0.0015–0.0035	0.0015–0.0032	NA	NA
	1	3.8 (3786)	45	45	210 @ 1.315 in.	1.690–1.720	0.0015–0.0035	0.0015–0.0032	NA	NA
1993–94	B	4.9 (4894)	45	45	214–232 @ 1.35 in.	NA	0.0010–0.0030	0.0020–0.0040	0.3413–0.3420	0.3401–0.3408
	9	4.6 (4573)	46	45	109 @ 0.823 in.	1.19	0.0010–0.0030	0.0020–0.0040	0.2331–0.2339	0.2331–0.2339
	L	3.8 (3786)	45	45	210 @ 1.315 in.	1.690–1.720	0.0015–0.0035	0.0015–0.0032	NA	NA
	1	3.8 (3786)	45	45	210 @ 1.315 in.	1.690–1.720	0.0015–0.0035	0.0015–0.0032	NA	NA

NA—Not available

PISTON AND RING SPECIFICATIONS

All measurements are given in inches.

Year	Engine ID/VIN	Engine Displacement Liters (cc)	Piston Clearance	Ring Gap Top Compression	Ring Gap Bottom Compression	Ring Gap Oil Control	Ring Side Clearance Top Compression	Ring Side Clearance Bottom Compression	Ring Side Clearance Oil Control
1990	C	3.8 (3786)	0.0004–0.0022	0.010–0.025	0.010–0.025	0.015–0.055	0.0013–0.0031	0.0013–0.0031	0.0011–0.0081
	3	4.5 (4474)	0.0010–0.0018	0.015–0.024	0.015–0.024	0.010–0.050	0.0016–0.0037	0.0016–0.0037	None (side sealing)
1991	C	3.8 (3786)	0.0004–0.0022	0.010–0.025	0.010–0.025	0.015–0.055	0.0013–0.0031	0.0013–0.0031	0.0011–0.0081
	L	3.8 (3786)	0.0004–0.0022	0.010–0.025	0.010–0.025	0.015–0.055	0.0013–0.0031	0.0013–0.0031	0.0011–0.0081
	B	4.9 (4894)	0.0004–0.0020	0.012–0.022	0.012–0.022	0.010–0.050	0.0016–0.0037	0.0016–0.0037	None (side sealing)

PISTON AND RING SPECIFICATIONS

All measurements are given in inches.

Year	Engine ID/VIN	Engine Displacement Liters (cc)	Piston Clearance	Ring Gap			Ring Side Clearance		
				Top Compression	Bottom Compression	Oil Control	Top Compression	Bottom Compression	Oil Control
1992	B	4.9 (4894)	0.0004–0.0020	0.012–0.022	0.012–0.022	0.010–0.050	0.0016–0.0037	0.0016–0.0037	None (side sealing)
	L	3.8 (3786)	0.0004–0.0022	0.010–0.025	0.010–0.025	0.015–0.055	0.0013–0.0031	0.0013–0.0031	0.0011–0.0081
	1	3.8 (3786)	0.0004–0.0022	0.010–0.025	0.010–0.025	0.015–0.055	0.0013–0.0031	0.0013–0.0031	0.0011–0.0081
1993-94	B	4.9 (4894)	0.0004–0.0020	0.012–0.022	0.012–0.022	0.004–0.020	0.0016–0.0037	0.0016–0.0037	None (side sealing)
	9	4.6 (4573)	0.0004–0.0020	NA	NA	NA	NA	NA	None (side sealing)
	L	3.8 (3786)	0.0004–0.0022	0.010–0.025	0.010–0.025	0.015–0.055	0.0013–0.0031	0.0013–0.0031	0.0011–0.0081
	1	3.8 (3786)	0.0004–0.0022	0.010–0.025	0.010–0.025	0.015–0.055	0.0013–0.0031	0.0013–0.0031	0.0011–0.0081

NA—Not available
① Skirt Top: 0.0007–0.0027
  Skirt Bottom: 0.0010–0.0045

TORQUE SPECIFICATIONS

All readings in ft. lbs.

Year	Engine ID/VIN	Engine Displacement Liters (cc)	Cylinder Head Bolts	Main Bearing Bolts	Rod Bearing Bolts	Crankshaft Damper Bolts	Flywheel Bolts	Manifold		Spark Plugs	Lug Nut
								Intake	Exhaust		
1990	C	3.8 (3786)	35	90	43	219	61	88④	41	20	100
	3	4.5 (4474)	①	85	24	65	70	②	18	11	100
1991	C	3.8 (3786)	⑥	⑦	⑧	③	61	88④	41	20	100
	L	3.8 (3786)	⑥	⑦	⑧	③	61	88④	41	20	100
	B	4.9 (4894)	①	85	25	70	70	②	18	23	100
1992	B	4.9 (4894)	①	85	25	70	70	②	18	23	100
	L	3.8 (3786)	⑥	⑦	⑧	③	61	88④	41	20	100
	1	3.8 (3786)	⑥	⑦	⑧	③	61	88④	41	20	100
1993-94	B	4.9 (4894)	①	85	25	70	70	②	16	23	100
	9	4.6 (4573)	NA	NA	NA	⑩	⑨	⑤	25	11	100
	L	3.8 (3786)	⑥	⑦	⑧	③	⑨	88④	37	20	100
	1	3.8 (3786)	⑥	⑦	⑧	③	⑨	88④	38	20	100

① Tighten in 3 steps:
  1. Tighten bolts in sequence to 38 ft. lbs.
  2. Tighten bolts in sequence to 68 ft. lbs.
  3. Tighten bolts 1, 3 and 4 to 90 ft. lbs.
② Tighten in 3 steps:
  1. Tighten 1, 2, 3, 4 in sequence to 8 ft. lbs.
  2. Tighten bolts 5 through 16 in sequence to 8 ft. lbs.
  3. Retighten all bolts in sequence to 12 ft. lbs.
③ 105 ± 7 (+56° ± 4)
④ Inch lbs.

⑤ 4 foot lbs. +120°
⑥ Tighten in 3 steps:
  1. Tighten bolts in sequence to 35 ft. lbs.
  2. Rotate each bolt an additional 130 degrees in sequence
  3. Rotate the center 4 bolts an additional 30 degrees in sequence
⑦ 26 ± 3 (+50° ± 3)
⑧ 20 ± 3 (+50° ± 3)
⑨ 11 ft. lbs. +50°
⑩ 105 ft. lbs. +120°

TORQUE SPECIFICATIONS

Component	English	Metric
Camshaft sprocket bolt		
3.8L (VIN C) engine:	26 ft. lbs.	35 Nm
3.8L (VIN L and 1) engines		
1990–91:	27 ft. lbs.	37 Nm
1992–94		
Step 1:	74 ft. lbs.	100 Nm
Step 2:	+ 105 degrees turn	+ 105 degrees turn
4.5L and 4.9L engines:	37 ft. lbs.	50 Nm
Connecting rod bearing cap bolts		
3.8L engine		
1990:	43 ft. lbs.	58 Nm
1991–94		
Step 1:	20 ft. lbs.	27 Nm
Step 2:	+ 50 degrees turn	+ 50 degrees turn
4.5L (VIN 3) engine *:	24 ft. lbs.	32 Nm
4.5L (VIN 5) engine:	22 ft. lbs.	30 Nm
4.9L engine:	25 ft. lbs.	33 Nm
* Note: Lubricate bolts with engine oil.		
Crankshaft damper		
3.8L engines		
1990:	220 ft. lbs.	297 Nm
1991–94		
Step 1:	105 ft. lbs.	140 Nm
Step 2:	+ 56 degrees turn	+ 56 degrees turn
4.5L engine:	65 ft. lbs.	90 Nm
4.9L engine:	70 ft. lbs.	95 Nm
Cylinder head bolt		
3.8L engine		
1990		
Step 1:	35 ft. lbs.	47 Nm
Step 2:	+ 130 degrees turn	+ 130 degrees turn
Step 3:	+ 30 degrees turn	+ 30 degrees turn
1991–94		
Step 1:	35 ft. lbs.	47 Nm
Step 2:	+ 130 degrees turn	+ 130 degrees turn
Step 3: 4 center bolts only	+ 30 degrees turn	+ 30 degrees turn
4.5L and 4.9L engines **		
Step 1:	38 ft. lbs.	50 Nm
Step 2:	68 ft. lbs.	90 Nm
Step 3: positions 1, 3, 4	90 ft. lbs.	120 Nm

* NOTE: If 60 ft. lbs. (81 Nm) is reached at any time during the sequence, STOP!; do not complete the balance of the 90 degrees turn on the bolt.

** Note: Lubricate bolts with engine oil.

Component	English	Metric
EGR valve-to-intake plenum		
3.8L (VIN C) engine		
1990:	18 ft. lbs.	24 Nm
4.5L and 4.9L engines:	18 ft. lbs.	24 Nm
Engine-to-transaxle:	55 ft. lbs.	75 Nm
Exhaust manifold		
3.8L engines:	41 ft. lbs.	55 Nm
4.5L engine:	18 ft. lbs.	25 Nm
4.9L engine:	16 ft. lbs.	21 Nm
Exhaust pipe-to-exhaust manifold nuts		
4.5L and 4.9L engines:	15 ft. lbs.	20 Nm
3.8L engines:	18 ft. lbs.	25 Nm

TORQUE SPECIFICATIONS

Component	English	Metric
Flywheel/flexplate-to-crankshaft bolts		
3.8L engine:	61 ft. lbs.	82 Nm
4.5L and 4.9L engines:	70 ft. lbs.	95 Nm
Flywheel-to-converter bolts:	46 ft. lbs.	62 Nm
Intake manifold		
3.8L (VIN C) engine:	89 inch lbs.	10 Nm
3.8L (VIN L and 1) engine		
Lower manifold:	89 inch lbs.	10 Nm
Upper manifold:	22 ft. lbs.	30 Nm
4.5L (VIN 3) and 4.9L engines		
Step 1 (positions 1, 2, 3, 4):	8 ft. lbs.	12 Nm
Step 2 (positions 5–16):	8 ft. lbs.	12 Nm
Step 3 (all bolts):	12 ft. lbs.	16 Nm
Step 4 (all bolts):	12 ft. lbs.	16 Nm
4.5L (VIN 5) engine		
Step 1 (positions 1, 2, 3, 4):	15 ft. lbs.	20 Nm
Step 2 (positions 5–16):	22 ft. lbs.	30 Nm
Step 3 (all bolts):	22 ft. lbs.	30 Nm
Step 4 (all bolts):	22 ft. lbs.	30 Nm
Main bearing cap bolts		
3.8L engine		
1990:	90 ft. lbs.	122 Nm
1991–94		
Step 1:	26 ft. lbs.	35 ft. lbs.
Step 2:	+ 50 degrees turn	+ 50 degrees turn
4.5L and 4.9L engines:	85 ft. lbs.	115 Nm
Oil pan		
3.8L engines:	124 inch lbs.	14 Nm
4.5L engine:	11 ft. lbs.	15 Nm
4.9L engine:	14 ft. lbs.	18 Nm
Oil pan drain plug		
3.8L engines		
1991:	18 ft. lbs.	25 Nm
1992–94:	30 ft. lbs.	40 Nm
4.5L and 4.9L engines:	22 ft. lbs.	30 Nm
Oil pump attaching bolts		
4.5L and 4.9L engines:	22 ft. lbs.	30 Nm
Oil pump cover screws		
3.8L engine:	97 inch lbs.	11 Nm
Rocker arm pivot bolt		
3.8L engines:	28 ft. lbs.	38 Nm
4.5L and 4.9L engines:	22 ft. lbs.	30 Nm
Rocker (valve) cover:	89 inch lbs.	10 Nm
Spark plug		
3.8L engine		
1991:	20 ft. lbs.	27 Nm
1992–94:	12 ft. lbs.	16 Nm
4.5L engine:	11 ft. lbs.	15 Nm
4.9L engine:	23 ft. lbs.	31 Nm
Starter-to-block:	35 ft. lbs.	47 Nm
Thermostat housing		
3.8L and 4.9L engines:	20 ft. lbs.	27 Nm
4.5L engine:	18 ft. lbs.	25 Nm
TBI fuel feed/return line:	17 ft. lbs.	23 Nm
TBI mounting bolts/nuts		
4.5L (VIN 3) and 4.9L engines:	14 ft. lbs.	19 Nm
4.5L (VIN 5) engine:	11 ft. lbs.	15 Nm

TORQUE SPECIFICATIONS

Component	English	Metric
Timing cover		
3.8L engine:	22 ft. lbs.	30 Nm
4.5L engine:	15 ft. lbs.	20 Nm
4.9L engine		
Upper (4):	30 ft. lbs.	40 Nm
Lower (4):	17 ft. lbs.	22 Nm
Water pump		
3.8L engine		
1990:	89 inch lbs.	10 Nm
1991–94:	126 inch lbs.	15 Nm
4.5L and 4.9L engines		
Water pump-to-block:	30 ft. lbs.	40 Nm
Water pump-to-front cover:	60 inch lbs.	7 Nm
Water pump pulley		
3.8L engine		
1990:	142 inch lbs.	16 Nm
1991–94:	114 inch lbs.	13 Nm
4.5L and 4.9L engines:	22 ft. lbs.	30 Nm

BRAKE SPECIFICATIONS

All measurements in inches unless noted.

Year	Model	Master Cylinder Bore	Brake Disc Original Thickness	Brake Disc Minimum Thickness	Brake Disc Maximum Runout	Brake Drum Diameter Original Inside Diameter	Brake Drum Diameter Max. Wear Limit	Brake Drum Diameter Maximum Machine Diameter	Minimum Lining Thickness Front	Minimum Lining Thickness Rear
1990	DeVille	0.937	1.043	0.972	0.004	8.860	0.006	8.880	0.030	0.030
	Fleetwood	0.937	1.043	0.972	0.004	8.860	0.006	8.880	0.030	0.030
	Electra	0.937	1.043	0.972	0.004	8.860	0.006	8.880	0.030	0.030
	Park Ave.	0.937	1.043	0.972	0.004	8.860	0.006	8.880	0.030	0.030
	LeSabre	0.937	1.043	0.972	0.004	8.860	0.006	8.880	0.030	0.030
	Ninety Eight	0.937	1.043	0.972	0.004	8.860	0.006	8.880	0.030	0.030
	Delta 88	0.937	1.043	0.972	0.004	8.860	0.006	8.880	0.030	0.030
	Bonneville	0.937	1.043	0.972	0.004	8.860	0.006	8.880	0.030	0.030
1991	DeVille	1.000	1.276	1.224	0.004	8.860	0.006	8.880	0.030	0.030
	Fleetwood	1.000	1.276	1.224	0.004	8.860	0.006	8.880	0.030	0.030
	Park Ave.	1.000	1.276	1.204	0.004	8.860	0.006	8.880	0.030	0.030
	LeSabre	1.000	1.043	0.972	0.004	8.860	0.006	8.880	0.030	0.030
	Ninety Eight	1.000	1.276	1.204	0.004	8.860	0.006	8.880	0.030	0.030
	88 Royale	1.000	1.043	0.972	0.004	8.860	0.006	8.880	0.030	0.030
	Bonneville	1.000	1.043	0.972	0.004	8.860	0.006	8.880	0.030	0.030
1992	DeVille	1.000	1.276	1.224	0.004	8.860	0.006	8.880	0.030	0.030
	Fleetwood	1.000	1.276	1.224	0.004	8.860	0.006	8.880	0.030	0.030
	Park Ave.	1.000	1.276	1.224	0.004	8.860	0.006	8.880	0.030	0.030
	LeSabre	1.000	1.276	1.224	0.004	8.860	0.006	8.880	0.030	0.030
	Ninety Eight	1.000	1.276	1.224	0.004	8.860	0.006	8.880	0.030	0.030
	88 Royale	1.000	1.276	1.224	0.004	8.860	0.006	8.880	0.030	0.030
	Bonneville	1.000	1.276	1.224	0.004	8.860	0.006	8.880	0.030	0.030

BRAKE SPECIFICATIONS

All measurements in inches unless noted.

| Year | Model | Master Cylinder Bore | Brake Disc | | | Brake Drum Diameter | | | Minimum Lining Thickness | |
			Original Thickness	Minimum Thickness	Maximum Runout	Original Inside Diameter	Max. Wear Limit	Maximum Machine Diameter	Front	Rear
1993–94	DeVille	1.000	1.276	1.224	0.004	8.860	0.006	8.880	0.030	0.030
	Park Ave.	1.000	1.276	1.224	0.004	8.860	0.006	8.880	0.030	0.030
	LeSabre	1.000	1.276	1.224	0.004	8.860	0.006	8.880	0.030	0.030
	Ninety Eight	1.000	1.276	1.224	0.004	8.860	0.006	8.880	0.030	0.030
	88 Royale	1.000	1.276	1.224	0.004	8.860	0.006	8.880	0.030	0.030
	Bonneville	1.000	1.276	1.224	0.004	8.860	0.006	8.880	0.030	0.030

WHEEL ALIGNMENT

| Year | Model | Caster | | Camber | | Toe-in (in.) | Steering Axis Inclination (deg.) |
		Range (deg.)	Preferred Setting (deg.)	Range (deg.)	Preferred Setting (deg.)		
1990	DeVille	2½P–3½P	3P	①	①	0	—
	Fleetwood	2½P–3½P	3P	①	①	0	—
	Electra	2½P–3½P	3P	$5/16$N–$11/16$P	$3/16$P	0	—
	Park Avenue	2½P–3½P	3P	$5/16$N–$11/16$P	$3/16$P	0	—
	LeSabre	2½P–3½P	3P	$5/16$N–$11/16$P	$3/16$P	0	—
	Ninety Eight	2½P–3½P	3P	$5/16$N–$11/16$P	$3/16$P	0	½P
	Delta 88	2½P–3½P	3P	$5/16$N–$11/16$P	$3/16$P	0	½P
	Bonneville	2½P–3½P	3P	$5/16$N–$11/16$P	$3/16$P	0	½P
1991	DeVille	2½P–3½P	3P	①	①	0	—
	Fleetwood	2½P–3½P	3P	①	①	0	—
	Park Avenue	2½P–3½P	3P	$5/16$N–$11/16$P	$3/16$P	0	—
	LeSabre	2½P–3½P	3P	$5/16$N–$11/16$P	$3/16$P	0	—
	Ninety Eight	2½P–3½P	3P	$5/16$N–$11/16$P	$3/16$P	0	½P
	88 Royale	2½P–3½P	3P	$5/16$N–$11/16$P	$3/16$P	0	½P
	Bonneville	2½P–3½P	3P	$5/16$N–$11/16$P	$3/16$P	0	½P
1992	DeVille	2½P–3½P	3P	①	①	0	—
	Fleetwood	2½P–3½P	3P	①	①	0	—
	Park Avenue	2½P–3½P	3P	$5/16$N–$11/16$P	$3/16$P	0	—
	LeSabre	2½P–3½P	3P	$5/16$N–$11/16$P	$3/16$P	0	—
	Ninety Eight	2½P–3½P	3P	$5/16$N–$11/16$P	$3/16$P	0	—
	88 Royale	2½P–3½P	3P	$5/16$N–$11/16$P	$3/16$P	0	—
	Bonneville	2½P–3½P	3P	$5/16$N–$11/16$P	$3/16$P	0	—
1993–94	DeVille	2¼P–3¾P	3P	①	①	0	—
	Park Avenue	2½P–3½P	3P	$5/16$N–$11/16$P	$3/16$P	0	—
	LeSabre	2½P–3½P	3P	$5/16$N–$11/16$P	$3/16$P	0	—
	Ninety Eight	2½P–3½P	3P	$5/16$N–$11/16$P	$3/16$P	0	—
	88 Royale	2½P–3½P	3P	$5/16$N–$11/16$P	$3/16$P	0	—
	Bonneville	2½P–3½P	3P	$5/16$N–$11/16$P	$3/16$P	0	—

N—Negative
P—Positive
① Left wheel

Min.—1N
Pref.—½N
Max.—0

Right wheel
Min.—0
Pref.—½P
Max.—1P

AIR CONDITIONING BELT TENSION

Year	Engine VIN	Engine Displacement Liters (cc)	Belt Type	Specifications New	Used
1990	8	4.5 (4563)	Serpentine		①
	C	3.8 (3788)	Serpentine		①
	1	3.8 (3788)	Serpentine		50–70 ②
1991	L	3.8 (3788)	Serpentine		①
	C	3.8 (3788)	Serpentine		①
	B	4.9 (4920)	Serpentine		①
1992	B	4.9 (4920)	Serpentine		①
	1	3.8 (3788)	Serpentine		50–70 ②
	L	3.8 (3788)	Serpentine		①
	C	3.8 (3788)	Serpentine		①
1993–94	B	4.9 (4920)	Serpentine		①
	L	3.8 (3788)	Serpentine		①
	1	3.8 (3788)	Serpentine		50–70 ②

① Equipped with automatic tensioner;
  no adjustment required.
② Equipped with automatic tensioner; however,
  the specification given (in pounds) is for testing
  whether the tensioner is maintaining its proper
  tension (specification given is the average of 3
  readings back-to-back).

REFRIGERANT CAPACITIES

Year	Model	Refrigerant (oz.)	Oil (fl. oz.)	Compressor Type
1990	Electra, Park Avenue, Park Avenue Ultra, Fleetwood, DeVille, 88 Royale, Ninety-Eight	46.0	8.0	HR-6
	LeSabre, Delta 88, Bonneville	38.5	8.0	HR-6
1991	Electra, Park Avenue, Park Avenue Ultra, Fleetwood, DeVille, 88 Royale, Ninety-Eight	46.0	8.0	HR-6
	LeSabre, Delta 88, Bonneville	38.5	8.0	HR-6
1992	Electra, Park Avenue, Park Avenue Ultra, Fleetwood, DeVille, 88 Royale, Ninety-Eight	38.7	8.0	HR-6, HR6-HE
	LeSabre, Delta 88, Bonneville	38.0	8.0	HR-6, HR6-HE
1993	Electra, Park Avenue, Park Avenue Ultra, Fleetwood, DeVille, 88 Royale, Ninety-Eight	38.0	8.0	HR-6, HR6-HE
	LeSabre, Delta 88, Bonneville	38.0	8.0	HR-6, HR6-HE

NOTE: At the time of publication, refrigerant capacity information relating to R-134a was not available from the manufacturer.

GENERAL MOTORS—"C AND H" BODY
BONNEVILLE • DELTA 88 • DEVILLE • ELECTRA • FLEETWOOD

MAINTENANCE INTERVALS—TYPE A: NORMAL SERVICE
Bonneville • Delta 88 • DeVille • Electra • Fleetwood • LeSabre • Ninety-Eight • Park Avenue • Park Avenue Ultra • 88 Royale

TO BE SERVICED	TYPE OF SERVICE	VEHICLE MILEAGE INTERVAL (X1000)							
		7.5	15	22.5	30	37.5	45	52.5	60
Oxygen Sensor	I				✔				✔
Ignition Timing	I①				✔				✔
Vacuum Lines and Hoses	I		✔		✔		✔		✔
Ignition Wires	I				✔				✔
Spark Plugs	R				✔				✔
Engine Oil	R	✔	✔	✔	✔	✔	✔	✔	✔
Engine Air Cleaner Element	R								✔
Crankcase Emission Filter	R②				✔				✔
PCV Valve	R				✔				✔
Fuel Filter	R								✔
Tire Rotation	I③	✔		✔		✔		✔	
Fuel/Vapor Return Lines	I				✔				✔
Fuel Tank Cap and Restrictor	I				✔				✔
Coolant System	R				✔				✔
Exhaust Pipe and Muffler	I				✔				✔
Brake Linings	I				✔				✔
Catalytic Converter and Shield	I				✔				✔
EGR System	I				✔				✔
Oil Filter	R	✔		✔		✔		✔	
Battery Connections	I		✔		✔		✔		✔
Automatic Transaxle Fluid	R④								
Coolant Hoses and Clamps	I		✔		✔		✔		✔
Idle Speed System	I⑤				✔				✔
Throttle Body Mounting Torque	I	✔							
Drive Belts	I⑥				✔				✔
Oil Maintenance Indicator	I⑦	✔	✔	✔	✔	✔	✔	✔	✔
Chassis Lubrication	L	✔	✔	✔	✔	✔	✔	✔	✔
CV-Joints and Boots	I	✔	✔	✔	✔	✔	✔	✔	✔
Parking Brake	I⑧	✔			✔		✔		✔
Seat Belt Operation	I⑧	✔			✔		✔		✔

FOR COMPLETE WARRANTY COVERAGE CONSULT INDIVIDUAL VEHICLE MANUFACTURER'S WARRANTY MAINTENANCE GUIDE.

I—Inspect
L—Lubricate
R—Replace
① Check and adjust timing on applicable models
② Replace as needed on applicable models
③ Rotate tires at 7,500 miles and then every 15,000 miles
④ Replace transmission fluid at 100,000 miles
⑤ Check and adjust as necessary
⑥ Inspect and replace as necessary
⑦ On applicable models reset indicator at every service as per owner's manual
⑧ Check, adjustment and lubricate cables as necessary

MAINTENANCE INTERVALS—TYPE B: SEVERE SERVICE
Bonneville • Delta 88 • DeVille • Electra • Fleetwood • LeSabre • Ninety-Eight • Park Avenue • Park Avenue Ultra • 88 Royale

TO BE SERVICED	TYPE OF SERVICE	VEHICLE MILEAGE INTERVAL (X1000)									
		3	6	9	12	15	18	21	24	27	30
Oxygen Sensor	I										✔
Ignition Timing	I①										✔
Vacuum Lines and Hoses	I					✔					✔
Ignition Wires	I										✔
Spark Plugs	R										✔
Engine Oil and Filter	R	✔	✔	✔	✔	✔	✔	✔	✔	✔	✔
Engine Air Cleaner Element	R					✔					✔
Crankcase Emission Filter	R					✔					✔
PCV Valve	R										✔
Fuel Filter	R					✔					✔
Tire Rotation	I②		✔					✔			
Fuel/Vapor Return Lines	I										✔
Fuel Tank Cap and Restrictor	I										✔
Coolant System	R										✔
Exhaust Pipe and Muffler	I										✔
Brake Linings	R					✔					✔
Catalytic Converter and Shield	I										✔
EGR System	I③										✔
Battery Connections	I					✔					
Coolant Hoses and Clamps	I					✔					✔
Automatic Transaxle Fluid	R					✔					✔
Idle Speed System	I④					✔					✔
Throttle Body Mounting Torque	I		✔								
Drive Belts	I					✔					✔
Oil Maintenance Indicator	I⑤										
Chassis Lubrication	L		✔		✔		✔		✔		✔
CV-Joints and Boots	I	✔	✔	✔	✔	✔	✔	✔	✔	✔	
Parking Brake	I⑥					✔					✔
Seat Belt Operation	I⑥					✔					✔

FOR COMPLETE WARRANTY COVERAGE CONSULT INDIVIDUAL VEHICLE MANUFACTURER'S WARRANTY MAINTENANCE GUIDE.

I—Inspect
L—Lubricate
R—Replace

① Check and adjust timing on applicable models
② Rotate tires at 6,000 miles and then every 15,000 miles
③ On applicable models
④ Adjust and lubricate as necessary
⑤ On applicable models reset indicator at every service as per owner's manual
⑥ Check, adjustment and lubricate cables as necessary

FIRING ORDERS

NOTE: To avoid confusion, always replace spark plug wires one at a time.

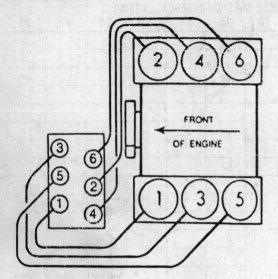

3.8L (VIN C and 1) Engines
Engine Firing Order: 1-6-5-4-3-2
Distributorless Ignition System

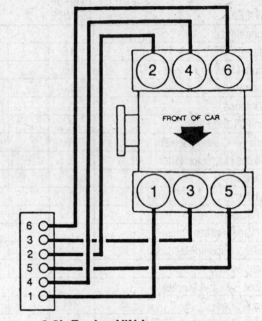

3.8L Engine VIN L
Engine Firing Order: 1–6–5–4–3–2
Distributorless Ignition System

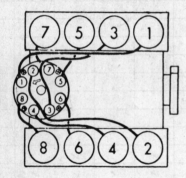

4.5L and 4.9L Engines
Engine Firing Order: 1–8–4–3–6–5–7–2
Distributor Rotation: Counterclockwise

CYLINDER HEAD TORQUE SEQUENCES

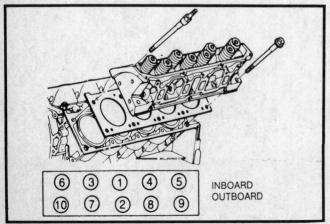

Cylinder head bolt tightening—4.5L and 4.9L engines

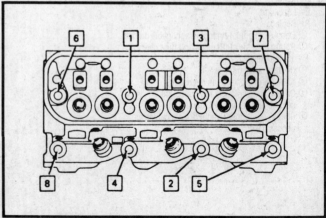

Cylinder head bolt tightening sequence—3.8L engine

TIMING MARK LOCATIONS

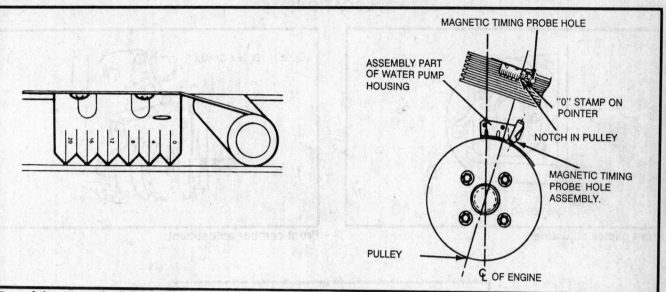

View of the magnetic timing probe hole—4.5L and 4.9L engines

TIMING CHAIN ALIGNMENT MARKS

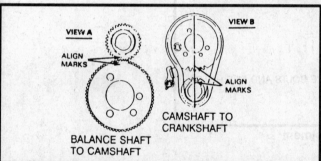

Timing chain alignment marks—3.8L engine

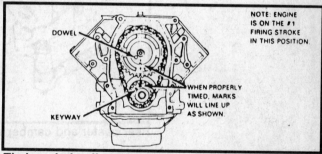

Timing chain alignment marks—4.5L and 4.9L engines

AIR CONDITIONING SERVICE VALVE LOCATIONS

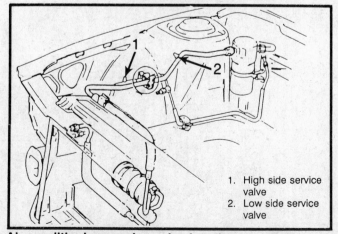

1. High side service valve
2. Low side service valve

Air conditioning service valve location

WHEEL ALIGNMENT ADJUSTMENT
LOCATIONS

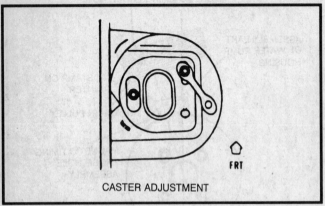

Front caster adjustment

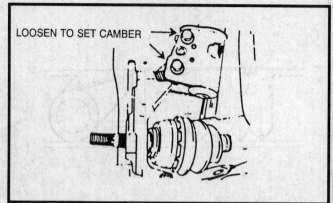

Front camber adjustment

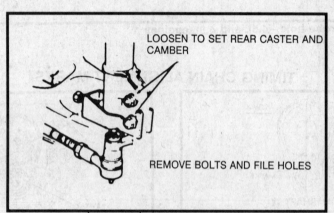

Rear caster and camber adjustment

SPECIFICATION CHARTS

VEHICLE IDENTIFICATION CHART

It is important for servicing and ordering parts to be certain of the vehicle and engine identification. The VIN (vehicle identification number) is a 17 digit number visible through the windshield on the driver's side of the dash and contains the vehicle and engine identification codes. The tenth digit indicates model year and the eighth digit indicates engine code. It can be interpreted as follows:

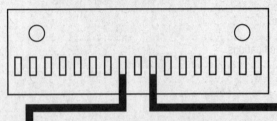

		Engine Code					Model Year	
Code	Liters	Cu. In. (cc)	Cyl.	Fuel Sys.	Eng. Mfg.		Code	Year
C	3.8	231 (3786)	6	SFI	Buick		L	1990
L	3.8	231 (3786)	6	SFI	Buick		M	1991
8	4.5	273 (4474)	8	SFI	Cadillac		N	1992
3	4.5	273 (4474)	8	SFI	Cadillac		P	1993
B	4.9	300 (4917)	8	SFI	Cadillac		R	1994
9	4.6	279 (4573)	8	SFI	Cadillac			
Y	4.6	279 (4573)	8	SFI	Cadillac			

SFI—Sequential Fuel Injection

ENGINE IDENTIFICATION

Year	Model	Engine Displacement Liters (cc)	Engine Series (ID/VIN)	Fuel System	No. of Cylinders	Engine Type
1990	Allante	4.5 (4474)	8	SFI	8	OHV
	Eldorado	4.5 (4474)	3	SFI	8	OHV
	Reatta	3.8 (3786)	C	SFI	6	OHV
	Riviera	3.8 (3786)	C	SFI	6	OHV
	Seville	4.5 (4474)	3	SFI	8	OHV
	Toronado	3.8 (3786)	C	SFI	6	OHV
	Trofeo	3.8 (3786)	C	SFI	6	OHV
1991	Allante	4.5 (4474)	8	SFI	8	OHV
	Eldorado	4.9 (4917)	B	SFI	8	OHV
	Reatta	3.8 (3786)	C	SFI	6	OHV
	Riviera	3.8 (3786)	C	SFI	6	OHV
	Seville	4.9 (4917)	B	SFI	8	OHV
	Toronado	3.8 (3786)	C	SFI	6	OHV
	Trofeo	3.8 (3786)	C	SFI	6	OHV
1992	Allante	4.5 (4474)	8	SFI	8	OHV
	Allante	4.6 (4573)	9	SFI	8	OHV
	Eldorado	4.9 (4917)	B	SFI	8	OHV
	Riviera	3.8 (3786)	L	SFI	6	OHV
	Seville	4.9 (4917)	B	SFI	8	OHV
	Toronado	3.8 (3786)	L	SFI	6	OHV

ENGINE IDENTIFICATION

Year	Model	Engine Displacement Liters (cc)	Engine Series (ID/VIN)	Fuel System	No. of Cylinders	Engine Type
1993-94	Allante	4.6 (4573)	9	SFI	8	OHV
	Deville Concours ①	4.6 (4573)	Y	SFI	8	OHV
	Sedan Deville ①	4.9 (4917)	B	SFI	8	OHV
	Eldorado	4.9 (4917)	B	SFI	8	OHV
	Eldorado	4.6 (4573)	9	SFI	8	OHV
	Eldorado	4.6 (4573)	Y	SFI	8	OHV
	Riviera	3.8 (3786)	L	SFI	8	OHV
	Seville	4.9 (4917)	B	SFI	8	OHV
	Seville	4.6 (4573)	Y	SFI	8	OHV
	Seville	4.6 (4573)	9	SFI	8	OHV

OHV—Overhead Valve
SFI—Sequential Fuel Injection
① In 1994, Deville Concours & Sedan Deville become K-body vehicles

GENERAL ENGINE SPECIFICATIONS

Year	Engine ID/VIN	Engine Displacement Liters (cc)	Fuel System Type	Net Horsepower @ rpm	Net Torque @ rpm (ft. lbs.)	Bore × Stroke (in.)	Compression Ratio	Oil Pressure @ rpm
1990	C	3.8 (3786)	SFI	165 @ 5200	210 @ 2000	3.800 × 3.400	8.5:1	37 @ 2400
	8	4.5 (4474)	SFI	200 @ 4400	230 @ 3200	3.620 × 3.310	9.0:1	①
	3	4.5 (4474)	SFI	180 @ 4000	245 @ 3000	3.620 × 3.310	9.5:1	①
1991	C	3.8 (3786)	SFI	165 @ 4800	210 @ 2000	3.800 × 3.400	8.5:1	40 @ 1850
	8	4.5 (4474)	SFI	200 @ 4400	270 @ 3200	3.620 × 3.310	9.0:1	①
	B	4.9 (4917)	SFI	200 @ 4100	275 @ 3000	3.620 × 3.620	9.5:1	53 @ 2000
1992	L	3.8 (3786)	SFI	170 @ 4800	220 @ 3200	3.800 × 3.400	8.5:1	60 @ 1850
	8	4.5 (4474)	SFI	200 @ 4400	270 @ 3200	3.620 × 3.310	9.0:1	①
	9	4.6 (4573)	SFI	290 @ 5600	290 @ 4400	3.660 × 3.310	10.3:1	35 @ 2000
	B	4.9 (4917)	SFI	200 @ 4100	275 @ 3000	3.620 × 3.620	9.5:1	53 @ 2000
1993-94	L	3.8 (3786)	SFI	170 @ 4800	220 @ 3200	3.800 × 3.400	8.5:1	60 @ 1850
	9	4.6 (4573)	SFI	295 @ 6000	290 @ 4400	3.660 × 3.310	10.3:1	35 @ 2000
	B	4.9 (4917)	SFI	200 @ 4100	275 @ 3000	3.620 × 3.620	9.5:1	53 @ 2000
	Y	4.6 (4573)	SFI	270 @ 5600	300 @ 4400	3.660 × 3.310	10.3:1	35 @ 2000

SFI—Sequential Fuel Injection
① 26–30 psi at 30 mph at normal operating temperature

GASOLINE ENGINE TUNE-UP SPECIFICATIONS

Year	Engine ID/VIN	Engine Displacement Liters (cc)	Spark Plugs Gap (in.)	Ignition Timing (deg.) MT	Ignition Timing (deg.) AT	Fuel Pump (psi)	Idle Speed (rpm) MT	Idle Speed (rpm) AT	Valve Clearance In.	Valve Clearance Ex.
1990	C	3.8 (3786)	0.060	—	①	②	—	①	Hyd.	Hyd.
	8	4.5 (4474)	0.060	—	①	40–50	—	①	Hyd.	Hyd.
	3	4.5 (4474)	0.060	—	①	40–50	—	①	Hyd.	Hyd.

GASOLINE ENGINE TUNE-UP SPECIFICATIONS

Year	Engine ID/VIN	Engine Displacement Liters (cc)	Spark Plugs Gap (in.)	Ignition Timing (deg.) MT	AT	Fuel Pump (psi)	Idle Speed (rpm) MT	AT	Valve Clearance In.	Ex.
1991	C	3.8 (3786)	0.060	—	①	②	—	①	Hyd.	Hyd.
	8	4.5 (4474)	0.060	—	①	40–50	—	①	Hyd.	Hyd.
	B	4.9 (4917)	0.060	—	①	40–50	—	①	Hyd.	Hyd.
1992	L	3.8 (3786)	0.060	—	①	②	—	①	Hyd.	Hyd.
	8	4.5 (4474)	0.060	—	①	40–50	—	①	Hyd.	Hyd.
	B	4.9 (4917)	0.060	—	①	40–50	—	①	Hyd.	Hyd.
1993	L	3.8 (3786)	0.060	—	①	②	—	①	Hyd.	Hyd.
	9	4.6 (4573)	0.060	—	①	40–50	—	①	Hyd.	Hyd.
	B	4.9 (4917)	0.060	—	①	40–50	—	①	Hyd.	Hyd.
1994	REFER TO UNDERHOOD SPECIFICATIONS STICKER									

NOTE: The lowest cylinder pressure should be within 75% of the highest cylinder pressure reading. For example, if the highest cylinder is 134 psi, the lowest should be 101. Engine should be at normal operating temperature with throttle valve in the wide open position.

The underhood specifications sticker often reflects tune-up specification changes in production. Sticker figures must be used if they disagree with those in this chart.

Hyd.—Hydraulic

① Controlled by ECM

② 1—Connect fuel pressure gauge, engine at normal operating temperature

2—Turn ignition switch ON

3—After approx. 2 seconds pressure should read 41–47 psi and hold steady

4—Start engine and idle, pressure should drop 3–10 psi from static pressure

CAPACITIES

Year	Model	Engine ID/VIN	Engine Displacement Liters (cc)	Engine Crankcase (qts.) with Filter	Transmission (pts.) 4-Spd	5-Spd	Auto.	Transfer case (pts.)	Drive Axle Front (pts.)	Rear (pts.)	Fuel Tank (gal.)	Cooling System (qts.)
1990	Allante	8	4.5 (4474)	5.5	—	—	13	—	—	—	22.0	12.1
	Eldorado	3	4.5 (4474)	5.5	—	—	13	—	—	—	18.8	12.1
	Reatta	C	3.8 (3786)	5.0	—	—	12	—	—	—	18.0	13.0
	Riviera	C	3.8 (3786)	5.0	—	—	12	—	—	—	18.0	13.0
	Seville	3	4.5 (4474)	5.5	—	—	13	—	—	—	18.8	12.1
	Toronado	C	3.8 (3786)	5.0	—	—	12	—	—	—	18.0	13.0
	Trofeo	C	3.8 (3786)	5.0	—	—	12	—	—	—	18.0	13.0
1991	Allante	8	4.5 (4474)	6.5	—	—	13	—	—	—	22.0	12.1
	Eldorado	B	4.5 (4474)	5.5	—	—	13	—	—	—	18.8	12.1
	Reatta	C	3.8 (3786)	5.0	—	—	12	—	—	—	18.0	13.0
	Riviera	C	3.8 (3786)	5.0	—	—	12	—	—	—	18.0	13.0
	Seville	B	4.9 (4917)	5.5	—	—	13	—	—	—	18.8	12.1
	Toronado	C	3.8 (3786)	5.0	—	—	12	—	—	—	18.0	13.0
	Trofeo	C	3.8 (3786)	5.0	—	—	12	—	—	—	18.0	13.0
1992	Allante	8	4.5 (4474)	6.5	—	—	13	—	—	—	22.0	12.1
	Allante	9	4.6 (4573)	7.5	—	—	13	—	—	—	22.0	12.5
	Eldorado	B	4.9 (4917)	5.5	—	—	13	—	—	—	18.8	12.1
	Riviera	L	3.8 (3786)	5.0	—	—	13	—	—	—	18.0	13.0
	Seville	B	4.9 (4917)	5.5	—	—	13	—	—	—	18.8	12.1
	Toronado	L	3.8 (3786)	5.0	—	—	13	—	—	—	18.0	13.0
	Trofeo	L	3.8 (3786)	5.0	—	—	13	—	—	—	18.0	13.0

CAPACITIES

Year	Model	Engine ID/VIN	Engine Displacement Liters (cc)	Engine Crankcase (qts.) with Filter	Transmission (pts.)			Transfer case (pts.)	Drive Axle		Fuel Tank (gal.)	Cooling System (qts.)
					4-Spd	5-Spd	Auto.		Front (pts.)	Rear (pts.)		
1993–94	Allante	9	4.6 (4573)	7.5	—	—	13	—	—	—	22.0	12.1
	Deville Concours ①	Y	4.6 (4573)	7.5	—	—	13	—	—	—	20.0	12.5
	Sedan Deville ①	B	4.9 (4917)	5.5	—	—	13	—	—	—	20.0	10.7
	Eldorado	9	4.6 (4573)	7.5	—	—	13	—	—	—	20.0	12.5
	Eldorado	B	4.9 (4917)	5.5	—	—	13	—	—	—	18.8	12.1
	Eldorado	Y	4.6 (4573)	7.5	—	—	13	—	—	—	20.0	12.5
	Riviera	L	3.8 (3786)	5.0	—	—	13	—	—	—	18.0	13.0
	Seville	9	4.9 (4917)	5.5	—	—	13	—	—	—	20.0	12.5
	Seville	Y	4.6 (4573)	7.5	—	—	13	—	—	—	20.0	12.5
	Seville	B	4.9 (4917)	5.5	—	—	13	—	—	—	20.0	12.5

① In 1994 Deville Concours and Sedan Deville become K-body vehicles

CAMSHAFT SPECIFICATIONS

All measurements given in inches.

Year	Engine ID/VIN	Engine Displacement Liters (cc)	Journal Diameter					Elevation		Bearing Clearance	Camshaft End Play
			1	2	3	4	5	In.	Ex.		
1990	C	3.8 (3786)	1.785–1.786	1.785–1.786	1.785–1.786	1.785–1.786	—	0.250	0.255	0.0005–0.0035	NA
	8	4.5 (4474)	NA	NA	NA	NA	NA	0.384	0.396	0.0018–0.0037	NA
	3	4.5 (4474)	NA	NA	NA	NA	NA	0.384	0.396	0.0018–0.0037	NA
1991	C	3.8 (3786)	1.785–1.786	1.785–1.786	1.785–1.786	1.785–1.786	—	0.250	0.255	0.0005–0.0035	NA
	8	4.5 (4474)	NA	NA	NA	NA	NA	0.384	0.396	0.0018–0.0037	NA
	B	4.9 (4917)	NA	NA	NA	NA	NA	0.384	0.396	0.0018–0.0037	NA
1992	L	3.8 (3786)	1.785–1.786	1.785–1.786	1.785–1.786	1.785–1.786	—	0.250	0.255	0.0005–0.0035	NA
	8	4.5 (4474)	NA	NA	NA	NA	NA	0.384	0.396	0.0018–0.0037	NA
	9	4.6 (4573)	1.061–1.062	1.061–1.062	1.061–1.062	1.061–1.062	1.061–1.062	0.370	0.339	0.0020–0.0030	NA
	B	4.9 (4917)	NA	NA	NA	NA	NA	0.384	0.396	0.0018–0.0037	NA
1993–94	L	3.8 (3786)	1.785–1.786	1.785–1.786	1.785–1.786	1.785–1.786	—	0.250	0.255	0.0005–0.0035	NA
	9	4.6 (4573)	1.061–1.062	1.061–1.062	1.061–1.062	1.061–1.062	1.061–1.062	0.370	0.339	0.0020–0.0030	NA
	B	4.9 (4917)	NA	NA	NA	NA	NA	0.384	0.396	0.0018–0.0037	NA
	Y	4.6 (4573)	1.061–1.062	1.061–1.062	1.061–1.062	1.061–1.062	1.061–1.062	0.339	0.339	0.0020–0.0030	NA

NA—Not available

CRANKSHAFT AND CONNECTING ROD SPECIFICATIONS

All measurements are given in inches.

Year	Engine ID/VIN	Engine Displacement Liters (cc)	Crankshaft				Connecting Rod		
			Main Brg. Journal Dia.	Main Brg. Oil Clearance	Shaft End-play	Thrust on No.	Journal Diameter	Oil Clearance	Side Clearance
1990	C	3.8 (3786)	2.4988–2.4998	0.0018–0.0030	0.003–0.011	2	2.2487–2.2499	0.0003–0.0028	0.003–0.015
	8	4.5 (4474)	2.6350–2.6360	0.0016–0.0039 ①	0.001–0.007	3	1.9270	0.0005–0.0028	0.008–0.020
	3	4.5 (4474)	2.6350–2.6360	0.0016–0.0039 ①	0.001–0.007	3	1.9270	0.0005–0.0028	0.008–0.020
1991	C	3.8 (3786)	2.4988–2.4998	0.0018–0.0030	0.003–0.011	2	2.2487–2.2499	0.0003–0.0028	0.003–0.015
	8	4.5 (4474)	2.6350–2.6360	0.0016–0.0039 ①	0.001–0.007	3	1.9270–1.9280	0.0005–0.0028	0.008–0.020
	B	4.9 (4917)	2.6350–2.6360	0.0016–0.0039 ①	0.001–0.008	3	1.9270–1.9280	0.0005–0.0028	0.008–0.020
1992	L	3.8 (3786)	2.4988–2.4998	0.0018–0.0030	0.003–0.011	2	2.2487–2.2499	0.0003–0.0028	0.003–0.015
	8	4.5 (4474)	2.6350–2.6360	0.0016–0.0039 ①	0.001–0.007	3	1.9270–1.9280	0.0005–0.0028	0.008–0.020
	9	4.6 (4573)	2.5195–2.5205	NA	0.002–0.019	3	NA	0.0010–0.0030	0.008–0.020
	B	4.9 (4917)	2.6350–2.6360	0.0016–0.0039 ①	0.001–0.008	3	1.9270–1.9280	0.0005–0.0028	0.008–0.020
1993–94	L	3.8 (3786)	2.4988–2.4998	0.0018–0.0030	0.003–0.011	2	2.2487–2.2499	0.0003–0.0028	0.003–0.015
	9	4.6 (4573)	2.5195–2.5205	NA	0.002–0.019	3	NA	0.0010–0.0030	0.008–0.020
	B	4.9 (4917)	2.6350–2.6360	0.0016–0.0039 ①	0.001–0.008	3	1.9270–1.9280	0.0005–0.0028	0.008–0.020
	Y	4.6 (4573)	2.5195–2.5205	NA	0.002–0.019	3	NA	0.0010–0.0030	0.008–0.020

NA—Not available
① No. 1—0.0008–0.0031

VALVE SPECIFICATIONS

Year	Engine ID/VIN	Engine Displacement Liters (cc)	Seat Angle (deg.)	Face Angle (deg.)	Spring Test Pressure (lbs. @ in.)	Spring Installed Height (in.)	Stem-to-Guide Clearance (in.)		Stem Diameter (in.)	
							Intake	Exhaust	Intake	Exhaust
1990	C	3.8 (3786)	45	45	200–220 @ 1.315 ①	1.690–1.750	0.0015–0.0035	0.0015–0.0032	NA	NA
	8	4.5 (4474)	45	44	204–221 @ 1.28 ①	2.216 ②	0.0010–0.0030	0.0010–0.0030	0.3413–0.3420	0.3401–0.3408
	3	4.5 (4474)	45	44	214–232 @ 1.35 ①	2.216 ②	0.0010–0.0030	0.0010–0.0030	0.3413–0.3420	0.3401–0.3408
1991	C	3.8 (3786)	45	45	200–220 @ 1.315 ①	1.690–1.720	0.0015–0.0035	0.0015–0.0032	NA	NA
	8	4.5 (4474)	45	44	204–221 @ 1.28	2.216 ②	0.0010–0.0030	0.0020–0.0040	0.3413–0.3420	0.3401–0.3408
	B	4.9 (4917)	45	45	214–232 @ 1.35	1.949 ②	0.0010–0.0030	0.0020–0.0040	0.3413–0.3420	0.3401–0.3408

VALVE SPECIFICATIONS

Year	Engine ID/VIN	Engine Displacement Liters (cc)	Seat Angle (deg.)	Face Angle (deg.)	Spring Test Pressure (lbs. @ in.)	Spring Installed Height (in.)	Stem-to-Guide Clearance (in.)		Stem Diameter (in.)	
							Intake	Exhaust	Intake	Exhaust
1992	L	3.8 (3786)	45	45	200–220 @ 1.315 ①	1.690–1.720	0.0015–0.0035	0.0015–0.0032	NA	NA
	8	4.5 (4474)	45	44	204–221 @ 1.28	2.216 ②	0.0010–0.0030	0.0020–0.0040	0.3413–0.3420	0.3401–0.3408
	9	4.6 (4573)	46	45	NA	1.190 ②	0.0010–0.0030	0.0020–0.0040	0.2331–0.2339	0.2331–0.2339
	B	4.9 (4917)	45	45	214–232 @ 1.35	1.949 ②	0.0010–0.0030	0.0020–0.0040	0.3413–0.3420	0.3401–0.3408
1993–94	L	3.8 (3786)	45	45	200–220 @ 1.315 ①	1.690–1.720	0.0015–0.0035	0.0015–0.0032	NA	NA
	9	4.6 (4573)	46	45	NA	1.190 ②	0.0010–0.0030	0.0020–0.0040	0.2331–0.2339	0.2331–0.2339
	B	4.9 (4917)	45	45	214–232 @ 1.35	1.949 ②	0.0010–0.0030	0.0020–0.0040	0.3413–0.3420	0.3401–0.3408
	Y	4.6 (4573)	46	45	NA	1.190 ②	0.0010–0.0030	0.0020–0.0040	0.2331–0.2339	0.2331–0.2339

NA—Not available
① Load open
② Free length

PISTON AND RING SPECIFICATIONS

All measurements are given in inches.

Year	Engine ID/VIN	Engine Displacement Liters (cc)	Piston Clearance	Ring Gap			Ring Side Clearance		
				Top Compression	Bottom Compression	Oil Control	Top Compression	Bottom Compression	Oil Control
1990	C	3.8 (3786)	0.0004–0.0022 ①	0.010–0.025	0.010–0.025	0.015–0.055	0.0013–0.0031	0.0013–0.0031	0.0011–0.0081
	8	4.5 (4474)	0.0010–0.0018	0.015–0.024	0.015–0.024	0.010–0.050	0.0016–0.0037	0.0016–0.0037	②
	3	4.5 (4474)	0.0010–0.0018	0.015–0.024	0.015–0.024	0.010–0.050	0.0016–0.0037	0.0016–0.0037	②
1991	C	3.8 (3786)	0.0004–0.0022 ①	0.010–0.025	0.010–0.025	0.015–0.055	0.0013–0.0031	0.0013–0.0031	0.0011–0.0081
	8	4.5 (4474)	0.0010–0.0018	0.015–0.024	0.015–0.024	0.010–0.050	0.0016–0.0037	0.0016–0.0037	②
	B	4.9 (4917)	0.0004–0.0020	0.012–0.022	0.012–0.022	0.004–0.020	0.0016–0.0037	0.0016–0.0037	②
1992	L	3.8 (3786)	0.0004–0.0022 ①	0.010–0.025	0.010–0.025	0.015–0.055	0.0013–0.0031	0.0013–0.0031	0.0011–0.0081
	8	4.5 (4474)	0.0010–0.0018	0.015–0.024	0.015–0.024	0.010–0.050	0.0016–0.0037	0.0016–0.0037	②
	9	4.6 (4573)	0.0004–0.0020	0.010–0.016	0.014–0.020	0.010–0.030	0.0020–0.0040	0.0020–0.0040	②
	B	4.9 (4917)	0.0004–0.0020	0.012–0.022	0.012–0.022	0.004–0.020	0.0016–0.0037	0.0016–0.0037	②

PISTON AND RING SPECIFICATIONS
All measurements are given in inches.

Year	Engine ID/VIN	Engine Displacement Liters (cc)	Piston Clearance	Ring Gap Top Compression	Ring Gap Bottom Compression	Ring Gap Oil Control	Ring Side Clearance Top Compression	Ring Side Clearance Bottom Compression	Ring Side Clearance Oil Control
1993–94	L	3.8 (3786)	0.0004–0.0022	0.010–0.025	0.010–0.025	0.015–0.055	0.0013–0.0031	0.0013–0.0031	0.0011–0.0081
	9	4.6 (4573)	0.0004–0.0020	0.010–0.016	0.014–0.020	0.010–0.030	0.0020–0.0040	0.0020–0.0040	②
	B	4.9 (4917)	0.0004–0.0020	0.012–0.022	0.012–0.022	0.004–0.020	0.0016–0.0037	0.0016–0.0037	②
	Y	4.6 (4573)	0.0004–0.0020	0.010–0.016	0.014–0.020	0.010–0.030	0.0020–0.0040	0.0020–0.0040	②

① 1.73 in. from top of piston
② None, side sealing

TORQUE SPECIFICATIONS
All readings in ft. lbs.

Year	Engine ID/VIN	Engine Displacement Liters (cc)	Cylinder Head Bolts	Main Bearing Bolts	Rod Bearing Bolts	Crankshaft Damper Bolts	Flywheel Bolts	Manifold Intake	Manifold Exhaust	Spark Plugs	Lug Nut
1990	C	3.8 (3786)	③	90	43	219⑤	61	88⑥	41	20	100
	8	4.5 (4474)	②	85	24④	18	70	⑧	18	11	100
	3	4.5 (4474)	②	85	24④	18	70	⑧	18	11	100
1991	C	3.8 (3786)	③	90	43	219⑤	61	88⑥	41	20	100
	8	4.5 (4474)	②	85	24④	18	70	⑧	18	11	100
	B	4.9 (4917)	②	85	25	70⑤	70	⑧	16	23	100
1992	L	3.8 (3786)	③	⑨	①	⑦	61	88⑥	38	12	100
	8	4.5 (4474)	②	85	24④	18	70	⑧	18	11	100
	9	4.6 (4573)	⑫	⑬	⑭	⑮	⑩	⑪	20	11	100
	B	4.9 (4917)	②	85	25	70⑤	70	⑧	16	23	100
1993–94	L	3.8 (3786)	③	⑨	①	⑦	61	88⑥	38	12	100
	9	4.6 (4573)	⑫	⑬	⑭	⑮	⑩	⑪	20	11	100
	B	4.9 (4917)	②	85	25	70⑤	70	⑧	16	23	100
	Y	4.6 (4573)	⑫	⑬	⑭	⑮	⑩	⑪	20	11	100

NA—Not available
① 20 ± 3 ft. lbs. + 50° ± 3°
② Torque in sequence to 38 ft. lbs.; then torque to 68 ft. lbs.; then torque No. 1, 3 and 4 bolts to 90 ft. lbs.
③ Torque in sequence to 35 ft. lbs.; then turn each bolt 10 degrees; then rotate each bolt an add'l. 30 degrees.
④ Lubricate with engine oil
⑤ Crankshaft balancer assembly
⑥ Inch lbs.
⑦ 105 ± 7 ft. lbs. + 56° ± 4°
⑧ Torque bolts 1, 2, 3 and 4 in sequence to 8 ft. lbs.; then tighten bolts 5 through 16 in sequence to 8 ft. lbs.; then retighten all bolts in sequence to 12 ft. lbs.; then retorque above step until torque level is maintained.

⑨ 26 ± 3 ft. lbs. + 50° ± 3°
⑩ 11 ft. lbs. + 50°
⑪ 4 ft. lbs. + 120°
⑫ Tighten in 3 steps:
 1. Tighten the ten 11 mm bolts in sequence to 22 ft. lbs.
 2. Turn each 11 mm bolt, in sequence an additional 90° turn
 3. Tighten the three 6 mm bolts to 10 ft. lbs.
⑬ Tighten in 3 steps:
 1. Main bearing bolts in sequence to 15 ft. lbs. + 65° turn
 2. Oil manifold bolts to 7 ft. lbs.
 3. Upper to lower crankcase bolts to 25 ft. lbs.
⑭ 20 ft. lbs. + 90° turn
⑮ 105 ft. lbs. + 120° turn

TORQUE SPECIFICATIONS

Component	English	Metric
Camshaft sprocket bolt		
Except 3.8L and 4.6L engines:	36 ft. lbs.	48 Nm
3.8L (VIN C) engine:	26 ft. lbs.	35 Nm
3.8L (VIN L) engine		
Step 1:	74 ft. lbs.	100 Nm.
Step 2:	+ 105 degrees turn	+ 105 degrees turn
4.6L engine		
Step 1:	15 ft. lbs.	20 Nm.
Step 2:	+ 45 degrees turn	+ 45 degrees turn
Connecting rod bearing cap bolts		
3.8L (VIN C) engine:	43 ft. lbs.	58 Nm.
3.8L (VIN L) engine		
Step 1:	20 ft. lbs.	27 Nm.
Step 2:	+ 50 degrees turn	+ 50 degrees turn
4.5L engine:	24 ft. lbs.	32 Nm.
4.6L engine		
Step 1:	20 ft. lbs.	27 Nm.
Step 2:	+ 90 degrees turn	+ 90 degrees turn
4.9L engine:	25 ft. lbs.	33 Nm.
Note: Lubricate bolts with engine oil.		
Crankshaft damper bolt		
3.8L (VIN C) engine:	220 ft. lbs.	297 Nm.
3.8L (VIN L) engine		
Step 1:	105 ft. lbs.	140 Nm.
Step 2:	+ 56 degrees turn	+ 56 degrees turn
4.5L engine:	65 ft. lbs.	90 Nm.
4.9L engine:	70 ft. lbs.	95 Nm.
Cylinder head bolt		
Except 3.8L and 4.6L engines		
Step 1:	38 ft. lbs.	50 Nm.
Step 2:	68 ft. lbs.	90 Nm.
Step 3 (positions 1, 3, 4):	90 ft. lbs.	120 Nm.
3.8L engine		
Step 1:	35 ft. lbs.	47 Nm.
Step 2:	+ 130 degrees turn	+ 130 degrees turn
Step 3:	+ 30 degrees turn	+ 30 degrees turn
EGR valve-to-intake plenum		
3.8L (VIN C) engine:	20 ft. lbs.	27 Nm.
4.5L and 4.9L engines:	18 ft. lbs.	24 Nm
4.6L engine:	20 ft. lbs.	27 Nm.
Engine-to-transmission:	55 ft. lbs.	75 Nm
Exhaust manifold		
Except 3.8L engine:	18 ft. lbs.	25 Nm
3.8L (VIN C) engine:	41 ft. lbs.	55 Nm
3.8L (VIN L) engine:	38 ft. lbs.	52 Nm
Exhaust pipe-to-exhaust manifold nuts		
Except 3.8L and 4.6L engines:	15 ft. lbs.	20 Nm
3.8L engine:	21 ft. lbs.	29 Nm
4.6L engine:	25 ft. lbs.	30 Nm
Flywheel/flexplate-to-crankshaft bolts		
3.8L (VIN C) engine:	61 ft. lbs.	82 Nm
3.8L (VIN L) engine		
Step 1:	11 ft. lbs.	15 Nm.
Step 2:	+ 50 degrees turn	+ 50 degrees turn
4.5L and 4.9L engines:	70 ft. lbs.	95 Nm
Flywheel-to-converter bolts		
Except 4.6L engine:	46 ft. lbs.	62 Nm
4.6L engine:	35 ft. lbs.	50 Nm

TORQUE SPECIFICATIONS

Component	English	Metric
Intake manifold		
3.8L (VIN C) engine:	89 inch lbs.	10 Nm
3.8L (VIN L) engine		
Lower manifold:	89 inch lbs.	10 Nm
Upper manifold:	22 ft. lbs.	30 Nm
4.5L (VIN 3) and 4.9L engines		
Step 1 (positions 1, 2, 3, 4):	8 ft. lbs.	12 Nm
Step 2 (positions 5–16):	8 ft. lbs.	12 Nm
Step 3 (all bolts):	12 ft. lbs.	16 Nm
Step 4 (all bolts):	12 ft. lbs.	16 Nm
4.5L (VIN 5)		
Step 1 (positions 1, 2, 3, 4):	15 ft. lbs.	20 Nm
Step 2 (positions 5–16):	22 ft. lbs.	30 Nm
Step 3 (all bolts):	22 ft. lbs.	30 Nm
Step 4 (all bolts):	22 ft. lbs.	30 Nm
4.5L (VIN 8)		
Lower manifold		
Step 1 (positions 1, 2, 3, 4):	8 ft. lbs.	12 Nm
Step 2 (positions 5–16):	8 ft. lbs.	12 Nm
Step 3 (all bolts):	12 ft. lbs.	16 Nm
Step 4 (all bolts):	12 ft. lbs.	16 Nm
Upper manifold:	15 ft. lbs.	20 Nm
4.6L engine		
Step 1:	6 ft. lbs.	4 ft. lbs.
Step 2:	+ 105 degrees turn	+ 105 degrees turn
Main bearing cap bolts		
3.8L (VIN C) engine:	90 ft. lbs.	122 Nm
3.8L (VIN L) engine		
Step 1:	26 ft. lbs.	35 ft. lbs.
Step 2:	+ 50 degrees turn	+ 50 degrees turn
4.5L and 4.9L engines:	85 ft. lbs.	115 Nm
Oil pan		
3.8L engine:	124 inch lbs.	14 Nm
4.5L engine:	11 ft. lbs.	15 Nm
4.6L engine:	7 ft. lbs.	10 Nm
4.9L engine:	14 ft. lbs.	18 Nm
Oil pan drain plug		
Except 3.8L and 4.6L engines:	22 ft. lbs.	30 Nm
3.8L (VIN C) engine:	18 ft. lbs.	25 Nm
3.8L (VIN L) engine:	30 ft. lbs.	40 Nm
4.6L engine:	15 ft. lbs.	20 Nm
Oil pump attaching bolts		
4.5L and 4.9L engines:	22 ft. lbs.	30 Nm
4.6L engine:	25 ft. lbs.	30 Nm
Oil pump cover screws		
3.8L engine:	97 inch lbs.	11 Nm
Rocker arm pivot bolt		
Except 3.8L engine:	22 ft. lbs.	30 Nm
3.8L engine:	28 ft. lbs.	38 Nm
Rocker (valve) cover:	89 inch lbs.	10 Nm
Spark plug		
3.8L (VIN C) engine:	20 ft. lbs.	27 Nm
3.8L (VIN L) engine:	12 ft. lbs.	16 Nm
4.5L and 4.6L engines:	11 ft. lbs.	15 Nm
4.9L engine:	23 ft. lbs.	31 Nm
Starter-to-block bolts		
3.8L and 4.9L engines:	35 ft. lbs.	47 Nm
4.5L engine:	34 ft. lbs.	46 Nm
4.6L engine:	25 ft. lbs.	30 Nm

TORQUE SPECIFICATIONS

Component	English	Metric
Thermostat housing		
3.8L engine:	20 ft. lbs.	27 Nm
4.5L engine:	18 ft. lbs.	25 Nm
4.6L engine:	7 ft. lbs.	10 Nm
4.9L engine:	20 ft. lbs.	27 Nm
TBI fuel meter cover screws:	27 inch lbs.	3 Nm
TBI-to-fuel meter body screws:	35 inch lbs.	4 Nm
TBI fuel feed/return line:	17 ft. lbs.	23 Nm
TBI mounting bolts/nuts		
4.5L (VIN 3) and 4.9L engines:	14 ft. lbs.	19 Nm
4.5L (VIN 5) engine:	11 ft. lbs.	15 Nm
Timing cover		
3.8L engine:	22 ft. lbs.	30 Nm
4.5L engine:	15 ft. lbs.	20 Nm
4.6L engine:	7 ft. lbs.	10 Nm
4.9L engine		
Upper (4):	30 ft. lbs.	40 Nm
Lower (4):	17 ft. lbs.	22 Nm
Water pump		
3.8L (VIN C) engine:	89 inch lbs.	10 Nm
3.8L (VIN L) engine		
Step 1:	11 ft. lbs.	15 ft. lbs.
Step 2:	+ 80 degrees turn	+ 80 degrees turn
4.5L and 4.9L engines:	60 inch lbs.	7 Nm
4.6L engine:	20 ft. lbs.	25 Nm
Water pump pulley		
3.8L (VIN C) engine:	142 inch lbs.	16 Nm
3.8L (VIN L) engine:	114 inch lbs.	13 Nm
4.5L engine:	25 ft. lbs.	35 Nm
4.9L engine:	22 inch lbs.	30 Nm

BRAKE SPECIFICATIONS

All measurements in inches unless noted.

Year	Model	Master Cylinder Bore	Brake Disc Original Thickness	Brake Disc Minimum Thickness	Brake Disc Maximum Runout	Brake Drum Diameter Original Inside Diameter	Brake Drum Diameter Max. Wear Limit	Brake Drum Diameter Maximum Machine Diameter	Minimum Lining Thickness Front	Minimum Lining Thickness Rear
1990	Allante	①	1.035④	0.971②	0.004③	NA	NA	NA	0.030	0.030
	Eldorado	①	1.035④	0.971②	0.004③	NA	NA	NA	0.030	0.030
	Reatta	①	1.035④	0.971②	0.004③	NA	NA	NA	0.030	0.030
	Riviera	①	1.035④	0.971②	0.004③	NA	NA	NA	0.030	0.030
	Seville	①	1.035④	0.971②	0.004③	NA	NA	NA	0.030	0.030
	Toronado	①	1.035④	0.971②	0.004③	NA	NA	NA	0.030	0.030
	Trofeo	①	1.035④	0.971②	0.004③	NA	NA	NA	0.030	0.030
1991	Allante	1.000	1.035④	0.971②	0.004③	NA	NA	NA	0.030	0.030
	Eldorado	1.000	1.035④	0.971②	0.004③	NA	NA	NA	0.030	0.030
	Reatta	1.000	1.035④	0.971②	0.004③	NA	NA	NA	0.030	0.030
	Riviera	1.000	1.035④	0.971②	0.004③	NA	NA	NA	0.030	0.030
	Seville	1.000	1.035④	0.971②	0.004③	NA	NA	NA	0.030	0.030
	Toronado	1.000	1.035④	0.971②	0.004③	NA	NA	NA	0.030	0.030
	Trofeo	1.000	1.035④	0.971②	0.004③	NA	NA	NA	0.030	0.030

BRAKE SPECIFICATIONS

All measurements in inches unless noted.

Year	Model	Master Cylinder Bore	Brake Disc			Brake Drum Diameter			Minimum Lining Thickness	
			Original Thickness	Minimum Thickness	Maximum Runout	Original Inside Diameter	Max. Wear Limit	Maximum Machine Diameter	Front	Rear
1992	Allante	1.000	1.260⑤⑦	1.250⑥⑧	0.002⑨	NA	NA	NA	0.030	0.030
	Eldorado	1.000	1.260⑤	1.250⑥	0.002	NA	NA	NA	0.030	0.030
	Riviera	1.000	1.260⑤	1.250⑥	0.002	NA	NA	NA	0.030	0.030
	Seville	1.000	1.260⑤	1.250⑥	0.002	NA	NA	NA	0.030	0.030
	Toronado	1.000	1.260⑤	1.250⑥	0.002	NA	NA	NA	0.030	0.030
	Trofeo	1.000	1.260⑤	1.250⑥	0.002	NA	NA	NA	0.030	0.030
1993–94	Allante	1.000	1.260⑤⑦	1.250⑥⑧	0.002⑨	NA	NA	NA	0.030	0.030
	Eldorado	1.000	1.260⑤	1.250⑥	0.002	NA	NA	NA	0.030	0.030
	Riviera	1.000	1.260⑤	1.250⑥	0.002	NA	NA	NA	0.030	0.030
	Seville	1.000	1.260⑤	1.250⑥	0.002	NA	NA	NA	0.030	0.030

NA—Not available
① Standard—1.126 in.
　 Quick Take-up—1.574 in.
　 Anti-Lock—1.000 in.
② Rear—0.444 in.
③ Rear—0.003 in.
④ Rear—0.494 in.
⑤ Rear—0.433 in.
⑥ Rear—0.423 in.
⑦ Original Thickness—1.035—Front
　　　　　　　　　0.494—Rear
⑧ Minimum Thickness—0.971—Front
　　　　　　　　　0.444—Rear
⑨ Maximum Runout—0.004—Front
　　　　　　　　　0.003—Rear

WHEEL ALIGNMENT

Year	Model		Caster		Camber		Toe-in (in.)	Steering Axis Inclination (deg.)
			Range (deg.)	Preferred Setting (deg.)	Range (deg.)	Preferred Setting (deg.)		
1990	Allante	Front	1¹³/₁₆P–2¹³/₁₆P	2⁵/₁₆P	¹³/₁₆N–¹³/₁₆P	0	³/₃₂	13⁵/₁₆
		Rear	—	—	½N–¹/₈P	³/₁₆N	³/₃₂	—
	Eldorado	Front	1⁵/₁₆P–3⁵/₁₆P	2⁵/₁₆P	¹³/₁₆N–¹³/₁₆P	0	0	13⁵/₁₆
		Rear	—	—	¹³/₃₂N–³/₁₆P	³/₃₂N	³/₃₂	—
	Reatta	Front	1¹³/₁₆P–3¹³/₁₆P	2¹³/₁₆P	¹³/₁₆N–¹³/₁₆P	0	0	NA
		Rear	—	—	0–1⁵/₁₆P	⁵/₈P	³/₃₂	—
	Riviera	Front	1⁵/₁₆P–3³/₁₆P	2⁵/₁₆P	¹³/₁₆N–¹³/₁₆P	0	0	NA
		Rear	—	—	0–1⁵/₁₆P	⁵/₈P	³/₃₂	—
	Seville	Front	1⁵/₁₆P–3⁵/₁₆P	2⁵/₁₆P	¹³/₁₆N–¹³/₁₆P	0	0	13⁵/₁₆
		Rear	—	—	¹³/₃₂N–³/₁₆P	³/₃₂N	³/₃₂	—
	Toronado	Front	1⁵/₁₆P–3⁵/₁₆P	2⁵/₁₆P	¹³/₁₆N–¹³/₁₆P	0	0	NA
		Rear	—	—	¹³/₃₂N–⁷/₃₂P	³/₃₂N	⁷/₆₄	—
	Trofeo	Front	1⁵/₁₆P–3⁵/₁₆P	2⁵/₁₆P	¹³/₁₆N–¹³/₁₆P	0	0	NA
		Rear	—	—	¹³/₃₂N–⁷/₃₂P	³/₃₂N	⁷/₆₄	—

WHEEL ALIGNMENT

Year	Model		Caster Range (deg.)	Caster Preferred Setting (deg.)	Camber Range (deg.)	Camber Preferred Setting (deg.)	Toe-in (in.)	Steering Axis Inclination (deg.)
1991	Allante	Front	$1^{13}/_{16}$P–$2^{13}/_{16}$P	$2^5/_{16}$P	$^{13}/_{16}$N–$^{13}/_{16}$P	0	0	$13^5/_{16}$
		Rear	—	—	$^{13}/_{32}$N–$^3/_{16}$P	$^3/_{32}$N	$^3/_{32}$	—
	Eldorado	Front	$1^5/_{16}$P–$3^5/_{16}$P	$2^5/_{16}$P	$^{13}/_{16}$N–$^{13}/_{16}$P	0	0	$13^5/_{16}$
		Rear	—	—	$^{13}/_{32}$N–$^3/_{16}$P	$^3/_{32}$N	$^3/_{32}$	—
	Reatta	Front	$1^{13}/_{16}$P–$3^{13}/_{16}$P	$2^{13}/_{16}$P	$^{13}/_{16}$N–$^{13}/_{16}$P	0	$^3/_{32}$	$13^5/_{16}$
		Rear	—	—	$^5/_8$N–$^3/_8$P	$^1/_8$N	$^3/_{32}$	—
	Riviera	Front	$1^5/_{16}$P–$3^5/_{16}$P	$2^5/_{16}$P	$^{13}/_{16}$N–$^{13}/_{16}$P	0	$^3/_{32}$	$13^5/_{16}$
		Rear	—	—	$^1/_2$N–$^1/_2$P	0	$^3/_{32}$	—
	Seville	Front	$1^5/_{16}$P–$3^5/_{16}$P	$2^5/_{16}$P	$^{13}/_{16}$N–$^{13}/_{16}$P	0	0	$13^5/_{16}$
		Rear	—	—	$^{13}/_{32}$N–$^3/_{16}$P	$^3/_{32}$N	$^3/_{32}$	—
	Toronado	Front	$1^5/_{16}$P–$3^5/_{16}$P	$2^5/_{16}$P	$^{13}/_{16}$N–$^{13}/_{16}$P	0	$^3/_{32}$	$13^{15}/_{16}$
		Rear	—	—	$^{11}/_{16}$N–$^5/_{16}$P	$^3/_{16}$N	$^3/_{32}$	—
	Trofeo	Front	$1^5/_{16}$P–$3^5/_{16}$P	$2^5/_{16}$P	$^{13}/_{16}$N–$^{13}/_{16}$P	0	$^3/_{32}$	$13^{15}/_{16}$
		Rear	—	—	$^{11}/_{16}$N–$^5/_{16}$P	$^3/_{16}$N	$^3/_{32}$	—
1992	Allante	Front	$1^{13}/_{16}$P–$2^{13}/_{16}$P	$2^5/_{16}$P	$^{13}/_{16}$N–$^{13}/_{16}$P	0	0	$13^5/_{16}$
		Rear	—	—	$^{13}/_{32}$N–$^3/_{16}$P	$^3/_{32}$N	$^3/_{32}$	—
	Eldorado	Front	$1^3/_{16}$P–$3^3/_{16}$P	$2^3/_{16}$P	$^{13}/_{16}$N–$^{13}/_{16}$P	0	$^3/_{32}$	$13^5/_{16}$
		Rear	—	—	$^{13}/_{16}$N–$^{13}/_{16}$P	0	$^3/_{32}$	—
	Riviera	Front	$1^5/_{16}$P–$3^5/_{16}$P	$2^5/_{16}$P	$^{13}/_{16}$N–$^{13}/_{16}$P	0	$^3/_{32}$	$13^5/_{16}$
		Rear	—	—	$^1/_2$N–$^1/_2$P	$^3/_{16}$N	$^3/_{32}$	—
	Seville	Front	$1^3/_{16}$P–$3^3/_{16}$P	$2^3/_{16}$P	$^{13}/_{16}$N–$^{13}/_{16}$P	0	$^3/_{32}$	$13^5/_{16}$
		Rear	—	—	$^{13}/_{16}$N–$^{13}/_{16}$P	0	$^3/_{32}$	—
	Toronado	Front	$1^5/_{16}$P–$3^5/_{16}$P	$2^5/_{16}$P	$^{13}/_{16}$N–$^{13}/_{16}$P	0	$^3/_{32}$	$13^{15}/_{16}$
		Rear	—	—	$^{11}/_{16}$N–$^5/_{16}$P	$^3/_{16}$N	$^3/_{32}$	—
	Trofeo	Front	$1^5/_{16}$P–$3^5/_{16}$P	$2^5/_{16}$P	$^{13}/_{16}$N–$^{13}/_{16}$P	0	$^3/_{32}$	$13^{15}/_{16}$
		Rear	—	—	$^{11}/_{16}$N–$^5/_{16}$P	$^3/_{16}$N	$^3/_{32}$	—
1993–94	Allante	Front	$1^{13}/_{16}$P–$2^{13}/_{16}$P	$2^5/_{16}$P	$^{13}/_{16}$N–$^{13}/_{16}$P	0	0	$13^5/_{16}$
		Rear	—	—	$^{13}/_{32}$N–$^3/_{16}$P	$^3/_{32}$N	$^3/_{32}$	—
	Eldorado	Front	$1^3/_{16}$P–$3^3/_{16}$P	$2^3/_{16}$P	$^{13}/_{16}$N–$^{13}/_{16}$P	0	$^3/_{32}$	$13^5/_{16}$
		Rear	—	—	$^{13}/_{16}$N–$^{13}/_{16}$P	0	$^3/_{32}$	—
	Riviera	Front	$1^5/_{16}$P–$3^5/_{16}$P	$2^5/_{16}$P	$^{13}/_{16}$N–$^{13}/_{16}$P	0	$^3/_{32}$	$13^5/_{16}$
		Rear	—	—	$^1/_2$N–$^1/_2$P	0	$^3/_{32}$	—
	Seville	Front	$1^3/_{16}$P–$3^3/_{16}$P	$2^3/_{16}$P	$^{13}/_{16}$N–$^{13}/_{16}$P	0	$^3/_{32}$	$13^5/_{16}$
		Rear	—	—	$^{13}/_{16}$N–$^{13}/_{16}$P	0	$^3/_{32}$	—

NA—Not available
N—Negative
P—Positive

AIR CONDITIONING BELT TENSION

Year	Engine VIN	Engine Displacement Liters (cc)	Belt Type	Specifications New	Used
1990	C	3.8 (3788)	Serpentine	①	①
	3	4.5 (4563)	Serpentine	①	①
	8	4.5 (4563)	Serpentine	①	①
1991	L	3.8 (3788)	Serpentine	①	①
	8	4.5 (4563)	Serpentine	①	①
	B	4.9 (4920)	Serpentine	①	①
1992	L	3.8 (3788)	Serpentine	50–70	②
	B	4.9 (4920)	Serpentine	①	①
	8	4.5 (4563)	Serpentine	①	①
1993–94	L	3.8 (3788)	Serpentine	①	②
	9	4.6 (4593)	Serpentine	①	①
	Y	4.6 (4593)	Serpentine	①	①
	B	4.9 (4920)	Serpentine	①	①

① Automatic dynamic tensioner

REFRIGERANT CAPACITIES

Year	Model	Refrigerant (oz.)	Oil (fl. oz.)	Compressor Type
1990	Riviera, Reatta, Eldorado, Toronado, Trofeo, Seville, Allante	38.0	8.0	HR-6
1991	Riviera, Reatta, Eldorado, Toronado, Trofeo, Seville, Allante	38.0	8.0	HR-6
1992	Riviera, Reatta, Eldorado, Toronado, Trofeo, Seville, Allante	38.0	8.0	HR-6-HE
1993	Riviera, Eldorado, Allante, Seville	38.0	8.0	HR-6-HE

NOTE: At the time of publication, refrigerant capacity information relating to R-134a was not available from the manufacturer.

MAINTENANCE INTERVALS—TYPE A: NORMAL SERVICE
Allante • Eldorado • Reatta • Riviera • Seville • Toronado • Trofeo

TO BE SERVICED	TYPE OF SERVICE	VEHICLE MILEAGE INTERVAL (X1000)							
		7.5	15	22.5	30	37.5	45	52.5	60
Oxygen Sensor	I				✔				✔
Ignition Timing	I①				✔				✔
Vacuum Lines and Hoses	I				✔				✔
Ignition Wires	I				✔				✔
Spark Plugs	R				✔				✔
Engine Oil	R②	✔	✔	✔	✔	✔	✔	✔	✔
Engine Air Cleaner Element	R				✔				✔
Crankcase Emission Filter	R				✔				✔
PCV Valve	R				✔				✔
Fuel Filter	R				✔				✔
Charcoal Canister	R				✔				✔
Fuel/Vapor Return Lines	I				✔				✔
Fuel Tank Cap and Restrictor	I				✔				✔
Coolant System	R				✔				✔
Exhaust Pipe and Muffler	I				✔				✔
Engine Oil Filter	R②	✔		✔		✔		✔	
Catalytic Converter and Shield	I				✔				✔
EGR System	I				✔				✔
Chassis Lubrication	L	✔	✔	✔	✔	✔	✔	✔	✔
Battery Connections	I		✔		✔		✔		✔
Automatic Transaxle Fluid	R③								
CV-Joints and Boots	I	✔	✔	✔	✔	✔	✔	✔	✔
Idle Speed System	I				✔				✔
Throttle Body Mounting Torque	I	✔							
Drive Belts	I								✔
Oil Maintenance Indicator	I④	✔	✔	✔	✔	✔	✔	✔	✔
Brake Linings	I		✔		✔		✔		✔
Parking Brake	I		✔		✔		✔		✔
Coolant Hoses and Clamps	I		✔		✔		✔		✔
Tire Rotation	I⑤								
Seat Belt Operation	I				✔				✔

FOR COMPLETE WARRANTY COVERAGE CONSULT INDIVIDUAL VEHICLE MANUFACTURER'S WARRANTY MAINTENANCE GUIDE.

I—Inspect
L—Lubricate
R—Replace
① Check and adjust timing as per engine emissions label on applicable vehicles
② Replace engine oil filter at first and every other oil change. (Note on Buick and Oldsmobile, change oil every 3,000 miles and oil filter every other oil change.)
③ Replace automatic transaxle fluid at 100,000 miles
④ Reset oil change soon light at every service—refer to the owners manual for proper procedure.
⑤ Rotate tires at 6,000 miles and then every 15,000 miles as necessary

MAINTENANCE INTERVALS—TYPE B: SEVERE SERVICE
Allante • Eldorado • Reatta • Riviera • Seville • Toronado • Trofeo

TO BE SERVICED	TYPE OF SERVICE	VEHICLE MILEAGE INTERVAL (X1000)									
		3	6	9	12	15	18	21	24	27	30
Oxygen Sensor	I										✔
Ignition Timing	I①										✔
Vacuum Lines and Hoses	I					✔					✔
Ignition Wires	I										✔
Spark Plugs	R										✔
Engine Oil	R	✔	✔	✔	✔	✔	✔	✔	✔	✔	✔
Engine Air Cleaner Element	R					✔					✔
PCV Valve	R										✔
Fuel Filter	R					✔					✔
Charcoal Canister	R										✔
Fuel/Vapor Return Lines	I										✔
Fuel Tank Cap and Restrictor	I										✔
Coolant System	R										✔
Exhaust Pipe and Muffler	I										✔
Tire Rotation	I②		✔								
Catalytic Converter and Shield	I										✔
EGR System	I										✔
Chassis Lubrication	L		✔		✔		✔		✔		✔
Battery Connections	I					✔					✔
Automatic Transaxle Fluid	R					✔					✔
CV-Joints and Boots	I	✔	✔	✔	✔	✔	✔	✔	✔	✔	✔
Idle Speed System	I										✔
Throttle Body Mounting Torque	I		✔								
Drive Belts	I										✔
Oil Maintenance Indicator	I③										
Brake Linings	I					✔					✔
Parking Brake	I					✔					✔
Coolant Hoses and Clamps	I		✔		✔		✔		✔		✔
Seat Belt Operation	I										✔

FOR COMPLETE WARRANTY COVERAGE CONSULT INDIVIDUAL VEHICLE MANUFACTURER'S WARRANTY MAINTENANCE GUIDE.

I—Inspect
L—Lubricate
R—Replace
① Check and adjust timing as per engine emissions label on applicable vehicles
② Rotate tires at 6,000 miles and then every 15,000 as necessary
③ Reset oil change light at every service—refer to the owners manual for proper procedure

FIRING ORDERS

NOTE: To avoid confusion, always replace spark plug wires one at a time.

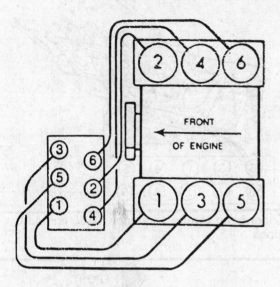

3.8L Engine VIN C
Engine Firing Order: 1–6–5–4–3–2
Distributorless Ignition System

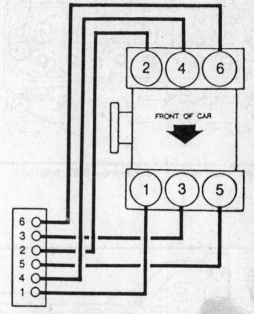

3.8L Engine VIN L
Engine Firing Order: 1–6–5–4–3–2
Distributorless Ignition System

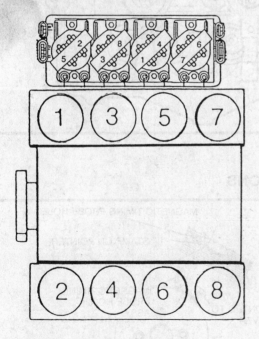

4.6L (VIN 9 and Y) Engine
Engine Firing Order: 1-2-7-3-4-5-6-8
Distributorless Ignition System

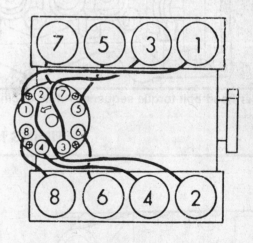

4.5L and 4.9L Engines
Engine Firing Order: 1-8-4-3-6-5-7-2
Distributor Rotation: Counterclockwise

CYLINDER HEAD TORQUE SEQUENCES

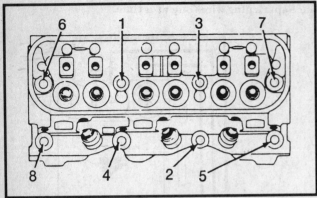

Cylinder head torque sequence—3.8L engine

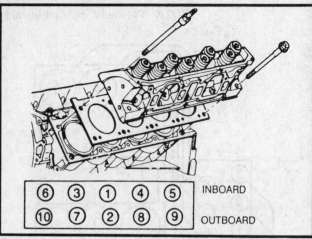

Cylinder head torque sequence—4.5L and 4.9L engines

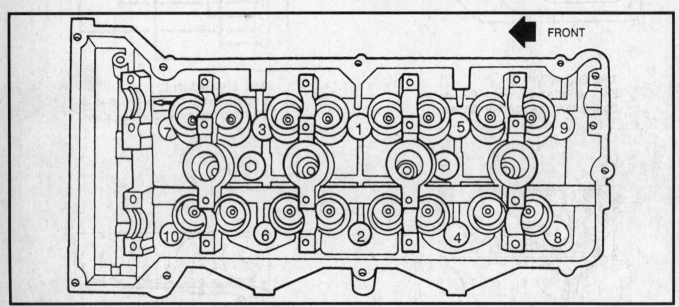

Cylinder head bolt torque sequence—4.6L engine

TIMING MARK LOCATIONS

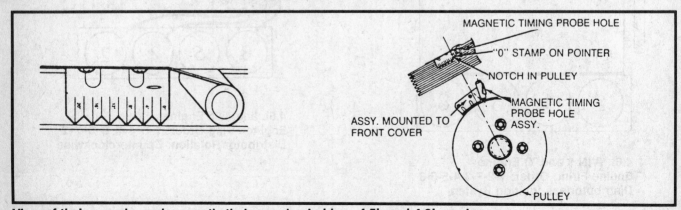

View of timing marks and magnetic timing probe holder—4.5L and 4.9L engines

TIMING CHAIN ALIGNMENT MARKS

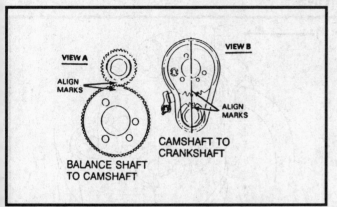

Timing chain alignment marks—3.8L engine

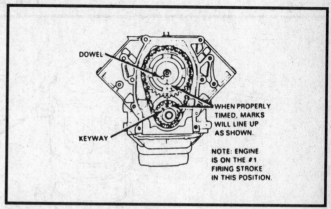

Timing chain alignment marks—4.5L and 4.9L engines

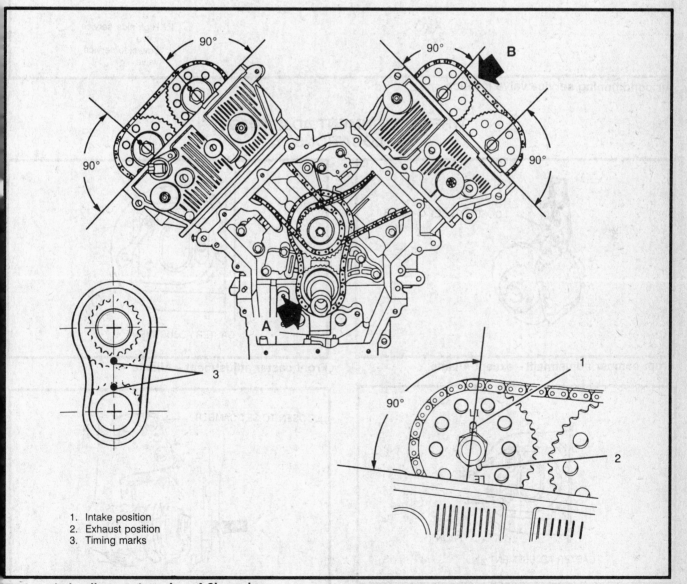

1. Intake position
2. Exhaust position
3. Timing marks

Timing chain alignment marks—4.6L engine

AIR CONDITIONING SERVICE VALVE LOCATIONS

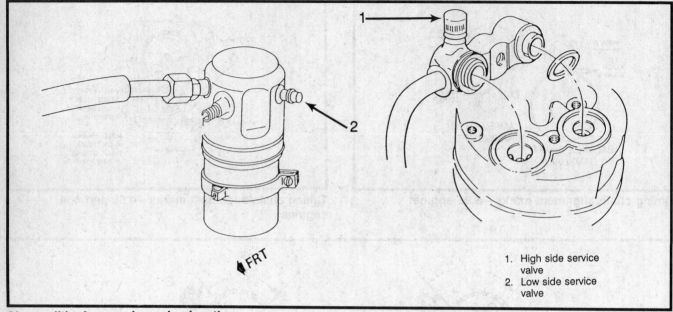

1. High side service valve
2. Low side service valve

Air conditioning service valve location

WHEEL ALIGNMENT ADJUSTMENT LOCATIONS

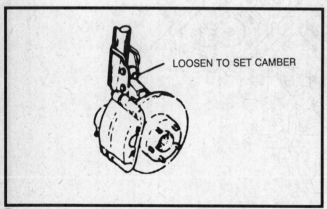

LOOSEN TO SET CAMBER

Front camber adjustment – except Allante

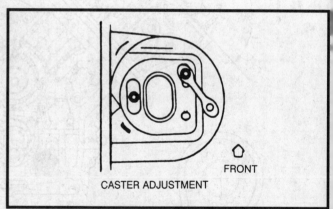

CASTER ADJUSTMENT

FRONT

Front caster adjustment – Allante

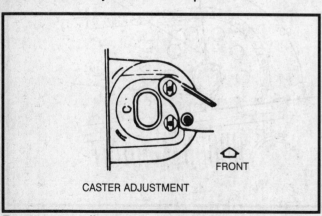

FRONT

CASTER ADJUSTMENT

Front caster adjustment – except Allante

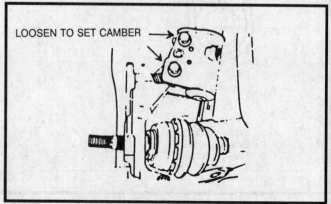

LOOSEN TO SET CAMBER

Front camber adjustment – Allante

WHEEL ALIGNMENT ADJUSTMENT LOCATIONS

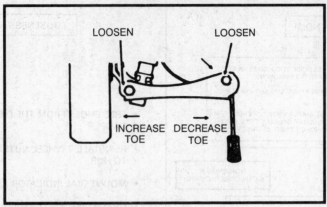

Rear toe adjustment

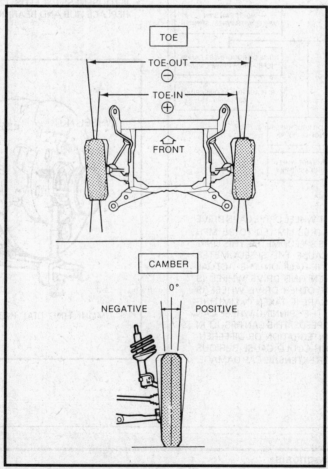

Front wheel alignment dimensions

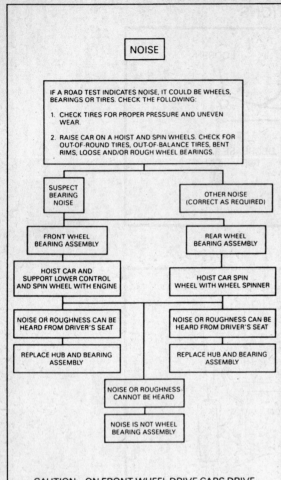

NOISE

IF A ROAD TEST INDICATES NOISE, IT COULD BE WHEELS, BEARINGS OR TIRES. CHECK THE FOLLOWING:

1. CHECK TIRES FOR PROPER PRESSURE AND UNEVEN WEAR.

2. RAISE CAR ON A HOIST AND SPIN WHEELS. CHECK FOR OUT-OF-ROUND TIRES, OUT-OF-BALANCE TIRES, BENT RIMS, LOOSE AND/OR ROUGH WHEEL BEARINGS.

SUSPECT BEARING NOISE

OTHER NOISE (CORRECT AS REQUIRED)

FRONT WHEEL BEARING ASSEMBLY

REAR WHEEL BEARING ASSEMBLY

HOIST CAR AND SUPPORT LOWER CONTROL AND SPIN WHEEL WITH ENGINE

HOIST CAR SPIN WHEEL WITH WHEEL SPINNER

NOISE OR ROUGHNESS CAN BE HEARD FROM DRIVER'S SEAT

NOISE OR ROUGHNESS CAN BE HEARD FROM DRIVER'S SEAT

REPLACE HUB AND BEARING ASSEMBLY

REPLACE HUB AND BEARING ASSEMBLY

NOISE OR ROUGHNESS CANNOT BE HEARD

NOISE IS NOT WHEEL BEARING ASSEMBLY

CAUTION: ON FRONT WHEEL DRIVE CARS DRIVE WHEEL SPIN SHOULD BE LIMITED TO 35 MPH AS INDICATED ON THE SPEEDOMETER. THIS LIMIT IS NECESSARY BECAUSE THE SPEEDOMETER ONLY INDICATES ONE-HALF ON THE ACTUAL WHEEL SPEED WHEN ONE DRIVE WHEEL IS SPINNING AND THE OTHER DRIVE WHEEL IS STOPPED. UNLESS CARE IS TAKEN IN LIMITING DRIVE WHEEL SPIN, THE SPINNING WHEEL CAN REACH EXCESSIVE SPEEDS. THIS CAN RESULT IN POSSIBLE TIRE DISINTEGRATION OR DIFFERENTIAL FAILURE, WHICH COULD CAUSE SERIOUS PERSONAL INJURY OR EXTENSIVE CAR DAMAGE.

LOOSENESS

- FREE SHOES FROM THE DISC OR REMOVE CALIPER

- REINSTALL 2 WHEEL NUTS TO SECURE DISC TO HUB

- MOUNT DIAL INDICATOR AS SHOWN

- GRASP DISC AND USE A PUSH-PULL MOVEMENT

- IF LOOSENESS EXCEEDS .127 MM (.005"), REPLACE HUB AND BEARING ASSEMBLY

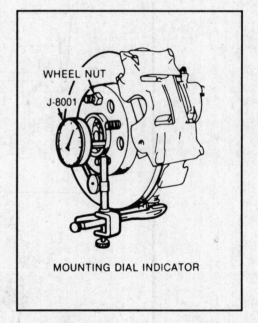

WHEEL NUT

J-8001

MOUNTING DIAL INDICATOR

Hub and bearing assembly diagnosis

SPECIFICATION CHARTS

VEHICLE IDENTIFICATION CHART

It is important for servicing and ordering parts to be certain of the vehicle and engine identification. The VIN (vehicle identification number) is a 17 digit number visible through the windshield on the driver's side of the dash and contains the vehicle and engine identification codes. The tenth digit indicates model year and the eighth digit indicates engine code. It can be interpreted as follows:

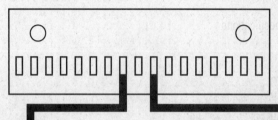

Engine Code							Model Year	
Code	Liters	Cu. In. (cc)	Cyl.	Fuel Sys.	Eng. Mfg.		Code	Year
K	2.0	121 (1998)	4	TBI	①		L	1990
M	2.0	121 (1998)	4	MFI Turbo	①		M	1991
H	2.0	121 (1998)	4	MFI	Pontiac		N	1992
G	2.2	134 (2190)	4	TBI	Chevrolet		P	1993
4	2.2	134 (2190)	4	MFI	Chevrolet		R	1994
T	3.1	192 (3136)	6	MFI	Chevrolet			

MFI—Multi-Port Fuel Injection
TBI—Throttle Body Injection
① Chevrolet-Pontiac-GM of Canada

ENGINE IDENTIFICATION

Year	Model	Engine Displacement Liters (cc)	Engine Series (ID/VIN)	Fuel System	No. of Cylinders	Engine Type
1990	Cavalier	2.2 (2190)	G	TBI	4	OHV
	Cavalier	3.1 (3136)	T	MFI	6	OHV
	Sunbird	2.0 (1998)	K	TBI	4	OHC
	Sunbird	2.0 (1998)	M	MFI Turbo	4	OHC
1991	Cavalier	2.2 (2190)	G	TBI	4	OHV
	Cavalier	3.1 (3136)	T	MFI	6	OHV
	Sunbird	2.0 (1998)	K	TBI	4	OHC
	Sunbird	3.1 (3136)	T	MFI	6	OHV
1992	Cavalier	2.2 (2190)	4	MFI	4	OHV
	Cavalier	3.1 (3136)	T	MFI	6	OHV
	Sunbird	2.0 (1998)	H	MFI	4	OHC
	Sunbird	3.1 (3136)	T	MFI	6	OHV
1993-94	Cavalier	2.2 (2190)	4	MFI	4	OHV
	Cavalier	3.1 (3136)	T	MFI	6	OHV
	Sunbird	2.0 (1998)	H	MFI	4	OHC
	Sunbird	3.1 (3136)	T	MFI	6	OHV

OHC—Overhead Cam
OHV—Overhead Valve
MFI—Multi-Port Fuel Injection
TBI—Throttle Body Injection

GENERAL ENGINE SPECIFICATIONS

Year	Engine ID/VIN	Engine Displacement Liters (cc)	Fuel System Type	Net Horsepower @ rpm	Net Torque @ rpm (ft. lbs.)	Bore × Stroke (in.)	Compression Ratio	Oil Pressure @ rpm
1990	K	2.0 (1998)	TBI	96 @ 4800	118 @ 3600	3.38 × 3.38	8.8:1	—
	M	2.0 (1998)	MFI-Turbo	165 @ 5500	175 @ 4000	3.38 × 3.38	8.0:1	—
	G	2.2 (2190)	TBI	95 @ 5200	120 @ 3200	3.50 × 3.46	9.0:1	56 @ 3000 ①
	T	3.1 (3136)	MFI	140 @ 4500	180 @ 3600	3.50 × 3.31	8.8:1	15 @ 1100 ②
1991	K	2.0 (1998)	TBI	96 @ 4800	118 @ 3600	3.38 × 3.38	8.8:1	—
	G	2.2 (2190)	TBI	95 @ 5200	120 @ 3200	3.50 × 3.46	9.0:1	56 @ 3000 ①
	T	3.1 (3136)	MFI	140 @ 4500	180 @ 3600	3.50 × 3.31	8.8:1	15 @ 1100 ②
1992	H	2.0 (1998)	MFI	111 @ 5200	125 @ 3600	3.38 × 3.38	9.2:1	—
	4	2.2 (2190)	MFI	110 @ 5200	130 @ 3200	3.50 × 3.46	9.0:1	56 @ 3000 ①
	T	3.1 (3136)	MFI	140 @ 4200	185 @ 3200	3.50 × 3.31	8.8:1	15 @ 1100 ②
1993-94	H	2.0 (1998)	MFI	110 @ 5200	124 @ 3600	3.39 × 3.39	9.2:1	—
	4	2.2 (2190)	MFI	110 @ 5200	130 @ 3200	3.50 × 3.46	9.0:1	56 @ 3000 ①
	T	3.1 (3136)	MFI	140 @ 4200	185 @ 3200	3.50 × 3.31	8.8:1	15 @ 1100 ②

MFI—Multi-Port Fuel Injection
TBI—Throttle Body Injection
① With oil at 150°F (60°C)
② At normal operating temperature

GASOLINE ENGINE TUNE-UP SPECIFICATIONS

Year	Engine ID/VIN	Engine Displacement Liters (cc)	Spark Plugs Gap (in.)	Ignition Timing (deg.) MT	Ignition Timing (deg.) AT	Fuel Pump (psi)	Idle Speed (rpm) MT	Idle Speed (rpm) AT	Valve Clearance In.	Valve Clearance Ex.
1990	K	2.0 (1998)	0.045	①	①	9–13	①	①	Hyd.	Hyd.
	M	2.0 (1998)	0.035	①	①	35–38	①	①	Hyd.	Hyd.
	G	2.2 (2190)	0.035	①	①	9–13	①	①	Hyd.	Hyd.
	T	3.1 (3136)	0.045	①	①	41–47 ②	①	①	Hyd.	Hyd.
1991	K	2.0 (1998)	0.045	①	①	9–13	①	①	Hyd.	Hyd.
	G	2.2 (2190)	0.035	①	①	9–13	①	①	Hyd.	Hyd.
	T	3.1 (3136)	0.045	①	①	41–47 ②	①	①	Hyd.	Hyd.
1992	H	2.0 (1998)	0.045	①	①	41–47 ②	①	①	Hyd.	Hyd.
	4	2.2 (2190)	0.045	①	①	41–47 ②	①	①	Hyd.	Hyd.
	T	3.1 (3136)	0.045	①	①	41–47 ②	①	①	Hyd.	Hyd.
1993	H	2.0 (1998)	0.045	①	①	41–47 ②	①	①	Hyd.	Hyd.
	4	2.2 (2190)	0.045	①	①	41–47 ②	①	①	Hyd.	Hyd.
	T	3.1 (3136)	0.045	①	①	41–47 ②	①	①	Hyd.	Hyd.
1994				SEE UNDERHOOD SPECIFICATIONS STICKER						

NOTE: The lowest cylinder pressure should be within 75% of the highest cylinder pressure reading. For example, if the highest cylinder is 134 psi, the lowest should be 101. Engine should be at normal operating temperature with throttle valve in the wide open position.
The underhood specifications sticker often reflects tune-up specification changes in production. Sticker figures must be used if they disagree with those in this chart.
Hyd.—Hydraulic
① See underhood Vehicle Emission Control
  information label
② Full system pressure with engine not running;
  3–10 psi lower with engine at idle

CAPACITIES

Year	Model	Engine ID/VIN	Engine Displacement Liters (cc)	Engine Crankcase with Filter (qts.)	Transmission (pts.)			Transfer case (pts.)	Drive Axle		Fuel Tank (gal.)	Cooling System (qts.)
					4-Spd	5-Spd	Auto.		Front (pts.)	Rear (pts.)		
1990	Cavalier	G	2.2 (2190)	4①	—	4	8②	—	—	—	13.6	8.5
	Cavalier	T	3.1 (3136)	4①	—	4	8②	—	—	—	13.6	11.0
	Sunbird	K	2.0 (1998)	4①	—	4	8②	—	—	—	13.6	8.5
	Sunbird	M	2.0 (1998)	4①	—	4	8②	—	—	—	13.6	8.5
1991	Cavalier	G	2.2 (2190)	4①	—	4	8②	—	—	—	13.6	11.7
	Cavalier	T	3.1 (3136)	4①	—	4	8②	—	—	—	13.6	14.2
	Sunbird	K	2.0 (1998)	4①	—	4	8②	—	—	—	13.6	11.7
	Sunbird	T	3.1 (3136)	4①	—	4	8②	—	—	—	13.6	14.2
1992	Cavalier	4	2.2 (2190)	4①	—	4	8②	—	—	—	13.6	9.2
	Cavalier	T	3.1 (3136)	4①	—	4	8②	—	—	—	13.6	13.1
	Sunbird	H	2.0 (1998)	4①	—	4	8②	—	—	—	13.6	11.7
	Sunbird	T	3.1 (3136)	4①	—	4	8②	—	—	—	13.6	14.2
1993-94	Cavalier	4	2.2 (2190)	4①	—	4	8②	—	—	—	13.6	11.7
	Cavalier	T	3.1 (3136)	4①	—	4	8②	—	—	—	13.6	14.2
	Sunbird	H	2.0 (1998)	4①	—	4	8②	—	—	—	13.6	11.7
	Sunbird	T	3.1 (3136)	4①	—	4	8②	—	—	—	13.6	14.2

① Check level after running engine
② Plus 4 pints when overhauling

CAMSHAFT SPECIFICATIONS

All measurements given in inches.

Year	Engine ID/VIN	Engine Displacement Liters (cc)	Journal Diameter					Elevation		Bearing Clearance	Camshaft End Play
			1	2	3	4	5	In.	Ex.		
1990	K	2.0 (1998)	1.6706–1.6712	1.6812–1.6818	1.6911–1.6917	1.7009–1.7015	1.7100–1.7106	0.2366	0.2515	0.0011–0.0035	0.0016–0.0063
	M	2.0 (1998)	1.6706–1.6712	1.6812–1.6818	1.6911–1.6917	1.7009–1.7015	1.7100–1.7106	0.2625	0.2625	0.0011–0.0035	0.0016–0.0063
	G	2.2 (2190)	1.8670–1.8690	1.8670–1.8690	1.8670–1.8690	1.8670–1.8690	1.8670–1.8690	0.2590	0.2590	0.0010–0.0039	NA
	T	3.1 (3136)	1.8677–1.8815	1.8677–1.8815	1.8677–1.8815	1.8677–1.8815	1.8677–1.8815	0.2626	0.2732	0.0010–0.0040	NA
1991	K	2.0 (1998)	1.6706–1.6712	1.6812–1.6818	1.6911–1.6917	1.7009–1.7015	1.7100–1.7106	0.2366	0.2515	0.0011–0.0035	0.0016–0.0063
	G	2.2 (2190)	1.8670–1.8690	1.8670–1.8690	1.8670–1.8690	1.8670–1.8690	1.8670–1.8690	0.2590	0.2590	0.0010–0.0039	NA
	T	3.1 (3136)	1.8677–1.8815	1.8677–1.8815	1.8677–1.8815	1.8677–1.8815	1.8677–1.8815	0.2626	0.2732	0.0010–0.0040	NA
1992	H	2.0 (1998)	1.6706–1.6712	1.6812–1.6818	1.6911–1.6917	1.7009–1.7015	1.7100–1.7106	0.2626	0.2626	0.0011–0.0035	0.0016–0.0063
	4	2.2 (2190)	1.8670–1.8690	1.8670–1.8690	1.8670–1.8690	1.8670–1.8690	1.8670–1.8690	0.2590	0.2500	0.0010–0.0039	NA
	T	3.1 (3136)	1.8677–1.8815	1.8677–1.8815	1.8677–1.8815	1.8677–1.8815	1.8677–1.8815	0.2626	0.2732	0.0010–0.0040	NA

CAMSHAFT SPECIFICATIONS

All measurements given in inches.

| Year | Engine ID/VIN | Engine Displacement Liters (cc) | Journal Diameter | | | | | Elevation | | Bearing Clearance | Camshaft End Play |
			1	2	3	4	5	In.	Ex.		
1993–94	H	2.0 (1998)	1.6706–1.6712	1.6812–1.6818	1.6911–1.6917	1.7009–1.7015	1.7100–1.7106	0.2626	0.2626	0.0011–0.0035	0.0016–0.0063
	4	2.2 (2190)	1.8670–1.8690	1.8670–1.8690	1.8670–1.8690	1.8670–1.8690	1.8670–1.8690	0.2590	0.2500	0.0010–0.0039	NA
	T	3.1 (3136)	2.0090–2.0110	1.9990–2.0010	1.9990–2.0010	1.9990–2.0010	2.0090–2.0110	0.2626	0.2732	0.0010–0.0040	NA

NA—Not available

CRANKSHAFT AND CONNECTING ROD SPECIFICATIONS

All measurements are given in inches.

| Year | Engine ID/VIN | Engine Displacement Liters (cc) | Crankshaft | | | | Connecting Rod | | |
			Main Brg. Journal Dia.	Main Brg. Oil Clearance	Shaft End-play	Thrust on No.	Journal Diameter	Oil Clearance	Side Clearance
1990	K	2.0 (1998)	2.2828–2.2833	0.0006–0.0016	0.0028–0.0118	3	1.9279–1.9287	0.0007–0.0025	0.0028–0.0095
	M	2.0 (1998)	2.2828–2.2833	0.0006–0.0016	0.0028–0.0118	3	1.9279–1.9287	0.0007–0.0025	0.0028–0.0095
	G	2.2 (2190)	2.4945–2.4954	0.0006–0.0019	0.0020–0.0070	4	1.9983–1.9994	0.0010–0.0031	0.0039–0.0149
	T	3.1 (3136)	2.6473–2.6483	0.0012–0.0030	0.0024–0.0083	3	1.9983–1.9994	0.0011–0.0034	0.0140–0.0270
1991	K	2.0 (1998)	2.2828–2.2833	0.0006–0.0016	0.0028–0.0118	3	1.9279–1.9287	0.0007–0.0025	0.0028–0.0095
	G	2.2 (2190)	2.4945–2.4954	0.0006–0.0019	0.0020–0.0070	4	1.9983–1.9994	0.0010–0.0031	0.0039–0.0149
	T	3.1 (3136)	2.6473–2.6483	0.0012–0.0030	0.0024–0.0083	3	1.9983–1.9994	0.0011–0.0034	0.0140–0.0270
1992	H	2.0 (1998)	2.2828–2.2833	0.0006–0.0016	0.0028–0.0118	3	1.9279–1.9287	0.0007–0.0025	0.0028–0.0095
	4	2.2 (2190)	2.4945–2.4954	0.0006–0.0019	0.0020–0.0070	4	1.9983–1.9994	0.0010–0.0031	0.0039–0.0149
	T	3.1 (3136)	2.6473–2.6483	0.0012–0.0030	0.0024–0.0083	3	1.9983–1.9994	0.0011–0.0034	0.0140–0.0270
1993–94	H	2.0 (1998)	2.2828–2.2833	0.0006–0.0016	0.0028–0.0118	3	1.9279–1.9287	0.0007–0.0025	0.0028–0.0095
	4	2.2 (2190)	2.4945–2.4954	0.0006–0.0019	0.0020–0.0070	4	1.9983–1.9994	0.0010–0.0031	0.0039–0.0149
	T	3.1 (3136)	2.6473–2.6483	0.0012–0.0030	0.0024–0.0083	3	1.9983–1.9994	0.0011–0.0037	0.0071–0.0173

VALVE SPECIFICATIONS

Year	Engine ID/VIN	Engine Displacement Liters (cc)	Seat Angle (deg.)	Face Angle (deg.)	Spring Test Pressure (lbs. @ in.)	Spring Installed Height (in.)	Stem-to-Guide Clearance (in.)		Stem Diameter (in.)	
							Intake	Exhaust	Intake	Exhaust
1990	K	2.0 (1998)	45	46	165–197 @ 1.043	NA	0.0006–0.0017	0.0012–0.0024	0.2760–0.2755	0.2753–0.2747
	M	2.0 (1998)	45	46	165–179 @ 1.043	NA	0.0006–0.0017	0.0012–0.0024	0.2760–0.2755	0.2753–0.2747
	G	2.2 (2190)	46	45	208–222 @ 1.22	NA	0.0011–0.0026	0.0014–0.0030	NA	NA
	T	3.1 (3136)	46	45	215 @ 1.291	1.575	0.0010–0.0027	0.0010–0.0027	NA	NA
1991	K	2.0 (1998)	45	46	165–197 @ 1.043	NA	0.0006–0.0017	0.0012–0.0024	0.2760–0.2755	0.2753–0.2747
	G	2.2 (2190)	46	45	208–222 @ 1.22	NA	0.0011–0.0026	0.0014–0.0031	NA	NA
	T	3.1 (3136)	46	45	215 @ 1.291	1.575	0.0010–0.0027	0.0010–0.0027	NA	NA
1992	H	2.0 (1998)	45	46	165–197 @ 1.043	NA	0.0006–0.0017	0.0012–0.0024	0.2760–0.2755	0.2753–0.2747
	4	2.2 (2190)	46	45	225–233 @ 1.247	NA	0.0011–0.0026	0.0014–0.0031	NA	NA
	T	3.1 (3136)	46	45	215 @ 1.291	1.575	0.0010–0.0027	0.0010–0.0027	NA	NA
1993–94	H	2.0 (1998)	45	46	165–197 @ 1.043	NA	0.0006–0.0017	0.0012–0.0024	0.2760–0.2755	0.2753–0.2747
	4	2.2 (2190)	46	45	225–233 @ 1.247	NA	0.0011–0.0026	0.0014–0.0031	NA	NA
	T	3.1 (3136)	46	45	215 @ 1.291	1.693	0.0008–0.0021	0.0014–0.0030	NA	NA

NA—Not available

PISTON AND RING SPECIFICATIONS

All measurements are given in inches.

Year	Engine ID/VIN	Engine Displacement Liters (cc)	Piston Clearance	Ring Gap			Ring Side Clearance		
				Top Compression	Bottom Compression	Oil Control	Top Compression	Bottom Compression	Oil Control
1990	K	2.0 (1998)	0.0004–0.0012	0.0098–0.0177	0.0118–0.0197	NA	0.0024–0.0036	0.0019–0.0032	NA
	M	2.0 (1998)	0.0012–0.0020	0.0098–0.0177	0.0118–0.0197	NA	0.0024–0.0036	0.0019–0.0032	NA
	G	2.2 (2190)	0.0007–0.0017	0.0100–0.0200	0.0100–0.0200	0.0100–0.0500	0.0019–0.0027	0.0019–0.0027	0.0019–0.0082
	T	3.1 (3136)	0.0009–0.0022	0.0100–0.0200	0.0200–0.0280	0.0100–0.0300	0.0020–0.0035	0.0020–0.0035	0.0080 Max.
1991	K	2.0 (1998)	0.0004–0.0012	0.0098–0.0177	0.0118–0.0197	NA	0.0024–0.0036	0.0019–0.0032	NA
	G	2.2 (2190)	0.0007–0.0017	0.0100–0.0200	0.0100–0.0200	0.0100–0.0500	0.0019–0.0027	0.0019–0.0027	0.0019–0.0082
	T	3.1 (3136)	0.0009–0.0022	0.0100–0.0200	0.0200–0.0280	0.0100–0.0300	0.0020–0.0035	0.0020–0.0035	0.0080 Max.

PISTON AND RING SPECIFICATIONS

All measurements are given in inches.

Year	Engine ID/VIN	Engine Displacement Liters (cc)	Piston Clearance	Ring Gap			Ring Side Clearance		
				Top Compression	Bottom Compression	Oil Control	Top Compression	Bottom Compression	Oil Control
1992	H	2.0 (1998)	0.0004–0.0012	0.0098–0.0177	0.0118–0.0197	NA	0.0024–0.0036	0.0019–0.0032	NA
	4	2.2 (2190)	0.0007–0.0017	0.0100–0.0200	0.0100–0.0200	0.0100–0.0500	0.0019–0.0027	0.0019–0.0027	0.0019–0.0082
	T	3.1 (3136)	0.0009–0.0022	0.0100–0.0200	0.0200–0.0280	0.0100–0.0300	0.0020–0.0035	0.0020–0.0035	0.0080 Max.
1993–94	H	2.0 (1998)	0.0004–0.0012	0.0098–0.0177	0.0118–0.0197	NA	0.0024–0.0036	0.0019–0.0032	NA
	4	2.2 (2190)	0.0007–0.0017	0.0100–0.0200	0.0100–0.0200	0.0100–0.0500	0.0019–0.0027	0.0019–0.0027	0.0019–0.0082
	T	3.1 (3136)	0.0009–0.0023	0.0071–0.0161	0.0200–0.0280	0.0100–0.0300	0.0020–0.0035	0.0020–0.0035	0.0080 Max.

NA—Not available

TORQUE SPECIFICATIONS

All readings in ft. lbs.

Year	Engine ID/VIN	Engine Displacement Liters (cc)	Cylinder Head Bolts	Main Bearing Bolts	Rod Bearing Bolts	Crankshaft Damper Bolts	Flywheel Bolts	Manifold		Spark Plugs	Lug Nut
								Intake	Exhaust		
1990	K	2.0 (1998)	②	44③	26④	114	⑪	16	10	15	100
	M	2.0 (1998)	②	44③	26④	114	⑪	18	10	15	100
	G	2.2 (2190)	⑩	70	38	85	⑦	18	⑥	7–15	100
	T	3.1 (3136)	33⑧	73	39	76	⑦	24①	18	7–15	100
1991	K	2.0 (1998)	②	44③	26④	114	⑪	16	10	20	100
	G	2.2 (2190)	⑨	70	38	77	⑦	18	10	11	100
	T	3.1 (3136)	33⑧	73	39	76	⑦	24①	18	11	100
1992	H	2.0 (1998)	②	44③	26④	114	⑪	16	16	20	100
	4	2.2 (2190)	⑨	70	38	77	55	22	10	11	100
	T	3.1 (3136)	33⑧	73	39	76	52	24①	18	11	100
1993–94	H	2.0 (1998)	②	44③	26④	114	⑪	16	16	20	100
	4	2.2 (2190)	⑨	70	38	77	55	22	10	11	100
	T	3.1 (3136)	33⑧	37⑤	37	76	52	24①	21	11	100

① Tighten in 2 steps
First step to 15 ft. lbs.

② Step 1—18 ft. lbs.
Step 2—Tighten additional 180 degrees in 3 steps of 60 degrees each
Step 3—Warm engine—tighten bolts additional 30–50 degree turn

③ Plus additional 40–50 degree turn

④ Plus additional 40–45 degree turn

⑤ Plus tighten bolts an additional 77 degree turn

⑥ Nuts—10 ft. lbs.
Studs—7 ft. lbs.

⑦ Auto. trans.—52
Manual trans.—55

⑧ Coat thread with sealer an additional 90 degree turn

⑨ Step 1—Tighten the long bolts—8, 4, 1, 5 and 9 to 46 ft. lbs.
Tighten the short bolts—7, 3, 2, 6 and 10 to 43 ft. lbs.
Step 2—Tighten all bolts an additional 90 degrees in sequence

⑩ Step 1—Tighten all bolts initially to 41 ft. lbs.
Step 2—Tighten all bolts an additional 45 degrees in sequence
Step 3—Tighten all bolts an additional 45 degrees in sequence
Step 4—Tighten the long bolts—8, 4, 1, 5 and 9 an additional 20 degrees and tighten the short bolts—7, 3, 2, 6 and 10 an additional 10 degrees

⑪ Auto. trans.—48 ft. lbs.—can reuse bolts.
Man. trans.—48 ft. lbs.—plus an additional 30 degrees—must use new bolts.

TORQUE SPECIFICATIONS

Component	English	Metric
Camshaft sprocket bolt		
2.0L engine:	33 ft. lbs.	45 Nm
2.2L engine:	77 ft. lbs.	105 Nm
3.1L engine		
1990:	18 ft. lbs.	24 Nm
1991–94:	21 ft. lbs.	28 Nm
Connecting rod bearing cap bolts		
2.0L engine		
Step 1:	26 ft. lbs.	35 Nm
Step 2:	+ 40–45 degrees turn	+ 40–45 degrees turn
2.2L engine:	38 ft. lbs.	52 Nm
3.1L engine:	37 ft. lbs.	50 Nm
Crankshaft damper bolt		
2.0L engine (sprocket):	114 ft. lbs.	155 Nm
2.2L engine:	77 ft. lbs.	105 Nm
3.1L engine:	76 ft. lbs.	103 Nm
Cylinder head		
2.0L engine		
Step 1:	18 ft. lbs.	25 Nm
Step 2:	+ 60 degrees turn	+ 60 degrees turn
Step 3:	+ 60 degrees turn	+ 60 degrees turn
Step 4:	+ 60 degrees turn	+ 60 degrees turn
Step 5 (after warm-up):	+ 30–50 degrees turn	+ 30–50 degrees turn
2.2L engine		
Step 1:	41 ft. lbs.	56 Nm
Step 2:	+ 45 degrees turn	+ 45 degrees turn
Step 3:	+ 45 degrees turn	+ 45 degrees turn
Step 4		
Long bolts:	+ 20 degrees turn	+ 20 degrees turn
Short bolts:	+ 10 degrees turn	+ 10 degrees turn
3.1L engine		
Step 1:	33 ft. lbs.	45 Nm
Step 2:	+ 90 degrees turn	+ 90 degrees turn
Engine-to-transmission:	55 ft. lbs.	75 Nm
Exhaust manifold		
2.0L engine:	16 ft. lbs.	25 Nm
2.2L engine:	115 inch lbs.	13 Nm
3.1L engine		
1990–92:	19 ft. lbs.	25 Nm
1993–94:	21 ft. lbs.	28 Nm
Exhaust pipe-to-exhaust manifold nuts		
Except 2.0L (VIN H) and 3.1L engines:	19 ft. lbs.	25 Nm
2.0L (VIN H) and 3.1L engines:	26 ft. lbs.	35 Nm
Flywheel/flexplate-to-crankshaft bolts		
2.0L engine		
Automatic transaxle:	48 ft. lbs.	65 Nm
Manual transaxle (new bolts only)		
Step 1:	48 ft. lbs.	65 Nm
Step 2:	+ 30 degrees turn	+ 30 degrees turn
2.2L engine		
Automatic transaxle		
1990–91:	52 ft. lbs.	70 Nm
1992–94:	55 ft. lbs.	75 Nm
Manual transaxle:	55 ft. lbs.	75 Nm
3.1L engine	52 ft. lbs.	70 Nm
Flexplate-to-converter bolt:	46 ft. lbs.	62 Nm

TORQUE SPECIFICATIONS

Component	English	Metric
Intake manifold-to-cylinder head		
2.0L (VIN K and H) engines:	16 ft. lbs.	22 Nm
2.0L (VIN M) engine:	20 ft. lbs.	27 Nm
2.2L (VIN G) engine:	15–22 ft. lbs.	20–30 Nm
2.2L (VIN 4) engine:	22 ft. lbs.	30 Nm
3.1L engine		
Upper manifold (plenum):	88 inch lbs.	10 Nm
Lower manifold		
Step 1:	15 ft. lbs.	20 Nm
Step 2:	24 ft. lbs.	33 Nm
Main bearing cap bolts		
2.0L engine		
Step 1:	44 ft. lbs.	60 Nm
Step 2:	+ 40–50 degrees turn	+ 40–50 degrees turn
2.2L engine:	70 ft. lbs.	95 Nm
3.1L engine		
1990–92:	73 ft. lbs.	99 Nm
1993–94		
Step 1:	37 ft. lbs.	50 Nm
Step 2:	+ 77 degrees turn	+ 77 degrees turn
Oil pan		
2.0L (VIN K and M) engines:	44 inch lbs.	5 Nm
2.0L (VIN H) engine:	97 inch lbs.	11 Nm
2.2L engine:	71 inch lbs.	6 Nm
3.1L engine		
Rear bolts (2):	18 ft. lbs.	25 Nm
All other fasteners:	89 inch lbs.	10 Nm
Oil pump attaching bolts		
2.0L engine:	62 inch lbs.	7 Nm
2.2L engine:	32 ft. lbs.	43 Nm
3.1L engine:	30 ft. lbs.	41 Nm
Pressure plate-to-flywheel		
Step 1:	Seat bolts in crosswise pattern	
Step 2:	12 ft. lbs.	16 Nm
Step 3		
Except 2.0L engine:	18 ft. lbs.	24 Nm
2.0L engine:	22 ft. lbs.	30 Nm
Step 4:	+ 30 degrees turn	+ 30 degrees turn
Rocker arm pivot bolt		
2.2L engine		
1990:	14 ft. lbs.	20 Nm
1991–94:	22 ft. lbs.	30 Nm
3.1L engine:	18 ft. lbs.	25 Nm
Rocker (valve) cover		
2.0L engine:	84 inch lbs.	9.5 Nm
2.2L engine:	89 inch lbs.	10 Nm
3.1L engine:	89 inch lbs.	10 Nm
Spark plug		
2.0L engine		
1990:	15 ft. lbs.	20 Nm
1991–94:	20 ft. lbs.	27 Nm
2.2L and 3.1L engines		
1990:	7–15 ft. lbs.	10–20 Nm
1991–94:	11 ft. lbs.	15 Nm
Thermostat housing		
2.0L engine:	20 ft. lbs.	27 Nm
2.2L engine:	89 inch lbs.	10 Nm
3.1L engine:	18 ft. lbs.	25 Nm

TORQUE SPECIFICATIONS

Component	English	Metric
Timing cover		
2.0L engine		
1990–91:	89 inch lbs.	10 Nm
1992–94:	62 inch lbs.	7 Nm
2.2L engine:	97 inch lbs.	11 Nm
3.1L engine		
1990–92:	20–28 ft. lbs.	27–38 Nm
1993–94		
Except 4 longer upper bolts:	15 ft. lbs.	21 Nm
4 longer upper bolts:	35 ft. lbs.	45 Nm
Water pump		
2.0L engine		
1990–91:	21 ft. lbs.	28 Nm
1992–94:	18 ft. lbs.	25 Nm
2.2L engine:	18 ft. lbs.	25 Nm
3.1L engine:	89 inch lbs.	10 Nm
Water pump pulley		
2.0L engine:	17 ft. lbs.	24 Nm
2.2L engine:	22 ft. lbs.	30 Nm
3.1L engine:	15 ft. lbs.	21 Nm

BRAKE SPECIFICATIONS

All measurements in inches unless noted.

Year	Model	Master Cylinder Bore	Brake Disc Original Thickness	Brake Disc Minimum Thickness	Maximum Runout	Brake Drum Diameter Original Inside Diameter	Brake Drum Diameter Max. Wear Limit	Brake Drum Diameter Maximum Machine Diameter	Minimum Lining Thickness Front	Minimum Lining Thickness Rear
1990	Cavalier	0.874	0.885	0.830①	0.004	7.879	7.929	7.899	1/8	1/8
	Sunbird	0.874	0.885	0.830①	0.004	7.879	7.929	7.899	1/8	1/8
1991	Cavalier	0.874	0.885	0.830①	0.004	7.879	7.929	7.899	1/8	1/8
	Sunbird	0.874	0.885	0.830①	0.004	7.879	7.929	7.899	1/8	1/8
1992	Cavalier	0.874	0.806	0.796①	0.004	7.899	7.929	7.879	1/8	1/8
	Sunbird	0.874	0.806	0.796①	0.004	7.879	7.929	7.899	1/8	1/8
1993–94	Cavalier	0.874	0.786	0.751①	0.004	7.874–7.890	7.929	7.879	1/8	1/8
	Sunbird	0.874	0.786	0.751①	0.004	7.874–7.890	7.929	7.899	1/8	1/8

① Specification is the minimum to which the disc
may be machined. The discard thickness is
slightly smaller and is cast into the disc.

WHEEL ALIGNMENT

Year	Model	Caster Range (deg.)	Caster Preferred Setting (deg.)	Camber Range (deg.)	Camber Preferred Setting (deg.)	Toe-in (in.)	Steering Axis Inclination (deg.)
1990	Cavalier	11/16P–2 11/16P	1 11/16P	11/16N–11/16P①	0①	0	13 1/2
	Sunbird	11/16P–2 11/16P	1 11/16P	11/16N–11/16P①	0①	0	13 1/2
1991	Cavalier	11/16P–2 11/16P	1 11/16P	11/16N–11/16P	0	0	13 1/2
	Sunbird	11/16P–2 11/16P	1 11/16P	11/16N–11/16P	0	0	13 1/2

WHEEL ALIGNMENT

Year	Model	Caster		Camber		Toe-in (in.)	Steering Axis Inclination (deg.)
		Range (deg.)	Preferred Setting (deg.)	Range (deg.)	Preferred Setting (deg.)		
1992	Cavalier	$^{11}/_{16}$P–$2^{11}/_{16}$P	$1^{11}/_{16}$P	$^{11}/_{16}$N–$^{11}/_{16}$P	0	0	$13^{1}/_{2}$
	Sunbird	$^{11}/_{16}$P–$2^{11}/_{16}$P	$1^{11}/_{16}$P	$^{11}/_{16}$N–$^{11}/_{16}$P	0	0	$13^{1}/_{2}$
1993–94	Cavalier	$^{5}/_{16}$P–$2^{5}/_{16}$P	$1^{5}/_{16}$P	$^{13}/_{16}$N–$^{9}/_{16}$P	$^{5}/_{32}$N	0	$13^{1}/_{2}$
	Sunbird	$^{5}/_{16}$P–$2^{5}/_{16}$P	$1^{5}/_{16}$P	$^{13}/_{16}$N–$^{9}/_{16}$P	$^{5}/_{32}$N	0	$13^{1}/_{2}$

N—Negative
P—Positive
① Specification given is for 224 or Pontiac with
16 in. wheels.
All others $^{1}/_{8}$P–$1^{1}/_{2}$P, Preferred $^{13}/_{16}$P

AIR CONDITIONING BELT TENSION

Year	Engine VIN	Engine Displacement Liters (cc)	Belt Type	Specifications	
				New	Used
1990	T	3.1 (3149)	Serpentine	①	
	G	2.2 (2198)	Serpentine	①	
	K	2.0 (1988)	Serpentine	①	
1991	T	3.1 (3149)	Serpentine	①	
	G	2.2 (2198)	Serpentine	①	
	K	2.0 (1988)	Serpentine	①	
1992	4	2.2 (2198)	Serpentine	67–77②	
	T	3.1 (3149)	Serpentine	50–70②	
	H	2.0 (1988)	Serpentine	36–44②	
1993–94	4	2.2 (2198)	Serpentine	50–70②	
	T	3.1 (3149)	Serpentine	50–70②	
	H	2.0 (1988)	Serpentine	①	

① Equipped with automatic tensioner;
no adjustment required.
② Equipped with automatic tensioner; however,
the specification given (in pounds) is for testing
whether the tensioner is maintaining its proper
tension (specification given is the average of 3
readings back-to-back).

REFRIGERANT CAPACITIES

Year	Model	Refrigerant (oz.)	Oil (fl. oz.)	Compressor Type
1990	Cavalier, Sunbird	36.0	8.0	V-5
1991	Cavalier, Sunbird	36.0	8.0	V-5
1992	Cavalier, Sunbird	36.0	8.0	V-5
1993	Cavalier, Sunbird	36.0	8.0	V-5

NOTE: At the time of publication, refrigerant capacity information relating to R-134a was not available from the manufacturer.

MAINTENANCE INTERVALS—TYPE A: NORMAL SERVICE
Cavalier • Sunbird

TO BE SERVICED	TYPE OF SERVICE	VEHICLE MILEAGE INTERVAL (X1000)							
		7.5	15	22.5	30	37.5	45	52.5	60
Oxygen Sensor	I				✔				✔
Ignition Timing	I①								
Vacuum Lines and Hoses	I		✔		✔		✔		✔
Ignition Wires	I				✔				✔
Spark Plugs	R				✔				✔
Engine Oil	R②	✔	✔	✔	✔	✔	✔	✔	✔
Engine Air Cleaner Element	R				✔				✔
Crankcase Emission Filter	R				✔				✔
PCV Valve	R				✔				✔
Fuel Filter	R				✔				✔
Engine Oil Filter	R③	✔		✔		✔		✔	
Fuel/Vapor Return Lines	I				✔				✔
Fuel Tank Cap and Restrictor	I				✔				✔
Coolant System Service	R				✔				✔
Exhaust Pipe and Muffler	I				✔				✔
Tire Rotation	I	✔		✔		✔		✔	
Catalytic Converter and Shield	I				✔				✔
EGR System	I								
Coolant Hoses and Clamps	I		✔		✔		✔		✔
Brake Linings	I		✔		✔		✔		✔
Parking Brake	I④		✔		✔		✔		✔
Timing Belt	R⑤								
Idle Speed System	I				✔				✔
Throttle Body Mounting Torque	I	✔							
Drive Belts	I				✔				✔
Chassis Lubrication	L	✔	✔	✔	✔	✔	✔	✔	✔
CV-Joints and Boots	I	✔	✔	✔	✔	✔	✔	✔	✔
Battery Connections	I	✔			✔		✔		✔
Automatic Transaxle Fluid	R								
Seat Belt Operation	I		✔		✔		✔		✔

FOR COMPLETE WARRANTY COVERAGE CONSULT INDIVIDUAL VEHICLE MANUFACTURER'S WARRANTY MAINTENANCE GUIDE.

I—Inspect
L—Lubricate
R—Replace
① Check and adjust timing as per engine emission label on applicable vehicles
② On Turbocharged engines, change oil every 3,000 miles
③ Replace oil filter at first and every other oil change
④ Adjust if necessary and lubricate cables
⑤ Replace timing belt at 60,000 miles

MAINTENANCE INTERVALS—TYPE B: SEVERE SERVICE
Cavalier • Sunbird

TO BE SERVICED	TYPE OF SERVICE	VEHICLE MILEAGE INTERVAL (X1000)									
		3	6	9	12	15	18	21	24	27	30
Oxygen Sensor	I										✔
Ignition Timing	I①										
Vacuum Lines and Hoses	I					✔					✔
Ignition Wires	I										✔
Spark Plugs	R										✔
Engine Oil and Filter	R	✔	✔	✔	✔	✔	✔	✔	✔	✔	✔
Engine Air Cleaner Element	R										✔
Crankcase Emission Filter	R										✔
PCV Valve	R										✔
Fuel Filter	R					✔					✔
Fuel/Vapor Return Lines	I										
Fuel Tank Cap and Restrictor	I										
Coolant System Service	R										
Exhaust Pipe and Muffler	I										✔
Tire Rotation	I②		✔								
Catalytic Converter and Shield	I										✔
EGR System	I										✔
Coolant Hoses and Clamps	I					✔					✔
Brake Linings	I					✔					✔
Parking Brake	I					✔					✔
Timing Belt	R										
Idle Speed System	I										✔
Throttle Body Mounting Torque	I		✔								
Drive Belts	I										✔
Chassis Lubrication	L		✔		✔		✔		✔		
CV-Joints and Boots	I	✔	✔	✔	✔	✔	✔	✔	✔	✔	✔
Battery Connections	I					✔					✔
Automatic Transaxle Fluid	R					✔					✔
Seat Belt Operation	I					✔					✔

FOR COMPLETE WARRANTY COVERAGE CONSULT INDIVIDUAL VEHICLE MANUFACTURER'S WARRANTY MAINTENANCE GUIDE.

I—Inspect
L—Lubricate
R—Replace
① Check and adjust timing as per engine emission label on applicable vehicles
② Rotate tires at 6,000 miles and then every 15,000 miles

FIRING ORDERS

NOTE: To avoid confusion, always replace spark plugs and wires one at a time.

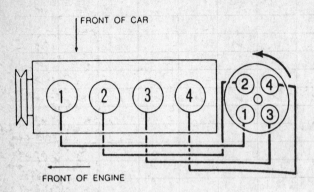

1990–91 2.0L (VIN K and M) Engines
Engine Firing Order: 1-3-4-2
Distributor Rotation: Counterclockwise

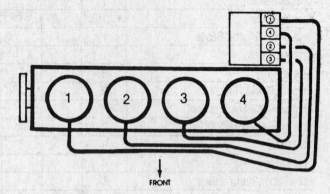

2.2L Engine
Engine Firing Order: 1-3-4-2
Distributorless Ignition System

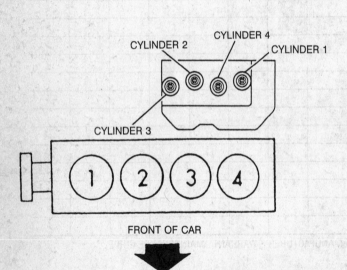

1992–94 2.0L (VIN H) Engine
Engine Firing Order: 1-3-4-2
Distributorless Ignition System

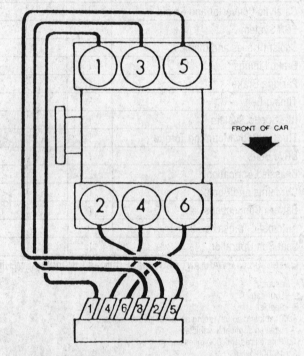

3.1L Engine
Engine Firing Order: 1-2-3-4-5-6
Distributorless Ignition System

CYLINDER HEAD TORQUE SEQUENCES

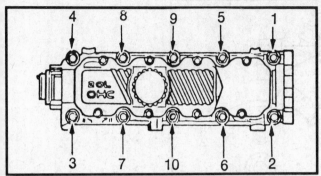

Camshaft carrier/cylinder head bolt loosening sequence—2.0L engine

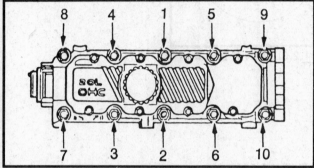

Camshaft carrier/cylinder head bolt torque sequence—2.0L engine

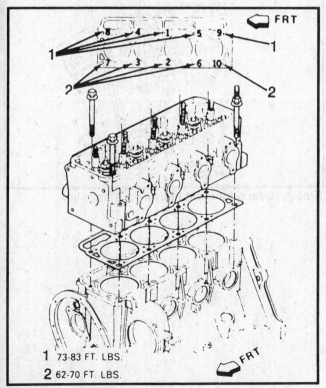

1. 73-83 FT. LBS.
2. 62-70 FT. LBS.

Cylinder head bolt torque sequence—1990 2.2L engine

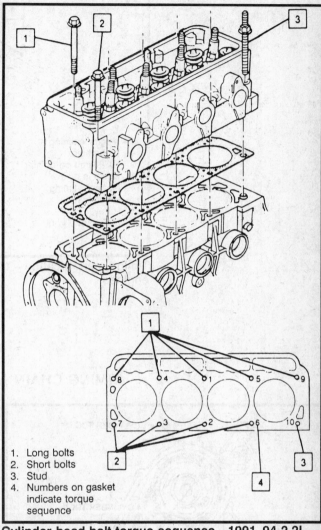

1. Long bolts
2. Short bolts
3. Stud
4. Numbers on gasket indicate torque sequence

Cylinder head bolt torque sequence—1991–94 2.2L engine

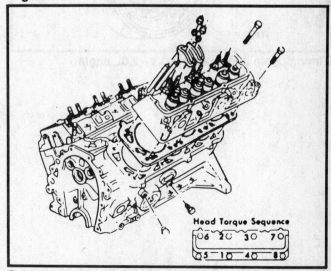

Cylinder head bolt torque sequence—3.1L engine

TIMING MARK LOCATIONS

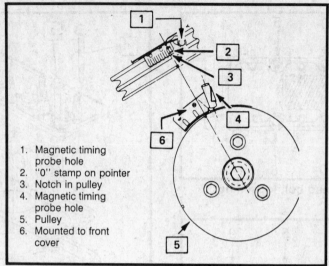

1. Magnetic timing probe hole
2. "0" stamp on pointer
3. Notch in pulley
4. Magnetic timing probe hole
5. Pulley
6. Mounted to front cover

Timing mark location—1990–91 2.0L (VIN K and M) engines

TIMING CHAIN ALIGNMENT MARKS

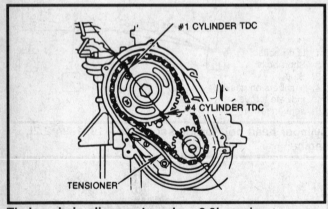

#1 CYLINDER TDC

#4 CYLINDER TDC

TENSIONER

Timing chain alignment marks—2.0L engine

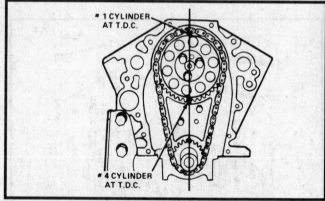

#1 CYLINDER AT T.D.C.

#4 CYLINDER AT T.D.C.

Timing chain alignment marks—3.1L engine

AIR CONDITIONING SERVICE VALVE
LOCATIONS

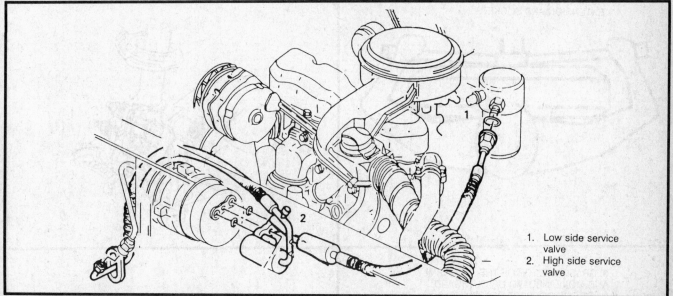

1. Low side service valve
2. High side service valve

Air conditioning service valve location

WHEEL ALIGNMENT ADJUSTMENT
LOCATIONS

LOOSEN TO SET CAMBER

Front camber adjustment

1. TOP VIEW: REACH AROUND THE TIRE AS SHOWN, USING APPROPRIATE EXTENSION AND SOCKETS

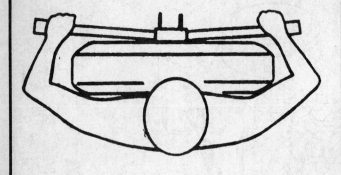

2. LOOSEN, BUT DO NOT REMOVE THE 2 STRUT BOLTS

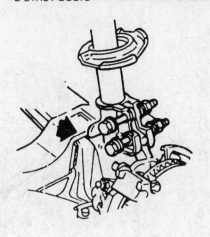

3. GRASP THE TOP OF THE TIRE FIRMLY AND MOVE INBOARD OR OUTBOARD UNTIL THE CORRECT READING IS OBTAINED

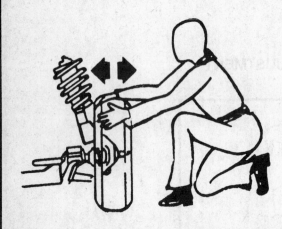

4. IF ACCESSIBILITY IS LIMITED, IT MAY BE NECESSARY TO REMOVE THE WHEEL AND TIRE. APPLY FINAL TORQUE TO BOLTS/NUTS TO RETAIN THE CORRECT CAMBER SETTING

Front wheel camber geometry

SPECIFICATION CHARTS

VEHICLE IDENTIFICATION CHART

It is important for servicing and ordering parts to be certain of the vehicle and engine identification. The VIN (vehicle identification number) is a 17 digit number visible through the windshield on the driver's side of the dash and contains the vehicle and engine identification codes. The tenth digit indicates model year and the eighth digit indicates engine code. It can be interpreted as follows:

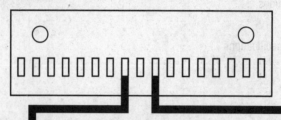

Engine Code							Model Year	
Code	Liters	Cu. In. (cc)	Cyl.	Fuel Sys.	Eng. Mfg.		Code	Year
G	2.2	133 (2180)	4	TBI	Chevrolet		L	1990
A	2.3	138 (2262)	4	PFI	Chevrolet		M	1991
T	3.1	191 (3130)	6	PFI	Chevrolet		N	1992
4	2.2	133 (2180)	4	PFI	Chevrolet		P	1993
							R	1994

PFI—Port Fuel Injection
TBI—Throttle Body Injection

ENGINE IDENTIFICATION

Year	Model	Engine Displacement Liters (cc)	Engine Series (ID/VIN)	Fuel System	No. of Cylinders	Engine Type
1990	Beretta	2.2 (2180)	G	TBI	4	OHV
	Beretta	2.3 (2262)	A	PFI	4	OHC
	Beretta	3.1 (3130)	T	PFI	6	OHV
	Corsica	2.2 (2180)	G	TBI	4	OHV
	Corsica	3.1 (3130)	T	PFI	6	OHV
1991	Beretta	2.2 (2180)	G	TBI	4	OHV
	Beretta	2.3 (2262)	A	PFI	4	OHC
	Beretta	3.1 (3130)	T	PFI	6	OHV
	Corsica	2.2 (2180)	G	TBI	4	OHV
	Corsica	3.1 (3130)	T	PFI	6	OHV
1992	Beretta	2.2 (2180)	4	PFI	4	OHV
	Beretta	2.3 (2262)	A	PFI	4	OHC
	Beretta	3.1 (3130)	T	PFI	6	OHV
	Corsica	2.2 (2180)	4	PFI	4	OHV
	Corsica	3.1 (3130)	T	PFI	6	OHV
1993-94	Beretta	2.2 (2180)	4	PFI	4	OHV
	Beretta	2.3 (2262)	A	PFI	4	OHC
	Beretta	3.1 (3130)	T	PFI	6	OHV
	Corsica	2.2 (2180)	4	PFI	4	OHV
	Corsica	3.1 (3130)	T	PFI	6	OHV

OHC—Overhead Cam
OHV—Overhead Valves
PFI—Port Fuel Injection
TBI—Throttle Body Injection

GENERAL ENGINE SPECIFICATIONS

Year	Engine ID/VIN	Engine Displacement Liters (cc)	Fuel System Type	Net Horsepower @ rpm	Net Torque @ rpm (ft. lbs.)	Bore × Stroke (in.)	Compression Ratio	Oil Pressure @ rpm
1990	G	2.2 (2180)	TBI	95 @ 5200	120 @ 3200	3.500 × 3.460	9.0:1	63–77 @ 1200
	A	2.3 (2262)	PFI	180 @ 6200	160 @ 5200	3.622 × 3.460	10.0:1	30 @ 2000
	T	3.1 (3130)	PFI	135 @ 4200	180 @ 3600	3.500 × 3.310	8.8:1	50–65 @ 2400
1991	G	2.2 (2180)	TBI	95 @ 5200	120 @ 3200	3.500 × 3.460	9.0:1	63–77 @ 1200
	A	2.3 (2262)	PFI	180 @ 6200	160 @ 5200	3.622 × 3.460	10.0:1	30 @ 2000
	T	3.1 (3130)	PFI	140 @ 4200	185 @ 3200	3.500 × 3.310	8.8:1	50–65 @ 2400
1992	4	2.2 (2180)	PFI	110 @ 5200	130 @ 2800	3.500 × 3.460	9.0:1	63–77 @ 1200
	A	2.3 (2262)	PFI	180 @ 6200	160 @ 5200	3.622 × 3.460	10.0:1	30 @ 2000
	T	3.1 (3130)	PFI	140 @ 4200	185 @ 3200	3.500 × 3.310	8.8:1	50–65 @ 2400
1993–94	4	2.2 (2180)	PFI	110 @ 5200	130 @ 2800	3.500 × 3.460	9.0:1	63–77 @ 1200
	A	2.3 (2262)	PFI	180 @ 6200	160 @ 5200	3.622 × 3.460	10.0:1	30 @ 2000
	T	3.1 (3130)	PFI	140 @ 4200	185 @ 3200	3.500 × 3.310	8.8:1	50–65 @ 2400

PFI—Port Fuel Injection
TBI—Throttle Body Injection

GASOLINE ENGINE TUNE-UP SPECIFICATIONS

Year	Engine ID/VIN	Engine Displacement Liters (cc)	Spark Plugs Gap (in.)	Ignition Timing (deg.) MT	AT	Fuel Pump (psi)	Idle Speed (rpm) MT	AT	Valve Clearance In.	Ex.
1990	G	2.2 (2180)	0.035	①	①	9–13	①	①	Hyd.	Hyd.
	A	2.3 (2262)	0.035	①	①	②	①	①	Hyd.	Hyd.
	T	3.1 (3130)	0.045	①	①	②	①	①	Hyd.	Hyd.
1991	G	2.2 (2180)	0.035	①	①	9–13	①	①	Hyd.	Hyd.
	A	2.3 (2262)	0.035	①	①	②	①	①	Hyd.	Hyd.
	T	3.1 (3130)	0.045	①	①	②	①	①	Hyd.	Hyd.
1992	4	2.2 (2180)	0.045	①	①	②	①	①	Hyd.	Hyd.
	A	2.3 (2262)	0.035	①	①	②	①	①	Hyd.	Hyd.
	T	3.1 (3130)	0.045	①	①	②	①	①	Hyd.	Hyd.
1993	4	2.2 (2180)	0.045	①	①	②	①	①	Hyd.	Hyd.
	A	2.3 (2262)	0.035	①	①	②	①	①	Hyd.	Hyd.
	T	3.1 (3130)	0.045	①	①	②	①	①	Hyd.	Hyd.
1994		SEE UNDERHOOD SPECIFICATIONS STICKER								

NOTE: The lowest cylinder pressure should be within 75% of the highest cylinder pressure reading. For example, if the highest cylinder is 134 psi, the lowest should be 101. Engine should be at normal operating temperature with throttle valve in the wide open position.
The underhood specifications sticker often reflects tune-up specification changes in production. Sticker figures must be used if they disagree with those in this chart.
Hyd.—Hydraulic
① Ignition timing and idle speed is controlled by the electronic control module. No adjustments are possible
② 1—Connect fuel pressure gauge, engine at normal operating temperature
2—Turn ignition switch on
3—After approx. 2 seconds; pressure should read 41–47 psi and hold steady
4—Start engine and idle; pressure should drop 3–10 psi from static pressure

CAPACITIES

Year	Model	Engine ID/VIN	Engine Displacement Liters (cc)	Engine Crankcase with Filter (qts.)	Transmission (pts.) 4-Spd	5-Spd	Auto.	Transfer case (pts.)	Drive Axle Front (pts.)	Rear (pts.)	Fuel Tank (gal.)	Cooling System (qts.)
1990	Beretta	G	2.2 (2180)	4.0①	NA	4.0	14.0③	—	—	—	15.6	④⑤
		A	2.3 (2262)	4.0①	NA	4.0	14.0③	—	—	—	15.6	⑤
		T	3.1 (3130)	4.0①	NA	4.0	14.0③	—	—	—	15.6	⑥
	Corsica	G	2.2 (2180)	4.0①	NA	4.0	14.0③	—	—	—	15.6	④⑤
		T	3.1 (3130)	4.0①	NA	4.0	14.0③	—	—	—	15.6	⑥
1991	Beretta	G	2.2 (2180)	4.0①	NA	4.2	14.0③	—	—	—	15.6	④⑤
		A	2.3 (2262)	4.0①	NA	4.2	14.0③	—	—	—	15.6	⑤
		T	3.1 (3130)	4.0①	NA	4.2	14.0③	—	—	—	15.6	⑥
	Corsica	G	2.2 (2180)	4.0①	NA	4.2	14.0③	—	—	—	15.6	④⑤
		T	3.1 (3130)	4.0①	NA	4.2	14.0③	—	—	—	15.6	⑥
1992	Beretta	4	2.2 (2180)	4.0①	NA	4.0	8.0②	—	—	—	15.6	9.2
		A	2.3 (2262)	4.0①	NA	4.0	8.0②	—	—	—	15.6	10.3
		T	3.1 (3130)	4.0①	NA	4.0	8.0②	—	—	—	15.6	13.1
	Corsica	4	2.2 (2180)	4.0①	NA	4.0	8.0②	—	—	—	15.6	9.2
		T	3.1 (3130)	4.0①	NA	4.0	8.0②	—	—	—	15.6	13.1
1993-94	Beretta	4	2.2 (2180)	4.0①	NA	4.0	8.0②	—	—	—	15.6	9.2
		A	2.3 (2262)	4.0①	NA	4.0	8.0②	—	—	—	15.6	10.3
		T	3.1 (3130)	4.0①	NA	4.0	8.0②	—	—	—	15.6	13.1
	Corsica	4	2.2 (2180)	4.0①	NA	4.0	8.0②	—	—	—	15.6	9.2
		T	3.1 (3130)	4.0①	NA	4.0	8.0②	—	—	—	15.6	13.1

NA—Not available
① Additional oil will be required if filter is changed.
② This figure is for drain and refill. After a complete overhaul, use 12.0 pts.
③ This figure is for drain and refill, if equipped with HM-3T40, after complete overhaul, use 18.0 pts.

④ Automatic transaxle
   With air conditioning—9.5 qts.
   Without air conditioning—9.6 qts.
⑤ Manual transaxle
   With or without air conditioning—9.5 qts.
⑥ Automatic transaxle—12.4 qts.
   Manual transaxle—11.8 qts.

CAMSHAFT SPECIFICATIONS

All measurements given in inches.

Year	Engine ID/VIN	Engine Displacement Liters (cc)	Journal Diameter 1	2	3	4	5	Elevation In.	Ex.	Bearing Clearance	Camshaft End Play
1990	G	2.2 (2180)	1.867–1.869	1.867–1.869	1.867–1.869	1.867–1.869	1.867–1.869	0.259	0.259	0.001–0.004	NA
	A	2.3 (2262)	1.572–1.573	1.375–1.376	1.375–1.376	1.375–1.376	1.375–1.376	0.410	0.410	0.002–0.004	0.0010–0.0090
	T	3.1 (3130)	1.868–1.881	1.868–1.881	1.868–1.881	1.868–1.881	—	0.263	0.273	0.001–0.004	NA
1991	G	2.2 (2180)	1.867–1.869	1.867–1.869	1.867–1.869	1.867–1.869	1.867–1.869	0.259	0.259	0.001–0.004	NA
	A	2.3 (2262)	1.572–1.573	1.375–1.376	1.375–1.376	1.375–1.376	1.375–1.376	0.410	0.410	0.002–0.004	0.0010–0.0090
	T	3.1 (3130)	1.868–1.881	1.868–1.881	1.868–1.881	1.868–1.881	—	0.263	0.273	0.001–0.004	NA

CAMSHAFT SPECIFICATIONS

All measurements given in inches.

Year	Engine ID/VIN	Engine Displacement Liters (cc)	Journal Diameter 1	2	3	4	5	Elevation In.	Ex.	Bearing Clearance	Camshaft End Play
1992	4	2.2 (2180)	1.867–1.869	1.867–1.869	1.867–1.869	1.867–1.869	1.867–1.869	0.259	0.259	0.001–0.004	NA
	A	2.3 (2262)	1.572–1.573	1.375–1.376	1.375–1.376	1.375–1.376	1.375–1.376	0.410	0.410	0.002–0.004	0.0009–0.0088
	T	3.1 (3130)	1.868–1.882	1.868–1.882	1.868–1.882	1.868–1.882	—	0.263	0.273	0.001–0.004	NA
1993–94	4	2.2 (2180)	1.867–1.869	1.867–1.869	1.867–1.869	1.867–1.869	1.867–1.869	0.259	0.259	0.001–0.004	NA
	A	2.3 (2262)	1.572–1.573	1.375–1.376	1.375–1.376	1.375–1.376	1.375–1.376	0.410	0.410	0.002–0.004	0.0009–0.0088
	T	3.1 (3130)	1.868–1.882	1.868–1.882	1.868–1.882	1.868–1.882	—	0.263	0.273	0.001–0.004	NA

NA—Not available

CRANKSHAFT AND CONNECTING ROD SPECIFICATIONS

All measurements are given in inches.

Year	Engine ID/VIN	Engine Displacement Liters (cc)	Crankshaft Main Brg. Journal Dia.	Main Brg. Oil Clearance	Shaft End-play	Thrust on No.	Connecting Rod Journal Diameter	Oil Clearance	Side Clearance
1990	G	2.2 (2180)	2.4945–2.4954	0.0006–0.0019	0.002–0.007	4	1.9983–1.9994	0.0010–0.0030	0.0040–0.0150
	A	2.3 (2262)	2.0470–2.0480	0.0005–0.0023	0.003–0.009	3	1.8887–1.8897	0.0005–0.0020	0.0059–0.0177
	T	3.1 (3130)	2.6473–2.6483	0.0012–0.0030	0.002–0.008	3	1.9983–1.9994	0.0010–0.0040	0.0140–0.0270
1991	G	2.2 (2180)	2.4945–2.4954	0.0006–0.0019	0.002–0.007	4	1.9983–1.9994	0.0010–0.0030	0.0040–0.0150
	A	2.3 (2262)	2.0470–2.0480	0.0005–0.0023	0.003–0.009	3	1.8887–1.8897	0.0005–0.0020	0.0059–0.0177
	T	3.1 (3130)	2.6473–2.6483	0.0012–0.0030	0.002–0.008	3	1.9983–1.9994	0.0010–0.0040	0.0140–0.0270
1992	4	2.2 (2180)	2.4945–2.4954	0.0006–0.0019	0.002–0.007	4	1.9983–1.9994	0.0010–0.0030	0.0040–0.0150
	A	2.3 (2262)	2.0470–2.0480	0.0005–0.0023	0.003–0.009	3	1.8887–1.8897	0.0005–0.0020	0.0059–0.0177
	T	3.1 (3130)	2.6473–2.6483	0.0012–0.0030	0.002–0.008	3	1.9983–1.9994	0.0010–0.0040	0.0140–0.0270
1993–94	4	2.2 (2180)	2.4945–2.4954	0.0006–0.0019	0.002–0.007	4	1.9983–1.9994	0.0010–0.0030	0.0040–0.0150
	A	2.3 (2262)	2.0470–2.0480	0.0005–0.0023	0.003–0.009	3	1.8887–1.8897	0.0005–0.0020	0.0059–0.0177
	T	3.1 (3130)	2.6473–2.6483	0.0012–0.0030	0.002–0.008	3	1.9983–1.9994	0.0010–0.0040	0.0140–0.0270

VALVE SPECIFICATIONS

Year	Engine ID/VIN	Engine Displacement Liters (cc)	Seat Angle (deg.)	Face Angle (deg.)	Spring Test Pressure (lbs. @ in.)	Spring Installed Height (in.)	Stem-to-Guide Clearance (in.)		Stem Diameter (in.)	
							Intake	Exhaust	Intake	Exhaust
1990	G	2.2 (2180)	46	45	208–222① @ 1.22	1.61②	0.0011–0.0026	0.0014–0.0030	NA	NA
	A	2.3 (2262)	45	44	193–207① @ 1.04	1.44②	0.0010–0.0027	0.0015–0.0032	0.274–0.275	0.274–0.275
	T	3.1 (3130)	46	45	90①	1.60②	0.0010–0.0027	0.0010–0.0027	NA	NA
1991	G	2.2 (2180)	46	45	208–222① @ 1.22	1.61②	0.0011–0.0026	0.0014–0.0031	NA	NA
	A	2.3 (2262)	46	45	193–207① @ 1.04	1.44②	0.0010–0.0027	0.0015–0.0032	0.274–0.275	0.274–0.275
	T	3.1 (3130)	46	45	215① @ 1.29	1.57②	0.0010–0.0027	0.0010–0.0027	NA	NA
1992	4	2.2 (2180)	46	45	225–233① @ 1.25	1.64②	0.0011–0.0026	0.0014–0.0031	NA	NA
	A	2.3 (2262)	46	45	193–207① @ 1.04	1.44②	0.0010–0.0027	0.0015–0.0032	0.274–0.275	0.274–0.275
	T	3.1 (3130)	46	45	215① @ 1.29	1.57②	0.0010–0.0027	0.0010–0.0027	NA	NA
1993–94	4	2.2 (2180)	46	45	225–233① @ 1.25	1.64②	0.0011–0.0026	0.0014–0.0031	NA	NA
	A	2.3 (2262)	46	45	193–207① @ 1.04	1.44②	0.0010–0.0027	0.0015–0.0032	0.274–0.275	0.274–0.275
	T	3.1 (3130)	46	45	215① @ 1.29	1.57②	0.0010–0.0027	0.0010–0.0027	NA	NA

NA—Not available
① With valve open
② With valve closed

PISTON AND RING SPECIFICATIONS

All measurements are given in inches.

Year	Engine ID/VIN	Engine Displacement Liters (cc)	Piston Clearance	Ring Gap			Ring Side Clearance		
				Top Compression	Bottom Compression	Oil Control	Top Compression	Bottom Compression	Oil Control
1990	G	2.2 (2180)	0.0007–0.0017	0.010–0.020	0.010–0.020	0.010–0.050	0.002–0.003	0.002–0.003	0.0020–0.0082
	A	2.3 (2262)	0.0007–0.0020	0.014–0.024	0.016–0.026	0.016–0.055	0.003–0.005	0.002–0.003	—
	T	3.1 (3130)	0.0009–0.0022	0.010–0.020	0.020–0.028	0.010–0.030	0.002–0.003	0.002–0.003	0.0080
1991	G	2.2 (2180)	0.0007–0.0017	0.010–0.020	0.010–0.020	0.010–0.050	0.002–0.003	0.002–0.003	0.0020–0.0082
	A	2.3 (2262)	0.0007–0.0020	0.014–0.024	0.016–0.026	0.016–0.055	0.003–0.005	0.002–0.003	—
	T	3.1 (3130)	0.0009–0.0022	0.010–0.020	0.020–0.028	0.010–0.030	0.002–0.003	0.002–0.003	0.0080

PISTON AND RING SPECIFICATIONS

All measurements are given in inches.

Year	Engine ID/VIN	Engine Displacement Liters (cc)	Piston Clearance	Ring Gap			Ring Side Clearance		
				Top Compression	Bottom Compression	Oil Control	Top Compression	Bottom Compression	Oil Control
1992	4	2.2 (2180)	0.0007–0.0017	0.010–0.020	0.010–0.020	0.010–0.050	0.002–0.003	0.002–0.003	0.0020–0.0082
	A	2.3 (2262)	0.0007–0.0020	0.014–0.024	0.016–0.026	0.016–0.055	0.003–0.005	0.002–0.003	—
	T	3.1 (3130)	0.0009–0.0022	0.010–0.020	0.020–0.028	0.010–0.030	0.002–0.003	0.002–0.003	0.0080
1993–94	4	2.2 (2180)	0.0007–0.0017	0.010–0.020	0.010–0.020	0.010–0.050	0.002–0.003	0.002–0.003	0.0020–0.0082
	A	2.3 (2262)	0.0007–0.0020	0.014–0.024	0.016–0.026	0.016–0.055	0.003–0.005	0.002–0.003	—
	T	3.1 (3130)	0.0009–0.0022	0.010–0.020	0.020–0.028	0.010–0.030	0.002–0.003	0.002–0.003	0.0080

TORQUE SPECIFICATIONS

All readings in ft. lbs.

Year	Engine ID/VIN	Engine Displacement Liters (cc)	Cylinder Head Bolts	Main Bearing Bolts	Rod Bearing Bolts	Crankshaft Damper Bolts	Flywheel Bolts	Manifold		Spark Plugs	Lug Nut
								Intake	Exhaust		
1990	G	2.2 (2180)	⑫	70	38	85④	52⑤	18	⑥	11	100
	A	2.3 (2262)	26⑦	15⑧	18⑨	74⑩	22⑪	18⑭	27①	17	100
	T	3.1 (3130)	③	73	39	66–85	45–59②	②	18	20	100
1991	G	2.2 (2180)	⑬	70	38	77④	52⑤	18	⑥	11	100
	A	2.3 (2262)	26⑦	15⑧	18⑨	74⑩	22⑪	18⑭	31①	17	100
	T	3.1 (3130)	③	73	39	76	52	②	18	18	100
1992	4	2.2 (2180)	⑬	70	38	77④	52⑤	22	⑥	11	100
	A	2.3 (2262)	26⑦	15⑧	18⑨	74⑩	22⑪	18⑭	31①	17	100
	T	3.1 (3130)	③	73	39	76	52	②	18	18	100
1993–94	4	2.2 (2180)	⑬	70	38	77④	52⑤	22	⑥	11	100
	A	2.3 (2262)	26⑦	15⑧	18⑨	74⑩	22⑪	18⑭	31①	17	100
	T	3.1 (3130)	③	73	39	76	52	②	18	18	100

① Cylinder head studs—106 inch lbs.
② Tighten all bolts to 15 ft. lbs. Then tighten all bolts to 24 ft. lbs.
③ Cylinder head bolts should first be torqued to 33 ft. lbs. Then tighten the bolts by rotating the torque wrench an additional 90 degrees.
④ Specification is for the crankshaft center bolt. Torque the pulley to hub bolts to 37 ft. lbs.
⑤ Specification is for automatic transaxle. Torque the manual transaxle bolts to 55 ft. lbs.
⑥ Nuts to 115 inch lbs.
   Studs to 89 inch lbs.
⑦ Cylinder head bolts should first be torqued in sequence to 26 ft. lbs. Then tighten the bolts by rotating the torque wrench an additional:
   100 degrees for short bolts.
   110 degrees for long bolts.
⑧ Main bearing bolts should first be torqued to 15 ft. lbs. Then tighten the bolts by rotating the torque wrench an additional 90 degrees.

⑨ Connecting rod bolts should first be torqued to 18 ft. lbs. Then tighten the bolts by rotating the torque wrench an additional 80 degrees.
⑩ Crankshaft balancer to crankshaft bolt should first be torqued to 74 ft. lbs. Then tighten an additional 90 degrees.
⑪ Flywheel bolts should first be torqued to 22 ft. lbs. Then tighten an additional 45 degrees.
⑫ Tighten all bolts in sequence to 41 ft. lbs. Then tighten all bolts 45 degrees in sequence. Then tighten all bolts an additional 45 degrees in sequence.
   Then tighten the long bolts (8, 4, 1 5 & 9) an additional 20 degrees and the short bolts (7, 3, 2, 6 & 10) an additional 10 degrees.
⑬ Tighten all bolts in sequence to: long bolts (8, 4, 1, 5 & 9) to 46 ft. lbs. amd short bolts (7, 3, 2, 6 & 10) to 43 ft. lbs. Then tighten all bolts an additional 90 degrees in sequence.
⑭ Cylinder head studs—96 inch lbs.

TORQUE SPECIFICATIONS

Component	English	Metric
Camshaft sprocket bolt		
2.2L engine:	77 ft. lbs.	105 Nm
2.3L engine:	40 ft. lbs.	54 Nm
2.8L engine:	18 ft. lbs.	25 Nm
3.1L engine:	21 ft. lbs.	28 Nm
Connecting rod bearing cap bolts		
2.2L engine:	38 ft. lbs.	52 Nm
2.3L engine		
Step 1:	18 ft. lbs.	25 Nm
Step 2:	+ 80 degrees turn	+ 80 degrees turn
2.8L engine:	37 ft. lbs.	50 Nm
3.1L engine:	39 ft. lbs.	53 Nm
Crankshaft damper bolt		
2.2L engine:	77 ft. lbs.	105 Nm
2.3L engine		
Step 1:	74 ft. lbs.	100 Nm
Step 2:	+ 90 degrees turn	+ 90 degrees turn
2.8L and 3.1L engines:	77 ft. lbs.	105 Nm
Cylinder head		
2.2L engine		
Long bolts:	46 ft. lbs.	63 Nm
Short bolts:	43 ft. lbs.	58 Nm
All bolts:	+ 90 degrees turn	+ 90 degrees turn
2.3L engine		
1990–91		
Step 1 (all bolts):	26 ft. lbs.	35 Nm
Step 2 (long bolts):	+ 110 degrees turn	+ 110 degrees turn
Step 3 (short bolts):	+ 100 degrees turn	+ 100 degrees turn
1992–94		
Step 1 (bolts 1–6):	26 ft. lbs.	35 Nm
Step 2 (bolts 7 & 8):	15 ft. lbs.	20 Nm
Step 3 (bolts 9 & 10):	22 ft. lbs.	30 Nm
2.8L and 3.1L engines		
Step 1:	33 ft. lbs.	45 Nm
Step 2:	+ 90 degrees turn	+ 90 degrees turn
EGR valve-to-intake plenum		
2.2L engine:	16 ft. lbs.	22 Nm
2.8L engine:	19 ft. lbs.	25 Nm
3.1L and 3.4L engines:	22 ft. lbs.	30 Nm
Engine-to-transmission:	55 ft. lbs.	75 Nm
Exhaust manifold		
2.2L engine:	115 inch lbs.	13 Nm
2.3L engine		
Nuts:	31 ft. lbs.	42 Nm
Studs:	106 inch lbs.	12 Nm
2.8L and 3.1L engines:	19 ft. lbs.	25 Nm
Exhaust pipe-to-exhaust manifold nuts:	19 ft. lbs.	25 Nm
Flywheel/flexplate-to-crankshaft bolts		
2.2L engine		
Automatic transmission:	52 ft. lbs.	70 Nm
Manual transmission:	55 ft. lbs.	75 Nm
2.3L engine		
Step 1:	22 ft. lbs.	30 Nm
Step 2:	+ 45 degrees turn	+ 45 degrees turn
2.8L and 3.1L engines:	52 ft. lbs.	70 Nm
Flywheel-to-converter bolt:	46 ft. lbs.	62 Nm

TORQUE SPECIFICATIONS

Component	English	Metric
Intake manifold-to-cylinder head		
2.2L and 2.3L engines:	18 ft. lbs.	25 Nm
2.8L and 3.1L engines		
Upper manifold:	16 ft. lbs.	21 Nm
Lower manifold		
Step 1:	15 ft. lbs.	20 Nm
Step 2:	24 ft. lbs.	33 Nm
Main bearing cap bolts		
2.2L and 2.8L engines:	70 ft. lbs.	95 Nm
2.3L engine		
Step 1:	15 ft. lbs.	23 Nm
Step 2:	+ 90 degrees turn	+ 90 degrees turn
3.1L engine:	73 ft. lbs.	99 Nm
Oil pan		
2.2L engine:	72 inch lbs.	8 Nm
2.3L engine		
M6 x 1.0 x 25:	106 inch lbs.	12 Nm
M8 x 1.25 x 25:	18 ft. lbs.	24 Nm
2.8L engine		
Rear bolts (2):	18 ft. lbs.	25 Nm
Studs:	13 ft. lbs.	17 Nm
All other bolts:	89 inch lbs.	10 Nm
3.1L engine		
Rear bolts (2):	18 ft. lbs.	25 Nm
All other bolts:	71 inch lbs.	8 Nm
Oil pan drain plug		
All except 1992–94 2.2L:	19 ft. lbs.	26 Nm
1992–94 2.2L:	35 ft. lbs.	45 Nm
Oil pump attaching bolts		
2.2L engines:	32 ft. lbs.	43 Nm
2.3L engine:	40 ft. lbs.	54 Nm
2.8L and 3.1L engines:	30 ft. lbs.	41 Nm
Pressure plate-to-flywheel		
2.8L engine:	15 ft. lbs.	20 Nm
2.2L and 3.1L engines:	18 ft. lbs.	25 Nm
2.3L engine:	22 ft. lbs.	30 Nm
Rocker arm pivot bolt		
2.2L engine:	22 ft. lbs.	30 Nm
2.8L and 3.1L engines:	18 ft. lbs.	25 Nm
Rocker (valve) cover		
2.2L engine:	89 inch lbs.	10 Nm
2.3L engine		
Except 2 intake-side rear bolts (short)		
Step 1:	11 ft. lbs.	15 Nm
Step 2:	+ 75 degrees turn	+ 75 degrees turn
2 intake side rear bolts (short)		
Step 1:	16 ft. lbs.	22 Nm
Step 2:	+ 25 degrees turn	+ 25 degrees turn
2.8L and 3.1L engines:	89 inch lbs.	10 Nm
Spark plug		
2.2L engine:	11 ft. lbs.	15 Nm
2.3L engine:	17 ft. lbs.	22 Nm
2.8L and 3.1L engines:	20 ft. lbs.	27 Nm
Starter-to-block bolts		
2.2L engine:	32 ft. lbs.	43 Nm
2.3L engine		
Motor-to-starter bolt:	71 ft. lbs.	96 Nm
Transaxle-to-starter bolt:	71 ft. lbs.	96 Nm
2.8L and 3.1L engines:	32 ft. lbs.	43 Nm

TORQUE SPECIFICATIONS

Component	English	Metric
Thermostat housing		
2.2L engine:	89 inch lbs.	10 Nm
2.3L engine:	19 ft. lbs.	26 Nm
2.8L and 3.1L engines:	18 ft. lbs.	25 Nm
TBI-to-fuel meter body screws:	31 inch lbs.	3.5 Nm
TBI fuel feed/return line:	33 ft. lbs.	45 Nm
TBI mounting bolts/nuts:	18 ft. lbs.	25 Nm
Timing cover		
2.2L engine:	97 ft. lbs.	11 Nm
2.3L engine:	106 inch lbs.	12 Nm
Water pump		
2.2L engine:	22 ft. lbs.	30 Nm
2.3L engine		
Studs and nuts::	19 ft. lbs.	26 Nm
Water pump cover-to-body:	125 inch lbs.	14 Nm
Water pump cover-to-engine block:	19 ft. lbs.	26 Nm
2.8L and 3.1L engines:	89 inch lbs.	10 Nm
Water pump pulley		
2.2L engine:	22 ft. lbs.	30 Nm
2.8L and 3.1L engines:	18 ft. lbs.	25 Nm

BRAKE SPECIFICATIONS

All measurements in inches unless noted.

Year	Model	Master Cylinder Bore	Brake Disc Original Thickness	Brake Disc Minimum Thickness	Brake Disc Maximum Runout	Brake Drum Diameter Original Inside Diameter	Brake Drum Diameter Max. Wear Limit	Brake Drum Diameter Maximum Machine Diameter	Minimum Lining Thickness Front	Minimum Lining Thickness Rear
1990	Beretta	0.875	0.885	0.830	0.004	7.879	7.929	7.899	3/32	3/32
	Corsica	0.875	0.885	0.830	0.004	7.879	7.929	7.899	3/32	3/32
1991	Beretta	0.875	0.885	0.830	0.004	7.879	7.929	7.899	3/32	3/32
	Corsica	0.875	0.885	0.830	0.004	7.879	7.929	7.899	3/32	3/32
1992	Beretta	0.874	0.806	0.736	0.003	7.879	7.929	7.899	3/32	3/32
	Corsica	0.874	0.806	0.736	0.003	7.879	7.929	7.899	3/32	3/32
1993-94	Beretta	0.874	0.806	0.736	0.003	7.879	7.929	7.899	3/32	3/32
	Corsica	0.874	0.806	0.736	0.003	7.879	7.929	7.899	3/32	3/32

WHEEL ALIGNMENT

Year	Model		Caster Range (deg.)	Caster Preferred Setting (deg.)	Camber Range (deg.)	Camber Preferred Setting (deg.)	Toe-in (in.)	Steering Axis Inclination (deg.)
1990	Beretta	Front	2/5P–19/10P	13/20P	0–12/10P	6/10P	0	—
		Rear	—	—	9/10N–4/10P	1/4N	5/16P	—
	Corsica	Front	2/5P–19/10P	13/20P	0–12/10P	6/10P	0	—
		Rear	—	—	8/10N–3/10P	1/4N	1/4P	—

WHEEL ALIGNMENT

Year	Model		Caster Range (deg.)	Caster Preferred Setting (deg.)	Camber Range (deg.)	Camber Preferred Setting (deg.)	Toe-in (in.)	Steering Axis Inclination (deg.)
1991	Beretta	Front	$2/5$P–$1^9/_{10}$P	$1^3/_{20}$P	②	③	①	14
		Rear	—	—	$^{13}/_{16}$N–$^5/_{16}$P	$^1/_4$N	$^1/_{16}$P	—
	Corsica	Front	$2/5$P–$1^9/_{10}$P	$1^3/_{20}$P	②	③	①	14
		Rear	—	—	$^7/_8$N–$^3/_8$P	$^1/_4$N	$^3/_{16}$P	—
1992	Beretta	Front	$2/5$P–$1^9/_{10}$P	$1^3/_{20}$P	②	③	①	14
		Rear	—	—	$^{13}/_{16}$N–$^5/_{16}$P	$^1/_4$N	$^1/_{16}$P	—
	Corsica	Front	$2/5$P–$1^9/_{10}$P	$1^3/_{20}$P	②	③	①	14
		Rear	—	—	$^7/_8$N–$^3/_8$P	$^1/_4$N	$^3/_{16}$P	—
1993–94	Beretta	Front	$2/5$P–$1^9/_{10}$P	$1^3/_{20}$P	②	③	①	14
		Rear	—	—	$^{13}/_{16}$N–$^5/_{16}$P	$^1/_4$N	$^1/_{16}$P	—
	Corsica	Front	$2/5$P–$1^9/_{10}$P	$1^3/_{20}$P	②	③	①	14
		Rear	—	—	$^7/_8$N–$^3/_8$P	$^1/_4$N	$^3/_{16}$P	—

N—Negative
P—Positive
① Not adjustable
② Except Beretta GTZ and Corsica w/Sport
   Susp.: $^9/_{16}$P–$^{13}/_{16}$P
   Beretta GTZ and Corsica w/Sport
   Susp.: $^{13}/_{16}$N–$^7/_{16}$P

③ Except Beretta GTZ and Corsica w/Sport
   Susp.: $^1/_8$P
   Beretta GTZ and Corsica w/Sport
   Susp.: $^{13}/_{16}$N

REFRIGERANT CAPACITIES

Year	Model	Refrigerant (oz.)	Oil (fl. oz.)	Compressor Type
1990	Beretta, Corsica	36.0	8.0	V-5
1991	Beretta, Corsica	36.0	8.0	V-5
1992	Beretta, Corsica	42.0	8.0	V-5
1993	Beretta, Corsica	42.0	8.0	V-5

NOTE: At the time of publication, refrigerant capacity information relating to R-134a was not available from the manufacturer.

AIR CONDITIONING BELT TENSION

Year	Engine VIN	Engine Displacement Liters (cc)	Belt Type	Specifications New	Specifications Used
1990	G	2.2 (2198)	Serpentine	63–77 ①	
	A	2.3 (2263)	Serpentine	50 ①	
	T	3.1 (3149)	Serpentine	50–70 ①	
1991	G	2.2 (2198)	Serpentine	63–77 ①	
	A	2.3 (2263)	Serpentine	50 ①	
	T	3.1 (3149)	Serpentine	50–70 ①	
1992	4	2.2 (2198)	Serpentine	67–77 ①	
	A	2.3 (2263)	Serpentine	50 ①	
	T	3.1 (3149)	Serpentine	50–70 ①	

AIR CONDITIONING BELT TENSION

Year	Engine VIN	Engine Displacement Liters (cc)	Belt Type	Specifications	
				New	Used
1993–94	4	2.2 (2198)	Serpentine	67–77 ①	
	A	2.3 (2263)	Serpentine	50 ①	
	T	3.1 (3149)	Serpentine	50–70 ①	

① Equipped with automatic tensioner; however, the specification given (in pounds) is for testing whether the tensioner is maintaining its proper tension (specification given is the average of 3 readings back-to-back).

MAINTENANCE INTERVALS—TYPE A: NORMAL SERVICE
Corsica • Beretta

TO BE SERVICED	TYPE OF SERVICE	VEHICLE MILEAGE INTERVAL (X1000)							
		7.5	15	22.5	30	37.5	45	52.5	60
Oxygen Sensor	I				✔				✔
Engine Oil Filter	R①	✔		✔		✔	✔		
Vacuum Lines and Hoses	I				✔				✔
Ignition Wires	I				✔				✔
Spark Plugs	R								✔
Engine Oil	R	✔	✔	✔	✔	✔	✔	✔	✔
Engine Air Cleaner Element	R				✔				✔
Crankcase Emission Filter	R				✔				✔
PCV Valve	R				✔				✔
Fuel Filter	R				✔				✔
Tire Rotation	I②	✔		✔		✔		✔	
Fuel/Vapor Return Lines	I				✔				✔
Fuel Tank Cap and Restrictor	I				✔				✔
Coolant System	R				✔				✔
Exhaust Pipe and Muffler	I				✔				✔
Chassis Lubrication	L	✔	✔	✔	✔	✔	✔	✔	✔
Catalytic Converter and Shield	I				✔				✔
EGR System	I				✔				✔
Battery Connections	I		✔		✔		✔		✔
Automatic Transaxle Fluid	R③								
Coolant Hoses and Bolts	I				✔		✔		✔
Brake Linings	I		✔		✔		✔		✔
Idle Speed System and Linkage	I				✔				✔
Throttle Body Mounting Torque	I	✔							
Drive Belts	I				✔				✔
CV-Joints and Boots	I	✔	✔	✔	✔	✔	✔	✔	✔
Parking Brake	I④	✔			✔		✔		✔
Seat Belt Operation	I		✔		✔		✔		✔

FOR COMPLETE WARRANTY COVERAGE CONSULT INDIVIDUAL VEHICLE MANUFACTURER'S WARRANTY MAINTENANCE GUIDE.

I—Inspect
L—Lubricate
R—Replace
① Replace oil filter at first oil change and then every other oil change

② Rotate tires at 7,500 miles and then every 15,000 miles
③ Replace transmission fluid and filter at 100,000 miles

④ Check, adjust and lubricate cables and mechanism as necessary

MAINTENANCE INTERVALS—TYPE B: SEVERE SERVICE
Corsica • Beretta

TO BE SERVICED	TYPE OF SERVICE	VEHICLE MILEAGE INTERVAL (X1000)									
		3	6	9	12	15	18	21	24	27	30
Oxygen Sensor	I										✔
Vacuum Lines and Hoses	I										✔
Ignition Wires	I										✔
Spark Plugs	I										✔
Engine Oil and Filter	R	✔	✔	✔	✔	✔	✔	✔	✔	✔	✔
Engine Air Cleaner Element	R					✔					✔
Crankcase Emission Filter	R										✔
PCV Valve	R										✔
Fuel Filter	R					✔					✔
Tire Rotation	I①										
Fuel/Vapor Return Lines	I										✔
Fuel Tank Cap and Restrictor	I										✔
Coolant System	R										✔
Exhaust Pipe and Muffler	I										✔
Chassis Lubrication	L		✔		✔		✔		✔		
Catalytic Converter and Shield	I										✔
EGR System	I										✔
Battery Connections	I					✔					✔
Automatic Transaxle Fluid	R					✔					✔
Coolant Hoses and Clamps	I					✔					✔
Brake Linings	I					✔					✔
Idle Speed System and Linkage	I										✔
Throttle Body Mounting Torque	I		✔								
Drive Belts	I										✔
CV-Joints and Boots	I		✔		✔		✔		✔		✔
Parking Brake	I②					✔					✔
Seat Belt Operation	I					✔					✔

FOR COMPLETE WARRANTY COVERAGE CONSULT INDIVIDUAL VEHICLE MANUFACTURER'S WARRANTY MAINTENANCE GUIDE.

I—Inspect
L—Lubricate
R—Replace
① Rotate tires at 6,000 miles and then every 15,000 miles
② Check, adjust and lubricate cables and mechanism as necessary

FIRING ORDERS

NOTE: To avoid confusion, always replace spark plugs and wires one at a time.

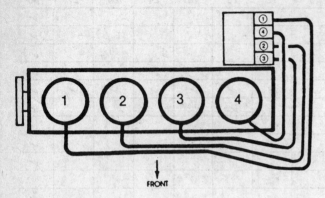

2.2L Engine
Engine Firing Order: 1-3-4-2
Distributorless Ignition System

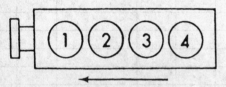

2.3L Engine
Engine Firing Order: 1-3-4-2
Distributorless Ignition System

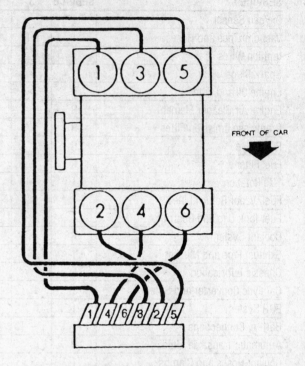

FRONT OF CAR

3.1L Engine
Engine Firing Order: 1-2-3-4-5-6
Distributorless Ignition System

CYLINDER HEAD TORQUE SEQUENCES

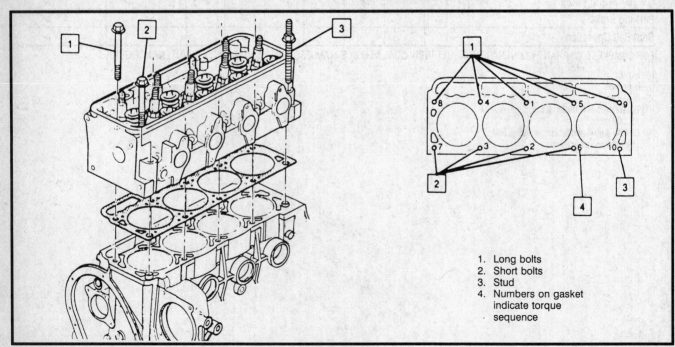

1. Long bolts
2. Short bolts
3. Stud
4. Numbers on gasket indicate torque sequence

Cylinder head bolt torque sequence—1991–94 2.2L engine

CYLINDER HEAD TORQUE SEQUENCES

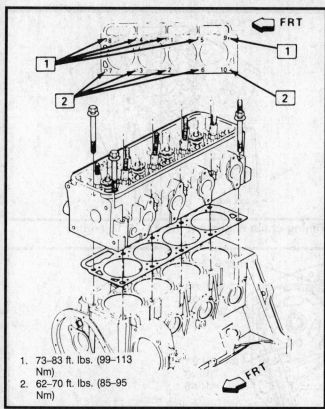

1. 73–83 ft. lbs. (99–113 Nm)
2. 62–70 ft. lbs. (85–95 Nm)

Cylinder head bolt torque sequence—1990 2.2L engine

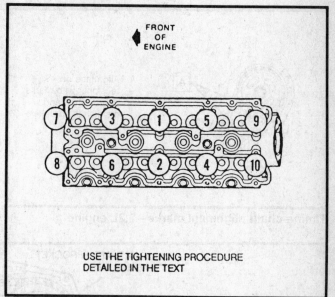

USE THE TIGHTENING PROCEDURE DETAILED IN THE TEXT

Cylinder head bolt torque sequence—1992–94 2.3L engine

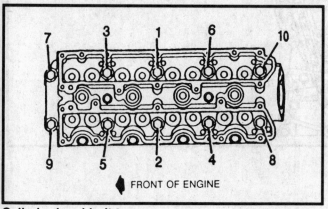

Cylinder head bolt torque sequence—1990–91 2.3L engine

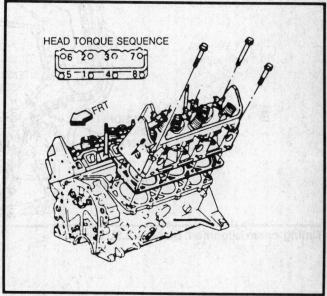

Cylinder head bolt torque sequence—3.1L engine

TIMING CHAIN ALIGNMENT MARKS

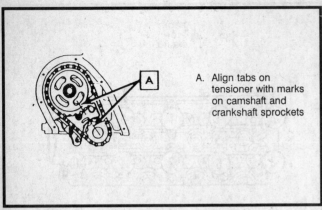

A. Align tabs on tensioner with marks on camshaft and crankshaft sprockets

Timing chain alignment marks—2.2L engine

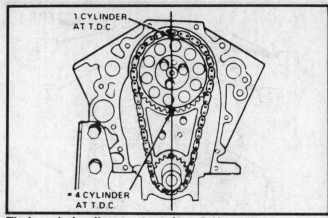

Timing chain alignment marks—3.1L engine

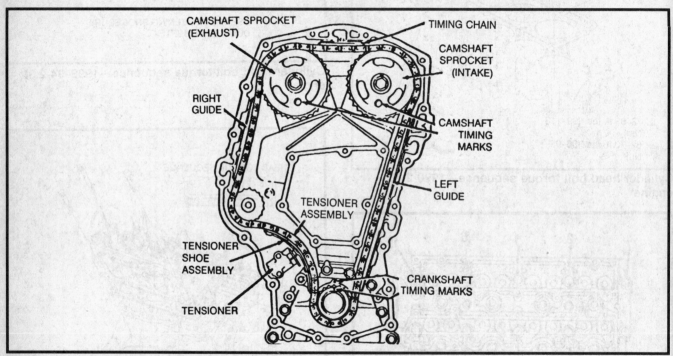

Timing chain alignment marks—2.3L engine

AIR CONDITIONING SERVICE VALVE LOCATIONS

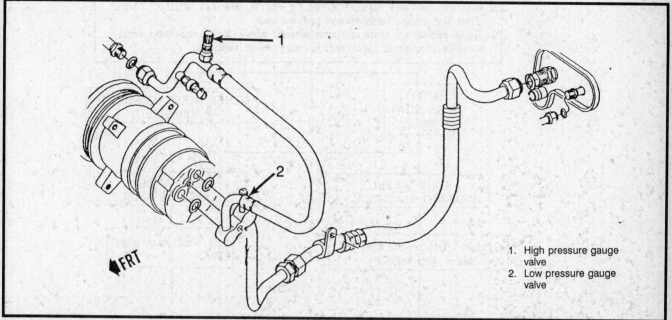

1. High pressure gauge valve
2. Low pressure gauge valve

Air conditioning service valve location

WHEEL ALIGNMENT ADJUSTMENT LOCATIONS

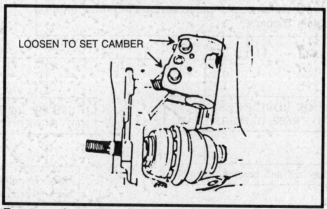

LOOSEN TO SET CAMBER

Front camber adjustment

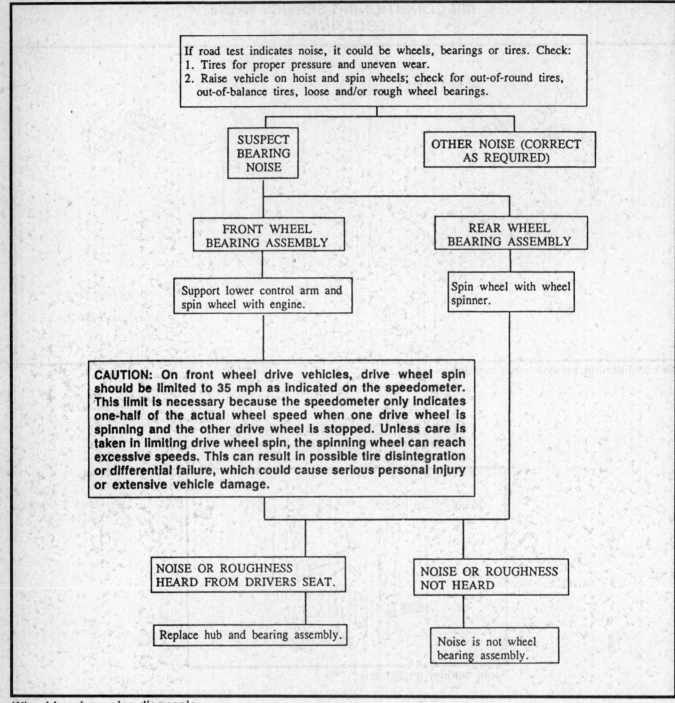

If road test indicates noise, it could be wheels, bearings or tires. Check:
1. Tires for proper pressure and uneven wear.
2. Raise vehicle on hoist and spin wheels; check for out-of-round tires, out-of-balance tires, loose and/or rough wheel bearings.

SUSPECT BEARING NOISE

OTHER NOISE (CORRECT AS REQUIRED)

FRONT WHEEL BEARING ASSEMBLY

REAR WHEEL BEARING ASSEMBLY

Support lower control arm and spin wheel with engine.

Spin wheel with wheel spinner.

CAUTION: On front wheel drive vehicles, drive wheel spin should be limited to 35 mph as indicated on the speedometer. This limit is necessary because the speedometer only indicates one-half of the actual wheel speed when one drive wheel is spinning and the other drive wheel is stopped. Unless care is taken in limiting drive wheel spin, the spinning wheel can reach excessive speeds. This can result in possible tire disintegration or differential failure, which could cause serious personal injury or extensive vehicle damage.

NOISE OR ROUGHNESS HEARD FROM DRIVERS SEAT.

NOISE OR ROUGHNESS NOT HEARD

Replace hub and bearing assembly.

Noise is not wheel bearing assembly.

Wheel bearing noise diagnosis

SPECIFICATION CHARTS

VEHICLE IDENTIFICATION CHART

It is important for servicing and ordering parts to be certain of the vehicle and engine identification. The VIN (vehicle identification number) is a 17 digit number visible through the windshield on the driver's side of the dash and contains the vehicle and engine identification codes. The tenth digit indicates model year and the eighth digit indicates engine code. It can be interpreted as follows:

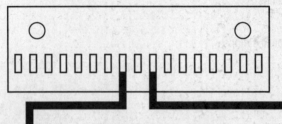

Engine Code						Model Year	
Code	Liters	Cu. In. (cc)	Cyl.	Fuel Sys.	Eng. Mfg.	Code	Year
A	2.3 HO	138 (2262)	4	PFI	Oldsmobile	L	1990
D	2.3	138 (2262)	4	PFI	Oldsmobile	M	1991
U	2.5	151 (2475)	4	TBI	Pontiac	N	1992
N	3.3	204 (3344)	6	PFI	Buick	P	1993
3	2.3	138 (2262)	4	PFI	Oldsmobile	R	1994
T	3.1	191 (3137)	6	PFI	Pontiac		

HO—High Output
PFI—Port Fuel Injection
TBI—Throttle Body Injection

ENGINE IDENTIFICATION

Year	Model	Engine Displacement Liters (cc)	Engine Series (ID/VIN)	Fuel System	No. of Cylinders	Engine Type
1990	Grand Am	2.3 (2262)	D	PFI	4	DOHC
	Grand Am	2.3 (2262)	A	PFI	4	DOHC-HO
	Grand Am	2.5 (2475)	U	TBI	4	OHV
	Calais	2.3 (2262)	D	PFI	4	DOHC
	Calais	2.3 (2262)	A	PFI	4	DOHC-HO
	Calais	2.5 (2475)	U	TBI	4	OHV
	Calais	3.3 (3344)	N	PFI	6	OHV
	Skylark	2.3 (2262)	D	PFI	4	DOHC
	Skylark	2.5 (2475)	U	TBI	4	OHV
	Skylark	3.3 (3344)	N	PFI	6	OHV
1991	Grand Am	2.3 (2262)	D	PFI	4	DOHC
	Grand Am	2.3 (2262)	A	PFI	4	DOHC-HO
	Grand Am	2.5 (2475)	U	TBI	4	OHV
	Calais	2.3 (2262)	D	PFI	4	DOHC
	Calais	2.3 (2262)	A	PFI	4	DOHC-HO
	Calais	2.5 (2475)	U	TBI	4	OHV
	Calais	3.3 (3344)	N	PFI	6	OHV
	Skylark	2.3 (2262)	D	PFI	4	DOHC
	Skylark	2.5 (2475)	U	TBI	4	OHV
	Skylark	3.3 (3344)	N	PFI	6	OHV

ENGINE IDENTIFICATION

Year	Model	Engine Displacement Liters (cc)	Engine Series (ID/VIN)	Fuel System	No. of Cylinders	Engine Type
1992	Grand Am	2.3 (2262)	D	PFI	4	DOHC
	Grand Am	2.3 (2262)	A	PFI	4	DOHC-HO
	Grand Am	2.3 (2262)	3	PFI	4	SOHC
	Grand Am	3.3 (3344)	N	PFI	6	OHV
	Achieva	2.3 (2262)	D	PFI	4	DOHC
	Achieva	2.3 (2262)	A	PFI	4	DOHC-HO
	Achieva	2.3 (2262)	3	PFI	4	SOHC
	Achieva	3.3 (3344)	N	PFI	6	OHV
	Skylark	2.3 (2262)	3	PFI	4	SOHC
	Skylark	3.3 (3344)	N	PFI	6	OHV
1993-94	Grand Am	2.3 (2262)	D	PFI	4	DOHC
	Grand Am	2.3 (2262)	A	PFI	4	DOHC-HO
	Grand Am	2.3 (2262)	3	PFI	4	SOHC
	Grand Am	3.3 (3344)	N	PFI	6	OHV
	Grand Am	3.1 (3137) ①	T	PFI	6	OHV
	Achieva	2.3 (2262)	D	PFI	4	DOHC
	Achieva	2.3 (2262)	A	PFI	4	DOHC-HO
	Achieva	2.3 (2262)	3	PFI	4	SOHC
	Achieva	3.3 (3344)	N	PFI	6	OHV
	Achieva	3.1 (3137)	T	PFI	6	OHV
	Skylark	2.3 (2262)	3	PFI	4	SOHC
	Skylark	3.3 (3344)	N	PFI	6	OHV
	Skylark	3.1 (3137) ①	T	PFI	6	OHV

DOHC—Double Overhead Cam
HO—High Output
OHC—Overhad Cam
OHV—Overhead Valve
PFI—Port Fuel Injection
TBI—Throttle Body Injection
① 1994 only

GENERAL ENGINE SPECIFICATIONS

Year	Engine ID/VIN	Engine Displacement Liters (cc)	Fuel System Type	Net Horsepower @ rpm	Net Torque @ rpm (ft. lbs.)	Bore × Stroke (in.)	Compression Ratio	Oil Pressure @ rpm
1990	A	2.3 (2262)	PFI	180 @ 6200	160 @ 5200	3.62 × 3.35	10.0:1	30 @ 2000
	D	2.3 (2262)	PFI	160 @ 6200	155 @ 5200	3.62 × 3.35	9.5:1	30 @ 2000
	U	2.5 (2475)	TBI	110 @ 5200	135 @ 3200	4.00 × 3.00	8.3:1	37 @ 2000
	N	3.3 (3344)	PFI	160 @ 5200	185 @ 3200	3.70 × 3.16	9.0:1	45 @ 2000
1991	A	2.3 (2262)	PFI	180 @ 6200	160 @ 5200	3.62 × 3.35	10.0:1	30 @ 2000
	D	2.3 (2262)	PFI	160 @ 6200	155 @ 5200	3.62 × 3.35	9.5:1	30 @ 2000
	U	2.5 (2475)	TBI	110 @ 5200	135 @ 3200	4.00 × 3.00	8.3:1	26 @ 800
	N	3.3 (3344)	PFI	160 @ 5200	185 @ 3200	3.70 × 3.16	9.0:1	60 @ 1850

GENERAL ENGINE SPECIFICATIONS

Year	Engine ID/VIN	Engine Displacement Liters (cc)	Fuel System Type	Net Horsepower @ rpm	Net Torque @ rpm (ft. lbs.)	Bore × Stroke (in.)	Compression Ratio	Oil Pressure @ rpm
1992	A	2.3 (2262)	PFI	180 @ 6200	160 @ 5200	3.62 × 3.35	10.0:1	30 @ 2000
	D	2.3 (2262)	PFI	160 @ 6200	155 @ 5200	3.62 × 3.35	9.5:1	30 @ 2000
	3	2.3 (2262)	PFI	120 @ 5200	140 @ 3200	3.62 × 3.35	9.5:1	30 @ 2000
	N	3.3 (3344)	PFI	160 @ 5200	185 @ 2000	3.70 × 3.16	9.0:1	60 @ 1850
1993-94	A	2.3 (2262)	PFI	175 @ 6200	155 @ 5200	3.63 × 3.35	10.0:1	30 @ 2000
	D	2.3 (2262)	PFI	155 @ 6000	150 @ 4800	3.63 × 3.35	9.5:1	30 @ 2000
	3	2.3 (2262)	PFI	115 @ 5200	140 @ 3200	3.63 × 3.35	9.5:1	30 @ 2000
	N	3.3 (3344)	PFI	160 @ 5200	185 @ 2000	3.70 × 3.16	9.0:1	60 @ 1850
	T	3.1 (3137)	PFI	155 @ 5200	185 @ 4000	3.50 × 3.30	9.5:1	NA

NA—Not available
PFI—Port Fuel Injection
TBI—Throttle Body Injection

GASOLINE ENGINE TUNE-UP SPECIFICATIONS

Year	Engine ID/VIN	Engine Displacement Liters (cc)	Spark Plugs Gap (in.)	Ignition Timing (deg.) MT	Ignition Timing (deg.) AT	Fuel Pump (psi)	Idle Speed (rpm) MT	Idle Speed (rpm) AT	Valve Clearance In.	Valve Clearance Ex.
1990	A	2.3 (2262)	0.035	③	③	②	①	①	Hyd.	Hyd.
	D	2.3 (2262)	0.035	③	③	②	①	①	Hyd.	Hyd.
	U	2.5 (2475)	0.060	③	③	9–13	①	①	Hyd.	Hyd.
	N	3.3 (3344)	0.060	—	③	②	—	①	Hyd.	Hyd.
1991	A	2.3 (2262)	0.035	③	③	②	①	①	Hyd.	Hyd.
	D	2.3 (2262)	0.035	③	③	②	①	①	Hyd.	Hyd.
	U	2.5 (2475)	0.060	③	③	9–13	①	①	Hyd.	Hyd.
	N	3.3 (3344)	0.060	—	③	②	—	①	Hyd.	Hyd.
1992	A	2.3 (2262)	0.035	③	③	②	①	①	Hyd.	Hyd.
	D	2.3 (2262)	0.035	③	③	②	①	①	Hyd.	Hyd.
	3	2.3 (2262)	0.035	③	③	②	①	①	Hyd.	Hyd.
	N	3.3 (3344)	0.060	—	③	②	—	①	Hyd.	Hyd.
1993	A	2.3 (2262)	0.035	③	③	②	①	①	Hyd.	Hyd.
	D	2.3 (2262)	0.035	③	③	②	①	①	Hyd.	Hyd.
	3	2.3 (2262)	0.035	③	③	②	①	①	Hyd.	Hyd.
	N	3.3 (3344)	0.060	—	③	②	—	①	Hyd.	Hyd.
1994			SEE UNDERHOOD SPECIFICATIONS STICKER							

NOTE: The lowest cylinder pressure should be within 75% of the highest cylinder pressure reading. For example, if the highest cylinder is 134 psi, the lowest should be 101. Engine should be at normal operating temperature with throttle valve in the wide open position.

The underhood specifications sticker often reflects tune-up specification changes in production. Sticker figures must be used if they disagree with those in this chart.

Hyd.—Hydraulic

① Idle speed is controlled by the ECM and is not adjustable

② 1—Connect fuel pressure guage, engine at normal operating temperature.
2—Turn ignition switch on.
3—After approx. 2 seconds; pressure should read 41–47 psi and hold steady.
4—Start engine and idle; pressure should drop 3–10 psi from static pressure.

③ Ignition timing is controlled by the ECM and is not adjustable

CAPACITIES

Year	Model	Engine ID/VIN	Engine Displacement Liters (cc)	Engine Crankcase with Filter (qts.) ①	Transmission (pts.) 4-Spd	5-Spd	Auto. ②	Transfer case (pts.)	Drive Axle Front (pts.)	Rear (pts.)	Fuel Tank (gal.)	Cooling System (qts.)
1990	Grand Am	A	2.3 (2262)	4	—	4	—	—	—	—	13.6	8
	Grand Am	D	2.3 (2262)	4	—	4	8	—	—	—	13.6	8
	Grand Am	U	2.5 (2475)	4	—	4	8	—	—	—	13.6	8
	Calais	A	2.3 (2262)	4	—	4	—	—	—	—	13.6	8
	Calais	D	2.3 (2262)	4	—	4	8	—	—	—	13.6	8
	Calais	U	2.5 (2475)	4	—	4	8	—	—	—	13.6	8
	Calais	N	3.3 (3344)	4	—	—	8	—	—	—	13.6	10
	Skylark	D	2.3 (2262)	4	—	—	8	—	—	—	13.6	8
	Skylark	U	2.5 (2475)	4	—	—	8	—	—	—	13.6	8
	Skylark	N	3.3 (3344)	4	—	—	8	—	—	—	13.6	10
1991	Grand Am	A	2.3 (2262)	4	—	4	8	—	—	—	13.6	10.4
	Grand Am	D	2.3 (2262)	4	—	4	8	—	—	—	13.6	10.4
	Grand Am	U	2.5 (2475)	4	—	4	8	—	—	—	13.6	10.7
	Calais	A	2.3 (2262)	4	—	4	—	—	—	—	13.6	10.4
	Calais	D	2.3 (2262)	4	—	4	8	—	—	—	13.6	10.4
	Calais	U	2.5 (2475)	4	—	4	8	—	—	—	13.6	10.7
	Calais	N	3.3 (3344)	4	—	—	8	—	—	—	13.6	12.7
	Skylark	D	2.3 (2262)	4	—	—	8	—	—	—	13.6	10.4
	Skylark	U	2.5 (2475)	4	—	—	8	—	—	—	13.6	10.7
	Skylark	N	3.3 (3344)	4	—	—	8	—	—	—	13.6	12.7
1992	Grand Am	D	2.3 (2262)	4	—	4	8	—	—	—	15.2	9.5
	Grand Am	A	2.3 (2262)	4	—	4	8	—	—	—	15.2	9.5
	Grand Am	3	2.3 (2262)	4	—	4	8	—	—	—	15.2	9.5
	Grand Am	N	3.3 (3344)	4	—	—	8	—	—	—	15.2	12.7
	Achieva	D	2.3 (2262)	4	—	—	8	—	—	—	15.2	9.5
	Achieva	A	2.3 (2262)	4	—	4	8	—	—	—	15.2	9.5
	Achieva	3	2.3 (2262)	4	—	4	8	—	—	—	15.2	9.5
	Achieva	N	3.3 (3344)	4	—	—	8	—	—	—	15.2	9.5
	Skylark	3	2.3 (2262)	4	—	—	8	—	—	—	15.2	9.5
	Skylark	N	3.3 (3344)	4	—	—	8	—	—	—	15.2	12.7
1993–94	Grand Am	D	2.3 (2262)	4	—	4	8	—	—	—	15.2	③
	Grand Am	A	2.3 (2262)	4	—	4	8	—	—	—	15.2	③
	Grand Am	3	2.3 (2262)	4	—	4	8	—	—	—	15.2	③
	Grand Am	N	3.3 (3344)	4	—	4	8	—	—	—	15.2	③
	Grand Am	T	3.1 (3137)	4	—	—	8	—	—	—	15.2	10.4
	Achieva	A	2.3 (2262)	4	—	4	8	—	—	—	15.2	③
	Achieva	D	2.3 (2262)	4	—	4	8	—	—	—	15.2	③
	Achieva	3	2.3 (2262)	4	—	4	8	—	—	—	15.2	③
	Achieva	N	3.3 (3344)	4	—	4	8	—	—	—	15.2	③
	Achieva	T	3.1 (3137)	4	—	—	8	—	—	—	15.2	10.4

CAPACITIES

Year	Model	Engine ID/VIN	Engine Displacement Liters (cc)	Engine Crankcase with Filter (qts.)①	Transmission (pts.) 4-Spd	Transmission (pts.) 5-Spd	Transmission (pts.) Auto.②	Transfer case (pts.)	Drive Axle Front (pts.)	Drive Axle Rear (pts.)	Fuel Tank (gal.)	Cooling System (qts.)
1993-94	Skylark	3	2.3 (2262)	4	—	4	8	—	—	—	15.2	③
	Skylark	N	3.3 (3344)	4	—	4	8	—	—	—	15.2	③
	Skylark	T	3.1 (3137)	4	—	—	8	—	—	—	15.2	10.4

① When changing the oil filter, additional oil may be needed to fill the crankcase. Normally, 1 qt.
② Drain and refill capacity shown. Dry capacity is 12 pts.
③ 1993 VIN D, A & 3—9.5 qts., VIN N—12.7 qts. 1994 All—10.4 qts.

CAMSHAFT SPECIFICATIONS
All measurements given in inches.

Year	Engine ID/VIN	Engine Displacement Liters (cc)	Journal Diameter 1	Journal Diameter 2	Journal Diameter 3	Journal Diameter 4	Journal Diameter 5	Elevation In.	Elevation Ex.	Bearing Clearance	Camshaft End Play
1990	D	2.3 (2262)	1.5720–1.5728	1.3751–1.3760	1.3751–1.3760	1.3751–1.3760	1.3751–1.3760	0.3400	0.3500	0.0019–0.0043	0.0060–0.0140
	A	2.3 (2262)	1.5720–1.5728	1.3751–1.3760	1.3751–1.3760	1.3751–1.3760	1.3751–1.3760	0.4100	0.4100	0.0019–0.0043	0.0060–0.0140
	U	2.5 (2475)	1.8690	1.8690	1.8690	1.8690	1.8690	0.2480	0.2480	0.0007–0.0027	0.0020–0.0090
	N	3.3 (3344)	1.7850–1.7860	1.7850–1.7860	1.7850–1.7860	1.7850–1.7860	—	0.2500	0.2550	0.0005–0.0035	NA
1991	D	2.3 (2262)	1.5720–1.5728	1.3751–1.3760	1.3751–1.3760	1.3751–1.3760	1.3751–1.3760	0.3750	0.3750	0.0019–0.0043	0.0009–0.0088
	A	2.3 (2262)	1.5720–1.5728	1.3751–1.3760	1.3751–1.3760	1.3751–1.3760	1.3751–1.3760	0.4100	0.4100	0.0019–0.0043	0.0009–0.0088
	U	2.5 (2475)	1.8690	1.8690	1.8690	1.8690	1.8690	0.2480	0.2480	0.0007–0.0027	0.0020–0.0090
	N	3.3 (3344)	1.7850–1.7860	1.7850–1.7860	1.7850–1.7860	1.7850–1.7860	—	0.2500	0.2550	0.0005–0.0035	NA
1992	D	2.3 (2262)	1.5720–1.5728	1.3751–1.3760	1.3751–1.3760	1.3751–1.3760	1.3751–1.3760	0.3750	0.3750	0.0019–0.0043	0.0009–0.0088
	A	2.3 (2262)	1.5720–1.5728	1.3751–1.3760	1.3751–1.3760	1.3751–1.3760	1.3751–1.3760	0.4100	0.4100	0.0019–0.0043	0.0009–0.0088
	3	2.3 (2262)	1.5720–1.5728	1.3751–1.3760	1.3751–1.3760	1.3751–1.3760	1.3751–1.3760	0.4100	0.4100	0.0019–0.0043	0.0009–0.0088
	N	3.3 (3344)	1.7850–1.7860	1.7850–1.7860	1.7850–1.7860	1.7850–1.7860	—	0.2500	0.2550	0.0005–0.0035	NA
1993-94	D	2.3 (2262)	1.5720–1.5728	1.3751–1.3760	1.3751–1.3760	1.3751–1.3760	1.3751–1.3760	0.3750	0.3750	0.0019–0.0043	0.0009–0.0088
	A	2.3 (2262)	1.5720–1.5728	1.3751–1.3760	1.3751–1.3760	1.3751–1.3760	1.3751–1.3760	0.4100	0.4100	0.0019–0.0043	0.0009–0.0088
	3	2.3 (2262)	1.5720–1.5728	1.3751–1.3760	1.3751–1.3760	1.3751–1.3760	1.3751–1.3760	0.4100	0.4100	0.0019–0.0043	0.0009–0.0088
	N	3.3 (3344)	1.7850–1.7860	1.7850–1.7860	1.7850–1.7860	1.7850–1.7860	—	0.2500	0.2550	0.0005–0.0035	NA
	T	3.1 (3137)	1.8677–1.8815	1.8677–1.8815	1.8677–1.8815	1.8677–1.8815	1.8677–1.8815	0.2626	0.2732	0.0010–0.0040	NA

NA—Not Available

CRANKSHAFT AND CONNECTING ROD SPECIFICATIONS

All measurements are given in inches.

Year	Engine ID/VIN	Engine Displacement Liters (cc)	Crankshaft Main Brg. Journal Dia.	Main Brg. Oil Clearance	Shaft End-play	Thrust on No.	Connecting Rod Journal Diameter	Oil Clearance	Side Clearance
1990	A	2.3 (2262)	2.0470–2.0480	0.0005–0.0023	0.0034–0.0095	3	1.8887–1.8897	0.0005–0.0020	0.0059–0.0177
	D	2.3 (2262)	2.0470–2.0480	0.0005–0.0023	0.0034–0.0095	3	1.8887–1.8897	0.0005–0.0020	0.0059–0.0177
	U	2.5 (2475)	2.3000	0.0005–0.0020	0.0060–0.0110	5	2.0000	0.0005–0.0030	0.0060–0.0240
	N	3.3 (3344)	2.4988–2.4998	0.0003–0.0018	0.0030–0.0110	2	2.2487–2.2499	0.0003–0.0026	0.0030–0.0150
1991	A	2.3 (2262)	2.0470–2.0480	0.0005–0.0023	0.0034–0.0095	3	1.8887–1.8897	0.0005–0.0020	0.0059–0.0177
	D	2.3 (2262)	2.0470–2.0480	0.0005–0.0023	0.0034–0.0095	3	1.8887–1.8897	0.0005–0.0020	0.0059–0.0177
	U	2.5 (2475)	2.3000	0.0005–0.0022	0.0060–0.0110	5	2.0000	0.0005–0.0030	0.0060–0.0240
	N	3.3 (3344)	2.4988–2.4998	0.0003–0.0018	0.0030–0.0110	2	2.2487–2.2499	0.0003–0.0026	0.0030–0.0150
1992	A	2.3 (2262)	2.0470–2.0480	0.0005–0.0023	0.0034–0.0095	3	1.8887–1.8897	0.0005–0.0020	0.0059–0.0177
	D	2.3 (2262)	2.0470–2.0480	0.0005–0.0023	0.0034–0.0095	3	1.8887–1.8897	0.0005–0.0020	0.0059–0.0177
	3	2.3 (2262)	2.0470–2.0480	0.0005–0.0023	0.0034–0.0095	3	1.8887–1.8897	0.0005–0.0020	0.0059–0.0177
	N	3.3 (3344)	2.4988–2.4998	0.0003–0.0018	0.0030–0.0110	2	2.2487–2.2499	0.0008–0.0022	0.0030–0.0150
1993–94	A	2.3 (2262)	2.0470–2.0480	0.0005–0.0023	0.0034–0.0095	3	1.8887–1.8897	0.0005–0.0020	0.0059–0.0177
	D	2.3 (2262)	2.0470–2.0480	0.0005–0.0023	0.0034–0.0095	3	1.8887–1.8897	0.0005–0.0020	0.0059–0.0177
	3	2.3 (2262)	2.0470 2.0480	0.0005–0.0023	0.0034–0.0095	3	1.8887 1.8897	0.0005–0.0020	0.0059–0.0177
	N	3.3 (3344)	2.4988–2.4998	0.0008–0.0022	0.0030–0.0110	2	2.2487–2.2499	0.0008–0.0022	0.0030–0.0150
	T	3.1 (3137)	2.6473–2.6483	0.0012–0.0030	0.0024–0.0083	3	1.9983–1.9994	0.0011–0.0034	0.0140–0.0270

VALVE SPECIFICATIONS

Year	Engine ID/VIN	Engine Displacement Liters (cc)	Seat Angle (deg.)	Face Angle (deg.)	Spring Test Pressure (lbs. @ in.)②	Spring Installed Height (in.)	Stem-to-Guide Clearance (in.) Intake	Exhaust	Stem Diameter (in.) Intake	Exhaust
1990	A	2.3 (2262)	45	①	193–207 @ 1.043 in.	1.420–1.440	0.0009–0.0027	0.0015–0.0032	0.2744–0.2751	0.2740–0.2747
	D	2.3 (2262)	45	①	193–207 @ 1.043 in.	1.420–1.440	0.0009–0.0027	0.0015–0.0032	0.2744–0.2751	0.2740–0.2747
	U	2.5 (2475)	46	45	173 @ 1.24 in.	1.680	0.0010–0.0026	0.0013–0.0041	NA	NA
	N	3.3 (3344)	45	45	200–220 @ 1.315 in.	1.690–1.750	0.0015–0.0035	0.0015–0.0032	NA	NA

VALVE SPECIFICATIONS

Year	Engine ID/VIN	Engine Displacement Liters (cc)	Seat Angle (deg.)	Face Angle (deg.)	Spring Test Pressure (lbs. @ in.)②	Spring Installed Height (in.)	Stem-to-Guide Clearance (in.) Intake	Exhaust	Stem Diameter (in.) Intake	Exhaust
1991	A	2.3 (2262)	45	44	193–207 @ 1.043 in.	0.980–③ 1.000	0.0010–0.0027	0.0015–0.0032	0.2744–0.2751	0.2740–0.2747
	D	2.3 (2262)	45	44	193–207 @ 1.043 in.	0.980–③ 1.000	0.0010–0.0027	0.0015–0.0032	0.2744–0.2751	0.2740–0.2747
	U	2.5 (2475)	46	45	173 @ 1.24 in.	1.680	0.0010–0.0026	0.0013–0.0041	NA	NA
	N	3.3 (3344)	45	45	210 @ 1.315 in.	1.690–1.750	0.0015–0.0035	0.0015–0.0032	NA	NA
1992	A	2.3 (2262)	45	44	193–207 @ 1.043 in.	0.980–③ 1.000	0.0010–0.0027	0.0015–0.0032	0.2744–0.2751	0.2740–0.2747
	D	2.3 (2262)	45	44	193–207 @ 1.043 in.	0.980–③ 1.000	0.0010–0.0027	0.0015–0.0032	0.2744–0.2751	0.2740–0.2747
	3	2.3 (2262)	45	44	193–207 @ 1.043 in.	0.980–③ 1.000	0.0010–0.0027	0.0015–0.0032	0.2744–0.2751	0.2740–0.2747
	N	3.3 (3344)	45	45	210 @ 1.315 in.	1.690–1.750	0.0015–0.0035	0.0015–0.0032	NA	NA
1993–94	A	2.3 (2262)	45	44	193–207 @ 1.043 in.	0.980–③ 1.000	0.0010–0.0027	0.0015–0.0032	0.2744–0.2751	0.2740–0.2747
	D	2.3 (2262)	45	44	193–207 @ 1.043 in.	0.980–③ 1.000	0.0010–0.0027	0.0015–0.0032	0.2744–0.2751	0.2740–0.2747
	3	2.3 (2262)	45	44	193–207 @ 1.043 in.	0.980–③ 1.000	0.0010–0.0027	0.0015–0.0032	0.2744–0.2751	0.2740–0.2747
	N	3.3 (3344)	45	45	210 @ 1.315 in.	1.690–1.750	0.0015–0.0035	0.0015–0.0032	NA	NA
	T	3.1 (3137)	46	45	215 @ 1.291 in.	1.575	0.0010–0.0027	0.0010–0.0027	NA	NA

NA—Not Available
① Intake: 44°
  Exhaust: 44.5°
② Load—open
③ Measured from top of valve stem to top of
  camshaft housing mounting surface

PISTON AND RING SPECIFICATIONS

All measurements are given in inches.

Year	Engine ID/VIN	Engine Displacement Liters (cc)	Piston Clearance	Ring Gap Top Compression	Bottom Compression	Oil Control	Ring Side Clearance Top Compression	Bottom Compression	Oil Control
1990	A	2.3 (2262)	0.0007–0.0020	0.014–0.024	0.016–0.026	0.016–0.055	0.003–0.005	0.002–0.003	NA
	D	2.3 (2262)	0.0007–0.0020	0.014–0.024	0.016–0.026	0.016–0.055	0.002–0.004	0.002–0.003	NA
	U	2.5 (2475)	0.0014–0.0022	0.010–0.020	0.010–0.020	0.020–0.060	0.002–0.003	0.001–0.003	0.0015–0.0055
	N	3.3 (3344)	0.0004–0.0022	0.010–0.025	0.010–0.025	0.010–0.040	0.001–0.003	0.001–0.003	0.001–0.008

PISTON AND RING SPECIFICATIONS
All measurements are given in inches.

Year	Engine ID/VIN	Engine Displacement Liters (cc)	Piston Clearance	Ring Gap			Ring Side Clearance		
				Top Compression	Bottom Compression	Oil Control	Top Compression	Bottom Compression	Oil Control
1991	A	2.3 (2262)	0.0007–0.0020	0.014–0.024	0.016–0.026	0.016–0.055	0.003–0.005	0.002–0.003	NA
	D	2.3 (2262)	0.0007–0.0020	0.014–0.024	0.016–0.026	0.016–0.055	0.002–0.004	0.002–0.003	NA
	U	2.5 (2475)	0.0014–0.0022	0.010–0.020	0.010–0.020	0.020–0.060	0.002–0.003	0.001–0.003	0.0015–0.0055
	N	3.3 (3344)	0.0004–① 0.0022	0.010–0.025	0.010–0.025	0.010–0.040	0.001–0.003	0.001–0.003	0.001–0.008
1992	A	2.3 (2262)	0.0007–0.0020	0.014–0.024	0.016–0.026	0.016–0.055	0.003–0.005	0.002–0.003	NA
	D	2.3 (2262)	0.0007–0.0020	0.014–0.024	0.016–0.026	0.016–0.055	0.002–0.004	0.002–0.003	NA
	3	2.3 (2262)	0.0007–0.0020	0.014–0.024	0.016–0.026	0.016–0.055	0.002–0.004	0.002–0.003	NA
	N	3.3 (3344)	0.0004–① 0.0022	0.010–0.025	0.010–0.025	0.015–0.055	0.001–0.003	0.001–0.003	0.001–0.008
1993–94	A	2.3 (2262)	0.0007–0.0020	0.014–0.024	0.016–0.026	0.016–0.055	0.002–0.004	0.002–0.003	NA
	D	2.3 (2262)	0.0007–0.0020	0.014–0.024	0.016–0.026	0.016–0.055	0.002–0.004	0.002–0.003	NA
	3	2.3 (2262)	0.0007–0.0020	0.014–0.024	0.016–0.026	0.016–0.055	0.002–0.004	0.002–0.003	NA
	N	3.3 (3344)	0.0004–① 0.0022	0.010–0.025	0.010–0.025	0.010–0.025	0.001–0.003	0.001–0.003	0.001–0.008
	T	3.1 (3137)	0.0009–0.0022	0.010–0.020	0.020–0.028	0.010–0.030	0.002–0.004	0.002–0.004	0.008–Max

NA—Not Available
① Measured 1.8 in. (44mm) down from top of piston

TORQUE SPECIFICATIONS
All readings in ft. lbs.

Year	Engine ID/VIN	Engine Displacement Liters (cc)	Cylinder Head Bolts	Main Bearing Bolts	Rod Bearing Bolts	Crankshaft Damper Bolts	Flywheel Bolts	Manifold		Spark Plugs	Lug Nut
								Intake	Exhaust		
1990	A	2.3 (2262)	⑮	15⑤	18⑬	74⑤	22②	18	⑦	17	100
	D	2.3 (2262)	⑮	15⑤	18⑬	74⑤	22②	18	⑦	17	100
	U	2.5 (2475)	⑫	65	29	162	⑨	25	⑩	15	100
	N	3.3 (3344)	⑭	90	20②	219	61	7	30	20	100
1991	A	2.3 (2262)	⑮	15⑤	18⑬	74⑤	22②	18	⑦	17	100
	D	2.3 (2262)	⑮	15⑤	18⑬	74⑤	22②	18	⑦	17	100
	U	2.5 (2475)	⑫	65	29	162	⑨	25	⑩	15	100
	N	3.3 (3344)	⑭	26⑯	20②	105④	89⑧⑤	89⑧	41	20	100

TORQUE SPECIFICATIONS
All readings in ft. lbs.

Year	Engine ID/VIN	Engine Displacement Liters (cc)	Cylinder Head Bolts	Main Bearing Bolts	Rod Bearing Bolts	Crankshaft Damper Bolts	Flywheel Bolts	Manifold Intake	Manifold Exhaust	Spark Plugs	Lug Nut
1992	A	2.3 (2262)	①	15 ⑤	18 ⑬	74 ⑤	22 ②	18	⑦	17	100
	D	2.3 (2262)	①	15 ⑤	18 ⑬	74 ⑤	22 ②	18	⑦	17	100
	3	2.3 (2262)	①	15 ⑤	18 ⑬	74 ⑤	22 ②	18	⑦	17	100
	N	3.3 (3344)	⑭	26 ③	20 ③	110 ⑥	11 ③	88 ⑧ ⑪	38	12	100
1993-94	A	2.3 (2262)	①	15 ⑤	18 ⑬	74 ⑤	22 ②	18	⑦	17	100
	D	2.3 (2262)	①	15 ⑤	18 ⑬	74 ⑤	22 ②	18	⑦	17	100
	3	2.3 (2262)	①	15 ⑤	18 ⑬	74 ⑤	22 ②	18	⑦	17	100
	N	3.3 (3344)	⑭	26 ③	20 ③	110 ⑥	11 ③	88 ⑧ ⑪	38	12	100
	T	3.1 (3137)	33 ⑰	73	39	76	52	⑱	18	11	100

① Bolts 1 through 6: 26 ft. lbs. + 90° turn
Bolts 7 and 8: 15 ft. lbs. + 90° turn
Bolts 9 through 10: 22 ft. lbs. + 90° turn
② Plus an additional 40–50° turn
③ Plus an additional 50° turn
④ Plus an additional 56° turn
⑤ Plus an additional 90° turn
⑥ Plus an additional 75° turn
⑦ Nuts: 27 ft. lbs.
Studs: 106 inch lbs.
⑧ Inch lbs.
⑨ Manual transaxle: 69 ft. lbs.
automatic transaxle: 55 ft. lbs.
⑩ Outer bolts: 26 ft. lbs.
Inner bolts: 37 ft. lbs.
⑪ Upper intake manifold to lower: 22 ft. lbs.

⑫ Step 1: 18 ft. lbs.
Step 2: 26 ft. lbs., except front bolt/stud
Step 3: Front bolt/stud to 18 ft. lbs.
Step 4: An additional 90° turn
⑬ Plus an additional 80° turn
⑭ Step 1: 35 ft. lbs.
Step 2: An additional 130° turn
Step 3: An additional 30° turn on center 4 bolts
⑮ Short bolts: 26 ft. lbs. plus an additional 100° turn
Long bolts: 26 ft. lbs. plus an additional 110° turn
⑯ Plus an additional 45° turn
⑰ Coat threads with sealer.
Turn an additional 90°
⑱ Tighten in sequence to 15 ft. lbs. and then to 24 ft. lbs.

TORQUE SPECIFICATIONS

Component	English	Metric
Camshaft sprocket bolt		
2.3L engine:	40 ft. lbs.	54 Nm
2.5L engine:	43 ft. lbs.	58 Nm
3.3L engine		
1990:	27 ft. lbs.	37 Nm
1991–94		
Step 1:	74 ft. lbs.	100 Nm
Step 2:	+ 105 degrees turn	+ 105 degrees turn
Connecting rod bearing cap bolts		
2.3L engine		
Step 1:	18 ft. lbs.	25 Nm
Step 2:	+ 80 degrees turn	+ 80 degrees turn
2.5L engine:	32 ft. lbs.	44 Nm
3.3L engine		
Step 1:	20 ft. lbs.	27 Nm
Step 2:	+ 50 degrees turn	+ 50 degrees turn
Crankshaft damper bolt		
2.3L engine		
Step 1:	74 ft. lbs.	100 Nm
Step 2:	+ 90 degrees turn	+ 90 degrees turn
2.5L engine:	162 ft. lbs.	220 Nm
3.3L engine		
Step 1:	105 ft. lbs.	140 Nm
Step 2:	+ 56 degrees turn	+ 56 degrees turn

TORQUE SPECIFICATIONS

Component	English	Metric
Cylinder head bolt/camshaft carrier		
2.3L engine		
1990–91		
Step 1 (all bolts):	26 ft. lbs.	35 Nm
Step 2 (except short bolts):	+ 110 degrees turn	+ 110 degrees turn
Step 3 (short bolts):	+ 100 degrees turn	+ 100 degrees turn
1992–94		
Step 1 (bolts 1 through 6):	26 ft. lbs.	35 Nm
Step 2 (bolts 7 and 8):	15 ft. lbs.	20 Nm
Step 3 (bolts 9 and 10):	22 ft. lbs.	30 Nm
2.5L engine		
Step 1 (all bolts):	18 ft. lbs.	26 Nm
Step 2 (except position "9 or i" (R/F):	26 ft. lbs.	35 Nm
Step 3 (retorque position "9 or i" (R/F):	18 ft. lbs.	26 Nm
Step 4 (all bolts):	+ 90 degrees turn	+ 90 degrees turn
3.3L engine		
Step 1:	35 ft. lbs.	47 Nm
Step 2:	+ 130 degrees turn	+ 130 degrees turn
Step 3:	+ 30 degrees turn on 4 center bolts	+ 30 degrees turn on 4 center bolts
EGR valve-to-intake manifold		
2.5L engine:	16 ft. lbs.	22 Nm
Engine-to-transmission		
Except 2.3L engine with automatic transaxle:	55 ft. lbs.	75 Nm
2.3L engine with automatic transaxle		
Positions No. 2, 3, 4, 5, 6:	71 ft. lbs.	96 Nm
Position No. 7 (stud):	115 inch lbs.	13 Nm
Position No. 7 (nut):	41 ft. lbs.	56 Nm
Position No. 8:	41 ft. lbs.	56 Nm
Exhaust manifold		
2.3L engine		
1990		
Stud:	106 inch lbs.	12 Nm
Nut:	27 ft. lbs.	37 Nm
1991–94		
Stud:	106 inch lbs.	12 Nm
Nut:	31 ft. lbs.	42 Nm
2.5L engine		
Inner bolt:	37 ft. lbs.	50 Nm
Outside bolt:	28 ft. lbs.	38 Nm
3.3L engine		
1990–91:	41 ft. lbs.	55 Nm
1992–94:	38 ft. lbs.	52 Nm
Exhaust pipe-to-exhaust manifold nuts		
2.3L engine:	19 ft. lbs.	26 Nm
2.5L and 3.3L engines:	22 ft. lbs.	30 Nm
Flywheel/flexplate-to-crankshaft bolts		
2.3L engine		
Step 1:	22 ft. lbs.	30 Nm
Step 2:	+ 45 degrees turn	+ 45 degrees turn
2.5L engine		
Automatic transaxle:	55 ft. lbs.	75 Nm
Manual transaxle:	69 ft. lbs.	93 Nm
3.3L engine		
1990–91		
Step 1:	89 inch lbs.	10 Nm
Step 2:	+ 90 degrees turn	+ 90 degrees turn
1992–94		
Step 1:	11 ft. lbs.	15 Nm
Step 2:	+ 50 degrees turn	+ 50 degrees turn

TORQUE SPECIFICATIONS

Component	English	Metric
Flywheel-to-converter bolt:	46 ft. lbs.	63 Nm
Intake manifold-to-cylinder head		
2.5L engine:	25 ft. lbs.	34 Nm
3.3L engine		
1990–91		
Step 1:	89 inch lbs.	10 Nm
Step 2:	89 inch lbs.	10 Nm
1992–94		
Lower half:	89 inch lbs.	10 Nm
Upper half to lower half:	22 ft. lbs.	30 Nm
Main bearing cap bolts		
2.3L engine		
Step 1:	15 ft. lbs.	20 Nm
Step 2:	+ 90 degrees turn	+ 90 degrees turn
2.5L engine:	65 ft. lbs.	88 Nm
3.3L engine		
Step 1:	26 ft. lbs.	35 Nm
Step 2:	+ 50 degrees turn	+ 45 degrees turn
Oil pan		
2.3L engine		
Side bolts:	106 inch lbs.	12 Nm
End bolts:	17 ft. lbs.	24 Nm
2.5L engine:	89 inch lbs.	10 Nm
3.3L engine:	124 inch lbs.	14 Nm
Oil pan drain plug		
2.3L engine:	19 ft. lbs.	26 Nm
2.5L engine:	25 ft. lbs.	34 Nm
3.3L engine:	30 ft. lbs.	40 Nm
Oil pump attaching bolts		
2.3L engine:	40 ft. lbs.	54 Nm
3.3L engine:	97 inch lbs.	11 Nm
Rocker arm pivot bolt		
2.5L engine:	20 ft. lbs.	27 Nm
3.3L engine:	28 ft. lbs.	38 Nm
Rocker (valve) cover		
2.3L engine		
Except 2 intake-side rear bolts (short)		
Step 1:	11 ft. lbs.	15 Nm
Step 2:	+ 75 degrees turn	+ 75 degrees turn
2 intake side rear bolts (short)		
Step 1:	16 ft. lbs.	22 Nm
Step 2:	+ 25 degrees turn	+ 25 degrees turn
2.5L engine:	45 inch lbs.	5 Nm
3.3L engine:	89 ft. lbs.	10 Nm
Spark plug		
2.5L engine		
With tapered seat:	15 ft. lbs.	20 Nm
Without tapered seat:	25 ft. lbs.	34 Nm
2.3L engine:	17 ft. lbs.	22 Nm
2.5L and 3.3L engines:	12 ft. lbs.	16 Nm
Starter-to-block bolts		
Except 2.3L engine:	35 ft. lbs.	48 Nm
2.3L engine:	71 ft. lbs.	96 Nm
Thermostat housing		
2.3L engine:	19 ft. lbs.	26 Nm
2.5L and 3.3L engines:	20 ft. lbs.	27 Nm
TBI-to-fuel meter body screws:	31 inch lbs.	3.5 Nm
TBI fuel feed/return line:	30 ft. lbs.	41 Nm
TBI mounting bolts/nuts:	18 ft. lbs.	25 Nm

TORQUE SPECIFICATIONS

Component	English	Metric
Timing cover		
2.3L engine:	106 inch lbs.	12 Nm
2.5L engine:	89 inch lbs.	10 Nm
3.3L engines:	22 ft. lbs.	30 Nm
Water pump		
2.3L engine		
Studs and nuts:	19 ft. lbs.	26 Nm
Water pump cover-to-body:	125 inch lbs.	14 Nm
Water pump cover-to-engine block:	19 ft. lbs.	26 Nm
2.5L engine:	24 ft. lbs.	33 Nm
3.3L engine		
Water pump to front cover top:	97 inch lbs.	11 Nm
Water pump to lower block/cover:	29 ft. lbs.	39 Nm

BRAKE SPECIFICATIONS

All measurements in inches unless noted.

Year	Model	Master Cylinder Bore	Brake Disc Original Thickness	Brake Disc Minimum Thickness	Maximum Runout	Brake Drum Diameter Original Inside Diameter	Brake Drum Diameter Max. Wear Limit	Brake Drum Diameter Maximum Machine Diameter	Minimum Lining Thickness Front	Minimum Lining Thickness Rear
1990	All	0.874	0.885	0.830	0.004	7.879	7.929	7.899	0.06	0.06
1991	All	0.874	0.806	0.736	0.003	7.879	7.929	7.899	0.06	0.06
1992	All	0.874	0.796	0.736	0.003	7.879	7.929	7.899	0.06	0.06
1993–94	All	0.874	0.786	0.736	0.003	7.879	7.929	7.899	0.06	0.06

WHEEL ALIGNMENT

Year	Model		Caster Range (deg.)	Caster Preferred Setting (deg.)	Camber Range (deg.)	Camber Preferred Setting (deg.)	Toe-in (in.)	Steering Axis Inclination (deg.)
1990	Calais	front	11/16P–2 11/16P	1 11/16P	1/8P–1 1/2P ②	13/16P ①	0	13 1/2
		rear	—	—	3/4N–1/4P	1/4N	1/4	—
	Grand Am	front	11/16P–2 11/16P	1 11/16P	1/8P–1 1/2P ②	13/16P ①	0	13 1/2
		rear	—	—	3/4N–1/4P	1/4N	1/4	—
	Skylark	front	11/16P–2 11/16P	1 11/16P	1/8P–1 1/2P ②	13/16P ①	0	13 1/2
		rear	—	—	3/4N–1/4P	1/4N	1/4	—
1991	Calais	front	11/16P–2 11/16P	1 11/16P	11/16N–11/16P	0	0	13 1/2
		rear	—	—	13/16N–5/16P	1/4N	1/8	—
	Grand Am	front	11/16P–2 11/16P	1 11/16P	11/16N–11/16P	0	0	13 1/2
		rear	—	—	13/16N–5/16P	1/4N	1/8	—
	Skylark	front	11/16P–2 11/16P	1 11/16P	11/16N–11/16P	0	0	13 1/2
		rear	—	—	3/4N–1/2P	1/4N	1/8	—
1992	Achieva	front	11/16P–2 11/16P	1 11/16P	11/16N–11/16P	0	0	13 1/2
		rear	—	—	13/16N–5/16P	1/4N	1/4	—
	Grand Am	front	11/16P–2 11/16P	1 11/16P	11/16N–11/16P	0	0	13 1/2
		rear	—	—	13/16N–5/16P	1/4N	1/4	—
	Skylark	front	11/16P–2 11/16P	1 11/16P	11/16N–11/16P	0	0	13 1/2
		rear	—	—	13/16N–5/16P	1/4N	1/4	—

WHEEL ALIGNMENT

Year	Model		Caster		Camber		Toe-in (in.)	Steering Axis Inclination (deg.)
			Range (deg.)	Preferred Setting (deg.)	Range (deg.)	Preferred Setting (deg.)		
1993-94	Achieva	front	7/16P–27/16P	17/16P	11/16N–11/16P	0	0	13½
		rear	—	—	13/16N–5/16P	¼N	0	—
	Grand Am	front	7/16P–27/16P	17/16P	11/16N–11/16P	0	0	13½
		rear	—	—	13/16N–5/16P	¼N	0	—
	Skylark	front	7/16P–27/16P	17/16P	11/16N–11/16P	0	0	13½
		rear	—	—	13/16N–11/16P	¼N	0	—

N—Negative
P—Positive
① with 16 in. wheels: 0
② with 16 in. wheels: 11/16N–11/16P

AIR CONDITIONING BELT TENSION

Year	Engine VIN	Engine Displacement Liters (cc)	Belt Type	Specifications	
				New	Used
1990	A	2.3 (2263)	Serpentine	50①	
	D	2.3 (2263)	Serpentine	50①	
	U	3.1 (3149)	Serpentine	50①	
1991	A	2.3 (2263)	Serpentine	50①	
	D	2.3 (2263)	Serpentine	50①	
	U	3.1 (3149)	Serpentine	50①	
1992	A	2.3 (2263)	Serpentine	50①	
	D	2.3 (2263)	Serpentine	50①	
	U	3.1 (3149)	Serpentine	50①	
	3	2.3 (2263)	Serpentine	50①	
	N	3.3 (3346)	Serpentine	67①	
1993	A	2.3 (2263)	Serpentine	50①	
	D	2.3 (2263)	Serpentine	50①	
	3	2.3 (2263)	Serpentine	50①	
	N	3.3 (3346)	Serpentine	67①	

① Equipped with automatic tensioner; however, the specification given (in pounds) is for testing whether the tensioner is maintaining its proper tension (specification given is the average of 3 readings back-to-back).

REFRIGERANT CAPACITIES

Year	Model	Refrigerant (oz.)	Oil (fl. oz.)	Compressor Type
1990	Skylark, Calais, Grand Am	36.0	8.0	V-5
1991	Skylark, Calais, Grand Am	36.0	8.0	V-5
1992	Skylark, Achieva, Grand Am	42.0	8.0	V-5
1993	Skylark, Achieva, Grand Am	42.0	8.0	V-5

NOTE: At the time of publication, refrigerant capacity information relating to R-134a was not available from the manufacturer.

MAINTENANCE INTERVALS—TYPE A: NORMAL SERVICE
Achieva • Calais • Grand Am • Skylark

TO BE SERVICED	TYPE OF SERVICE	VEHICLE MILEAGE INTERVAL (X1000)							
		7.5	15	22.5	30	37.5	45	52.5	60
Oxygen Sensor	I				✔				✔
Vacuum Lines and Hoses	I		✔		✔		✔		✔
Ignition Wires	I				✔				✔
Spark Plugs	R				✔				✔
Engine Oil	R	✔	✔	✔	✔	✔	✔	✔	✔
Engine Air Cleaner Element	R				✔				✔
Crankcase Emission Filter	R				✔				✔
PCV Valve	R				✔				✔
Fuel Filter	R				✔				✔
Engine Oil Filter	R①	✔		✔		✔		✔	
Fuel/Vapor Return Lines	I				✔				✔
Fuel Tank Cap and Restrictor	I				✔				✔
Coolant System Service	R				✔				✔
Exhaust Pipe and Muffler	I				✔				✔
Tire Rotation	I②	✔		✔		✔		✔	
Catalytic Converter and Shield	I				✔				✔
EGR System	I				✔				✔
Automatic Transaxle Fluid	R③								
Battery Connections	I		✔		✔		✔		✔
Chassis Lubrication	L	✔	✔	✔	✔	✔	✔	✔	✔
CV-Joints and Boots	I	✔	✔	✔	✔	✔	✔	✔	✔
Idle Speed System	I				✔				✔
Throttle Body Mounting Torque	I	✔							
Drive Belts	I				✔				✔
Brake Linings	I		✔		✔		✔		✔
Parking Brake	I		✔		✔		✔		✔
Coolant Hoses and Clamps	I		✔		✔		✔		✔
Seat Belt Operation	I				✔				✔

FOR COMPLETE WARRANTY COVERAGE CONSULT INDIVIDUAL VEHICLE MANUFACTURER'S WARRANTY MAINTENANCE GUIDE.

I—Inspect
L—Lubricate
R—Replace
① Replace oil filter at first and every other oil change
② Rotate tires at 7,500 miles and then every 15,000 miles, as necessary
③ Replace automatic transaxle fluid and filter at 100,000 miles

MAINTENANCE INTERVALS—TYPE B: SEVERE SERVICE
Achieva • Calais • Grand Am • Skylark

TO BE SERVICED	TYPE OF SERVICE	VEHICLE MILEAGE INTERVAL (X1000)									
		3	6	9	12	15	18	21	24	27	30
Oxygen Sensor	I										✔
Vacuum Lines and Hoses	I					✔					✔
Ignition Wires	I										✔
Spark Plugs	R										✔
Engine Oil and Filter	R	✔	✔	✔	✔	✔	✔	✔	✔	✔	✔
Engine Air Cleaner Element	R					✔					✔
Crankcase Emission Filter	R					✔					✔
PCV Valve	R					✔					✔
Fuel Filter	R					✔					✔
Fuel/Vapor Return Lines	I										✔
Fuel Tank Cap and Restrictor	I										✔
Coolant System	R										✔
Exhaust Pipe and Muffler	I										✔
Tire Rotation	I ①		✔								
Catalytic Converter and Shield	I										
Automatic Transaxle Fluid	R					✔					✔
Battery Connections	I					✔					✔
Chassis Lubrication	L		✔		✔		✔		✔		✔
CV-Joints and Boots	I	✔	✔	✔	✔	✔	✔	✔	✔	✔	✔
Idle Speed System	I					✔					✔
Throttle Body Mounting Torque	I		✔								
Drive Belts	I										✔
Brake Linings	I					✔					✔
Parking Brake	I					✔					✔
Coolant Hoses and Clamps	I					✔					✔
Seat Belt Operation	I										✔

FOR COMPLETE WARRANTY COVERAGE CONSULT INDIVIDUAL VEHICLE MANUFACTURER'S WARRANTY MAINTENANCE GUIDE.

I—Inspect
L—Lubricate
R—Replace
① Rotate tires at 6,000 miles and then every
   15,000 miles, as necessary

FIRING ORDERS

NOTE: To avoid confusion, always replace spark plugs and wires one at a time.

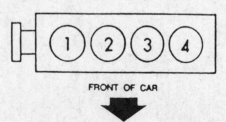

FRONT OF CAR

2.3L Engine
Engine Firing Order: 1–3–4–2
Distributorless Ignition System

FIRING ORDERS

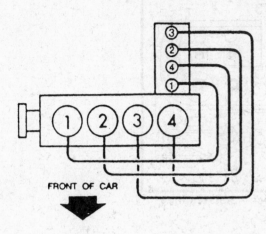

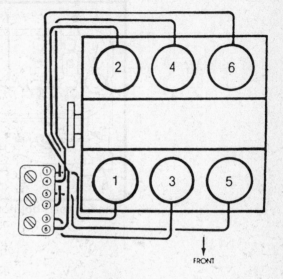

2.5L Engine
Engine Firing Order: 1–3–4–2
Distributorless Ignition System

3.3L Engine
Engine Firing Order: 1–6–5–4–3–2
Distributorless Ignition System

CYLINDER HEAD TORQUE SEQUENCES

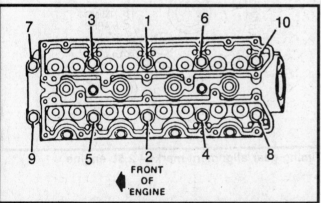

Cylinder head bolt torque sequence – 1990–91 2.3L engine

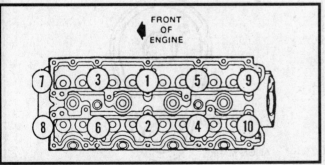

Cylinder head bolt torque sequence – 1992–94 2.3L engine

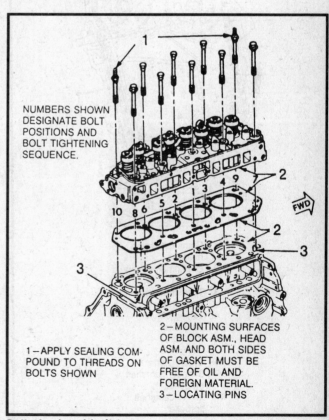

NUMBERS SHOWN DESIGNATE BOLT POSITIONS AND BOLT TIGHTENING SEQUENCE.

1 – APPLY SEALING COMPOUND TO THREADS ON BOLTS SHOWN

2 – MOUNTING SURFACES OF BLOCK ASM., HEAD ASM. AND BOTH SIDES OF GASKET MUST BE FREE OF OIL AND FOREIGN MATERIAL.
3 – LOCATING PINS

Cylinder head bolt torque sequence – 2.5L engine

CYLINDER HEAD TORQUE SEQUENCES

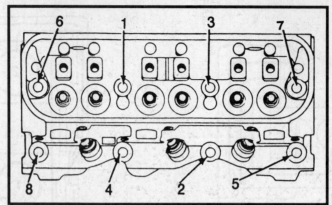

Cylinder head bolt torque sequence—3.3L engine

TIMING CHAIN ALIGNMENT MARKS

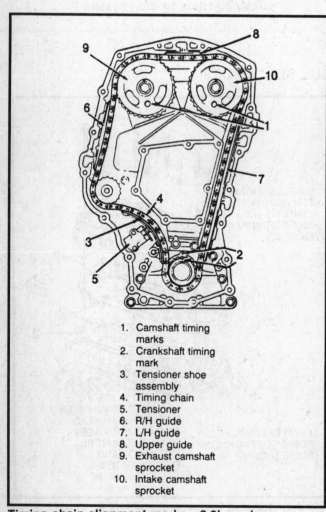

1. Camshaft timing marks
2. Crankshaft timing mark
3. Tensioner shoe assembly
4. Timing chain
5. Tensioner
6. R/H guide
7. L/H guide
8. Upper guide
9. Exhaust camshaft sprocket
10. Intake camshaft sprocket

Timing chain alignment marks—2.3L engine

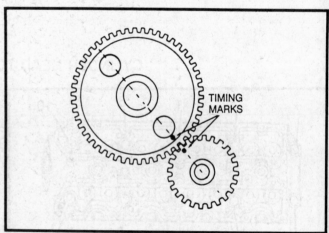

Timing gear alignment marks—2.5L engine

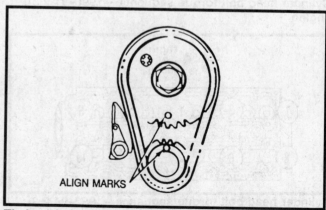

Timing chain alignment marks—3.3L engine

AIR CONDITIONING SERVICE VALVE LOCATIONS

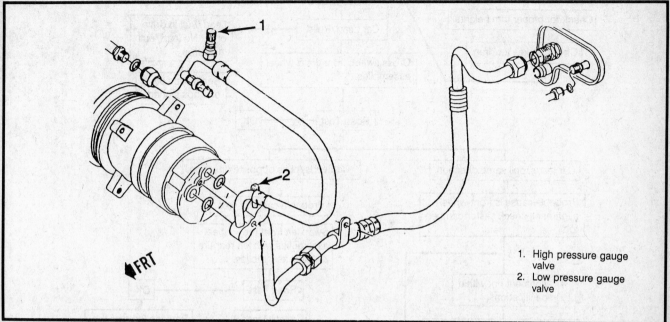

1. High pressure gauge valve
2. Low pressure gauge valve

Air conditioning service valve location

WHEEL ALIGNMENT ADJUSTMENT LOCATIONS

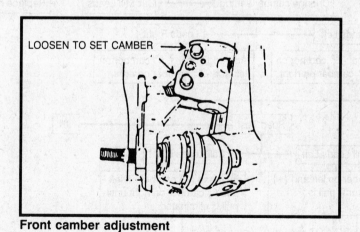

LOOSEN TO SET CAMBER

Front camber adjustment

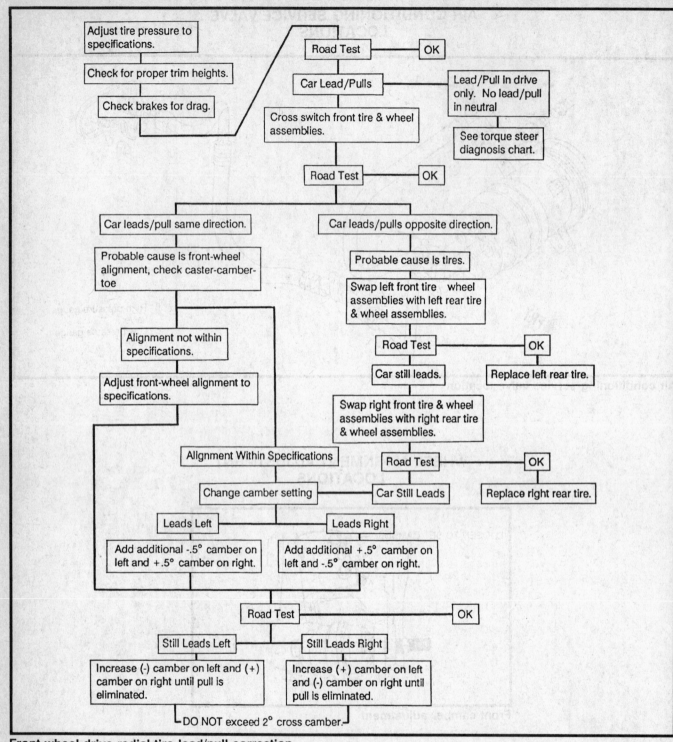

Front wheel drive radial tire lead/pull correction

SPECIFICATION CHARTS

VEHICLE IDENTIFICATION CHART

It is important for servicing and ordering parts to be certain of the vehicle and engine identification. The VIN (vehicle identification number) is a 17 digit number visible through the windshield on the driver's side of the dash and contains the vehicle and engine identification codes. The tenth digit indicates model year and the eighth digit indicates engine code. It can be interpreted as follows:

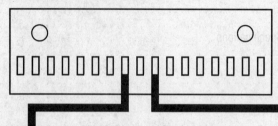

Engine Code					
Code	Liters	Cu. In. (cc)	Cyl.	Fuel Sys.	Eng. Mfg.
6	1.6	98 (1598)	4	TBI	GM
K	2.0	121 (1998)	4	TBI	GM

TBI—Throttle body injection

Model Year	
Code	Year
L	1990
M	1991
N	1992
P	1993

ENGINE IDENTIFICATION

Year	Model	Engine Displacement Liters (cc)	Engine Series (ID/VIN)	Fuel System	No. of Cylinders	Engine Type
1990	Lemans	1.6 (1598)	6	TBI	4	OHC
	Lemans	2.0 (1998)	K	TBI	4	OHC
1991	Lemans	1.6 (1598)	6	TBI	4	OHC
	Lemans	2.0 (1998)	K	TBI	4	OHC
1992	Lemans	1.6 (1598)	6	TBI	4	OHC
1993	Lemans	1.6 (1598)	6	TBI	4	OHC

OHC—Overhead cam
TBI—Throttle Body Injection

GENERAL ENGINE SPECIFICATIONS

Year	Engine ID/VIN	Engine Displacement Liters (cc)	Fuel System Type	Net Horsepower @ rpm	Net Torque @ rpm (ft. lbs.)	Bore × Stroke (in.)	Compression Ratio	Oil Pressure @ rpm
1990	6	1.6 (1598)	TBI	74 @ 5600	90 @ 2800	3.11 × 3.21	8.5:1	55 @ 2000
	K	2.0 (1998)	TBI	96 @ 4800	118 @ 3600	3.39 × 3.39	8.8:1	55 @ 2000
1991	6	1.6 (1598)	TBI	74 @ 5600	90 @ 2800	3.11 × 3.21	8.5:1	55 @ 2000
	K	2.0 (1998)	TBI	96 @ 4800	118 @ 3600	3.39 × 3.39	8.8:1	55 @ 2000
1992	6	1.6 (1598)	TBI	74 @ 5600	90 @ 2800	3.11 × 3.21	8.5:1	55 @ 2000
1993	6	1.6 (1598)	TBI	74 @ 5600	90 @ 2800	3.11 × 3.21	8.5:1	55 @ 2000

TBI—Throttle body injection

ENGINE TUNE-UP SPECIFICATIONS

Year	Engine ID/VIN	Engine Displacement Liters (cc)	Spark Plugs Gap (in.)	Ignition Timing (deg.) MT	Ignition Timing (deg.) AT	Fuel Pump (psi)	Idle Speed (rpm) MT	Idle Speed (rpm) AT	Valve Clearance In.	Valve Clearance Ex.
1990	6	1.6 (1598)	0.045	①	①	18–27	600	500	Hyd.	Hyd.
	K	2.0 (1998)	0.045	①	①	18–27	600	600	Hyd.	Hyd.
1991	6	1.6 (1598)	0.045	①	①	18–27	600	500	Hyd.	Hyd.
	K	2.0 (1998)	0.045	①	①	18–27	600	600	Hyd.	Hyd.
1992	6	1.6 (1598)	0.045	①	①	18–27	600	500	Hyd.	Hyd.
1993	6	1.6 (1598)	0.045	①	①	18–27	600	500	Hyd.	Hyd.

NOTE: The lowest cylinder pressure should be within 75% of the highest cylinder pressure reading. For example, if the highest cylinder is 134 psi, the lowest should be 101. Engine should be at normal operating temperature with throttle valve in the wide open position.
The underhood specifications sticker often reflects tune-up specification changes in production. Sticker figures must be used if they disagree with those in this chart.
Hyd.—Hydraulic
① See underhood specifications sticker.

CAPACITIES

Year	Model	Engine ID/VIN	Engine Displacement Liters (cc)	Engine Crankcase with Filter (qts.)	Transmission (pts.) 4-Spd.	Transmission (pts.) 5-Spd.	Transmission (pts.) Auto.	Drive Axle (pts.)	Fuel Tank (gal.)	Cooling System (qts.)
1990	Lemans	6	1.6 (1598)	4.0	3.5	3.5	8①	—	13.0	8.1
	Lemans	K	2.0 (1998)	4.0	3.5	4.5	8①	—	13.0	8.1
1991	Lemans	6	1.6 (1598)	4.0	3.4	3.4	8①	—	13.0	8.1
	Lemans	K	2.0 (1998)	4.0	3.4	4.4	8①	—	13.0	8.1
1992	Lemans	6	1.6 (1598)	4.0	3.4	3.4	8①	—	13.0	8.1
1993	Lemans	6	1.6 (1598)	4.0	3.4	3.4	8①	—	13.0	8.1

① Overhaul—12 pts.

CAMSHAFT SPECIFICATIONS

All measurements given in inches.

Year	Engine ID/VIN	Engine Displacement Liters (cc)	Journal Diameter 1	Journal Diameter 2	Journal Diameter 3	Journal Diameter 4	Journal Diameter 5	Elevation In.	Elevation Ex.	Bearing Clearance	Camshaft End Play
1990	6	1.6 (1598)	1.552–1.553	1.562–1.563	1.572–1.573	1.582–1.583	1.592–1.593	0.220	0.241	0.0018–0.0035	0.0035–0.0083
	K	2.0 (1998)	1.670–1.671	1.671–1.672	1.691–1.692	1.701–1.702	1.710–1.711	0.237	0.252	0.0011–0.0035	0.0016–0.0063
1991	6	1.6 (1598)	1.552–1.553	1.562–1.563	1.572–1.573	1.582–1.583	1.592–1.593	0.220	0.241	0.0018–0.0035	0.0035–0.0083
	K	2.0 (1998)	1.670–1.671	1.671–1.672	1.691–1.692	1.701–1.702	1.710–1.711	0.237	0.252	0.0011–0.0035	0.0016–0.0063
1992	6	1.6 (1598)	1.552–1.553	1.562–1.563	1.572–1.573	1.582–1.583	1.592–1.593	0.220	0.241	0.0018–0.0035	0.0035–0.0083
1993	6	1.6 (1598)	1.552–1.553	1.562–1.563	1.572–1.573	1.582–1.583	1.592–1.593	0.220	0.241	0.0018–0.0035	0.0035–0.0083

CRANKSHAFT AND CONNECTING ROD SPECIFICATIONS

All measurements are given in inches.

Year	Engine ID/VIN	Engine Displacement Liters (cc)	Crankshaft				Connecting Rod		
			Main Brg. Journal Dia.	Main Brg. Oil Clearance	Shaft End-play	Thrust on No.	Journal Diameter	Oil Clearance	Side Clearance
1990	6	1.6 (1598)	2.1653	0.0006–0.0020	0.0047–0.0138	3	1.6918–1.6920	0.0007–0.0025	0.0028–0.0095
	K	2.0 (1998)	2.2828–2.2833	0.0006–0.0016	0.0028–0.0118	3	1.9279–1.9287	0.0007–0.0025	0.0028–0.0095
1991	6	1.6 (1598)	2.1700	0.0006–0.0020	0.0047–0.0138	3	1.6918–1.6920	0.0018–0.0035	0.0028–0.0095
	K	2.0 (1998)	2.2828–2.2833	0.0006–0.0016	0.0028–0.0118	3	1.9279–1.9287	0.0007–0.0025	0.0028–0.0095
1992	6	1.6 (1598)	2.1700	0.0006–0.0020	0.0047–0.0138	3	1.6918–1.6920	0.0018–0.0035	0.0028–0.0095
1993	6	1.6 (1598)	2.1700	0.0006–0.0020	0.0047–0.0138	3	1.6918–1.6920	0.0018–0.0035	0.0028–0.0095

VALVE SPECIFICATIONS

Year	Engine ID/VIN	Engine Displacement Liters (cc)	Seat Angle (deg.)	Face Angle (deg.)	Spring Test Pressure (lbs. @ in.)	Spring Installed Height (in.)	Stem-to-Guide Clearance (in.)		Stem Diameter (in.)	
							Intake	Exhaust	Intake	Exhaust
1990	6	1.6 (1598)	46	46	140 @ 0.85	1.24	0.0008–0.0020	0.0016–0.0028	0.276	0.275
	K	2.0 (1998)	45	46	165–197 @ 1.043	1.48	0.0006–0.0017	0.0012–0.0024	0.276	0.275
1991	6	1.6 (1598)	46	46	140 @ 0.85	1.24	0.0008–0.0020	0.0016–0.0028	0.276	0.275
	K	2.0 (1998)	45	46	165–197 @ 1.043	1.48	0.0006–0.0017	0.0012–0.0024	0.276	0.275
1992	6	1.6 (1598)	46	46	140 @ 0.85	1.24	0.0008–0.0020	0.0016–0.0028	0.276	0.275
1993	6	1.6 (1598)	46	46	140 @ 0.85	1.24	0.0008–0.0020	0.0016–0.0028	0.276	0.275

PISTON AND RING SPECIFICATIONS

All measurements are given in inches.

Year	Engine ID/VIN	Engine Displacement Liters (cc)	Piston Clearance	Ring Gap			Ring Side Clearance		
				Top Compression	Bottom Compression	Oil Control	Top Compression	Bottom Compression	Oil Control
1990	6	1.6 (1598)	0.0008	0.012–0.020	0.012–0.020	0.016–0.055	0.0024–0.0036	0.0019–0.0032	NA
	K	2.0 (1998)	0.0004–0.0012	0.010–0.018	0.012–0.020	0.010–0.050	0.0024–0.0036	0.0019–0.0032	0.0019–0.0082
1991	6	1.6 (1598)	0.0008	0.012–0.020	0.012–0.020	NA	0.0024–0.0036	0.0019–0.0032	NA
	K	2.0 (1998)	0.0004–0.0012	0.010–0.018	0.012–0.020	0.010–0.050	0.0024–0.0036	0.0019–0.0032	0.0019–0.0082

PISTON AND RING SPECIFICATIONS

All measurements are given in inches.

Year	Engine ID/VIN	Engine Displacement Liters (cc)	Piston Clearance	Ring Gap			Ring Side Clearance		
				Top Compression	Bottom Compression	Oil Control	Top Compression	Bottom Compression	Oil Control
1992	6	1.6 (1598)	0.0008	0.012–0.020	0.012–0.020	NA	0.0024–0.0036	0.0019–0.0032	NA
1993	6	1.6 (1598)	0.0008	0.012–0.020	0.012–0.020	NA	0.0024–0.0036	0.0019–0.0032	NA

NA—Not available

TORQUE SPECIFICATIONS

All readings in ft. lbs.

Year	Engine ID/VIN	Engine Displacement Liters (cc)	Cylinder Head Bolts	Main Bearing Bolts	Rod Bearing Bolts	Crankshaft Damper Bolts	Flywheel Bolts	Manifold		Spark⑦ Plugs	Lug Nuts
								Intake	Exhaust		
1990	6	1.6 (1598)	18①	37②	18③	41	25④	16	10	15	66
	K	2.0 (1998)	18①	44⑥	26④	13	⑤	16	10	15	66
1991	6	1.6 (1598)	18①	37②	18③	41	26④	16	16	15	65
	K	2.0 (1998)	18①	44⑥	26④	13	⑤	16	10	15	65
1992	6	1.6 (1598)	18①	37②	18③	41	26④	16	16	15	65
1993	6	1.6 (1598)	18①	37②	18③	41	26④	16	16	15	65

① Cold—plus 2 turns of 60 degrees each and 1 turn of 30 degrees
② Plus a 45–60 degree turn
③ Plus a 30 degree turn
④ Plus a 30–45 degree turn
⑤ Automatic—52 ft. lbs.
 Manual —55 ft. lbs.
⑥ Plus a 40–50 degree turn
⑦ Only replace spark plugs with the cylinder head cold.

TORQUE SPECIFICATIONS

Component	English	Metric
Camshaft carrier/cylinder head bolt		
1.6L engine		
Step 1:	18 ft. lbs.	25 Nm
Step 2:	+ 60 degrees turn	+ 60 degrees turn
Step 3:	+ 60 degrees turn	+ 60 degrees turn
Step 4:	+ 30 degrees turn	+ 30 degrees turn
2.0L engine		
Step 1:	18 ft. lbs.	25 Nm
Step 2:	+ 60 degrees turn	+ 60 degrees turn
Step 3:	+ 60 degrees turn	+ 60 degrees turn
Step 4:	+ 60 degrees turn	+ 60 degrees turn
Step 5:	+ 30–50 degrees after engine warm-up	+ 30–50 degrees after engine warm-up
Camshaft sprocket bolt:	33 ft. lbs.	45 Nm
Connecting rod bolts		
1.6L engine		
Step 1:	18 ft. lbs.	25 Nm
Step 2:	+ 30 degrees turn	+ 30 degrees turn
2.0L engine		
Step 1:	26 ft. lbs.	35 Nm
Step 2:	+ 40–45 degrees turn	+ 40–45 degrees turn

TORQUE SPECIFICATIONS

Component	English	Metric
Crankshaft pulley bolt		
1.6L engine:	41 ft. lbs.	55 Nm
2.0L engine		
1990–91:	150 inch lbs.	17 Nm
Crankshaft sprocket bolt:	33 ft. lbs.	45 Nm
EGR valve-to-intake plenum:	14 ft. lbs.	18 Nm
Engine-to-transmission:	55 ft. lbs.	75 Nm
Exhaust manifold:	16 ft. lbs.	22 Nm
Exhaust pipe-to-exhaust manifold nuts		
1.6L engine		
1990–93:	115 inch lbs.	13 Nm
2.0L engine:	19 ft. lbs.	25 Nm
Flywheel/flexplate-to-crankshaft bolts		
1.6L engine		
Step 1:	26 ft. lbs.	35 Nm
Step 2:	+ 30–45 degrees turn	+ 30–45 degrees turn
2.0L engine		
Manual transaxle:	55 ft. lbs.	75 Nm
Automatic transaxle:	52 ft. lbs.	70 Nm
Flywheel-to-converter bolts:	44 ft. lbs.	60 Nm
Intake manifold:	16 ft. lbs.	22 Nm
Main bearing cap bolts		
1.6L engine		
Step 1:	37 ft. lbs.	50 Nm
Step 2:	+ 45–60 degrees turn	+ 45–60 degrees turn
2.0L engine		
Step 1:	44 ft. lbs.	60 Nm
Step 2:	+ 40–50 degrees turn	+ 40–50 degrees turn
Oil pan		
1.6L engine:	71 inch lbs.	8 Nm
2.0L engine:	44 inch lbs.	5 Nm
Oil pan drain plug:	33 ft. lbs.	45 Nm
Oil pump attaching bolts:	62 inch lbs.	7 Nm
Rocker (camshaft carrier) cover:	80 inch lbs.	9 Nm
Spark plug:	15 ft. lbs.	20 Nm
Starter-to-block bolts		
1990–91:	33 ft. lbs.	45 Nm
1992–93:	29 ft. lbs.	39 Nm
Thermostat housing:	89 inch lbs.	10 Nm
TBI-to-fuel meter body screws:	53 inch lbs.	6 Nm
TBI fuel feed/return line:	20 ft. lbs.	27 Nm
TBI mounting bolts/nuts:	12 ft. lbs.	17 Nm
Timing cover		
1.6L engine:	71 inch lbs.	8 Nm
2.0L engine:	89 inch lbs.	10 Nm
Water pump:	71 inch lbs.	8 Nm

BRAKE SPECIFICATIONS

All measurements in inches unless noted.

Year	Model	Master Cylinder Bore	Original Thickness	Brake Disc Minimum Thickness	Maximum Runout	Brake Drum Diameter Original Inside Diameter	Max. Wear Limit	Maximum Machine Diameter	Minimum Lining Thickness Front	rear
1990	Lemans	0.874	0.50	0.42①	0.004	7.87	7.90	7.90	0.28③	0.02④
1991	Lemans	0.874	0.50	0.42①	0.004	7.87	7.90	7.90	0.28③	0.02④

BRAKE SPECIFICATIONS

All measurements in inches unless noted.

| Year | Model | Master Cylinder Bore | Brake Disc | | | Brake Drum Diameter | | | Minimum Lining Thickness | |
			Original Thickness	Minimum Thickness	Maximum Runout	Original Inside Diameter	Max. Wear Limit	Maximum Machine Diameter	Front	rear
1992	Lemans	0.874	0.94	0.86 ②	0.004	7.87	7.90	7.90	0.28 ③	0.02 ④
1993	Lemans	0.874	0.94	0.86 ②	0.004	7.87	7.90	7.90	0.28 ③	0.02 ④

① Specification is minimum refinish thickness. Discard rotor at 0.38 in.

② Specification is minimum refinish thickness. Discard rotor at 0.83 in.

③ Shoe and lining together
④ Above any rivet head

WHEEL ALIGNMENT

| Year | Model | | Caster | | Camber | | Toe-in (in.) | Steering Axis Inclination (deg.) |
			Range (deg.)	Preferred Setting (deg.)	Range (deg.)	Preferred Setting (deg.)		
1990	Lemans	Front	3/4P–2 3/4P	NA	1N–1/2P	NA	0	—
		Rear	—	—	1N	NA	NA	—
1991	Lemans	Front	3/4P–2 3/4P	NA	1N–1/2P	NA	0	—
		Rear	—	—	1N	NA	NA	—
1992	Lemans	Front	3/4P–2 3/4P	NA	1 1/4N–1/4P	NA	0	—
		Rear	—	—	1N–0	NA	NA	—
1993	Lemans	Front	3/4P–2 3/4P	NA	1 1/4N–1/4P	NA	0	—
		Rear	—	—	1N–0	NA	NA	—

NA—Not adjustable
N—Negative
P—Positive

AIR CONDITIONING BELT TENSION

| Year | Engine VIN | Engine Displacement Liters (cc) | Belt Type | Specifications | |
				New	Used
1990	6	1.6 (1595)	Serpentine	①	
	K	2.0 (1988)	Serpentine	①	
1991	6	1.6 (1595)	Serpentine	①	
	K	2.0 (1988)	Serpentine	①	
1992	6	1.6 (1595)	Serpentine	①	
	K	2.0 (1988)	Serpentine	①	
1993	6	1.6 (1595)	Serpentine	①	

① Equipped with automatic tensioner; no adjustment required.

REFRIGERANT CAPACITIES

Year	Model	Refrigerant (oz.)	Oil (fl. oz.)	Compressor Type
1990	Lemans	35.0	8.0	V-5
1991	Lemans	35.0	8.0	V-5
1992	Lemans	35.0	8.0	V-5
1993	Lemans	35.0	8.0	V-5

NOTE: At the time of publication, refrigerant capacity information relating to R-134a was not available from the manufacturer.

MAINTENANCE INTERVALS—TYPE A: NORMAL SERVICE
LeMans

TO BE SERVICED	TYPE OF SERVICE	VEHICLE MILEAGE INTERVAL (X1000)							
		7.5	15	22.5	30	37.5	45	52.5	60
Oxygen Sensor	I				✔				✔
Ignition Timing	I				✔				✔
Vacuum Lines and Hoses	I		✔		✔		✔		✔
Ignition Wires	I				✔				✔
Spark Plugs	R				✔				✔
Engine Oil and Filter	R	✔	✔	✔	✔	✔	✔	✔	✔
Engine Air Cleaner Element	R				✔				✔
Crankcase Emission Filter	R				✔				✔
Tire Rotation	I①	✔							
Fuel Filter	R				✔				✔
Coolant Hoses and Clamps	I		✔		✔		✔		✔
Fuel/Vapor Return Lines	I				✔				✔
Fuel Tank Cap and Restrictor	I				✔				✔
Coolant System	R				✔				✔
Exhaust Pipe and Muffler	I				✔				✔
Battery Connections	I		✔		✔		✔		✔
Catalytic Converter and Shield	I				✔				✔
EGR System	I				✔				✔
CV-Joints and Boots	I	✔	✔	✔	✔	✔	✔	✔	✔
Body Lubrication	L				✔				✔
Automatic Transaxle Fluid	R②								
Timing Belt	R③								✔
Idle Speed System	I				✔				✔
Throttle Body Mounting Torque	I	✔							
Drive Belts	I				✔				✔
Brake Linings	I		✔		✔		✔		✔
Parking Brake	I		✔		✔		✔		✔
Thermostatically Controlled Air Cleaner	I					✔			✔
PCV Valve	R				✔				✔
Clutch Pedal Adjust	I	✔	✔	✔	✔	✔	✔	✔	✔
Seat Belt Operation	I				✔				✔

FOR COMPLETE WARRANTY COVERAGE CONSULT INDIVIDUAL VEHICLE MANUFACTURER'S WARRANTY MAINTENANCE GUIDE.

I—Inspect
L—Lubricate
R—Replace
① Rotate tires at 7,500 miles and then every 15,000 miles
② Replace automatic transaxle fluid at 100,000 miles
③ Replace timing belt at 60,000 miles

MAINTENANCE INTERVALS—TYPE B: SEVERE SERVICE
LeMans

TO BE SERVICED	TYPE OF SERVICE	VEHICLE MILEAGE INTERVAL (X1000)									
		3	6	9	12	15	18	21	24	27	30
Oxygen Sensor	I										✔
Ignition Timing	I										✔
Vacuum Lines and Hoses	I					✔					✔
Ignition Wires	I										✔
Spark Plugs	R										✔
Engine Oil and Filter	R	✔	✔	✔	✔	✔	✔	✔	✔	✔	✔
Engine Air Cleaner Element	R					✔					✔
Crankcase Emission Filter	R					✔					✔
Tire Rotation	I①		✔								
Fuel Filter	R					✔					✔
Battery Connections	I					✔					✔
Fuel/Vapor Return Lines	I										✔
Fuel Tank Cap and Restrictor	I										✔
Coolant System	R										✔
Exhaust Pipe and Muffler	I										✔
Coolant Hoses and Clamps	I					✔					✔
Catalytic Converter and Shield	I					✔					✔
EGR System	I										✔
CV-Joints and Boots	I	✔	✔	✔	✔	✔	✔	✔	✔		
Body Lubrication	L										✔
Automatic Transaxle Fluid	R					✔					✔
Timing Belt	R②										
Idle Speed System	I										✔
Throttle Body Mounting Torque	I		✔								
Drive Belts	I					✔					✔
Brake Linings	I					✔					✔
Parking Brake	I					✔					✔
Thermostatically Controlled Air Cleaner	I										
PCV Valve	R										✔
Clutch Pedal Adjust	I		✔		✔		✔		✔		✔
Seat Belt Operation	I										✔

FOR COMPLETE WARRANTY COVERAGE CONSULT INDIVIDUAL VEHICLE MANUFACTURER'S WARRANTY MAINTENANCE GUIDE.

I—Inspect
L—Lubricate
R—Replace
① Rotate tires at 6,000 miles and then every 15,000 miles as necessary
② Replace timing belt at 60,000 miles

FIRING ORDERS

NOTE: To avoid confusion, always replace spark plugs and wires one at a time.

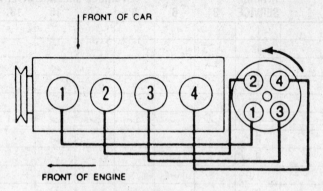

1.6L and 2.0L Engines
Engine Firing Order: 1–3–4–2
Distributor Rotation: Counterclockwise

TIMING MARK LOCATIONS

Timing mark location

CYLINDER HEAD TORQUE SEQUENCES

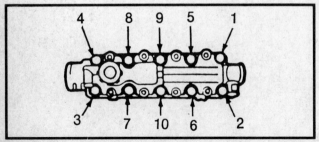

Camshaft carrier/cylinder head loosening sequence

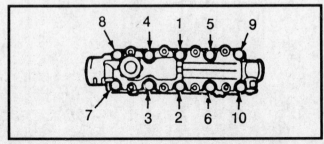

Camshaft carrier/cylinder head torque sequence

TIMING BELT ALIGNMENT MARKS

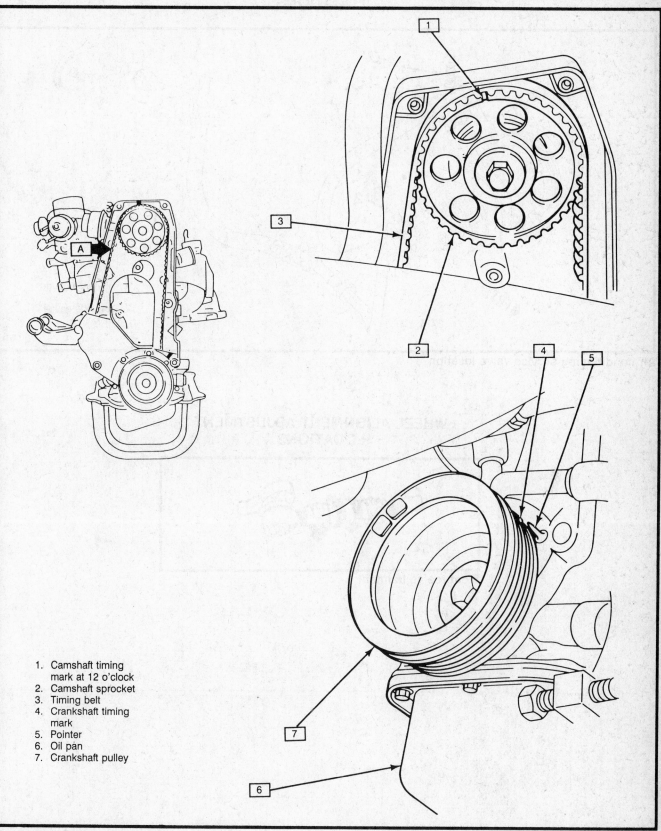

1. Camshaft timing mark at 12 o'clock
2. Camshaft sprocket
3. Timing belt
4. Crankshaft timing mark
5. Pointer
6. Oil pan
7. Crankshaft pulley

Timing belt alignment marks

AIR CONDITIONING SERVICE VALVE LOCATIONS

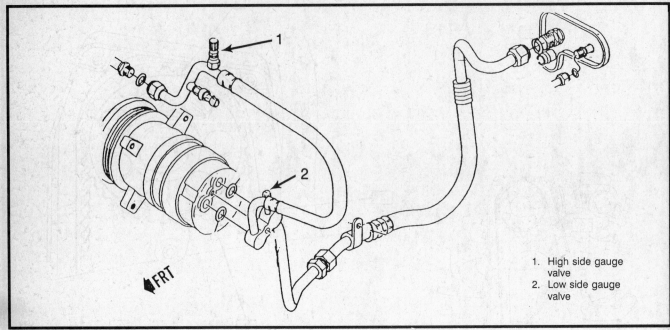

1. High side gauge valve
2. Low side gauge valve

Air conditioning service valve location

WHEEL ALIGNMENT ADJUSTMENT LOCATIONS

Front toe adjustment

SPECIFICATION CHARTS

VEHICLE IDENTIFICATION CHART

It is important for servicing and ordering parts to be certain of the vehicle and engine identification. The VIN (vehicle identification number) is a 17 digit number visible through the windshield on the driver's side of the dash and contains the vehicle and engine identification codes. The tenth digit indicates model year and the eighth digit indicates engine code. It can be interpreted as follows:

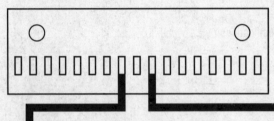

		Engine Code					Model Year	
Code	Liters	Cu. In. (cc)	Cyl.	Fuel Sys.	Eng. Mfg.	Code		Year
4	2.2	133 (2180)	4	MPFI	CPC	L		1990
A①	2.3	138 (2300)	4	MPFI	BOC	M		1991
D	2.3	138 (2300)	4	MPFI	BOC	N		1992
R	2.5	151 (2500)	4	TBI	CPC	P		1993
V②	3.1	191 (3100)	6	MPFI	CPC	R		1994
T	3.1	191 (3100)	6	MPFI	CPC			
X	3.4	204 (3400)	6	MPFI	CPC			
L	3.8	231 (3800)	6	TPI	BOC			

CPC—Chevrolet/Pontiac/Canada
BOC—Buick/Oldsmobile/Cadillac
TBI—Throttle Body Injection
TPI—Tuned Port Injection
MPFI—Multi-Port Fuel Injection
① Supercharged Engine
② Turbocharged Engine

ENGINE IDENTIFICATION

Year	Model	Engine Displacement Liters (cc)	Engine Series (ID/VIN)	Fuel System	No. of Cylinders	Engine Type
1990	Grand Prix	2.3 (2300)	D	MPFI	4	DOHC
	Grand Prix	3.1 (3100)	T	MPFI	6	OHV
	Grand Prix	3.1 (3100)	V①	MPFI	6	OHV
	Cutlass Supreme	2.3 (2300)	A②	MPFI	4	DOHC
	Cutlass Supreme	2.3 (2300)	D	MPFI	4	DOHC
	Cutlass Supreme	3.1 (3100)	T	MPFI	6	OHV
	Regal	3.1 (3100)	T	MPFI	6	OHV
	Regal	3.8 (3800)	L	TPI	6	OHV
	Lumina	2.5 (2500)	R	TBI	4	OHV
	Lumina	3.1 (3100)	T	MPFI	6	OHV

ENGINE IDENTIFICATION

Year	Model	Engine Displacement Liters (cc)	Engine Series (ID/VIN)	Fuel System	No. of Cylinders	Engine Type
1991	Grand Prix	2.3 (2300)	D	MPFI	4	DOHC
	Grand Prix	3.1 (3100)	T	MPFI	6	OHV
	Grand Prix	3.4 (3400)	X	MPFI	6	DOHC
	Cutlass Supreme	2.3 (2300)	D	MPFI	4	DOHC
	Cutlass Supreme	3.1 (3100)	T	MPFI	6	OHV
	Cutlass Supreme	3.4 (3400)	X	MPFI	6	DOHC
	Regal	3.1 (3100)	T	MPFI	6	OHV
	Regal	3.8 (3800)	L	TPI	6	OHV
	Lumina	2.5 (2500)	R	TBI	4	OHV
	Lumina	3.1 (3100)	T	MPFI	6	OHV
	Lumina	3.4 (3400)	X	MPFI	6	DOHC
1992	Grand Prix	3.1 (3100)	T	MPFI	6	OHV
	Grand Prix	3.4 (3400)	X	MPFI	6	DOHC
	Cutlass Supreme	3.1 (3100)	T	MPFI	6	OHV
	Cutlass Supreme	3.4 (3400)	X	MPFI	6	DOHC
	Regal	3.1 (3100)	T	MPFI	6	OHV
	Regal	3.8 (3800)	L	TPI	6	OHV
	Lumina	2.5 (2500)	R	TBI	4	OHV
	Lumina	3.1 (3100)	T	MPFI	6	OHV
	Lumina	3.4 (3400)	X	MPFI	6	DOHC
1993-94	Grand Prix	3.1 (3100)	T	MPFI	6	OHV
	Grand Prix	3.4 (3400)	X	MPFI	6	DOHC
	Cutlass Supreme	3.1 (3100)	T	MPFI	6	OHV
	Cutlass Supreme	3.4 (3400)	X	MPFI	6	DOHC
	Regal	3.1 (3100)	T	MPFI	6	OHV
	Regal	3.8 (3800)	L	TPI	6	OHV
	Lumina	2.2 (2180)	4	MPFI	4	OHV
	Lumina	3.1 (3100)	T	MPFI	6	OHV
	Lumina	3.4 (3400)	X	MPFI	6	DOHC

DOHC—Double Overhead Camshaft
MPFI—Multi-Port Fuel Injection
OHV—Overhead Valve
TBI—Throttle Body Injection
TPI—Tuned Port Injection
① Turbocharged Engine
② Supercharged Engine

GENERAL MOTORS – "W" BODY
CUTLASS SUPREME • GRAND PRIX • LUMINA • REGAL

GENERAL ENGINE SPECIFICATIONS

Year	Engine ID/VIN	Engine Displacement Liters (cc)	Fuel System Type	Net Horsepower @ rpm	Net Torque @ rpm (ft. lbs.)	Bore × Stroke (in.)	Compression Ratio	Oil Pressure @ rpm
1990	D	2.3 (2300)	MPFI	160 @ 6200	155 @ 5200	3.620 × 3.350	9.5:1	30 @ 2000
	A①	2.3 (2300)	MPFI	180 @ 6200	160 @ 5200	3.620 × 3.350	10.0:1	30 @ 2000
	R	2.5 (2500)	TBI	105 @ 4800	135 @ 3200	4.000 × 3.000	8.3:1	26 @ 800
	T	3.1 (3100)	MPFI	140 @ 4200	185 @ 3600	3.500 × 3.310	8.8:1	15 @ 1100
	V②	3.1 (3100)	MPFI	205 @ 4800	220 @ 3000	3.500 × 3.310	8.9:1	15 @ 1100
	L	3.8 (3800)	TPI	170 @ 4800	220 @ 3200	3.800 × 3.400	8.5:1	60 @ 1850
1991	D	2.3 (2300)	MPFI	160 @ 6200	155 @ 5200	3.620 × 3.350	9.5:1	30 @ 2000
	R	2.5 (2500)	TBI	105 @ 4800	135 @ 3200	4.000 × 3.000	8.3:1	26 @ 800
	T	3.1 (3100)	MPFI	140 @ 4200	185 @ 3600	3.500 × 3.310	8.8:1	15 @ 1100
	X	3.4 (3400)	MPFI	210 @ 5200	215 @ 4000	3.620 × 3.310	9.25:1	15 @ 1100
	L	3.8 (3800)	TPI	170 @ 4800	220 @ 3200	3.800 × 3.400	8.5:1	60 @ 1850
1992	R	2.5 (2500)	TBI	105 @ 4800	135 @ 3200	4.000 × 3.000	8.3:1	26 @ 800
	T	3.1 (3100)	MPFI	140 @ 4200	185 @ 3600	3.500 × 3.310	8.8:1	15 @ 1100
	X	3.4 (3400)	MPFI	210 @ 5200	215 @ 4000	3.620 × 3.310	9.25:1	15 @ 1100
	L	3.8 (3800)	TPI	170 @ 4800	220 @ 3200	3.800 × 3.400	8.5:1	60 @ 1850
1993–94	4	2.2 (2180)	MPFI	110 @ 5200	130 @ 3200	3.500 × 3.460	9.0:1	63–77 @ 1200
	T	3.1 (3100)	MPFI	140 @ 4200	185 @ 3600	3.510 × 3.310	8.9:1	50–65 @ 2400
	X	3.4 (3400)	MPFI	③	215 @ 4000	3.620 × 3.300	9.25:1	40 @ 2000
	L	3.8 (3800)	TPI	170 @ 4800	225 @ 3200	3.800 × 3.400	9.0:1	60 @ 1850

MPFI—Multi-Port Fuel Injection
TBI—Throttle Body Injection
TPI—Tuned Port Injection
① High Output Engine
② Turbocharged Engine
③ 200 hp @ 5000 rpm w/M13 4 speed automatic transmission
210 hp @ 5200 rpm w/M27 5 speed manual transmission

GASOLINE ENGINE TUNE-UP SPECIFICATIONS

Year	Engine ID/VIN	Engine Displacement Liters (cc)	Spark Plugs Gap (in.)	Ignition Timing (deg.) MT	Ignition Timing (deg.) AT	Fuel Pump① (psi)	Idle Speed (rpm) MT	Idle Speed (rpm) AT	Valve Clearance In.	Valve Clearance Ex.
1990	D	2.3 (2300)	0.035	①	①	40–47	①	①	Hyd.	Hyd.
	A	2.3 (2300)	0.035	①	①	40–47	①	①	Hyd.	Hyd.
	R	2.5 (2500)	0.060	①	①	26–32	①	①	Hyd.	Hyd.
	T	3.1 (3100)	0.045	①	①	41–47	①	①	Hyd.	Hyd.
	V	3.1 (3100)	0.045	①	①	41–47	①	①	Hyd.	Hyd.
	L	3.8 (3800)	0.045	①	①	41–47	①	①	Hyd.	Hyd.
1991	D	2.3 (2300)	0.035	①	①	41–47	①	①	Hyd.	Hyd.
	R	2.5 (2500)	0.060	①	①	26–32	①	①	Hyd.	Hyd.
	T	3.1 (3100)	0.045	①	①	41–47	①	①	Hyd.	Hyd.
	X	3.4 (3400)	0.045	①	①	41–47	①	①	Hyd.	Hyd.
	L	3.8 (3800)	0.060	①	①	40–47	①	①	Hyd.	Hyd.

GASOLINE ENGINE TUNE-UP SPECIFICATIONS

Year	Engine ID/VIN	Engine Displacement Liters (cc)	Spark Plugs Gap (in.)	Ignition Timing (deg.) MT	AT	Fuel Pump① (psi)	Idle Speed (rpm) MT	AT	Valve Clearance In.	Ex.
1992	R	2.5 (2500)	0.060	①	①	26–32	①	①	Hyd.	Hyd.
	T	3.1 (3100)	0.045	①	①	41–47	①	①	Hyd.	Hyd.
	X	3.4 (3400)	0.045	①	①	41–47	①	①	Hyd.	Hyd.
	L	3.8 (3800)	0.060	①	①	40–47	①	①	Hyd.	Hyd.
1993	4	2.2 (2180)	0.045	①	①	41–47	①	①	Hyd.	Hyd.
	T	3.1 (3100)	0.045	①	①	41–47	①	①	Hyd.	Hyd.
	X	3.4 (3400)	0.045	①	①	41–47	①	①	Hyd.	Hyd.
	L	3.8 (3800)	0.060	①	①	40–47	①	①	Hyd.	Hyd.
1994			SEE UNDERHOOD SPECIFICATIONS STICKER							

NOTE: The lowest cylinder pressure should be within 75% of the highest cylinder pressure reading. For example, if the highest cylinder is 134 psi, the lowest should be 101. Engine should be at normal operating temperature with throttle valve in the wide open position.
The underhood specifications sticker often reflects tune-up specification changes in production. Sticker figures must be used if they disagree with those in this chart.
Hyd.—Hydraulic
① Ignition timing and engine speed are controlled
by the Electronic Control Module. No adjustment is necessary.

CAPACITIES

Year	Model	Engine ID/VIN	Engine Displacement Liters (cc)	Engine Crankcase with Filter (qts.)①	Transmission (pts.) 4-Spd	5-Spd	Auto.	Transfer Case (pts.)	Drive Axle Front (pts.)	Rear (pts.)	Fuel Tank (gal.)	Cooling System (qts.)
1990	Grand Prix	D	2.3 (2300)	4.0	—	4.2	②	—	—	—	16.5	9.2
	Grand Prix	T	3.1 (3100)	4.0	—	4.2	②	—	—	—	16.5	12.5
	Grand Prix	V	3.1 (3100)	4.0	—	4.2	②	—	—	—	16.5	13.2
	Cutlass Supreme	A	2.3 (2300)	4.0	—	4.4	②	—	—	—	16.5	8.9
	Cutlass Supreme	D	2.3 (2300)	4.0	—	4.4	②	—	—	—	16.5	9.2
	Cutlass Supreme	T	3.1 (3100)	4.0	—	4.4	②	—	—	—	16.5	12.5
	Regal	T	3.1 (3100)	4.0	—	—	②	—	—	—	16.5	12.5
	Regal	L	3.8 (3800)	4.0	—	—	②	—	—	—	16.5	11.1
	Lumina	R	2.5 (2500)	4.0	—	—	②	—	—	—	16.0	9.4
	Lumina	T	3.1 (3100)	4.0	—	—	②	—	—	—	16.0	12.6
1991	Grand Prix	D	2.3 (2300)	4.0	—	4.2	②	—	—	—	16.5	9.2
	Grand Prix	T	3.1 (3100)	4.0	—	4.2	②	—	—	—	16.5	12.5
	Grand Prix	X	3.4 (3400)	5.0	—	4.0	②	—	—	—	16.5	12.7
	Cutlass Supreme	D	2.3 (2300)	4.0	—	4.4	②	—	—	—	16.5	9.2
	Cutlass Supreme	T	3.1 (3100)	4.0	—	4.4	②	—	—	—	16.5	12.5
	Cutlass Supreme	X	3.4 (3400)	5.0	—	4.0	②	—	—	—	16.5	12.7
	Regal	T	3.1 (3100)	4.0	—	—	②	—	—	—	16.5	12.5
	Regal	L	3.8 (3800)	4.0	—	—	②	—	—	—	16.5	11.1
	Lumina	R	2.5 (2500)	4.0	—	—	②	—	—	—	16.0	9.4
	Lumina	T	3.1 (3100)	4.0	—	—	②	—	—	—	16.0	12.6
	Lumina	X	3.4 (3400)	5.0	—	—	②	—	—	—	16.5	12.7

GENERAL MOTORS—"W" BODY
CUTLASS SUPREME • GRAND PRIX • LUMINA • REGAL

CAPACITIES

Year	Model	Engine ID/VIN	Engine Displacement Liters (cc)	Engine Crankcase with Filter (qts.)①	Transmission (pts.) 4-Spd	5-Spd	Auto.	Transfer Case (pts.)	Drive Axle Front (pts.)	Rear (pts.)	Fuel Tank (gal.)	Cooling System (qts.)
1992	Grand Prix	T	3.1 (3100)	4.0	—	4.2	②	—	—	—	16.5	12.6
	Grand Prix	X	3.4 (3400)	5.0	—	4.2	②	—	—	—	16.5	12.6
	Cutlass Supreme	T	3.1 (3100)	4.0	—	4.4	②	—	—	—	16.5	12.6
	Cutlass Supreme	X	3.4 (3400)	5.0	—	4.4	②	—	—	—	16.5	12.6
	Regal	T	3.1 (3100)	5.0	—	—	②	—	—	—	16.5	12.6
	Regal	L	3.8 (3800)	5.0	—	—	②	—	—	—	16.5	11.1
	Lumina	R	2.5 (2500)	4.0	—	—	②	—	—	—	16.4	9.1
	Lumina	T	3.1 (3100)	4.0	—	—	②	—	—	—	16.4	12.0
	Lumina	X	3.4 (3400)	5.0	—	4.2	②	—	—	—	16.4	12.6
1993-94	Grand Prix	T	3.1 (3100)	4.0	—	—	②	—	—	—	16.5	③
	Grand Prix	X	3.4 (3400)	5.0	—	4.5	②	—	—	—	16.5	④
	Cutlass Supreme	T	3.1 (3100)	4.0	—	—	②	—	—	—	16.5	③
	Cutlass Supreme	X	3.4 (3400)	5.0	—	—	②	—	—	—	16.5	12.7
	Regal	T	3.1 (3100)	4.0	—	—	②	—	—	—	16.5	12.6
	Regal	L	3.8 (3800)	4.0	—	—	②	—	—	—	16.5	11.1
	Lumina	4	2.2 (2180)	4.0	—	—	②	—	—	—	17.1	11.7
	Lumina	T	3.1 (3100)	4.0	—	—	②	—	—	—	16.5	③
	Lumina	X	3.4 (3400)	5.0	—	4.5	②	—	—	—	16.5	④

① Add fluid as required to fill to the appropriate level.
② 3T40: drain and refill only—8 pts., overhaul—14 pts.
   4T60: drain and refill only—12 pts., overhaul—16 pts.
   4T60E: drain and refill only—14.8 pts., overhaul—20 pts.
③ With 3T40 trans.—12.7 qts.
   With 4T60E trans.—12.5 qts.
④ With manual trans.—12.9 qts.
   With 4T60E trans.—12.7 qts.

CAMSHAFT SPECIFICATIONS
All measurements given in inches.

Year	Engine ID/VIN	Engine Displacement Liters (cc)	Journal Diameter 1	2	3	4	5	Elevation In.	Ex.	Bearing Clearance	Camshaft End Play
1990	D	2.3 (2300)	1.572–1.573	1.375–1.376	1.375–1.376	1.375–1.376	1.375–1.376	0.375	0.375	0.0019–0.0043	0.0009–0.0088
	A	2.3 (2300)	1.572–1.573	1.375–1.376	1.375–1.376	1.375–1.376	1.375–1.376	0.410	0.410	0.0019–0.0043	0.0009–0.0088
	R	2.5 (2500)	1.869	1.869	1.869	1.869	—	0.248	0.248	0.0007–0.0027	0.0014–0.0050
	T	3.1 (3100)	1.868–1.882	1.868–1.882	1.868–1.882	1.868–1.882	—	0.262	0.273	0.0010–0.0040	NA
	V	3.1 (3100)	1.868–1.882	1.868–1.882	1.868–1.882	1.868–1.882	—	0.262	0.273	0.0010–0.0040	NA
	L	3.8 (3800)	1.785–1.786	1.785–1.786	1.785–1.786	1.785–1.786	—	0.250	0.255	0.0005–0.0035	NA

CAMSHAFT SPECIFICATIONS

All measurements given in inches.

Year	Engine ID/VIN	Engine Displacement Liters (cc)	Journal Diameter					Elevation		Bearing Clearance	Camshaft End Play
			1	2	3	4	5	In.	Ex.		
1991	D	2.3 (2300)	1.572–1.573	1.375–1.376	1.375–1.376	1.375–1.376	1.375–1.376	0.375	0.375	0.0019–0.0043	0.0009–0.0088
	R	2.5 (2500)	1.869	1.869	1.869	1.869	—	0.248	0.248	0.0007–0.0027	0.0014–0.0050
	T	3.1 (3100)	1.868–1.882	1.868–1.882	1.868–1.882	1.868–1.882	—	0.262	0.273	0.0010–0.0040	NA
	X	3.4 (3400)	2.165–2.166	2.165–2.166	2.165–2.166	2.165–2.166	—	0.370	0.370	0.0015–0.0035	NA
	L	3.8 (3800)	1.785–1.786	1.785–1.786	1.785–1.786	1.785–1.786	—	0.250	0.255	0.0005–0.0035	NA
1992	R	2.5 (2500)	1.869	1.869	1.869	1.869	—	0.248	0.248	0.0007–0.0027	0.0009–0.0088
	T	3.1 (3100)	1.868–1.882	1.868–1.882	1.868–1.882	1.868–1.882	—	0.262	0.273	0.0010–0.0040	0.0014–0.0050
	X	3.4 (3400)	2.165–2.166	2.165–2.166	2.165–2.166	2.165–2.166	—	0.370	0.370	0.0015–0.0035	NA
	L	3.8 (3800)	1.785–1.786	1.785–1.786	1.785–1.786	1.785–1.786	—	0.250	0.255	0.0005–0.0035	NA
1993–94	4	2.2 (2180)	1.867–1.869	1.867–1.869	1.867–1.869	1.867–1.869	—	0.259	0.250	0.0010–0.0039	NA
	T	3.1 (3100)	1.868–1.882	1.868–1.882	1.868–1.882	1.868–1.882	—	0.263	0.273	0.0010–0.0040	NA
	X	3.4 (3400)	2.164–2.165	2.164–2.165	2.164–2.165	2.164–2.165	—	0.370	0.370	0.0019–0.0040	NA
	L	3.8 (3800)	1.785–1.786	1.785–1.786	1.785–1.786	1.785–1.786	—	0.250	0.255	0.0005–0.0035	NA

NA—Not available

CRANKSHAFT AND CONNECTING ROD SPECIFICATIONS

All measurements are given in inches.

Year	Engine ID/VIN	Engine Displacement Liters (cc)	Crankshaft				Connecting Rod		
			Main Brg. Journal Dia.	Main Brg. Oil Clearance	Shaft End-play	Thrust on No.	Journal Diameter	Oil Clearance	Side Clearance
1990	D	2.3 (2300)	2.0470–2.0480	0.0005–0.0023	0.0034–0.0095	3	1.8887–1.8897	0.0005–0.0020	0.0054–0.0177
	A	2.3 (2300)	2.0470–2.0480	0.0005–0.0023	0.0034–0.0095	3	1.8887–1.8897	0.0005–0.0020	0.0054–0.0177
	R	2.5 (2500)	2.3000	0.0005–0.0022	0.0005–0.0180	5	2.0000	0.0005–0.0030	0.0060–0.0240
	T	3.1 (3100)	2.6473–2.6483	0.0024–0.0027	0.0012–0.0083	3	1.9983–1.9994	0.0014–0.0036	0.0140–0.0270
	V	3.1 (3100)	2.6473–2.6483	0.0024–0.0027	0.0012–0.0083	3	1.9983–1.9994	0.0014–0.0036	0.0140–0.0270
	L	3.8 (3800)	2.4988–2.4998	0.0018–0.0030	0.0030–0.0110	3	2.2487–2.2499	0.0003–0.0026	0.0030–0.0150

CRANKSHAFT AND CONNECTING ROD SPECIFICATIONS

All measurements are given in inches.

Year	Engine ID/VIN	Engine Displacement Liters (cc)	Crankshaft				Connecting Rod		
			Main Brg. Journal Dia.	Main Brg. Oil Clearance	Shaft End-play	Thrust on No.	Journal Diameter	Oil Clearance	Side Clearance
1991	D	2.3 (2300)	2.0470–2.0480	0.0005–0.0023	0.0034–0.0095	3	1.8887–1.8897	0.0005–0.0020	0.0054–0.0177
	R	2.5 (2500)	2.3000	0.0005–0.0022	0.0005–0.0180	5	2.0000	0.0005–0.0030	0.0060–0.0240
	T	3.1 (3100)	2.6473–2.6483	0.0024–0.0027	0.0012–0.0083	3	1.9983–1.9994	0.0014–0.0036	0.0140–0.0270
	X	3.4 (3400)	2.6473–2.6479	0.0013–0.0030	0.0024–0.0083	3	1.9987–1.9994	0.0011–0.0032	0.0140–0.0250
	L	3.8 (3800)	2.4988–2.4998	0.0018–0.0030	0.0030–0.0110	3	2.2487–2.2499	0.0003–0.0026	0.0030–0.0150
1992	R	2.5 (2500)	2.3000	0.0005–0.0022	0.0005–0.0180	5	2.0000	0.0005–0.0030	0.0060–0.0240
	T	3.1 (3100)	2.6473–2.6483	0.0024–0.0027	0.0012–0.0083	3	1.9983–1.9994	0.0014–0.0036	0.0140–0.0270
	X	3.4 (3400)	2.6473–2.6479	0.0013–0.0030	0.0024–0.0083	3	1.9987–1.9994	0.0011–0.0032	0.0140–0.0250
	L	3.8 (3800)	2.4988–2.4998	0.0018–0.0030	0.0030–0.0110	3	2.2487–2.2499	0.0003–0.0026	0.0030–0.0150
1993–94	4	2.2 (2180)	2.4945–2.4954	0.0006–0.0019	0.0020–0.0070	4	1.9983–1.9994	0.0098–0.0031	0.0039–0.0149
	T	3.1 (3100)	2.6473–2.6479	0.0013–0.0030	0.0024–0.0083	3	1.9987–1.9994	0.0011–0.0032	0.0071–0.0173
	X	3.4 (3400)	2.6472–2.6479	0.0013–0.0030	0.0024–0.0083	3	1.9987–1.9994	0.0011–0.0032	0.0071–0.0173
	L	3.8 (3800)	2.4988–2.4998	0.0008–0.0022	0.0030–0.0110	3	2.2487–2.2499	0.0008–0.0022	0.0030–0.0150

VALVE SPECIFICATIONS

Year	Engine ID/VIN	Engine Displacement Liters (cc)	Seat Angle (deg.)	Face Angle (deg.)	Spring Test Pressure (lbs. @ in.)	Spring Installed Height (in.)	Stem-to-Guide Clearance (in.)		Stem Diameter (in.)	
							Intake	Exhaust	Intake	Exhaust
1990	D	2.3 (2300)	45	①	76 @ 1.43	NA	0.0010–0.0027	0.0010–0.0027	NA	NA
	A	2.3 (2300)	45	①	76 @ 1.43	NA	0.0010–0.0027	0.0010–0.0027	NA	NA
	R	2.5 (2500)	45	46	75 @ 1.68	1.68	0.0010–0.0026	0.0013–0.0041	NA	NA
	T	3.1 (3100)	46	45	90 @ 1.70	1.57	0.0010–0.0027	0.0010–0.0027	NA	NA
	V	3.1 (3100)	46	45	90 @ 1.70	1.57	0.0010–0.0027	0.0010–0.0027	NA	NA
	L	3.8 (3800)	45	45	80 @ 1.75	1.70	0.0015–0.0035	0.0015–0.0032	NA	NA

VALVE SPECIFICATIONS

Year	Engine ID/VIN	Engine Displacement Liters (cc)	Seat Angle (deg.)	Face Angle (deg.)	Spring Test Pressure (lbs. @ in.)	Spring Installed Height (in.)	Stem-to-Guide Clearance (in.) Intake	Stem-to-Guide Clearance (in.) Exhaust	Stem Diameter (in.) Intake	Stem Diameter (in.) Exhaust
1991	D	2.3 (2300)	45	①	76 @ 1.43	NA	0.0010–0.0027	0.0010–0.0027	NA	NA
	R	2.5 (2500)	45	46	75 @ 1.68	1.68	0.0010–0.0026	0.0013–0.0041	NA	NA
	T	3.1 (3100)	46	45	90 @ 1.70	1.57	0.0010–0.0027	0.0010–0.0027	NA	NA
	X	3.4 (3400)	46	45	75 @ 1.40	1.40	0.0011–0.0026	0.0014–0.0031	NA	NA
	L	3.8 (3800)	45	45	80 @ 1.75	1.70	0.0015–0.0035	0.0015–0.0032	NA	NA
1992	R	2.5 (2500)	45	46	75 @ 1.68	1.68	0.0010–0.0026	0.0013–0.0041	NA	NA
	T	3.1 (3100)	46	45	90 @ 1.70	1.57	0.0010–0.0027	0.0010–0.0027	NA	NA
	X	3.4 (3400)	46	45	75 @ 1.40	1.40	0.0011–0.0026	0.0014–0.0031	NA	NA
	L	3.8 (3800)	45	45	80 @ 1.75	1.70	0.0015–0.0035	0.0015–0.0032	NA	NA
1993–94	4	2.2 (2180)	46	45	79–85 @ 1.63	NA	0.0011–0.0026	0.0014–0.0031	NA	NA
	T	3.1 (3100)	46	45	90 @ 1.69	1.69	0.0008–0.0021	0.0014–0.0030	NA	NA
	X	3.4 (3400)	46	45	65 @ 1.40	1.40	0.0011–0.0026	0.0018–0.0033	NA	NA
	L	3.8 (3800)	45	45	80 @ 1.75	1.70	0.0015–0.0035	0.0015–0.0032	NA	NA

NA—Not available
① Intake—44 degrees; Exhaust—44.5 degrees

PISTON AND RING SPECIFICATIONS
All measurements are given in inches.

Year	Engine ID/VIN	Engine Displacement Liters (cc)	Piston Clearance	Ring Gap Top Compression	Ring Gap Bottom Compression	Ring Gap Oil Control	Ring Side Clearance Top Compression	Ring Side Clearance Bottom Compression	Ring Side Clearance Oil Control
1990	D	2.3 (2300)	0.0007–0.0020	0.013–0.023	0.015–0.025	0.015–0.055	0.002–0.003	0.001–0.003	0.002–0.003
	A	2.3 (2300)	0.0007–0.0020	0.013–0.023	0.015–0.025	0.015–0.055	0.002–0.004	0.001–0.004	0.002–0.003
	R	2.5 (2500)	0.0014–0.0022	0.010–0.020	0.010–0.020	0.020–0.060	0.002–0.003	0.001–0.003	0.002–0.006
	T	3.1 (3100)	0.0009–0.0022	0.010–0.020	0.010–0.028	0.010–0.030	0.002–0.003	0.002–0.003	0.001–0.008
	V	3.1 (3100)	0.0009–0.0022	0.010–0.020	0.010–0.028	0.010–0.030	0.002–0.003	0.002–0.003	0.001–0.008
	L	3.8 (3800)	0.0004–0.0022	0.010–0.025	0.010–0.025	0.015–0.055	0.001–0.003	0.001–0.003	0.001–0.008

PISTON AND RING SPECIFICATIONS

All measurements are given in inches.

Year	Engine ID/VIN	Engine Displacement Liters (cc)	Piston Clearance	Ring Gap			Ring Side Clearance		
				Top Compression	Bottom Compression	Oil Control	Top Compression	Bottom Compression	Oil Control
1991	D	2.3 (2300)	0.0007–0.0020	0.013–0.023	0.015–0.025	0.015–0.055	0.002–0.003	0.001–0.003	0.002–0.003
	R	2.5 (2500)	0.0014–0.0022	0.010–0.020	0.010–0.020	0.020–0.060	0.002–0.003	0.001–0.003	0.002–0.006
	T	3.1 (3100)	0.0009–0.0022	0.010–0.020	0.010–0.028	0.010–0.030	0.002–0.003	0.002–0.003	0.001–0.008
	X	3.4 (3400)	0.0009–0.0023	0.012–0.022	0.019–0.029	0.010–0.030	0.002–0.004	0.002–0.004	0.002–0.008
	L	3.8 (3800)	0.0004–0.0022	0.010–0.025	0.010–0.025	0.015–0.055	0.001–0.003	0.001–0.003	0.001–0.008
1992	R	2.5 (2500)	0.0014–0.0022	0.010–0.020	0.010–0.020	0.020–0.060	0.002–0.003	0.001–0.003	0.002–0.006
	T	3.1 (3100)	0.0009–0.0022	0.010–0.020	0.010–0.028	0.010–0.030	0.002–0.003	0.002–0.003	0.001–0.008
	X	3.4 (3400)	0.0009–0.0023	0.012–0.022	0.019–0.029	0.010–0.030	0.002–0.004	0.002–0.004	0.002–0.008
	L	3.8 (3800)	0.0004–0.0022	0.010–0.025	0.010–0.025	0.015–0.055	0.001–0.003	0.001–0.003	0.001–0.008
1993–94	4	2.2 (2180)	0.0007–0.0017	0.010–0.020	0.010–0.020	0.010–0.050	0.002–0.003	0.002–0.003	0.002–0.008
	T	3.1 (3100)	0.0009–0.0023	0.007–0.016	0.020–0.028	0.010–0.029	0.002–0.003	0.002–0.003	0.001–0.008
	X	3.4 (3400)	0.0013–0.0027	0.009–0.019	0.019–0.029	0.010–0.029	0.002–0.003	0.002–0.003	0.002–0.008
	L	3.8 (3800)	0.0004–0.0022	0.010–0.025	0.010–0.025	0.015–0.055	0.002–0.003	0.002–0.003	0.001–0.008

TORQUE SPECIFICATIONS

All readings in ft. lbs.

Year	Engine ID/VIN	Engine Displacement Liters (cc)	Cylinder Head Bolts	Main Bearing Bolts	Rod Bearing Bolts	Crankshaft Damper Bolts	Flywheel Bolts	Manifold		Spark Plugs	Lug Nut
								Intake	Exhaust		
1990	D	2.3 (2300)	⑤	⑥	⑦	⑧	⑨	18	27	17	100
	A	2.3 (2300)	⑤	⑥	⑦	⑧	⑨	18	27	17	100
	R	2.5 (2500)	②	65	29	162	55	25	④	18	100
	T	3.1 (3100)	①	73	39	76	60	③	18	18	100
	V	3.1 (3100)	①	73	39	76	60	③	18	18	100
	L	3.8 (3800)	⑩	⑪	⑫	⑬	⑭	⑮	41	20	100
1991	D	2.3 (2300)	⑤	⑥	⑦	⑧	⑨	18	27	17	100
	R	2.5 (2500)	②	65	29	162	55	25	④	11	100
	T	3.1 (3100)	①	73	39	76	60	③	18	11	100
	X	3.4 (3400)	⑯	⑰	39	78	61	18	⑱	11	100
	L	3.8 (3800)	⑩	⑪	⑫	⑬	⑭	⑮	41	20	100

TORQUE SPECIFICATIONS

All readings in ft. lbs.

Year	Engine ID/VIN	Engine Displacement Liters (cc)	Cylinder Head Bolts	Main Bearing Bolts	Rod Bearing Bolts	Crankshaft Damper Bolts	Flywheel Bolts	Manifold		Spark Plugs	Lug Nut
								Intake	Exhaust		
1992	R	2.5 (2500)	②	65	29	162	55	25	④	11	100
	T	3.1 (3100)	①	73	39	76	44	③	18	11	100
	X	3.4 (3400)	⑯	⑰	39	78	61	18	⑱	11	100
	L	3.8 (3800)	⑩	⑪	⑫	⑬	⑭	⑮	41	20	100
1993-94	4	2.2 (2180)	⑲	70	38	77	55	22	⑱	11	100
	T	3.1 (3100)	①	⑰	37	76	52	③	21	11	100
	X	3.4 (3400)	⑯	⑰	37	80	61	⑳	13	11	100
	L	3.8 (3800)	⑩	⑪	⑫	⑬	⑭	⑮	38	20	100

① Torque in 2 steps:
  1st step—33 ft. lbs.
  2nd step—Turn an additional 90 degrees (¼ turn)
② Torque in 3 steps:
  1st step—18 ft. lbs.
  2nd step—Bolts "A" through "J" except "I" to 26 ft. lbs. Tighten bolt "I" to 18 ft. lbs.
  3rd step—Turn an additional 90 degrees (¼ turn)
③ Torque in 2 steps:
  1st step—15 ft. lbs.
  2nd step—24 ft. lbs.
④ Torque inner bolts to 37 ft. lbs. and outer bolts to 26 ft. lbs.
⑤ Torque in 2 steps:
  1st step—Torque all bolts in sequence to 26 ft. lbs.
  2nd step—Torque in sequence bolts number 7 and 9 an additional 100 degrees and the remaining bolts 110 degrees
⑥ 15 ft. lbs. plus an additional 90 degree turn
⑦ 18 ft. lbs. plus an additional 80 degree turn
⑧ 74 ft. lbs. plus an additional 90 degree turn
⑨ 22 ft. lbs. plus an additional 45 degree turn

⑩ Torque in 3 steps:
  1st step—Tighten all bolts in sequence to 35 ft. lbs.
  2nd step—Tighten all bolts in sequence an additional 130 degrees
  3rd step—Tighten the center 4 bolts an additional 30 degrees
⑪ 26 ft. lbs. plus an additional 45 degree turn
⑫ 20 ft. lbs. plus an additional 50 degree turn
⑬ 105 ft. lbs. plus an additional 56 degree turn
⑭ 89 inch lbs. plus an additional 90 degree turn
⑮ Intake manifold to cylinder head (lower)—89 inch lbs.
⑯ Torque in 2 steps:
  1st step—Torque all bolts in sequence to 37 ft. lbs.
  2nd step—Turn an additional 90 degrees (¼ turn)
⑰ 37 ft. lbs. plus an additional 75 degree turn
⑱ 115 inch lbs.
⑲ Long bolts—46 ft. lbs. plus an additional 90 degree turn
  Short bolts and stud—43 ft. lbs. plus an additional 90 degree turn
⑳ Upper intake manifold mount bolt—97 inch lbs. Upper intake manifold retaining bolt and nut—18 ft. lbs.

TORQUE SPECIFICATIONS

Component	English	Metric
Camshaft sprocket bolt		
2.3L engine:	40 ft. lbs.	54 Nm
2.5L engine:	43 ft. lbs.	58 Nm
2.8L and 3.1L engines:	21 ft. lbs.	28 Nm
3.4L engine:	81 ft. lbs.	110 Nm
3.8L engine		
Step 1:	74 ft. lbs.	100 Nm
Step 2:	+ 105 degree turn	+ 105 degree turn
Connecting rod bearing cap bolts		
2.3L engine		
Step 1:	18 ft. lbs.	25 Nm
Step 2:	+ 80 degree turn	+ 80 degree turn
2.5L engine:	29 ft. lbs.	40 Nm
2.8L engine:	37 ft. lbs.	50 Nm
3.1L and 3.4L engines:	39 ft. lbs.	53 Nm
3.8L engine		
Step 1:	20 ft. lbs.	27 Nm
Step 2:	+ 50 degree turn	+ 50 degree turn

TORQUE SPECIFICATIONS

Component	English	Metric
Crankshaft damper bolt		
2.3L engine		
Step 1:	74 ft. lbs.	100 Nm
Step 2:	+ 90 degree turn	+ 90 degree turn
2.5L engine:	162 ft. lbs.	220 Nm
2.8L, 3.1L and 3.4L engines:	77 ft. lbs.	105 Nm
3.8L engine		
Step 1:	110 ft. lbs.	150 Nm
Step 2:	+ 76 degree turn	+ 76 degree turn
Cylinder head bolt		
2.3L engine		
Step 1 (All bolts):	26 ft. lbs.	35 Nm
Step 2 (Except short bolts):	+ 110 degree turn	+ 110 degree turn
Step 3 (Short bolts):	+ 100 degree turn	+ 100 degree turn
2.5L engine		
Step 1 (all bolts):	18 ft. lbs.	26 Nm
Step 2 (all except position "i" (R/F):	26 ft. lbs.	35 Nm
Step 3 (retorque position "i" (R/F):	18 ft. lbs.	26 Nm
Step 4 (all bolts:	+ 90 degree turn	+ 90 degree turn
2.8L and 3.1L engines		
Step 1:	33 ft. lbs.	45 Nm
Step 2:	+ 90 degrees	+ 90 degrees
3.4L engines		
Step 1:	37 ft. lbs.	50 Nm
Step 2:	+ 90 degree turn	+ 90 degree turn
3.8L engine		
Step 1:	35 ft. lbs.	47 Nm
Step 2:	+ 130 degree turn	+ 130 degree turn
Step 3:	+ 30 degree turn	+ 30 degree turn
	4 center bolts	4 center bolts
EGR valve-to-intake plenum		
2.3L engine:	18 ft. lbs.	26 Nm
2.5L engine:	16 ft. lbs.	22 Nm
2.8L engine:	19 ft. lbs.	25 Nm
3.1L and 3.4L engine:	22 ft. lbs.	30 Nm
Engine-to-transmission		
Except 2.3L engine with automatic transaxle:	55 ft. lbs.	75 Nm
2.3L engine with automatic transaxle		
Positions No. 2, 3, 4, 5, 6:	71 ft. lbs.	96 Nm
Position No. 7 (stud):	115 inch lbs.	13 Nm
Position No. 7 (nut):	41 ft. lbs.	56 Nm
Position No. 8:	37 ft. lbs.	50 Nm
Exhaust manifold		
2.3L engine		
Nuts:	27 ft. lbs.	Nm
Studs:	106 inch lbs.	12 Nm
2.5L engine		
Inner bolt:	37 ft. lbs.	50 Nm
Outer bolt:	28 ft. lbs.	38 Nm
2.8L and 3.1L engines:	19 ft. lbs.	25 Nm
3.4L engine		
Nuts:	116 inch lbs.	13 Nm
Studs:	13 ft. lbs.	17 Nm
3.8L engine:	41 ft. lbs.	55 Nm
Exhaust pipe-to-exhaust manifold nuts:	19 ft. lbs.	25 Nm

TORQUE SPECIFICATIONS

Component	English	Metric
Flywheel/flexplate-to-crankshaft bolts		
2.3L engine		
Step 1:	22 ft. lbs.	30 Nm
Step 2:	+ 45 degree turn	+ 45 degree turn
2.5L engine:	55 ft. lbs.	75 Nm
2.8L and 3.1L engines:	52 ft. lbs.	70 Nm
3.4L engine:	61 ft. lbs.	83 Nm
3.8L engine		
Step 1:	11 ft. lbs.	15 Nm
Step 2:	+ 50 degree turn	+ 50 degree turn
Flywheel-to-converter bolt:	46 ft. lbs.	63 Nm
Intake manifold-to-cylinder head		
2.3L engine:	18 ft. lbs.	25 Nm
2.5L engine:	25 ft. lbs.	34 Nm
2.8L and 3.1L engines:	24 ft. lbs.	33 Nm
3.4L engine:	18 ft. lbs.	25 Nm
3.8L engine:	89 inch. lbs.	10 Nm
Intake manifold-to-plenum		
2.8L and 3.1L engine:	24 ft. lbs.	33 Nm
3.4L engine:	89 inch lbs.	10 Nm
3.8L engine:	22 ft. lbs.	30 Nm
Main bearing cap bolts		
2.3L engine		
Step 1:	15 ft. lbs.	23 Nm
Step 2:	+ 90 degree turn	+ 90 degree turn
2.5L engine:	65 ft. lbs.	88 Nm
2.8L and 3.1L engines:	73 ft. lbs.	99 Nm
3.4L engine		
Step 1:	37 ft. lbs.	50 Nm
Step 2:	+ 75 degree turn	+ 75 degree turn
3.8L engine		
Step 1:	26 ft. lbs.	35 Nm
Step 2:	+ 45 degree turn	+ 45 degree turn
Oil pan		
2.3L engine		
Except rear bolts:	89 inch lbs.	10 Nm
Rear bolts:	18 ft. lbs.	25 Nm
2.5L engine:	89 inch lbs.	10 Nm
2.8L engine		
Rear bolts (2):	18 ft. lbs.	25 Nm
Studs and nuts (4):	13 ft. lbs.	17 Nm
All other bolts:	89 inch lbs.	10 Nm
3.1L engine		
Rear bolts (2):	18 ft. lbs.	25 Nm
All other bolts:	71 inch lbs.	8 Nm
3.4L engine		
Rear bolts (2):	18 ft. lbs.	25 Nm
All other bolts:	89 inch lbs.	10 Nm
3.8L engine:	124 inch lbs.	14 Nm
Oil pan drain plug		
Except 2.5 and 3.8L engine:	19 ft. lbs.	26 Nm
2.5L engine:	25 ft. lbs.	34 Nm
3.8L engine:	30 ft. lbs.	40 Nm
Oil pump attaching bolts		
2.3L engine:	33 ft. lbs.	45 Nm
3.4L engines:	40 ft. lbs.	54 Nm
2.8L and 3.1L engines:	30 ft. lbs.	41 Nm
3.8L engine:	97 inch lbs.	11 Nm
Rocker arm pivot bolt		
2.5L engine:	20 ft. lbs.	27 Nm
2.8L and 3.1L engines:	18 ft. lbs.	24 Nm
3.8L engine:	28 ft. lbs.	38 Nm

TORQUE SPECIFICATIONS

Component	English	Metric
Rocker (valve) cover		
2.3L engine		
Except 2 intake-side rear bolts (short)		
Step 1:	11 ft. lbs.	15 Nm
Step 2:	+ 75 degree turn	+ 75 degree turn
2 intake side rear bolts (short)		
Step 1:	16 ft. lbs.	22 Nm
Step 2:	+ 25 degree turn	+ 25 degree turn
2.5L engine:	80 inch lbs.	9 Nm
2.8L and 3.1L engines:	96 inch lbs.	11 Nm
3.4L and 3.8L engines:	89 ft. lbs.	10 Nm
Spark plug		
2.3L engine:	17 ft. lbs.	22 Nm
2.5L and 3.8L engines:	20 ft. lbs.	27 Nm
2.8L, 3.1L and 3.4L engines:	18 ft. lbs.	24 Nm
Starter-to-block bolts		
2.3L engine:	71 ft. lbs.	96 Nm
2.5L, 2.8L, 3.1L and 3.4L engines:	32 ft. lbs.	43 Nm
3.8L engine:	35 ft. lbs.	48 Nm
Thermostat housing		
2.3L engine:	19 ft. lbs.	26 Nm
2.5L engine:	17 ft. lbs.	23 Nm
2.8L, 3.1L and 3.4L engines:	18 ft. lbs.	25 Nm
3.8L engine:	20 ft. lbs.	27 Nm
TBI-to-fuel meter body screws:	31 inch lbs.	3.5 Nm
TBI fuel feed/return line:	30 ft. lbs.	41 Nm
TBI mounting bolts/nuts:	18 ft. lbs.	25 Nm
Timing cover		
2.3L engine:	106 inch lbs.	12 Nm
2.5L and 3.4L engines:	89 inch lbs.	10 Nm
3.8L engine:	22 ft. lbs.	30 Nm
Water Pump		
2.3L engine		
Studs and nuts:	19 ft. lbs.	26 Nm
Water pump cover-to-body:	125 inch lbs.	14 Nm
Water pump cover-to-engine block:	19 ft. lbs.	26 Nm
2.5L engine:	24 ft. lbs.	33 Nm
2.8L, 3.1L and 3.4L engines:	89 inch lbs.	10 Nm
3.8L engine		
Long bolts:	22 ft. lbs.	30 Nm
Short bolts:	18 ft. lbs.	13 Nm

BRAKE SPECIFICATIONS

All measurements in inches unless noted.

Year	Model		Master Cylinder Bore	Brake Disc Original Thickness	Brake Disc Minimum Thickness	Brake Disc Maximum Runout	Brake Drum Diameter Original Inside Diameter	Brake Drum Diameter Max. Wear Limit	Brake Drum Diameter Maximum Machine Diameter	Minimum Lining Thickness Front	Minimum Lining Thickness Rear
1990	Grand Prix	Front	0.945	1.040	0.972	0.004	—	—	—	0.003	0.003
		Rear	—	0.492	0.429	0.004	—	—	—	0.003	0.003
	Cutlass Supreme	Front	0.945	1.040	0.972	0.004	—	—	—	0.003	0.003
		Rear	—	0.492	0.429	0.004	—	—	—	0.003	0.003
	Regal	Front	0.945	1.040	0.972	0.004	—	—	—	0.003	0.003
		Rear	—	0.492	0.429	0.004	—	—	—	0.003	0.003
	Lumina	Front	0.945	1.040	0.972	0.004	—	—	—	0.003	0.003
		Rear	—	0.492	0.429	0.004	—	—	—	0.003	0.003

BRAKE SPECIFICATIONS

All measurements in inches unless noted.

Year	Model		Master Cylinder Bore	Brake Disc Original Thickness	Brake Disc Minimum Thickness	Brake Disc Maximum Runout	Brake Drum Diameter Original Inside Diameter	Brake Drum Diameter Max. Wear Limit	Brake Drum Diameter Maximum Machine Diameter	Minimum Lining Thickness Front	Minimum Lining Thickness Rear
1991	Grand Prix	Front	0.945	1.040	0.972	0.004	—	—	—	0.003	0.003
		Rear	—	0.492	0.429	0.004	—	—	—	0.003	0.003
	Cutlass Supreme	Front	0.945	1.040	0.972	0.004	—	—	—	0.003	0.003
		Rear	—	0.492	0.429	0.004	—	—	—	0.003	0.003
	Regal	Front	0.945	1.040	0.972	0.004	—	—	—	0.003	0.003
		Rear	—	0.492	0.429	0.004	—	—	—	0.003	0.003
	Lumina	Front	0.945	1.040	0.972	0.004	—	—	—	0.003	0.003
		Rear	—	0.492	0.429	0.004	—	—	—	0.003	0.003
1992	Grand Prix	Front	0.945	1.040	0.972	0.004	—	—	—	0.003	0.003
		Rear	—	0.492	0.429	0.004	—	—	—	0.003	0.003
	Cutlass Supreme	Front	0.945	1.040	0.972	0.004	—	—	—	0.003	0.003
		Rear	—	0.492	0.429	0.004	—	—	—	0.003	0.003
	Regal	Front	0.945	1.040	0.972	0.004	—	—	—	0.003	0.003
		Rear	—	0.492	0.429	0.004	—	—	—	0.003	0.003
	Lumina	Front	0.945	1.040	0.972	0.004	—	—	—	0.003	0.003
		Rear	—	0.492	0.429	0.004	—	—	—	0.003	0.003
1993–94	Grand Prix	Front	0.945	1.040	0.972	0.004	—	—	—	0.003	0.003
		Rear	—	0.492	0.429	0.004	—	—	—	0.003	0.003
	Cutlass Supreme	Front	0.945	1.040	0.972	0.004	—	—	—	0.003	0.003
		Rear	—	0.492	0.429	0.004	—	—	—	0.003	0.003
	Regal	Front	0.945	1.040	0.972	0.004	—	—	—	0.003	0.003
		Rear	—	0.492	0.429	0.004	—	—	—	0.003	0.003
	Lumina	Front	0.945	1.040	0.972	0.004	—	—	—	0.003	0.003
		Rear	—	0.492	0.429	0.004	—	—	—	0.003	0.003

WHEEL ALIGNMENT

Year	Model	Caster Range (deg.)	Caster Preferred Setting (deg.)	Camber Range (deg.)	Camber Preferred Setting (deg.)	Toe-in (in.)	Steering Axis Inclination (deg.)
1990	Cutlass Supreme	$1\frac{1}{2}$P–$2\frac{1}{2}$P	2P	$\frac{3}{16}$P–$1\frac{3}{16}$P	$\frac{11}{16}$P	$\frac{3}{32}$N–$\frac{3}{32}$P	NA
	Grand Prix	$1\frac{5}{16}$P–$2\frac{5}{16}$P	$1\frac{13}{16}$P	$\frac{3}{16}$P–$1\frac{3}{16}$P	$\frac{11}{16}$P	$\frac{3}{32}$N–$\frac{3}{32}$P	NA
	Regal	$1\frac{1}{2}$P–$2\frac{1}{2}$P	2P	$\frac{3}{16}$P–$1\frac{3}{16}$P	$\frac{11}{16}$P	$\frac{3}{32}$N–$\frac{3}{32}$P	NA
	Lumina	$1\frac{1}{2}$P–$2\frac{1}{2}$P	2P	$\frac{3}{16}$P–$1\frac{3}{16}$P	$\frac{11}{16}$P	$\frac{3}{32}$N–$\frac{3}{32}$P	NA
1991	Cutlass Supreme	$1\frac{1}{2}$P–$2\frac{1}{2}$P	2P	$\frac{3}{16}$P–$1\frac{3}{16}$P	$\frac{11}{16}$P	$\frac{3}{32}$N–$\frac{3}{32}$P	NA
	Grand Prix	$1\frac{1}{2}$P–$2\frac{1}{2}$P	2P	$\frac{3}{16}$P–$1\frac{3}{16}$P	$\frac{11}{16}$P	$\frac{3}{32}$N–$\frac{3}{32}$P	NA
	Regal	$1\frac{1}{2}$P–$2\frac{1}{2}$P	2P	$\frac{3}{16}$P–$1\frac{3}{16}$P	$\frac{11}{16}$P	$\frac{3}{32}$N–$\frac{3}{32}$P	NA
	Lumina	$1\frac{1}{2}$P–$2\frac{1}{2}$P	2P	$\frac{3}{16}$P–$1\frac{3}{16}$P	$\frac{11}{16}$P	$\frac{3}{32}$N–$\frac{3}{32}$P	NA
1992	Cutlass Supreme	$1\frac{1}{2}$P–$2\frac{1}{2}$P	2P	$\frac{3}{16}$P–$1\frac{3}{16}$P	$\frac{11}{16}$P	$\frac{3}{32}$N–$\frac{3}{32}$P	NA
	Grand Prix	$1\frac{1}{2}$P–$2\frac{1}{2}$P	2P	$\frac{3}{16}$P–$1\frac{3}{16}$P	$\frac{11}{16}$P	$\frac{3}{32}$N–$\frac{3}{32}$P	NA
	Regal	$1\frac{1}{2}$P–$2\frac{1}{2}$P	2P	$\frac{3}{16}$P–$1\frac{3}{16}$P	$\frac{11}{16}$P	$\frac{3}{32}$N–$\frac{3}{32}$P	NA
	Lumina	$1\frac{1}{2}$P–$2\frac{1}{2}$P	2P	$\frac{3}{16}$P–$1\frac{3}{16}$P	$\frac{11}{16}$P	$\frac{3}{32}$N–$\frac{3}{32}$P	NA

WHEEL ALIGNMENT

Year	Model	Caster Range (deg.)	Caster Preferred Setting (deg.)	Camber Range (deg.)	Camber Preferred Setting (deg.)	Toe-in (in.)	Steering Axis Inclination (deg.)
1993-94	Cutlass Supreme	1½P–2½P	2P	$^3/_{16}$P–1$^3/_{16}$P	$^{11}/_{16}$P	$^3/_{32}$N–$^3/_{32}$P	NA
	Grand Prix	1½P–2½P	2P	$^3/_{16}$P–1$^3/_{16}$P	$^{11}/_{16}$P	$^3/_{32}$N–$^3/_{32}$P	NA
	Regal	1½P–2½P	2P	$^3/_{16}$P–1$^3/_{16}$P	$^{11}/_{16}$P	$^3/_{32}$N–$^3/_{32}$P	NA
	Lumina	1½P–2½P	2P	$^3/_{16}$P–1$^3/_{16}$P	$^{11}/_{16}$P	$^3/_{32}$N–$^3/_{32}$P	NA

NA—Not available
N—Negative
P—Positive

AIR CONDITIONING BELT TENSION

Year	Engine VIN	Engine Displacement Liters (cc)	Belt Type	Specifications New	Specifications Used
1990	T	3.1 (3149)	Serpentine	①	①
	R	2.5 (2476)	Serpentine	①	①
	A	2.3 (2263)	Serpentine	①	①
	D	2.3 (2263)	Serpentine	50②	50②
	V	3.1 (3149)	Serpentine	①	①
1991	T	3.1 (3149)	Serpentine	①	①
	L	3.8 (3788)	Serpentine	①	①
	R	2.5 (2476)	Serpentine	①	①
	X	3.4 (3362)	Serpentine	①	①
	D	2.3 (2263)	Serpentine	50②	50②
1992	R	2.5 (2476)	Serpentine	①	①
	T	3.1 (3149)	Serpentine	50–70②	50–70②
	X	3.4 (3362)	Serpentine	①	①
	L	3.8 (3788)	Serpentine	50–70②	50–70②
1993-94	T	3.1 (3149)	Serpentine	50–70②	50–70②
	L	3.8 (3788)	Serpentine	50–70②	50–70②
	4	2.2 (2198)	Serpentine	50–70②	50–70②
	X	3.4 (3362)	Serpentine	①	①

① Equipped with automatic tensioner;
no adjustment required.
② Equipped with automatic tensioner; however,
the specification given (in pounds) is for testing
whether the tensioner is maintaining its proper
tension (specification given is the average of 3
readings back-to-back).

REFRIGERANT CAPACITIES

Year	Model	Refrigerant (oz.)	Oil (fl. oz.)	Compressor Type
1990	Regal, Lumina, Cutlass Supreme, Grand Prix	44.0②	8.0	HR-6
1991	Regal, Lumina, Cutlass Supreme, Grand Prix	44.0②	8.0	HR-6

REFRIGERANT CAPACITIES

Year	Model	Refrigerant (oz.)	Oil (fl. oz.)	Compressor Type
1992	Regal, Lumina, Cutlass Supreme, Grand Prix	36.0①	9.0	V5, HR-6①
1993	Regal, Lumina, Cutlass Supreme, Grand Prix	36.0①	9.0	V5, HR6-HE①

NOTE: At the time of publication, refrigerant capacity information relating to R-134a was not available from the manufacturer.
① HR-6 and V-5 compressors
② Refrigerant capacity 36.0 oz. with V-5 compressor

MAINTENANCE INTERVALS—TYPE A: NORMAL SERVICE
Cutlass Supreme • Grand Prix • Lumina • Regal

TO BE SERVICED	TYPE OF SERVICE	VEHICLE MILEAGE INTERVAL (X1000)							
		7.5	15	22.5	30	37.5	45	52.5	60
Oxygen Sensor	I				✔				✔
Vacuum Lines and Hoses	I		✔		✔		✔		✔
Ignition Wires	I				✔				✔
Spark Plugs	R				✔				✔
Engine Oil	R	✔	✔	✔	✔	✔	✔	✔	✔
Engine Air Cleaner Element	R								✔
PCV Valve	R								✔
Fuel Filter	R								✔
Engine Oil Filter	R①	✔		✔		✔		✔	
Fuel/Vapor Return Lines	I				✔				✔
Fuel Tank Cap and Restrictor	I				✔				✔
Coolant System Service	R				✔				✔
Exhaust Pipe and Muffler	I				✔				✔
Tire Rotation	I②	✔		✔		✔		✔	
Catalytic Converter and Shield	I				✔				✔
EGR System	I								✔
Automatic Transaxle Fluid	R③								
Battery Connections	I		✔		✔		✔		✔
Chassis Lubrication	L	✔	✔	✔	✔	✔	✔	✔	✔
CV-Joints and Boots	I	✔	✔	✔	✔	✔	✔	✔	✔
Idle Speed System	I				✔				✔
Throttle Body Mounting Torque	I	✔							
Drive Belts	I								✔
Brake Linings	I		✔		✔		✔		✔
Parking Brake	I		✔		✔		✔		✔
Coolant Hoses and Clamps	I		✔		✔		✔		✔
Seat Belt Operation	I		✔		✔		✔		✔

FOR COMPLETE WARRANTY COVERAGE CONSULT INDIVIDUAL VEHICLE MANUFACTURER'S WARRANTY MAINTENANCE GUIDE.

I—Inspect
L—Lubricate
R—Replace
① Replace oil filter at first and every other oil change
② Rotate tires at 7,500 miles, then every 15,000 miles
③ Replace automatic transmission fluid and filter at 100,000 miles

MAINTENANCE INTERVALS—TYPE B: SEVERE SERVICE
Cutlass Supreme • Grand Prix • Lumina • Regal

TO BE SERVICED	TYPE OF SERVICE	VEHICLE MILEAGE INTERVAL (X1000)									
		3	6	9	12	15	18	21	24	27	30
Oxygen Sensor	I										✔
Vacuum Lines and Hoses	I					✔					✔
Ignition Wires	I										✔
Spark Plugs	R										✔
Engine Oil and Filter	R	✔	✔	✔	✔	✔	✔	✔	✔	✔	✔
Engine Air Cleaner Element	R										✔
PCV Valve	R					✔					✔
Fuel Filter	R					✔					✔
Fuel/Vapor Return Lines	I										✔
Fuel Tank Cap and Restrictor	I										✔
Coolant System Service	R										✔
Exhaust Pipe and Muffler	I										✔
Tire Rotation	I ①		✔					✔			
Catalytic Converter and Shield	I										✔
EGR System	I										✔
Automatic Transaxle Fluid	R					✔					✔
Battery Connections	I					✔					
Chassis Lubrication	L		✔		✔		✔		✔		
CV-Joints and Boots	I	✔	✔	✔	✔	✔	✔	✔	✔	✔	✔
Idle Speed System	I					✔					✔
Throttle Body Mounting Torque	I		✔								
Drive Belts	I										✔
Brake Linings	I					✔					✔
Parking Brake	I					✔					✔
Coolant Hoses and Clamps	I					✔					✔
Seat Belt Operation	I					✔					✔

FOR COMPLETE WARRANTY COVERAGE CONSULT INDIVIDUAL VEHICLE MANUFACTURER'S WARRANTY MAINTENANCE GUIDE.

I—Inspect
L—Lubricate
R—Replace
① Rotate tires at 6,000 miles, then every 15,000 miles

FIRING ORDERS

NOTE: To avoid confusion, always replace spark plug wires one at a time.

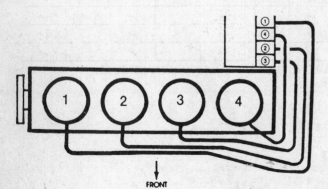

1993–94 2.2L (VIN 4) and 1990–92 2.5L (VIN R) Engines
Engine Firing Order: 1-3-4-2
Distributorless Ignition System

FIRING ORDERS

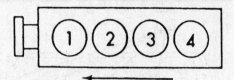

FRONT OF ENGINE

2.3L Engine
Engine Firing Order: 1–3–4–2
Distributorless Ignition System

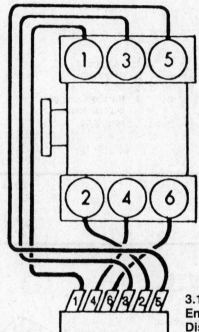

3.1L and 3.4L Engines
Engine Firing Order: 1-2-3-4-5-6
Distributorless Ignition System

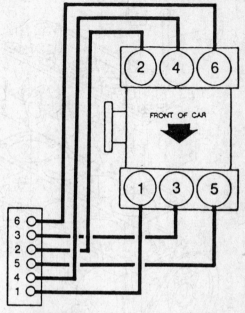

FRONT OF CAR

3.8L Engine
Engine Firing Order: 1–6–5–4–3–2
Distributorless Ignition System

CYLINDER HEAD TORQUE SEQUENCES

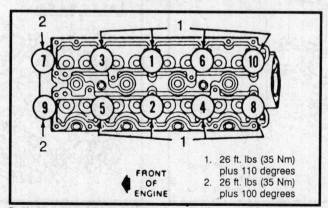

FRONT OF ENGINE

1. 26 ft. lbs (35 Nm) plus 110 degrees
2. 26 ft. lbs (35 Nm) plus 100 degrees

Cylinder head bolt torque sequence—2.3L engine

CYLINDER HEAD TORQUE SEQUENCES

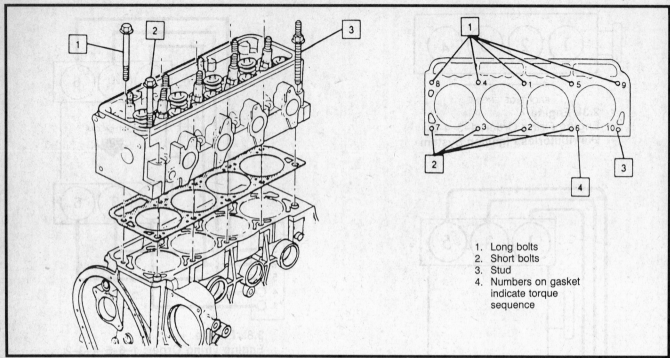

1. Long bolts
2. Short bolts
3. Stud
4. Numbers on gasket indicate torque sequence

Cylinder head bolt torque sequence—2.2L engine

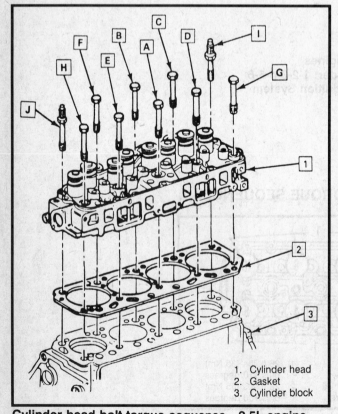

1. Cylinder head
2. Gasket
3. Cylinder block

Cylinder head bolt torque sequence—2.5L engine

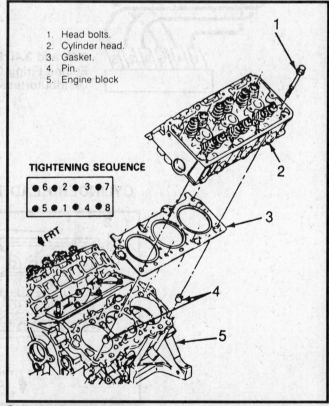

1. Head bolts.
2. Cylinder head.
3. Gasket.
4. Pin.
5. Engine block.

TIGHTENING SEQUENCE

Cylinder head bolt torque sequence—3.4L engine

CYLINDER HEAD TORQUE SEQUENCES

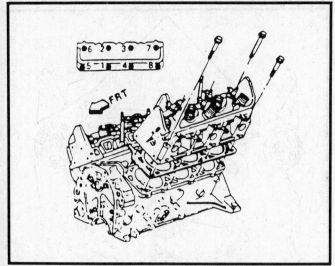

Cylinder head bolt torque sequence—3.1L engine

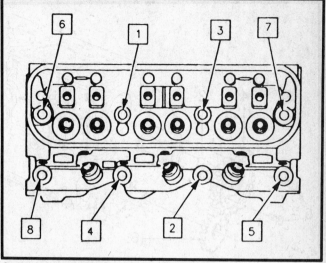

Cylinder head bolt torque sequence—3.8L engine

TIMING CHAIN ALIGNMENT MARKS

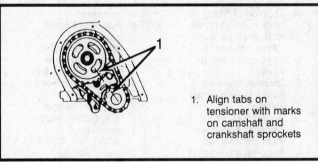

1. Align tabs on tensioner with marks on camshaft and crankshaft sprockets

Timing chain alignment marks—2.2L engine

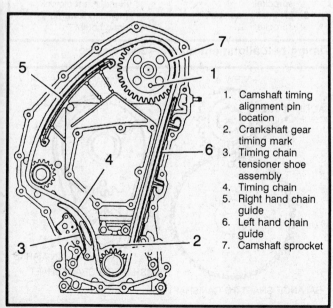

1. Camshaft timing alignment pin location
2. Crankshaft gear timing mark
3. Timing chain tensioner shoe assembly
4. Timing chain
5. Right hand chain guide
6. Left hand chain guide
7. Camshaft sprocket

Timing chain alignment marks—2.3L SOHC engine

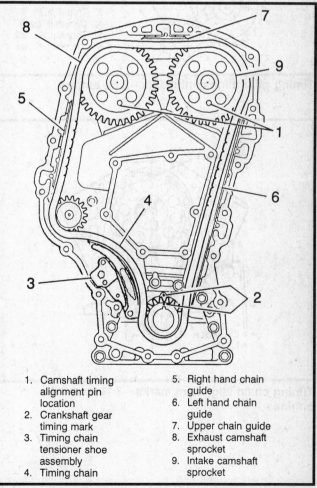

1. Camshaft timing alignment pin location
2. Crankshaft gear timing mark
3. Timing chain tensioner shoe assembly
4. Timing chain
5. Right hand chain guide
6. Left hand chain guide
7. Upper chain guide
8. Exhaust camshaft sprocket
9. Intake camshaft sprocket

Timing chain alignment marks—2.3L DOHC engine

TIMING CHAIN ALIGNMENT MARKS

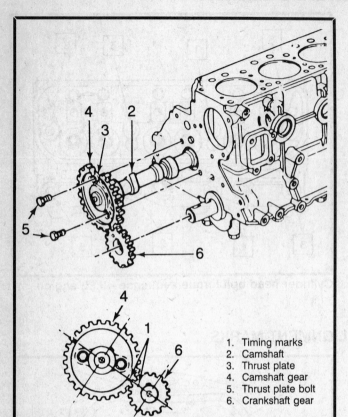

1. Timing marks
2. Camshaft
3. Thrust plate
4. Camshaft gear
5. Thrust plate bolt
6. Crankshaft gear

Timing gear alignment marks—2.5L engine

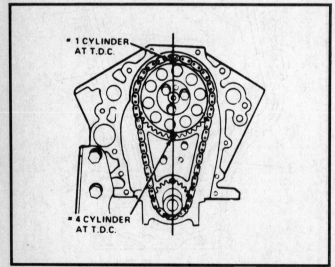

Timing chain alignment marks—3.1L and 3.4L engines

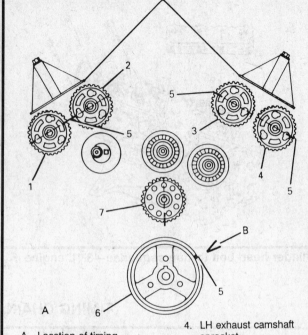

A. Location of timing marks with camshaft hold-down tools J–38613 installed
B. Front cover timing marks
C. Location of timing marks with drive belt installed
D. Location where camshaft hold-down tools are installed
1. RH exhaust camshaft sprocket
2. RH intake camshaft sprocket
3. LH intake camshaft sprocket
4. LH exhaust camshaft sprocket
5. Permanent marks painted dots. Remove previous marks if timing is being changed and mark again if these locations
6. Torsional damper
7. Intermediate shaft sprocket
NOTE: This TDC for No. 1 exhaust. Intermediate shaft belt sprocket timing mark is at 6 o'clock (pointing towards drain notch).

Timing belt alignment marks—3.4L engine

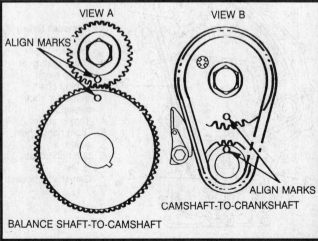

Timing gear and chain alignment marks—3.8L engine

AIR CONDITIONING SERVICE VALVE
LOCATIONS

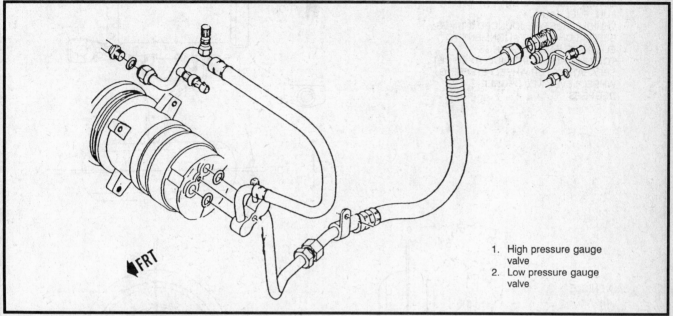

1. High pressure gauge valve
2. Low pressure gauge valve

Air conditioning service valve location

WHEEL ALIGNMENT ADJUSTMENT
LOCATIONS

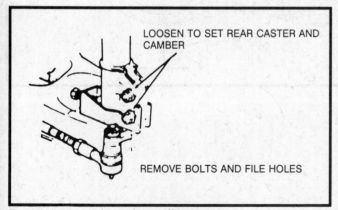

LOOSEN TO SET REAR CASTER AND CAMBER

REMOVE BOLTS AND FILE HOLES

Rear caster and camber adjustment

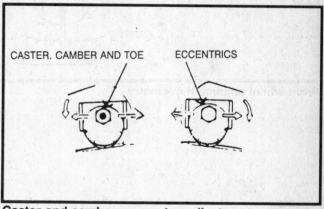

CASTER. CAMBER AND TOE   ECCENTRICS

Caster and camber or rear toe adjustment

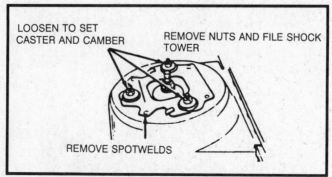

LOOSEN TO SET CASTER AND CAMBER

REMOVE NUTS AND FILE SHOCK TOWER

REMOVE SPOTWELDS

Front caster and camber adjustment

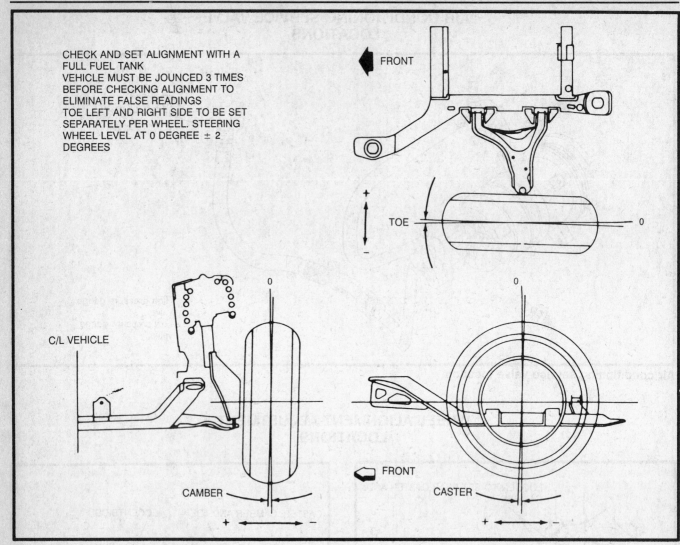

CHECK AND SET ALIGNMENT WITH A
FULL FUEL TANK
VEHICLE MUST BE JOUNCED 3 TIMES
BEFORE CHECKING ALIGNMENT TO
ELIMINATE FALSE READINGS
TOE LEFT AND RIGHT SIDE TO BE SET
SEPARATELY PER WHEEL. STEERING
WHEEL LEVEL AT 0 DEGREE ± 2
DEGREES

FRONT

TOE

0

C/L VEHICLE

0

CAMBER

0

FRONT

CASTER

Front wheel alignment geometry

SPECIFICATION CHARTS

VEHICLE IDENTIFICATION CHART

It is important for servicing and ordering parts to be certain of the vehicle and engine identification. The VIN (vehicle identification number) is a 17 digit number visible through the windshield on the driver's side of the dash and contains the vehicle and engine identification codes. The tenth digit indicates model year and the eighth digit indicates engine code. It can be interpreted as follows:

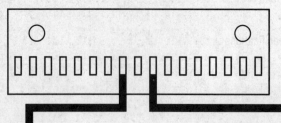

		Engine Code					Model Year	
Code	Liters	Cu. In. (cc)	Cyl.	Fuel Sys.	Eng. Mfg.	Code		Year
7	1.9	116 (1901)	4	MFI	Saturn	M		1991
9	1.9	116 (1901)	4	TBI	Saturn	N		1992
						P		1993
						R		1994

MFI—Multi-Point Fuel Injection
TBI—Throttle Body Injection

ENGINE IDENTIFICATION

Year	Model	Engine Displacement Liters (cc)	Engine Series Identification (ID/VIN)	Fuel System	No. of Cylinders	Engine Type
1991	Sedan	1.9 (1901)	7	MFI	4	DOHC
	Sedan	1.9 (1901)	9	TBI	4	SOHC
	Coupe	1.9 (1901)	7	MFI	4	DOHC
1992	Sedan	1.9 (1901)	7	MFI	4	DOHC
	Sedan	1.9 (1901)	9	TBI	4	SOHC
	Coupe	1.9 (1901)	7	MFI	4	DOHC
1993-94	Wagon	1.9 (1901)	7	MFI	4	DOHC
	Wagon	1.9 (1901)	9	TBI	4	SOHC
	Sedan	1.9 (1901)	7	MFI	4	DOHC
	Sedan	1.9 (1901)	9	TBI	4	SOHC
	Coupe	1.9 (1901)	7	MFI	4	DOHC
	Coupe	1.9 (1901)	9	TBI	4	SOHC

DOHC—Dual Overhead Cam
SOHC—Single Overhead Cam
MFI—Multi-Point Fuel Injection
TBI—Throttle Body Injection

GENERAL ENGINE SPECIFICATIONS

Year	Engine ID/VIN	Engine Displacement Liters (cc)	Fuel System Type	Net Horsepower @ rpm	Net Torque @ rpm (ft. lbs.)	Bore × Stroke (in.)	Compression Ratio	Oil Pressure @ rpm
1991	7	1.9 (1901)	MFI	124 @ 5600	122 @ 4800	3.23 × 3.54	9.5:1	29 @ 2000
	9	1.9 (1901)	TBI	85 @ 5000	107 @ 2400	3.23 × 3.54	9.3:1	36 @ 2000
1992	7	1.9 (1901)	MFI	124 @ 5600	122 @ 4800	3.23 × 3.54	9.5:1	29 @ 2000
	9	1.9 (1901)	TBI	85 @ 5000	107 @ 2400	3.23 × 3.54	9.3:1	36 @ 2000
1993–94	7	1.9 (1901)	MFI	124 @ 5600	122 @ 4800	3.23 × 3.54	9.5:1	29 @ 2000
	9	1.9 (1901)	TBI	85 @ 5000	107 @ 2400	3.23 × 3.54	9.3:1	36 @ 2000

MFI—Multi Point Fuel Injection
TBI—Throttle Body Injection

ENGINE TUNE-UP SPECIFICATIONS

Year	Engine ID/VIN	Engine Displacement Liters (cc)	Spark Plugs Gap (in.)	Ignition Timing (deg.) MT	Ignition Timing (deg.) AT	Fuel Pump③ (psi)	Idle Speed (rpm)② MT	Idle Speed (rpm)② AT	Valve Clearance In.	Valve Clearance Ex.
1991	7	1.9 (1901)	0.040	①	①	31–36	850	750	Hyd.	Hyd.
	9	1.9 (1901)	0.040	①	①	26–31	750	650	Hyd.	Hyd.
1992	7	1.9 (1901)	0.040	①	①	31–36	850	750	Hyd.	Hyd.
	9	1.9 (1901)	0.040	①	①	26–31	750	650	Hyd.	Hyd.
1993	7	1.9 (1901)	0.040	①	①	31–36	850	750	Hyd.	Hyd.
	9	1.9 (1901)	0.040	①	①	26–31	750	650	Hyd.	Hyd.
1994		SEE UNDERHOOD SPECIFICATIONS STICKER								

NOTE: The lowest cylinder pressure should be within 75% of the highest cylinder pressure reading. For example, if the highest cylinder is 134 psi, the lowest should be 101. Engine should be at normal operating temperature with throttle valve in the wide open position.
The underhood specifications sticker often reflects tune-up specification changes in production. Sticker figures must be used if they disagree with those in this chart.
Hyd.—Hydraulic

① These engines are equipped with an ECM controlled Distributorless Ignition System (DIS), therefore the ignition timing is not adjustable.

② Manual speed with transmission in N
Automatic speed with transmission in D
③ Pressure measured at idle

CAPACITIES

Year	Model	Engine ID/VIN	Engine Displacement Liters (cc)	Engine Crankcase with Filter (qts.)	Transmission (pts.) 4-Spd	Transmission (pts.) 5-Spd	Transmission (pts.) Auto.	Drive Axle (pts.)	Fuel Tank (gal.)	Cooling System (qts.)
1991	Sedan	7	1.9 (1901)	4.0	—	5.2	7.5	—	12.8	7.0
	Sedan	9	1.9 (1901)	4.0	—	5.2	7.5	—	12.8	7.0
	Coupe	7	1.9 (1901)	4.0	—	5.2	7.5	—	12.8	7.0
1992	Sedan	7	1.9 (1901)	4.0	—	5.2	7.5	—	12.8	7.0
	Sedan	9	1.9 (1901)	4.0	—	5.2	7.5	—	12.8	7.0
	Coupe	7	1.9 (1901)	4.0	—	5.2	7.5	—	12.8	7.0
1993–94	Wagon	7	1.9 (1901)	4.0	—	5.2	7.5	—	13.2	7.0
	Wagon	9	1.9 (1901)	4.0	—	5.2	7.5	—	13.2	7.0
	Sedan	7	1.9 (1901)	4.0	—	5.2	7.5	—	13.2	7.0
	Sedan	9	1.9 (1901)	4.0	—	5.2	7.5	—	13.2	7.0
	Coupe	7	1.9 (1901)	4.0	—	5.2	7.5	—	13.2	7.0
	Coupe	9	1.9 (1901)	4.0	—	5.2	7.5	—	13.2	7.0

CAMSHAFT SPECIFICATIONS

All measurements given in inches.

Year	Engine ID/VIN	Engine Displacement Liters (cc)	Journal Diameter					Elevation		Bearing Clearance	Camshaft End Play
			1	2	3	4	5	In.	Ex.		
1991	7	1.9 (1901)	1.1398–1.1406	1.1398–1.1406	1.1398–1.1406	1.1398–1.1406	1.1398–1.1406	0.3528–0.3559	0.3409–0.3441	0.0012–0.0030	0.0020–0.0080
	9	1.9 (1901)	1.7480–1.7490	1.7480–1.7490	1.7480–1.7490	1.7480–1.7490	1.7480–1.7490	0.2531–0.2556	0.2531–0.2556	0.0020–0.0040	0.0028–0.0079
1992	7	1.9 (1901)	1.1398–1.1406	1.1398–1.1406	1.1398–1.1406	1.1398–1.1406	1.1398–1.1406	0.3528–0.3559	0.3409–0.3441	0.0012–0.0030	0.0020–0.0080
	9	1.9 (1901)	1.7480–1.7490	1.7480–1.7490	1.7480–1.7490	1.7480–1.7490	1.7480–1.7490	0.2531–0.2556	0.2531–0.2556	0.0020–0.0040	0.0028–0.0079
1993-94	7	1.9 (1901)	1.1398–1.1406	1.1398–1.1406	1.1398–1.1406	1.1398–1.1406	1.1398–1.1406	0.3528–0.3559	0.3409–0.3441	0.0012–0.0030	0.0020–0.0080
	9	1.9 (1901)	1.7480–1.7490	1.7480–1.7490	1.7480–1.7490	1.7480–1.7490	1.7480–1.7490	0.2531–0.2556	0.2531–0.2556	0.0020–0.0040	0.0028–0.0079

CRANKSHAFT AND CONNECTING ROD SPECIFICATIONS

All measurements are given in inches.

Year	Engine ID/VIN	Engine Displacement Liters (cc)	Crankshaft				Connecting Rod		
			Main Brg. Journal Dia.	Main Brg. Oil Clearance	Shaft End-play	Thrust on No.	Journal Diameter	Oil Clearance	Side Clearance
1991	7	1.9 (1901)	2.2438–2.2444	0.0002–0.0020	0.002–0.008	3	1.8500–1.8508	0.0001–0.0021	0.0065–0.1713
	9	1.9 (1901)	2.2438–2.2444	0.0002–0.0020	0.002–0.008	3	1.8500–1.8508	0.0001–0.0021	0.0065–0.1713
1992	7	1.9 (1901)	2.2438–2.2444	0.0002–0.0020	0.002–0.008	3	1.8500–1.8508	0.0001–0.0021	0.0065–0.1713
	9	1.9 (1901)	2.2438–2.2444	0.0002–0.0020	0.002–0.008	3	1.8500–1.8508	0.0001–0.0021	0.0065–0.1713
1993-94	7	1.9 (1901)	2.2438–2.2444	0.0002–0.0020	0.002–0.008	3	1.8500–1.8508	0.0001–0.0021	0.0065–0.1713
	9	1.9 (1901)	2.2438–2.2444	0.0002–0.0020	0.002–0.008	3	1.8500–1.8508	0.0001–0.0021	0.0065–0.1713

VALVE SPECIFICATIONS

Year	Engine ID/VIN	Engine Displacement Liters (cc)	Seat Angle (deg.)	Face Angle (deg.)	Spring Test Pressure (lbs. @ in.)	Spring Installed Height (in.)	Stem-to-Guide Clearance (in.)		Stem Diameter (in.)	
							Intake	Exhaust	Intake	Exhaust
1991	7	1.9 (1901)	44.5–45.5	45.0–45.5	163–180 @ 0.984	①	0.0010–0.0025	0.0015–0.0032	0.2736–0.2740	0.2729–0.2736
	9	1.9 (1901)	44.5–45.5	45.0–45.5	202–211 @ 1.280	①	0.0010–0.0025	0.0015–0.0032	0.2736–0.2741	0.2736–0.2740
1992	7	1.9 (1901)	44.5–45.5	45.0–45.5	163–180 @ 0.984	①	0.0010–0.0025	0.0015–0.0032	0.2736–0.2740	0.2729–0.2736
	9	1.9 (1901)	44.5–45.5	45.0–45.5	202–211 @ 1.280	①	0.0010–0.0025	0.0015–0.0032	0.2736–0.2741	0.2736–0.2740

VALVE SPECIFICATIONS

Year	Engine ID/VIN	Engine Displacement Liters (cc)	Seat Angle (deg.)	Face Angle (deg.)	Spring Test Pressure (lbs. @ in.)	Spring Installed Height (in.)	Stem-to-Guide Clearance (in.)		Stem Diameter (in.)	
							Intake	Exhaust	Intake	Exhaust
1993–94	7	1.9 (1901)	44.5–45.5	45.0–45.5	163–180 @ 0.984	①	0.0010–0.0025	0.0015–0.0032	0.2736–0.2740	0.2729–0.2736
	9	1.9 (1901)	44.5–45.5	45.0–45.5	202–211 @ 1.280	①	0.0010–0.0025	0.0015–0.0032	0.2736–0.2741	0.2736–0.2740

① Installed height—not available
Free length—SOHC: 1.8898–1.9134
DOHC: 1.6100

PISTON AND RING SPECIFICATIONS

All measurements are given in inches.

Year	Engine ID/VIN	Engine Displacement Liters (cc)	Piston Clearance	Ring Gap			Ring Side Clearance		
				Top Compression	Bottom Compression	Oil Control	Top Compression	Bottom Compression	Oil Control
1991	7	1.9 (1901)	①	0.0098–0.0197	0.0098–0.0197	0.0098–0.0492	0.0016–0.0035	0.0012–0.0031	Snug
	9	1.9 (1901)	①	0.0098–0.0197	0.0098–0.0197	0.0098–0.0492	0.0016–0.0035	0.0012–0.0031	Snug
1992	7	1.9 (1901)	①	0.0098–0.0197	0.0098–0.0197	0.0098–0.0492	0.0016–0.0035	0.0012–0.0031	Snug
	9	1.9 (1901)	①	0.0098–0.0197	0.0098–0.0197	0.0098–0.0492	0.0016–0.0035	0.0012–0.0031	Snug
1993–94	7	1.9 (1901)	①	0.0098–0.0197	0.0098–0.0197	0.0098–0.0492	0.0016–0.0035	0.0012–0.0031	Snug
	9	1.9 (1901)	①	0.0098–0.0197	0.0098–0.0197	0.0098–0.0492	0.0016–0.0035	0.0012–0.0031	Snug

① Bore 1, 2, 3: 0.0002–0.0017
Bore 4: 0.0006–0.0021

TORQUE SPECIFICATIONS

All readings in ft. lbs.

Year	Engine ID/VIN	Engine Displacement Liters (cc)	Cylinder Head Bolts	Main Bearing Bolts	Rod Bearing Bolts	Crankshaft Damper Bolts	Flywheel ④ Bolts	Manifold		Spark Plugs	Lug Nut
								Intake	Exhaust		
1991	7	1.9 (1901)	②	37	33	159	59	22 ③	23 ③	20	103
	9	1.9 (1901)	①	37	33	159	59	15 ③	16 ③	20	103
1992	7	1.9 (1901)	②	37	33	159	59	22 ③	23 ③	20	103
	9	1.9 (1901)	①	37	33	159	59	15 ③	16 ③	20	103
1993–94	7	1.9 (1901)	②	37	33	159	59	22 ③	23 ③	20	103
	9	1.9 (1901)	①	37	33	159	59	15 ③	16 ③	20	103

① 1st step: 22 ft. lbs.
2nd step: 33 ft. lbs.
3rd step: 90 degrees torquing angle
② 1st step: 22 ft. lbs.
2nd step: 37 ft. lbs.
3rd step: 90 degrees torquing angle
③ Studs—106 inch lbs.
④ Flexplate specification is 44 ft. lbs.

23–5

TORQUE SPECIFICATIONS

Component	English	Metric
Belt idler pulley:	33 ft. lbs.	45 Nm
Belt tensioner:	22 ft. lbs.	30 Nm
Camshaft bearing cap DOHC engine:	124 inch lbs.	14 Nm
Camshaft sprocket:	75 ft. lbs.	102 Nm
Camshaft thrust bearing SOHC engine:	19 ft. lbs.	25 Nm
Connecting rod bearing cap bolts:	33 ft. lbs.	45 Nm
Crankshaft damper bolt:	159 ft. lbs.	215 Nm
Crankshaft rear oil seal carrier:	97 inch lbs.	11 Nm
Cylinder head bolt SOHC engine Step 1: Step 2: Step 3: DOHC engine Step 1: Step 2: Step 3:	 22 ft. lbs. 33 ft. lbs. + 90 degrees turn 22 ft. lbs. 37 ft. lbs. + 90 degrees turn	 30 Nm 45 Nm + 90 degrees turn 30 Nm 50 Nm + 90 degrees turn
EGR valve-to-intake manifold Nut: Stud:	 21 ft. lbs. 62 inch lbs.	 28 Nm 7 Nm
Engine-to-transaxle Lower bolts: Upper bolts/studs:	 96 ft. lbs. 66 ft. lbs.	 130 Nm 90 Nm
Engine cradle-to-body:	151 ft. lbs.	205 Nm
Exhaust manifold-to-cylinder head Bolts SOHC engine: DOHC engine: Studs:	 16 ft. lbs. 23 ft. lbs. 106 inch lbs.	 22 Nm 31 Nm 12 Nm
Exhaust pipe-to-manifold:	115 ft. lbs.	13 Nm
Flexplate-to-crankshaft:	44 ft. lbs.	60 Nm
Flywheel-to-crankshaft:	59 ft. lbs.	80 Nm
Flexplate-to-converter bolts:	41 ft. lbs.	55 Nm
Fuel rail-to-manifold:	22 ft. lbs.	30 Nm
Intake manifold SOHC engine: DOHC engine:	 188 inch lbs. 22 ft. lbs.	 20 Nm 30 Nm
Main bearing cap bolts:	37 ft. lbs.	50 Nm
Oil pan:	80 inch lbs.	9 Nm
Oil pan drain plug:	26 ft. lbs.	35 Nm
Oil pump cover:	97 inch lbs.	11 Nm
Rocker arm shaft SOHC engine:	19 ft. lbs.	25 Nm
Rocker/camshaft cover SOHC engine: DOHC engine:	 22 ft. lbs. 89 inch lbs.	 30 Nm 10 Nm
Spark plug:	20 ft. lbs.	27 Nm
Starter-to-block bolts:	27 ft. lbs.	37 Nm
Thermostat housing:	22 ft. lbs.	30 Nm
Timing chain guides SOHC engine: DOHC engine:	 19 ft. lbs. 21 ft. lbs.	 26 Nm 28 Nm
Timing chain tensioner:	168 inch lbs.	19 Nm

TORQUE SPECIFICATIONS

Component	English	Metric
Timing chain cover		
Perimeter bolts and 1992–94 top center bolt for DOHC engines:	19 ft. lbs.	25 Nm
Lower center bolt:	89 inch lbs.	10 Nm
Timing chain cover studs 1992–94 torque axis mount system:	18 ft. lbs.	25 Nm
Throttle body-to-intake manifold:	24 ft. lbs.	33 Nm
Transaxle mount-to-transaxle		
Lower mount:	23 ft. lbs.	31 Nm
Rear mount:	36 ft. lbs.	49 Nm
Pitch restrictor:	42 ft. lbs.	55 Nm
Transaxle mount-to-cradle:	41 ft. lbs.	55 Nm
Water pump:	22 ft. lbs.	30 Nm
Water pump pulley:	19 ft. lbs.	25 Nm

BRAKE SPECIFICATIONS

All measurements in inches unless noted.

Year	Model	Master Cylinder Bore	Brake Disc			Brake Drum Diameter			Minimum Lining Thickness	
			Original Thickness	Minimum Thickness	Maximum Runout	Original Inside Diameter	Max. Wear Limit	Maximum Machine Diameter	Front	Rear
1991	All	NA	0.710①	0.633②	0.0024③	7.87	7.93	7.90	0.08	0.04
1992	All	NA	0.710①	0.633②	0.0024③	7.87	7.93	7.90	0.08	0.04
1993–94	All	NA	0.710①	0.633②	0.0024③	7.87	7.93	7.90	0.08	0.04

NA—Not available
① Rear Disc: 0.430 in.
② Rear Disc: 0.370 in.
  NOTE: Both front and rear disc specifications are minimums to which the rotors may be machined. The discard wear limit is 0.625 in. for front discs and 0.350 in. for rear discs.
③ Maximum thickness variation—0.0005 in.

WHEEL ALIGNMENT

Year	Model	Caster		Camber		Toe-in (in.)	Steering Axis Inclination (deg.)
		Range (deg.)	Preferred Setting (deg.)	Range (deg.)	Preferred Setting (deg.)		
1991	All models	1.20P–2.70P	1.70P	1.20N–0.65P①	0.00	0.20P②	NA
1992	All models	1.20P–2.70P	1.70P	1.20N–0.65P①	0.00	0.20P②	NA
1993–94	All models	1.20P–2.70P	1.70P	1.20N–0.65P①	0.00	0.20P②	NA

NA—Not available
N—Negative
P—Positive
① Rear 1.55N–0.00
  Preferred 0.60N
② Specification is total toe front or rear

AIR CONDITIONING BELT TENSION

Year	Model	Engine Displacement Liters (cc)	Belt Type	Specifications New ①	Used ①
1991	Sedan SL/SL1	1.9 (1901) ②	Serpentine	50–65 lbs.	45 lbs. min.
	Sedan SL2	1.9 (1901) ③	Serpentine	50–65 lbs.	45 lbs. min.
	Coupe SC	1.9 (1901) ③	Serpentine	50–65 lbs.	45 lbs. min.
1992	Sedan SL/SL1	1.9 (1901) ②	Serpentine	50–65 lbs.	45 lbs. min.
	Sedan SL2	1.9 (1901) ③	Serpentine	50–65 lbs.	45 lbs. min.
	Coupe SC	1.9 (1901) ③	Serpentine	50–65 lbs.	45 lbs. min.
1993–94	Sedan SL/SL1	1.9 (1901) ②	Serpentine	50–65 lbs.	45 lbs. min.
	Sedan SL2	1.9 (1901) ③	Serpentine	50–65 lbs.	45 lbs. min.
	Wagon SW1	1.9 (1901) ②	Serpentine	50–65 lbs.	45 lbs. min.
	Wagon SW2	1.9 (1901) ③	Serpentine	50–65 lbs.	45 lbs. min.
	Coupe SC1	1.9 (1901) ②	Serpentine	50–65 lbs.	45 lbs. min.
	Coupe SC2	1.9 (1901) ③	Serpentine	50–65 lbs.	45 lbs. min.

① Inches of deflection at midpoint of the belt
② SOHC engine
③ DOHC engine

REFRIGERANT CAPACITIES

Year	Model	Refrigerant (oz.)	Oil (cc)	Compressor Type
1991	Sedan SL/SL1	36.0	200	Variable displacement; rotary vane
	Sedan SL2	36.0	200	Variable displacement; rotary vane
	Coupe SC	36.0	200	Variable displacement; rotary vane
1992	Sedan SL/SL1	36.0	200	Variable displacement; rotary vane
	Sedan SL2	36.0	200	Variable displacement; rotary vane
	Coupe SC	36.0	200	Variable displacement; rotary vane
1993	Sedan SL/SL1	34.0	200	Variable displacement; rotary vane
	Sedan SL2	34.0	200	Variable displacement; rotary vane
	Wagon SW1	34.0	200	Variable displacement; rotary vane
	Wagon SW2	34.0	200	Variable displacement; rotary vane
	Coupe SC1	34.0	200	Variable displacement; rotary vane
	Coupe SC2	34.0	200	Variable displacement; rotary vane

NOTE: At the time of publication, refrigerant capacity information relating to R-134a was not available from the manufacturer.

MAINTENANCE INTERVALS—TYPE A: NORMAL SERVICE
Saturn

TO BE SERVICED	TYPE OF SERVICE	3	6	9	12	15	18	21	24	27	30	33	36	39	42	45	48	51	54	57	60
CV-Joints and Boots	I		✔		✔		✔		✔		✔		✔		✔		✔		✔		✔
Body Lubrication	I①		✔		✔		✔		✔		✔		✔		✔		✔		✔		✔
Vacuum Lines and Hoses	I										✔										✔
Ignition Wires	I										✔										✔
Spark Plugs	R										✔										✔
Engine Oil and Filter	R		✔		✔		✔		✔		✔		✔		✔		✔		✔		✔
Engine Air Cleaner Element	R										✔										✔
Automatic Transaxle Fluid	R										✔										✔
Automatic Transaxle Filter	R②										✔										
Fuel Filter	R																				✔
Manual Transaxle Fluid	R③																				
Fuel/Vapor Return Lines	I										✔										✔
Fuel Tank Cap and Restrictor	I										✔										✔
Coolant System	R												✔								
Exhaust Pipe and Muffler	I		✔		✔		✔		✔		✔		✔		✔		✔		✔		✔
Drive Belts	I				✔								✔						✔		
Catalytic Converter and Shield	I		✔		✔		✔		✔		✔		✔		✔		✔		✔		✔
Brake Linings	I				✔				✔				✔				✔				✔
Parking Brake	I				✔				✔				✔				✔				✔
Tire Rotation	I		✔				✔				✔				✔				✔		
Battery Connections	I				✔				✔				✔				✔				✔
Coolant Hoses and Clamps	I				✔								✔						✔		
Seat Belt Operation	I										✔										✔

FOR COMPLETE WARRANTY COVERAGE CONSULT INDIVIDUAL VEHICLE MANUFACTURER'S WARRANTY MAINTENANCE GUIDE.

I—Inspect
R—Replace
① Includes passive restraint tracks, door hinges, check links, hood sunroof and headlamp door assemblies
② Replace filter at 30,000 miles and then every 60,000 miles
③ Replace fluid at 6,000 miles only

MAINTENANCE INTERVALS—TYPE B: SEVERE SERVICE
Saturn

TO BE SERVICED	TYPE OF SERVICE	VEHICLE MILEAGE INTERVAL (X1000)																			
		3	6	9	12	15	18	21	24	27	30	33	36	39	42	45	48	51	54	57	60
CV-Joints and Boots	I		✔		✔		✔		✔		✔		✔		✔		✔		✔		✔
Body Lubrication	I①		✔		✔		✔		✔		✔		✔		✔		✔		✔		✔
Vacuum Lines and Hoses	I										✔										✔
Ignition Wires	I										✔										✔
Spark Plugs	R										✔										✔
Engine Oil and Filter	R	✔	✔	✔	✔	✔	✔	✔	✔	✔	✔	✔	✔	✔	✔	✔	✔	✔	✔	✔	✔
Engine Air Cleaner Element	R										✔										✔
Automatic Transaxle Fluid	R										✔										
Automatic Transaxle Filter	R②										✔										✔
Fuel Filter	R										✔										✔
Manual Transaxle Fluid	R③																				
Fuel/Vapor Return Lines	I										✔										✔
Fuel Tank Cap and Restrictor	I										✔										✔
Coolant System	R												✔								
Exhaust Pipe and Muffler	I		✔		✔		✔		✔		✔		✔		✔		✔		✔		✔
Drive Belts	I					✔							✔						✔		
Catalytic Converter and Shield	I		✔		✔		✔		✔		✔		✔		✔		✔		✔		✔
Brake Linings	I				✔				✔				✔				✔				✔
Parking Brake	I				✔				✔				✔				✔				✔
Tire Rotation	I		✔			✔					✔				✔				✔		
Battery Connections	I				✔				✔				✔				✔				✔
Coolant Hoses and Clamps	I					✔							✔						✔		
Seat Belt Operation	I				✔						✔					✔					✔

FOR COMPLETE WARRANTY COVERAGE CONSULT INDIVIDUAL VEHICLE MANUFACTURER'S WARRANTY MAINTENANCE GUIDE.

I—Inspect
R—Replace
① Includes passive restraint tracks, door hinges, check links, hood sunroof and headlamp door assemblies
② Replace filter at 30,000 miles and then every 60,000 miles
③ Replace fluid at 6,000 miles only

FIRING ORDERS

NOTE: To avoid confusion, always replace spark plugs and wires one at a time.

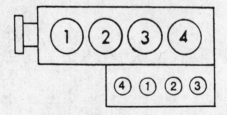

1.9L Engine
Engine Firing Order: 1–3–4–2
Distributorless Ignition System

CYLINDER HEAD TORQUE SEQUENCES

Intake Side				
3	7	10	6	2
4	8	9	5	1
Exhaust Side				

Cylinder head loosening sequence—all engines

INTAKE SIDE				
8	4	1	5	9
7	3	2	6	10
EXHAUST SIDE				

Cylinder head bolt torque sequence—all engines

TIMING CHAIN ALIGNMENT MARKS

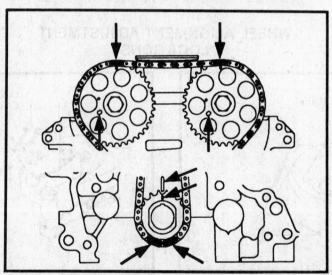

Timing chain alignment marks—DOHC engine

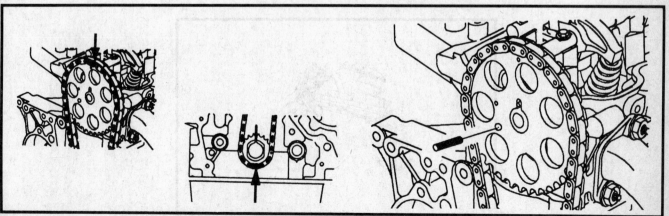

Timing chain alignment marks—SOHC engine

AIR CONDITIONING SERVICE VALVE LOCATIONS

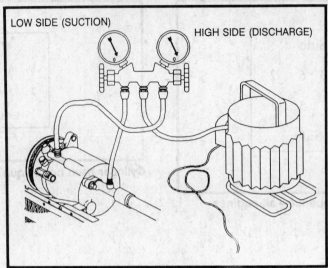

LOW SIDE (SUCTION)

HIGH SIDE (DISCHARGE)

Air conditioning charge port location

WHEEL ALIGNMENT ADJUSTMENT LOCATIONS

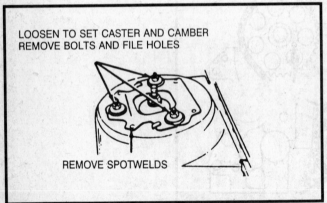

LOOSEN TO SET CASTER AND CAMBER
REMOVE BOLTS AND FILE HOLES

REMOVE SPOTWELDS

Front caster and camber adjustment at the top of the strut

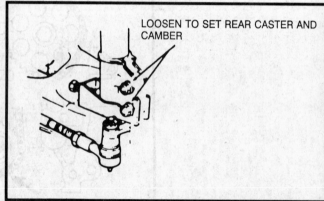

LOOSEN TO SET REAR CASTER AND CAMBER

Front and caster and camber adjustment at the steering knuckle

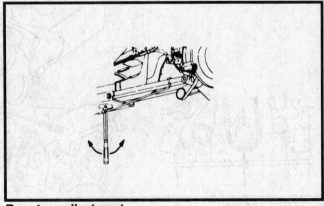

Rear toe adjustment

SPECIFICATION CHARTS

VEHICLE IDENTIFICATION CHART

It is important for servicing and ordering parts to be certain of the vehicle and engine identification. The VIN (vehicle identification number) is a 17 digit number visible through the windshield on the driver's side of the dash and contains the vehicle and engine identification codes. The tenth digit indicates model year and the eighth digit indicates engine code. It can be interpreted as follows:

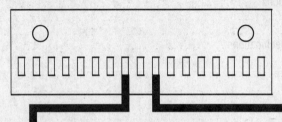

Engine Code						Model Year	
Code	Liters	Cu. In. (cc)	Cyl.	Fuel Sys.	Eng. Mfg.	Code	Year
Y	5.0	307 (5032)	8	Carburetor	B.O.C.	L	1990
E	5.0	305 (5011)	8	TBI	C.P.C.	M	1991
7	5.7	350 (5733)	8	TBI	C.P.C.	N	1992
P	5.7	350 (5733)	8	SFI	C.P.C.	P	1993
						R	1994

SFI—Sequential Fuel Injection
TBI—Throttle Body Injection
B.O.C.—Buick, Oldsmobile, Cadillac
C.P.C.—Chevrolet, Pontiac, Canada

ENGINE IDENTIFICATION

Year	Model	Engine Displacement Liters (cc)	Engine Series (ID/VIN)	Fuel System	No. of Cylinders	Engine Type
1990	Brougham	5.0 (5032)	Y	Carbureted	8	OHV
	Brougham	5.7 (5733)	7	TBI	8	OHV
1991	Brougham	5.0 (5011)	E	TBI	8	OHV
	Brougham	5.7 (5733)	7	TBI	8	OHV
1992	Brougham	5.0 (5011)	E	TBI	8	OHV
	Brougham	5.7 (5733)	7	TBI	8	OHV
1993	Fleetwood Brougham	5.7 (5733)	7	TBI	8	OHV
1994	Fleetwood Brougham	5.7 (5733)	P	SFI	8	OHV

OHV—Overhead valves
SFI—Sequential Fuel Injection
TBI—Throttle Body Injection

GENERAL ENGINE SPECIFICATIONS

Year	Engine ID/VIN	Engine Displacement Liters (cc)	Fuel System Type	Net Horsepower @ rpm	Net Torque @ rpm (ft. lbs.)	Bore × Stroke (in.)	Compression Ratio	Oil Pressure @ rpm
1990	Y	5.0 (5032)	4 bbl	140 @ 3200	255 @ 2000	3.800 × 3.385	8.0:1	30–45 ①
	7	5.7 (5733)	TBI	185 @ 3800	300 @ 2400	4.000 × 3.480	9.3:1	18 ②
1991	E	5.0 (5011)	TBI	170 @ 4200	255 @ 2400	3.740 × 3.480	9.3:1	18 ②
	7	5.7 (5733)	TBI	185 @ 3800	300 @ 2400	4.000 × 3.480	9.3:1	18 ②

GENERAL ENGINE SPECIFICATIONS

Year	Engine ID/VIN	Engine Displacement Liters (cc)	Fuel System Type	Net Horsepower @ rpm	Net Torque @ rpm (ft. lbs.)	Bore × Stroke (in.)	Compression Ratio	Oil Pressure @ rpm
1992	E	5.0 (5011)	TBI	170 @ 4200	255 @ 2400	3.740 × 3.480	9.3:1	18②
	7	5.7 (5733)	TBI	185 @ 3800	300 @ 2400	4.000 × 3.480	9.8:1	18②
1993	7	5.7 (5733)	TBI	185 @ 3800	300 @ 2400	4.000 × 3.480	9.8:1	18②
1994	P	5.7 (5733)	SFI	260 @ 5000	NA	4.000 × 3.480	10.5:1	18②

NA—Not available
SFI—Sequential Fuel Injection
TBI—Throttle Body Injection
① @ 1500 rpm
② @ 2000 rpm

GASOLINE ENGINE TUNE-UP SPECIFICATIONS

Year	Engine ID/VIN	Engine Displacement Liters (cc)	Spark Plugs Gap (in.)	Ignition Timing (deg.) MT	Ignition Timing (deg.) AT	Fuel Pump (psi)	Idle Speed (rpm) MT	Idle Speed (rpm) AT	Valve Clearance In.	Valve Clearance Ex.
1990	Y	5.0 (5032)	0.060	—	①	6.0–7.5	—	①	Hyd.	Hyd.
	7	5.7 (5733)	0.035	—	①	9.0–13.0	—	①	Hyd.	Hyd.
1991	E	5.0 (5011)	0.035	—	①	9.0–13.0	—	①	Hyd.	Hyd.
	7	5.7 (5733)	0.035	—	①	9.0–13.0	—	①	Hyd.	Hyd.
1992	E	5.0 (5011)	0.035	—	①	9.0–13.0	—	①	Hyd.	Hyd.
	7	5.7 (5733)	0.035	—	①	9.0–13.0	—	①	Hyd.	Hyd.
1993	7	5.7 (5733)	0.035	—	①	9.0–13.0	—	①	Hyd.	Hyd.
1994	SEE UNDERHOOD SPECIFICATIONS STICKER									

NOTE: The lowest cylinder pressure should be within 75% of the highest cylinder pressure reading. For example, if the highest cylinder is 134 psi, the lowest should be 101. Engine should be at normal operating temperature with throttle valve in the wide open position.
The underhood specifications sticker often reflects tune-up specification changes in production. Sticker figures must be used if they disagree with those in this chart.
Hyd.—Hydraulic
① Use data on underhood vehicle specification sticker

CAPACITIES

Year	Model	Engine ID/VIN	Engine Displacement Liters (cc)	Engine Crankcase (qts.) with Filter	Transmission (pts.) 4-Spd	Transmission (pts.) 5-Spd	Transmission (pts.) Auto.	Drive Axle (pts.)	Fuel Tank (gal.)	Cooling System (qts.)
1990	Brougham	Y	5.0 (5032)	5.0	—	—	②	④	25.0	15.2①
	Brougham	7	5.7 (5733)	5.0	—	—	③	④	25.0	16.5
1991	Brougham	E	5.0 (5011)	5.0	—	—	⑤	④	25.0	16.7
	Brougham	7	5.7 (5733)	5.0	—	—	⑤	④	25.0	16.5
1992	Brougham	E	5.0 (5011)	5.0	—	—	⑤	④	25.0	17.6
	Brougham	7	5.7 (5733)	5.0	—	—	⑤	④	25.0	17.6
1993	Fleetwood Brougham	7	5.7 (5733)	5.0	—	—	⑤	④	23.0	17.6
1994	Fleetwood Brougham	P	5.7 (5733)	4.5	—	—	⑥	④	23.0	15⑦

All capacities shown are approximate. Add fluid as necessary to bring to proper level
① Heavy duty—15.6
② Pan 6.0, overhaul 20.0
③ Pan 9.0, overhaul 20.0
④ Fill to Flush or ¼" (6mm) of Filler Hole
⑤ Pan 10.0, overhaul 22.4
⑥ Pan 10.0, overhaul 21.6
⑦ With HD Rad.: 15.7

CAMSHAFT SPECIFICATIONS

All measurements given in inches.

Year	Engine ID/VIN	Engine Displacement Liters (cc)	Journal Diameter 1	2	3	4	5	Elevation In.	Ex.	Bearing Clearance	Camshaft End Play
1990	Y	5.0 (5032)	2.0352–2.0365	2.0152–2.0166	1.9952–1.9965	1.9752–1.9765	1.9552–1.9565	0.247	0.251	0.0020–0.0058	0.006–0.022
	7	5.7 (5733)	1.8682–1.8692	1.8682–1.8692	1.8682–1.8692	1.8682–1.8692	1.8682–1.8692	0.257	0.269	NA	0.004–0.012
1991	E	5.0 (5011)	1.8682–1.8690	1.8682–1.8692	1.8682–1.8692	1.8682–1.8692	1.8682–1.8692	0.234	0.251	NA	0.004–0.012
	7	5.7 (5733)	1.8682–1.8692	1.8682–1.8692	1.8682–1.8692	1.8682–1.8692	1.8682–1.8692	0.257	0.269	NA	0.004–0.012
1992	E	5.0 (5011)	1.8682–1.8690	1.8682–1.8692	1.8682–1.8692	1.8682–1.8692	1.8682–1.8692	0.234	0.251	NA	0.004–0.012
	7	5.7 (5733)	1.8682–1.8692	1.8682–1.8692	1.8682–1.8692	1.8682–1.8692	1.8682–1.8692	0.257	0.269	NA	0.004–0.012
1993	7	5.7 (5733)	1.8682–1.8692	1.8682–1.8692	1.8682–1.8692	1.8682–1.8692	1.8682–1.8692	0.233	0.256	NA	0.004–0.012
1994	P	5.7 (5733)	1.8682–1.8692	1.8682–1.8692	1.8682–1.8692	1.8682–1.8692	1.8682–1.8692	0.298–0.302	0.298–0.302	NA	0.004–0.012

NA—Not available

CRANKSHAFT AND CONNECTING ROD SPECIFICATIONS

All measurements are given in inches.

Year	Engine ID/VIN	Engine Displacement Liters (cc)	Crankshaft Main Brg. Journal Dia.	Main Brg. Oil Clearance	Shaft Endplay	Thrust on No.	Connecting Rod Journal Diameter	Oil Clearance	Side Clearance
1990	Y	5.0 (5032)	2.4985–2.4995②	0.0005–0.0021①	0.004–0.014	3	2.1238–2.1248	0.0004–0.0033	0.006–0.020
	7	5.7 (5733)	2.4481–2.4490④	0.0011–0.0020③	0.001–0.007	5	2.0893–2.0998	0.0013–0.0035	0.006–0.014
1991	E	5.0 (5011)	2.4481–2.4490④	0.0011–0.0020③	0.001–0.007	5	2.0893–2.0998	0.0013–0.0035	0.006–0.014
	7	5.7 (5733)	2.4481–2.4490④	0.0011–0.0020③	0.001–0.007	5	2.0893–2.0998	0.0013–0.0035	0.006–0.014
1992	E	5.0 (5011)	2.4481–2.4490④	0.0011–0.0020③	0.001–0.007	5	2.0893–2.0998	0.0013–0.0035	0.006–0.014
	7	5.7 (5733)	2.4481–2.4490④	0.0011–0.0020③	0.001–0.007	5	2.0893–2.0998	0.0013–0.0035	0.006–0.014
1993	7	5.7 (5733)	2.4481–2.4490④	0.0011–0.0020③	0.001–0.007	5	2.0893–2.0998	0.0013–0.0035	0.006–0.014
1994	P	5.7 (5733)	2.4481–2.4490⑤	0.0011–0.0020③	0.001–0.007	5	2.0893–2.0998	0.0013–0.0035	0.006–0.014

① No. 5—0.0015–0.0031
② No. 1—2.4988–2.4998
③ No. 1—0.0008–0.0020
No. 5—0.0017–0.0032
④ No. 1—2.4488–2.4493
No. 5—2.4481–2.4488
⑤ Front: 2.4484–2.4493
Rear: 2.4481–2.4488

VALVE SPECIFICATIONS

Year	Engine ID/VIN	Engine Displacement Liters (cc)	Seat Angle (deg.)	Face Angle (deg.)	Spring Test Pressure (lbs. @ in.)	Spring Installed Height (in.)	Stem-to-Guide Clearance (in.)		Stem Diameter (in.)	
							Intake	Exhaust	Intake	Exhaust
1990	Y	5.0 (5032)	45①	44①	180–194 @ 1.27	1⁴³/₆₄	0.0010–0.0027	0.0015–0.0032	0.3425–0.3432	0.3420–0.3427
	7	5.7 (5733)	46	45	194–206 @ 1.25	1²³/₃₂	0.0011–0.0027	0.0011–0.0027	NA	NA
1991	E	5.0 (5011)	46	45	194–206 @ 1.25	1²³/₃₂	0.0011–0.0027	0.0011–0.0027	NA	NA
	7	5.7 (5733)	46	45	194–206 @ 1.25	1²³/₃₂	0.0011–0.0027	0.0011–0.0027	NA	NA
1992	E	5.0 (5011)	46	45	194–206 @ 1.25	1²³/₃₂	0.0011–0.0027	0.0011–0.0027	NA	NA
	7	5.7 (5733)	46	45	194–206 @ 1.25	1²³/₃₂	0.0011–0.0027	0.0011–0.0027	NA	NA
1993	7	5.7 (5733)	46	45	194–206 @ 1.25	1²³/₃₂	0.0011–0.0027	0.0011–0.0027	NA	NA
1994	P	5.7 (5733)	46	45	252–272 @ 1.305	1.78	0.0011–0.0027	0.0011–0.0027	NA	NA

NA—Not available
① Exhaust Valve—31° Seat, 30° Face

PISTON AND RING SPECIFICATIONS
All measurements are given in inches.

Year	Engine ID/VIN	Engine Displacement Liters (cc)	Piston Clearance	Ring Gap			Ring Side Clearance		
				Top Compression	Bottom Compression	Oil Control	Top Compression	Bottom Compression	Oil Control
1990	Y	5.0 (5032)	0.0008–0.0017①	0.009–0.019	0.009–0.019	0.015–0.055	0.0018–0.0038	0.0018–0.0038	0.001–0.005
	7	5.7 (5733)	0.0007–0.0021	0.010–0.020	0.010–0.025	0.015–0.055	0.0012–0.0032	0.0012–0.0032	0.002–0.007
1991	E	5.0 (5011)	0.0007–0.0021	0.010–0.020	0.010–0.025	0.015–0.055	0.0012–0.0032	0.0012–0.0032	0.002–0.007
	7	5.7 (5733)	0.0007–0.0021	0.010–0.020	0.010–0.025	0.015–0.065	0.0012–0.0032	0.0012–0.0032	0.002–0.007
1992	E	5.0 (5011)	0.0007–0.0021	0.010–0.020	0.010–0.025	0.015–0.055	0.0012–0.0032	0.0012–0.0032	0.002–0.007
	7	5.7 (5733)	0.0007–0.0021	0.010–0.020	0.010–0.025	0.015–0.065	0.0012–0.0032	0.0012–0.0032	0.002–0.007
1993	7	5.7 (5733)	0.0007–0.0021	0.010–0.020	0.010–0.025	0.015–0.065	0.0012–0.0032	0.0012–0.0032	0.002–0.007
1994	P	5.7 (5733)	0.0010–0.0027	0.010–0.020	0.018–0.026	0.010–0.030	0.0012–0.0032	0.0012–0.0032	0.002–0.007

① Clearance to bore (selective)

TORQUE SPECIFICATIONS
All readings in ft. lbs.

Year	Engine ID/VIN	Engine Displacement Liters (cc)	Cylinder Head Bolts	Main Bearing Bolts	Rod Bearing Bolts	Crankshaft Damper Bolts	Flywheel Bolts	Manifold		Spark Plugs	Lug Nut
								Intake	Exhaust		
1990	Y	5.0 (5032)	40①③	70⑤	18④	255	60	40①	25	25	100
	7	5.7 (5733)	70	75	45	70	75	35	26②	22	100
1991	E	5.0 (5011)	70	75	45	70	75	35	26②	22	100
	7	5.7 (5733)	70	75	45	70	75	35	26②	22	100
1992	E	5.0 (5011)	70	75	45	70	75	35	26②	11	100
	7	5.7 (5733)	65	75	45	70	75	35	26②	11	100
1993	7	5.7 (5733)	65	75	45	70	75	35	26②	11	100
1994	P	5.7 (5733)	65	78	45	60	74	35⑥	26	11	100

① Dip bolt in oil before installation
② Stud 20
③ Rotate bolts 1–7 and 9—120°
   Roate bolts 8 and 10—95°
④ Rotate 70°
⑤ Rear main bearing torque 105
⑥ Tighten in 2 passes:
   1st pass—71 in. lbs.

TORQUE SPECIFICATIONS

Component	English	Metric
Camshaft sprocket bolt		
Except 5.0L (VIN Y) engine:	21 ft. lbs.	28 Nm
5.0L (VIN Y) engine:	65 ft. lbs.	88 Nm
Carburetor-to-manifold bolts:	12 ft. lbs.	16 Nm
Connecting rod bearing cap bolts		
1990–93 except 5.0L (VIN Y) engine:	44 ft. lbs.	60 Nm
5.0L (VIN Y) engine		
Step 1:	18 ft. lbs.	24 Nm
Step 2:	+ 70 degrees turn	+ 70 degrees turn
5.7L (VIN P) engine:	47 ft. lbs.	64 Nm
Crankshaft damper bolt		
1990–93 except 5.0L (VIN Y) engine:	70 ft. lbs.	95 Nm
5.0L (VIN Y) engine:	255 ft. lbs.	345 Nm
5.7L (VIN P with damper/pulley assembly) engine:	60 ft. lbs.	81 Nm
Crankshaft hub bolt		
5.7L (VIN P) engine:	75 ft. lbs.	102 Nm
Crankshaft pulley bolt		
1990–93 except 5.0L (VIN Y) engine:	45 ft. lbs.	60 Nm
5.0L (VIN Y) engine:	28 ft. lbs.	40 Nm
5.7L (VIN P with damper/pulley assembly) engine:	60 ft. lbs.	81 Nm
Cylinder head bolts		
1990 5.0L (VIN Y) engine*		
Step 1:	40 ft. lbs.	54 Nm
Step 2 (positions 1 to 7 & 9):	+ 120 degrees turn	+ 120 degrees turn
Step 3 (positions 8 & 10):	+ 95 degrees turn	+ 95 degrees turn
5.0L (VIN E) and 5.7L (VIN 8) engine:	70 ft. lbs.	95 Nm
5.7L (VIN P) engine**:	68 ft. lbs.	92 Nm

* NOTE: Clean and dip entire bolt in 5W30 engine oil prior to installation

** Tighten using at least 3 passses of the proper torque sequence

TORQUE SPECIFICATIONS

Component	English	Metric
Engine-to-transmission		
Except 5.0L (VIN Y) and 5.7L (VIN P) engines:	55 ft. lbs.	75 Nm
5.0L (VIN Y) and 5.7L (VIN P) engines:	35 ft. lbs.	47 Nm
Exhaust manifold		
1990–93 except 5.0L (VIN Y) engine		
Nuts on studs:	20 ft. lbs.	27 Nm
Bolts and studs:	25 ft. lbs.	34 Nm
5.0L (VIN Y) engine:	25 ft. lbs.	34 Nm
5.7L (VIN P) engine:	26 ft. lbs.	35 Nm
Exhaust pipe-to-exhaust manifold nuts:	15 ft. lbs.	20 Nm
Flywheel/flexplate-to-crankshaft bolts		
Except 5.0L (VIN Y) engine:	75 ft. lbs.	100 Nm
5.0L (VIN Y) engine:	60 ft. lbs.	81 Nm
Flywheel-to-converter bolts		
Except 5.0L (VIN Y) and 5.7L (VIN P) engines:	35 ft. lbs.	47 Nm
5.0L (VIN Y) and 5.7L (VIN P) engines:	46 ft. lbs.	63 Nm
Fuel pump-to-block:	25 ft. lbs.	34 Nm
Intake manifold		
1990–93 except 5.0L (VIN Y) engine:	35 ft. lbs.	47 Nm
5.0L (VIN Y) engine*:	40 ft. lbs.	54 Nm
5.7L (VIN P) engine		
Step 1:	71 inch lbs.	8 Nm
Step 2:	35 ft. lbs.	48 Nm
* NOTE: Clean and dip entire bolt in 5W30 engine oil prior to installation		
Main bearing cap bolts		
1990–93 except 5.0L (VIN Y) engine:	77 ft. lbs.	105 Nm
5.0L (VIN Y) engine		
Bearing cap No. 1, 2, 3, 4:	80 ft. lbs.	108 Nm
Bearing cap No. 5:	120 ft. lbs.	163 Nm
5.7L (VIN P) engine:	78 ft. lbs.	106 Nm
Oil pan		
1990–93 except 5.0L (VIN Y) engine		
Nuts:	17 ft. lbs.	24 Nm
Bolts:	120 inch lbs.	14 Nm
5.0L (VIN Y) engine		
Nuts:	17 ft. lbs.	24 Nm
5.7L (VIN P) engine		
Corner fasteners:	15 ft. lbs.	20 Nm
Remaining fasteners:	100 inch lbs.	11 Nm
Bolts:	95 inch lbs.	11 Nm
Oil pan drain plug:		
Except 5.7L (VIN P) engine:	30 ft. lbs.	41 Nm
5.7L (VIN P) engine:	16 ft. lbs.	22 Nm
Oil pump attaching bolts		
1990–93 except 5.0L (VIN Y) engine:	80 ft. lbs.	105 Nm
5.0L (VIN Y) engine:	35 ft. lbs.	47 Nm
5.7L (VIN P) engine:	65 ft. lbs.	88 Nm
Rocker arm pivot bolt		
5.0L (VIN Y) engine:	22 ft. lbs.	28 Nm
Rocker (valve) cover		
1990–93 except 5.0L (VIN Y) engine:	95 inch lbs.	11 Nm
5.0L (VIN Y) engine:	90 inch lbs.	10 Nm
5.7L (VIN P) engine:	96 inch lbs.	11 Nm
Spark plug		
1990–93 except 5.0L (VIN Y) engine:	22 ft. lbs.	30 Nm
5.0L (VIN Y) engine:	25 ft. lbs.	34 Nm
5.7L (VIN P) engine:	11 ft. lbs.	15 Nm

TORQUE SPECIFICATIONS

Component	English	Metric
Starter-to-block bolts:	35 ft. lbs.	47 Nm
Thermostat housing		
Except 5.0L (VIN Y) engine:	21 ft. lbs.	28 Nm
5.0L (VIN Y) engine:	32 ft. lbs.	44 Nm
Timing cover		
Except 5.0L (VIN Y) engine:	100 inch lbs.	11 Nm
5.0L (VIN Y) engine:	35 ft. lbs.	47 Nm
Water pump pulley:	18 ft. lbs.	24 Nm

BRAKE SPECIFICATIONS
All measurements in inches unless noted.

Year	Model	Master Cylinder Bore	Brake Disc Original Thickness	Brake Disc Minimum ① Thickness	Maximum Runout	Brake Drum Diameter Original Inside Diameter	Brake Drum Diameter Max. Wear Limit	Brake Drum Diameter Maximum Machine Diameter	Minimum Lining Thickness Front	Minimum Lining Thickness Rear
1990	Brougham	1.125	1.032	0.972	0.0005	11.00	11.09	11.06	0.030	0.030
1991	Brougham	1.125	1.032	0.972	0.0005	11.00	11.09	11.06	0.030	0.030
1992	Brougham	1.125	1.032	0.972	0.0005	11.00	11.09	11.06	0.030	0.030
1993	Fleetwood Brougham	1.125	1.043	0.980	0.004	11.00	11.09	11.06	0.030	0.030
1994	Fleetwood Brougham	1.125	1.043	0.980	0.004	11.00	11.09	11.06	0.030	0.030

① Figure given is Minimum Refinishing Thickness.
  All rotors have a discard thickness cast into
  them. This dimension is usually smaller than
  the refinish dimension. Do not cut a rotor to the
  discard thickness.

WHEEL ALIGNMENT

Year	Model	Caster Range (deg.)	Caster Preferred Setting (deg.)	Camber Range (deg.)	Camber Preferred Setting (deg.)	Toe-in (in.)	Steering Axis Inclination (deg.)
1990	Brougham	2P–4P	3P	5/16N–5/16P	0	3/64	NA
1991	Brougham	2P–4P	3P	5/16N–5/16P	0	3/64	NA
1992	Brougham	2P–4P	3P	5/16N–5/16P	0	3/64	NA
1993	Fleetwood Brougham	2½P–4½P	3½P	1N–1P	0	1/32	NA
1994	Fleetwood Brougham	2½P–4½P	3½P	1N–1P	0	1/32	NA

NA—Not available
N—Negative
P—Positive

AIR CONDITIONING BELT TENSION

Year	Model	Engine Displacement Liters (cc)	Belt Type	Specifications (lbs.) New	Used
1990	Brougham	5.0 (5032)	V-Belt	169	112
	Brougham, Fleetwood Brougham	5.7 (5733)	Serpentine	①	①
1991	Brougham, Fleetwood Brougham	5.0 (5011)	Serpentine	①	①
		5.7 (5733)	Serpentine	①	①
1992	Brougham, Fleetwood Brougham	5.0 (5011)	Serpentine	99–121	99–121
		5.7 (5733)	Serpentine	99–121	99–121
1993–94	Brougham, Fleetwood Brougham	5.0 (5011)	Serpentine	99–121	99–121
		5.7 (5733)	Serpentine	99–121	99–121

① Equipped with automatic tensioner; however, the specification given (in pounds) is for testing whether the tensioner is maintaining its proper tension (specification given is the average of 3 readings back-to-back).

REFRIGERANT CAPACITIES

Year	Model	Refrigerant (oz.)	Oil (fl. oz.)	Compressor Type
1990	Brougham, Fleetwood Brougham	53.0	6.0	R-4
1991	Brougham, Fleetwood Brougham	49.6	6.0	R-4
1992	Brougham, Fleetwood Brougham	49.6	6.0	R-4
1993–94	Brougham, Fleetwood Brougham	49.6	6.0	R-4

NOTE: At the time of publication, refrigerant capacity information relating to R-134a was not available from the manufacturer.

MAINTENANCE INTERVALS—TYPE A: NORMAL SERVICE
Brougham • Fleetwood Brougham

TO BE SERVICED	TYPE OF SERVICE	VEHICLE MILEAGE INTERVAL (X1000) 7.5	15	22.5	30	37.5	45	52.5	60
Oxygen Sensor	I				✔				✔
Ignition Timing	I				✔				✔
Vacuum Lines and Hoses	I		✔		✔		✔		✔
Ignition Wires	I				✔				✔
Spark Plugs	R				✔				✔
Engine Oil	R	✔	✔	✔	✔	✔	✔	✔	✔
Engine Air Cleaner Element	R				✔				✔
Crankcase Emission Filter	R				✔				✔
PCV Valve	R				✔				✔
Fuel Filter	R				✔				✔
Engine Oil Filter	R①	✔		✔		✔		✔	
Fuel/Vapor Return Lines	I				✔				✔
Fuel Tank Cap and Restrictor	I				✔				✔
Coolant System Service	I				✔				✔
Exhaust Pipe and Muffler	I				✔				✔

MAINTENANCE INTERVALS—TYPE A: NORMAL SERVICE
Brougham • Fleetwood Brougham

TO BE SERVICED	TYPE OF SERVICE	VEHICLE MILEAGE INTERVAL (X1000)							
		7.5	15	22.5	30	37.5	45	52.5	60
Chassis Lubrication	L	✔	✔	✔	✔	✔	✔	✔	✔
Catalytic Converter and Shield	I				✔				✔
EGR System	I				✔				✔
Air Pump Filter	R				✔				✔
Air Pump and Connections	I				✔				✔
Tire Rotation	I②	✔		✔		✔		✔	
Seat Belt Operation	I		✔		✔		✔		✔
Idle Speed System	I				✔				
Throttle Body Mounting Torque	I	✔							
Drive Belts	I				✔				✔
Coolant Hoses and Clamps	I		✔		✔		✔		✔
Rear Axle Lubricant	R③	✔	✔	✔	✔	✔	✔	✔	✔
Front Wheel Bearings	L				✔				✔
Brake Linings	I		✔		✔		✔		✔
Parking Brake	I		✔		✔		✔		✔
Battery Connections	I		✔		✔		✔		✔
Automatic Transmission Fluid	R④								

FOR COMPLETE WARRANTY COVERAGE CONSULT INDIVIDUAL VEHICLE MANUFACTURER'S WARRANTY MAINTENANCE GUIDE.

I—Inspect
L—Lubricate
R—Replace
① Replace oil filter at first and every other oil change
② Rotate tires at 7,500 miles, then every 15,000 miles as necessary
③ If vehicle is used to pull a trailer, change the gear lubricant every 7,500 miles
④ Replace automatic transmission fluid and filter every 100,000 miles

MAINTENANCE INTERVALS—TYPE B: SEVERE SERVICE
Brougham • Fleetwood Brougham

TO BE SERVICED	TYPE OF SERVICE	VEHICLE MILEAGE INTERVAL (X1000)									
		3	6	9	12	15	18	21	24	27	30
Oxygen Sensor	I										✔
Ignition Timing	I										✔
Vacuum Lines and Hoses	I					✔					✔
Ignition Wires	I										✔
Spark Plugs	R										✔
Engine Oil	R	✔	✔	✔	✔	✔	✔	✔	✔	✔	✔
Engine Air Cleaner Element	R										✔
Crankcase Emission Filter	R										✔
PCV Valve	R					✔					✔
Fuel Filter	R					✔					✔
Engine Oil Filter	R	✔	✔	✔	✔	✔	✔	✔	✔	✔	✔
Fuel/Vapor Return Lines	I										✔
Fuel Tank Cap and Restrictor	I										✔

MAINTENANCE INTERVALS—TYPE B: SEVERE SERVICE
Brougham • Fleetwood Brougham

TO BE SERVICED	TYPE OF SERVICE	3	6	9	12	15	18	21	24	27	30
Coolant System Service	R										✔
Exhaust Pipe and Muffler	I										✔
Chassis Lubrication	L		✔		✔		✔		✔		✔
Catalytic Converter and Shield	I										✔
EGR System	I										✔
Air Pump Filter	R										✔
Air Pump and Connections	I										✔
Tire Rotation	I ①		✔					✔			
Seat Belt Operation	I					✔					✔
Idle Speed System	I					✔					✔
Throttle Body Mounting Torque	I		✔								
Drive Belts	I										✔
Coolant Hoses and Clamps	I					✔					✔
Rear Axle Lubricant	R ②		✔		✔		✔		✔		✔
Front Wheel Bearings	L										✔
Brake Linings	I					✔					✔
Parking Brake	I					✔					✔
Battery Connections	I					✔					✔
Automatic Transmission Fluid	R					✔					✔

FOR COMPLETE WARRANTY COVERAGE CONSULT INDIVIDUAL VEHICLE MANUFACTURER'S WARRANTY MAINTENANCE GUIDE.

I—Inspect
L—Lubricate
R—Replace
① Rotate tires at 6,000 miles, then every 15,000 miles as necessary
② If vehicle is used to pull a trailer, change the gear lubricant every 7,500 miles

FIRING ORDERS

NOTE: To avoid confusion, always replace spark plugs and wires one at a time.

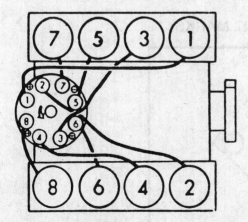

5.0L (VIN Y) Engine
Engine Firing Order: 1–8–4–3–6–5–7–2
Distributor Rotation: Counterclockwise

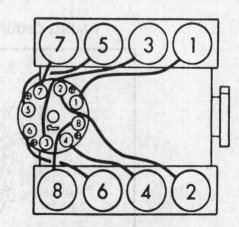

5.0L (VIN E) and 5.7L Engines
Engine Firing Order: 1–8–4–3–6–5–7–2
Distributor Rotation: Clockwise

CYLINDER HEAD TORQUE SEQUENCES

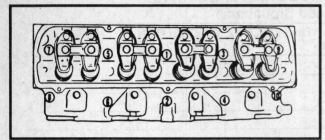

Cylinder head bolt torque sequence—5.0L (VIN Y) engine

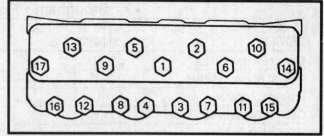

Cylinder head bolt torque sequence—5.0L (VIN E) and 5.7L engines

TIMING MARK LOCATIONS

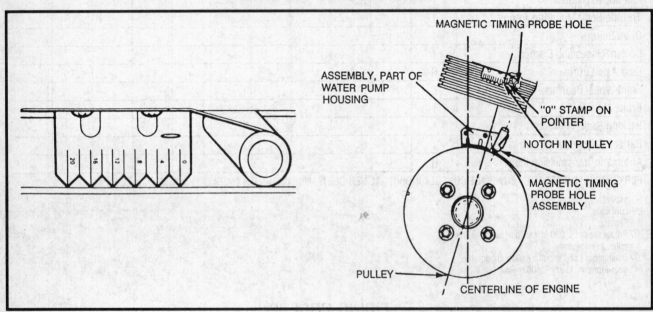

Timing mark location

TIMING CHAIN ALIGNMENT MARKS

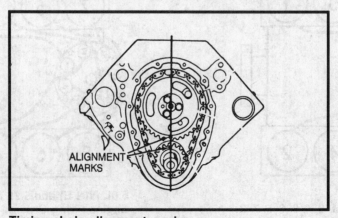

Timing chain alignment marks

AIR CONDITIONING SERVICE VALVE LOCATIONS

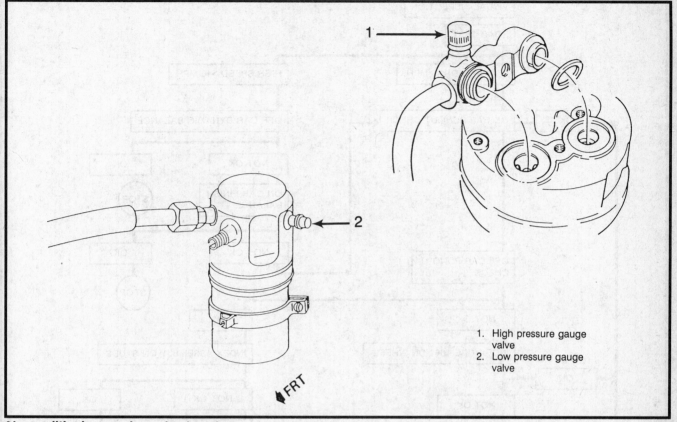

1. High pressure gauge valve
2. Low pressure gauge valve

Air conditioning service valve location

WHEEL ALIGNMENT ADJUSTMENT LOCATIONS

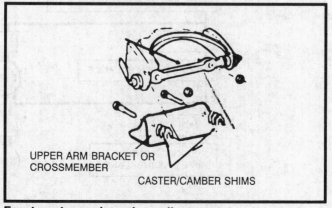

UPPER ARM BRACKET OR CROSSMEMBER

CASTER/CAMBER SHIMS

Front caster and camber adjustment

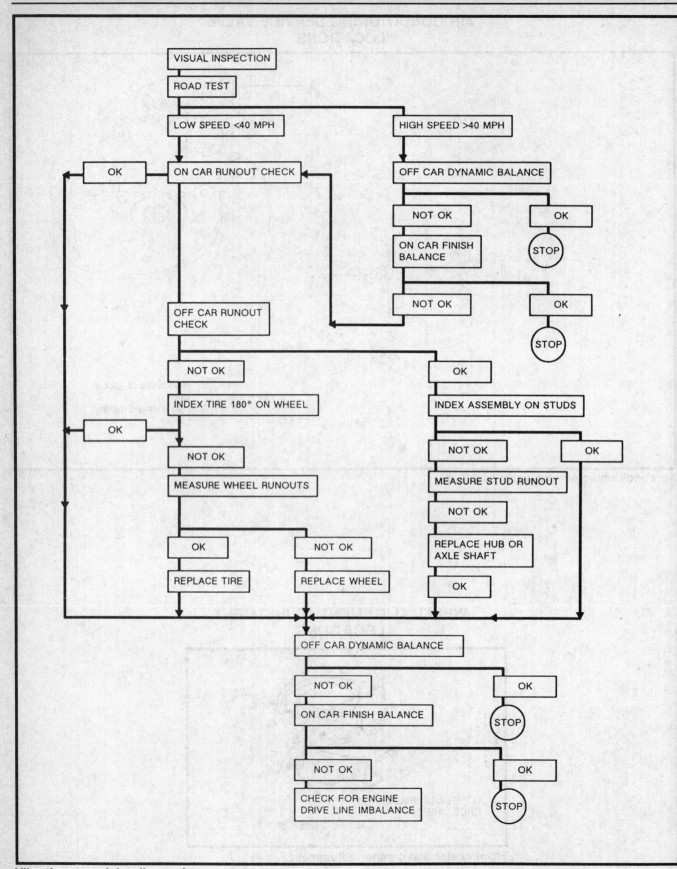

Vibration complaint diagnosis

SPECIFICATION CHARTS

VEHICLE IDENTIFICATION CHART

It is important for servicing and ordering parts to be certain of the vehicle and engine identification. The VIN (vehicle identification number) is a 17 digit number visible through the windshield on the driver's side of the dash and contains the vehicle and engine identification codes. The tenth digit indicates model year and the eighth digit indicates engine code. It can be interpreted as follows:

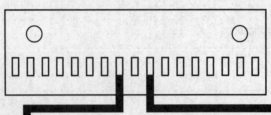

Engine Code						Model Year	
Code	Liters	Cu. In. (cc)	Cyl.	Fuel Sys.	Eng. Mfg.	Code	Year
Z	4.3	262 (4300)	6	TBI	C.P.C.	L	1990
T	4.3	264 (4300)	8	SFI	C.P.C.	M	1991
E	5.0	305 (5011)	8	TBI	C.P.C.	N	1992
Y	5.0	305 (5011)	8	4 bbl	B.O.C.	P	1993
P	5.7	350 (5733)	8	SFI	C.P.C.	R	1994
7	5.7	350 (5733)	8	TBI	C.P.C.		

B.O.C.—Buick, Oldsmobile, Cadillac
C.P.C.—Chevrolet, Pontiac, Canada
SFI—Sequential Fuel Injection
TBI—Throttle Body Injection

ENGINE IDENTIFICATION

Year	Model	Engine Displacement Liters (cc)	Engine Series (ID/VIN)	Fuel System	No. of Cylinders	Engine Type
1990	Estate Wagon	5.0 (5011)	Y	4 bbl.	8	OHV
	Caprice Sedan ①	4.3 (4300)	Z	TBI	6	OHV
	Caprice Sedan	5.0 (5011)	E	TBI	8	OHV
	Caprice Wagon	5.0 (5011)	Y	4 bbl.	8	OHV
	Caprice Sedan ②	5.7 (5733)	7	TBI	8	OHV
	Custom Cruiser	5.0 (5011)	Y	4 bbl.	8	OHV
1991	Roadmaster Sedan	5.7 (5733)	7	TBI	8	OHV
	Roadmaster Estate Wagon	5.0 (5011)	E	TBI	8	OHV
	Caprice Sedan	5.0 (5011)	E	TBI	8	OHV
	Caprice Wagon	5.0 (5011)	E	TBI	8	OHV
	Caprice Sedan ②	5.7 (5733)	7	TBI	8	OHV
	Custom Cruiser Sedan	5.0 (5011)	E	TBI	8	OHV
	Custom Cruiser Sedan	5.7 (5733)	7	TBI	8	OHV
	Custom Cruiser Wagon	5.0 (5011)	E	TBI	8	OHV
	Custom Cruiser Wagon	5.7 (5733)	7	TBI	8	OHV

ENGINE IDENTIFICATION

Year	Model	Engine Displacement Liters (cc)	Engine Series (ID/VIN)	Fuel System	No. of Cylinders	Engine Type
1992	Roadmaster Sedan	5.7 (5733)	7	TBI	8	OHV
	Roadmaster Estate Wagon	5.7 (5733)	7	TBI	8	OHV
	Caprice Sedan ③	4.3 (4300)	Z	TBI	6	OHV
	Caprice Sedan	5.0 (5011)	E	TBI	8	OHV
	Caprice Wagon	5.0 (5011)	E	TBI	8	OHV
	Caprice Wagon	5.7 (5733)	7	TBI	8	OHV
	Caprice Sedan ②	5.7 (5733)	7	TBI	8	OHV
	Custom Cruiser Sedan	5.0 (5011)	E	TBI	8	OHV
	Custom Cruiser Sedan	5.7 (5733)	7	TBI	8	OHV
	Custom Cruiser Wagon	5.0 (5011)	E	TBI	8	OHV
	Custom Cruiser Wagon	5.7 (5733)	7	TBI	8	OHV
1993	Roadmaster Sedan	5.7 (5733)	7	TBI	8	OHV
	Roadmaster Wagon	5.7 (5733)	7	TBI	8	OHV
	Caprice Sedan ③	4.3 (4300)	Z	TBI	6	OHV
	Caprice Sedan	5.0 (5011)	E	TBI	8	OHV
	Caprice Wagon	5.0 (5011)	E	TBI	8	OHV
	Caprice Sedan	5.7 (5733)	7	TBI	8	OHV
	Caprice Sedan ②	5.7 (5733)	7	TBI	8	OHV
	Caprice Wagon	5.7 (5733)	7	TBI	8	OHV
1994	Roadmaster Sedan	5.7 (5733)	P	SFI	8	OHV
	Roadmaster Wagon	5.7 (5733)	P	SFI	8	OHV
	Caprice Sedan	4.3 (4300)	T	SFI	8	OHV
	Caprice Wagon	4.3 (4300)	T	SFI	8	OHV
	Caprice Sedan	5.7 (5733)	P	SFI	8	OHV
	Caprice Wagon	5.7 (5733)	P	SFI	8	OHV

OHV—Overhead Valves
SFI—Sequential Fuel Injection
TBI—Throttle Body Injection
① Fleet only
② Police
③ Taxi

GENERAL ENGINE SPECIFICATIONS

Year	Engine ID/VIN	Engine Displacement Liters (cc)	Fuel System Type	Net Horsepower @ rpm	Net Torque @ rpm (ft. lbs.)	Bore × Stroke (in.)	Compression Ratio	Oil Pressure @ rpm
1990	Z	4.3 (4300)	TBI	140 @ 4000	225 @ 2000	4.000 × 3.480	9.3:1	18 @ 2000
	E	5.0 (5011)	TBI	170 @ 4400	255 @ 2400	3.740 × 3.480	9.3:1	18 @ 2000
	Y	5.0 (5011)	4 bbl	140 @ 3200	255 @ 2000	3.800 × 3.385	8.0:1	18 @ 2000
	7	5.7 (5733)	TBI	195 @ 4200	295 @ 2400	4.000 × 3.500	9.8:1	18 @ 2000
1991	E	5.0 (5011)	TBI	170 @ 4200	255 @ 2400	3.740 × 3.480	9.3:1	18 @ 2000
	7	5.7 (5733)	TBI	195 @ 4200	295 @ 2400	4.000 × 3.500	9.8:1	18 @ 2000
1992	Z	4.3 (4300)	TBI	140 @ 4000	225 @ 2000	4.000 × 3.480	9.3:1	18 @ 2000
	E	5.0 (5011)	TBI	170 @ 4200	255 @ 2400	3.738 × 3.480	9.1:1	18 @ 2000
	7	5.7 (5733)	TBI	195 @ 4200	295 @ 2400	4.001 × 3.480	9.8:1	18 @ 2000

GENERAL MOTORS—"B" BODY

CAPRICE • CUSTOM CRUISER • ESTATE WAGON • ROADMASTER

GENERAL ENGINE SPECIFICATIONS

Year	Engine ID/VIN	Engine Displacement Liters (cc)	Fuel System Type	Net Horsepower @ rpm	Net Torque @ rpm (ft. lbs.)	Bore × Stroke (in.)	Compression Ratio	Oil Pressure @ rpm
1993	Z	4.3 (4300)	TBI	145 @ 4000	220 @ 2800	4.000 × 3.480	9.3:1	18 @ 2000
	E	5.0 (5011)	TBI	170 @ 4200	255 @ 2400	3.738 × 3.480	9.1:1	18 @ 2000
	7	5.7 (5733)	TBI	180 @ 4000	300 @ 2400	4.001 × 3.480	9.8:1	18 @ 2000
1994	T	4.3 (4300)	SFI	200 @ 5200	NA	3.740 × 3.000	9.8:1	NA
	P	5.7 (5733)	SFI	260 @ 5000	NA	4.000 × 3.480	10.5:1	18 @ 2000

NA—Not available
SFI—Sequential Fuel Injection
TBI—Throttle Body Injection

GASOLINE ENGINE TUNE-UP SPECIFICATIONS

Year	Engine ID/VIN	Engine Displacement Liters (cc)	Spark Plug Gap (in.)	Ignition Timing (deg.) MT	Ignition Timing (deg.) AT	Fuel Pump (psi)	Idle Speed (rpm) MT	Idle Speed (rpm) AT	Valve Clearance In.	Valve Clearance Ex.
1990	Z	4.3 (4300)	0.035	—	①	9–13	—	①	Hyd.	Hyd.
	E	5.0 (5011)	0.035	—	①	9–13	—	①	Hyd.	Hyd.
	Y	5.0 (5011)	0.060	—	①	6.0–7.5	—	①	Hyd.	Hyd.
	7	5.7 (5733)	0.035	—	①	9–13	—	①	Hyd.	Hyd.
1991	E	5.0 (5011)	0.035	—	①	9–13	—	①	Hyd.	Hyd.
	7	5.7 (5733)	0.035	—	①	9–13	—	①	Hyd.	Hyd.
1992	Z	4.3 (4300)	0.035	—	①	9–13	—	①	Hyd.	Hyd.
	E	5.0 (5011)	0.035	—	①	9–13	—	①	Hyd.	Hyd.
	7	5.7 (5733)	0.035	—	①	9–13	—	①	Hyd.	Hyd.
1993	Z	4.3 (4300)	0.035	—	①	9–13	—	①	Hyd.	Hyd.
	E	5.0 (5011)	0.035	—	①	9–13	—	①	Hyd.	Hyd.
	7	5.7 (5733)	0.035	—	①	9–13	—	①	Hyd.	Hyd.
1994	SEE UNDERHOOD SPECIFICATIONS STICKER									

NOTE: The lowest cylinder pressure should be within 75% of the highest cylinder pressure reading. For example, if the highest cylinder is 134 psi, the lowest should be 101. Engine should be at normal operating temperature with throttle valve in the wide open position.
The underhood specifications sticker often reflects tune-up specification changes in production. Sticker figures must be used if they disagree with those in this chart.
Hyd.—Hydraulic
① See the Emission Control Label

CAPACITIES

Year	Model	Engine ID/VIN	Engine Displacement Liters (cc)	Engine Crankcase with Filter (qts.)	Transmission (pts.) 4-Spd	Transmission (pts.) 5-Spd	Transmission (pts.) Auto. ①	Drive Axle (pts.)	Fuel Tank (gal.)	Cooling System (qts.)
1990	Estate Wagon	Y	5.0 (5011)	5	—	—	7③	②	22	16.4
	Caprice Sedan ⑥	Z	4.3 (4300)	4⑧	—	—	7③	②	24.5	12.0
	Caprice Sedan	E	5.0 (5011)	5	—	—	7③	②	24.5	16.7
	Caprice Wagon	Y	5.0 (5011)	5	—	—	7③	②	24.5	16.7
	Caprice Sedan ⑦	7	5.7 (5733)	5	—	—	7③	②	22	14.8
	Custom Cruiser	Y	5.0 (5011)	5	—	—	7③	②	22	16.4

CAPACITIES

Year	Model	Engine ID/VIN	Engine Displacement Liters (cc)	Engine Crankcase with Filter (qts.)	Transmission (pts.)			Drive Axle (pts.)	Fuel Tank (gal.)	Cooling System (qts.)
					4-Spd	5-Spd	Auto. ①			
1991	Roadmaster Sedan	7	5.7 (5733)	5	—	—	10	②	23	14.6
	Roadmaster Estate Wagon	E	5.0 (5011)	5	—	—	10	②	23	16.7⑤
	Caprice Sedan	E	5.0 (5011)	5	—	—	10	②	23	16.7⑤
	Caprice Wagon	E	5.0 (5011)	5	—	—	10	②	23	16.7⑤
	Caprice Sedan ⑦	7	5.7 (5733)	5	—	—	10	②	23	14.6
	Custom Cruiser	E	5.0 (5011)	5	—	—	10	②	23	16.7⑤
1992	Roadmaster Sedan	7	5.7 (5733)	5	—	—	10	②	23	16.7⑤
	Roadmaster Estate Wagon	7	5.7 (5733)	5	—	—	10	②	22	16.7⑤
	Caprice Sedan	Z	4.3 (4300)	4⑧	—	—	10	②	23	12.6⑤
	Caprice Sedan	E	5.0 (5011)	5	—	—	10	②	23	16.7⑤
	Caprice Sedan ⑦	7	5.7 (5733)	5	—	—	10	②	23	14.6⑤
	Caprice Wagon	E	5.0 (5011)	5	—	—	10	②	22	16.7⑤
	Caprice Wagon	7	5.7 (5733)	5	—	—	10	②	22	14.6⑤
	Custom Cruiser Sedan	E	5.0 (5011)	5	—	—	10	②	23	16.7⑤
	Custom Cruiser Sedan	7	5.7 (5733)	5	—	—	10	②	23	16.7⑤
	Custom Cruiser Wagon	E	5.0 (5011)	5	—	—	10	②	22	16.7⑤
	Custom Cruiser Wagon	7	5.7 (5733)	5	—	—	10	②	22	16.7⑤
1993	Roadmaster Sedan	7	5.7 (5733)	4.5	—	—	10	⑨	23	14.5⑤
	Roadmaster Wagon	7	5.7 (5733)	4.5	—	—	10	⑨	22	14.5⑤
	Caprice Sedan ④	Z	4.3 (4300)	4.5	—	—	10	⑨	23	12.6⑤
	Caprice Sedan	E	5.0 (5011)	4.5	—	—	10	⑨	23	16.7⑤
	Caprice Wagon	E	5.0 (5011)	4.5	—	—	10	⑨	22	16.7⑤
	Caprice Sedan	7	5.7 (5733)	4.5	—	—	10	⑨	23	14.5
	Caprice Sedan ⑦	7	5.7 (5733)	4.5	—	—	10	⑨	23	15.1
	Caprice Wagon	7	5.7 (5733)	4.5	—	—	10	⑨	22	14.5
1994	Roadmaster Sedan	P	5.7 (5733)	5.0	—	—	10	⑨	23	⑧
	Roadmaster Wagon	P	5.7 (5733)	5.0	—	—	10	⑨	22	⑧
	Caprice Sedan	T	4.3 (4300)	NA	—	—	10	⑨	23	⑧
	Caprice Wagon	T	4.3 (4300)	NA	—	—	10	⑨	22	⑧
	Caprice Sedan	P	5.7 (5733)	5.0	—	—	10	⑨	23	⑧
	Caprice Wagon	P	5.7 (5733)	5.0	—	—	10	⑨	22	⑧

NA—Not available
① Additional transmission fluid may be required to bring level to full mark if overhauled or torque converter drained
② 7½ in. ring gear—3.5 pts.
   8½ in. ring gear—4.25 pts.
   8¾ in. ring gear—5.4 pts.
③ Hydra-matic 4L60-10.0 pts.
④ Taxi
⑤ With Heavy Duty Radiator add 0.6 qts.
⑥ Fleet only
⑦ Police
⑧ Add as necessary to bring to appropriate level.
⑨ 7½ in. ring gear—2.9 pts.
   8½ in. ring gear—3.5 pts.
   + add 4 ounces of limited slip additive to all rear axles

CAMSHAFT SPECIFICATIONS

Year	Engine ID/VIN	Engine Displacement Liters (cc)	Journal Diameter 1	2	3	4	5	Elevation In.	Ex.	Bearing Clearance	End Play
1990	Z	4.3 (4300)	1.8682–1.8692	1.8682–1.8692	1.8682–1.8692	1.8682–1.8692	1.8682–1.8692	0.234	0.257	NA	0.004–0.012
	E	5.0 (5011)	1.8682–1.8692	1.8682–1.8692	1.8682–1.8692	1.8682–1.8692	1.8682–1.8692	0.234	0.257	NA	0.004–0.012
	Y	5.0 (5011)	2.0362	2.0360	1.9959	1.9759	1.9559	0.247	0.251	0.0038	0.006–0.022
	7	5.7 (5733)	1.8682–1.8692	1.8682–1.8692	1.8682–1.8692	1.8682–1.8692	1.8682–1.8692	0.257	0.269	NA	0.004–0.012
1991	E	5.0 (5011)	1.8682–1.8692	1.8682–1.8692	1.8682–1.8692	1.8682–1.8692	1.8682–1.8692	0.234	0.257	NA	0.004–0.012
	7	5.7 (5733)	1.8682–1.8692	1.8682–1.8692	1.8682–1.8692	1.8682–1.8692	1.8682–1.8692	0.257	0.269	NA	0.004–0.012
1992	Z	4.3 (4300)	1.8682–1.8692	1.8682–1.8692	1.8682–1.8692	1.8682–1.8692	1.8682–1.8692	0.234	0.257	NA	0.001–0.009
	E	5.0 (5011)	1.8682–1.8692	1.8682–1.8692	1.8682–1.8692	1.8682–1.8692	1.8682–1.8692	0.234	0.257	NA	0.004–0.012
	7	5.7 (5733)	1.8682–1.8692	1.8682–1.8692	1.8682–1.8692	1.8682–1.8692	1.8682–1.8692	0.233	0.256	NA	0.004–0.012
	7①	5.7 (5733)	1.8682–1.8692	1.8682–1.8692	1.8682–1.8692	1.8682–1.8692	1.8682–1.8692	0.257	0.269	NA	0.004–0.012
1993	Z	4.3 (4300)	1.8682–1.8692	1.8682–1.8692	1.8682–1.8692	1.8682–1.8692	1.8682–1.8692	0.233	0.257	NA	0.004–0.012
	E	5.0 (5011)	1.8682–1.8692	1.8682–1.8692	1.8682–1.8692	1.8682–1.8692	1.8682–1.8692	0.233	0.257	NA	0.004–0.012
	7	5.7 (5733)	1.8682–1.8692	1.8682–1.8692	1.8682–1.8692	1.8682–1.8692	1.8682–1.8692	0.233	0.257	NA	0.004–0.012
1994	P	5.7 (5733)	1.8682–1.8692	1.8682–1.8692	1.8682–1.8692	1.8682–1.8692	1.8682–1.8692	0.2980–0.3020	0.2980–0.3020	NA	0.004–0.012

NA—Not available
① Police

CRANKSHAFT AND CONNECTING ROD SPECIFICATIONS

All measurements are given in inches.

Year	Engine ID/VIN	Engine Displacement Liters (cc)	Crankshaft Main Brg. Journal Dia.	Main Brg. Oil Clearance	Shaft End-play	Thrust on No.	Connecting Rod Journal Diameter	Oil Clearance	Side Clearance
1990	Z	4.3 (4300)	2.4484–2.4493①	0.0008–0.0020③	0.002–0.006	4	2.2487–2.2498	0.0013–0.0035	0.006–0.014
	E	5.0 (5011)	2.4481–2.4490④	0.0011–0.0020②	0.001–0.007	5	2.0893–2.0998	0.0013–0.0035	0.006–0.014
	Y	5.0 (5011)	2.4985–2.4995①	0.0005–0.0021③	0.003–0.013	3	2.1238–2.1248	0.0004–0.0033	0.006–0.020
	7	5.7 (5733)	2.4481–2.4990④	0.0011–0.0020②	0.001–0.007	5	2.0893–2.0998	0.0013–0.0035	0.006–0.014
1991	E	5.0 (5011)	2.4481–2.4490④	0.0011–0.0020②	0.001–0.007	5	2.0893–2.0998	0.0013–0.0035	0.006–0.014
	7	5.7 (5733)	2.4481–2.4490④	0.0011–0.0020②	0.001–0.007	5	2.0893–2.0998	0.0013–0.0035	0.006–0.014

CRANKSHAFT AND CONNECTING ROD SPECIFICATIONS

All measurements are given in inches.

Year	Engine ID/VIN	Engine Displacement Liters (cc)	Crankshaft Main Brg. Journal Dia.	Crankshaft Main Brg. Oil Clearance	Crankshaft Shaft End-play	Crankshaft Thrust on No.	Connecting Rod Journal Diameter	Connecting Rod Oil Clearance	Connecting Rod Side Clearance
1992	Z	4.3 (4300)	2.4485–2.4494 ⑤	0.0011–0.0023 ⑥	0.002–0.007	4	2.2487–2.2498	0.0013–0.0035	0.006–0.014
	E	5.0 (5011)	2.4481–2.4490 ④	0.0011–0.0020 ②	0.001–0.007	5	2.0893–2.0998	0.0013–0.0035	0.006–0.014
	7	5.7 (5733)	2.4481–2.4490 ④	0.0011–0.0020 ②	0.001–0.007	5	2.0893–2.0998	0.0013–0.0035	0.006–0.014
1993	Z	4.3 (4300)	2.4481–2.4490 ④	0.0011–0.0020 ⑥	0.001–0.007	4	2.0893–2.0998	0.0013–0.0035	0.006–0.014
	E	5.0 (5011)	2.4481–2.4490 ④	0.0011–0.0020 ②	0.001–0.007	5	2.0893–2.0998	0.0013–0.0035	0.006–0.014
	7	5.7 (5733)	2.4481–2.4490 ④	0.0011–0.0020 ②	0.001–0.007	5	2.0893–2.0998	0.0013–0.0035	0.006–0.014
1994	P	5.7 (5733)	2.4481–2.4490 ⑦	0.0011–0.0020 ⑧	0.001–0.007	5	2.0893–2.0998	0.0013–0.0035	0.006–0.014

① Intermediate—2.4481–2.4490
  Rear—2.4479–2.4488
② Rear: 0.0020–0.0032
③ Intermediate—0.0011–0.0034
  Rear—0.0015–0.0031
④ Front: 2.4488–2.4493
  Rear: 2.4481–2.4488
⑤ Front: 2.4488–2.4493
  Rear: 2.4480–2.4489
⑥ Front: 0.0008–0.0020
  Rear: 0.0017–0.0032
⑦ Front: 2.4484–2.4493
  Rear: 2.4481–2.4488
⑧ Front: 0.0008–0.0020
  Rear: 0.0017–0.0032

VALVE SPECIFICATIONS

Year	Engine ID/VIN	Engine Displacement Liters (cc)	Seat Angle (deg.)	Face Angle (deg.)	Spring Test Pressure (lbs. @ in.)	Spring Installed Height (in.)	Stem-to-Guide Clearance (in.) Intake	Stem-to-Guide Clearance (in.) Exhaust	Stem Diameter (in.) Intake	Stem Diameter (in.) Exhaust
1990	Z	4.3 (4300)	46	45	194–206 @ 1.25	1.70	0.0010–0.0027	0.0010–0.0027	0.3414	0.3414
	E	5.0 (5011)	46	45	194–206 @ 1.25	1.70	0.0011–0.0027	0.0011–0.0027	NA	NA
	Y	5.0 (5011)	①	②	180–194 @ 1.27	1.70	0.0010–0.0027	0.0015–0.0032	0.3425–0.3432	0.3420–0.3427
	7	5.7 (5733)	46	45	194–206 @ 1.25	1.70	0.0011–0.0027	0.0011–0.0027	NA	NA
1991	E	5.0 (5011)	46	45	194–206 @ 1.25	1.70	0.0011–0.0027	0.0011–0.0027	NA	NA
	7	5.7 (5733)	46	45	194–206 @ 1.25	1.70	0.0011–0.0027	0.0011–0.0027	NA	NA
1992	Z	4.3 (4300)	46	45	194–206 @ 1.25	1.69–1.71	0.0011–0.0027	0.0011–0.0027	NA	NA
	E	5.0 (5011)	46	45	194–206 @ 1.25	1.70	0.0011–0.0027	0.0011–0.0027	NA	NA
	7	5.7 (5733)	46	45	194–206 @ 1.25	1.70	0.0011–0.0027	0.0011–0.0027	NA	NA

VALVE SPECIFICATIONS

Year	Engine ID/VIN	Engine Displacement Liters (cc)	Seat Angle (deg.)	Face Angle (deg.)	Spring Test Pressure (lbs. @ in.)	Spring Installed Height (in.)	Stem-to-Guide Clearance (in.)		Stem Diameter (in.)	
							Intake	Exhaust	Intake	Exhaust
1993	Z	4.3 (4300)	46	45	194–206 @ 1.25	1.67–1.73	0.0011–0.0027	0.0011–0.0027	NA	NA
	E	5.0 (5011)	46	45	194–206 @ 1.25	1.67–1.73	0.0011–0.0027	0.0011–0.0027	NA	NA
	7	5.7 (5733)	46	45	194–206 @ 1.25	1.67–1.73	0.0011–0.0027	0.0011–0.0027	NA	NA
1994	P	5.7 (5733)	46	45	252–272 @ 1.305	1.78	0.0011–0.0027	0.0011–0.0027	NA	NA

NA—Not available
① Intake—45°, Exhaust—31°
② Intake—44°, Exhaust—30°

PISTON AND RING SPECIFICATIONS

Year	Engine ID/VIN	Engine Displacement Liters (cc)	Piston Clearance	Ring Gap			Ring Side Clearance		
				Top Compression	Bottom Compression	Oil Control	Top Compression	Bottom Compression	Oil Control
1990	Z	4.3 (4300)	0.0012–0.0021	0.010–0.020	0.010–0.020	0.015–0.055	0.0012–0.0032	0.0012–0.0032	0.0020–0.0070
	E	5.0 (5011)	0.0007–0.0021	0.010–0.020	0.010–0.025	0.015–0.055	0.0012–0.0032	0.0012–0.0032	0.0020–0.0070
	Y	5.0 (5011)	0.0008–0.0018	0.009–0.019	0.009–0.019	0.015–0.055	0.0018–0.0038	0.0018–0.0038	0.0010–0.0050
	7	5.7 (5733)	0.0007–0.0021	0.010–0.020	0.010–0.025	0.015–0.055	0.0012–0.0032	0.0012–0.0032	0.0020–0.0070
1991	E	5.0 (5011)	0.0007–0.0021	0.010–0.020	0.010–0.025	0.015–0.055	0.0012–0.0032	0.0012–0.0032	0.0020–0.0070
	7	5.7 (5733)	0.0007–0.0021	0.010–0.020	0.010–0.025	0.015–0.055	0.0012–0.0032	0.0012–0.0032	0.0020–0.0070
1992	Z	4.3 (4300)	0.0007–0.0017	0.010–0.020	0.017–0.025	0.015–0.055	0.0014–0.0032	0.0014–0.0032	0.0014–0.0032
	E	5.0 (5011)	0.0007–0.0021	0.010–0.020	0.018–0.026	0.015–0.055	0.0012–0.0032	0.0012–0.0032	0.0020–0.0070
	7	5.7 (5733)	0.0005–0.0022	0.010–0.020	0.018–0.026	0.015–0.055	0.0012–0.0032	0.0012–0.0032	0.0020–0.0070
1993	Z	4.3 (4300)	0.0005–0.0022	0.010–0.020	0.018–0.026	0.015–0.055	0.0012–0.0032	0.0012–0.0032	0.0020–0.0070
	E	5.0 (5011)	0.0005–0.0022	0.010–0.020	0.018–0.026	0.015–0.055	0.0012–0.0032	0.0012–0.0032	0.0020–0.0070
	7	5.7 (5733)	0.0005–0.0022	0.010–0.020	0.018–0.026	0.015–0.055	0.0012–0.0032	0.0012–0.0032	0.0020–0.0070
1994	P	5.7 (5733)	0.0010–0.0027	0.010–0.020	0.018–0.026	0.010–0.030	0.0012–0.0032	0.0012–0.0032	0.0020–0.0070

TORQUE SPECIFICATIONS

All readings in ft. lbs.

Year	Engine ID/VIN	Engine Displacement Liters (cc)	Cylinder Head Bolts	Main Bearing Bolts	Rod Bearing Bolts	Crankshaft Damper Bolts	Flywheel Bolts	Manifold Intake	Manifold Exhaust	Spark Plugs	Lug⑧ Nut
1990	Z	4.3 (4300)	65	65	44	70②	70	35	⑥	22	100⑨
	E	5.0 (5011)	68	77	44	70②	74	35	⑥	22	100⑨
	Y	5.0 (5011)	40④	①	18⑤	200–310	60	40③	25	25	100⑨
	7	5.7 (5733)	68	77	44	70②	74	35	⑥	22	100⑨
1991	E	5.0 (5011)	68	77	44	70②	74	35	⑥	22	100
	7	5.7 (5733)	68	77	44	70②	74	35	⑥	22	100
1992	Z	4.3 (4300)	68	77	44	70②	74	35	20⑦	11	100
	E	5.0 (5011)	68	77	44	70②	74	35	20⑦	11	100
	7	5.7 (5733)	68	77	44	70②	74	35	20⑦	11	100
1993	Z	4.3 (4300)	68	77	44	70②	74	35⑧	20⑦	11	100
	E	5.0 (5011)	68	77	44	70②	74	35⑧	20⑦	11	100
	7	5.7 (5733)	68	77	44	70②	74	35⑧	20⑦	11	100
1994	P	5.7 (5733)	65	78	45	60	74	35⑩	26	11	100

① 80 ft. lbs. on Nos. 1–4; 120 ft. lbs. on No. 5
② Torque listed is for torsioner damper, crankshaft pulley is 43 ft. lbs.
③ Dip in clean engine oil before tightening
④ Rotate position 1, 7 & 9—120°
Rotate position 8 & 10—95°
⑤ Torque in 2 steps:
1st step—18 ft.lbs.
2nd step—additional 70 degrees turn further

⑥ Bolts—26 ft. lbs.
Studs—20 ft. lbs.
⑦ Two inner—26 ft. lbs.
⑧ Torque in 2 steps, 1st pass tighten to 124 inch lbs.
⑨ Chevy, sedan—81 ft. lbs.
Wagon and Police—103 ft. lbs.
⑩ Tighten in 2 passes
1st pass torque to 71 inch lbs.

TORQUE SPECIFICATIONS

Component	English	Metric
Camshaft retainer bolt 1990–93:	106 inch lbs.	12 Nm
Camshaft sprocket bolt 1990–93		
Except 5.0L (VIN Y) engine:	21 ft. lbs.	28 Nm
5.0L (VIN Y) engine:	65 ft. lbs.	88 Nm
Carburetor-to-manifold bolts:	12 ft. lbs.	16 Nm
Connecting rod bearing cap bolts 1990–93		
Except 5.0L (VIN Y) engine:	44 ft. lbs.	60 Nm
5.0L (VIN Y) engine *:	18 ft. lbs.	24 Nm
5.7L (VIN P) engine:	47 ft. lbs.	64 Nm
* Plus rotate 70 degrees		
Crankshaft damper bolt 1990–93		
Except 5.0L (VIN Y) engine:	95 ft. lbs.	70 Nm
5.0L (VIN Y) engine:	200–310 ft. lbs.	271–420 Nm
5.7L (VIN P) engine With damper/pulley assembly:	60 ft. lbs.	81 Nm
Crankshaft hub bolt 5.7L (VIN P) engine:	75 ft. lbs.	102 Nm

TORQUE SPECIFICATIONS

Component	English	Metric
Crankshaft pulley bolt		
1990–93		
Except 5.0L (VIN Y) engine:	43 ft. lbs.	58 Nm
5.0L (VIN Y) engine:	28 ft. lbs.	40 Nm
5.7L (VIN P) engine		
With damper/pulley assembly:	60 ft. lbs.	81 Nm
Cylinder head bolt		
1990–93		
Except 5.0L (VIN Y) engine:	68 ft. lbs.	92 Nm
1990 5.0L (VIN Y) engine *		
Step 1:	40 ft. lbs.	54 Nm
Step 2 (positions 1 to 7 and 9):	+ 120 degree turn	+ 120 degree turn
Step 3 (positions 8 and 10):	+ 95 degree turn	+ 95 degree turn
5.7L (VIN P) engine**:	68 ft. lbs.	92 Nm

* NOTE: Clean and dip entire bolt in clean
engine oil prior to installation

** Tighten using at least 3 passses of the
proper torque sequence

Component	English	Metric
EGR valve-to-intake plenum		
1990–93		
Except 5.0L (VIN Y) engine:	16 ft. lbs.	22 Nm
5.0L (VIN Y) engine:	20 ft. lbs.	27 Nm
Engine-to-transmission:	35 ft. lbs.	47 Nm
Exhaust manifold		
Except 5.7L (VIN P) engine		
1990–91		
Studs:	20 ft. lbs.	27 Nm
Bolts:	26 ft. lbs.	35 Nm
1992–93		
Front/rear fasteners:	20 ft. lbs.	27 Nm
Center fasteners:	26 ft. lbs.	35 Nm
5.7L (VIN P) engine:	26 ft. lbs.	35 Nm
Exhaust pipe-to-exhaust manifold nuts	15 ft. lbs.	20 Nm
Flywheel/flexplate-to-crankshaft bolts		
1990–93		
Except 5.0L (VIN Y) engine:	74 ft. lbs.	100 Nm
5.0L (VIN Y) engine:	60 ft. lbs.	81 Nm
Flywheel-to-converter bolts	46 ft. lbs.	63 Nm
Fuel pump-to-block:	25 ft. lbs.	34 Nm
Intake manifold		
1990–93		
Except 5.0L (VIN Y) engine		
Step 1:	10 ft. lbs.	11 Nm
Step 2:	35 ft. lbs.	47 Nm
5.0L (VIN Y) engine *		
Step 1:	15 ft. lbs.	20 Nm
Step 2:	40 ft. lbs.	54 Nm
5.7L (VIN P) engine		
Step 1:	71 inch lbs.	8 Nm
Step 2:	35 ft. lbs.	48 Nm

* NOTE: Clean and dip entire bolt in clean
engine oil prior to installation

TORQUE SPECIFICATIONS

Component	English	Metric
Main bearing cap bolts		
1990–93		
Except 5.0L (VIN Y) engine:	77 ft. lbs.	105 Nm
5.0L (VIN Y) engine		
Bearing cap No. 1, 2, 3, 4:	80 ft. lbs.	108 Nm
Bearing cap No. 5:	120 ft. lbs.	163 Nm
5.7L (VIN P) engine:	78 ft. lbs.	106 Nm
Oil pan		
1990–93		
Nuts:	17 ft. lbs.	23 Nm
Bolts		
Except 5.0L (VIN Y) engine:	97 inch lbs.	11 Nm
5.0L (VIN Y) engine:	10 ft. lbs.	14 Nm
5.7L (VIN P) engine		
Corner fasteners:	15 ft. lbs.	20 Nm
Remaining fasteners:	100 inch lbs.	11 Nm
Oil pan drain plug		
Except 5.0L (VIN Y) engine:	16 ft. lbs.	22 Nm
5.0L (VIN Y) engine:	30 ft. lbs.	41 Nm
Oil pump attaching bolts		
1990–93		
Except 5.0L (VIN Y) engine:	77 ft. lbs.	105 Nm
5.0L (VIN Y) engine:	35 ft. lbs.	47 Nm
5.7L (VIN P) engine:	65 ft. lbs.	88 Nm
Rocker arm pivot bolt		
5.0L (VIN Y) engine:	22 ft. lbs.	28 Nm
Rocker (valve) cover		
1990		
Except 5.0L (VIN Y) engine:	75 inch lbs.	8.5 Nm
5.0L (VIN Y) engine:	90 inch lbs.	10 Nm
1991–93:	95 inch lbs.	11 Nm
5.7L (VIN P) engine:	96 inch lbs.	11 Nm
Spark plug		
1990–91		
Except 5.0L (VIN Y) engine:	22 ft. lbs.	30 Nm
5.0L (VIN Y) engine:	25 ft. lbs.	34 Nm
1992–94:	11 ft. lbs.	15 Nm
Starter-to-block bolts		
Except 5.7L (VIN P) engine		
1990–92:	35 ft. lbs.	47 Nm
1993:	32 ft. lbs.	43 Nm
5.7L (VIN P) engine:	35 ft. lbs.	47 Nm
Thermostat housing	21 ft. lbs.	28 Nm
Timing cover		
1990–93		
Except 5.0L (VIN Y) engine:	97 inch lbs.	11 Nm
5.0L (VIN Y) engine		
Upper bolts:	22 ft. lbs.	28 Nm
Lower 3 bolts:	35 ft. lbs.	47 Nm
TIming indicator stud:	35 ft. lbs.	47 Nm
5.7L (VIN P) engine:	100 inch lbs.	11 Nm
Water pump pulley		
1990–93:	18 ft. lbs.	24 Nm

BRAKE SPECIFICATIONS
All measurements in inches unless noted.

Year	Model	Master Cylinder Bore	Brake Disc			Brake Drum Diameter			Minimum Lining Thickness ①	
			Original Thickness	Minimum Thickness	Maximum Runout	Original Inside Diameter	Max. Wear Limit	Maximum Machine Diameter	Front	Rear
1990	Estate Wagon	1.125	1.043	0.980②	0.004	11.00	11.090	11.060	0.030	0.030
	Caprice	1.125	1.043	0.980②	0.004	11.00	11.090	11.060	0.030	0.030
	Custom Cruiser	1.125	1.043	0.980②	0.004	11.00	11.090	11.060	0.030	0.030
1991	Roadmaster	1.125	1.043	0.980②	0.004	11.00	11.090	11.060	0.030	0.030
	Caprice	1.125	1.043	0.980②	0.004	11.00	11.090	11.060	0.030	0.030
	Custom Cruiser	1.125	1.043	0.980②	0.004	11.00	11.090	11.060	0.030	0.030
1992	Roadmaster	1.125	1.043	0.980②	0.004	11.00	11.090	11.060	0.030	0.030
	Caprice	1.125	1.043	0.980②	0.004	11.00	11.090	11.060	0.030	0.030
	Custom Cruiser	1.125	1.043	0.980②	0.004	11.00	11.090	11.060	0.030	0.030
1993–94	Roadmaster	1.125	1.043	0.980②	0.003	11.00	11.090	11.060	0.030	0.030
	Caprice	1.125	1.043	0.980②	0.003	11.00	11.090	11.060	0.030	0.030

① Replace when lining is within 0.030 in. of rivet or backing
② Specification is the minimum to which the disc may be cut. All rotors have a discard dimension cast into them which is the minimum the rotor may be allowed to wear in use.

WHEEL ALIGNMENT

Year	Model	Caster		Camber		Toe-in (in.)	Steering Axis Inclination (deg.)
		Range (deg.)	Preferred Setting (deg.)	Range (deg.)	Preferred Setting (deg.)		
1990	Estate Wagon	2P–4P	3P	0–1⅝P	¹³/₁₆P	¹/₃₂	9¾
	Custom Cruiser	2P–4P	3P	0–1⅝P	¹³/₁₆P	¹/₃₂	9²⁵/₃₂
	Caprice	2P–4P	3P	0–1⅝P	¹³/₁₆P	¹/₃₂	9²⁵/₃₂
1991	Custom Cruiser	2½P–4½P	3½P	0–1⅝P	¹³/₁₆P	¹/₃₂	0
	Roadmaster	2½P–4½P	3½P	0–1⅝P	¹³/₁₆P	¹/₃₂	0
	Caprice	2½P–4½P	3½P	0–1⅝P	¹³/₁₆P	¹/₃₂	0
1992	Custom Cruiser	2½P–4½P	3½P	0–1⅝P	¹³/₁₆P	¹/₃₂	0
	Roadmaster	2½P–4½P	3½P	0–1⅝P	¹³/₁₆P	¹/₃₂	0
	Caprice	2½P–4½P	3½P	0–1⅝P	¹³/₁₆P	¹/₃₂	0
1993–94	Roadmaster	2½P–4½P	3½P	1N–1P	0	¹/₃₂	0
	Caprice	2½P–4½P	3½P	1N–1P	0	¹/₃₂	0

NA—Not available
N—Negative
P—Positive

AIR CONDITIONING BELT TENSION

Year	Model	Engine Displacement Liters (cc)	Belt Type	Specifications New	Used
1990	Caprice	4.3 (4300)	V-Belt ①	②	③
		5.0 (5011)	V-Belt ①	②	③
		5.7 (5733)	V-Belt ①	②	③
	Estate Wagon	5.0 (5011)	V-Belt ①	②	③
	Custom Cruiser	5.0 (5011)	V-Belt ①	②	③
1991	Caprice	5.0 (5011)	Serpentine	①	①
		5.7 (5733)	Serpentine	①	①
	Estate Wagon	5.0 (5011)	Serpentine	①	①
	Custom Cruiser	5.0 (5011)	Serpentine	①	①
	Buick Roadmaster	5.0 (5011)	Serpentine	①	①
1992	Estate Wagon	5.0 (5011)	Serpentine	105–127	105–127
		5.7 (5733)	Serpentine	105–127	105–127
	Buick Roadmaster	5.0 (5011)	Serpentine	105–127	105–127
	Caprice	4.3 (4300)	Serpentine	105–127	105–127
		5.0 (5011)	Serpentine	105–127	105–127
		5.7 (5733)	Serpentine	105–127	105–127
	Custom Cruiser	5.0 (5011)	Serpentine	105–127	105–127
		5.7 (5733)	Serpentine	105–127	105–127
1993–94	Buick Roadmaster	5.0 (5011)	Serpentine	105–127	105–127
	Caprice	4.3 (4300)	Serpentine	105–127	105–127
		5.0 (5011)	Serpentine	105–127	105–127
		5.7 (5733)	Serpentine	105–127	105–127
	Estate Wagon	5.0 (5011)	Serpentine	105–127	105–127
		5.7 (5733)	Serpentine	105–127	105–127

① Lbs.
② If equipped with serpentine belt—no adjustment necessary

③ New belts:
5/16" wide—80 lbs.
3/8" & 13/32" wide—140 lbs.
7/16" wide—165 lbs.

③ Used belts:
5/16" wide—50 lbs.
3/8" & 13/32" wide—740 lbs.
7/16" wide—90 lbs.

REFRIGERANT CAPACITIES

Year	Model	Refrigerant (oz.)	Oil (fl. oz.)	Compressor Type
1990	Caprice	56.0	6.0	R-4
	Estate Wagon	56.0	6.0	R-4
	Custom Cruiser	56.0	6.0	R-4
1991	Caprice	49.6	6.0	R-4
	Buick Roadmaster	49.6	6.0	R-4
	Custom Cruiser	49.6	6.0	R-4
1992	Caprice	49.6	6.0	R-4
	Buick Roadmaster	49.6	6.0	R-4
	Custom Cruiser	49.6	6.0	R-4
1993	Buick Roadmaster	49.6	6.0	R-4
	Caprice	49.6	6.0	R-4
	Custom Cruiser	49.6	6.0	R-4

NOTE: At the time of publication, refrigerant capacity information relating to R-134a was not available from the manufacturer.

MAINTENANCE INTERVALS—TYPE A: NORMAL SERVICE
Caprice • Custom Cruiser • Estate Wagon • Roadmaster

TO BE SERVICED	TYPE OF SERVICE	VEHICLE MILEAGE INTERVAL (X1000)							
		7.5	15	22.5	30	37.5	45	52.5	60
Oxygen Sensor	I				✓				✓
Ignition Timing	I①				✓				✓
Vacuum Lines and Hoses	I		✓		✓		✓		✓
Ignition Wires	I				✓				✓
Spark Plugs	R				✓				✓
Engine Oil	R	✓	✓	✓	✓	✓	✓	✓	✓
Engine Air Cleaner Element	R				✓				✓
Crankcase Emission Filter	R				✓				✓
PCV Valve	R				✓				✓
Fuel Filter	R				✓				✓
Charcoal Canister	R				✓				✓
Fuel/Vapor Return Lines	I				✓				✓
Fuel Tank Cap and Restrictor	I				✓				✓
Coolant System	R				✓				✓
Exhaust Pipe and Muffler	I				✓				✓
Engine Oil Filter	R②	✓		✓		✓		✓	
Catalytic Converter and Shield	I				✓				✓
EGR System	I				✓				✓
Tire Rotation	I④								
Chassis Lubrication	L	✓	✓	✓	✓	✓	✓	✓	✓
Battery Connections	I		✓		✓		✓		✓
Automatic Transmission Fluid	R③								
Idle Speed System	I				✓				✓
Throttle Body Mounting Torque	I	✓							
Drive Belts	I				✓				✓
Brake Linings	I		✓		✓		✓		✓
Parking Brake	I		✓		✓		✓		✓
Seat Belt Operation	I				✓				✓
Coolant Hoses and Clamps	I				✓				✓

FOR COMPLETE WARRANTY COVERAGE CONSULT INDIVIDUAL VEHICLE MANUFACTURER'S WARRANTY MAINTENANCE GUIDE.

I—Inspect
L—Lubricate
R—Replace
① Check and adjust timing as per engine emission label on applicable vehicles
② Change oil filter at 7,500 miles and then every other oil change

③ Replace automatic transmission fluid at 100,000 miels
④ Rotate tires at 7,500 miles then every 15,000 miles as necessary

MAINTENANCE INTERVALS—TYPE B: SEVERE SERVICE
Caprice • Custom Cruiser • Estate Wagon • Roadmaster

TO BE SERVICED	TYPE OF SERVICE	VEHICLE MILEAGE INTERVAL (X1000)									
		3	6	9	12	15	18	21	24	27	30
Oxygen Sensor	I										✓
Ignition Timing	I①										✓
Vacuum Lines and Hoses	I					✓					✓
Ignition Wires	I										✓

MAINTENANCE INTERVALS—TYPE B: SEVERE SERVICE
Caprice • Custom Cruiser • Estate Wagon • Roadmaster

TO BE SERVICED	TYPE OF SERVICE	3	6	9	12	15	18	21	24	27	30
		VEHICLE MILEAGE INTERVAL (X1000)									
Spark Plugs	R										✔
Engine Oil and Filter	R	✔	✔	✔	✔	✔	✔	✔	✔	✔	✔
Engine Air Cleaner Element	R					✔					✔
Crankcase Emission Filter	R					✔					✔
PCV Valve	R					✔					✔
Fuel Filter	R					✔					✔
Charcoal Canister	R					✔					✔
Fuel/Vapor Return Lines	I										✔
Fuel Tank Cap and Restrictor	I										✔
Coolant System	R										✔
Exhaust Pipe and Muffler	I										✔
Tire Rotation	I②		✔								
Catalytic Converter and Shield	I										✔
EGR System	I										
Chassis Lubrication	L		✔		✔		✔		✔		✔
Battery Connections	I										
Automatic Transmission Fluid	R					✔					✔
Coolant Hoses and Clamps	I					✔					✔
Idle Speed System	I										✔
Throttle Body Mounting Torque	I		✔								
Drive Belts	I										✔
Seat Belt Operation	I										✔

FOR COMPLETE WARRANTY COVERAGE CONSULT INDIVIDUAL VEHICLE MANUFACTURER'S WARRANTY MAINTENANCE GUIDE.

I—Inspect
L—Lubricate
R—Replace
① Check and adjust timing as per engine emissions label on applicable vehicles
② Rotate tires at 6,000 miles and then every 15,000 miles as necessary

FIRING ORDERS

NOTE: To avoid confusion, always replace spark plug wires one at a time.

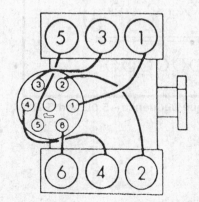

4.3L Engine
Engine Firing Order: 1–6–5–4–3–2
Distributor Rotation: Clockwise

FIRING ORDERS

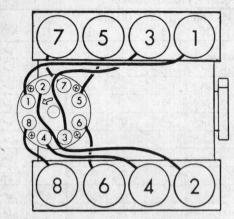

5.0L (VIN Y) Engine
Engine Firing Order: 1–8–4–3–6–5–7–2
Distributor Rotation: Counterclockwise

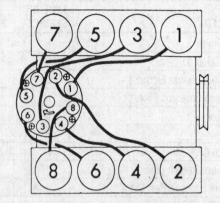

5.0L (VIN E) and 5.7L Engines
Engine Firing Order: 1–8–4–3–6–5–7–2
Distributor Rotation: Clockwise

CYLINDER HEAD TORQUE SEQUENCES

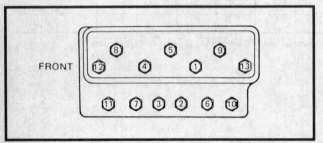

Cylinder head bolt torque sequence—4.3L engine

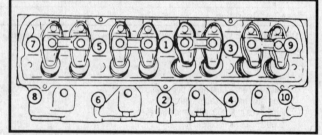

Cylinder head bolt torque sequence—5.0L (VIN Y) engine

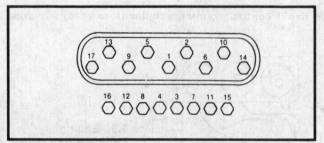

Cylinder head bolt torque sequence—5.0L and 5.7L engines (VIN E, 7)

TIMING MARK LOCATIONS

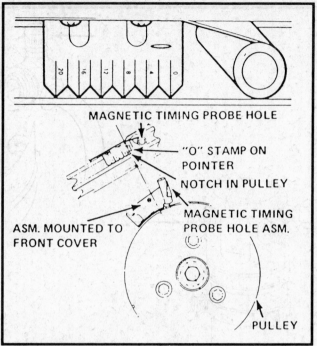

Timing mark location

TIMING CHAIN ALIGNMENT MARKS

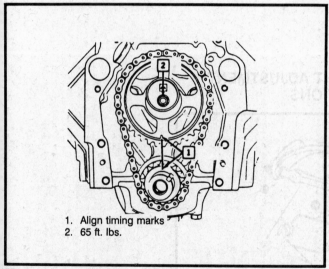

1. Align timing marks
2. 65 ft. lbs.

Timing chain alignment marks — 5.0L (VIN Y) engine

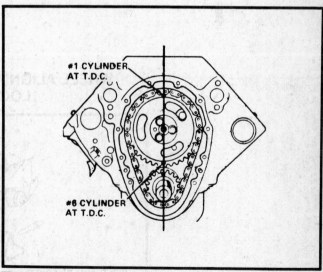

Timing chain alignment marks — 4.3L, 5.0L (VIN E) and 5.7L engines

AIR CONDITIONING SERVICE VALVE LOCATIONS

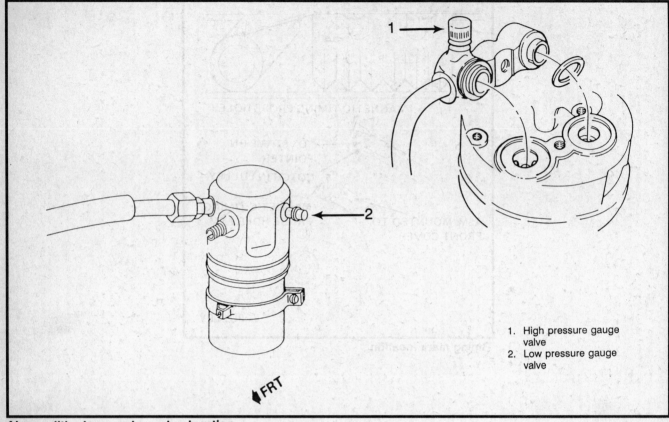

1. High pressure gauge valve
2. Low pressure gauge valve

FRT

Air conditioning service valve location

WHEEL ALIGNMENT ADJUSTMENT LOCATIONS

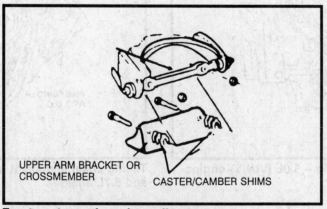

UPPER ARM BRACKET OR CROSSMEMBER

CASTER/CAMBER SHIMS

Front caster and camber adjustment

SPECIFICATION CHARTS

VEHICLE IDENTIFICATION CHART

It is important for servicing and ordering parts to be certain of the vehicle and engine identification. The VIN (vehicle identification number) is a 17 digit number visible through the windshield on the driver's side of the dash and contains the vehicle and engine identification codes. The tenth digit indicates model year and the eighth digit indicates engine code. It can be interpreted as follows:

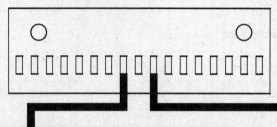

Engine Code

Code	Liters	Cu. In. (cc)	Cyl.	Fuel Sys.	Eng. Mfg.
T	3.1	191 (3136)	6	MFI	CPC
S	3.4	205 (3350)	6	SFI	CPC
F	5.0	305 (5011)	8	TPI	CPC
E	5.0	305 (5011)	8	TBI	CPC
8	5.7	350 (5733)	8	TPI	CPC
P	5.7	350 (5733)	8	①	CPC

Model Year

Code	Year
L	1990
M	1991
N	1992
P	1993
R	1994

MFI—Multi Port Fuel Injection
SFI—Sequential Fuel Injection
TBI—Throttle Body Injection
TPI—Tuned Port Injection
① MFI for 1993
  SFI for 1994

ENGINE IDENTIFICATION

Year	Model	Engine Displacement Liter (cc)	Engine Series (ID/VIN)	Fuel System	No. of Cylinders	Engine Type
1990	Camaro	3.1 (3136)	T	MFI	6	OHV
	Firebird	3.1 (3136)	T	MFI	6	OHV
	Camaro	5.0 (5011)	F	TPI	8	OHV
	Firebird	5.0 (5011)	F	TPI	8	OHV
	Camaro	5.0 (5011)	E	TBI	8	OHV
	Firebird	5.0 (5011)	E	TBI	8	OHV
	Camaro	5.7 (5733)	8	TPI	8	OHV
	Firebird	5.7 (5733)	8	TPI	8	OHV
1991	Camaro	3.1 (3136)	T	MFI	6	OHV
	Firebird	3.1 (3136)	T	MFI	6	OHV
	Camaro	5.0 (5011)	F	TPI	8	OHV
	Firebird	5.0 (5011)	F	TPI	8	OHV
	Camaro	5.0 (5011)	E	TBI	8	OHV
	Firebird	5.0 (5011)	E	TBI	8	OHV
	Camaro	5.7 (5733)	8	TPI	8	OHV
	Firebird	5.7 (5733)	8	TPI	8	OHV

ENGINE IDENTIFICATION

Year	Model	Engine Displacement Liter (cc)	Engine Series (ID/VIN)	Fuel System	No. of Cylinders	Engine Type
1992	Camaro	3.1 (3136)	T	MFI	6	OHV
	Firebird	3.1 (3136)	T	MFI	6	OHV
	Camaro	5.0 (5011)	F	TPI	8	OHV
	Firebird	5.0 (5011)	F	TPI	8	OHV
	Camaro	5.0 (5011)	E	TBI	8	OHV
	Firebird	5.0 (5011)	E	TBI	8	OHV
	Camaro	5.7 (5733)	8	TPI	8	OHV
	Firebird	5.7 (5733)	8	TPI	8	OHV
1993	Camaro	3.4 (3350)	S	SFI	6	OHV
	Firebird	3.4 (3350)	S	SFI	6	OHV
	Camaro	5.7 (5733)	P	MFI	8	OHV
	Firebird	5.7 (5733)	P	MFI	8	OHV
1994	Camaro	3.4 (3350)	S	SFI	6	OHV
	Firebird	3.4 (3350)	S	SFI	6	OHV
	Camaro	5.7 (5733)	P	SFI	8	OHV
	Firebird	5.7 (5733)	P	SFI	8	OHV

OHV—Overhead Valve
MFI—Mult-Port Fuel Injection
TBI—Throttle Body Injection
TPI—Tuned Port Injection
SFI—Sequential Fuel Injection

GENERAL ENGINE SPECIFICATIONS

Year	Engine ID/VIN	Engine Displacement Liter (cc)	Fuel System Type	Net Horsepower @ rpm	Net Torque @ rpm (ft. lbs.)	Bore × Stroke (in.)	Compression Ratio	Oil Pressure @ rpm
1990	T	3.1 (3136)	MFI	140 @ 4400	180 @ 3600	3.503 × 3.312	8.8:1	55 @ 2000
	F	5.0 (5011)	TPI	230 @ 4400	300 @ 3200	3.740 × 3.480	9.3:1	18 @ 2000
	E	5.0 (5011)	TBI	170 @ 4000	255 @ 2400	3.740 × 3.480	9.3:1	18 @ 2000
	8	5.7 (5733)	TPI	240 @ 4400	345 @ 3200	4.000 × 3.480	9.3:1	18 @ 2000
1991	T	3.1 (3136)	MFI	140 @ 4400	180 @ 3600	3.503 × 3.312	8.5:1	8 @ 600
	F	5.0 (5011)	TPI	140 @ 4400	300 @ 3200	3.740 × 3.480	9.3:1	18 @ 2000
	E	5.0 (5011)	TPI	170 @ 4000	255 @ 2400	3.740 × 3.480	9.3:1	18 @ 2000
	8	5.7 (5733)	TPI	240 @ 4400	345 @ 3200	4.000 × 3.480	9.75:1	18 @ 2000
1992	T	3.1 (3136)	MFI	140 @ 4400	180 @ 3600	3.503 × 3.312	8.5:1	8 @ 600
	F	5.0 (5011)	TPI	140 @ 4400	300 @ 3200	3.740 × 3.480	9.3:1	18 @ 2000
	E	5.0 (5011)	TPI	170 @ 4000	255 @ 2400	3.740 × 3.480	9.3:1	18 @ 2000
	8	5.7 (5733)	TPI	240 @ 4400	345 @ 3200	4.000 × 3.480	9.75:1	18 @ 2000
1993	S	3.4 (3350)	SFI	160 @ 4600	200 @ 3600	3.623 × 3.312	9.0:1	15 @ 1100
	P	5.7 (5733)	MFI	275 @ 5000	325 @ 2400	4.000 × 3.480	10.5:1	18 @ 2000
1994	S	3.4 (3350)	SFI	160 @ 4600	200 @ 3600	3.623 × 3.312	9.0:1	15 @ 1100
	P	5.7 (5733)	MFI	275 @ 5000	325 @ 2400	4.000 × 3.480	10.5:1	18 @ 2000

MFI—Multi-Port Fuel Injection
SFI—Sequential Fuel Injection
TBI—Throttle Body Injection
TPI—Tuned Port Injection

GASOLINE ENGINE TUNE-UP SPECIFICATIONS

Year	Engine ID/VIN	Engine Displacement Liter (cc)	Spark Plugs Gap (in.)	Ignition Timing (deg.) MT	Ignition Timing (deg.) AT	Fuel Pump (psi)	Idle Speed (rpm) MT	Idle Speed (rpm) AT	Valve Clearance In.	Valve Clearance Ex.
1990	T	3.1 (3136)	0.045	10	10	34–47	①	①	Hyd.	Hyd.
	F	5.0 (5011)	0.035	6	6	34–47	①	①	Hyd.	Hyd.
	E	5.0 (5011)	0.035	0	0	9.0–13.0	①	①	Hyd.	Hyd.
	8	5.7 (5733)	0.035	6	6	34–47	①	①	Hyd.	Hyd.
1991	T	3.1 (3136)	0.045	10	10	34–47	①	①	Hyd.	Hyd.
	F	5.0 (5011)	0.035	6	6	34–47	①	①	Hyd.	Hyd.
	E	5.0 (5011)	0.035	0	0	9.0–13.0	①	①	Hyd.	Hyd.
	8	5.7 (5733)	0.035	6	6	34–47	①	①	Hyd.	Hyd.
1992	T	3.1 (3136)	0.045	10	10	34–47	①	①	Hyd.	Hyd.
	F	5.0 (5011)	0.035	6	6	34–47	①	①	Hyd.	Hyd.
	E	5.0 (5011)	0.035	0	0	9.0–13.0	①	①	Hyd.	Hyd.
	8	5.7 (5733)	0.035	6	6	34–47	①	①	Hyd.	Hyd.
1993	S	3.4 (3350)	0.045	②	②	41–47	③	③	Hyd.	Hyd.
	P	5.7 (5733)	0.050	②	②	41–47	③	③	Hyd.	Hyd.
1994				REFER TO UNDERHOOD STICKER						

NOTE: The lowest cylinder pressure should be within 75% of the highest cylinder pressure reading. For example, if the highest cylinder is 134 psi, the lowest should be 101. Engine should be at normal operating temperature with throttle valve in the wide open position.
The underhood specifications sticker often reflects tune-up specification changes in production. Sticker figures must be used if they disagree with those in this chart.
Hyd.—Hydraulic
① See Underhood Emission Decal
② Ignition timing is controlled by the ECM through the Opti-Spark Distributor Ignition System. No adjustment is necessary or possible.
③ ECM controlled—non-adjustable

CAPACITIES

Year	Model	Engine ID/VIN	Engine Displacement Liter (cc)	Engine Crankcase with Filter (qts.)①	Transmission (pts.) 5-Spd	Transmission (pts.) 6-Spd	Transmission (pts.) Auto.	Drive Axle (pts.)	Fuel Tank (gal.)	Cooling System (qts.)
1990	Camaro	T	3.1 (3136)	4.0	5.9	—	10	3.5	15.5	14.5
	Camaro	F	5.0 (5011)	5.0	5.9	—	10	3.5	15.5	17.5
	Camaro	E	5.0 (5011)	5.0	5.9	—	10	3.5	15.5	17.5
	Camaro	8	5.7 (5733)	5.0	5.9	—	10	3.5	15.5	16.5
	Firebird	T	3.1 (3136)	4.0	5.9	—	10	3.5	15.5	14.5
	Firebird	F	5.0 (5011)	5.0	5.9	—	10	3.5	15.5	17.5
	Firebird	E	5.0 (5011)	5.0	5.9	—	10	3.5	15.5	17.5
	Firebird	8	5.7 (5733)	5.0	5.9	—	10	3.5	15.5	16.5
1991	Camaro	T	3.1 (3136)	4.0	5.9	—	10	3.5	15.5	14.8
	Camaro	F	5.0 (5011)	5.0	5.9	—	10	3.5	15.5	18.0
	Camaro	E	5.0 (5011)	5.0	5.9	—	10	3.5	15.5	18.0
	Camaro	8	5.7 (5733)	5.0	5.9	—	10	3.5	15.5	16.7
	Firebird	T	3.1 (3136)	4.0	5.9	—	10	3.5	15.5	14.8
	Firebird	F	5.0 (5011)	5.0	5.9	—	10	3.5	15.5	18.0
	Firebird	E	5.0 (5011)	5.0	5.9	—	10	3.5	15.5	18.0
	Firebird	8	5.7 (5733)	5.0	5.9	—	10	3.5	15.5	16.7

CAPACITIES

Year	Model	Engine ID/VIN	Engine Displacement Liter (cc)	Engine Crankcase with Filter (qts.)①	Transmission (pts.) 5-Spd	6-Spd	Auto.	Drive Axle (pts.)	Fuel Tank (gal.)	Cooling System (qts.)
1992	Camaro	T	3.1 (3136)	4.0	5.9	—	10	3.5	15.5	14.8
	Camaro	F	5.0 (5011)	5.0	5.9	—	10	3.5	15.5	18.0
	Camaro	E	5.0 (5011)	5.0	5.9	—	10	3.5	15.5	18.0
	Camaro	8	5.7 (5733)	5.0	5.9	—	10	3.5	15.5	16.7
	Firebird	T	3.1 (3136)	4.0	5.9	—	10	3.5	15.5	14.8
	Firebird	F	5.0 (5011)	5.0	5.9	—	10	3.5	15.5	18.0
	Firebird	E	5.0 (5011)	5.0	5.9	—	10	3.5	15.5	18.0
	Firebird	8	5.7 (5733)	5.0	5.9	—	10	3.5	15.5	16.7
1993–94	Camaro	S	3.4 (3350)	4.0	5.9	—	10	3.5	15.5	12.5
	Camaro	P	5.7 (5733)	4.5	—	8.0	10	3.5	15.5	15.2
	Firebird	S	3.4 (3350)	4.0	5.9	—	10	3.5	15.5	12.5
	Firebird	P	5.7 (5733)	4.5	—	8.0	10	3.5	15.5	15.2

① Check dipstick and add additional oil, as necessary, before operating engine.

CAMSHAFT SPECIFICATIONS

All measurements given in inches.

Year	Engine ID/VIN	Engine Displacement Liter (cc)	Journal Diameter 1	2	3	4	5	Elevation In.	Ex.	Bearing Clearance	Camshaft End Play
1990	T	3.1 (3136)	1.8678–1.8697	1.8678–1.8697	1.8678–1.8697	1.8678–1.8697	1.8678–1.8697	0.2626	0.2732	0.0010–0.0040	NA
	F	5.0 (5011)	1.8682–1.8692	1.8682–1.8692	1.8682–1.8692	1.8682–1.8692	1.8682–1.8692	0.2690	0.2760	NA	0.004–0.012
	E	5.0 (5011)	1.8682–1.8692	1.8682–1.8692	1.8682–1.8692	1.8682–1.8692	1.8682–1.8692	0.2340	0.2570	NA	0.004–0.012
	8	5.7 (5733)	1.8682–1.8692	1.8682–1.8692	1.8682–1.8692	1.8682–1.8692	1.8682–1.8692	0.2730	0.2820	NA	0.004–0.012
1991	T	3.1 (3136)	1.8678–1.8697	1.8678–1.8697	1.8678–1.8697	1.8678–1.8697	1.8678–1.8697	0.2626	0.2732	0.0010–0.0040	NA
	F	5.0 (5011)	1.8682–1.8692	1.8682–1.8692	1.8682–1.8692	1.8682–1.8692	1.8682–1.8692	0.2750	0.2850	NA	0.004–0.012
	E	5.0 (5011)	1.8682–1.8692	1.8682–1.8692	1.8682–1.8692	1.8682–1.8692	1.8682–1.8692	0.2340	0.2570	NA	0.004–0.012
	8	5.7 (5733)	1.8682–1.8692	1.8682–1.8692	1.8682–1.8692	1.8682–1.8692	1.8682–1.8692	0.2750	0.2850	NA	0.004–0.012
1992	T	3.1 (3136)	1.8678–1.8697	1.8678–1.8697	1.8678–1.8697	1.8678–1.8697	1.8678–1.8697	0.2626	0.2732	0.0010–0.0040	NA
	F	5.0 (5011)	1.8682–1.8692	1.8682–1.8692	1.8682–1.8692	1.8682–1.8692	1.8682–1.8692	0.2750	0.2850	NA	0.004–0.012
	E	5.0 (5011)	1.8682–1.8692	1.8682–1.8692	1.8682–1.8692	1.8682–1.8692	1.8682–1.8692	0.2340	0.2570	NA	0.004–0.012
	8	5.7 (5733)	1.8682–1.8692	1.8682–1.8692	1.8682–1.8692	1.8682–1.8692	1.8682–1.8692	0.2750	0.2850	NA	0.004–0.012
1993–94	S	3.4 (3350)	1.8680–1.8710	1.8680–1.8710	1.8680–1.8710	1.8680–1.8710	1.8680–1.8710	0.2626	0.2732	0.0010–0.0040	NA
	P	5.7 (5733)	1.8682–1.8692	1.8682–1.8692	1.8682–1.8692	1.8682–1.8692	1.8682–1.8692	0.2980–0.3020	0.2980–0.3020	NA	0.004–0.012

NA—Not available

CRANKSHAFT AND CONNECTING ROD SPECIFICATIONS

All measurements are given in inches.

Year	Engine ID/VIN	Engine Displacement Liter (cc)	Crankshaft Main Brg. Journal Dia.	Crankshaft Main Brg. Oil Clearance	Crankshaft Shaft End-play	Crankshaft Thrust on No.	Connecting Rod Journal Diameter	Connecting Rod Oil Clearance	Connecting Rod Side Clearance
1990	T	3.1 (3136)	2.6473–2.6483	③	0.0024–0.0083	3	1.9983–1.9994	0.0014–0.0036	0.0140–0.0290
	F	5.0 (5011)	①	②	0.0010–0.0070	5	2.0890–2.0990	0.0013–0.0035	0.0060–0.0140
	E	5.0 (5011)	①	②	0.0010–0.0070	5	2.0890–2.0990	0.0013–0.0035	0.0060–0.0140
	8	5.7 (5733)	①	②	0.0010–0.0070	5	2.0890–2.0990	0.0013–0.0035	0.0060–0.0140
1991	T	3.1 (3136)	2.6473–2.6483	④	0.0024–0.0083	3	1.9983–1.9994	0.0011–0.0033	0.0140–0.0290
	F	5.0 (5011)	①	②	0.0010–0.0070	5	2.0890–2.0990	0.0013–0.0035	0.0060–0.0140
	E	5.0 (5011)	①	②	0.0010–0.0070	5	2.0890–2.0990	0.0013–0.0035	0.0060–0.0140
	8	5.7 (5733)	①	②	0.0010–0.0070	5	2.0890–2.0990	0.0013–0.0035	0.0060–0.0140
1992	T	3.1 (3136)	2.6473–2.6483	④	0.0024–0.0083	3	1.9983–1.9994	0.0011–0.0033	0.0080–0.0170
	F	5.0 (5011)	①	②	0.0010–0.0070	5	2.0890–2.0990	0.0013–0.0035	0.0060–0.0140
	E	5.0 (5011)	①	②	0.0010–0.0070	5	2.0890–2.0990	0.0013–0.0035	0.0060–0.0140
	8	5.7 (5733)	①	②	0.0010–0.0070	5	2.0890–2.0990	0.0013–0.0035	0.0060–0.0140
1993–94	S	3.4 (3350)	2.6473–2.6483	0.0012–0.0030	0.0024–0.0083	3	1.9987–1.9994	0.0011–0.0032	0.0070–0.0170
	P	5.7 (5733)	2.4481–⑤2.4490	②	0.0010–0.0070	5	2.0893–2.0998	0.0013–0.0035	0.0060–0.0140

① No. 1—2.4484–2.4493
Nos. 2, 3, 4—2.4481–2.4490
No. 5—2.4479–2.4488
② No. 1—0.0008–0.0020
Nos. 2, 3, 4—0.0011–0.0020
No. 5—0.0017–0.0032
③ Main Bearing Clearance—0.0012–0.0027
Main Thrust Bearing Clearance—0.0016–0.0027
④ Main Bearing Clearance—0.0012–0.0030
Main Thrust Bearing Clearance—0.0016–0.0030
⑤ Front: 2.4484–2.4493
Rear: 2.4481–2.4488

VALVE SPECIFICATIONS

Year	Engine ID/VIN	Engine Displacement Liter (cc)	Seat Angle (deg.)	Face Angle (deg.)	Spring Test Pressure (lbs. @ in.)	Spring Installed Height (in.)	Stem-to-Guide Clearance (in.) Intake	Stem-to-Guide Clearance (in.) Exhaust	Stem Diameter (in.) Intake	Stem Diameter (in.) Exhaust
1990	T	3.1 (3136)	46	45	190 @ 1.20	1.60	0.0014–0.0025	0.0016–0.0029	NA	NA
	F	5.0 (5011)	46	45	194–206 @ 1.25	①	0.0011–0.0027	0.0011–0.0027	NA	NA
	E	5.0 (5011)	46	45	194–206 @ 1.25	①	0.0011–0.0027	0.0011–0.0027	NA	NA
	8	5.7 (5733)	46	45	194–206 @1.25	①	0.0011–0.0027	0.0011–0.0027	NA	NA

VALVE SPECIFICATIONS

Year	Engine ID/VIN	Engine Displacement Liter (cc)	Seat Angle (deg.)	Face Angle (deg.)	Spring Test Pressure (lbs. @ in.)	Spring Installed Height (in.)	Stem-to-Guide Clearance (in.) Intake	Stem-to-Guide Clearance (in.) Exhaust	Stem Diameter (in.) Intake	Stem Diameter (in.) Exhaust
1991	T	3.1 (3136)	46	45	190 @ 1.20	1.61	0.0014–0.0025	0.0016–0.0029	NA	NA
	F	5.0 (5011)	46	45	194–206 @ 1.25	①	0.0011–0.0027	0.0011–0.0027	NA	NA
	E	5.0 (5011)	46	45	194–206 @ 1.25	①	0.0011–0.0027	0.0011–0.0027	NA	NA
	8	5.7 (5733)	46	45	194–206 @1.25	①	0.0011–0.0027	0.0011–0.0027	NA	NA
1992	T	3.1 (3136)	46	45	190 @ 1.20	1.61	0.0014–0.0025	0.0016–0.0029	NA	NA
	F	5.0 (5011)	46	45	194–206 @ 1.25	1.70	0.0011–0.0027	0.0011–0.0027	NA	NA
	E	5.0 (5011)	46	45	194–206 @ 1.25	1.70	0.0011–0.0027	0.0011–0.0027	NA	NA
	8	5.7 (5733)	46	45	194–206 @1.25	1.70	0.0011–0.0027	0.0011–0.0027	NA	NA
1993–94	S	3.4 (3350)	46	45	190 @ 1.20	1.61	0.0014–0.0027	0.0015–0.0029	NA	NA
	P	5.7 (5733)	46	45	252–272 @ 1.305	1.78	0.0011–0.0027	0.0011–0.0027	NA	NA

NA—Not available
① Intake—1.72
Exhaust—1.59

PISTON AND RING SPECIFICATIONS

All measurements are given in inches.

Year	Engine ID/VIN	Engine Displacement Liter (cc)	Piston Clearance	Ring Gap Top Compression	Ring Gap Bottom Compression	Ring Gap Oil Control	Ring Side Clearance Top Compression	Ring Side Clearance Bottom Compression	Ring Side Clearance Oil Control
1990	T	3.1 (3136)	0.0012–0.0028	0.010–0.020	0.010–0.020	0.010–0.030	0.0020–0.0035	0.0020–0.0035	0.0075 Max.
	F	5.0 (5011)	0.0007–0.0021	0.010–0.020	0.010–0.025	0.015–0.055	0.0012–0.0032	0.0012–0.0032	0.0020–0.0070
	E	5.0 (5011)	0.0007–0.0021	0.010–0.020	0.010–0.025	0.015–0.055	0.0012–0.0032	0.0012–0.0032	0.0020–0.0070
	8	5.7 (5733)	0.0007–0.0021	0.010–0.020	0.018–0.026	0.015–0.055	0.0012–0.0032	0.0012–0.0032	0.0020–0.0070
1991	T	3.1 (3136)	0.0012–0.0028	0.010–0.020	0.020–0.028	0.010–0.030	0.0020–0.0035	0.0020–0.0035	0.0070 Max.
	F	5.0 (5011)	0.0007–0.0021	0.010–0.020	0.010–0.025	0.010–0.030	0.0012–0.0032	0.0012–0.0032	0.0020–0.0070
	E	5.0 (5011)	0.0007–0.0021	0.010–0.020	0.010–0.025	0.010–0.030	0.0012–0.0032	0.0012–0.0032	0.0020–0.0070
	8	5.7 (5733)	0.0007–0.0021	0.010–0.020	0.018–0.026	0.010–0.030	0.0012–0.0032	0.0012–0.0032	0.0020–0.0070

PISTON AND RING SPECIFICATIONS

All measurements are given in inches.

Year	Engine ID/VIN	Engine Displacement Liter (cc)	Piston Clearance	Ring Gap Top Compression	Ring Gap Bottom Compression	Ring Gap Oil Control	Ring Side Clearance Top Compression	Ring Side Clearance Bottom Compression	Ring Side Clearance Oil Control
1992	T	3.1 (3136)	0.0012–0.0026	0.007–0.016	0.020–0.028	0.010–0.030	0.0020–0.0035	0.0020–0.0035	0.0070 Max.
	F	5.0 (5011)	0.0007–0.0021	0.010–0.020	0.018–0.026	0.010–0.030	0.0012–0.0032	0.0012–0.0032	0.0020–0.0070
	E	5.0 (5011)	0.0007–0.0021	0.010–0.020	0.018–0.026	0.010–0.030	0.0012–0.0032	0.0012–0.0032	0.0020–0.0070
	8	5.7 (5733)	0.0007–0.0021	0.010–0.020	0.018–0.026	0.010–0.030	0.0012–0.0032	0.0012–0.0032	0.0020–0.0070
1993–94	S	3.4 (3350)	0.0011–0.0024	0.007–0.016	0.019–0.029	0.010–0.030	0.0020–0.0035	0.0020–0.0035	0.0080 Max.
	P	5.7 (5733)	0.0010–0.0027	0.010–0.020	0.018–0.026	0.010–0.030	0.0012–0.0032	0.0012–0.0032	0.0020–0.0070

NA—Not available

TORQUE SPECIFICATIONS

All readings in ft. lbs.

Year	Engine ID/VIN	Engine Displacement Liter (cc)	Cylinder Head Bolts	Main Bearing Bolts	Rod Bearing Bolts	Crankshaft Damper Bolts	Flywheel Bolts	Manifold Intake	Manifold Exhaust	Spark Plugs	Lug Nut
1990	T	3.1 (3136)	③	73	39	70	52	④	25	25	100
	F	5.0 (5011)	68	77	44	70	74	35	②	22	100
	E	5.0 (5011)	68	77	44	70	74	35	②	22	100
	8	5.7 (5733)	68	77	44	70	74	35	②	22	100
1991	T	3.1 (3136)	③	73	39	70	52	④	25	25	100
	F	5.0 (5011)	68	77	44	70	74	35	②	22	100
	E	5.0 (5011)	68	77	44	70	74	35	②	22	100
	8	5.7 (5733)	68	77	44	70	74	35	②	22	100
1992	T	3.1 (3136)	③	73	39	70	52	④	25	25	100
	F	5.0 (5011)	68	77	44	70	74	⑤	②	11	100
	E	5.0 (5011)	68	77	44	70	74	⑤	②	11	100
	8	5.7 (5733)	68	77	44	70	74	⑤	②	11	100
1993–94	S	3.4 (3350)	③	37①	37	58	61	⑦	18	23	100
	P	5.7 (5733)	65	78	47	60	74	35⑥	26	11	100

① Plus an additional 77 degrees turn
② Outer bolts—26 ft. lbs.
  Center bolts—20 ft. lbs.
③ Torque in 2 steps:
  1st step: Tighten to 40 ft. lbs.
  2nd step: Rotate wrench an additional 90 degrees.
④ Lower intake manifold—19 ft. lbs.
  Center intake manifold—15 ft. lbs.
⑤ Torque in 2 steps:
  1st step: 89 inch lbs.
  2nd step: 35 ft. lbs.
⑥ Tighten in 2 steps:
  First step tighten to 71 inch lbs.
⑦ Upper manifold—18 ft. lbs.
  Lower manifold bolt/nut—22 ft. lbs.
  Upper manifold stud—89 inch lbs.

TORQUE SPECIFICATIONS

Component	English	Metric
Camshaft sprocket bolt		
Except 3.4L engine:	21 ft. lbs.	28 Nm
3.4L engine:	18 ft. lbs.	24 Nm
Connecting rod bearing cap bolts		
3.1L engine:	39 ft. lbs.	53 Nm
3.4L engine:	37 ft. lbs.	50 Nm
5.0L and 5.7L (VIN 8) engines:	44 ft. lbs.	60 Nm
5.7L (VIN P) engine:	47 ft. lbs.	64 Nm
Crankshaft damper bolt		
3.1L engine:	70 ft. lbs.	95 Nm
3.4L engine:	58 ft. lbs.	79 Nm
5.0L and 5.7L (VIN 8) engines:	70 ft. lbs.	95 Nm
5.7L (VIN P with damper/pulley assembly) engine:	60 ft. lbs.	81 Nm
Crankshaft hub bolt		
5.7L (VIN P) engine:	75 ft. lbs.	102 Nm
Crankshaft pulley bolt		
1990–92:	43 ft. lbs.	58 Nm
3.4L engine:	37 ft. lbs.	50 Nm
5.7L (VIN P with damper/pulley assembly) engine:	60 ft. lbs.	81 Nm
Cylinder head bolt		
3.1L engine		
Step 1:	40 ft. lbs.	55 Nm
Step 2:	+ 90 degree turn	+ 90 degree turn
3.4L engine		
Step 1:	41 ft. lbs.	55 Nm
Step 2:	+ 90 degree turn	+ 90 degree turn
5.0L and 5.7L (VIN 8) engines:	68 ft. lbs.	92 Nm
5.7L (VIN P) engine*:	68 ft. lbs.	92 Nm

* Tighten using at least 3 passses of the proper torque sequence

NOTE: For all engines, clean the bolt threads, then coat with fresh sealant

Component	English	Metric
Exhaust manifold		
3.1L engine:	25 ft. lbs.	34 Nm
3.4L engine:	18 ft. lbs.	25 Nm
5.0L and 5.7L (VIN 8) engines		
Outer bolts:	20 ft. lbs.	27 Nm
Inner bolts:	26 ft. lbs.	35 Nm
5.7L (VIN P) engine:	26 ft. lbs.	35 Nm
Exhaust pipe nuts:	15 ft. lbs.	20 Nm
Flywheel/flexplate-to-crankshaft bolts		
3.1L engine:	52 ft. lbs.	71 Nm
3.4L engine:	61 ft. lbs.	83 Nm
5.0L and 5.7L engines:	74 ft. lbs.	100 Nm
Flywheel-to-converter bolts:	46 ft. lbs.	63 Nm
Flywheel-to-pressure plate		
3.1L engine:	15 ft. lbs.	21 Nm
3.4L engine		
Step 1:	15 ft. lbs.	21 Nm
Step 2:	+30 degree turn	+30 degree turn
5.0L and 5.7L (VIN 8) engines:	30 ft. lbs.	40 Nm
5.7L (VIN P) engine:	22 ft. lbs.	30 Nm

TORQUE SPECIFICATIONS

Component	English	Metric
Intake manifold		
3.1L engine		
Manifold:	19 ft. lbs.	26 Nm
Center manifold:	15 ft. lbs.	21 Nm
3.4L engine		
Manifold:	22 ft. lbs.	30 Nm
Upper manifold:	18 ft. lbs.	25 Nm
5.0L (VIN E) engine		
Step 1:	89 inch lbs.	10 Nm
Step 2:	35 ft. lbs.	47 Nm
5.0L (VIN F) and 5.7L (VIN 8) engines		
Intake-to-engine		
Step 1:	89 inch lbs.	10 Nm
Step 2:	35 ft. lbs.	47 Nm
Intake-to-runners:	25 ft. lbs.	34 Nm
Runners-to-plenum:	25 ft. lbs.	34 Nm
5.7L (VIN P) engine		
Step 1:	71 inch lbs.	8 Nm
Step 2:	35 ft. lbs.	48 Nm
Main bearing cap bolts		
3.1L engine:	73 ft. lbs.	99 Nm
3.4L engine		
Step 1:	37 ft. lbs.	50 Nm
Step 2:	+ 30 degree turn	+ 30 degree turn
5.0L and 5.7L (VIN 8) engines:	77 ft. lbs.	105 Nm
5.7L (VIN P) engine:	78 ft. lbs.	106 Nm
Oil pan		
3.1L engine		
Except 2 rear bolts:	89 inch lbs.	10 Nm
2 rear bolts:	18 ft. lbs.	25 Nm
3.4L engine		
Front corner nuts:	24 ft. lbs.	33 Nm
Rear corner bolts:	18 ft. lbs.	25 Nm
Side rail bolts:	89 inch lbs.	10 Nm
Oil pan studs:	53 inch lbs.	6 Nm
1990–92 5.0L and 5.7L (VIN 8) engines		
Bolt:	101 inch lbs.	11 Nm
Nut:	17 ft. lbs.	23 Nm
5.7L (VIN P) engine		
Corner fasteners:	15 ft. lbs.	20 Nm
Remaining fasteners:	100 inch lbs.	11 Nm
Oil pan drain plug		
V6 engines:	18 ft. lbs.	25 Nm
V8 engines:	16 ft. lbs.	22 Nm
Oil pump attaching bolts		
V6 engines:	30 ft. lbs.	41 Nm
V8 engines:	65 ft. lbs.	88 Nm
Rocker (valve) cover		
3.1L engine:	120 inch lbs.	14 Nm
3.4L engine:	89 inch lbs.	10 Nm
5.0L and 5.7L (VIN 8) engines:	96 inch lbs.	11 Nm
5.7L (VIN P) engine:	96 inch lbs.	11 Nm
Spark plug		
3.1L engine:	25 ft. lbs.	34 Nm
3.4L engine:	23 ft. lbs.	31 Nm
5.0L and 5.7L (VIN 8) engines:	22 ft. lbs.	30 Nm
5.7L (VIN P) engine:	11 ft. lbs.	15 Nm
Starter-to-block bolts:	35 ft. lbs.	47 Nm

TORQUE SPECIFICATIONS

Component	English	Metric
Thermostat housing		
3.1L engine:	15 ft. lbs.	21 Nm
5.0L (VIN E) engine:	21 ft. lbs.	28 Nm
5.0L (VIN F) and 5.7L (VIN 8) engines:	25 ft. lbs.	34 Nm
3.4L and 5.7L (VIN P) engines:	21 ft. lbs.	28 Nm
Timing cover		
V6 engines:	15 ft. lbs.	21 Nm
V8 engines:	100 inch lbs.	11 Nm
Transmission (automatic) bolts		
Except 3.4L engine:	35 ft. lbs.	47 Nm
3.4L engine:	70 ft. lbs.	95 Nm
Transmission (manual) bolts		
Except 5.7L (VIN P) engine:	55 ft. lbs.	75 Nm
5.7L (VIN P) engine:	26 ft. lbs.	35 Nm
Water pump pulley		
Except 3.4L engine:	23 ft. lbs.	31 Nm
3.4L engine:	18 ft. lbs.	25 Nm

BRAKE SPECIFICATIONS

All measurements in inches unless noted.

Year	Model	Master Cylinder Bore	Brake Disc Original Thickness	Brake Disc Minimum ④ Thickness	Maximum Runout	Brake Drum Diameter Original Inside Diameter	Brake Drum Diameter Max. Wear Limit	Brake Drum Diameter Maximum Machine Diameter	Minimum Lining Thickness Front	Minimum Lining Thickness Rear
1990	Camaro	①	②	③	0.005	9.500	9.590	9.560	0.030	0.030
	Firebird	①	②	③	0.005	9.500	9.590	9.560	0.030	0.030
1991	Camaro	①	②	③	0.005	9.500	9.590	9.560	0.030	0.030
	Firebird	①	②	③	0.005	9.500	9.590	9.560	0.030	0.030
1992	Camaro	①	②	③	0.005	9.500	9.590	9.560	0.030	0.030
	Firebird	①	②	③	0.005	9.500	9.590	9.560	0.030	0.030
1993–94	Camaro	1.00	1.260⑤	1.250⑥	0.005⑦	9.500	9.590	9.560	0.030	0.030
	Firebird	1.00	1.260⑤	1.250⑥	0.005⑦	9.500	9.590	9.560	0.030	0.030

① Rear Drum—0.945
　 Rear Disc—1.00
② Front—1.043
　 Rear—0.795
③ Front—0.980
　 Rear—0.744

④ Specification is the minimum to which a rotor may be refinished; a small discard dimension is cast into the rotor itself
⑤ Rear—0.787
⑥ Rear—0.733
⑦ Rear—0.006

WHEEL ALIGNMENT

Year	Model	Caster Range (deg.)	Caster Preferred Setting (deg.)	Camber Range (deg.)	Camber Preferred Setting (deg.)	Toe-in (in.)	Steering Axis Inclination (deg.)
1990	Camaro	4.2P–5.2P	4.7P	0.2N–0.8P	0.3P	0	NA
	Firebird	4.2P–5.2P	4.7P	0.2N–0.8P	0.3P	0	NA
1991	Camaro	4.3P–5.3P	4.8P	0.2N–0.8P	0.3P	0	NA
	Firebird	4.3P–5.3P	4.8P	0.2N–0.8P	0.3P	0	NA

WHEEL ALIGNMENT

Year	Model	Caster Range (deg.)	Caster Preferred Setting (deg.)	Camber Range (deg.)	Camber Preferred Setting (deg.)	Toe-in (in.)	Steering Axis Inclination (deg.)
1992	Camaro	4.3P–5.3P	4.8P	0.2N–0.8P	0.3P	0	NA
	Firebird	4.3P–5.3P	4.8P	0.2N–0.8P	0.3P	0	NA
1993–94	Camaro	3.9P–4.9P	4.4P	0.1N–0.9P①	0.4P①	0	0
	Firebird	3.9P–4.9P	4.4P	0.1N–0.9P①	0.4P①	0	0

NA—Not available
N—Negative
P—Positive
① Rear camber range—0.6N–0.6P
   Preferred Setting—0

AIR CONDITIONING BELT TENSION

Year	Model	Engine Displacement Liters (cc)	Belt Type	Specifications (lbs.) New①	Specifications (lbs.) Used①
1990	Camaro	3.1 (3136)	V-Belt	②	③
		5.0 (5011)	V-Belt	②	③
		5.7 (5733)	V-Belt	②	③
	Firebird	3.1 (3136)	Serpentine	①	①
		5.0 (5011)	Serpentine	①	①
		5.7 (5733)	Serpentine	①	①
1991	Camaro	3.1 (3136)	Serpentine	①	①
		5.0 (5011)	Serpentine	①	①
		5.7 (5733)	Serpentine	①	①
	Firebird	3.1 (3136)	Serpentine	①	①
		5.0 (5011)	Serpentine	①	①
		5.7 (5733)	Serpentine	①	①
1992	Camaro	3.1 (3136)	Serpentine	85–110	④
	Firebird	3.1 (3136)	Serpentine	85–110	④
	Camaro	5.0 (5011)	Serpentine	99–121	④
		5.7 (5733)	Serpentine	99–121	④
	Firebird	5.0 (5011)	Serpentine	99–121	④
		5.7 (5733)	Serpentine	99–121	④
1993–94	Camaro	3.4 (3350)	Serpentine	85–110	④
	Firebird	3.4 (3350)	Serpentine	85–110	④
	Camaro	5.7 (5733)	Serpentine	99–121	④
	Firebird	5.7 (5733)	Serpentine	99–121	④

① If equipped with serpentine belt—
   no adjustment necessary
② New belts
   5/16" wide—80 lbs.
   3/8" & 13/32" wide—140 lbs.
   7/16" wide—165 lbs.
③ Used belts
   5/16" wide—50 lbs.
   3/8" & 13/32" wide—740 lbs.
   7/16" wide—90 lbs.
④ Specification given with A/C; if no A/C:
   95–140 lbs.

REFRIGERANT CAPACITIES

Year	Model	Refrigerant (oz.)	Oil (fl. oz.)	Compressor Type
1990	Camaro	36.0	6.0	R-4
	Firebird	36.0	6.0	R-4
1991	Camaro	36.0	6.0	R-4
	Firebird	36.0	6.0	R-4
1992	Camaro	36.0	6.0	R-4
	Firebird	36.0	6.0	R-4
1993–94	Camaro	32.0①	8.0	HD6/HR6-HE
	Firebird	32.0①	8.0	HD6/HR6-HE

① Use R-134a refrigerant and PAG refrigerant oil.
   Do not mix, in any amount, with R-12 or R-12
   system oil or components.

MAINTENANCE INTERVALS—TYPE A: NORMAL SERVICE
Camaro • Firebird

TO BE SERVICED	TYPE OF SERVICE	VEHICLE MILEAGE INTERVAL (X1000)							
		7.5	15	22.5	30	37.5	45	52.5	60
Oxygen Sensor	I				✔				✔
Ignition Timing	I①								
Vacuum Lines and Hoses	I		✔		✔		✔		✔
Ignition Wires	I								✔
Spark Plugs	R②				✔				✔
Engine Oil	R	✔	✔	✔	✔	✔	✔	✔	✔
Engine Air Cleaner Element	R				✔				✔
Crankcase Emission Filter	R				✔				✔
PCV Valve	R				✔				✔
Fuel Filter	R				✔				✔
Tire Rotation	I③				✔				✔
Fuel/Vapor Return Lines	I				✔				✔
Fuel Tank Cap and Restrictor	I				✔				✔
Coolant System	R				✔				✔
Exhaust Pipe and Muffler	I				✔				✔
Coolant Hoses and Clamps	I		✔		✔		✔		✔
Catalytic Converter and Shield	I				✔				✔
EGR System	I				✔				✔
Automatic Transmission Fluid	R④								
Chassis Lubrication	L	✔	✔	✔	✔	✔	✔	✔	✔
Brake Linings	I		✔		✔		✔		✔
Parking Brake	I		✔		✔		✔		✔
Idle Speed System	I				✔				✔
Throttle Body	I				✔				✔
Drive Belts	I				✔				✔
Wheel Bearings	L				✔				✔
Thermostatically Controlled Air Cleaner	I				✔				✔
Battery Connections	I		✔		✔		✔		✔

MAINTENANCE INTERVALS—TYPE A: NORMAL SERVICE
Camaro • Firebird

TO BE SERVICED	TYPE OF SERVICE	VEHICLE MILEAGE INTERVAL (X1000)							
		7.5	15	22.5	30	37.5	45	52.5	60
Engine Oil Filter	R⑤	✔		✔		✔		✔	
Seat Belt Operation	I				✔				✔

FOR COMPLETE WARRANTY COVERAGE CONSULT INDIVIDUAL VEHICLE MANUFACTURER'S WARRANTY MAINTENANCE GUIDE.

I—Inspect
L—Lubricate
R—Replace
① Check and adjust timing as per engine emission label on applicable vehicles
② Replace spark plugs at 30,000 miles—except for 1993–94 5.7 LTI—replace at 100,000 miles
③ Rotate tires at 7,500 miles and then every 15,000 miles
④ Replace transmission fluid at 100,000 miles
⑤ Replace oil filter at first and every other oil change

MAINTENANCE INTERVALS—TYPE B: SEVERE SERVICE
Camaro • Firebird

TO BE SERVICED	TYPE OF SERVICE	VEHICLE MILEAGE INTERVAL (X1000)									
		3	6	9	12	15	18	21	24	27	30
Oxygen Sensor	I										✔
Ignition Timing	I①										
Vacuum Lines and Hoses	I					✔					✔
Ignition Wires	I										✔
Spark Plugs	R②										✔
Engine Oil and Filter	R	✔	✔	✔	✔	✔	✔	✔	✔	✔	✔
Engine Air Cleaner Element	R					✔					✔
Crankcase Emission Filter	R					✔					✔
PCV Valve	R					✔					✔
Fuel Filter	R					✔					✔
Tire Rotation	I③		✔								
Fuel/Vapor Return Lines	I										✔
Fuel Tank Cap and Restrictor	I										✔
Coolant System	R										✔
Exhaust Pipe and Muffler	I										✔
Coolant Hoses and Clamps	I					✔					✔
Catalytic Converter and Shield	I										✔
EGR System	I										✔
Automatic Transmission Fluid	R					✔					✔
Chassis Lubrication	L		✔		✔		✔		✔		✔
Brake Linings	I					✔					✔
Parking Brake	I					✔					✔
Idle Speed System	I		✔								
Throttle Body Mounting Torque	I										✔
Drive Belts	I										✔
Wheel Bearings	L					✔					✔

MAINTENANCE INTERVALS—TYPE B: SEVERE SERVICE
Camaro • Firebird

TO BE SERVICED	TYPE OF SERVICE	VEHICLE MILEAGE INTERVAL (X1000)									
		3	6	9	12	15	18	21	24	27	30
Thermostatically Controlled Air Cleaner	I ④										✔
Battery Connections	I					✔					✔
Seat Belt Operation	I					✔					✔

FOR COMPLETE WARRANTY COVERAGE CONSULT INDIVIDUAL VEHICLE MANUFACTURER'S WARRANTY MAINTENANCE GUIDE.

I—Inspect
L—Lubricate
R—Replace
① Check and adjust timing as per engine emission label on applicable vehicles
② Replace spark plugs at 30,000 miles except for 1993–94 5.7 LTI—replace at 100,000 miles
③ Rotate tires at 6,000 miles and then every 15,000 miles
④ On applicable models

FIRING ORDERS

NOTE: To avoid confusion, always replace spark plugs and wires one at a time.

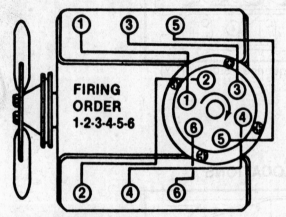

3.1L Engine
Engine Firing Order: 1-2-3-4-5-6
Distributor Rotation: Clockwise

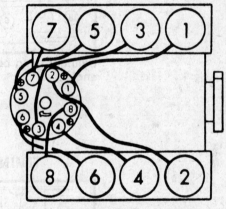

5.0L and 5.7L Engines
Engine Firing Order: 1-8-4-3-6-5-7-2
Distributor Rotation: Clockwise

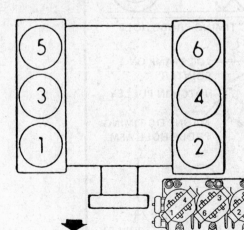

FRONT OF CAR

3.4L Engine
Engine Firing Order: 1-2-3-4-5-6
Distributorless Ignition System

CYLINDER HEAD TORQUE SEQUENCES

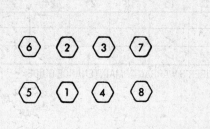

Cylinder head torque sequence—3.1L and 3.4L engines

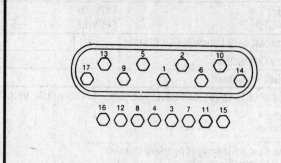

Cylinder head bolt torque sequence—5.0L and 5.7L engines (VIN E, 7)

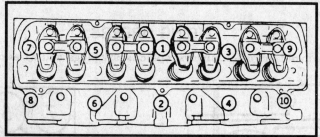

Cylinder head bolt torque sequence—5.0L (VIN Y) engine

TIMING MARK LOCATIONS

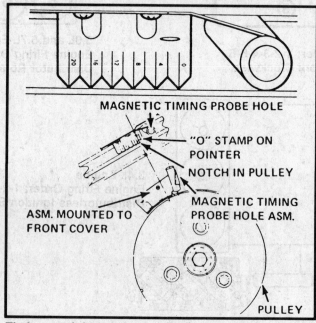

MAGNETIC TIMING PROBE HOLE

"O" STAMP ON POINTER

NOTCH IN PULLEY

MAGNETIC TIMING PROBE HOLE ASM.

ASM. MOUNTED TO FRONT COVER

PULLEY

Timing mark location—8 cylinder engine

TIMING CHAIN ALIGNMENT MARKS

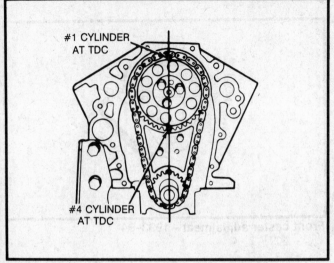

Timing chain alignment marks—V6 engine

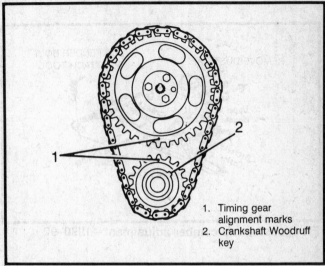

1. Timing gear alignment marks
2. Crankshaft Woodruff key

Timing chain alignment marks—V8 engine

AIR CONDITIONING SERVICE VALVE LOCATIONS

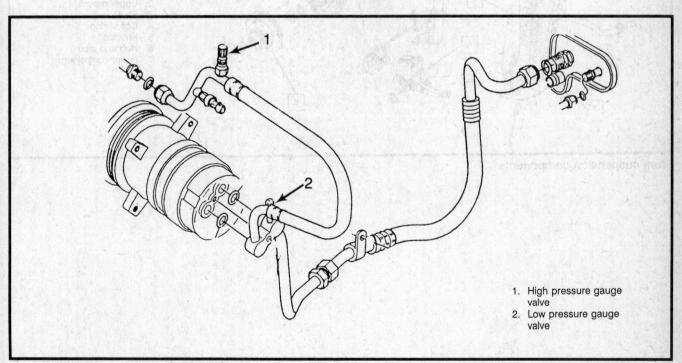

1. High pressure gauge valve
2. Low pressure gauge valve

Air conditioning service valve location

WHEEL ALIGNMENT ADJUSTMENT
LOCATIONS

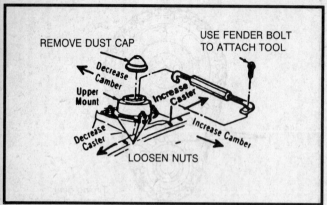

Front caster and camber adjustment—1990–92

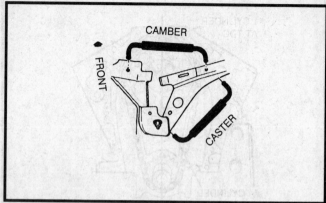

Front caster adjustment—1993–94

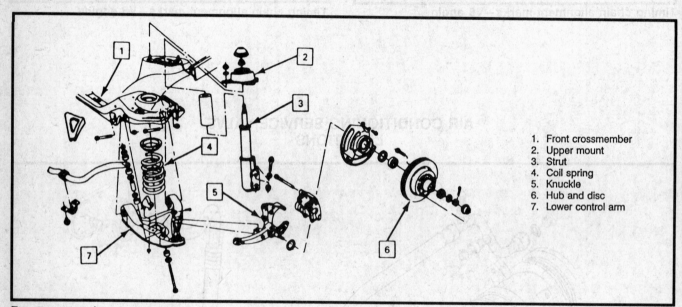

1. Front crossmember
2. Upper mount
3. Strut
4. Coil spring
5. Knuckle
6. Hub and disc
7. Lower control arm

Front suspension components

SPECIFICATION CHARTS

VEHICLE IDENTIFICATION CHART

It is important for servicing and ordering parts to be certain of the vehicle and engine identification. The VIN (vehicle identification number) is a 17 digit number visible through the windshield on the driver's side of the dash and contains the vehicle and engine identification codes. The tenth digit indicates model year and the eighth digit indicates engine code. It can be interpreted as follows:

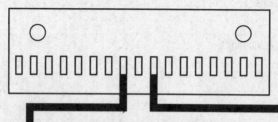

Engine Code						Model Year	
Code	Liters	Cu. In. (cc)	Cyl.	Fuel Sys.	Eng. Mfg.	Code	Year
8	5.7	350 (5733)	8	MFI	Chevrolet	L	1990
P	5.7	350 (5733)	8	MFI	Chevrolet	M	1991
J	5.7	350 (5727)	8	SFI	Chevrolet	N	1992
						P	1993
						R	1994

MFI—Multi-Port Fuel Injection
SFI—Sequential Fuel Injection

ENGINE IDENTIFICATION

Year	Model	Engine Displacement Liters (cc)	Engine Series (ID/VIN)	Fuel System	No. of Cylinders	Engine Type
1990	Corvette	5.7 (5733)	8	MFI	8	OHV
	Corvette ZR-1	5.7 (5727)	J	SFI	8	DOHC
1991	Corvette	5.7 (5733)	8	MFI	8	OHV
	Corvette ZR-1	5.7 (5727)	J	SFI	8	DOHC
1992	Corvette	5.7 (5733)	P	MFI	8	OHV
	Corvette ZR-1	5.7 (5727)	J	SFI	8	DOHC
1993-94	Corvette	5.7 (5733)	P	MFI	8	OHV
	Corvette ZR-1	5.7 (5727)	J	SFI	8	DOHC

DOHC—Dual Overhead Camshafts
OHV—Overhead Valves
MFI—Multi-Port Fuel Injection
SFI—Sequential Fuel Injection

GENERAL ENGINE SPECIFICATIONS

Year	Engine ID/VIN	Engine Displacement Liters (cc)	Fuel System Type	Net Horsepower @ rpm	Net Torque @ rpm (ft. lbs.)	Bore × Stroke (in.)	Compression Ratio	Oil Pressure @ rpm [1]
1990	8	5.7 (5733)	MFI	245 @ 4000	340 @ 3200	4.000 × 3.480	10.25:1	18 @ 2000
	J	5.7 (5727)	SFI	375 @ 5800	370 @ 4500	3.897 × 3.661	11:1	40 @ 3000 [2]
1991	8	5.7 (5733)	MFI	245 @ 4000	340 @ 3200	4.000 × 3.480	10.25:1	18 @ 2000
	J	5.7 (5727)	SFI	375 @ 5800	370 @ 4800	3.897 × 3.661	11:1	40 @ 3000 [2]

GENERAL ENGINE SPECIFICATIONS

Year	Engine ID/VIN	Engine Displacement Liters (cc)	Fuel System Type	Net Horsepower @ rpm	Net Torque @ rpm (ft. lbs.)	Bore × Stroke (in.)	Compression Ratio	Oil Pressure @ rpm ①
1992	P	5.7 (5733)	MFI	300 @ 5000	330 @ 4000	4.000 × 3.480	10.25:1	18 @ 2000
	J	5.7 (5727)	SFI	375 @ 5800	370 @ 4800	3.897 × 3.661	11:1	40 @ 3000 ②
1993–94	P	5.7 (5733)	MFI	300 @ 5000	340 @ 3600	4.000 × 3.480	10.5:1	18 @ 2000
	J	5.7 (5727)	SFI	405 @ 5800	385 @ 5200	3.897 × 3.661	11:1	40 @ 3000 ②

MFI—Multi-Port Fuel Injection
SFI—Sequential Fuel Injection
① Measurement is the minimum with the engine HOT
② Minimum RPM for pressure reading

GASOLINE ENGINE TUNE-UP SPECIFICATIONS

Year	Engine ID/VIN	Engine Displacement Liters (cc)	Spark Plugs Gap (in.)	Ignition Timing (deg.) MT	Ignition Timing (deg.) AT	Fuel Pump (psi) ②	Idle Speed (rpm) MT	Idle Speed (rpm) AT	Valve Clearance In.	Valve Clearance Ex.
1990	8	5.7 (5733)	0.035	①	①	41–47	①	①	Hyd.	Hyd.
	J	5.7 (5727)	0.035	①	①	48–55	①	①	Hyd.	Hyd.
1991	8	5.7 (5733)	0.035	①	①	41–47	①	①	Hyd.	Hyd.
	J	5.7 (5727)	0.035	①	①	48–55	①	①	Hyd.	Hyd.
1992	P	5.7 (5733)	0.050	①	①	41–47	①	①	Hyd.	Hyd.
	J	5.7 (5727)	0.035	①	①	48–55	①	①	Hyd.	Hyd.
1993	P	5.7 (5733)	0.050	①	①	41–47	①	①	Hyd.	Hyd.
	J	5.7 (5727)	0.035	①	①	48–55	①	①	Hyd.	Hyd.
1994			SEE UNDERHOOD SPECIFICATIONS STICKER							

NOTE: The lowest cylinder pressure should be within 75% of the highest cylinder pressure reading. For example, if the highest cylinder is 134 psi, the lowest should be 101. Engine should be at normal operating temperature with throttle valve in the wide open position.
The underhood specifications sticker often reflects tune-up specification changes in production. Sticker figures must be used if they disagree with those in this chart.
Hyd.—Hydraulic
① Refer to Vehicle Emission Control Information label for ignition timing and idle specifications. If no specifications are shown, no adjustment is required.
② Ignition ON, engine not running

CAPACITIES

Year	Model	Engine ID/VIN	Engine Displacement Liters (cc)	Engine Crankcase without Filter (qts.)	Transmission (pts.) 5-Spd	Transmission (pts.) 6-Spd	Transmission (pts.) Auto.	Drive Axle (pts.)	Fuel Tank (gal.)	Cooling System (qts.)
1990	Corvette	8	5.7 (5733)	5.0	—	4.4	10	3.75 ①	20	17.8
	Corvette ZR-1	J	5.7 (5727)	8.6	—	4.4	—	3.75 ①	20	14.7
1991	Corvette	8	5.7 (5733)	5.0	—	4.4	10	①	20	17.8
	Corvette ZR-1	J	5.7 (5727)	8.6	—	4.4	—	①	20	14.7
1992	Corvette	P	5.7 (5733)	5.0	—	4.4	10	①	20	17.8
	Corvette ZR-1	J	5.7 (5727)	8.6	—	4.4	—	①	20	14.7
1993–94	Corvette	P	5.7 (5733)	4.5	—	4.4	10	①	20	17.8
	Corvette ZR-1	J	5.7 (5727)	8.6	—	4.4	—	①	20	14.7

① Fluid level should be no lower than a ¼ in. (6mm) below filler plug opening.

CAMSHAFT SPECIFICATIONS

All measurements given in inches.

Year	Engine ID/VIN	Engine Displacement Liters (cc)	Journal Diameter					Elevation		Bearing Clearance	Camshaft End Play
			1	2	3	4	5	In.	Ex.		
1990	8	5.7 (5733)	1.8682–1.8692	1.8682–1.8692	1.8682–1.8692	1.8682–1.8692	1.8682–1.8692	0.2730–0.2770	0.2836–0.2876	—	0.004–0.012
	J	5.7 (5727)	1.1400–1.1410	1.1400–1.1410	1.1400–1.1410	1.1400–1.1410	1.1400–1.1410	0.3878–0.3918–	0.3878–0.3918–	—	0.006–0.014
1991	8	5.7 (5733)	1.8682–1.8692	1.8682–1.8692	1.8682–1.8692	1.8682–1.8692	1.8682–1.8692	0.2730–0.2770	0.2836–0.2876	—	0.004–0.012
	J	5.7 (5727)	1.1400–1.1410	1.1400–1.1410	1.1400–1.1410	1.1400–1.1410	1.1400–1.1410	0.3878–0.3918–	0.3878–0.3918–	—	0.006–0.014
1992	P	5.7 (5733)	1.8682–1.8692	1.8682–1.8692	1.8682–1.8692	1.8682–1.8692	1.8682–1.8692	0.2980–0.3020	0.2980–0.3020	—	0.004–0.012
	J	5.7 (5727)	1.1400–1.1410	1.1400–1.1410	1.1400–1.1410	1.1400–1.1410	1.1400–1.1410	0.3878–0.3918–	0.3878–0.3918–	—	0.006–0.014
1993–94	P	5.7 (5733)	1.8682–1.8692	1.8682–1.8692	1.8682–1.8692	1.8682–1.8692	1.8682–1.8692	0.2980–0.3020	0.2980–0.3020	—	0.004–0.012
	J	5.7 (5727)	1.1400–1.1410	1.1400–1.1410	1.1400–1.1410	1.1400–1.1410	1.1400–1.1410	0.3878–0.3918–	0.3878–0.3918–	—	0.006–0.014

CRANKSHAFT AND CONNECTING ROD SPECIFICATIONS

All measurements are given in inches.

Year	Engine ID/VIN	Engine Displacement Liters (cc)	Crankshaft				Connecting Rod		
			Main Brg. Journal Dia.	Main Brg. Oil Clearance	Shaft End-play	Thrust on. No.	Journal Diameter	Oil Clearance	Side Clearance
1990	8	5.7 (5733)	2.4484–2.4493①	0.0008–0.0030④	0.0020–0.0060	5	2.0988–2.0998	0.0035③	0.006–0.014
	J	5.7 (5727)	2.7550–2.7560	0.0007–0.0023	0.0006–0.0010	3	2.0993–2.1000	0.0007–0.0027	0.008–0.028
1991	8	5.7 (5733)	2.4484–2.4493①	0.0008–0.0030④	0.0020–0.0060	5	2.0988–2.0998	0.0035③	0.006–0.014
	J	5.7 (5727)	2.7550–2.7560	0.0007–0.0023	0.0063–0.0140	3	2.0993–2.1000	0.0007–0.0027	0.008–0.028
1992	P	5.7 (5733)	2.4484–2.4493①	0.0008–0.0020②	0.0010–0.0070	5	2.0893–2.0998	0.0013–0.0035	0.006–0.014
	J	5.7 (5727)	2.7550–2.7560	0.0007–0.0023	0.0063–0.0140	3	2.0993–2.1000	0.0007–0.0027	0.008–0.028
1993–94	P	5.7 (5733)	2.4484–2.4493①	0.0008–0.0020②	0.0010–0.0070	5	2.0893–2.0998	0.0013–0.0035	0.006–0.014
	J	5.7 (5727)	2.7550–2.7560	0.0007–0.0023	0.0063–0.0140	3	2.0993–2.1000	0.0007–0.0027	0.008–0.028

① Specification applies to the No. 1 bearing.
  Nos. 2, 3, 4—2.4481–2.4490
  VIN 8 No. 5—2.4479–2.4488
  VIN P No. 5—2.4481–2.4488
② Specification applies to the No. 1 bearing.
  Nos 2, 3, 4—0.0011–0.0020
  No. 5—0.0017–0.0032
  Specifications shown apply to new components
③ Maximum clearance
④ Specification applies to the No. 1 bearing.
  Nos 2, 3, 4—0.0011–0.0033
  No. 5—0.0017–0.0042

VALVE SPECIFICATIONS

Year	Engine ID/VIN	Engine Displacement Liters (cc)	Seat Angle (deg.)	Face Angle (deg.)	Spring Test Pressure (lbs. @ in.)	Spring Installed Height (in.)	Stem-to-Guide Clearance (in.)		Stem Diameter (in.)	
							Intake	Exhaust	Intake	Exhaust
1990	8	5.7 (5733)	46	45	194–206 @ 1.25	1.72	0.0010–0.0037	0.0010–0.0047	NA	NA
	J	5.7 (5727)	44	45	146.8–166.4 @ 0.95 ①	1.34②	0.0012–0.0026	0.0014–0.0030	NA	NA
1991	8	5.7 (5733)	46	45	194–206 @ 1.25	1.72	0.0010–0.0037	0.0010–0.0047	NA	NA
	J	5.7 (5727)	44	45	146.8–166.4 @ 0.95 ①	1.34②	0.0012–0.0026	0.0014–0.0030	NA	NA
1992	P	5.7 (5733)	46	45	252–272 @ 1.305	1.78	0.0011–0.0027	0.0011–0.0027	NA	NA
	J	5.7 (5727)	44	45	146.8–166.4 @ 0.95 ①	1.34②	0.0012–0.0026	0.0014–0.0030	NA	NA
1993–94	P	5.7 (5733)	46	45	252–272 @ 1.305	1.78	0.0011–0.0027	0.0011–0.0027	NA	NA
	J	5.7 (5727)	44	45	146.8–166.4 @ 0.95 ①	1.34②	0.0012–0.0026	0.0014–0.0030	NA	NA

NA—Not available
① Inner spring—75.5–81.8 lb. @ 0.79 in.
② Inner spring—1.18 in.

PISTON AND RING SPECIFICATIONS

All measurements are given in inches.

Year	Engine ID/VIN	Engine Displacement Liters (cc)	Piston Clearance	Ring Gap			Ring Side Clearance		
				Top Compression	Bottom Compression	Oil Control	Top Compression	Bottom Compression	Oil Control
1990	8	5.7 (5733)	①	0.010–0.030	0.013–0.027	0.010–0.040	0.0012–0.0039	0.0012–0.0039	0.0012–0.0039
	J	5.7 (5727)	—	0.016–0.026	0.031–0.039	0.012–0.024	0.0020–0.0030	0.0020–0.0030	0.0010–0.0020
1991	8	5.7 (5733)	①	0.010–0.030	0.013–0.027	0.010–0.040	0.0012–0.0039	0.0012–0.0039	0.0012–0.0039
	J	5.7 (5727)	—	0.016–0.026	0.031–0.039	0.012–0.024	0.0020–0.0030	0.0020–0.0030	0.0010–0.0020
1992	P	5.7 (5733)	0.0007–0.0021①	0.010–0.020	0.018–0.026	0.010–0.030	0.0012–0.0032	0.0012–0.0032	0.0020–0.0070
	J	5.7 (5727)	—	0.016–0.026	0.031–0.039	0.012–0.024	0.0020–0.0030	0.0020–0.0030	0.0010–0.0020
1993–94	P	5.7 (5733)	0.0010–0.0027	0.010–0.020	0.018–0.026	0.010–0.030	0.0012–0.0032	0.0012–0.0032	0.0020–0.0070
	J	5.7 (5727)	—	0.016–0.026	0.031–0.039	0.012–0.024	0.0020–0.0030	0.0020–0.0030	0.0010–0.0020

① 0.0027 maximum

TORQUE SPECIFICATIONS
All readings in ft. lbs.

Year	Engine ID/VIN	Engine Displacement Liters (cc)	Cylinder Head Bolts	Main Bearing Bolts	Rod Bearing Bolts	Crankshaft Damper Bolts	Flywheel Bolts	Manifold Intake	Manifold Exhaust	Spark Plugs	Lug Nut
1990	8	5.7 (5733)	67	80	45	70	74	35②	19	22	100
	J	5.7 (5727)	③	⑤	22⑥	148	74	④	22①	15	100
1991	8	5.7 (5733)	67	80	45	70	74	35②	19	22	100
	J	5.7 (5727)	③	⑤	22⑥	148	74	④	22①	19	100
1992	P	5.7 (5733)	65	68⑦	47	60	74	35⑧	26	11	100
	J	5.7 (5727)	③	⑤	22⑥	148	66	④	22⑨	15	100
1993–94	P	5.7 (5733)	65	68⑦	45	60	74	35⑧	26	11	100
	J	5.7 (5727)	③	⑩	22⑥	148	66	④	22⑨	15	100

① Manifold studs only, all others; 11 ft. lbs.
② All except Nos. 1 and 4; 1 and 4, 45 ft. lbs.
③ Torque bolts in 3 steps: 1st at 45 ft. lbs.; 2nd at 74 ft. lbs.; and final at 118 ft. lbs.
④ Injector Housing Bolts and Fuel Rail Bolts; 20 ft. lbs.
⑤ Torque bolts on No. 1, 3 and 5 to 30 ft. lbs. (40 Nm) plus 45–50° turn
Torque bolts on No. 2 and 4 to 15 ft. lbs. (20 Nm), plus 77.5–82.5° turn

⑥ Plus 80–85° turn
⑦ Inboard bolts on 4-bolt cap—78 ft. lbs.
⑧ Tighten in 2 passes. 1st pass torque to 71 inch lbs.
⑨ Studs only, tigthen bolts to 18 ft. lbs.
⑩ All bolts initially to 15 ft. lbs., then inner main bearings an additial 65–70° turn (M10 bolts) outer main bearings an additial 50–55° turn (M8 bolts)

TORQUE SPECIFICATIONS

Component	English	Metric
Clutch housing-to-engine		
5.7L (VIN 8) engine:	30 ft. lbs.	40 Nm
5.7L (VIN J and VIN P) engines:	37 ft. lbs.	50 Nm
Camshaft sprocket bolt		
5.7L (VIN 8) engine:	20 ft. lbs.	27 Nm
5.7L (VIN P) engine:	21 ft. lbs.	28 Nm
5.7L (VIN J) engine Idler sprocket:	19 ft. lbs.	26 Nm
Connecting rod bearing cap bolts		
5.7L (VIN 8) engine:	45 ft. lbs.	60 Nm
5.7L (VIN P) engine:	47 ft. lbs.	64 Nm
5.7L (VIN J) engine Step 1:	22 ft. lbs.	30 Nm
Step 2:	+ 80–85 degree turn	+ 80–85 degree turn
Crankshaft damper bolt		
5.7L (VIN 8) engine:	70 ft. lbs.	95 Nm
5.7L (VIN P) engine:	60 ft. lbs.	81 Nm
5.7L (VIN J) engine:	148 ft. lbs.	200 Nm
Crankshaft pulley bolt		
5.7L (VIN 8) engine:	32 ft. lbs.	43 Nm
Cylinder head bolt		
5.7L (VIN 8) engine:	67 ft. lbs.	91 Nm
5.7L (VIN P) engine:	65 ft. lbs.	88 Nm
5.7L (VIN J) engine Step 1:	45 ft. lbs.	60 Nm
Step 2:	74 ft. lbs.	100 Nm
Step 3:	118 ft. lbs.	160 Nm
EGR valve-to-intake (manifold or plenum)		
5.7L (VIN 8 and VIN P) engines:	16 ft. lbs.	22 Nm
Engine-to-transmission:	35 ft. lbs.	47 Nm

TORQUE SPECIFICATIONS

Component	English	Metric
Engine mount through bolt		
5.7L (VIN P) engine:	77 ft. lbs.	105 Nm
5.7L (VIN 8 and VIN J) engines:	40 ft. lbs.	54 Nm
Engine mount-to-cylinder case bolt		
5.7L (VIN 8 and VIN P) engines:	41 ft. lbs.	56 Nm
5.7L (VIN J) engine:	38 ft. lbs.	52 Nm
Engine mount-to-crossmember nut:	40 ft. lbs.	54 Nm
Exhaust manifold		
5.7L (VIN 8) engine:	19 ft. lbs.	26 Nm
5.7L (VIN P) engine:	26 ft. lbs.	35 Nm
5.7L (VIN J) engine		
1990–91:	11 ft. lbs.	15 Nm
1992–94:	18 ft. lbs.	24 Nm
Flywheel/flexplate-to-crankshaft bolts:	74 ft. lbs.	100 Nm
Flywheel-to-converter bolts:	46 ft. lbs.	62 Nm
Flywheel-to-pressure plate:	30 ft. lbs.	41 Nm
Intake manifold		
5.7L (VIN 8) engine		
Intake-to-engine *:	35 ft. lbs.	47 Nm
Intake-to-runners:	25 ft. lbs.	34 Nm
Runners-to-plenum:	25 ft. lbs.	34 Nm
5.7L (VIN P) engine		
Intake bolt/stud		
1st pass:	71 inch lbs.	8 Nm
2nd pass:	35 ft. lbs.	48 Nm
5.7L (VIN J) engine		
Injector housing-to-cylinder head:	20 ft. lbs.	26 Nm
Injector housing-to-plenum:	20 ft. lbs.	26 Nm
* NOTE: Spedification is for alll bolts, except positions 1 and 4. These 2 bolts should be tightened to 45 ft. lbs. (61 Nm)		
Main bearing cap bolts		
5.7L (VIN 8) engine:	80 ft. lbs.	108 Nm
5.7L (VIN P) engine		
Inboard 4-bolt cap:	78 ft. lbs.	106 Nm
All other bolts:	68 ft. lbs.	92 Nm
5.7L (VIN J) engine		
1990–92		
Journals 1, 3 and 5:	30 ft. lbs.	40 Nm
Journals 1, 3 and 5:	+ 45–50 degree turn	+ 45–50 degree turn
Journals 2 and 4:	15 ft. lbs.	20 Nm
Journals 2 and 4:	+ 77½–82½ degree turn	+ 77½–82½ degree turn
1993–94		
Step 1 (all bolts):	15 ft. lbs.	20 Nm
Step 2 (inner bolts):	+ 65–70 degree turn	+ 65–70 degree turn
Step 3 (outer bolts):	+ 50–55 degree turn	+ 50–55 degree turn
Oil pan		
5.7L (VIN 8) engine		
Front and rear corners:	16 ft. lbs.	22 Nm
Remaining bolts:	8 ft. lbs.	11 Nm
5.7L (VIN P) engine		
1992		
Front and rear corners:	17 ft. lbs.	23 Nm
Remaining bolts:	8 ft. lbs.	11 Nm
1993–94		
Front and rear corners:	15 ft. lbs.	20 Nm
Remaining bolts:	8 ft. lbs.	11 Nm

TORQUE SPECIFICATIONS

Component	English	Metric
5.7L (VIN J) engine		
1990		
Front screws:	89 inch lbs.	10 Nm
Bolts:	19 ft. lbs.	26 Nm
1991–94		
Front screws:	106 inch lbs.	12 Nm
Bolts:	23 ft. lbs.	31 Nm
Oil pan drain plug		
5.7L (VIN 8 and P) engines:	16 ft. lbs.	22 Nm
5.7L (VIN J) engine:	38 ft. lbs.	52 Nm
Oil pump attaching bolts		
5.7L (VIN 8 and VIN P) engines:	65 ft. lbs.	88 Nm
5.7L (VIN J) engine:	19 ft. lbs.	26 Nm
Spark plug		
5.7L (VIN 8) engine:	22 ft. lbs.	30 Nm
5.7L (VIN P) engine:	11 ft. lbs.	15 Nm
5.7L (VIN J) engine		
1991:	19 ft. lbs.	26 Nm
Except 1991:	15 ft. lbs.	20 Nm
Starter-to-block bolts		
5.7L (VIN 8 and VIN P) engines:	34 ft. lbs.	47 Nm
5.7L (VIN J) engine:	38 ft. lbs.	52 Nm
Thermostat housing		
5.7L (VIN P) engine:	8 ft. lbs.	10 Nm
5.7L (VIN 8 and VIN J) engines:	25 ft. lbs.	34 Nm
TBI-to-plenum bolts:	18 ft. lbs.	24 Nm
Timing cover		
5.7L (VIN 8) engine:	99 inch lbs.	11 Nm
5.7L (VIN P) engine:	100 inch lbs.	11 Nm
5.7L (VIN J) engine:	20 ft. lbs.	28 Nm
Nuts:	21 ft. lbs.	28 Nm
Bolts:	19 ft. lbs.	26 Nm
Valve (rocker or camshaft) cover		
5.7L (VIN 8) engine:	90 inch lbs.	10 Nm
5.7L (VIN P) engine		
1992:	75 inch lbs.	8 Nm
1993–94:	100 inch lbs.	11 Nm
5.7L (VIN J) engine		
M8 bolts:	15 ft. lbs.	20 Nm
M6 screws:	90 inch lbs.	10 Nm
Water pump		
5.7L (VIN 8 and VIN P) engines:	30 ft. lbs.	40 Nm
5.7L (VIN J) engine:	20 ft. lbs.	26 Nm
Water pump pulley		
5.7L (VIN 8) engine:	22 ft. lbs.	30 Nm
5.7L (VIN J) engine:	89 inch lbs.	10 Nm

BRAKE SPECIFICATIONS

All measurements in inches unless noted.

Year	Model	Master Cylinder Bore	Brake Disc Original Thickness	Brake Disc Minimum Thickness ①	Brake Disc Maximum Runout	Brake Drum Diameter Original Inside Diameter	Brake Drum Diameter Max. Wear Limit	Brake Drum Diameter Maximum Machine Diameter	Minimum Lining Thickness Front	Minimum Lining Thickness Rear
1990	Corvette	—	0.795 ④	0.744 ③	0.006	—	—	—	0.062	0.062
1991	Corvette	—	0.795 ④	0.744 ③	0.006	—	—	—	0.062	0.062
1992	Corvette	—	0.795 ④	0.744 ③	0.006	—	—	—	0.030 ②	0.030 ②
1993–94	Corvette	—	0.795 ④	0.744 ③	0.006	—	—	—	0.030 ②	0.030 ②

① All rotors have a discard dimension cast into them. This is a wear, not refinish, dimension. Only cut rotors to the minimum thickness specification listed here.

② Minimum thickness of lining as measured to pad backing or rivet, as applicable
③ Heavy duty—1.059
④ Heavy duty—1.110

WHEEL ALIGNMENT

Year	Model		Caster Range (deg.)	Caster Preferred Setting (deg.)	Camber Range (deg.)	Camber Preferred Setting (deg.)	Toe-in (deg.)	Axis Inclination (deg.)
1990	Corvette	Front	5½P–6½P	6P	0–1P	½P	1/10N–1/10P	—
		Rear	—	—	½N–½P	0	0	—
1991	Corvette	Front	5½P–6½P	6P	0–1P	½P	1/10N–1/10P	—
		Rear	—	—	½N–½P	0	0	—
1992	Corvette	Front	5½P–6½P	6P	0–1P	½P	1/10N–1/10P	—
		Rear	—	—	½N–½P	0	0	—
1993–94	Corvette	Front	5½P–6½P	6P	0–1P	½P	1/10N–1/10P	—
		Rear	—	—	½N–½P	0	0	—

N—Negative
P—Positive

AIR CONDITIONING BELT TENSION

Year	Model	Engine Displacement Liters (cc)	Belt Type	Specifications New	Used
1990	Corvette	5.7 (5733) (5727 ①)	Serpentine	Automatic tensioner	
1991	Corvette	5.7 (5733) (5727 ①)	Serpentine	Automatic tensioner	
1992	Corvette	5.7 (5733) (5727 ①)	Serpentine	Automatic tensioner	
1993–94	Corvette	5.7 (5733) (5727 ①)	Serpentine	Automatic tensioner	

① ZR-1 Engine

REFRIGERANT CAPACITIES

Year	Model	Refrigerant (oz.)	Oil (fl. oz.)	Compressor Type
1990	Corvette	36.0	8.0	10PA17/10PA20 ①
1991	Corvette	36.0	8.0	10PA17/10PA20 ①
1992	Corvette	36.0	8.0	10PA17/10PA20 ①
1993	Corvette	36.0	8.0	10PA17/10PA20 ①

NOTE: At the time of publication, refrigerant capacity information relating to R-134a was not available from the manufacturer.
① 10PA17 used with Vin J engine (ZR-1)

MAINTENANCE INTERVALS—TYPE A: NORMAL SERVICE
1990-91 Corvette

TO BE SERVICED	TYPE OF SERVICE	VEHICLE MILEAGE INTERVAL (X1000)							
		7.5	15	22.5	30	37.5	45	52.5	60
Oxygen Sensor	I				✔				✔
Ignition Timing	I			✔			✔		
Engine Oil Filter	R①	✔		✔		✔	✔	✔	
Ignition Wires	I			✔			✔		
Spark Plugs	R		✔			✔			
Engine Oil	R	✔	✔	✔	✔	✔	✔	✔	✔
Engine Air Cleaner Element	R			✔			✔		
Crankcase Emission Filter	R			✔			✔		
PCV Valve	R			✔			✔		
Fuel Filter	R			✔			✔		
Charcoal Canister	I			✔			✔		
Fuel/Vapor Return Lines	I			✔			✔		
Fuel Tank Cap and Restrictor	I			✔			✔		
Coolant System	R				✔				✔
Exhaust Pipe and Muffler	I				✔				✔
Manifold Heat Control Valve	I				✔				✔
Catalytic Converter and Shield	I				✔				✔
EGR System	I				✔				✔
Tire Rotation	I②								
Throttle Body Mounting Torque	I	✔							
Drive Belts	I		✔				✔		
Chassis Lubrication	L	✔	✔	✔	✔	✔	✔	✔	✔
Automatic Transmission Fluid	R③								
Oil Maintenance Indicator	I④								
Battery Connections	I		✔		✔		✔		✔
Seat Belt Operation	I		✔		✔		✔		✔

FOR COMPLETE WARRANTY COVERAGE CONSULT INDIVIDUAL VEHICLE MANUFACTURER'S WARRANTY MAINTENANCE GUIDE.

I—Inspect
L—Lubricate
R—Replace
① Replace oil filter at first and every other oil change
② Rotate tires at 7,500 miles and then every 15,000 miles as necessary. Do not rotate tires on the RPO ZR1 performance coupe.
③ Service transmission at 100,000 miles
④ **NOTICE:** When your oil is changed, be sure that the Engine Oil Life Monitor is reset before you drive your vehicle. Reset it whether the **CHANGE OIL** light came on or not. The Engine Oil Life Monitor will not work correctly unless it is reset when the oil is changed.

Resetting the Engine Oil Life Monitor:
a. Turn the key to the **Run** position, but don't start the engine.
b. Press the **ENG MET** button on the Trip Monitor. Within five seconds, press the **ENG MET** button again.
c. Within five seconds of step 2, press and hold the **GAUGES** button on the Trip Monitor. The **CHANGE OIL** light will flash.
d. Hold the **GAUGES** button until the **CHANGE OIL** light stops flashing and goes out. This should take about ten seconds. When the light goes out, the Engine Oil Life Monitor is reset. If it doesn't reset, turn the ignition to **Off** and repeat the procedure.

MAINTENANCE INTERVALS—TYPE B: SEVERE SERVICE
1990-91 Corvette

TO BE SERVICED	TYPE OF SERVICE	VEHICLE MILEAGE INTERVAL (X1000)									
		3	6	9	12	15	18	21	24	27	30
Oxygen Sensor	I										✓
Ignition Timing	I										✓
Automatic Transmission Fluid	R					✓					✓
Ignition Wires	I										✓
Spark Plugs	R										✓
Engine Oil and Filter	R	✓	✓	✓	✓	✓	✓	✓	✓	✓	✓
Engine Air Cleaner Element	R										
Crankcase Emission Filter	R										
PCV Valve	I										✓
Fuel Filter	R					✓					✓
Charcoal Canister	I										✓
Fuel/Vapor Return Lines	I										✓
Fuel Tank Cap and Restrictor	I										✓
Coolant System	R										✓
Exhaust Pipe and Muffler	I										✓
Manifold Heat Control Valve	I										✓
Catalytic Converter and Shield	I										✓
EGR System	I										✓
Throttle Body Mounting Torque	I		✓								
Drive Belts	I										✓
Chassis Lubrication	L		✓		✓		✓		✓		✓
Brake Linings	I					✓					✓
Wheel Bearings	I										✓
Tire Rotation	I①		✓								
Oil Maintenance Indicator	X②										
Seat Belt Operation	I					✓					✓

FOR COMPLETE WARRANTY COVERAGE CONSULT INDIVIDUAL VEHICLE MANUFACTURER'S WARRANTY MAINTENANCE GUIDE.

I—Inspect
L—Lubricate
R—Replace

① Rotate tires at 6,000 miles and then every 15,000 miles as necessary. Do not rotate tires on the RPO ZR1 special performance coupe.

② *NOTICE:* When your oil is changed, be sure that the Engine Oil Life Monitor is reset before you drive your vehicle. Reset it whether the CHANGE OIL light came on or not. The Engine Oil Life Monitor will not work correctly unless it is reset when the oil is changed.

Resetting the Engine Oil Life Monitor:

a. Turn the key to the **Run** position, but don't start the engine.

b. Press the **ENG MET** button on the Trip Monitor. Within five seconds, press the **ENG MET** button again.

c. Within five seconds of step 2, press and hold the **GAUGES** button on the Trip Monitor. The **CHANGE OIL** light will flash.

d. Hold the **GAUGES** button until the **CHANGE OIL** light stops flashing and goes out. This should take about ten seconds. When the light goes out, the Engine Oil Life Monitor is reset. If it doesn't reset, turn the ignition to **Off** and repeat the procedure.

MAINTENANCE INTERVALS—TYPE A: NORMAL SERVICE
1992-94 Corvette

TO BE SERVICED	TYPE OF SERVICE	VEHICLE MILEAGE INTERVAL (X1000)						
		7.5	15	22.5	30	37.5	45	60
Tire Rotation	I③	✔						
Engine Oil Filter	R②	✔		✔		✔		✔
Ignition Wires	I				✔			✔
Spark Plugs	R①							
Engine Oil	R	✔	✔	✔	✔	✔	✔	✔
Engine Air Cleaner Element	R				✔			✔
Crankcase Emission Filter	R				✔			✔
PCV Valve	R				✔			✔
Fuel Filter	R				✔			✔
Charcoal Canister	I				✔			✔
Fuel/Vapor Return Lines	I				✔			✔
Fuel Tank Cap and Restrictor	I				✔			✔
Coolant System	R				✔			✔
Exhaust Pipe and Muffler	I				✔			✔
Manifold Heat Control Valve	I				✔			✔
Catalytic Converter and Shield	I				✔			✔
EGR System	I				✔			✔
Coolant Hoses and Belts	I				✔			✔
Automatic Transmission Fluid	R④							
Brake Linings	I				✔			✔
Throttle Body Mounting Torque	I	✔						
Drive Belts	I				✔			✔
Oil Maintenance Indicator	I⑤							
Chassis Lubrication	L	✔		✔		✔		✔
Battery Connections	I		✔		✔			✔
Seat Belt Operation	I		✔		✔		✔	✔

FOR COMPLETE WARRANTY COVERAGE CONSULT INDIVIDUAL VEHICLE MANUFACTURER'S WARRANTY MAINTENANCE GUIDE.

I—Inspect
L—Lubricate
R—Replace

① Replace spark plugs at 100,000 miles on VIN P, every 30,000 miles on VIN J
② Replace oil filter at first and every other oil change
③ Rotate tires at 7,500 miles and then every 15,000 miles as necessary. Do not rotate tires on RPO ZR1 special performance coupe
④ Service transmission at 100,000 miles
⑤ *NOTICE:* When your oil is changed, be sure that the Engine Oil Life Monitor is reset before you drive your vehicle. Reset it whether the **CHANGE OIL** light came on or not. The Engine Oil Life Monitor will not work correctly unless it is reset when the oil is changed.

Resetting the Engine Oil Life Monitor:
a. Turn the key to the **Run** position, but don't start the engine.
b. Press the **ENG MET** button on the Trip Monitor. Within five seconds, press the **ENG MET** button again.
c. Within five seconds of step 2, press and hold the **GAUGES** button on the Trip Monitor. The **CHANGE OIL** light will flash.
d. Hold the **GAUGES** button until the **CHANGE OIL** light stops flashing and goes out. This should take about ten seconds. When the light goes out, the Engine Oil Life Monitor is reset. If it doesn't reset, turn the ignition to **Off** and repeat the procedure.

MAINTENANCE INTERVALS—TYPE B: SEVERE SERVICE
1992–94 Corvette

TO BE SERVICED	TYPE OF SERVICE	VEHICLE MILEAGE INTERVAL (X1000)									
		3	6	9	12	15	18	21	24	27	30
Oxygen Sensor	I										✔
Tire Rotation	I①		✔								
Brake Linings	I					✔					✔
Ignition Wires	I										✔
Spark Plugs	R②										
Engine Oil and Filter	R	✔	✔	✔	✔	✔	✔	✔	✔	✔	✔
Engine Air Cleaner Element	R										✔
Crankcase Emission Filter	R										✔
PCV Valve	R										✔
Fuel Filter	R					✔					✔
Charcoal Canister	I										✔
Fuel/Vapor Return Lines	I										✔
Fuel Tank Cap and Restrictor	I										✔
Coolant System	R										✔
Exhaust Pipe and Muffler	I										✔
Manifold Heat Control Valve	I										✔
Catalytic Converter and Shield	I										✔
EGR System	I										✔
Coolant Hoses and Belts	I					✔					✔
Automatic Transmission Fluid	R					✔					✔
Throttle Body Mounting Torque	I		✔								
Drive Belts	I										✔
Oil Maintenance Indicator	I③										
Chassis Lubrication	L		✔		✔		✔		✔		✔
Battery Connections	I					✔					✔
Seat Belt Operation	I					✔					✔

FOR COMPLETE WARRANTY COVERAGE CONSULT INDIVIDUAL VEHICLE MANUFACTURER'S WARRANTY MAINTENANCE GUIDE.

I—Inspect
L—Lubricate
R—Replace

① Rotate tires at 6,000 miles and then every 15,000 miles as necessary. Do not rotate on ZR1 special performance coupe.
② Replace spark plugs at 100,000 miles on VIN P, every 30,000 on VIN J
③ **NOTICE:** When your oil is changed, be sure that the Engine Oil Life Monitor is reset before you drive your vehicle. Reset it whether the **CHANGE OIL** light came on or not. The Engine Oil Life Monitor will not work correctly unless it is reset when the oil is changed.

Resetting the Engine Oil Life Monitor:
a. Turn the key to the **Run** position, but don't start the engine.
b. Press the **ENG MET** button on the Trip Monitor. Within five seconds, press the **ENG MET** button again.
c. Within five seconds of step 2, press and hold the **GAUGES** button on the Trip Monitor. The **CHANGE OIL** light will flash.
d. Hold the **GAUGES** button until the **CHANGE OIL** light stops flashing and goes out. This should take about ten seconds. When the light goes out, the Engine Oil Life Monitor is reset. If it doesn't reset, turn the ignition to **Off** and repeat the procedure.

FIRING ORDERS

NOTE: To avoid confusion, always replace spark plug wires one at a time.

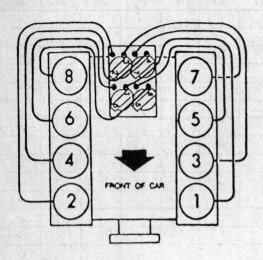

5.7L (VIN J) Engine
Engine Firing Order: 1-8-4-3-6-5-7-2
Distributorless Ignition System

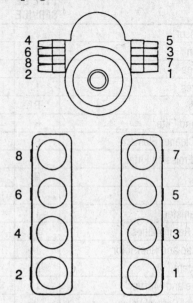

5.7L (VIN P) Engine
Engine Firing Order: 1-8-4-3-6-5-7-2
Distributor Rotation: Clockwise

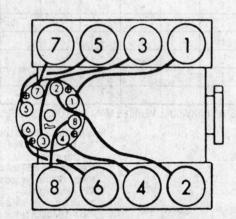

5.7L (VIN 8) Engine
Engine Firing Order: 1-8-4-3-6-5-7-2
Distributor Rotation: Clockwise

CYLINDER HEAD TORQUE SEQUENCES

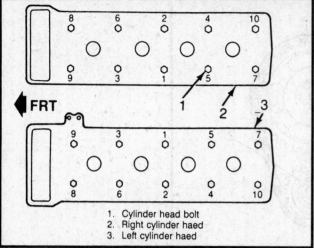

1. Cylinder head bolt
2. Right cylinder haed
3. Left cylinder haed

Cylinder head bolt torque sequence — 5.7L (VIN J) engine

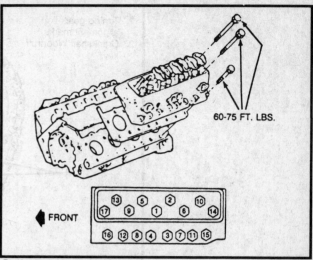

Cylinder head bolt torque sequence — 5.7L (VIN 8) engine

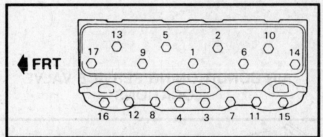

Cylinder head bolt torque sequence — 5.7L (VIN P) engine

TIMING MARK LOCATIONS

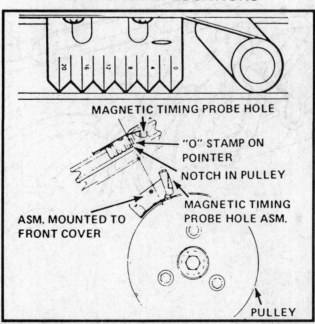

MAGNETIC TIMING PROBE HOLE

"O" STAMP ON POINTER

NOTCH IN PULLEY

MAGNETIC TIMING PROBE HOLE ASM.

ASM. MOUNTED TO FRONT COVER

PULLEY

Timing mark location

TIMING CHAIN ALIGNMENT MARKS

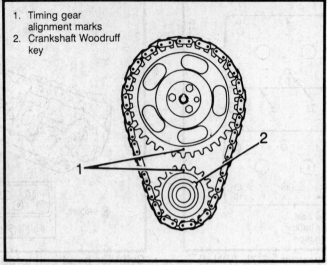

1. Timing gear alignment marks
2. Crankshaft Woodruff key

Timing chain alignment marks

AIR CONDITIONING SERVICE VALVE LOCATIONS

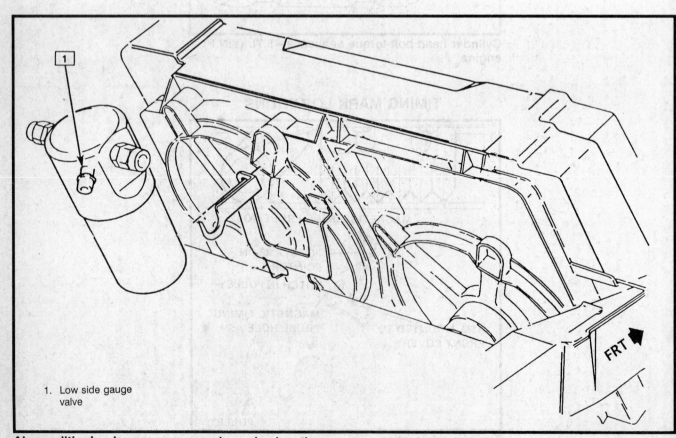

1. Low side gauge valve

FRT

Air conditioning low pressure service valve location

AIR CONDITIONING SERVICE VALVE LOCATIONS

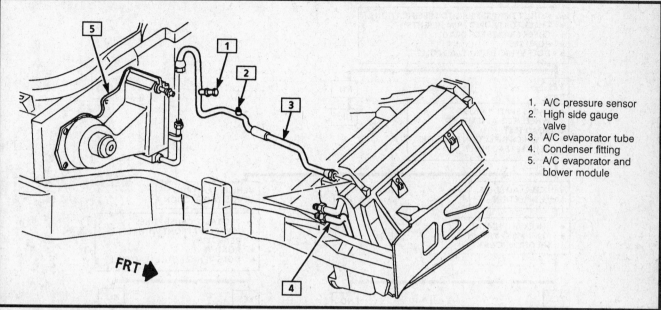

1. A/C pressure sensor
2. High side gauge valve
3. A/C evaporator tube
4. Condenser fitting
5. A/C evaporator and blower module

Air conditioning high pressure service valve location

WHEEL ALIGNMENT ADJUSTMENT LOCATIONS

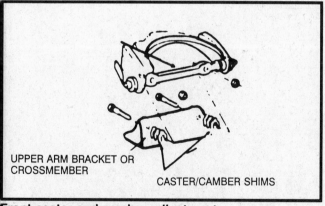

UPPER ARM BRACKET OR CROSSMEMBER

CASTER/CAMBER SHIMS

Front caster and camber adjustment

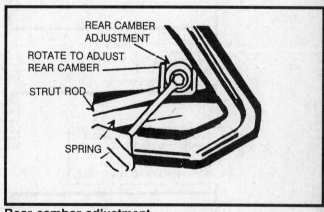

REAR CAMBER ADJUSTMENT

ROTATE TO ADJUST REAR CAMBER

STRUT ROD

SPRING

Rear camber adjustment

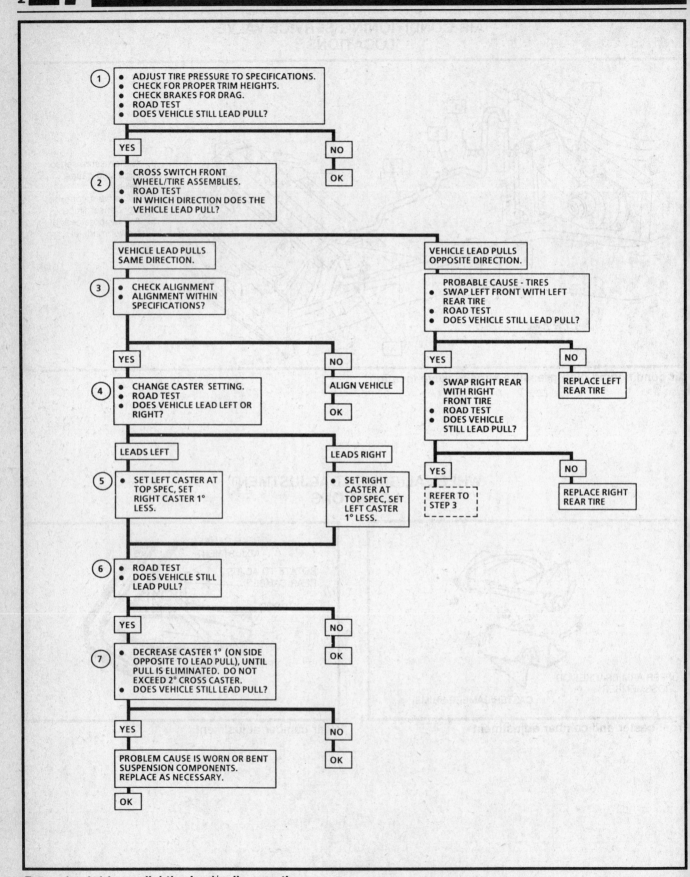

1
- ADJUST TIRE PRESSURE TO SPECIFICATIONS.
- CHECK FOR PROPER TRIM HEIGHTS.
- CHECK BRAKES FOR DRAG.
- ROAD TEST
- DOES VEHICLE STILL LEAD PULL?

YES — NO → OK

2
- CROSS SWITCH FRONT WHEEL/TIRE ASSEMBLIES.
- ROAD TEST
- IN WHICH DIRECTION DOES THE VEHICLE LEAD PULL?

VEHICLE LEAD PULLS SAME DIRECTION.

VEHICLE LEAD PULLS OPPOSITE DIRECTION.

3
- CHECK ALIGNMENT
- ALIGNMENT WITHIN SPECIFICATIONS?

PROBABLE CAUSE - TIRES
- SWAP LEFT FRONT WITH LEFT REAR TIRE
- ROAD TEST
- DOES VEHICLE STILL LEAD PULL?

YES — NO → ALIGN VEHICLE → OK

YES
- SWAP RIGHT REAR WITH RIGHT FRONT TIRE
- ROAD TEST
- DOES VEHICLE STILL LEAD PULL?

NO → REPLACE LEFT REAR TIRE

4
- CHANGE CASTER SETTING.
- ROAD TEST
- DOES VEHICLE LEAD LEFT OR RIGHT?

LEADS LEFT

LEADS RIGHT

YES → REFER TO STEP 3

NO → REPLACE RIGHT REAR TIRE

5
- SET LEFT CASTER AT TOP SPEC, SET RIGHT CASTER 1° LESS.

- SET RIGHT CASTER AT TOP SPEC, SET LEFT CASTER 1° LESS.

6
- ROAD TEST
- DOES VEHICLE STILL LEAD PULL?

YES — NO → OK

7
- DECREASE CASTER 1° (ON SIDE OPPOSITE TO LEAD PULL), UNTIL PULL IS ELIMINATED. DO NOT EXCEED 2° CROSS CASTER.
- DOES VEHICLE STILL LEAD PULL?

YES — NO → OK

PROBLEM CAUSE IS WORN OR BENT SUSPENSION COMPONENTS. REPLACE AS NECESSARY.

OK

Rear wheel drive radial tire lead/pull correction

CHRYSLER CORPORATION/JEEP–EAGLE

Acclaim, Aries, Caravelle, Horizon, Lancer, LeBaron, Omni, Shadow, Spirit, Sundance, TC

GENERAL DESCRIPTION

FRONT WINDSHIELD WIPER AND WASHER

The windshield wipers can be operated with the windshield wiper switch only when the ignition switch is in the **ACC** or **IGN** position. A fuse, located in the fuse block, protects the circuitry of the wiper system and the vehicle.

The wiper motor has permanent magnet fields. The speeds are determined by current flow to the appropriate set of brushes.

The intermittent wipe system, in addition to low and high speed, has a delay mode. The delay mode has a range of 2–15 seconds. This is accomplished by a variable resistor in the wiper switch and is controlled electrically by a relay.

The wiper system completes the wipe cycle when the switch is turned OFF. The blades park in the lowest portion of the wipe pattern.

TESTING

Front Wiper Motor

WILL NOT RUN IN ANY SWITCH POSITION

1. Check for blown fuse in fuse block.
   a. If fuse is good, proceed to Step 2.
   b. If fuse is bad, replace and check motor operation in all switch positions.
   c. If motor is still inoperative and the fuse does not blow, proceed to Step 2.
   d. If replacement fuse blows, disconnect motor wiring connector and replace fuse. If fuse does not blow, motor is defective. If fuse blows, switch or wiring is at fault.
2. Place switch in **LOW** speed position. Listen to motor. If motor cannot be heard running, proceed to Step 3. If it is running, check motor output shaft. If output shaft is not turning, replace motor. If it is turning with drive link to output shaft or linkage is disconnected, replace worn parts.
3. If motor could not be heard running, connect a voltmeter between motor terminal **3** and the ground strap. If there is no voltage or less than 1 volt, move the negative test lead from the ground to the negative battery terminal.
   a. If an increase in voltage is noticed, the problem is a bad ground circuit. Make sure the motor mounting is free of paint and the nuts or bolts are tight.
   b. If there still is no indication of voltage, the problem is an open circuit in the wiring harness or wiper switch.
   c. If no noticeable increase (greater then 3 volts) in voltage is observed, the problem is a faulty motor assembly.

MOTOR RUNS SLOWLY AT ALL SPEEDS

1. Disconnect the wiring harness connector at the motor. Remove the wiper arms and blades. Connect an ammeter between the battery and terminal **3** on the motor.
   a. If the motor runs and average ammeter reading is more than 6 amps, proceed to Step 2.
   b. If the motor runs and average ammeter reading is less than 6 amps, proceed to Step 3.
2. Check to see if the wiper linkage or pivots are binding or caught. Disconnect the drive link from the motor.

   a. If the motor now runs and draws less than 3 amps, repair wiper linkage system.
   b. If motor continues to draw more than 3 amps, replace the motor assembly.
3. Check the motor wiring harness for shorting between high and low speed as follows:
   a. Connect a voltmeter or test light to motor ground strap.
   b. Set wiper switch to **LOW** position.
   c. Connect other lead of voltmeter or test light to terminal **4** of the wiring harness.
   d. If voltage is present, there is a short in the wiring or wiper switch. If no voltage is present proceed to the next step.
   e. Set wiper switch to **HIGH** position.
   f. Move voltmeter or test light lead from terminal **4** to terminal **3** of the wiring harness.
   g. If voltage is present, there is a short in the wiring or wiper switch.

MOTOR WILL RUN AT HIGH SPEED, BUT NOT LOW SPEED
MOTOR WILL RUN AT LOW SPEED, BUT NOT HIGH SPEED

1. If motor will not run on high speed, put the switch in **HIGH** position and connect a test light between motor terminal **4** and ground. If the motor will not run on low speed, put the switch in **LOW** position and connect a test light between motor terminal **3** and ground.
2. If a test light will not turn ON at the motor terminal, there is an open in the wiring or switch. If the test light turns ON at the motor terminal, replace the motor assembly.

MOTOR WILL KEEP RUNNING WITH SWITCH IN OFF POSITION

1. Remove the wiring harness connector. Connect a jumper wire from terminal **1** to terminal **3** of the wiper motor.
2. Connect a second jumper wire from terminal **2** to the battery. If motor runs to the PARK position and stops, the wiper switch is faulty. If the motor keeps running and does not park, replace the motor assembly.

MOTOR WILL STOP ANYWHERE; WIPERS DO NOT PARK

1. Remove the motor wiring connector and clean the terminals. Reconnect electrical connector and clean the terminals. Reconnect electrical connector and test motor. If problem persists, proceed to Step 2.
2. Set wiper switch to **OFF** position. Disconnect motor wiring connector. Connect a voltmeter or test light to the motor ground strap. Connect the other lead to terminal **2** of the wiring connector.
   a. If voltage is not present, check for an open circuit in the wiring harness or wiper control switch.
   b. If voltage is present, proceed to Step 3.
3. Connect an ohmmeter or continuity tester between terminals **3** and **1**.
   a. If there is continuity between these terminals the problem is a defective motor.
   b. If there is no continuity, the problem is an open circuit in the wiper control switch or wiring harness.

Intermittent Function Tests

─── **CAUTION** ───

On vehicles equipped with the airbag restraint system, follow proper procedures to disarm the system when working around the steering column checking or servicing the intermittent wiper module. Failure to do so could cause accidental deployment of the airbag and possible personal injury.

IN DELAY MODE, WIPERS RUN CONTINUALLY WHEN WASH IS OPERATED BUT DO NOT PROVIDE EXTRA WIPE WHEN WASH CONTROL IS RELEASED

1. Turn wipers to **DELAY**. Confirm problem.
2. If wipers run when wash is activated but do not provide extra when wash is released, control unit is defective.
3. Replace the intermittent control unit.

WIPERS START ERRATICALLY DURING DELAY MODE

1. Verify that the ground at the instrument panel is making good connection, free from paint and mounting is tight.
2. Verify that the motor ground strap is making good contact and that the motor mounting bolts are tight.
3. Verify that the wiring ground connections for the intermittent wipe control unit and the wiper switch are tight.

INTERMITTENT WIPE SWITCH CONTINUITY CHART, NON-TILT COLUMN
CHRYSLER CORP. LEBARON LANDAU, SPIRIT, ACCLAIM, OMNI, HORIZON, SHADOW, SUNDANCE

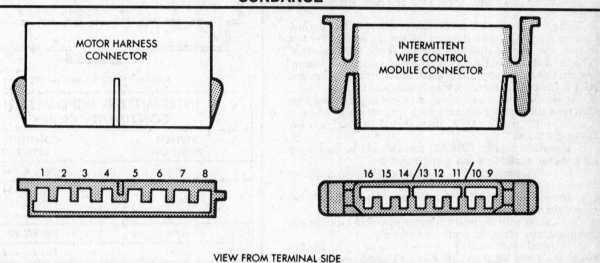

VIEW FROM TERMINAL SIDE

SWITCH POSITION	CONTINUITY BETWEEN
OFF	PIN 1-13, PIN 3-10, PIN 4-11, PIN 5-12
DELAY	PIN 1-13, PIN 3-10, PIN 4-16, PIN 4-11, PIN 4-9, PIN 5-12, PIN 8-15, PIN 9-16, PIN 11-16, PIN 9-11
LOW	PIN 1-13, PIN 3-10, PIN 4-7, PIN 4-11, PIN 5-12, PIN 7-11
HIGH	PIN 1-13, PIN 3-10, PIN 4-6, PIN 4-11, PIN 5-12, PIN 6-11

MULTI-FUNCTION SWITCH CONNECTOR AND INTERMITTENT WIPE CONTINUITY CHART, TILT COLUMN— CHRYSLER CORP. LEBARON LANDAU, SPIRIT, ACCLAIM, OMNI, HORIZON, SHADOW, SUNDANCE

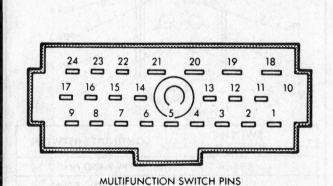

MULTIFUNCTION SWITCH PINS

INTERMITTENT WIPE SWITCH CONTINUITY CHART

SWITCH POSITION	CONTINUITY BETWEEN
OFF	PIN 6 & PIN 7
DELAY	PIN 8 & PIN 9 PIN 2 & PIN 4 PIN 1 & PIN 2
LOW	PIN 4 & PIN 6
HIGH	PIN 4 & PIN 5

*RESISTANCE AT MAXIMUM DELAY POSITION SHOULD BE BETWEEN 270,000 OHMS AND 300,000 OHMS.
*RESISTANCE AT MINIMUM DELAY POSITION SHOULD BE ZERO WITH OHMMETER SET ON HIGH OHM SCALE.

4. If condition is not corrected, replace the control unit.

EXCESSIVE DELAY (MORE THAN 30 SECONDS) OR INADEQUATE VARIATION IN DELAY

1. Variations in delay should be as follows:

a. Minimum delay with control to extreme counterclockwise position before 1st detent: ½–2 seconds.

b. Maximum delay with control to extreme clockwise position before OFF detent: 10–30 seconds.

2. If there is excessive delay or no variations in delay, perform Intermittent Wipe Switch Test.

Intermittent Wiper Switch Test

1. Disconnect the switch wires from the body wiring at the connector.

2. Using a continuity tester or an ohmmeter, test for continuity (no resistance) between the terminals of the switch. For test purposes, the first or clockwise position is the **OFF** position. Next is the slide for the **DELAY** wipe, with counterclockwise rotation reducing the delay. **LOW** is the next detent position and **HIGH** is the full counterclockwise detent position.

3. On vehicles with the multi-function and intermittent wipe switch on a tilt steering column, check for continuity when:

a. In switch position **OFF**, there should be continuity between pin **6 and 7**.

b. In switch position **DELAY**, there should be continuity between pin **8 and 9, 2 and 4 and 1 and 2**.

c. In switch position **LOW**, there should be continuity between pin **4 and 6**.

d. In switch position **HIGH**, there should be continuity between pin **4 and 5**.

4. On vehicles with the intermittent wipe switch on a non-tilt steering column, check for continuity when:

a. In switch position **OFF**, there should be continuity between pin **1 and 13, 3 and 10, 4 and 11 and 5 and 12**.

b. In switch position **DELAY**, there should be continuity between pin **1 and 13, 3 and 10, 4 and 16, 4 and 11, 4 and 9, 5 and 12, 8 and 15, 9 and 16, 11 and 16 and 9 and 11**.

c. In switch position **LOW**, there should be continuity between pin **1 and 13, 3 and 10, 4 and 7, 4 and 11, 5 and 12 and 7 and 11**.

d. In switch position **HIGH**, there should be continuity between pin **1 and 13, 3 and 10, 4 and 6, 4 and 11, 5 and 12 and 6 and 11**.

4. In any wiper mode, if the knob is pushed all the way in, the washer circuit will be completed.

Daytona, Dynasty, Imperial, LeBaron, New Yorker, New Yorker 5th Avenue

GENERAL DESCRIPTION

FRONT WINDSHIELD WIPER AND WASHER

Since the 2-speed functions of all wiper motors are identical, refer to the wiper tests in the preceeding section for diagnosis of problems which do not involve the delay function. If the problem occurs only in the **DELAY** mode, the following tests may be performed.

The intermittent wipe function on vehicles covered in this section is controlled by the body controller located in the passenger compartment behind the right side kick panel.

WIPERS DO NOT COME ON WHEN SWITCH IS IN DELAY POSITION

1. Disconnect the black 25-way connector from the body controller.

2. Place the wiper control switch in maximum **DELAY** position.

MULTI-FUNCTION SWITCH CONNECTOR AND INTERMITTENT WIPE CONTINUITY CHART— CHRYSLER CORP. NEW YORKER, NEW YORKER 5TH AVE., DYNASTY, IMPERIAL

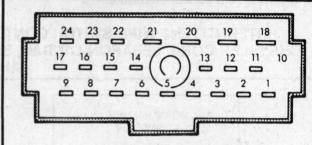

MULTIFUNCTION SWITCH PINS

INTERMITTENT WIPE SWITCH CONTINUITY CHART

SWITCH POSITION	CONTINUITY BETWEEN
OFF	PIN 6 & PIN 7
DELAY	PIN 8 & PIN 9 PIN 2 & PIN 4 PIN 1 & PIN 2
LOW	PIN 4 & PIN 6
HIGH	PIN 4 & PIN 5

*RESISTANCE AT MAXIMUM DELAY POSITION SHOULD BE BETWEEN 270,000 OHMS AND 300,000 OHMS.

*RESISTANCE AT MINIMUM DELAY POSITION SHOULD BE ZERO WITH OHMMETER SET ON HIGH OHM SCALE.

FRONT WIPER CONTINUITY CHART— CHRYSLER CORP. DAYTONA, LEBARON

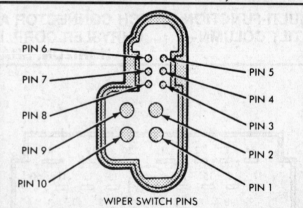

WIPER SWITCH PINS

SWITCH POSITION	CONTINUITY BETWEEN
OFF	PIN 9 AND PIN 10
DELAY	PIN 1 AND PIN 5
LOW	PIN 1 AND PIN 10
HIGH	PIN 1 AND PIN 2

MULTI-FUNCTION SWITCH CONNECTOR AND INTERMITTENT WIPE CONTINUITY CHART — CHRYSLER CORP. LEBARON LANDAU, SPIRIT, ACCLAIM, NEW YORKER, NEW YORKER 5TH AVE., DYNASTY, SHADOW, SUNDANCE, IMPERIAL

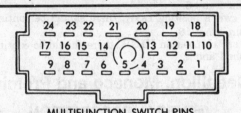

MULTIFUNCTION SWITCH PINS

SWITCH POSITION	CONTINUITY BETWEEN
OFF	PIN 6 AND PIN 7
DELAY	PIN 8 AND PIN 9 PIN 2 AND PIN 4 PIN 1 AND PIN 2 PIN 1 AND PIN 4
LOW	PIN 4 AND PIN 6
HIGH	PIN 4 AND PIN 5
WASH	PIN 3 AND PIN 4

*RESISTANCE AT MAXIMUM DELAY POSITION SHOULD BE BETWEEN 270,000 OHMS AND 330,000 OHMS.

*RESISTANCE AT MINIMUM DELAY POSITION SHOULD BE ZERO WITH OHMMETER SET ON HIGH OHM SCALE.

FRONT WIPER CONTINUITY CHART — CHRYSLER CORP. DAYTONA, LEBARON

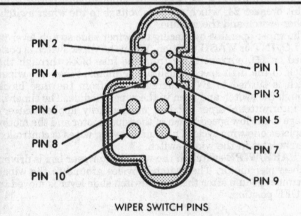

WIPER SWITCH PINS

SWITCH POSITION	CONTINUITY BETWEEN
OFF	PIN 8 AND PIN 10
DELAY	PIN 1 AND PIN 9
LOW	PIN 9 AND PIN 10
HIGH	PIN 9 AND PIN 7

3. Connect the positive lead of a voltmeter to pin **9** of the black connector and the negative lead to the metal case of the body computer.

a. If the voltmeter reads zero, check the control switch and wiring for an open circuit.

b. If the voltmeter reads 10–15 volts, connect the positive voltmeter lead to pin **22** of the black connector and the negative voltmeter lead to a good ground.

c. If the voltmeter reads zero, check the fuses and wiring for an open circuit.

d. If the voltmeter reads 10–15 volts, reconnect the body controller and proceed to Step 4.

4. Connect the positive voltmeter lead to pin **24** of the black connector and the negative lead to the metal case of the body computer. Disconnect the wiring harness from the wiper motor and set the control switch to the minimum delay mode.

a. If the voltmeter reads zero, check the wiring from the intermittent wipe switch to the body controller for an open circuit.

b. If the voltmeter reads 10–15 volts, proceed to Step 5.

5. Connect the voltmeter to pin **L** of the intermittent wiper switch. Place the switch in the maximum **DELAY** position.

a. If the voltmeter reads zero volts, change the intermittent wiper switch.

b. If the voltmeter reads 10–15 volts, check the wiring harness from the intermittent wiper switch to the wiper motor for an open circuit.

6. If all tests have been performed and the problem was not found, the factory recommends replacing the body controller.

WIPERS START TO WIPE BUT STOP BEFORE ONE COMPLETE CYCLE — WIPERS DO NOT RETURN TO PARK

1. Verify that motor will park when the column switch is put in the **OFF** position.

2. Set wiper control switch to maximum **DELAY** and allow motor to run until it stops during the wipe cycle. When the motor stops, disconnect the 25-way black connector from the body computer.

3. Connect the positive voltmeter lead to pin **20** of the black connector and the negative lead to the metal case of the body controller.

a. If the voltmeter reads zero, check wiring for an open circuit.

b. If the voltmeter reads 10–15 volts, proceed to Step 4.

4. Using an ohmmeter or continuity tester:

a. Check for continuity between pins **20** and **24** of the black connector of the body computer.

b. Reverse the ohmmeter leads on pins **20** and **24** of the black connector of the body computer, again checking for continuity.

c. If continuity between pins **20** and **24** is not observed in both Steps a and b, replace the body controller.

EXCESSIVE DELAY OF MORE THAN 30 SECONDS OR INADEQUATE VARIATION IN DELAY

1. Variations in delay should be as follows:

a. Minimum delay with the delay control to the extreme counterclockwise position before the first detent, ½–2 seconds.

b. Maximum delay with the delay control to the extreme clockwise position before the **OFF** detent, 15–25 seconds.

2. If there is excessive delay or no variations in delay, remove the wiper motor wiring harness while the motor is parked, in the **OFF** position.

3. Remove the black 25-way connector from the body controller.

4. Set the wiper control switch to the maximum **DELAY** position.

5. With the ignition switch in the **ON** position, measure the voltage between pin **9** of the black connector and a good ground.

a. If the voltmeter reads zero, proceed to Step 6.

b. If the voltmeter reads 10–15 volts, proceed to Step 7.

6. Set the wiper control switch to minimum **DELAY** position

and measure voltage between pin **9** of the black connector and a good ground. If the voltmeter reads zero, check for an open circuit in the intermittent wipe wiring harness.

7. Remove the wiper motor circuit fuse.

8. Using an ohmmeter, measure the resistance between pins **9** and **22** of the black body controller 25-way connector and the wiper control switch first set to minimum **DELAY** and then maximum **DELAY**.

    a. If the resistance reading at minimum **DELAY** setting is between 0–15 ohms and at maximum **DELAY** setting the resistance is between 240–330 kilo-ohms, replace the body computer.

    b. If the resistance values above are not obtained, replace the wiper control switch.

WIPERS DO NOT RUN CONTINUALLY WHEN WASH CONTROL IS OPERATED DURING DELAY MODE

1. Disconnect the black 25-way connector from the body computer.

2. Using a voltmeter, connect the positive lead to pin **10** of the black connector. Connect the negative voltmeter lead to the body computer metal case.

3. Set the wiper control switch to the DELAY position.

4. Depress the wash switch.

5. If voltage reads zero, check the switch relay and wiring.

6. If voltage is between 10–15 volts, the problem is in the body controller.

IN DELAY MODE, WIPERS RUN CONTINUALLY WHEN WASH IS OPERATED, BUT DO NOT PROVIDE THE FOUR EXTRA WIPES WHEN THE WASH CONTROL IS RELEASED

1. Place wipers in **DELAY** mode.

2. Test system to verify complaint.

3. If wipers do not provide the extra wipes when wash control is released, body controller is defective.

4. Replace the body controller.

WIPERS START ERRATICALLY DURING DELAY MODE

1. Verify that the ground connection at the instrument panel is making a good connection, free of paint and is tight.

2. Verify that the motor ground strap is making good contact and that the motor mounting bolts are tight.

3. Verify that the wiring connections to the body computer, wiper motor and wiper motor switch are tight and free of corrosion.

4. If condition is not corrected after these checks, the problem is with the body controller.

Intermittent Wipe Switch Test

DYNASTY, IMPERIAL, NEW YORKER, NEW YORKER 5TH AVENUE

To test the switch, first disconnect the switch wires from the body wiring in the steering column. Using an ohmmeter, test for continuity between the terminals of the switch.

There should be continuity when:

1. In switch position **OFF**, there should be continuity between pin **6** and **7**.

2. In switch position **DELAY**, there should be continuity between pin **8** and **9**, **2** and **4** and **1** and **2**.

3. In switch position **LOW**, there should be continuity between pin **4** and **6**.

4. In switch position **HIGH**, there should be continuity between pin **4** and **5**.

For test purposes, the first position is the **OFF** position, next is the slide for the **DELAY** wipe. **LOW** is the next detent position and **HIGH** is the full counterclockwise detent position.

In any wiper mode, if the knob is pushed all the way in, the washer circuit will be completed.

DAYTONA, LEBARON

To test the switch, remove the switch pod from the instrument panel. Using an ohmmeter, test for continuity between the terminals of the switch.

There should be continuity when:

1. In switch position **OFF**, there should be continuity between pin **9** and **10**.

2. In switch position **DELAY**, there should be continuity between pin **1** and **5**.

3. In switch position **LOW**, there should be continuity between pin **1** and **10**.

4. In switch position **HIGH**, there should be continuity between pin **1** and **2**.

Medallion, Monaco and Premier

GENERAL DESCRIPTION

Two-speed intermittent electric windshield wipers and electric washers are standard equipment. The intermittent part of the wiper system provides a pause between wipe cycles for use during light rain.

The controls for the windshield wipers on the Monaco and Premier are part of the control switch module mounted on the switch pod located on the left side of the steering column. The Medallion uses a steering column mounted switch.

The electric wipers are operated by moving the wipe switch slide lever to the far side. For intermittent operation move the wiper switch slide lever slightly to the right to the desired intermittent position.

To activate the washer system, push the wiper switch lever knob in. Activating the washer also turns the wiper ON.

The windshield wiper arms and blades must not be moved manually from side to side or damage may result.

The intermittent wiper/washer circuit contains 4 major components—wiper switch, wiper module, wiper motor and washer pump.

The intermittent wiper/washer is supplied with power from circuit breaker 24, which supplies voltage to the wiper switch, washer switch and the module.

The wiper operates by placing the wiper slide switch lever in **HI**, **LO**, **INT** or **WASH** position. When the wiper switch is positioned on **HI**, current flows from the fuse block through the switch to the high speed brush of the motor. When the wiper switch is turned to **INT**, current flows from the fuse block through the switch and then to the wiper module. The timer in the intermittent wiper module momentarily applies battery voltage to the low speed brush of the wiper motor and the motor completes one wipe cycle. The time between wipes is controlled by a rheostat in the wiper switch.

A **PARK/WIPE** switch in the wiper motor gear box is driven by the wiper motor. The switch provides ground to the wiper electronic module after the wiper switch slide lever is moved to the OFF position.

Laser, Summit, Summit Wagon, Talon and Stealth

GENERAL DESCRIPTION

FRONT WINDSHIELD WIPER AND WASHER

Two-speed intermittent electric windshield wipers and electric washers are standard equipment on Laser, Talon, Stealth and Summit Wagon, optional on Summit. The intermittent part of the wiper system provides a pause between wipe cycles for use during light rain.

When the wiper switch is placed in the **LO** position with the ignition switch in the **ACC** or **ON** position, wipers operate continuously at low speed. Placing the wiper switch in the **HI** position causes the wipers to operate at high speed.

When the wiper switch is placed in the **OFF** position, the cam contacts of the wiper motor cause current to flow through the auto wiper stop circuit, allowing the wiper blades to cycle before they reach the stop positions.

When the wiper switch is placed in the **INT** position, with the ignition switch in **ACC** or **ON** position, the intermittent wiper relay is energized, causing the intermittent wiper relay contacts to close and open repeatedly. When the contacts are closed, the wiper motor is energized. When the wiper motor is energized, the relay contacts open; however the cam contacts keep the wiper motor energized until the wiper blades return to the stop position.

When the washer switch is turned **ON**, the intermittent wiper relay contacts close causing the wipers to cycle 2–3 times.

REAR WINDOW WIPER AND WASHER

When the rear wiper switch is placed in the **ON** position with the ignition switch in the **ACC** or **ON** position, the wiper will operate continuously at low speed.

When the rear wiper switch is placed in the **OFF** position, the cam contacts of the wiper motor cause current to flow through the auto wiper stop circuit allowing the wiper blade to cycle before reaching the stop position.

When the rear window wiper switch is placed in the **INT** position with the ignition switch in the **ACC** or **ON** position, the rear intermittent wiper relay is energized causing the rear intermittent wiper relay contacts to close and open repeatedly. When the contacts are closed, the wiper motor is energized. When the rear wiper motor is energized, the rear intermittent wiper relay contacts open. However, the cam contacts keep the rear wiper motor energized until the wiper blades return to their stop position.

FORD MOTOR COMPANY

Delay Wiper System

GENERAL DESCRIPTION

Interval Governor

All vehicles except Capri with interval wipers have a separate electronic governor to activate the wipers at the timed interval selected at the switch. The switch testing procedure includes the governor tests and the governor is available as a replacement part. This unit is always screwed in place and is considered a sensitive electronic device which must be handled carefully when being removed or installed. Before removing the governor, disconnect the negative battery cable.

GOVERNOR LOCATION

On most vehicles, the interval governor is to the left of or above the steering column, attached to the column brace or attached to the rear of the instrument panel in the same area. On the Mark VII, it is attached to the left kick panel above the knee bolster. On the Taurus, Sable and Town Car, it is in the center of the dash panel, below the radio or attached to the center brace.

TROUBLE DIAGNOSIS

- On all vehicles, when trouble shooting the wiper system, test the motor first, then work back towards the switch to test the delay governor, power circuits and the switch itself.
- In most of the tests described here, a volt-ohmmeter is required, although a test light can also be useful. For testing the motor, a 0–15 amp DC ammeter is required.
- When the test calls for a voltage check, the ignition switch must be in the **ON** or **ACC** position.
- When testing for continuity or resistance values, turn the ignition switch to the **OFF** position and/or disconnect the negative battery cable.
- Improper or careless testing can cause permanent damage to the vehicle's electronic circuits and to test equipment. Carefully follow the test equipment manufacturer's instructions.

COMPONENT REPLACEMENT

Testing

WIPER MOTOR

Except Probe and Festiva

NOTE: The motors in these vehicles contain perma-

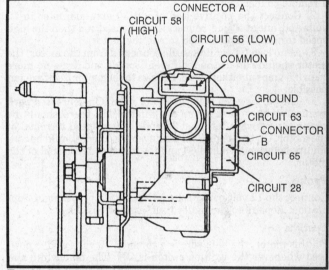

Ford wiper motor Type A

nent magnets made of ceramic, which can shatter like glass if the motor is dropped or hit with a hammer. When removing the wiper motor, handle with care.

1. To test the motor itself for proper operation, unplug the wiring connectors. On motor types A and C, the common terminal is 12 volts and terminals **56** and **58** are grounds for low and

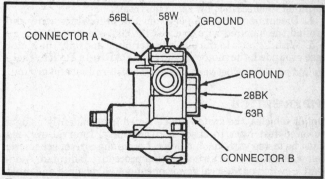

Ford wiper motor Type B

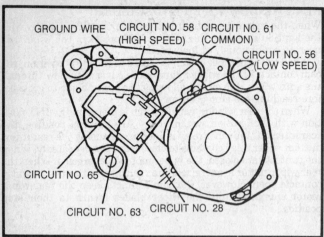

GROUND WIRE   CIRCUIT NO. 58   CIRCUIT NO. 61
(HIGH SPEED)   (COMMON)

CIRCUIT NO. 56
(LOW SPEED)

CIRCUIT NO. 65

CIRCUIT NO. 63   CIRCUIT NO. 28

Ford wiper motor Type C

high speed. On motor type B, the common terminal is a ground and terminals **56** and **58** are 12 volt feeds for low and high speeds. The motor for the Escort is similar to the others but has a remote connector.

2. Connect the positive lead of a 0–30 amp ammeter to 12 volts and, one at a time, connect the low speed and then the high speed terminals as indicated to run the motor.

3. At no load (wiper linkage disconnected from the motor) the motor should run at the 2 different speeds and draw no more than 3.5 amps at either speed. Repairs to the motor itself are not possible.

4. The park switch is in the motor itself. On depressed park systems (wipers park below the windshield), there should be continuity between terminal **65** and the low speed terminal of the motor. On non-depressed park systems, there should be continuity between terminal **63** and the low speed terminal of the motor.

Probe

Connect the 12 volt power source to check for proper motor operation. Repairs to the motor itself are not possible.

Festiva

On this motor, the blue wire is a common 12 volts and is powered whenever the ignition switch is **ON**. The blue/white and blue/red wires are ground circuits for the low and high speeds. The blue/black wire connects to the motor's internal park switch and, when the wipers are in the park position, should have continuity with the blue wire terminal on the motor to feed 12 volts to the wiper switch.

1. To test the motor, turn the ignition switch **OFF** and unplug the wiper motor connector.

2. Carefully use a jumper wire to feed 12 volts to the blue wire terminal on the motor plug.

3. Use a jumper wire to carefully ground the blue/white wire terminal to check for low speed operation.

4. Disconnect the jumper from the blue/white wire and ground the blue/red wire to check for high speed operation.

5. With 12 volts to the blue wire terminal and only the motor case grounded, the motor should go to **PARK**. In **PARK**, there should be 12 volts between the blue/black terminal and ground.

WIPER SWITCH

On all vehicles, the switch can be tested independently using a powered test light to check for continuity. Interval systems must be tested with an ohmmeter. Locate the correct schematic below and follow the switch testing procedure indicated. A defective switch or interval governor cannot be repaired and must be replaced.

WASHER MECHANISM

All vehicles have a washer pump mounted on the washer fluid reservoir. It is a simple 12 volt DC motor that gets current directly from the switch. If the washer does not work, the pump can be tested without being removed by putting 12 volts to a terminal on the pump and grounding the other. The motor should draw 2–4 amps when pumping fluid. The pump can be removed and tested or replaced separately. On some vehicles, the reservoir must be removed to gain access to the pump. This information also applies to vehicles with a rear window wiper/washer.

Removal and Installation

EXCEPT FESTIVA

1. Disconnect the hoses and wires to the pump and, if necessary, drain and remove the fluid reservoir.

2. Carefully pry off the retaining ring without distorting it.

3. Use pliers to carefully grip one wall around the electrical connector and pull the pump, seal and impeller straight out of the reservoir. The impeller may come off but can easily be pushed back on.

To install:

4. Before installing the pump, apply a dry lubricant to the rubber seal to prevent tearing it during installation.

5. When inserting the pump, be sure to align the small tab on the side of the motor housing with the slot in the reservoir.

6. Use a 1 in. socket to press the retaining ring against the motor endplate.

FESTIVA

On this vehicle, the pump is attached to the reservoir with 2 screws. The blue wire feeds 12 volts to the pump whenever the ignition switch is on and the washer switch completes the circuit to ground. The pump can be tested without being removed by putting 12 volts to the terminal farthest from the mounting screw and grounding the other. The motor should draw 2–4 amps when pumping fluid. The pump can be removed and tested or replaced separately but the reservoir must be removed first.

1. Disconnect the negative battery cable. Removing the battery may make this procedure easier.

2. Remove the reservoir filler neck attaching bolt.

3. Remove the cap from the coolant expansion reservoir, remove the nuts the coolant expansion reservoir.

4. Disconnect the washer pump electrical connector.

5. Raise and safely support the vehicle and remove the left front wheel and inner fender splash shield.

6. Detach the hose from the pump and clips and drain the reservoir.

7. Unbolt the reservoir and remove it from the vehicle. The filler neck will stay in fender.

8. Remove the attaching screws and lift the pump out of the reservoir.

To install:

9. Position the filler neck and bolt it in place.

10. Route the washer pump wiring, attach the reservoir to the filler neck and bolt it in place.

11. Attach the hose and electrical connector and clip the hose in place.

12. Reinstall the splash shield, wheel, coolant reservoir and battery and test the system.

CAPRI

General Description

The windshield wiper system used on the Capri is a conventional system with the wiper motor located in the engine compartment and connected directly to the wiper linkage. The motor is a 2-speed permanent magnet non-depressed park type. It is operated by a lever-type switch mounted on the steering column. Intermittent operation is adjustable by a rotary knob mounted on the stalk. One touch operation is achieved by pushing on the control for a single pass. Note that the intermittent control module is located inside the vehicle to the lower left of the underside of the instrument panel.

Testing

When troubleshooting wiper problems, first visually inspect the components. Check for blown 20 amp fuse, loose or corroded connections, damaged wiring harness, damaged wiper motor or switch. Also check for binding wiper arms, damaged wiper motor or linkage or damaged switch.

To aid in troubleshooting, turn the ignition switch **ON**, place the wiper switch in each position and observe if the wiper is functioning. If the problem, such as damaged wires or broken linkage is not evident, use the following list of conditions with their possible causes to start troubleshooting.

WIPERS NOT WORKING

1. Wiper fuse—See Check 1
2. Governor ground—See Check 9
3. Wiper motor ground—See Check 10
4. Electrical circuit—See Check 4

LOW WIPER SPEED NOT WORKING

1. Wiper switch—See Check 5
2. Wiper governor—See Check 8
3. Wiper motor—See Check 12
4. Electrical circuit—See Check 4

HIGH WIPER SPEED NOT WORKING

1. Wiper switch—See Check 5
2. Wiper motor—See Check 12
3. Electrical circuit—See Check 4

INTERMITTENT WIPER SPEED NOT WORKING

1. Wiper switch—See Check 14
2. Wiper governor—See Check 15
3. Wiper motor—See Check 12
4. Electrical circuit—See Check 4

WIPER NOT WORKING WITH WASHER WORKING

1. Wiper motor—See Check 12
2. Wiper governor—See Check 8
3. Electrical circuit—See Check 4

PARK NOT WORKING

1. Wiper switch—See Check 5
2. Wiper governor—See Check 8
3. Wiper motor—See Check 13
4. Electrical circuit—See Check 4

CHECK 1: FRONT WIPER FUSE CHECK

1. Confirm that wipers are inoperative.
2. Check 20 amp wiper fuse
   a. If okay, go to Check 4
   b. If fuse is bad, go to Check 2

CHECK 2: WIPER SWITCH, GOVERNOR AND WIPER MOTOR PARK SWITCH SUPPLY CHECK

1. Replace fuse, confirm fuse is good.
2. Turn ignition switch **ON** and check wiper fuse does not blow.
   a. If fuse is okay, go to Check 4
   b. If fuse is bad, go to Check 3

CHECK 3: WIPER SWITCH, GOVERNOR AND WIPER MOTOR PARK SWITCH SUPPLY SHORT CHECK

1. Turn ignition switch **OFF**.
2. Disconnect **BL** wire connectors from wiper switch, governor and wiper motor.
3. Measure the resistance of the **BL** wire between each component connector, the wiper switch, the governor and wiper motor and ground.
   a. If resistance is greater than 10,000 ohms, go to Check 4.

b. If resistance is not greater than 10,000 ohms, service each affected **BL** wire between the component connector and the fuse.

CHECK 4: CHECK SUPPLY AT WIPER SWITCH, WIPER GOVERNOR AND WIPER MOTOR

1. Access the wiper switch, wiper governor and the wiper motor connectors.
2. Turn the ignition switch **ON**.
3. Measure the voltage on the **BL** wire at the wiper motor connectors.
   a. If the voltage is greater than 10 volts, go to Check 5.
   b. If the voltage is less than 10 volts, service the **BL** wire being checked.

CHECK 5: WIPER SWITCH CHECK

1. Turn ignition switch **OFF**.
2. Disconnect the wiper switch connector and measure the resistance between the **BL** terminal and the following terminals at the switch:
   a. In switch position **OFF**, at all wires the resistance should be greater than 10,000 ohms.
   b. In switch position **INTERMITTENT**, at terminal **BR/W** the resistance should be less than 5 ohms and at all other terminals, the resistance should be greater than 10,000 ohms.
   c. In switch position **LOW**, at terminal **GN** the resistance should be less than 5 ohms and at all other terminals, the resistance should be greater than 10,000 ohms.
   d. In switch position **HI**, at terminal **GN** and **BL/R** the resistance should be less than 5 ohms and at all other terminals, the resistance should be greater than 10,000 ohms.
3. Are the resistances correct?
   a. If the resistances are correct, go to Check 6.
   b. If the resistances are not correct, replace the wiper switch.

CHECK 6: CHECK LEADS BETWEEN WIPER SWITCH AND WIPER GOVERNOR

1. Access the wiper governor.
2. Measure the resistance of the following wires between the wiper switch and the wiper governor: **O, Y/R, GN, BR/W.** On all wires the resistance should be less than 5 ohms.
   a. If the resistances are correct, go to Check 7.
   b. If the resistances are not correct, service the problem wire.

CHECK 7: CHECK WIPER GOVERNOR GROUND

1. Set ohmmeter to read low scale.
2. Measure the resistance of the **BK** wire between the governor and ground. The resistance should be less than 5 ohms:
   a. If the resistances are correct, go to Check 8.
   b. If the resistances are not correct, service the **BK** wire.

CHECK 8: CHECK WIPER GOVERNOR

1. Turn ignition switch **ON**.
2. Disconnect the wiper governor operation by measuring the voltage on the following terminal at the wiper governor connector in the stated wiper switch position.
   a. In switch position **OFF**, at terminal colors **BL/W, BL/BK**, the voltage should be less than 1 volt.
   b. In switch position **LOW**, at terminal colors **BL/W, BL/BK**, the voltage should be greater than 10 volts, less than 1 volt during each cycle.
   c. In switch position **HI**, at terminal colors **BL/W, BL/BK, BL/R**, the voltage should be greater than 10 volts, less than 1 volt during each cycle.
   d. In switch position **INTERMITTENT**, at terminal colors **BL/W, BL/BK**, the voltage should be greater than 10 volts, less than 1 volt during each cycle.
3. Are the voltages correct?
   a. If the voltages are correct, go to Check 9.

b. If the voltages are not correct, replace the wiper governor.

CHECK 9: CHECK HI–SPEED LEAD BETWEEN WIPER SWITCH AND WIPER MOTOR

1. Disconnect the wiper motor connector.
2. Measure the voltage on the **BL/R** wire at the harness connector.
   a. If the voltage is greater than 10 volts, go to Check 10.
   b. If the voltage is less than 10 volts, service the **BL/R** wire.

CHECK 10: CHECK LEADS BETWEEN WIPER GOVERNOR AND WIPER MOTOR

1. Turn the ignition switch **OFF**.
2. Measure the resistance of the **BL/W** and **BL/BK** wires between the wiper governor and the wiper motor.
   a. If the resistance is less than 5 ohms, go to Check 11.
   b. If the resistance is more than 5 ohms, service the problem wire.

CHECK 11: CHECK WIPER MOTOR GROUND

1. Set ohmmeter to low scale.
2. Measure the resistance of the **BK** wire between the wiper motor and ground.
   a. If the resistance is less than 5 ohms, go to Check 12.
   b. If the resistance is more than 5 ohms, service the **BK** wire.

CHECK 12: CHECK WIPER MOTOR

1. Turn the ignition switch **ON**.
2. Turn the wiper switch to the **LOW** position.
   a. If the wipers operate, go to Check 13.
   b. If the wipers do not operate, replace the wiper motor.
3. Turn the wiper switch to the **HIGH** position.
   a. If the wipers operate faster, go to Check 13.
   b. If the wipers do not operate faster, replace the wiper motor.

CHECK 13: CHECK WIPER MOTOR PARK SYSTEM

1. Turn the ignition switch **ON**.
2. Turn the wiper switch to **LOW**.

3. Turn the wiper switch to **OFF** while the wiper is not in the **PARK** position.
4. Measure the voltage on the **BL/W** wire until the wiper reaches the **PARK** position.
   a. If the voltage is greater than 10 volts when not in the **PARK** position, go to Check 14.
   b. If the voltage is not greater than 10 volts when not in the **PARK** position, replace the wiper motor.

CHECK 14: CHECK THE INTERVAL WIPER SWITCH

1. Turn the wiper interval switch to the following positions and measure the resistance of the **Y/R** terminal to the **O** terminal at the wiper switch for each position listed below.
   a. At switch position **SLOW**, the resistance should be 1.5 kilo-ohms, ± 10–15 percent
   b. At switch position **1**, the resistance should be 9.3 kilo-ohms, ± 10–15 percent
   c. At switch position **2**, the resistance should be 7.6 kilo-ohms, ± 10–15 percent
   d. At switch position **3**, the resistance should be 5.8 kilo-ohms, ± 10–15 percent
   e. At switch position **4**, the resistance should be 4.2 kilo-ohms, ± 10–15 percent
   f. At switch position **5**, the resistance should be 2.4 kilo-ohms, ± 10–15 percent
   g. At switch position **FAST**, the resistance should be 750 kilo-ohms
2. If the readings are similar to those listed, go to Check 15.
3. If the readings are not similar to those listed, replace the wiper switch.

CHECK 15: CHECK WIPER GOVERNOR

1. Turn the ignition switch **ON**.
2. Move the wiper switch to the **INTERMITTENT** position.
3. Move the interval switch to the first position. The wipers should operate intermittently. If not, replace the wiper governor.
4. Turn the interval switch to increase the time interval. The length of time between wipe cycles should increase. If not, replace the wiper governor.

TO TEST	Connect Self-Powered Test Lamp or Ohmmeter to Terminals	Move Switch to These Positions	A Good Switch Will Indicate
Wiper Circuit (Interval)	C213 BL/W, (D) *and* C213 BL/BK, (E)	OFF INT LOW HIGH	Closed Circuit* Closed Circuit* Open Circuit Open Circuit
Wiper Circuit (Lo Speed)	C213 BK, (C) *and* C213 BL/W, (D)	OFF INT LOW HIGH	Open Circuit Open Circuit Closed Circuit Open Circuit
Wiper Circuit (Hi Speed)	C213 BK, (C) and C213 BL/R, (F)	OFF INT LOW HIGH	Open Circuit Open Circuit Open Circuit Closed Circuit
Washer Circuit	C213 BK, (C) and C213 BL/R, (A)	OFF ON	Open Circuit Closed Circuit

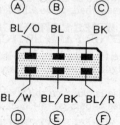

TERMINAL LOCATIONS

WIPER/WASHER SWITCH

(A) (B) (C)
BL/O BL BK

BL/W BL/BK BL/R
(D)   (E)   (F)

Festiva switch test

TO TEST	Connect Self-Powered Test Lamp or Ohmmeter to Terminals	Move Switch to These Positions	A Good Switch Will Indicate
Washer Switch Circuit	BL *and* BL/O	Push Washer Switch / Release Washer Switch	Closed Circuit / Open Circuit
Wiper Switch Circuit	R/Y *and* BK	Lo and Hi positions / All other positions	Closed Circuit / Open Circuit
	BK *and* BL/W	INT / All other positions	Closed Circuit / Open Circuit
	BK *and* BL/R	Hi / All other positions	Closed Circuit / Open Circuit
Interval Time Adjust	R/Y *and* BK	Rotate control clockwise. Ohmeter will show smoothly increasing resistance from 420 - 880 ohms (minimum), to 7,000 - 13,000 ohms (maximum). All positions are closed circuits	

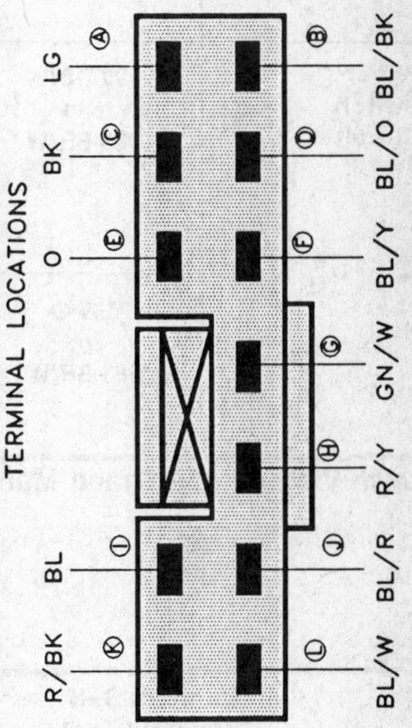

TERMINAL LOCATIONS

LG — BK — O — BL — R/BK

BL/BK — BL/O — BL/Y — GN/W — R/Y — BL/R — BL/W

Probe switch test

TO TEST	Connect Self Powered Test Light or Ohmmeter to Terminals	Move Switch to These Positions	A Good Switch Will Indicate
Washer Switch Circuit	65 DG (B +) *and* 941 BK/W (W)	Pull washer lever .... / Release washer lever	Closed Circuit / Open Circuit
Wiper Switch Circuit	61 Y/R (C) *and* 65 DG (B)	Off .... / Lo .... / Hi	Open Circuit / Closed Circuit / Closed Circuit
	57 BK (G) *and* 58 W (H)	Off .... / Lo .... / Hi	Open Circuit / Open Circuit / Closed Circuit
	61 Y/R (C) *and* 63 R (D)	Off .... / Lo .... / Hi	Closed Circuit / Open Circuit / Open Circuit
	57 BK (G) *and* 56 DB/O (L)	Off .... / Lo .... / Hi	Open Circuit / Closed Circuit / Open Circuit
	28 BK/PK (F) *and* 56 DB/O (L)	Off .... / Lo .... / Hi	Closed Circuit / Open Circuit / Open Circuit

61 Y/R   941 BK/W

56 DB/O   65 DG

C   W
L   H   B
F   G   D   58 W

28 BK/PK   57 BK   33 R

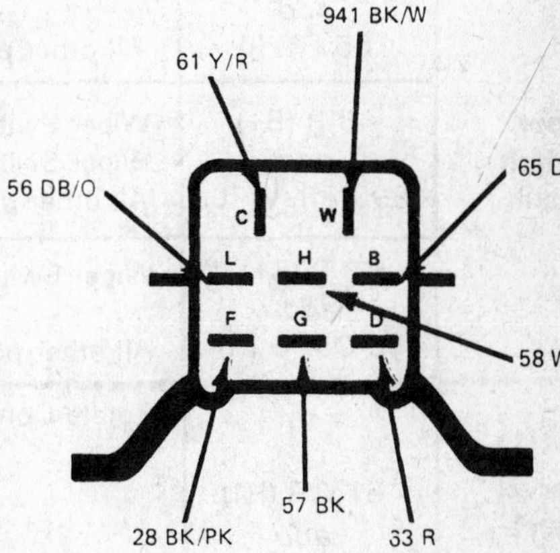

Tempo and Topaz with interval wipers—switch test

TO TEST	Connect Ohmmeter to Terminals	Move Switch to These Positions	A Good Switch Will Indicate
Washer Switch Circuit	590 DB/W and 993 BR/W	Push Washer Lever	Closed Circuit
		Release Washer Lever	Open Circuit
Wiper Switch Circuit	590 DB/W and 993 BR/W	OFF	103.3K
		INT MAX	103.3K
		INT MIN	3.3K
		LO	3.3K
		HI	3.3K
	589 O and 993 BR/W	OFF	47.6K
		INT MAX	11.33K
		INT MIN	11.33K
		LO	4.08K
		HI	O

589 (O) / 188 (W/BK) / 12 (LG/BK) / 590 (DB/W)

15 (R/Y) / 993 (BR/W) / 196 (DB/O)

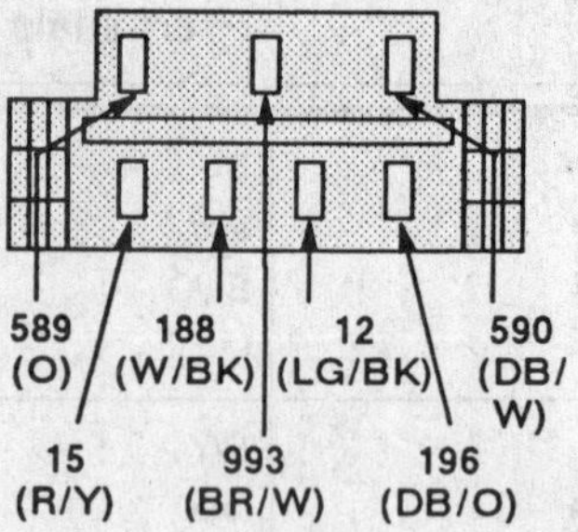

Crown Victoria and Grand Marquis—switch test

TO TEST	Connect Self Powered Test Light or Ohmmeter to Terminals	Move Switch to These Positions	A Good Switch Will Indicate
Washer Switch Circuit	941 BK/W (W) and 63 R (B+)	Pull Washer Lever . . . . Closed Circuit	
		Release Washer Lever . . . . . . .Open Circuit	
	63 R (B+) and 65 DG (I)	Wiper Switch to INT position . Closed Circuit	
		All other positions . . . . Open Circuit	
Wiper Switch Circuit	63 R (B+) and 993 BR/W (L)	Wiper Switch to Lo position . . Closed Circuit	
		Wiper Switch to Hi position . . Closed Circuit	
		All other positions . . . . Open Circuit	
	63 R (B+) and 56 DB/O (H)	Wiper Switch to Hi position . . Closed Circuit	
		All other positions . . . . Open Circuit	
Interval Adjust	61 Y/R (R1) and 589 O (R2)	Rotate Control Clockwise . . . . . Ohmmeter will indicate smoothly increasing resistance from 420/880 Ohms minimum to 7000/13,000 Ohms maximum.	

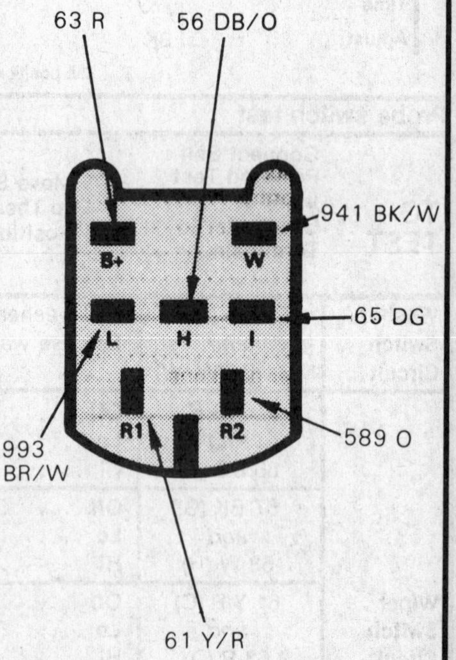

63 R / 56 DB/O

941 BK/W

65 DG

589 O

993 BR/W

61 Y/R

Mustang switch test

TO TEST	Connect Self-Powered Test Lamp or Ohmmeter to Terminals	Move Switch to These Positions	A Good Switch Will Indicate
Washer Switch Circuit	63(R) (B+) and 941(BK/W) (W)	Push in washer switch Release washer switch	Closed Circuit Open Circuit
Wiper Switch Circuit	993(BR/W) (L) and 63(R) (B+)	Lo and Hi All other positions	Closed Circuit Open Circuit
	63(R) (B+) and 65(DG) (I)	INT All other positions	Closed Circuit Open Circuit
	63(R) (B+) and 56(DB/O) (H)	Hi All other positions	Closed Circuit Open Circuit
Interval Time Adjust	589(O) (R2) and 61(Y/R) (R1)	All positions	Rotate control clockwise. Ohmmeter will show smoothly increasing resistance from 420-880 ohms min. to 7000-13,000 ohms max.

Thunderbird and Cougar with interval wipers—switch test

TO TEST	Connect Self-Powered Test Lamp or Ohmmeter to Terminals	Move Switch to These Positions	A Good Switch Will Indicate
Washer Switch Circuit	63 (R) (B) and 941 (BK/W) (W)	(Wiper Switch In LO or HI)	
		Pull Release	Closed circuit Open circuit
Wiper Switch Circuit	63 (R) (B) and 58 (W) (L)	Off Lo Hi	Open circuit Closed circuit Open circuit
	63 (R) (B) and 56 (DB/O) (H)	Off Lo Hi	Open circuit Open circuit Closed circuit
	58 (W) (L) and 28 (BK/PK) (P)	Off Lo Hi	Closed circuit Open circuit Open circuit

Escort without interval wipers—switch test

TO TEST	Connect Self-Powered Test Lamp or Ohmmeter to Terminals	Move Switch to These Positions	A Good Switch Will Indicate
Washer Switch Circuit	590 (DB/W) and 993 (BR/W)	Pull Washer Switch / Release Washer Switch	Closed Circuit (0Ω) / Open Circuit
Wiper Switch Circuit	589 (O) and 933 (BR/W)	Off / Int Max / Int Min / LO / HI	47.6 KΩ / 11.33KΩ / 11.33KΩ / 4.08KΩ / 0 Ω
Interval Time Adjust	590 (DB/W) and 993 (BR/W)	Off / Int Max / Int Min / LO / HI	103.3 KΩ / 103.3KΩ / 3.3KΩ / 3.3KΩ / 3.3KΩ

Terminals: 590 (DB/W), 993 (BR/W), 589 (O), 196 (DB/O), 12 (LG/BK), 13 (R/BK), 15 (R/Y)

Taurus and Sable—switch test

TO TEST	Connect Self-Powered Test Lamp or Ohmmeter to Terminals	Move Switch to These Positions	A Good Switch Will Indicate
Washer Switch Circuit	65 DG (B+) and 941 BK/W (W)	Pull washer switch / Release washer switch	Closed Circuit / Open Circuit
Wiper Switch Circuit	993 BR/W (F) and 56 DB/O (L)	Off / All other positions	Closed Circuit / Open Circuit
	589 O (P) and 57 BK (G)	Off / All other positions	Closed Circuit / Open Circuit
	58 W (H) and 57 BK (G)	HI / All other positions	Closed Circuit / Open Circuit
	56 DB/O (L) and 57 BK (G)	Lo / Int / All other positions	Closed Circuit / Closed Circuit / Open Circuit
Interval Time Adjust	590 DB/W (R) and 57 BK (G)	Int and Off / Lo and HI	Rotate Control clockwise. Ohmmeter Will Show Smoothly Increasing Resistance from 420-880 ohms min. to 7000-13,000 ohms max. / Closed Circuit

Terminals: 56 (DB/O), 58 (W), 57 (BK), 993 (BR/W), 65 (DG), 941 (BK/W), 589 (O), 590 (DB/W)

Continental switch test

TO TEST	Connect Self-Powered Test Lamp or Ohmmeter to Terminals	Move Switch to These Positions	A Good Switch Will Indicate
Washer Switch Circuit	941 (BK/W) (W) and 63 (R) (B)	Pull Release	Closed circuit Open circuit
Wiper Switch Circuit	63 (R) (B) and 65 (DG) (I)	INT All other positions	Closed circuit Open circuit
	63 (R) (B) and 993 (BR/W) (L)	Lo Hi All other positions	Closed circuit Closed circuit Open circuit
	63 (R)(B) and 56 (DB/O) (H)	Hi All other positions	Closed circuit Open circuit
Interval Time Adjust	61 (Y/R) (R2) and 589 (O) (R1)	Rotate Control Clockwise...Ohmmeter will indicate smoothly increasing resistance from 420/880 Ohms minimum to 7,000/13,000 Ohms maximum	

Escort with interval wipers—switch test

TO TEST	Connect Self-Powered Test Light or Ohmmeter to Terminals	Move Switch to These Positions	A Good Switch Will Indicate
Washer Switch Circuit	590 (DB/W) and 993 (BR/W)	Push washer switch Release washer switch	Closed Circuit Open Circuit
Wiper Switch Circuit	589 (O) and 993 (BR/W)	OFF INT LO HI	47.6 K ohms 11.33 K ohms 4.08 K ohms Closed Circuit
Interval Time Adjust	593 (DB/W) and 993 (BR/W)	Int and Off	Rotate Control clockwise. Ohmmeter Will Show Smoothly Increasing Resistance from 33 K ohm min. to 10,660 ohms max.
		LO and HI	3.3 K ohms

Town car switch test

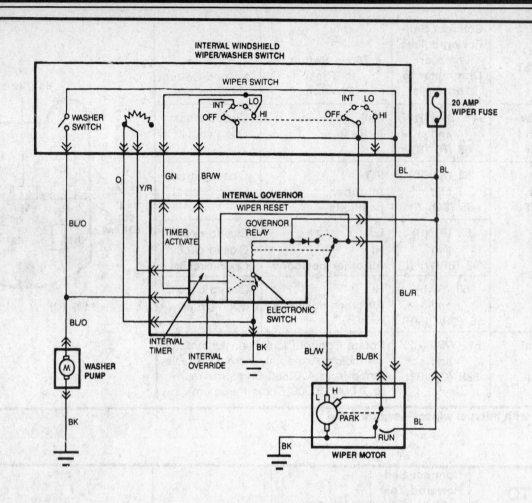

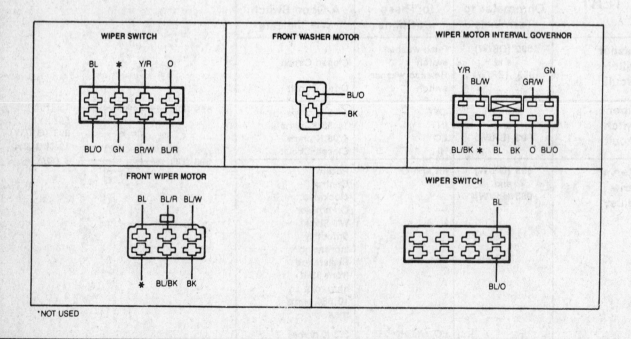

Windshield wiper wiring diagram—Capri

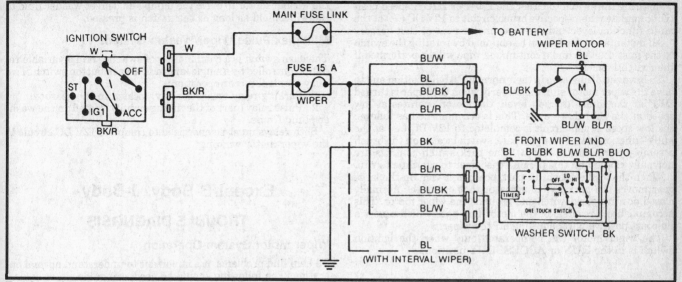

Festiva wiper wiring schematic

GENERAL MOTORS CORPORATION

General Information

General Motors Corporation uses several basic wiper motor types. Most common and used across the entire GM domestic vehicle line, is a round-type motor with 9 terminals. This is a Permanent Magnet Depressed Park (PMDP) windshield wiper-washer system consists of a depressed park wiper motor and an integral flex-vane washer motor packaged in the same unit.

Based on the type of control switch used and whether an optional electronic printed circuit board is attached to the wiper cover, the system can serve as either a pulse-type wiper-washer system or a standard 2-speed type windshield wiper. Pulse timing and demand wash functions are controlled electronically on pulse windshield wipers.

The other basic wiper type has a roughly square-type cover on the motor case. It has 4 terminals and a separate, remote washer motor. This motor is used primarily on J-Body vehicles (Chevrolet Cavalier, Buick Skyhawk and Pontiac Sunbird).

FOUR TERMINAL WIPER MOTOR

Wiper System

This wiper motor is a 2-speed motor designed for a non-depressed wiper park system. It uses a permanent magnet positive park wiper motor with a dynamic brake and separate washer pump assembly.

When equipped for delay or pulse type operation, the pulse windshield wiper and washer system uses a turn signal type wiper/washer switch. The pulse and demand wash functions are controlled by a plug-in printed circuit board enclosed in the wiper's die-cast aluminum housing.

Internal parts such as field magnet, armature, drive gear, park switch actuator and brush holder assembly are enclosed in the aluminum housing. The cover is attached with rivets. A radio interference suppressor is located in the terminal connector on the wiper motor. A strap attached to one of the motor bolt hole grommets provides a ground for the suppressor. An automatic reset-type circuit breaker located on the motor brush

holder assembly protects the motor while a fuse in the fuse block protects the vehicle wiring.

Power and control are through a 4-terminal connector. Use care when disconnecting the lock-type connectors that attach the vehicle wiring to the wiper.

The wiper motor has 3 brushes: common, low speed and high speed. When the ignition switch is **ON**, a 12V (+) circuit is applied to both the low and high speed fixed contacts in the multi-function lever. The low and high speed brushes are connected to the multi-function lever through terminals **C** and **D**. The armature is grounded through the common brush via the ground strap.

Washer System

The washer system consists of a solvent container, pump, washer hose and nozzle.

The fluidic washer system is controlled by a small plastic element designed into the washer nozzle. As water is forced through this insert, the design of the mechanism creates an oscillating power stream, designed to more widely disperse the washer fluid for better cleaning. A correctly operating wiper-washer system has a spray pattern that cleans 75 percent of the wipe pattern within 10 wiper cycles.

If the nozzle becomes plugged, apply air pressure. If nozzle remains plugged, the nozzle must be replaced. If the spray pattern is too low or too high on the windshield, wedge-type adjustment shims can be used. Placement of a shim under the nozzle mounting bracket will raise the pattern about 3 degrees. Reverse installation of the same shim will lower the pattern 3 degrees.

WIPER AND WASHER OPERATION

The electronic printed circuit board controls all the timing and washer commands. When the wash button is pushed for more than 0.3 second, a demand wash is performed in 1.5 second intervals for as long as the button is held, followed by approximately 6 seconds of dry wipes and a shut off.

Rotating the switch to either the **LOW** or **HIGH** speed position completes the respective brush circuit to 12V DC (+) at the multi-function lever and the wiper motor runs at that speed.

An instantaneous wipe can be obtained by rotating the switch to the mist position and a continuous wipe will be performed if the switch is held.

To have the blades stop in their normal **PARK** position and to have the wiper motor shut off properly when the wiper is turned **OFF** at the multi-function lever, the motor operates at low speed at the shut-down cycle. This is accomplished as follows: the low speed brush circuit is completed to 12V DC (+) at the multi-function lever through a park switch located on the brush assembly (terminals **A** and **B**). The park switch contacts are normally closed and this permits the wiper to continue to run.

When the blades reach the park position, a cam on the large gear moves the park switch actuator that opens the normally closed positive park switch and grounds the wiper motor. This accomplishes a reversal of the motor flux path which causes a no-coast positive park, shutting off the wiper.

The wiper motor can be operated only when the ignition switch is in the **RUN** or **ACCESSORY** position.

Nine Terminal Wiper Motor

GENERAL INFORMATION

The basic 9-terminal windshield wiper/washer system is available in several configurations. On some vehicles, such as 1989–90 B-Body vehicles, it consists of a depressed park wiper motor and an integral washer motor packaged in the same unit. On other vehicles, the washer pump is mounted remotely on the solvent container.

Depending on the type of control switch used and whether an optional electronic printed circuit board is attached to the wiper cover, the system can serve as either a pulse-type wiper/washer system or a standard type 2-speed windshield wiper. Pulse timing and demand wash functions are controlled electronically on pulse windshield wipers.

Standard wound field (non-pulse) motors are about 4½ in. (114mm) in length. The motor and gearbox assembly electrical leads (black and black with pink stripe) are routed internally through a cavity in the gearbox casting. These leads, formerly exposed on a past model design, are routed through a grommet in the motor casting.

Both standard system and multiplex pulse system styles use similar motors. Multiplex pulse wipers use a green pulse relay case. Multiplex pulse wipers can also be identified by a single electrical lead (black with pink stripe wire) leading to the timing circuit.

The multiplex pulse wiper system provides a controlled wiping action. It uses a wound field motor and wiper blades that park below the hoodline. The wiper switch in the **DELAY** mode can be turned from a **MIN** (minimum) to a **MAX** (maximum) position. Turning the control knob from the **MIN** to **MAX** position varies the amount of time the wiper will delay between each wipe. The delay ranges between 0–12 seconds depending on the position of the knob. Minimum delay or 0 seconds between wipes provides the equivalent of low speed continuous operation.

WIPER AND WASHER OPERATION

Standard Wiper/Washer System

The standard system is controlled by the multi-function lever switch and the wipers can be driven at 2 speeds, either **HIGH** or **LOW**. When pushed, the **WASH** switch on the lever energizes the washer motor to drive the pump and deliver washer fluid to the windshield as long as the switch is pressed.

Multiplex Pulse Wiper/Washer System

The dash switch is a combination of switches and a variable resistor controlled by a single knob and a wash button switch. Two relays control motor operation:
1. Parking relay (gearbox relay) located in the gearbox.
2. Pulse relay (part of the timing circuit) located on the washer pump frame.

Both relays must be energized to complete 12V DC circuit to the wiper motor windings.

Except B-Body, J-Body

TROUBLE DIAGNOSIS

Wiper Motor System Operation

To help find problems, it's important to understand normal operation. The following should be used as a guide:
1. With the ignition switch in **ACCY** or **RUN**, press the washer switch to **ON** for less than 1 second. Look for:
    a. Normal operation is for the washer to spray the windshield for approximately 2½ seconds.
    b. The wiper should run at low speed and continue to run at low speed until the washer button is released.
    c. After the button is released, wipers run for approximately 6 seconds and then return to park.
2. With the wiper switch turned to **PULSE** or Delay Mode, look for:
    a. Wipers should make 1 complete stroke, then pause for 0–25 seconds before making the next stroke.
    b. The wait time should be adjustable by turning the wiper switch through the delay range.
3. With the wiper switch in **PULSE**, hold the washer switch ON for 1–2 seconds. Look for:
    a. Washer should spray windshield as long as washer button is held **ON**.
    b. Pulse function is overridden and the wipers run at low speed during the spray period.
    c. After the washer stops, the wipers continue to run for 6 seconds.
    d. Wipers return to Pulse operation.
4. With the wiper switch in **HIGH**, hold the washer switch for 1–2 seconds. Look for: Same operation at low speed wash except that wipers run at high speed.
5. Turn wiper switch to **LOW**. Look for: Wipers should run continuously at low speed.
6. Turn wiper switch to **HIGH**. Look for: Wipers should run continuously at high speed.
7. Turn wiper switch **OFF**. Look for: Wipers should return to the park position at low speed, then shut off.
8. Turn the wiper switch to **MIST**. Look for: Wipers should make 1 complete stroke and then park.
In addition, check the following:
1. Check the wiper fuse.
2. Check that the wiper/washer switch connector and wiper/washer motor connectors are mated correctly.
3. If the washer does not operate check that:
    a. The washer reservoir is filled.
    b. The hoses are not pinched or kinked.
    c. The hoses are correctly attached.
    d. The nozzles are not clogged.
4. If the wipers cycle in and out of park position in **HIGH** but do not operate in **LOW**, **MIST** or **PULSE**, check the yellow wire of an open.
5. If the wiper motor runs but the wiper blades do not, check the wiper linkage at the wiper crank arm.

NOTE: THE FOLLOWING PROCEDURES ASSUME THAT THE TECHNICIAN HAS CHECKED THE FOLLOWING:

1. CONTINUITY OF ALL HARNESS WIRES
2. WIPER MOTOR TO DASH MOUNTING SCREWS TIGHT
3. FUSES

WIPER MOTOR

CHECK FOR MOTOR OPERATION BEFORE REMOVING FROM VEHICLE. DISCONNECT ALL WIRING FROM WIPER AND PERFORM THE FOLLOWING CHECKS IN THIS ORDER:

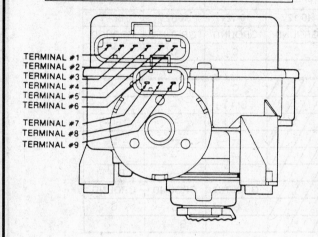

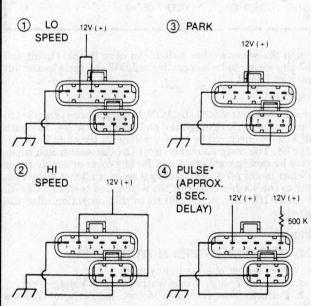

IF WIPER MOTOR FUNCTIONS IN ALL MODES, GO TO WIPER/WASHER SWITCH CHECK CHART.

*IF A STANDARD TYPE MOTOR IS WIRED FOR THE PULSE CHECK, THE PARK RELAY WILL CLICK SHUT BUT THERE WILL BE NO OBSERVABLE MOTOR ACTION.

Terminal identification for wiper system on-car check—9-terminal wiper motor, Corsica/Beretta shown, but typical of G.M. non–B-Body vehicles

CHECK FOR WASHER PUMP OPERATION BEFORE REMOVING FROM VEHICLE. REMOVE COVER HARNESS CONNECTOR AND APPLY 12V(+) TO #4 TERMINAL OF WIRING HARNESS, GROUND #5 TERMINAL AS SHOWN.

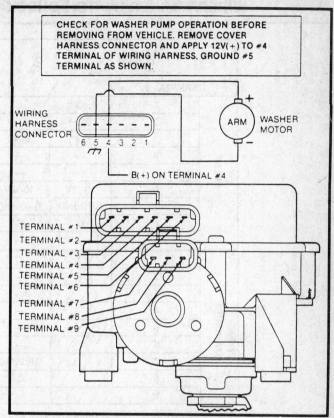

Terminal identification for washer pump on-car check—9-terminal wiper motor, Corsica/Beretta shown, but typical of G.M. non–B-Body vehicles

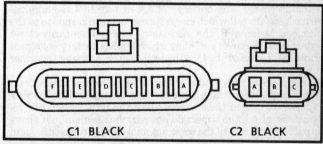

Wiper motor assembly electrical connectors—9-terminal wiper motor—General Motors

Circuit Operation

In addition to the features of a conventional non-pulse wiper system (2-speed, low and high) the pulse-type windshield wiper/washer system includes an operating mode in which the wipers make a single stroke with an adjustable time interval between strokes. The time interval is controlled by a solid state timer in the wiper motor assembly. The duration of the delay interval is determined by the delay rheostat in the wiper switch assembly.

The wiper motor is protected by a circuit breaker. If the wipers are blocked (by snow or ice, for example) the circuit breaker will open the circuit. The circuit breaker resets automatically when it cools.

PULSE OPERATION

With the wiper/washer switch in **PULSE**, battery voltage is applied to the wiper motor assembly at terminal **B** of connector C1

WIPER/WASHER SWITCH CHECK CHART – STANDARD AND PULSE

SWITCH MODE / TERMINAL #	MIST	OFF	PULSE	LO	HI †	WASH
PULSE 1	C	C	C	C	C	C
2	B(+)	—	B(+)	B(+)	—	*B(+)
3	B(+)	B(+)	—	B(+)	—	*B(+)
4	—					
5	—					
6	10-12V	10-12V	10-12V	10-12V	10-12V	B(+)
7	GROUND	GROUND	GROUND	GROUND	GROUND	GROUND
8	C	C	C	C	C	C
9	—	—	—	—	B(+)	—
STANDARD 1		C		C	C	C
2		—		B(+)	—	*B(+)
3		B(+)		B(+)	—	*B(+)
4						
5						
6		—		—	—	B(+)
7		GROUND		GROUND	GROUND	GROUND
8		C		C	C	C
9		—		—	B(+)	—

C = CONTINUITY   † TERMINALS #2 & #3 CONNECTED TOGETHER.   *EXCEPT ON HI.

through the gray wire. Voltage is also applied to terminal **F** through the pink wire and the pulse delay resistor in the wiper switch assembly. The battery voltage at terminal **B** energizes the park switch coil which closes its contacts. In response to the voltage at terminal **F**, the solid state timer momentarily closes contact **A** on the cover assembly which applies battery voltage at terminal **B** to the contacts of the park switch, starting the wiper motor.

A mechanical arm (end of sweep input) operates contacts on the cover assembly which cause contact **A** to open when the wipers have completed their sweep. Since the park switch coil remains energized, the wipers do not park but remain just above the park position until the cover assembly closes contact **A** again to start another sweep.

The length of delay time between sweeps is controlled by the variable pulse delay resistor. The delay is adjustable from 0–25 seconds.

LOW SPEED

With the wiper switch in **LOW**, battery voltage is applied at the wiper motor assembly connector C1, terminals **B** and **C** through the dark green and gray wires. The park switch coil is again energized and battery voltage is applied to the park switch contacts and the wiper motor which runs continuously.

HIGH SPEED

With the wiper switch in **HIGH**, battery voltage is applied directly to the wiper motor at terminal **A** without passing through the park switch contacts. Terminal **A** is connected to a separate wiper motor brush for high speed operation. The park switch coil remains energized in the **HIGH** position because of the voltage that is present at the low speed wiper motor brush when voltage is applied to the high speed brush. The current path from the low speed brush to the park switch coil is completed

through the wiper/washer switch. An open in this circuit will cause the wipers to be inoperative in **LOW** and cycle in and out of park in **HIGH**.

WASHER

When the washer switch is held ON, battery voltage is applied to the cover assembly through the pink and gray wires. The park switch coil is energized by battery voltage at terminal **B** of connector C1. The cover assembly turns ON the washer and wiper motors by closing contacts **A** and **B**. The cover assembly turns the wiper motor off approximately 6 seconds after it interrupts power to the washer motor. If the wipers had been in **PULSE**, **LO** or **HIGH**, they would return to that operation after the wash cycle.

Testing

SYMPTOM TEST – WIPER MOTOR: PULSE

1. Wipers do not operate in any mode
   a. Perform Test A: Wiper/Washer Switch Voltage Test
   b. Perform Test B: Wiper Motor Module Input Voltage Test
   c. Perform Test E: Wiper Motor Module Current Draw Test
2. Wipers run at **LOW** speed only (no HIGH speed). Perform Test B: Wiper Motor Module Input Voltage Test
3. Wipers cycle in and out of park when in **HIGH**
   a. Perform Test B: Wiper Motor Module Input Voltage Test
   b. Perform Test C: Wiper Motor Module Resistance Test
4. Wipers cycle in and out of park when in **OFF** and operate in **LOW**. Replace the Park Switch.
5. Wipers will not shut off. Perform Test B: Wiper Motor Module Input Voltage Test.

6. No delay in **PULSE** mode or **PULSE** mode does not operate correctly
    a. Perform Test B: Wiper Motor Module Input Voltage Test
    b. Perform Test D: Wiper/Washer Pulse Control Resistance Test
7. Wipers operate very slowly or intermittently. Perform Test E: Wiper Motor Module Current Draw Test
8. Wipers do not park. Perform Test F: Complete Mechanical Inspection
9. Washer will not operate or runs continuously
    a. Perform Test B: Wiper Motor Module Input Voltage Test
    b. Perform Test G: Washer Motor Voltage Test
10. Wipers stay in delay during wash cycle. Replace cover assembly.

Troubleshooting Tests

TEST A: WIPER/WASHER SWITCH VOLTAGE TEST

1. Measure the voltage at the wiper/washer switch connector (disconnected).
2. Turn the ignition switch to **ACCY**.
3. Measure the voltage between terminal **D** of the white wire and ground. It should read battery voltage.
    a. If voltage is correct, recheck symptoms.
    b. If no voltage is present, check the white wire and the wiper fuse for an open.

TEST B: WIPER MOTOR MODULE INPUT VOLTAGE TEST

1. Measure the voltage at the wiper motor module connectors C1 and C2 (disconnected).
2. Turn the ignition switch to **ACCY**.
3. With the wiper switch in position **OFF**, connect between connector C2, terminal **A** (purple wire) and ground.
    a. There should be no voltage.
    b. If there is voltage, check the associated wiring for a short to voltage.
    c. If wiring is good, replace the wiper/washer switch.
4. With the wiper switch in position **OFF**, connect between connector C1, terminal **B** (gray wire) and ground.
    a. There should be no voltage.
    b. If there is voltage, check the associated wiring for a short to voltage.
    c. If wiring is good, replace the wiper/washer switch.
5. With the wiper switch in position **OFF**, connect between connector C1, terminal **C** (dark green wire) and ground.
    a. There should be battery voltage.
    b. If there is no voltage, check the associated wiring to the wiper/washer switch for an open or short to ground.
    c. If the wiring is good, replace the wiper/washer switch.
6. With the wiper switch in position **OFF**, connect between connector C1, terminal **F** (pink wire) and ground.
    a. There should be battery voltage.
    b. If there is no voltage, check the associated wiring to the wiper/washer switch for an open or short to ground.
    c. If the wiring is good, replace the wiper/washer switch.
7. With the wiper switch in position **MIST**, connect between connector C2, terminal **A** (purple wire) and ground.
    a. There should be no voltage.
    b. If there is voltage, check the associated wiring for a short to voltage.
    c. If wiring is good, replace the wiper/washer switch.
8. With the wiper switch in position **MIST**, connect between connector C1, terminal **B** (gray wire) and ground.
    a. There should be battery voltage.
    b. If there is no voltage, check the associated wiring for an open or a short to ground.
    c. If the wiring is good, replace the wiper/washer switch.

9. With the wiper switch in position **MIST**, connect between connector C1, terminal **C** (dark green wire) and ground.
    a. There should be battery voltage.
    b. If there is no voltage, check the associated wiring for an open or a short to ground.
    c. If the wiring is good, replace the wiper/washer switch.
10. With the wiper switch in position **MIST**, connect between connector C1, terminal **F** (pink wire) and ground.
    a. There should be battery voltage.
    b. If there is no voltage, check the associated wiring for an open or a short to ground.
    c. If the wiring is good, replace the wiper/washer switch.
11. With the wiper switch in position **PULSE**, connect between connector C2, terminal **A** (purple wire) and ground.
    a. There should be no voltage.
    b. If there is voltage, check the associated wiring for a short to voltage.
    c. If wiring is good, replace the wiper/washer switch.
12. With the wiper switch in position **PULSE**, connect between connector C1, terminal **B** (gray wire) and ground.
    a. There should be battery voltage.
    b. If there is no voltage, check the associated wiring for an open or a short to ground.
    c. If the wiring is good, replace the wiper/washer switch.
13. With the wiper switch in position **PULSE**, connect between connector C1, terminal **C** (dark green wire) and ground.
    a. There should be no voltage.
    b. If there is voltage, check the associated wiring for a short to voltage.
    c. If wiring is good, replace the wiper/washer switch.
14. With the wiper switch in position **PULSE**, connect between connector C1, terminal **F** (pink wire) and ground.
    a. There should be battery voltage.
    b. If there is no voltage, check the associated wiring for an open or a short to ground.
    c. If the wiring is good, replace the wiper/washer switch.
15. With the wiper switch in position **LOW**, connect between connector C2, terminal **A** (purple wire) and ground.
    a. There should be no voltage.
    b. If there is voltage, check the associated wiring for a short to voltage.
    c. If wiring is good, replace the wiper/washer switch.
16. With the wiper switch in position **LOW**, connect between connector C1, terminal **B** (gray wire) and ground.
    a. There should be battery voltage.
    b. If there is no voltage, check the associated wiring for an open or a short to ground.
    c. If the wiring is good, replace the wiper/washer switch.
17. With the wiper switch in position **LOW**, connect between connector C1, terminal **C** (dark green wire) and ground.
    a. There should be battery voltage.
    b. If there is no voltage, check the associated wiring for an open or a short to ground.
    c. If the wiring is good, replace the wiper/washer switch.
18. With the wiper switch in position **LOW**, connect between connector C1, terminal **F** (pink wire) and ground.
    a. There should be battery voltage.
    b. If there is no voltage, check the associated wiring for an open or a short to ground.
    c. If the wiring is good, replace the wiper/washer switch.
19. With the wiper switch in position **HIGH**, connect between connector C2, terminal **A** (purple wire) and ground.
    a. There should be battery voltage.
    b. If there is no voltage, check the associated wiring for an open or a short to ground.
    c. If the wiring is good, replace the wiper/washer switch.
20. With the wiper switch in position **HIGH**, connect between connector C1, terminal **B** (gray wire) and ground.
    a. There should be no voltage.
    b. If there is voltage, check the associated wiring for a short to voltage.

c. If wiring is good, replace the wiper/washer switch.

21. With the wiper switch in position **OFF** and washer switch **ON**, connect between connector C2, terminal **A** (purple wire) and ground.

    a. There should be no voltage.

    b. If there is voltage, check the associated wiring for a short to voltage.

    c. If wiring is good, replace the wiper/washer switch.

22. With the wiper switch in position **OFF** and washer switch **ON**, connect between connector C1, terminal **B** (gray wire) and ground.

    a. There should be battery voltage.

    b. If there is no voltage, check the associated wiring for an open or a short to ground.

    c. If the wiring is good, replace the wiper/washer switch.

23. With the wiper switch in position **OFF** and washer switch **ON**, connect between connector C1, terminal **C** (dark green wire) and ground.

    a. There should be battery voltage.

    b. If there is no voltage, check the associated wiring for an open or a short to ground.

    c. If the wiring is good, replace the wiper/washer switch.

24. With the wiper switch in position **OFF** and washer switch **ON**, connect between connector C1, terminal **F** (pink wire) and ground.

    a. There should be battery voltage.

    b. If there is no voltage, check the associated wiring for an open or a short to ground.

    c. If the wiring is good, replace the wiper/washer switch.

    d. If all measurements are correct and the wiper motor is ON all the time, replace the cover assembly. Otherwise, review symptoms.

TEST C: WIPER MOTOR MODULE RESISTANCE TEST

1. Measure the resistance at the wiper motor assembly connectors C1 and C2 (disconnected).

2. Turn the ignition switch **OFF** and the wiper switch to **HIGH**. Measure the resistance between connector C1, terminal **C** of the dark green wire and terminal **B** of the gray wire. It should read less than 0.5 ohms.

    a. If resistance is not as specified, check the dark green wire and gray wire for a short to ground, to each other or opens.

    b. If wires are okay, replace wiper switch assembly.

3. Turn the ignition switch **OFF** and the wiper switch to **OFF, PULSE**. Measure the resistance between connector C1, terminal **C** of the dark green wire and terminal **B** of the gray wire. It should read infinite resistance.

    a. If resistance is not as specified, check the dark green wire and gray wire for a short to ground, to each other or opens.

    b. If wires are okay, replace wiper switch assembly.

4. Turn the ignition switch **OFF** and the wiper switch to **OFF, PULSE**. Measure the resistance between connector C1, terminal **A** of the yellow wire which is a jumper between the connectors and connector C2, terminal **B** of the other end of the yellow wire. It should read less than 0.5 ohms. If resistance is not as specified, check the yellow wire an open.

5. Turn the ignition switch **OFF** and the wiper switch to **OFF, PULSE**. Measure the resistance between connector C1, terminal **A** of the yellow wire and ground. It should read infinite resistance. If resistance is not as specified, check the yellow wire for a short to ground.

TEST D: WIPER/WASHER PULSE CONTROL RESISTANCE TEST

1. Measure the resistance at the wiper motor assembly connector C1 (disconnected).

2. Turn the ignition switch **OFF**, disconnect the negative battery cable and turn the wiper switch to **LOW**. Measure the

resistance between terminal **B** of the gray wire and terminal **F** of the pink wire. It should read approximately 24 kilo-ohms.

    a. If resistance is not as specified, check the pink wire and gray wire for an open.

    b. If the wires are okay, replace wiper switch assembly.

3. Turn the ignition switch **OFF**, disconnect the negative battery cable and turn the wiper switch through the delay range to the maximum delay position. Measure the resistance between terminal **B** of the gray wire and terminal **F** of the pink wire. It should read approximately 1.2 mega-ohms.

    a. If resistance is not as specified, check the pink wire and gray wire for an open.

    b. If the wires are okay, replace wiper switch assembly.

    c. If both resistances are correct, but the pulse mode does not operate, replace the cover assembly.

TEST E: WIPER MOTOR MODULE CURRENT DRAW TEST

1. Remove the wiper fuse.

2. Connect an ammeter (30 amp range or higher) across fuse terminals.

3. Turn the ignition switch to **RUN**, wet the windshield and turn the wiper switch to **HIGH**.

4. Read the ammeter. Current will vary. Look for the lowest reading. If the lowest reading is less than 3.5 amps or if the reading cycles between any value and zero, check:

    a. Motor grounds

    b. Brush/commutator condition

    c. Circuit breaker, which should be closed

    d. Armature.

5. If the ammeter reading is greater than 6.5 amps:

    a. Replace the wiper blades

    b. Retest

6. After replacing the wiper blades and retesting, if the reading is less then 6.5 amps system is okay. The wiper blades were causing the problem.

7. After replacing the wiper blades and retesting, if the reading is greater then 6.5 amps:

    a. Disconnect the linkage from the motor crank.

    b. Retest.

    c. If current draw is still greater than 6.5 amps, remove the wiper motor assembly for repair.

    d. If the current draw is now less than 6.5 amps, the linkage is binding. Remove and repair as required.

TEST F: MECHANICAL INSPECTION

1. Remove the wiper motor cover.

2. Reconnect the motor without the cover.

3. Turn the wiper switch to **LOW**.

4. Observe the spring loaded latch arm and drive pawl which rotates with the big gear.

5. Turn the wiper switch **OFF**.

    a. Does the latch arm spring out and catch drive pawl to shift to park?

    b. If latch arm doesn't spring out, replace the park switch.

    c. If latch arm does spring out, check for bent pawl or shaft end-play.

TEST G: WASHER MOTOR VOLTAGE TEST

1. Measure the voltage at the washer motor connector (disconnected).

2. Turn the ignition switch to **ACCY** and the washer switch to **ON** and hold.

3. Measure the voltage between terminal **A** of the red wire and terminal **B** of the dark blue wire. It should read battery voltage.

    a. If measurement does not read battery voltage, check the red wire and dark blue wire for an open.

    b. If the wires are okay, check the terminal control between the park switch and cover assembly.

    c. If the contact is good, replace the cover assembly.

4. Turn the ignition switch to **ACCY** and turn the washer switch to **OFF**.

5. Measure the voltage between terminal **A** of the red wire and terminal **B** of the dark blue wire. It should read 0 voltage.

   a. If voltage is present, check the red wire for a short to voltage.

   b. If the wire is okay, replace the cover assembly.

   c. If all voltage checks are okay and washer does not work, replace washer motor.

UNIT REPAIR

Removal and Installation

WASHER PUMP

Standard Wiper Motor

1. Remove the washer hoses from the pump.
2. Disconnect the wires from the pump relay.
3. Remove the plastic pump cover.
4. Remove the attaching screws securing the pump frame to the motor gearbox and remove the pump and frame.

To install:

5. Installation is the reverse of the removal procedure. The wiper motor gear must be in park position to assemble the pump to the wiper motor.

6. Rotate the 4-lobe cam until the index hole in the cam is aligned with the hole in the pump mounting plate. Insert a pin through both holes to maintain cam in position.

7. Position the pump on the wiper so the slot in the 4-lobe cam fits over the gear drive pin which is part of the lock pawl. Secure the pump to gear housing and remove the locator pin. Temporarily connect the wiring connector.

8. Turn the wiper motor **ON** and use the washer pump to check pump operation. A loud knocking noise would indicate that the pump cam has not engaged the drive pin properly.

9. Install pump cover.

Multiplex Pulse Wiper Motor

1. Remove the complete wiper/washer assembly from the vehicle.
2. Pull the plastic cover off the mounting post.
3. Disconnect the green lead from terminal **1A**, the yellow and red leads from the pulse relay terminals and unsolder the black with pink stripe wire from the remaining relay terminal.

4. If just the pump assembly is being removed from the motor and gearbox (wiper motor still on vehicle), cut the black with pink stripe lead 4 in. from the motor grommet. Depending on the type of repair required, it will be necessary to splice this lead to the replacement relay lead or to the original relay lead after the pump is reinstalled.

5. Remove the 3 screws that attach the pump to the gearbox.

To install:

6. Installation is the reverse of the removal procedure. Make sure the wiper gearbox is in the park position.

7. Install a locator pin in the pump mechanism through the hole in the 4-lobe cam. If it is necessary to rotate the cam to install the locator pin, be sure to turn the cam counterclockwise.

8. Position the pump assembly on the gearbox and install the 3 attaching screws. Remove the locator pin.

9. Route and attach the leads. Solder the black and pink stripe wire back into place.

10. Position the cover on the washer pump and mechanism and snap it over the mounting pin.

11. Reinstall wiper in vehicle, attach wiring and hoses. Test system.

RELAY SWITCH AND TERMINAL BOARD ASSEMBLY

Multiplex Pulse Wiper Motor

1. Remove the washer pump.
2. The wiper gear mechanism must be out of the park posi-

tion to remove the relay switch and terminal board assembly. If the wiper gear mechanism is not in the park position, drive pawl away from the latch arm, use the following procedure:

   a. To move the wiper gear drive pawl out of the park position, manually trip the latch arm toward the coil and apply feed current to the center terminal of the relay switch and terminal board and ground the motor case. The wiper motor should turn the gear, moving the drive pawl out of the park position in the relay switch slot.

   b. If applying feed current to the center terminal does not energize the motor, it is possible to remove some of the insulation from the black with pink stripe wire between the motor and the relay switch and apply feed current at this point. Be sure to cover the exposed wire with tape after the repair is complete.

3. Remove the relay switch and terminal board attaching screw and carefully lift the assembly out of the gearbox. Unsolder leads as required.

To install:

4. Installation is the reverse of the removal procedure. Resolder leads to relay switch and terminal board assembly as required. Solder black wire to terminal 3 and the black with pink stripe wire to the fixed contact post. Use care to route the wires in such a manner as to avoid having them pinched between the relay switch and wiper housing.

5. Position the relay switch and terminal board assembly in the housing and attach with screw.

6. Install the washer pump to the wiper motor.

7. Install assembly into vehicle and test system.

PARK SWITCH REPLACEMENT

1. Remove the wiper motor cover.
2. If the motor is in the park position, operate the motor as required to remove the pawl from the relay slot.
3. Remove the park switch assembly.

To install:

4. Installation is the reverse of the removal procedure. Install the new park switch assembly. When installing the new wiper cover, always install the cover assembly with the wiper in the park position and the drive pin in the large angled open area of the cam. Do not try to put the drive pin in the slot of the cam. Place it in the open area only.

5. Tighten the cover screws to 18 inch lbs.

WIPER MOTOR REPLACEMENT

1. Raise the hood and remove the cowl screen.
2. Loosen the transmission drive link-to-motor crank arm attaching nuts.
3. Remove the transmission drive link from the motor crank arm.
4. Disconnect the wiring and washer hoses.
5. Remove the 3 motor attaching screws.
6. Remove the motor while guiding crank arm through hole.

To install:

7. Installation is the reverse of the removal procedure. Note that the motor must be in the park position before assembling the crank arm to the transmission.

8. Connect wiring and hoses. Test system.

B-Body

GENERAL INFORMATION

The windshield wiper system used on these vehicles is similar to the system listed above. There are some differences in wiring color codes that will affect troubleshooting.

Before beginning troubleshooting, check fuse 10. If open, check for short to ground in the white wire that runs from the fuse block to the wiper/washer switch. Make sure all connectors are firmly mated.

If the washer does not operate, check that the washer reservoir is filled, the hoses correctly attached, hoses are not cut, kinked or pinches, the nozzles are not clogged and the connector seal at the washer motor is not damaged or missing.

If the washer does not operate and wipers run in HIGH only (low speed inoperative), check the gray wire that runs from the washer/wiper switch to the windshield wiper motor module for an open.

Other problem areas could be binding or broken wiper arm linkage or missing or damaged connector seal at the windshield wiper motor module.

CIRCUIT OPERATION

In addition to the features of a conventional (non-pulse) wiper system (mist, low and high speed), the pulse-type wiper/washer system includes an operating mode in which the wipers make single strokes with an adjustable time interval between strokes. The time interval is controlled by a solid state timer in the wiper motor assembly, often referred to as the wiper motor "module" since it contains not only the wiper motor itself, but also the solid state electronic components that make up the delay timer as well as the park relay and self-resetting circuit breaker. The duration of the delay interval is determined by the pulse delay resistor in the windshield wiper/washer switch assembly.

Note that in the following information, connector C1 and C2 refers to the connectors at the wiper motor.

PULSE OPERATION

With the wiper/washer switch in PULSE, voltage is applied to the windshield wiper motor at connector C1, terminal F through the pink wire. Voltage is also applied to connector C1, terminal B through the gray wire.

The variable resistance seen through the pulse delay resistor is used by the wiper motor module to determine the delay time between sweeps.

LOW SPEED

In the LOW position, the wiper/washer switch applies battery voltage to the wiper motor module at connector C1 terminal C through the dark green wire to connector C1 terminal B through the gray wire. Voltage is also applied from a 24 kilo-ohm resistor inside the wiper/washer switch to connector C1 terminal F through the pink wire.

The wiper motor assembly module supplies power through connector C1 terminal A through the yellow jumper wire to connector C2 terminal B to the wiper motor, which runs continuously.

HIGH SPEED

In the HIGH position, the wiper/washer switch applies battery voltage to the wiper motor assembly at connector C1 terminal C through the dark green wire and to connector C1 terminal B through the gray wire.

The wiper motor assembly supplies power from connector C1 terminal A through the yellow jumper wire to connector C2 terminal B to the wiper motor. The wiper motor also has voltage applied from the wiper/washer switch to connector C2 terminal A through the purple wire to a separate armature brush for high speed operation.

OFF POSITION

When turned OFF from any position, the wipers complete the last sweep and park. When the wiper/washer switch is OFF, the wiper motor assembly module has battery voltage applied through connector C1, terminal C through the dark green wire and connector C1 terminal F through the pink wire. The wiper motor module controls power through the park relay to connector C1 terminal A through the yellow jumper wire to connector C2, terminal B to the wiper motor, which runs until the park relay is opened.

The park relay is controlled both electronically and mechanically. The relay is held closed mechanically until the wipers reach the park position and the wiper request is no longer present. Whenever wiper request is present, the relay is held closed electronically.

WASHER OPERATION

When the washer switch is turned ON, the wipers operate at low speed using the same circuit operation as low speed or the same as high speed only if HIGH speed is selected.

When the washer switch is held ON, the wiper motor assembly module will keep the washer motor ON only as long as the washer switch is held ON.

If the wipers had been in PULSE, LOW or HIGH, they would return to that operation after the wash cycle. If not, they then return to the PARK position.

MIST

When the wiper/washer switch is moved to MIST and released, the wipers make 1 sweep at low speed and return to PARK. The circuit operation is the same as that of low speed.

TROUBLE DIAGNOSIS

Wiper Motor System Operation

To help find problems, it's important to understand normal operation. The following should be used as a guide:

1. With the ignition switch in RUN, turn the wiper/washer switch to WASHER. Normal operation is for the wipers to operate at low speed. The washer sprays the windshield as long as the washer switch is held in the WASHER position. After releasing the switch, the washer stops and the wipers return to park.

2. With the ignition switch in RUN, turn the wiper/washer switch to PULSE. Normal operation is for the wipers to make 1 complete stroke then pause for 1–10 seconds before making the next stroke. The pause time is adjusted by turning the wiper switch through the delay range.

3. With the ignition switch in RUN, turn the wiper/washer switch to PULSE and turn the washer switch to ON. Look for:
   a. Normal operation is for the washer to spray the windshield as long as the washer switch is held ON.
   b. Wipers run at low speed while spraying and continue until the washer switch is released. Wipers then return to pulse operation.

4. With the ignition switch in RUN, turn the wiper/washer switch to LOW. Normal operation is for the wipers to run continuously at low speed.

5. With the ignition switch in RUN, turn the wiper/washer switch to HIGH. Normal operation is for the wipers to run continuously at HIGH speed.

6. With the ignition switch in RUN, turn the wiper/washer switch OFF. Normal operation is for the wipers to run at low speed and return to PARK.

7. With the ignition switch in RUN, turn the wiper/washer switch to MIST and then release. Normal operation is for the wipers to make one complete stroke then return to the PARK position.

Testing

SYMPTOM TEST – WIPER/MOTOR: PULSE

1. Wipers do not operate in any mode. Perform Test A: Wiper/Washer Switch Voltage Test.
2. Wipers run at high speed only (low speed inoperative). Perform Test B: High Speed Test.
3. Wipers run at low speed only (high speed inoperative). Perform Test C: Low Speed Test.
4. Wipers will not run. Perform Test D: Wiper Module Voltage Test.

5. Pulse delay operates incorrectly or not at all. Perform Test E: Pulse Resistance Check.

6. Washer will not operate. Perform Test F: Washer Voltage Check.

TEST A: WIPER/WASHER SWITCH VOLTAGE TEST WIPERS DO NOT OPERATE IN ANY MODE

1. Disconnect the 7 cavity connector for the washer/wiper switch. This connector is flat and gray in color and is located at the base of the steering column. Turn ignition switch to **RUN**. Connect test light to terminal **B** of the connector, (white wire). Is test light ON?

   a. If test light is not ON, check for open fuse 10 or open in white wire. If fuse and wire are okay but test light is not ON, check for open power feed in the heavy brown wire from the **RUN** side of the ignition switch.

   b. If test light is ON, go to Step 2.

2. Disconnect the windshield wiper motor module connector C2. Connect a test light from connector C2, terminal **C** (pink wire) to battery voltage. Is test light ON?

a. If test light is not ON, repair open in ground circuit (black wire).

   b. If test light is ON, go to Step 3.

3. Reconnect the 7 cavity connector for the washer/wiper switch. Disconnect the windshield wiper motor connector C1. Connect a test light from connector C1, terminal **C** (dark green wire) to ground. Is test light ON?

   a. If test light is not ON, check for a poor connection at the wiper/washer switch or at the wiper motor or an open in the dark green wire between the switch and motor. If all are okay, replace the wiper/washer switch.

   b. If test light is ON, go to Step 4.

4. Turn wiper switch to **LOW**. Connect a test light from connector C1 terminal **B** (gray wire) to ground. Is test light ON?

   a. If test light is not ON, check for a poor connection at the wiper/washer switch or at the 37 cavity connector joining the body harness to engine compartment harness which should be behind the right side of the instrument panel between the blower motor and instrument panel compartment or an open

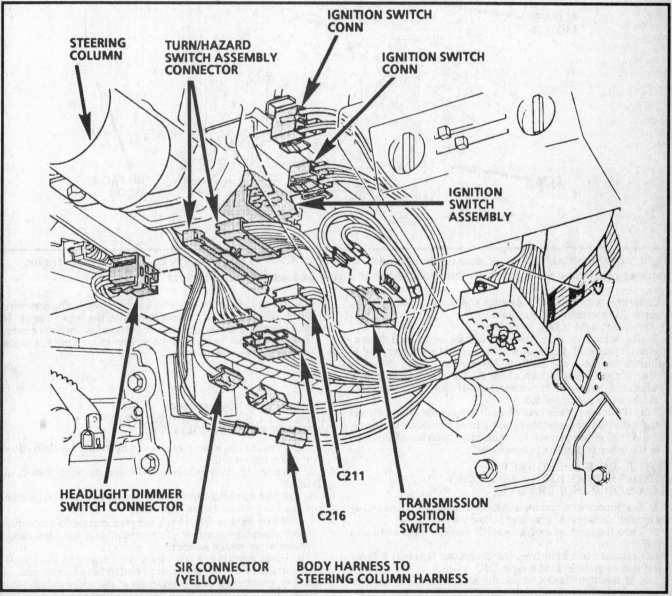

Left side underdash wiring at base of steering column. Connector C216 is the 7-way wiper/washer switch connector—General Motors

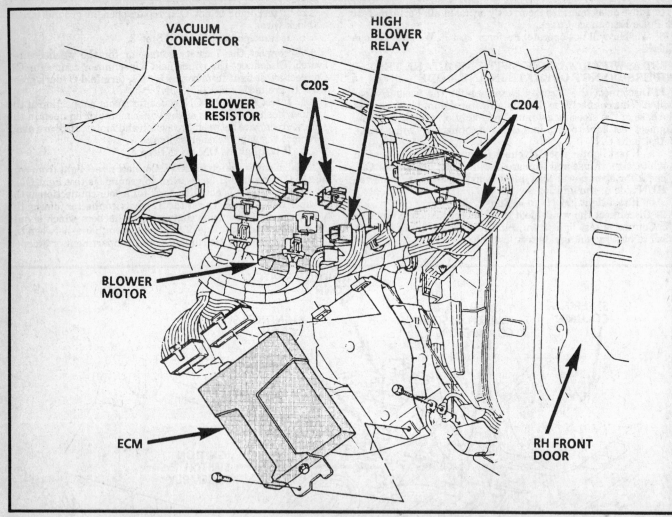

VACUUM CONNECTOR

HIGH BLOWER RELAY

C205

BLOWER RESISTOR

C204

BLOWER MOTOR

ECM

RH FRONT DOOR

Right side underdash wiring at passenger kickpad. Connector C204 is the 37 cavity body harness to engine harness connector through which the wiper/ washer wiring passes—General Motors

in the gray wire between the switch and motor. If all are okay, replace the wiper/washer switch.

b. If test light is ON, go to Step 5.

5. Check for continuity from windshield wiper module connector C1 terminal **A** (yellow wire) to connector C2 terminal **B** (which is the other end of the yellow wire).

a. If there is continuity, check for poor connection at the windshield wiper motor connectors. If okay, replace windshield wiper motor module.

b. If there is no continuity, repair open in the yellow wire on the wiper motor assembly running from connector C1 terminal **A** (yellow jumper wire) to connector C2 terminal **B** (which is the other end of the yellow wire).

TEST B: HIGH SPEED TEST
WIPERS RUN AT HIGH SPEED ONLY
(LOW SPEED INOPERATIVE)

1. Disconnect wiper motor assembly connector C1 (connector with pink, dark green, gray and yellow wire).

2. Turn the ignition switch to **RUN** and the wiper switch to **LOW**.

3. Connect a test light from the connector, terminal **B** (gray wire) and to ground. Is test light ON?

a. If test light is ON, check for poor connection at wiper motor assembly connector. If connection and wires are okay, replace wiper motor assembly.

b. If test light is not ON, check for an open in the gray wire which runs from the column switch to the wiper motor. If okay, check for a poor connection at the wiper switch connector or the 37 cavity body harness connector. If okay, replace wiper/washer switch.

TEST C: LOW SPEED TEST
WIPERS RUN AT LOW SPEED ONLY
(HIGH SPEED INOPERATIVE)

1. Disconnect the wiper motor assembly connector C2 (yellow wire and purple wire).

2. Turn the ignition switch to **RUN** and the wiper switch to **HIGH**.

3. Connect a test light from the connector, terminal **A** (purple wire) and to ground. Is test light ON?

a. If test light is ON, check for poor connection at wiper motor assembly connector. If connection and wires are okay, replace wiper motor assembly.

b. If test light is not ON, check for an open in the purple wire which runs from the column switch to the wiper motor. If okay, check for a poor connection at the wiper switch connector or the 37 cavity body harness connector. If okay, replace wiper/washer switch.

TEST D: WIPER MODULE VOLTAGE TEST (WIPERS WILL NOT TURN OFF)

1. Disconnect windshield wiper motor assembly connector C1 (pink, dark green, gray and yellow wires).
2. Turn the ignition switch to **RUN** and the wiper switch to **OFF**.
3. Using a digital voltmeter measure the voltage from connector C1, terminal **B** (gray wire) to ground. What is the voltage reading?

   a. If there is battery voltage, check for a short to voltage somewhere along the gray wire. If okay, replace the wiper/washer switch.

   b. If there is no voltage, disconnect the wiper motor assembly connector C2 (purple and yellow wires). Using a digital voltmeter, measure the voltage from connector C2 terminal **A** (yellow wire) and ground. If there is battery voltage, check for a short to voltage somewhere along the purple wire. If okay, replace the wiper/washer switch.

   c. If there is no voltage, replace the wiper motor assembly.

TEST E: PULSE RESISTANCE CHECK (PULSE DELAY OPERATES INCORRECTLY OR NOT AT ALL)

1. Turn ignition switch **OFF** and disconnect the 7-way wiper/washer switch connector at the base of the steering column.
2. Turn the windshield wiper/washer switch to **PULSE**.
3. With a digital voltmeter set to the ohms scale, measure the resistance through the wiper/washer switch at the switch connector from terminal **B** (white wire) to terminal **F** (pink wire). Move the wiper switch through the entire delay range. Does the resistance vary from approximately 1.2 mega-ohms to 24 kilo-ohms.

   a. If the resistance changes as specified, check the pink wire for an open or poor connection. If okay, replace the wiper motor assembly.

   b. If the resistance does not change as specified, replace the wiper/washer switch.

TEST F: WASHER VOLTAGE CHECK (WASHER WILL NOT OPERATE)

1. Disconnect the windshield washer motor.
2. Turn the ignition to **RUN**.
3. Connect a test light between terminal **A** (red wire) and terminal **B** (dark blue) of the windshield washer pump motor. Activate the washer switch with observing the test light. Is the test light ON? If the test light is ON, check for a poor connection at the washer motor connector. If okay, replace the windshield washer motor.
4. If the test light is not ON, connect a test light from the washer motor terminal **A** (red wire) and ground. Activate the washer switch while observing the test light. Is the test light ON? If the test light is ON, check for a poor connection or an open in the dark blue wire. If okay, replace the windshield wiper motor since there is an internal ground that's open.
5. If the test light is not ON, turn the ignition to **RUN**. Using a digital voltmeter, backprobe the 7-way windshield wiper switch connector at the base of the steering column, checking terminal **F** (pink wire) to ground. Activate the washer switch while observing the voltmeter.

   a. If there is no voltage, check for an open or poor connection along the pink wire between the 7-way connector and the wiper motor. If okay, replace the windshield wiper/washer switch.

   b. If there is battery voltage, check for a poor connection at the 7-way connector of the 37-cavity body harness connector and the windshield wiper motor connector. Also check for an open along the pink wire. If all okay, replace the windshield wiper assembly.

UNIT REPAIR

Removal and Installation

WASHER PUMP

1. Remove the washer solvent from the reservoir.
2. Disconnect the electrical connector and washer hose from washer pump.
3. Remove the washer pump from the reservoir.

To install:

4. Installation is the reverse of the removal procedure. Install the washer pump to the reservoir. Note that the new washer pump must be pushed all the way into the solvent container recess and gasket.
5. Connect the electric connector and the washer hose.
6. Refill with washer solvent and test system.

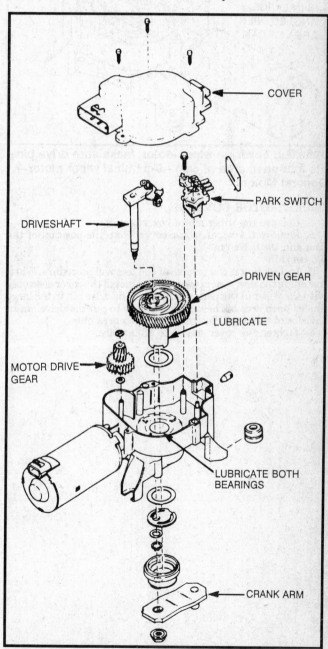

Exploded view of 9-terminal wiper motor, remote pump system—typical—General Motors

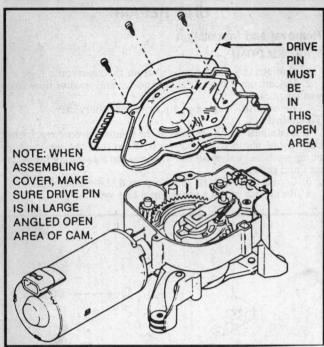

Installing cover on wiper motor, make sure drive pin fits into open area of cam—9-terminal wiper motor—General Motors

WIPER MOTOR COVER

1. Remove the wiper motor cover screws.
2. Remove the wiper motor cover. Note the position of the cam and the drive pin.
To install:
3. Installation is the reverse of the removal procedure. When installing the new wiper cover, always install the cover assembly with the wiper in the park position and the drive pin in the large angled open area of the cam. Do not try to put the drive pin in the slot of the cam. Place it in the open area only.
4. Tighten the cover screws to 18 inch lbs.

PARK SWITCH REPLACEMENT

1. Remove the wiper motor cover.
2. If the motor is in the park position, operate the motor as required to remove the pawl from the relay slot.
3. Remove the park switch assembly.
To install:
4. Installation is the reverse of the removal procedure. Install the new park switch assembly. When installing the new wiper cover, always install the cover assembly with the wiper in the park position and the drive pin in the large angled open area of the cam. Do not try to put the drive pin in the slot of the cam. Place it in the open area only.
5. Tighten the cover screws to 18 inch lbs.

WIPER MOTOR REPLACEMENT

1. Remove the right side wiper arm and hose.

NOTE: To prevent possible windshield damage, the left side cowl vent screen must be removed before the right side cowl vent screen is removed.

2. Remove the left and right side cowl vent screens.
3. Remove the wiper linkage access hole cover screws and remove the cover.
4. Disconnect the wiper drive link from the motor crank arm.
5. Disconnect the electrical connectors, remove the motor attaching bolts and remove the wiper motor, guiding the crank arm through the hole.
To install:
6. Installation is the reverse of the removal procedure. Install the wiper motor guiding the crank arm through the hole. Tighten the mounting bolts to 70–89 inch lbs.
7. Install the electrical connectors.
8. Connect the motor drive link to the motor crank arm. Tighten the socket nuts to 20–30 inch lbs.
9. Apply a suitable body sealer to the edges of the access hole cover and reinstall the cover. Tighten the cover screws to 8–14 inch lbs.
10. To avoid damage to the windshield, the right side cowl vent screen must be installed before the left side cowl vent screen. Install the vent screens.
11. Connect the right side wiper arm and hose.
12. Test system.

FUSES, CIRCUIT BREAKERS AND RELAYS

Laser, Stealth, Summit, Summit Wagon and Talon

Location

SUMMIT AND SUMMIT WAGON

Fuses and Fusible Links

Main fuse panel—passenger's side, under the hood, just behind the battery.

Main relay bank—passenger's side, under the hood, just behind the battery.

Fuse links—passenger's side, under the hood, just behind the battery.

Air conditioning control relay center—driver's side, under the hood, up front behind the headlight.

Multi-purpose fuse block—inside the vehicle, on the left side behind the driver's knee protector.

Relays

Headlight relay, power window relay, radiator fan motor relay and alternator relay—passenger's side, under the hood, just behind the battery.

Air conditioner compressor relay, the condenser fan motor relay and the condenser fan motor control relay—under the hood, up front behind the headlight.

Intermittent wiper relay—incorporated into the column switch.

Seat belt warning timer relay—behind the instrument panel to the right of the center air conditioning outlets.

Multi-Point Injection control relay—inside the passenger compartment behind the right kick panel on Summit Wagon or behind the forward part of the console, on the left side on Summit.

Starter relay—right side of the vehicle in the relay box.

Defogger relay—under the driver's left side knee protector.

Door lock relay—behind the driver's side kick panel, at the bottom.

Heater relay, the turn signal and hazard flasher unit and the defogger timer—located in the multi-purpose fuse panel located under the driver's left side knee protector

Automatic seatbelt motor relay—located in the driver's side windshield post on Summit hatchback, and inside the trim panel on the driver's side rear quarter panel, just behind the front door post on Summit Sedan and Summit Wagon.

LASER AND TALON

Fuses and Fusible Links

MPI circuit—20 amp fuse link—under the hood in a centralized junction with the battery positive cable clamp.

Radiator fan motor circuit—30 amp fuse link—under the hood in a centralized junction with the battery positive cable clamp.

Ignition switch circuit—30 amp fuse link—under the hood in a centralized junction with the battery positive cable clamp.

Secondary fuse panel—located on the passenger side, under the hood, just forward of the strut tower.

Secondary fuse panel—driver's side, under the hood, back against the firewall.

Multi-purpose fuse block—located inside the vehicle, on the left side behind the driver's knee protector.

Relays

Taillight relay, headlight relay, radiator fan motor relay, pop-up (retractable light) motor relay, power window relay, alternator relay and fog light relay.—passenger side of vehicle, under the hood, just forward of the strut tower.

Air conditioning condenser fan relays and air conditioning compressor clutch relay—driver's side of vehicle, under the hood, just forward of the strut tower.

Door lock relay, starter relay, defogger timer—interior relay box inside the vehicle passanger compartment.

STEALTH

Fuses and Fusible Links

Main fuse panel—located on the passenger side, under the hood, just forward of the air flow box. This panel also contains several fusible links.

Multipurpose fuse block—located under the instrument panel, on the left side behind the driver's knee protector.

Relays

Radiator fan relay, air conditioning system relays—centralized fuse/relay panel on the driver side, under the hood, just forward of the strut tower.

Taillight relay, headlight relay, pop-up (retractable light) motor relay, horn relay, alternator relay and fog light relay—engine compartment in front of the air flow box.

Blower motor and theft alarm horn.—inside the vehicle, above the fuse box.

Computers

Location

SUMMIT AND SUMMIT WAGON

Multi-Point Injection (MPI) control unit—located under the instrument panel at the top of the passenger side kick panel, next to the blower motor.

Air conditioning control unit—mounted behind the glove box.

Automatic transaxle control unit—mounted on the floor at the very front of the console.

Cruise control unit—under the instrument panel behind the driver's side knee protector.

Electric door lock control unit—fastened to the body structure behind the driver's side kick panel.

Automatic seat belt control unit—under the console next to hand brake handle.

ELC 4-speed automatic transaxle control unit—under the instrument panel at center of dash.

Anti-lock Braking System (ABS) control unit—under the instrument panel at center of dash.

LASER AND TALON

Multi-Point Injection (MPI) control unit—located under the instrument panel at the front of the center console.

Air conditioning control unit—mounted behind the glove box.

Automatic transaxle control unit—mounted on the floor at the very front of the console.

Cruise control unit—mounted at top of instrument panel structure near where the dash pad and windshield meet.

Electric door lock control unit or theft-alarm control unit—fastened to the body structure behind the passenger's side kick panel.

Automatic seat belt control unit—fastened to the body structure under the trim panel at the base of the driver's side door latch pillar.

Anti-Lock Brake control unit—mounted behind the right side rear quarter trim panel.

STEALTH

Multi-Point Injection (MPI) control unit—located under the instrument panel at the front of the center console.

Automatic transaxle control unit—mounted on the floor at the very front of the console.

Air conditioning control unit—mounted at the front of the center console just above the MPI control unit.

Air conditioner compressor lock controller—mounted on the bottom of the heater core housing under the right side of the instrument panel.

Cruise control unit—located behind the right side kick panel.

Electronic Timing and Control System (ETACS) unit—located just to the left of the the steering column.

Air bag diagnosis unit—located under the arm rest in the console.

Electronic Suspension Control (ECS) control unit—mounted behind the right rear trim panel behind an access door.

Anti-Lock Brake control unit—mounted behind the right side rear quarter trim panel.

Active exhaust control unit—located in the rear luggage compartment, behind the left side trim panel.

Flashers

Location

SUMMIT, SUMMIT WAGON, LASER AND TALON

Turn signal and hazard flasher unit—located in the multi-purpose fuse panel located under the driver's left side knee protector.

Cruise Control

For further information, please refer to Chilton's Chassis Electronics Service Manual.

Adjustment

Before starting adjustments, turn air conditioner and lights **OFF.** Warm engine until the idle is stable and the rpm is correct. Stop engine and set the ignition switch to **OFF.** On 1.5L engine and Laser equipped with 1.8L engine, turn the ignition switch to the **ON** position, without starting the engine. Leave in the position for approximately 15 seconds. Confirm there are no sharp bends in the accelerator, throttle and cruise control cables. Check the inner cables for correct slack. If too loose or too tight, adjust with the following procedure:

1. Remove the air cleaner. If equipped with a protective cover over the actuator, remove it.

2. First, adjust the accelerator cable on the throttle valve side. After loosening the adjustment bolts at the air intake plenum side and freeing the inner cable, use the adjusting bolts that secure the plate so the free-play of the inner cable becomes 0.040–0.080 in. (1–2mm). If there is excessive play of the accelerator cable, when climbing a hill the vehicle speed will drop substantially. If there is no play, the idling speed will increase.

3. After adjusting the accelerator cable, confirm that the throttle lever touches the idle position switch.

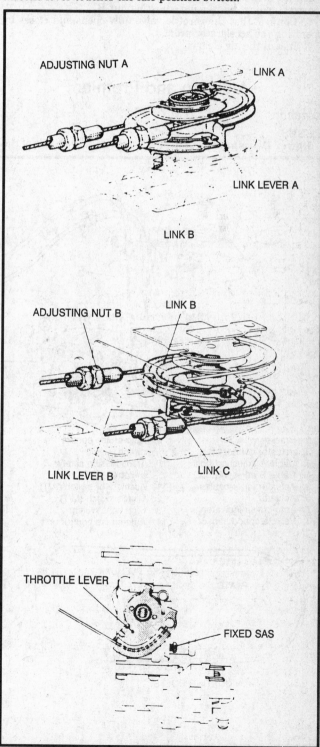

Common cable adjusting points—1992 Stealth

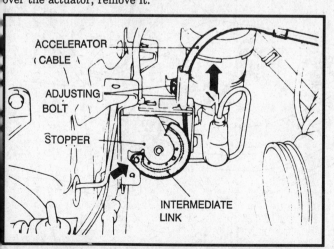

Common cable adjusting point—1990 Summit

4. Next, adjust accelerator cable on the accelerator pedal side. Loosen the adjusting bolt or locknut. While keeping the intermediate link of the actuator in close contact with the stop, adjust the inner cable play of accelerator cable **A** to 0–0.040 in. (0–1mm) for manual transaxle vehicles or 0.080–0.120 in. (2–3mm) for automatic transaxle vehicles.

5. After making the adjustment of the cable, make sure the throttle lever at the engine side moves 0.040–0.080 in. (1–2mm) when the actuator link is turned. If throttle lever movement is incorrect, adjust by turning adjusting nut **B**.

6. Confirm that the throttle valve fully opens and closes by operating the accelerator pedal.

7. Install the air cleaner.

Monaco and Premier

Location
FUSES
Power Distribution Center—located on the left side of the engine compartment on vehicles built on or after October 9, 1991.

Main fuse panel—located under the instrument panel, above the parking brake release lever.

FUSIBLE LINKS
Fusible links are used to prevent major wire harness damage in the event of a short circuit or an overload condition in the wiring circuits which are normally not fused, due to carrying high amperage loads or because of their locations within the wiring harness. The fuse links are located in the wiring harness near the battery. Each fusible link is of a fixed value for a specific electrical load and should a link fail, the cause of the failure must be determined and repaired prior to installing a new fusible link of the same value.

CIRCUIT BREAKERS
Circuit breakers are an integral part of the headlight switch, the wiper switch and the air conditioning circuit. They are used to protect each circuit from an overload. Other circuit breakers are on the fuse panel.

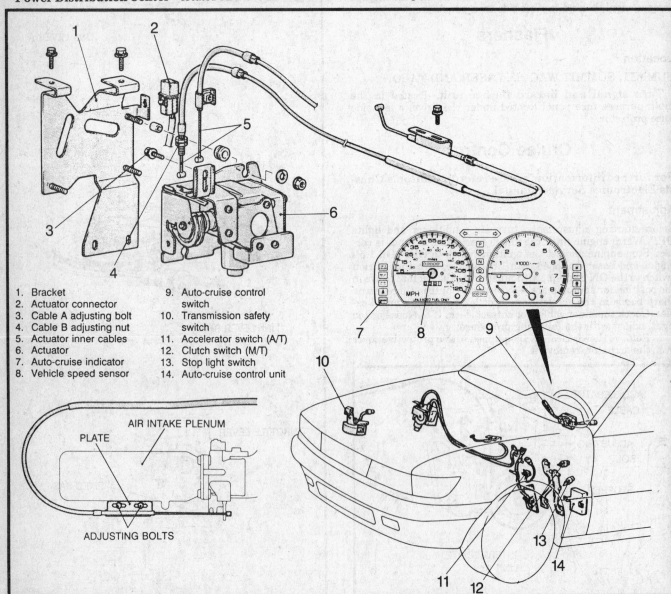

1. Bracket
2. Actuator connector
3. Cable A adjusting bolt
4. Cable B adjusting nut
5. Actuator inner cables
6. Actuator
7. Auto-cruise indicator
8. Vehicle speed sensor
9. Auto-cruise control switch
10. Transmission safety switch
11. Accelerator switch (A/T)
12. Clutch switch (M/T)
13. Stop light switch
14. Auto-cruise control unit

AIR INTAKE PLENUM
PLATE
ADJUSTING BOLTS

Main cruise control components—Summit

RELAYS

Relays are used throughout the system in various locations. When replacing a protective electrical relay, be very sure to install the same type of relay. Verify that the schematic imprinted on the original and replacement relays are identical. Relay part numbers may change. Do not rely on them for identification. Instead, use the schematic imprinted on the relay for positive identification.

On vehicles built before October 9, 1991, a relay bank is located on the left side of the engine compartment. On vehicles built on or after October 9, 1991, the Power Distribution Center is used in the same location and is equipped with additional fuses. Additional relay locations are as follows:

Power door lock relay—on the right side kick panel.
Passive restraint relays—under the seats.
Light outage module—behind the right side speaker in the trunk.
Passive restraint control module—on the left side of the trunk.
Headlight module—under the left side of the instrument panel.
Daytime running light module—in the right front area of the engine compartment.
Climate control relays and module—under the right side of the instrument panel.
Sun roof relay—near the sun roof motor.

Computers

Location

Engine Control Unit (except vehicles built after October 9, 1991)—under the right side of the instrument panel.
Single Board Engine Controller (vehicles built on or after October 9, 1991)—in the left front area of the engine compartment.
Transmission Controller—in the right front area of the engine compartment.
Anti Lock Brakes Controller—on the front of the right front strut tower in the engine compartment.

Flashers

Location

Turn Signal Flasher—behind the left side of the instrument panel.
Hazard Flasher—behind the left side of the instrument panel.

Acclaim, Aries, Daytona, LeBaron, Shadow, Spirit, Sundance and TC

Location

ARIES AND RELIANT

The fuse block is located behind a removeable access panel, below the steering column. The hazard and turn signal flashers along with the time delay and horn relays are also located behind the panel. Additional relays are mounted on the inner fender panel near the battery.

SPIRIT, ACCLAIM, SHADOW AND SUNDANCE

The fuse block is located behind the steering column cover, accessible by removing the fuse access panel above the hood latch release lever. The relay and flasher module is located behind an access panel in the glovebox. Included in the module are the hazard and turn signal flashers along with the time delay and horn

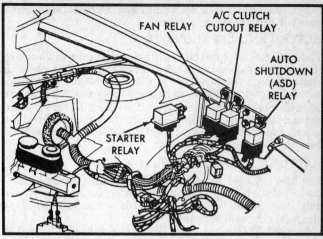

Relay identification—1990 vehicles and early 1991 Shadow Convertible

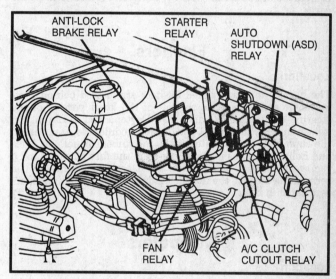

Relay identification—1991 vehicles without Power Distribution Center

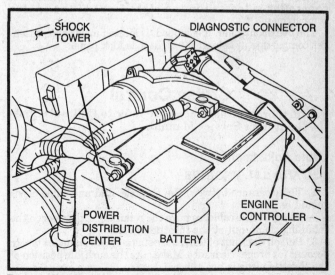

Power distribution center—Daytona

relays. Additional relays are mounted on the inner fender panel near the battery and strut tower.

LANCER AND LEBARON GTS

The fuse block is located behind the glove box door, accessible by removing the fuse access panel. The relay and flasher module is located behind the cupholder in the center of the instrument panel. The entire module can be removed by pushing it up and off of its mounting bracket. Included in the module are the hazard and turn signal flashers along with the time delay and horn relays. Additional relays are mounted on the inner fender panel near the battery and strut tower.

DAYTONA, LEBARON AND TC

The fuse block is located behind a removeable access panel to the left of the lower portion of the steering column. On TC and 1990 Daytona and LeBaron, the time delay and horn relays are also located behind the panel.

On 1990–93 Daytona and LeBaron, a relay bank is located on the left side kick panel. The Power Distribution Center, which contains additional relays and fuses, is located in the engine compartment behind the battery. Each item is identified on the cover.

Flashers

Location

The hazard and turn signal flashers are located behind a removeable access panel to the left of the lower portion of the steering column on TC and 1990 Daytona and LeBaron. On Lancer and LeBaron GTS, the flasher module is located behind the cupholder in the center of the instrument panel. On Aries and Reliant, the flashers are located in the fuse block behind a removeable access panel, below the steering column. On the remaining models, the flasher module is located behind an access panel in the glovebox.

Computers

Location

The Single Board Engine Controller (SBEC) is located in engine compartment, to the left of the battery.

If equipped with the A604 automatic transaxle, the transaxle controller is located in the right front of the engine compartment.

The body controller, if equipped, is located inside the passenger compartment, behind the right side kick panel.

Cruise Control

For further information, please refer to Chilton's Chassis Electronics Service Manual.

Cable Adjustment

2.2L AND 2.5L ENGINES

1. The clearance between the throttle stud and cable clevis should be $\frac{1}{16}$ in.
2. To adjust the cable, remove the retaining clip or loosen the retaining clamp nut at the throttle bracket.
3. Pull all slack out of the cable using a $\frac{1}{16}$ in. diameter tool to account for proper clearance. Make sure the curb idle position of the throttle blade is not affected.
4. Reinstall the retaining clip or nut.

3.0L ENGINE

1. Grip the cable core and lightly push toward the servo.
2. While holding the position, mark the core wire next to the protective sleeve.
3. Pull the core wire away from the servo. There should be a 0.24 in. (6mm) gap between the mark on the core wire and the protective sleeve.
4. If the gap is not correct, remove the adjustment clip from the throttle bracket and move the sleeve to bring the gap into specification.
5. Reinstall the clip.

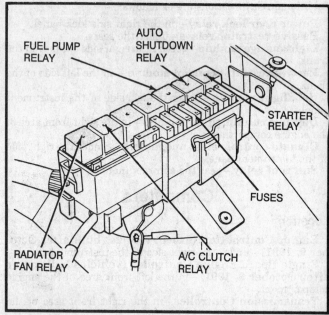

Relay identification – Daytona

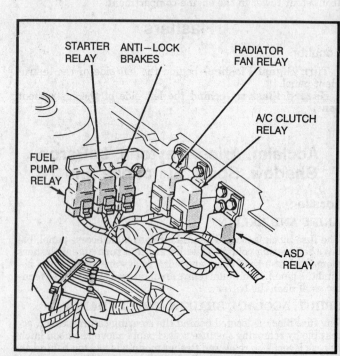

Power identification – LeBaron, Spirit, Acclaim, Shadow, Sundance

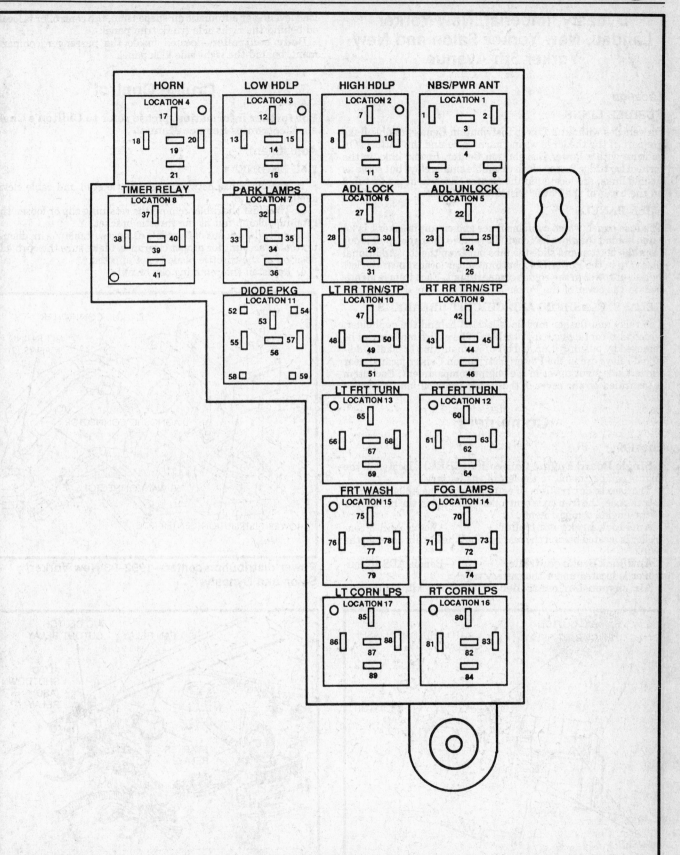

Relay identification. Wire-end view of the relay bank on the left side kick panel – 1990–92 Daytona and LeBaron

Dynasty, Imperial, New Yorker Landau, New Yorker Salon and New Yorker 5th Avenue

Location

FUSIBLE LINKS

On vehicles without a Power Distribution Center, fusible links are part of the the large wiring harness behind the battery. On vehicles with a Power Distribution Center, fusible links in the form of cartridge fuses, which resemble small relays but serve as fusible links, are located in the Center. Each item is identified on the cover of the Power Distribution Center.

FUSE PANELS

The fuse panel, which contains fuses and circuit breakers, is located behind the glove box door. To remove the panel, pull it out from the bottom and slide the tabs out from the top. Additional fuses are in the Power Distribution Center located near the left side strut tower in the engine compartment. Each item is identified on the cover of the Power Distribution Center.

RELAYS, FLASHERS AND CIRCUIT BREAKERS

The relay and flasher module is located behind the cupholder, which also contains circuit breakers. The entire module can be removed by pushing it up and off of its mounting bracket. Additional relays are in the Power Distribution Center located near the left side strut tower in the engine compartment. Each item is identified on the cover of the Power Distribution Center.

Computers

Location

Single Board Engine Controller (SBEC)—located in the engine compartment, to the left of the battery.

Transaxle controller—if equipped with the A604 automatic transaxle, the transaxle controller is located in the right front of the engine compartment.

Anti-lock brake controller —Bosch ABS 3 controller is located behind the rear seat bulkhead trim panel in the trunk.

Anti-lock brake controller —Bendix ABS 10 controller is located under the battery tray.

Air suspension controller—if equipped with automatic load leveling or automatic air suspension, the controller is located behind the right side trunk trim panel.

Body controller—located inside the passenger compartment, behind the right side kick panel.

Cruise Control

For further information, please refer to Chilton's Chassis Electronics Service Manual.

Adjustment

2.5L ENGINE

1. The clearance between the throttle stud and cable clevis should be $\frac{1}{16}$ in.

2. To adjust the cable, remove the retaining clip or loosen the retaining clamp nut at the throttle bracket.

3. Pull all slack out of the cable using a suitable $\frac{1}{16}$ in. diameter tool to account for proper clearance. Make sure the curb idle position of the throttle blade is not affected.

4. Reinstall the retaining clip or nut.

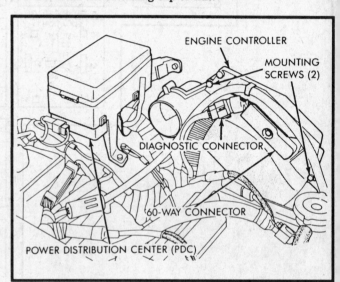

Power distribution center—1992–93 New Yorker/ Salon and Dynasty

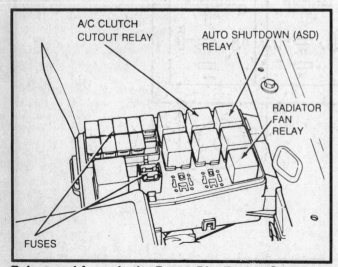

Relays and fuses in the Power Distribution Center

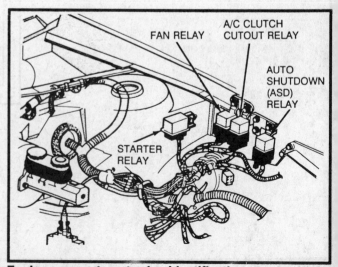

Engine compartment relay identification

3.0L, 3.3L AND 3.8L ENGINES

1. Grip the cable core and lightly push toward the servo.
2. While holding the position, mark the core wire next to the protective sleeve.
3. Pull the core wire away from the servo. There should be a 0.24 in. (6mm) gap between the mark on the core wire and the protective sleeve.
4. If the gap is not correct, remove the adjustment clip from the throttle bracket and move the sleeve to bring the gap into specification.
5. Reinstall the clip.

Omni and Horizon

Location

FUSES, CIRCUIT BREAKER AND FLASHERS

The fuse block, which contains the fuses, circuit breaker and flashers, is located on the left side kick panel, below the left side of the instrument panel.

RELAYS

A/C Clutch Cutout Relay—located on the left front inner fender just in front of the strut tower.
Automatic Shutdown (ASD) Relay—located on the left front inner fender just in front of the strut tower.
Cooling Fan Motor Relay—located on the left front inner fender just in front of the strut tower.
Horn Relay—located on the upper right side of the fuse block.
Rear Window Defroster Timer—part of the defroster switch.
Seatbelt Warning Buzzer—located on the fuse block.
Starter Relay—located on the left front strut tower.
Time Delay Relay—taped to the wiring harness near the fuse block.

Computers

Location

The Single Board Engine Controller (SBEC) is located in the engine compartment, to the left of the battery.

The Airbag System Diagnostic Module (ASDM), if equipped, is located under the instrument panel, to the right of the front of the console.

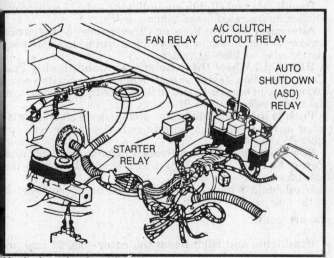

FAN RELAY
A/C CLUTCH CUTOUT RELAY
AUTO SHUTDOWN (ASD) RELAY
STARTER RELAY

Underhood relay identification

Cruise Control

For further information, please refer to Chilton's Chassis Electronics Service Manual.

Adjustment

1. The clearance between the throttle stud and cable clevis should be $\frac{1}{16}$ in.
2. To adjust the cable, remove the retaining clip or loosen the retaining clamp nut at the throttle bracket.
3. Pull all slack out of the cable using a suitable $\frac{1}{16}$ in. diameter tool to account for proper clearance. Make sure the curb idle position of the throttle blade is not affected.
4. Reinstall the retaining clip or nut.

Concorde, Intrepid, LHS, New Yorker and Vision

Location

FUSES

Power Distribution Center—located on the left side of the engine compartment at the firewall.
Multi-Purpose Fuse Block—inside the vehicle, on the left side behind the driver's knee protector.

FUSIBLE LINKS

Fuse Links—in the engine compartment, just behind the battery.

RELAYS

Hazard Flasher Relay—located on the left side of the passenger compartment, between the junction block and the brake pedal.
Anti-Lock Brake System Relays—left side of the engine compartment, mounted on the side of the power distribution center.
Horn Relay—multi-purpose fuse block inside the vehicle, on the left side behind the driver's knee protector.
Door Lock Relay—multi-purpose fuse block inside the vehicle, on the left side behind the driver's knee protector.
Cruise Control Relay—multi-purpose fuse block inside the vehicle, on the left side behind the driver's knee protector.
Engine Starter Relay—located in the power distribution center on the left side of the engine compartment at the firewall.
Fuel Pump Relay—located in the power distribution center on the left side of the engine compartment at the firewall.
Intermittent Wiper Relay—located in the power distribution center on the left side of the engine compartment at the firewall.
Radiator Fan Relay—located in the power distribution center on the left side of the engine compartment at the firewall.
Anti-Lock Brake System (ABS) Pump Rrelay—located in the power distribution center on the left side of the engine compartment at the firewall.

Computers

Location

Engine Controller—inside the engine compartment, mounted on the right front fender.
Body Control Module—right side of pasenger compartment, behind the kick panel.
Daytime Running Lamp Module—inside the engine compartment, the right front area of the engine compartment.

Transmission Control Module – inside the engine compartment, mounted on the left front fender, behind the battery.

Anti-Lock Brake System (ABS) Controller – left front of engine compartment, on the right side of the battery.

Climate Control Module – under the right side of the instrument panel.

Air Bag Control Module – under the left side of the instrument panel.

Remote Keyless Entry Module – under the right side of the instrument panel.

Cruise Control

For further information, please refer to Chilton's Chassis Electronics Service Manual.

Adjustment

If the cruise control system is functioning improperly, inspect the control cable to assure both ends are securely attached. If either end is loose, the cruise control system will be inoperative.

Escort, Tempo and Topaz

Location

FUSES

On all vehicles, a fuse panel is located under the instrument panel to the left of the steering column. On 1991–94 Escort, a fuse block is mounted in the left-hand side of the engine compartment.

FUSIBLE LINKS

Fusible links are used to prevent major wire harness damage in the event of a short circuit or an overload condition in the wiring circuits that are normally not fused, due to carrying high amperage loads or because of their locations within the wiring harness. Each fusible link is of a fixed value for a specific electrical load and should a fusible link fail, the cause of the failure must be determined and repaired prior to installing a new fusible link of the same value. Please be advised that the color coding of replacement fusible links may vary from the production color coding that is outlined in the text that follows.

Gray 12 Gauge Wire – on 1992–94 Tempo and Topaz, there is 1 link located in the charging circuit near the starter motor relay.

Dark Green 14 Gauge Wire – on 1990–91 Tempo and Topaz and 1990 Escort, there is 1 link located in the charging circuit near the starter motor relay. On 1992–94 Tempo and Topaz, there is 1 link for the cooling fan relay in the wiring assembly on the starter motor relay.

Black 16 Gauge Wire – on 1990 Escort, there is 1 link for the rear window defogger located in the engine compartment on the starter relay. On Tempo, Topaz and 1990 Escort, there is 1 link for the headlight feed located in the engine compartment on the starter relay and 1 link for the ignition feed near the starter relay. On 1990–91 Tempo and Topaz, there is 1 link for the cooling fan relay located in the wiring assembly on the starter relay.

Brown 18 Gauge Wire – on Tempo and Topaz, there is 1 link used to protect the rear window defogger and the fuel door release. On 1991–94 Tempo and Topaz, there is 1 link in the charging circuit near the starter relay. On 1992–94 Tempo and Topaz, there is 1 link near the starter motor relay to protect the EEC module. On the 1990 Escort, there is 1 link used to protect the cooling fan motor circuit and 1 link for the EEC system power relay on the starter relay.

Dark Blue 20 Gauge Wire – on 1990 Escort, there are 4 links in the engine compartment near the starter for the shift indicator light module, ignition coil and distributor, passive restraint module and fuel pump relay. On 1990–91 Tempo and Topaz, there is 1 link for the fan and air conditioning clutch in the wiring assembly on the starter. On all Tempo and Topaz, there is 1 link for the air bag module in the engine compartment near the starter relay. On 1991–94 Tempo and Topaz, there is 1 link for the passive restraint module located in the engine compartment on the starter relay, 1 link for the heated oxygen sensor, 4-wheel drive and air conditioning fan controller located near the left shock tower and 1 link for the ignition coil, TFI module and ECA relay located near the left shock tower. On 1992–94 Tempo and Topaz, there is 1 link in the wiring assembly near the starter motor relay for the EEC power relay and fuel pump relay.

NOTE: Always disconnect the negative battery cable before servicing the high current fuses or serious personal injury may result.

FUSE LINK CARTRIDGE

Fuse link cartridges are used on 1991–94 Escort. Fuse link cartridges have a colored plastic housing with a clear "window" at the top. To check a fuse cartridge, look at the fuse element through the clear "window". The fuse link cartridges are located in the engine compartment fuse box. The following fuse link cartridges are listed according to their labels in the fuse box.

FUEL INJ – Pink 30 amp: to protect the electronic engine control circuit.

HEAD – Pink 30 amp: to protect the headlight circuit and the daytime running lights circuit.

MAIN – Black 80 amp for 1.8L engine or Dark Blue 100 amp for 1.9L engine: to protect all circuits, except starter and starter solenoid circuits.

BTN – Yellow 60 amp for 1.8L engine or Green 40 amp for 1.9L engine: to protect the courtesy lights, electronic automatic transaxle, electronic engine control, exterior lights, horn, interior lights, passive restraint, power door locks, radio, shift lock and warning chime circuits.

COOLING FAN – Pink 20 amp for 1.8L engine or Green 40 amp for 1.9L engine: to protect cooling fans circuit.

CIRCUIT BREAKERS

Circuit breakers are used to protect the various components of the electrical system, such as headlights and windshield wipers. The circuit breakers are located either in the control switch or mounted on or near the fuse panel.

Tempo and Topaz

Headlights and Highbeam Indicator – one 22 amp circuit breaker incorporated in the lighting switch.

Alternator Voltage Sensing Circuit – one 18 amp circuit breaker located in engine compartment wiring assembly near starter relay on 1990–91 vehicles.

HEGO, All Wheel Drive Relays, Air Conditioning Fan Controller, Fan Tester and All Wheel Drive Switch – one 20 amp circuit breaker located in the engine compartment near the starter relay on 1990–91 vehicles.

Passive Restraint Module – one 20 amp circuit breaker located in the engine compartment near the starter relay on 1990–91 vehicles.

Power Windows, Power Seats, Power Door Locks and Power Lumbar – one 20 amp circuit breaker located in the fuse panel.

Windshield Wipers – one 8.25 amp circuit breaker located in the fuse panel.

Escort

Headlights and High Beam Indicator – one 22 amp circuit breaker incorporated in the lighting switch, on 1990 vehicles.

Liftgate Wiper—one 4.5 amp circuit breaker located in the instrument panel, to the left of the radio, on 1990 vehicles.

Windshield Wiper and Wiper Pump Circuit—one 8.25 amp circuit breaker located in the fuse panel, on 1990 vehicles.

Engine Cooling Fan Motor, Without A/C—one 12 amp circuit breaker located in the fuse panel on 1990 vehicles.

Heater Blower Motor—one 30 amp circuit breaker located in the fuse panel under the dash, to the left of the steering column, on 1991–94 vehicles.

VARIOUS RELAYS

Tempo and Topaz

All Wheel Drive Relays—located behind the right side of the instrument panel.

Door Lock Control Relay—located below the left side of the instrument panel, near the fuse panel.

Cooling Fan Relay—located in the left front of the engine compartment.

Electronic Engine Control Power Relay—located behind the right side of the instrument panel.

Fuel Pump Relay—located behind the right side of the instrument panel.

Horn Relay—located behind the left side of the instrument panel, above the fuse panel.

Starter Relay—located on the left front fender apron in front of the strut tower.

Rear Window Defrost Relay—located behind the left side of the instrument panel, to the right of the steering column.

Shift Indicator Dimmer Relay—located behind the left side of the instrument panel, near the steering column on 1990–91 vehicles or on the right side of the brake pedal support on 1992–94 vehicles.

Window Safety Relay—located behind the left side of the instrument panel, above the fuse panel.

1990 Escort

Cooling Fan Relay—located in the left front of the engine compartment, near the left headlight.

Electronic Engine Control (EEC) Power Relay—located behind the left side of the instrument panel.

Fuel Pump Relay—located behind the left side of the instrument panel.

Horn Relay—located behind the left side of the instrument panel, to the right of the steering column.

Shift Indicator Dimmer Relay—located behind the right side of the instrument panel.

Starter Relay—located on the left side of the fender apron in front of the shock tower.

1991–94 Escort

Air Conditioning Relay—located on the rear of the right fender apron on 1991 vehicles or in the right rear corner of the engine compartment, on the firewall on 1992–94 vehicles.

Cooling Fan Lo and Hi Speed Relays—located on the front of the left fender apron.

Cooling Fan Relay—located on top of the left front wheel well, in the engine compartment fuse block.

Door Lock Relay—located above the left cowl on 1991 vehicles or behind the left side of the instrument panel, near the cowl on 1992–94 vehicles.

Daytime Running Lights Relay—located behind the right side of the instrument panel, near the blower motor.

Electronic Engine Control Power Relay—located behind the center of the instrument panel.

Fuel Pump Relay—located behind the center of the instrument panel.

Headlight Relay—located above the left cowl on 1991 vehicles or behind the left side of the instrument panel, near the cowl on 1992–94 vehicles.

Horn Relay—located above the left cowl on 1991 vehicles or behind the left side of the instrument panel, near the cowl on 1992–94 vehicles.

Ignition Relay—located on top of the left front wheel well, in the engine compartment fuse block.

Parking Light Relay—located behind the left side of the instrument panel.

Vane Air Flow Meter Relay—located behind the center of the instrument panel.

Wide Open Throttle Cutout Relay—located on the rear of the right fender apron on 1991 vehicles or in the right rear corner of the engine compartment, on the firewall on 1992–94 vehicles.

Computers

Location

The Electronic Engine Control (EEC) module is located behind the left side of the instrument panel on all except 1991–94 Escort. On the 1991–94 Escort, the EEC module is located behind the center of the instrument panel.

Turn Signal/Hazard Warning Flashers

Location

EXCEPT 1991–94 ESCORT

The turn signal flasher is located on the front side of the fuse panel. The hazard flasher is located on the rear of the fuse panel behind the turn signal flasher.

1991–94 ESCORT

The turn signal and hazard flasher switch use the same flasher unit. The flasher unit is located with the combination switch.

Cruise Control

Adjustment
ACTUATOR CABLE

1.8L and 1991–94 1.9L Engines

1. Remove the cable adjusting clip from the cable housing.
2. Pull tightly on the cable until all of the slack is taken out.
3. Install the cable adjusting clip.

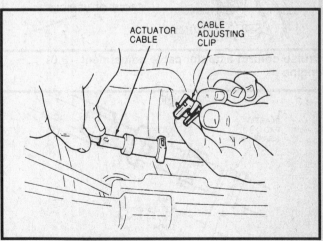

Cruise control actuator cable adjustment—1.8L and 1991–94 1.9L engines

2.3L and 1990 1.9L Engines

1. With engine **OFF**, set the throttle linkage so the throttle plate is closed.
2. Remove the locking pin.
3. Pull the bead chain through the adjuster.
4. Insert the locking pin in the best hole of the adjuster to draw the bead chain tight without opening the throttle plate.

3.0L Engine

1. Remove the actuator cable retaining clip.
2. Pull the actuator cable through the adjuster until slight tension is felt.
3. Insert the cable retaining clip and snap into place.

VACUUM DUMP VALVE

1. Firmly depress the brake pedal and hold in position.

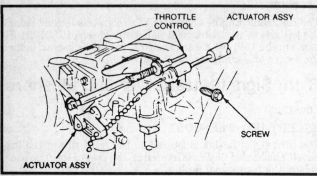

Cruise control actuator cable adjustment—2.3L and 1990 1.9L engines

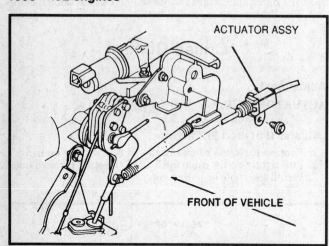

Cruise control actuator cable adjustment—3.0L engine

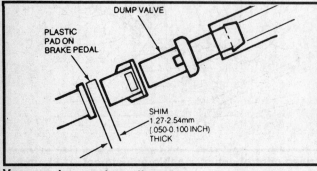

Vacuum dump valve adjustment

2. Push in the dump valve until the valve collar bottoms against the retaining clip.
3. Place a 0.050–0.10 in. (1.27–2.54mm) shim between the white button of the valve and the pad on the brake pedal.
4. Firmly pull the brake pedal rearward to its normal position, allowing the dump valve to ratchet backwards in the retaining clip.

CLUTCH SWITCH

Except 1991–94 Escort

1. Prop the clutch pedal in the full-up position—pawl fully released from the sector.
2. Loosen the switch mounting screw.
3. Slide the switch forward toward the clutch pedal until the switch plunger cap is 0.030 in. (0.76mm) from contacting the switch housing. Tighten the attaching screw.
4. Remove the prop from the clutch pedal and test drive for clutch cancellation of cruise control.

1991–94 Escort

1. Measure the distance from the bulkhead to the upper center of the clutch pedal pad. The distance should be 7.72–8.03 in. (196–204mm). If not proceed to Step 2.
2. Disconnect the clutch switch electrical connector.
3. Loosen the switch locknut and turn the switch until the specified distance is achieved. Tighten the locknut to 10–13 ft. lbs. (14–18 Nm).
4. Push the clutch pedal down by hand until clutch resistance is felt.
5. Measure the distance between the upper pedal height and where resistance is felt. The free-play should be 0.20–0.51 in. (5–13mm). If not, proceed to Step 6.
6. Loosen the pushrod locknut and turn the pushrod until the specified free-play is achieved.
7. Check that disengagement height is correct when the pedal is fully depressed. Minimum disengagement height is 1.6 in. (41mm).
8. Tighten the pushrod locknut to 9–12 ft. lbs. (12–17mm) and connect the clutch switch electrical connector.

Festiva

Location

FUSES

The fuse panel is located in the passenger compartment, to the left of the steering column. It is concealed behind an access panel that clips into position on the instrument panel. The fuses are the cartridge type that must be removed for inspection. When making replacements, install only cartridge type fuses with the same amperage rating as the fuse that was removed.

FUSIBLE LINKS

The main fuse links are located in the engine compartment on the front of the left strut tower. The main fuse link panel contains 3 fusible links—**PTC** on carbureted engine or **EGI** on EFI engine, as well as **MAIN**, and **HEAD**. The ends of the fusible links are connected to the main fuse panel through standard push-on connectors. To remove a link, grasp the insulator and pull until the connector separates from the panel. Install the new link by reversing the removal procedure.

RELAYS

Air Conditioning Relays—located in the left front corner of the engine compartment, left of the cooling fan. There are 3 air conditioning relays, the main relay, the wide open throttle cut-off relay and the condenser fan relay.

Cooling Fan Relay—located on the fender apron, behind the left headlight.

Daytime Running Light Relay—located on the fender apron, behind the left headlight on Canadian vehicles only.

FUSE CHART—1990–91 VEHICLES

Fuse	Item for Circuit Affected	Fuse	Item for Circuit Affected
TAIL (15A)	License lamp, Parking/side marker lamps, Front parking lamps, Illumination lamps and taillamps	F. WIPER (15A)	Front wiper and washer
STOP (15A)	Horn, Stoplamps and Hi-mount Stoplamp	ENG. (10A)	Charging system and Emission control system
HAZARD (15A)	Seat belt warning, Interior light, Luggage compartment lamp, Turn and hazard flasher lamps, Ignition key reminder buzzer and Radio system	METER (10A)	Seat belt warning, Turn and hazard flasher lamps, Cooling fan system, Backup lamp and cluster and warning lamps
CIGAR (15A)	Radio system, Cigar lighter and remote control mirror	R. DEF. (15A)	Rear window defroster
R. WIPER (15A)	Rear wiper and washer		
HEATER (15A)	Heater and Air conditioner		
FAN (15A)	Heater and Air conditioner and Cooling fan system		

FUSE CHART—1992–93 VEHICLES

Fuse	Item for Circuit Affected	Fuse	Item for Circuit Affected
TAIL (15A)	License lamp, Parking/side marker lamps, Front parking lamps, Illumination lamps and tail lamps	F. WIPER (15A)	Front wiper and washer
STOP (15A)	Horn, Stoplamps and Hi-mount Stoplamp	ENG. (10A)	Charging system and Emission control system
HAZARD (15A)	Seat belt warning, Interior light, Luggage compartment lamp, Turn and hazard flasher lamps, Ignition key reminder buzzer and Radio system	METER (10A)	Seat belt warning, Turn and hazard flasher lamps, Cooling fan system, Backup lamp and cluster and warning lamps
CIGAR (15A)	Radio system, Cigar lighter and remote control mirror	R. DEF. (15A)	Rear window defroster
R. WIPER (15A)	Rear wiper and washer	R. DEF. (15A)	Rear window defroster
HEATER (15A)	Heater and Air conditioner	BELT (30A)	Passive Restraint System
FAN (15A)	Heater and Air conditioner and Cooling fan system	BELT (30A)	Passive Restraint System

MAIN FUSE LINK CHART

Main Fuse	Item for Circuit Affected
PTC or EGI Fusible Link (Brown, 15A)	EFE Heater (carbureted engine) or EFI (EFI engine)
Main Fusible Link (Red, 25A)	Parking/side marker lamps, Illumination lamps, Tail lamps, Horn & stop-lamps, Interior lamp, Luggage compartment lamp, Turn & hazard flasher lamps, Radio, Charging system, Cigar lighter, Rear wiper & washer, Air conditioning & heater, Cooling fan system, Front wiper & washer, Emission control system, Backup lamps, Cluster & warning lights, Rear window defroster, Ignition system, Starting system
Head Fusible Link (Brown, 15A)	Headlamp

EFE Relay—located in the passenger compartment mounted on a bracket behind the left upper corner of the instrument panel, on carbureted vehicles only.

Fuel Pump Relay—located on the left side of the instrument panel, to the left of the electronic control unit, on EFI vehicles only.

Headlight Relay—located on the fender apron, behind the left headlight.

Horn Relay—located behind left corner of instrument panel.

Main Relay—located in the left front corner of the engine compartment, attached to the fender apron.

Parking Light Relay—located in the right front corner of the engine compartment, on the fender apron.

Computers

Location

The electronic control unit is located behind the instrument panel on the drivers side of the vehicle.

Flashers

Location

The turn signal and hazard flashers are controlled by a single flasher unit. The flasher unit is located under the instrument panel, behind the electronic control unit.

Probe

Location

FUSES

The main fuse block is located in the left side of the engine compartment near the battery. The interior fuse block is located above the left side kick panel on 1990–92 vehicles or behind the left side kick panel on 1993–94 vehicles.

CIRCUIT BREAKERS

A bimetal circuit breaker, used to protect the rear window defroster circuit, is located in the joint box, which is just above the interior fuse panel on 1990–92 vehicles.

RELAYS

1990–92

The main relay box is located in the engine compartment on the upper left side of the firewall (bulkhead). There is also a relay box located inside the vehicle under the left side of the instrument panel.

EFI Main Relays (2)—located in the main relay box
Horn Relay—located in the main relay box
Cooling Fan Relay No. 1—located in the main relay box
Cooling Fan Relay No. 2—located in the main relay box
Turn Signal/Hazard Flasher Relay—located in the relay box
Fuel pump Relay—located in the relay box
Rear Window Defroster Relay—located in the relay box
Intermittent Wiper Relay—located in the relay box

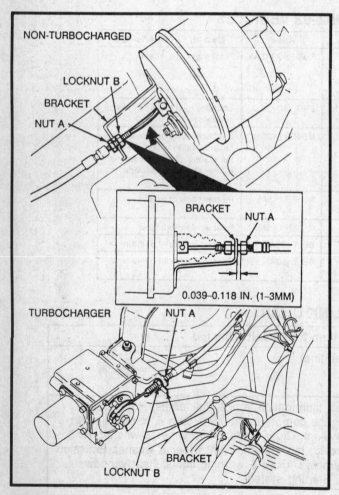

Cruise control actuator cable adjustment—2.2L engines

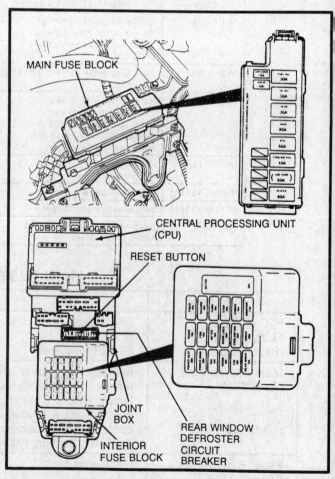

Main and interior fuse blocks—1990–92

Stoplight/Tail Light Checker Relay—located in the relay box

Fog Light Relay—located in the relay box

ABS Relay—located in the engine compartment, near the master cylinder

Air Conditioning Relay—on Probe LX only, located behind the right side of the instrument panel, to the left of the blower motor

Blower Motor Relay—located in the engine compartment, forward of the battery

Condenser Fan Relay—on Probe GL and Probe GT only, located in the engine compartment, on right front of condenser

Dimmer Relay—located in the engine compartment, forward of the washer reservoir

Power Door Lock Relay—located behind the left interior rear quarter trim panel

NOTE: Cooling fan relay No. 1 is used only on vehicles equipped with the electronically controlled 4EAT automatic transaxle.

1993–94

Several main relays are located within the main fuse block. These include the starter relay, main relay, fuel pump relay, parking light/turn signal relay, horn relay, daytime running light relay, A/C relay, headlight relay and fog light relay.

Computers

Location

The computer controlling engine operation, the Electronic Control Assembly (ECA), is located behind the instrument panel, forward of the center console.

On 1990–92 vehicles, the control units for the anti-lock brake system and the variable assist power steering are both located under the driver's seat. On 1993–94 vehicles, the control unit for the anti-lock brake system is located behind the left side kick panel and air bag diagnostic monitor is located under the left side of the instrument panel.

A central processing unit is located directly above the interior fuse block. This microprocessor controls the warning chime systems and the theft warning and illuminated entry systems, if equipped.

Flashers

Location

The turn/signal flasher relay is located in the relay box under the instrument panel on 1990–92 vehicles and in the main fuse block on 1993–94 vehicles.

Cruise Control

Adjustment

2.2L ENGINE

Non-Turbocharged Engine

1. Loosen the locknut and adjusting nuts.
2. Pull on the cable housing without moving the actuator rod.
3. Position adjusting nut A until there is 0.039–0.118 in. (1–3mm) clearance between nut A and the bracket.
4. Tighten locknut B securely.

Turbocharged Engine

1. Remove the plastic cover.
2. Loosen the locknut and adjusting nuts.

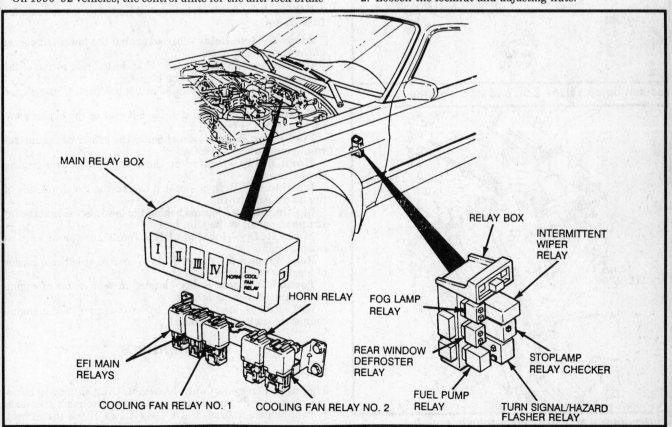

Main relay box and relay box contents and locations—1990–92

3. Pull on the cable housing without moving the actuator spool.

4. Position adjusting nut A until there is 0.039–0.118 in. (1–3mm) clearance between nut A and the bracket.

5. Tighten locknut B securely.

6. Install the plastic cover.

2.0L AND 2.5L ENGINES

Actuator Cable

1. Remove the cable adjusting clip from the cable housing.
2. Pull lightly on the cable until all of the slack is taken out.
3. Install the cable adjusting clip.

Vacuum Dump Valve

1. Disconnect the dump valve-to-actuator vacuum hose at the actuator.

2. Connect a suitable vacuum tester to the end of the hose at the actuator.

3. Pump up the vacuum to approximately 10–15 in.

NOTE: If vacuum cannot be obtained, check the hose and vacuum dump valve for leaks.

4. Depress the brake pedal and the vacuum should release.

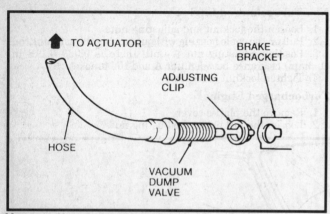

Vacuum dump valve—2.0L and 2.5L engines

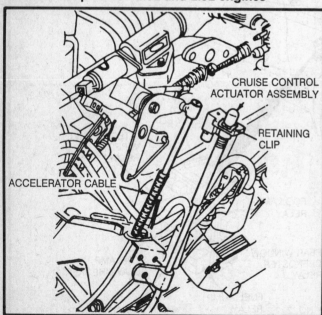

Cruise control actuator cable adjustment—3.0L engine

5. If the vacuum does not release, adjust the vacuum dump valve as follows:

   a. When the brake pedal is released and in the upright position, the vacuum dump valve plunger should protrude 4–5mm from the body.

   b. If the plunger protrudes more than 5mm, move the vacuum dump valve position in the adjusting clip until the plunger is within specification.

6. Repeat Steps 2–4. If the vacuum does not release, replace the vacuum dump valve.

3.0L ENGINE

1. Remove the cruise control actuator cable retaining clip.
2. Push the actuator cable through the adjuster until slight tension is felt.
3. Insert the cable retaining clip and snap into place.

Capri

Location

FUSES

The vehicle is equipped with 2 fuse panels. The main fuse panel protects the high current circuits and is located on the driver's side of the engine compartment. The interior fuse panel protects the lower current circuits and is located under the left side of the instrument panel.

CIRCUIT BREAKERS

A 30 amp circuit breaker, used to protect the blower motor circuit, is attached to the interior fuse panel.

RELAYS

NOTE: A relay block is located just above the interior fuse panel.

Audio System Relay—located behind the lower left corner of the instrument panel.

Condenser Fan Relay—located at the left rear corner of the engine compartment, at the bulkhead.

Cooling Fan Relay—located at the left front of the engine compartment.

Foglight Relay—located at the left rear of the engine compartment, at the bulkhead.

Fuel Pump Relay—located below the center of the instrument panel, under the ECA.

Horn Relay—located at the left front of the engine compartment.

Ignition Key Relays—located behind the lower left side of the instrument panel.

Ignition Relay—located behind the lower left side of the instrument panel, at the joint box.

Main Relay—located at left front corner of engine compartment.

Rear Window Defroster Relay—located at left rear corner of luggage compartment.

Turbo Overboost Relay—located in rear center of engine compartment, near bulkhead.

WAC Relay—located at the left rear corner of the engine compartment, at the bulkhead.

Computers

Location

The engine Electronic Control Assembly (ECA) is located below the center of the instrument panel. The automatic transaxle control module is located at the right side of the instrument panel, above the glove box. The air bag diagnostic module is located behind the left corner of the instrument panel.

Flashers

Location

The turn signal/hazard flasher is located on the relay panel, which is located above the interior fuse panel.

Cruise Control

For further information, please refer to Chilton's Chassis Electronics Service Manual.

Adjustment
ACTUATOR CABLE

NOTE: A setting tool must be fabricated to properly adjust the cruise control cables.

Cable at Throttle Body

1. Disconnect the cable from the cruise control actuator.
2. Slightly loosen the cable retaining nuts at the bracket on the cylinder head cover.
3. Insert the setting tool between nut **B** and the bracket.
4. Tighten both nuts to eliminate all cable slack.
5. Loosen nut **A** only enough to remove the tool. Do not adjust nut **B**.
6. Tighten nut **A** without moving nut **B**.

Cable at Actuator

NOTE: To be performed after throttle body end adjustment.

1. Slightly loosen the cable retaining nuts at the bracket.
2. Insert the setting tool between bracket and nut **D**.
3. Tighten both nuts to eliminate all slack at the throttle body end of the cable.
4. Loosen nut **C** only enough to remove the setting tool. Do not adjust nut **D**.
5. Tighten nut **C** without moving nut **D**.

CLUTCH PEDAL HEIGHT

Measure the distance from the center of the clutch pedal to the lower dash panel, the front area of the footwell. The pedal height must be 8.44–8.64 in. (214.5–219.5mm). If necessary, adjust as follows:
1. Loosen the locknut and turn the clutch switch until the desired pedal height is obtained.
2. Tighten the locknut when the clutch pedal height is achieved.

BRAKE PEDAL HEIGHT

Check the distance from the brake pedal to the stoplight switch screw. The distance should be 0.078 in. (2mm). If necessary, adjust as follows:
1. Disconnect the negative battery cable. Disconnect the connector to the stoplight switch.

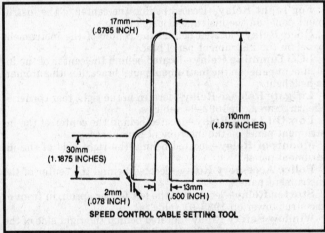

Cruise control cable adjustment tool dimensions

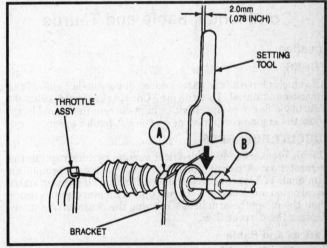

Cruise control cable adjustment—cable at throttle body

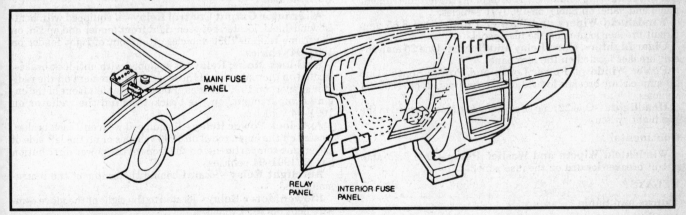

Fuse panel locations

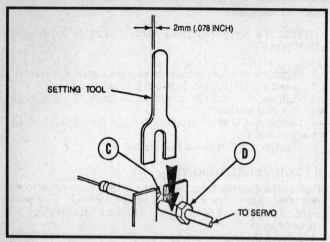

Cruise control cable adjustment—cable at actuator

2. Loosen the locknut.
3. Adjust the distance by rotating the stoplight switch. Rotate the switch until the distance is within specification.
4. Tighten the locknut and connect the electrical connector.
5. Connect the negative battery cable. Check the operation of the stoplight switch and rear lights.

Continental, Sable and Taurus

Location

FUSES

All vehicles have a fuse panel located under the left side of the instrument panel. In addition, Continental and 1992-94 Taurus/Sable are equipped with a high-current fuse panel located in the engine compartment on the left fender apron.

CIRCUIT BREAKERS

Circuit breakers protect electrical circuits by interrupting the current flow. A circuit breaker conducts current through an arm made of 2 types of metal bonded together. If the arm starts to carry too much current, it heats up. As 1 metal expands faster than the other the arm bends, opening the contacts and interrupting the current flow.

Taurus and Sable

Station Wagon Rear Window/Washer—One 4.5 amp circuit breaker located on the instrument panel brace, on the left side of the steering column on Taurus or on the left instrument panel end panel on Sable, on 1990-91 vehicles.
Windshield Wipers and Washer Pump—One 8.25 amp circuit breaker located on the fuse panel.
Cigar Lighters, Horn Relay and Horns—One 20 amp circuit breaker located on the fuse panel.
Power Windows, Power Locks and Power Seats—One 20 amp circuit breaker located on the fuse panel, on 1990-94 vehicles.
Headlights—One 22 amp circuit breaker incorporated in the headlight switch.

Continental

Windshield Wipers and Washer Pump—One 8.25 amp circuit breaker located on the fuse panel.

RELAYS

Taurus and Sable

Alternator Output Control Relay—located between the

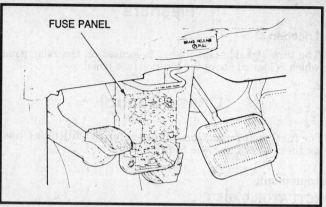

Fuse panel location—Continental

right front inner fender and fender splash shield on 1990-91 vehicles, if equipped with 3.0L or 3.8L engines and heated windshield.
Anti-lock Motor Relay—located in lower left front of engine compartment, if equipped with anti-lock brakes.
Anti-lock Power Relay—located in left rear corner of engine compartment on 1990-91 vehicles, right rear of engine compartment on firewall on early 1992 vehicles or on front of left front fender apron on late 1992-94 vehicles, if equipped with anti-lock brakes.
Autolight Dual Coil Relay—located behind the center of the instrument panel on the instrument panel brace, if with automatic headlights.
Fog Light Relay—located behind the center of the instrument panel on the instrument panel brace.
Horn Relay—located behind the center of the instrument panel on the instrument panel brace.
LCD Dimming Relay—located behind the center of the instrument panel on the instrument panel brace, if with automatic headlights.
Liftgate Release Relay—located in the right rear corner of the cargo area, on 1992-94 vehicles.
Low Oil Level Relay—located behind the center of the instrument panel on the instrument panel brace.
Moonroof Relay—located behind the right side of the instrument panel.
Police Accessory Relay—located behind the center of the instrument panel.
Starter Relay—located on the left fender apron, in front of the strut tower on 1989-91 vehicles.
Window Safety Relay—located behind the right side of the instrument panel on 1990-91 vehicles.

Continental

Alternator Output Control Relay—if equipped with heated windshield, located between right front fender and apron, on the frame rail, on 1990 vehicles or in front of right fender on 1991-94 vehicles.
Anti-lock Motor Relay—if equipped with anti-lock brakes, located on the right side of the engine compartment on the radiator support on 1990 vehicles or on the lower left front of the engine compartment, on the bracket behind the radiator on 1991-94 vehicles.
Anti-lock Power Relay—if equipped with anti-lock brakes, located on the engine cowl on 1990 vehicles or on the left side of the engine compartment, on the front of the power distribution box on 1991-94 vehicles.
Autolight Relay—located behind the center of the instrument panel.
Blower Motor Relay—located to the right of the glove compartment on 1990 vehicles.
Compressor Relay—located on the engine cowl or on the

left side of the engine compartment on 1990 vehicles or on the front of the power distribution box on 1991–94 vehicles.

Hard Shock Relay – located below the left side of the rear package tray.

Hi-Lo Beam Relay – located behind the left side of the instrument panel on 1990 vehicles or behind the center of the instrument panel on 1991–94 vehicles.

Horn Relay – located behind the center of the instrument panel on 1990 vehicles or behind the lower center of the instrument panel, near the left side of the warning chime module, on 1991–94 vehicles.

Interior Light Relay – located behind the right side of the instrument panel on 1990 vehicles.

LCD Dimming Relay – located behind the center of the instrument panel.

Soft Shock Relay – located below the left side of rear package tray.

Starter Relay – located on the left fender apron.

Window Safety Relay – located behind the center of the instrument panel.

Computers

Location

TAURUS AND SABLE

Electronic Engine Control Module – located on the passenger side of the firewall.

Anti-lock Brake Control Module – located at the front of the engine compartment next to the passenger side fender, except on Taurus SHO where it is located at the front of the engine compartment on the driver's side.

Automatic Temperature Control Module – located behind the center of the instrument panel.

Heated Windshield Control Module – located behind the left side of the instrument panel, to the right of the steering column.

Integrated Control Module – located at the front of the engine compartment, on the upper radiator support.

Air Bag Diagnostic Module – located behind the right side of the instrument panel, above the glove box.

CONTINENTAL

Electronic Engine Control Module – located on the passenger side of the firewall.

Anti-lock Brake Control Module – located in the trunk on the passenger side under the package tray.

Air Bag Diagnostic Module – located behind the left side of the instrument panel, above the fuse panel.

Automatic Temperature Control Module – located behind the center of the instrument panel.

Heated Windshield Control Module – located behind the left side of the instrument panel.

Integrated Control Module – located at the front of the engine compartment, on the upper radiator support.

Air Suspension Control Module – located in left side of trunk.

Flashers

Location

An electronic combination turn signal and emergency warning flasher is attached to the lower left instrument panel reinforcement above the fuse panel.

Cruise Control

Adjustment

ACTUATOR CABLE

2.5L Engine

1. Remove locking pin.
2. Pull bead chain through adjuster.
3. Insert locking pin in best hole of adjuster for tight bead chain without opening throttle plate.

3.0L and 3.8L Engines

1. Remove cable retaining clip.
2. Push actuator cable through adjuster until slight tension is felt.
3. Insert cable retaining clip and snap into place.

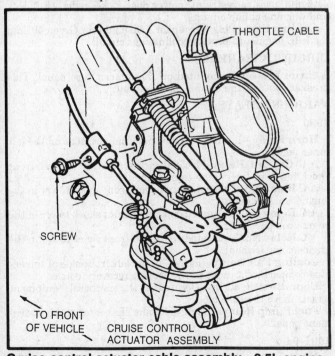

Cruise control actuator cable assembly – 2.5L engine

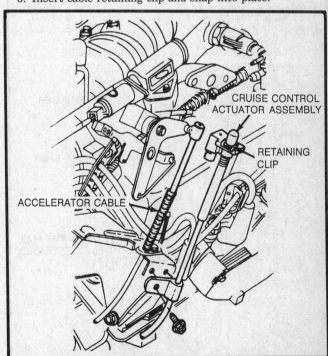

Cruise control circuator cable assembly – 3.0L engine

VACUUM DUMP VALVE

The vacuum dump valve is adjustable in its mounting bracket. It should be adjusted so it is closed (no vacuum leak) when the brake pedal is in the normal release position (not depressed) and

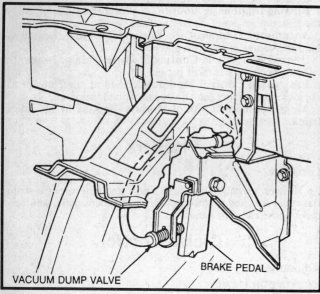

VACUUM DUMP VALVE

BRAKE PEDAL

Vacuum dump valve location

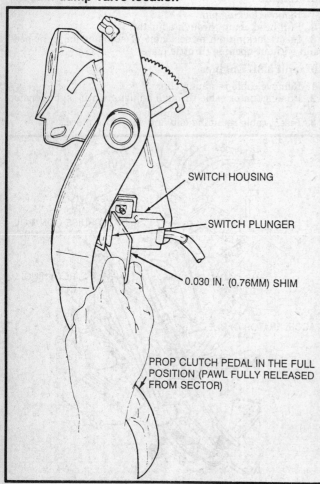

SWITCH HOUSING

SWITCH PLUNGER

0.030 IN. (0.76MM) SHIM

PROP CLUTCH PEDAL IN THE FULL POSITION (PAWL FULLY RELEASED FROM SECTOR)

Cruise control clutch switch adjustment

open when the pedal is depressed. Use a hand vacuum pump or equivalent to make this adjustment.

CLUTCH SWITCH

1. Prop the clutch pedal in the full-up position. The pawl should be fully released from the sector.
2. Loosen the switch retaining screw.
3. Slide the switch forward toward the clutch pedal until the switch plunger cap is 0.030 in. (0.76mm) from contacting the switch housing. Tighten the retaining screw.
4. Remove the prop from the clutch pedal and test drive for clutch switch cancellation of cruise control.

Tracer

Location

FUSES

All vehicles are equipped with a fuse panel mounted inside the vehicle, under the left side of the instrument panel as well as a fuse box mounted in the engine compartment.

FUSE LINK CARTRIDGE

Fuse link cartridges are used on 1991–94 vehicles. Fuse link cartridges have a colored plastic housing with a clear "window" at the top. To check a fuse cartridge, look at the fuse element through the clear "window". The fuse link cartridges are located in the engine compartment fuse box. The following fuse link cartridges are listed according to their labels in the fuse box.

Fuel Inj – Pink 30 amp: to protect the electronic engine control circuit.

Head – Pink 30 amp: to protect the headlight circuit and in Canada, the daytime running lights circuit.

Main – Black 80 amp for 1.8L engine or Dark Blue 100 amp for 1.9L engine: to protect all circuits, except starter and starter solenoid circuits.

BTN – Yellow 60 amp for 1.8L engine or Green 40 amp for 1.9L engine: to protect the courtesy lights, electronic automatic transaxle, electronic engine control, exterior lights, horn, interior lights, passive restraint, power door locks, radio, shift lock and warning chime circuits.

Cooling Fan – Pink 30 amp for 1.8L engine or Green 40 amp for 1.9L engine: to protect cooling fans circuit.

CIRCUIT BREAKERS

A circuit breaker is mounted on the interior fuse panel. This breaker controls the blower motor circuit.

VARIOUS RELAYS

1990

Horn Relay – located in the engine compartment on the left inner fender.

A/C Cut-out Relay – located in the front of the left front shock tower in the engine compartment.

A/C Relay No. 1 – located on the left front shock tower in the engine compartment.

A/C Relay No. 2 – located on the left front shock tower in the engine compartment.

A/C Relay No. 3 – located on the left front shock tower in the engine compartment.

Cooling Fan Relay – located in the left front side of the engine compartment, next to the coolant recovery bottle.

Door Buzzer Relay – located in the electrical equipment panel, above the fuse block.

Fuel Pump Relay – mounted under the center of the instrument panel.

1991–94

Air Conditioning Relay – located on the rear of the right fender apron on 1991 vehicles or in the right rear corner of the engine compartment, on the firewall on 1992–94 vehicles.

Cooling Fan Lo and Hi Speed Relays—located on the front of the left fender apron.

Cooling Fan Relay—located on top of the left front wheel well, in the engine compartment fuse block.

Door Lock Relay—located above the left cowl on 1991 vehicles or behind the left side of the instrument panel, near the cowl on 1992–94 vehicles.

Daytime Running Lights Relay—located behind the right side of the instrument panel, near the blower motor.

Electronic Engine Control Power Relay—located behind the center of the instrument panel.

Fuel Pump Relay—located behind the center of the instrument panel.

Headlight Relay—located above the left cowl on 1991 vehicles or behind the left side of the instrument panel, near the cowl on 1992–94 vehicles.

Horn Relay—located above the left cowl on 1991 vehicles or behind the left side of the instrument panel, near the cowl on 1992–94 vehicles.

Ignition Relay—located on top of the left front wheel well, in the engine compartment fuse block.

Parking Light Relay—located behind the left side of the instrument panel.

Vane Air Flow Meter Relay—located behind the center of the instrument panel.

Wide Open Throttle Cutout Relay—located on the rear of

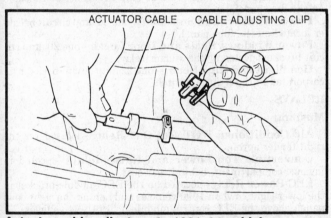

Actuator cable adjustment—1991–94 vehicles

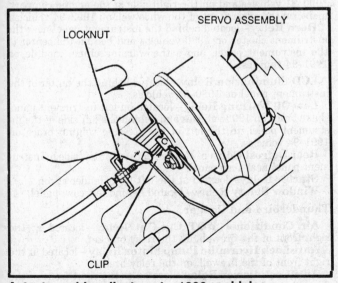

Actuator cable adjustment—1990 vehicles

the right fender apron on 1991 vehicles or in the right rear corner of the engine compartment, on the firewall on 1992–94 vehicles.

Computers

Location

The Electronic Control Unit (ECU) is located behind the center of the instrument panel.

Flashers

Location

On 1990 vehicles, the turn signal/hazard flasher is located on the interior fuse panel. On 1991–94 vehicles, the flasher unit is located with the combination switch.

Cruise Control

Adjustment
ACTUATOR CABLE
1990

1. With the engine off, remove the clip from the actuator cable and adjust the locknut while pressing down on the cable until free-play is 0.04–0.12 in. (1–3mm).
2. Check the system operation and adjust as needed.

1991–94

1. Remove the cable adjusting clip from the cable housing.
2. Pull tightly on the cable until all of the slack is taken out.
3. Install the cable adjusting clip.

CLUTCH PEDAL HEIGHT
1990

Pedal height is the distance from the cowl to the center of the clutch pedal pad.

1. Remove the necessary instrument panel components which block access to the clutch pedal.
2. Loosen the clutch pedal locknut.
3. Turn the stop bolt to obtain the correct pedal height of 8.44–8.64 in. (214.5–219.5mm). Tighten the locknut.
4. If components from the instrument panel were removed, reinstall them.

BRAKE PEDAL HEIGHT
1990

Measure the distance from the center of the brake pedal to lower dash panel. Pedal height must be 8.62–8.82 in. (219–224mm). If the brake pedal height is not within these specifications, adjust as follows:

1. Disconnect the negative battery cable.
2. Adjust the pedal height by adjusting the stoplight switch.
3. Disconnect the connector on the stoplight switch.
4. Loosen the stoplight switch locknut and rotate the switch until the pedal height is 8.62–8.82 in. (219–224mm).
5. Tighten the switch locknut.
6. Connect the stoplight switch connector.
7. Connect the negative battery cable and check stoplight operation.

VACUUM DUMP VALVE
1991–94

1. Firmly depress the brake pedal and hold in position.
2. Push in the dump valve until the valve collar bottoms against the retaining clip.

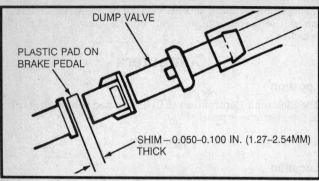

DUMP VALVE

PLASTIC PAD ON BRAKE PEDAL

SHIM—0.050–0.100 IN. (1.27–2.54MM) THICK

Vacuum dump valve adjustment—1991–94 vehicles

3. Place a 0.050–0.10 in. (1.27–2.54mm) shim between the white button of the valve and the pad on the brake pedal.

4. Firmly pull the brake pedal rearward to its normal position, allowing the dump valve to ratchet backwards in the retaining clip.

CLUTCH SWITCH

1991–94

1. Measure the distance from the bulkhead to the upper center of the clutch pedal pad. The distance should be 7.72–8.03 in. (196–204mm). If not proceed to Step 2.

2. Disconnect the clutch switch electrical connector.

3. Loosen the switch locknut and turn the switch until the specified distance is achieved. Tighten the locknut to 10–13 ft. lbs. (14–18 Nm).

4. Push the clutch pedal down by hand until clutch resistance is felt.

5. Measure the distance between the upper pedal height and where resistance is felt. The free-play should be 0.20–0.51 in. (5–13mm). If not, proceed to Step 6.

6. Loosen the pushrod locknut and turn the pushrod until the specified free-play is achieved.

7. Check that disengagement height is correct when the pedal is fully depressed. Minimum disengagement height is 1.6 in. (41mm).

8. Tighten the pushrod locknut to 9–12 ft. lbs. (12–17mm) and connect the clutch switch electrical connector.

Cougar, Mark VII, Mark VIII, Mustang and Thunderbird

Location

FUSES

All vehicles are equipped with a fuse panel located on the left side of the lower instrument panel. In addition, Thunderbird and Cougar are equipped with a high-current fuse box located in the engine compartment on the left fender apron.

FUSE LINKS

Fuse links are used to protect the main wiring harness and selected branches from complete burn-out, should a short circuit or electrical overload occur. A fuse link is a short length of insulated wire, integral with the engine compartment wiring harness. It is several wire gauges smaller than the circuit it protects and generally located in-line directly from the positive terminal of the battery.

CIRCUIT BREAKERS

Circuit breakers are used on certain electrical components requiring high amperage. The advantage of the circuit breaker is its ability to open and close the electrical circuit as the load demands, rather than the necessity of a part replacement.

Mustang

Windshield Wiper Circuit—one 8.25 amp circuit breaker located on the fuse panel.

Power Windows—one 20 amp circuit breaker located on the fuse panel.

Power Windows, Power Seats, Power Door Locks—one 20 amp circuit breaker located at the starter relay.

Headlight and High Beam—one 22 amp circuit breaker incorporated in the lighting switch.

Convertible Top—one 25 amp circuit breaker located at the lower instrument panel-reinforcement.

Thunderbird and Cougar

Windshield Wiper Circuit—one 8.25 amp circuit breaker located on the fuse panel.

Power Windows and Moon Roof Motor—one 20 amp circuit breaker located on the fuse panel.

Power Seats, Door Locks and Fuel Door Release Solenoid—one 20 amp circuit breaker located on the fuse panel.

Cigar Lighter and High Beam—one 20 amp circuit breaker located on the fuse panel.

Mark VII

Windshield Wiper Circuit—one 6 amp circuit breaker located on the fuse panel.

Cigar Lighters/Horns—one 20 amp circuit breaker located on the fuse panel.

Power Windows and Sun Roof—one 20 amp circuit breaker located on the fuse panel.

Power Windows, Seats and Door Locks—one 20 amp circuit breaker located at the starter relay.

Headlight and High Beam—one 22 amp circuit breaker incorporated in the lighting switch.

RELAYS

Mustang

Air Conditioner WOT Cut-Out Relay—located on the right fender apron.

Convertible Top Lower and Raise Relays—located in luggage compartment, behind rear seat.

EEC Power Relay—located on the EEC module bracket in the lower right cowl on 1990 vehicles and behind the right cowl panel, above the EEC control module on 1991–94 vehicles.

Fuel Pump Relay—located under the driver's seat on 1990–91 vehicles and on the right side of the engine compartment, on the lower front of the wheelwell on 1992–94 vehicles.

Horn Relay—located behind the instrument panel near the instrument cluster on 1990 vehicles and behind the center of the instrument panel, above the warning chime module on 1991–94 vehicles.

LCD illumination Relay—located behind the center of the instrument panel on 1990–94 vehicles.

Low Oil Warning Relay—located on left instrument panel shake brace on 1990 vehicles and behind the left side of the instrument panel, to the left of the steering column brace on 1991–94 vehicles.

Rear Defrost Control Relay—located at left side of instrument panel near fuse panel.

Starter Relay—located at the left front fender apron.

Window Safety Relay—located behind left cowl panel.

Thunderbird and Cougar

Air Conditioner WOT Cut-Out Relay—located at the right front of the firewall, on the relay bracket.

Anti-Lock Hydraulic Pump Motor Relay—located at the right front of the firewall, on the relay bracket.

Anti-Lock Power Relay—located at the right front of the firewall, on the relay bracket.

Autolamp Dual Coil Relay—located behind the center of the instrument panel, to the left of the glove box on 1990 vehicles and at the left side of the instrument panel, to the right of the steering column on 1991–94 vehicles.

EEC Power Relay—located at the left fender apron, inside the power distribution box.

Fuel Pump Relay—located in the left side of the trunk, behind the wheel well.

Hard Ride Relay—located under the rear package tray.

Hi-Lo Beam Relay—located behind the left side of the instrument panel, to the right of the steering column on 1990 vehicles.

Horn Relay—located in the left side of the engine compartment, inside the power distribution box.

LCD Illumination Relay—located behind the left side of the instrument panel, near the steering column.

Soft Ride Relay—located under the rear package tray.

Starter Relay—located on the left fender apron.

Starter Interrupt Relay—located under the left side of the instrument panel on 1990 vehicles.

Mark VII

Air Conditioning WOT Cut-Out Relay—located on the left fender apron, near the shock tower.

Air Suspension Compressor Relay—located on the left fender apron, near the shock tower.

Anti-Lock Brake Hydraulic Pump Motor Relay—located in front of the firewall, behind the brake master cylinder.

Anti-Lock Power Relay—located in front of the firewall, behind the brake master cylinder.

Anti-Theft Alarm Relay—located under the right side of the rear package tray on 1990 vehicles.

Anti-Theft Inverter Relay—located under the right side of the rear package tray on 1990 vehicles.

Anti-Theft Starter Interrupt Relay—located under the left side of the instrument panel near the ground bus bracket on 1990 vehicles.

ATC Feedback Isolation Relay—located behind the right side of the instrument panel, near the rear of the glove box on 1990 vehicles and behind the left side of the instrument panel, to the right of the steering column on 1991–94 vehicles.

Autolamp Relay—located to the left of the panel defrost actuator on 1990 vehicles and behind the left side of the instrument panel, to the right of the steering column on 1991–94 vehicles.

EEC Power Relay—located on the right fender apron on 1990 vehicles and in the right rear of the engine compartment on 1991–94 vehicles.

Fuel Pump Relay—located at the outside of the left deck lid hinge support.

Hi-Lo Beam Relay—located to the right of the steering column, behind the instrument panel.

Horn Relay—located on the right fender apron, near the right front height sensor on 1990–91 vehicles and in the right rear corner of the engine compartment on the firewall on 1992–94 vehicles.

Keyless/Anti-Theft Disarm Relay—located under right side of rear package tray on 1990 vehicles.

Low Oil Level Relay—located at the right of the instrument panel, behind the glove compartment on 1990 vehicles and behind the left side of the instrument panel on 1991–94 vehicles.

Moonroof Relay—located at the center rear of the roof, above the headliner, on 1991–94 vehicles.

Starter Relay—located on the left fender apron.

Computers

Location

The engine electronic control module is located behind the right cowl panel. The anti-lock brake control module is located under the center of the rear package tray. The automatic temperature control module is located behind the center of the instrument panel. The air bag diagnostic module is located behind the lower center of the instrument panel on Mustang and 1990 Mark VII and behind the top right side of the instrument panel, above the glove compartment, on 1991–94 Mark VII and VIII.

Turn Signal and Hazard Flashers

Location

The turn signal and hazard flashers are attached to the fuse panel, or the instrument panel reinforcement over the fuse panel, on Mustang and Mark VII. On Thunderbird and Cougar, an electronic flasher is located behind the left side of the instrument panel, to the right of the steering column.

Cruise Control

Adjustment

ACTUATOR CABLE

1. Remove the cable retaining clip.
2. Push the cable through the adjuster until a slight tension is felt.
3. Insert the cable retaining clip and snap into place.

VACUUM DUMP VALVE

The vacuum dump valve is movable in its mounting bracket. It should be adjusted so it is closed (no vacuum leaks) when the brake pedal is in its normal release position (not depressed) and open when the pedal is depressed. Use a hand vacuum pump to make this adjustment.

CLUTCH SWITCH

Mustang

1. Prop the clutch pedal in the full-up position, pawl fully released from the sector.
2. Loosen the switch retaining screw.
3. Slide the switch forward toward the clutch pedal until the switch plunger cap is 0.030 in. (0.76mm) from contacting the switch housing. Then, tighten the retaining screw.
4. Remove the prop from the clutch pedal and test drive for clutch switch cancellation of cruise control.

Thunderbird

1. Disconnect the wiring harness from the switch.
2. Using a volt-ohmmeter, probe the switch terminals with the switch installed and the clutch pedal at the up, or clutch engaged position.

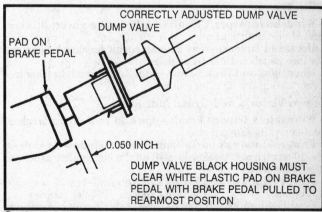

Cruise control dump valve adjustment

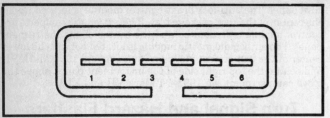

Clutch switch terminal locations—Thunderbird

3. The EFI switch, terminals 5 and 6, should be normally open and close within approximately 2 in. (50mm) of clutch pedal travel.

4. The cruise control release switch, terminals 3 and 4, should be normally closed and open within approximately 2 in. (50mm) of clutch travel.

5. The clutch interlock switch, terminals 1 and 2, should be normally open and close when the clutch pedal has been moved to approximately 1 in. (25mm) from full travel.

6. Replace the clutch switch if any of the conditions in Steps 3, 4 and 5 are not as specified.

Crown Victoria, Grand Marquis and Town Car

Location

FUSES

All vehicles are equipped with a fuse panel located on the left side of the lower instrument panel. In addition, 1990–94 Town Car and 1992–94 Crown Victoria and Grand Marquis are equipped with a fuse box located in the right front of the engine compartment.

FUSE LINKS

Fuse links are used to protect the main wiring harness and selected branches from complete burn-out, should a short circuit or electrical overload occur. A fuse link is a short length of insulated wire, integral with the engine compartment wiring harness. It is several wire gauges smaller than the circuit it protects and generally located in-line directly from the positive terminal of the battery.

CIRCUIT BREAKERS

Circuit breakers are used on certain electrical components requiring high amperage. The advantage of the circuit breaker is its ability to open and close the electrical circuit as the load demands, rather than the necessity of a part replacement.

Town Car

Windshield Wiper Circuit—one 8.25 amp circuit breaker located on the fuse panel.

Deck Lid Release—one 20 amp circuit breaker located on the fuse panel on 1990–94 vehicles.

Headlight and High Beam—one 22 amp circuit breaker incorporated in the lighting switch.

Crown Victoria and Grand Marquis

Windshield Wiper Circuit—one 8.25 amp circuit breaker located on the fuse panel.

Power Windows and Tailgate Power Window Switch—one 20 amp circuit breaker located on the instrument panel on 1990–91 vehicles.

Power Windows and Trunk Lid Release—one 20 amp circuit breaker located on the fuse panel on 1992–94 vehicles.

Headlight and High Beam—one 22 amp circuit breaker incorporated in the lighting switch.

Power Seats and Door Locks—one 30 amp circuit breaker located on the fuse panel on 1988–91 vehicles, located in the engine compartment fuse box on 1992–94 vehicles.

RELAYS

Town Car

Air Conditioner WOT Cut-Out Relay—located at the left fender apron.

Alternator Output Control Relay—located on the right side of the engine compartment on 1990–94 vehicles.

Anti-Lock Brake Motor Relay—located in the left front of the engine compartment on 1990–94 vehicles.

Anti-Lock Brakes Relay—located in the right front of the engine compartment, in the engine compartment fuse box on 1990–94 vehicles.

Compressor Relay—located on the right side of the engine compartment, in the engine compartment fuse box.

Delayed Exit Relay—located behind the left side of the instrument panel.

EEC Power Relay—located at the left fender apron.

Fuel Pump Relay—located at the left fender apron.

Hi-Lo Beam Relay—located behind the left side of the instrument panel.

Horn Relay—located in the right front of the engine compartment, in the engine compartment fuse box on 1990 vehicles.

Moonroof Relay—located at the center of the headliner, behind the moonroof on 1991–94 vehicles.

Starter Relay—located on the right front fender apron.

Trailer Battery Charging Relay—located in the trunk, on the left wheel well.

Trailer Exterior Lamps Relay—located in the trunk, on the left wheel well.

Trailer Left Hand Turn Lamp Relay—located in the trunk, on the left wheel well.

Trailer Right Hand Turn Relay—located in the trunk, on the left wheel well.

Unlock Relay—located behind the right cowl panel.

Window Safety Relay—located behind the right cowl panel on 1990 vehicles and behind the right side of the instrument panel on 1991–94 vehicles.

Crown Victoria and Grand Marquis

Alternator Output Control Relay—located in the right front of the engine compartment.

Anti-Lock Brake Motor Relay—located on lower left front of engine compartment, on bracket near front of ABS hydraulic control unit.

Anti-Lock Brake Relay—located in right front of engine compartment, in engine compartment fuse box.

Autolamp Relay—located to the right of the steering column on 1990 vehicles, behind the lower left side of the instrument panel on 1991 vehicles and behind the center of the instrument panel on 1992–94 vehicles.

Compressor Relay—located on the left fender apron on 1990–91 vehicles and in the right front of the engine compartment, in the engine compartment fuse box on 1992–94 vehicles.

EEC Power Relay—located in the left side of the engine compartment in the relay center on 1991–94 vehicles.

Fuel Pump Relay—located on the left side of the engine compartment.

Horn Relay—located near the blower motor on 1990–91 vehicles and in the right front of the engine compartment, in the engine compartment fuse box on 1992–94 vehicles.

LCD Dimming Relay—located at the left side of the instrument panel, to the right of the steering column on 1990–91 vehicles and behind the center of the instrument panel on 1992–94 vehicles.

Police Power Relay—located behind the glove box on 1990–91 vehicles.

Starter Relay—located on the right fender apron.

Thermactor Control Relay—located on front of left fender apron on 1990–91 vehicles.

Thermactor Dump Relay—located on front of left fender apron on 1990–91 vehicles.

Throttle Kicker Control Relay—located in right side of engine compartment, above the wheel well on 1990–91 vehicles.

Trailer Battery Charging Relay—located near right rear wheel well on 1990 sedan, left side of trunk on 1991–94 sedan and above left rear wheel well on wagon.

Trailer Exterior Lamps Relay—located near right rear wheel well on 1990 sedan, left side of trunk on 1991–94 sedan and above left rear wheel well on wagon.

Trailer Left Turn Lamp Relay—located near right rear wheel well on 1990 sedan, left side of trunk on 1991–94 sedan and above left rear wheel well on wagon.

Trailer Right Turn Lamp Relay—located near right rear wheel well on 1990 sedan, left side of trunk on 1991–94 sedan and above left rear wheel well on wagon.

Window Safety Relay—located behind the glove box on 1990–91 vehicles.

WOT Cutout Relay—located in left side of the engine compartment in the relay center on 1991–94 vehicles.

Computers

Location

The engine electronic control unit is located in the engine compartment, attached to the firewall on the driver's side, near the master cylinder. The anti-lock brake control module is located in the left front of the engine compartment, on the front of the upper radiator support on Crown Victoria and Grand Marquis and in the right front of the engine compartment, under the radiator support on Town Car. The air bag diagnostic module is located behind the right side of the instrument panel, above the glove compartment on Crown Victoria and Grand Marquis and behind the left side of the instrument panel on Town Car. The automatic temperature control module is located behind the center of the instrument panel.

Turn Signal and Hazard Flashers

Location

The turn signal and hazard flashers are attached to the fuse panel.

Cruise Control

Adjustment

ACTUATOR CABLE

1. Remove the cable retaining clip.
2. Make sure the throttle is in the closed position.
3. Pull on the actuator cable end tube to take up any slack. Maintain a light tension on the cable.
4. Insert the cable retaining clip and snap into place.
5. Check that the throttle linkage operates freely and smoothly.

VACUUM DUMP VALVE

The vacuum dump valve is movable in its mounting bracket. It should be adjusted so it is closed, no vacuum leaks, when the brake pedal is in its normal release position. Adjust the dump valve as follows:
1. Hold the brake pedal down and push the dump valve forward through its adjustment collar.
2. Install a 0.05 in. (1.27mm) shim on the surface of the adapter and pull the brake pedal fully rearward.
3. Release the brake pedal and remove the shim. The adapter

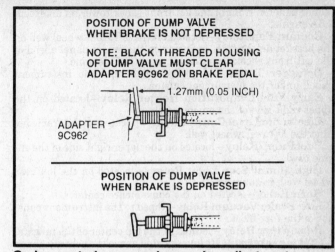

POSITION OF DUMP VALVE
WHEN BRAKE IS NOT DEPRESSED

NOTE: BLACK THREADED HOUSING
OF DUMP VALVE MUST CLEAR
ADAPTER 9C962 ON BRAKE PEDAL

1.27mm (0.05 INCH)

ADAPTER
9C962

POSITION OF DUMP VALVE
WHEN BRAKE IS DEPRESSED

Cruise control vacuum dump valve adjustment

should be in contact with the yellow dump valve plunger and not with the black dump valve housing.
4. Use a hand vacuum pump to check the vacuum dump valve for sealing off vacuum.

Celebrity, Century, Cutlass Ciera, Cutlass Cruiser and 6000

Location

FUSIBLE LINKS

There are several locations where fusible links can be found. They are located ahead of the left side front shock tower, near the positive battery connection or at the starter solenoid near the front of the engine.

CIRCUIT BREAKERS

Circuit breakers are used along with the fusible links to protect the various components of the electrical system, such as headlights, the windshield wipers and electric windows. The circuit breakers are located either in the switch or mounted on or near the lower lip of the instrument panel, to the right or left of the steering column.

FUSE PANEL

The fuse panel is located on the left side of the vehicle. It is under the instrument panel assembly. In order to gain access to the fuse panel, it may be necessary to first remove the under dash padding.

RELAYS

Except Century

Air Conditioner Compressor Relay—located on the upper right corner of the engine cowl.

Air Conditioner Delay Relay—located in the upper right corner of the engine cowl.

Air Conditioner/Heater Blower Relay—located on the plenum, on the right side of the firewall.

Altitude Advance Relay—located on the left inner fender, in front of the shock tower.

Charging System Relay—located behind the instrument panel, near the fuse block.

Constant Run Relay—located on the left inner fender wheel well.

Coolant Fan Low-Speed Relay—located on the left inner fender wheel well, on a bracket on the 2.5L engine or on the fender panel in front of the left front shock tower on all except 2.5L engine.

Coolant Fan Relay—located on the left front wheel well on the bracket on the 2.5L engine or on the fender panel ahead of the left front shock tower on all except 2.5L engine.

Defogger Timer Relay—located behind the instrument panel, under the instrument cluster.

Early Fuel Evaporation Heater Relay—located on the upper right side of the engine cowl.

Electronic Level Control Relay—located on the frame behind the left rear wheel well.

Fuel Pump Relay—located on the upper right side of the engine cowl.

High Mount Stop Light Relays—located on the left rear wheel well, in the trunk.

Horn Relay—located on the convenience center.

Low Brake Vacuum Relay—taped to the instrument panel above the fuse block.

Rear Wiper Relay—located in the top center of the tailgate.

Starter Interrupt Relay—located above the ashtray, taped to the instrument panel harness.

Century

Air Conditioner Coolant Fan Relay (2.5L engine)—located on the right side of the firewall.

Blower Relay—located on the right side of the firewall.

Coolant Fan Delay Relay (SFI)—located in front of the left front shock tower, on a bracket.

Coolant Fan Relay—located in front of the left front shock tower.

Fuel Pump Relay (2.5L engine)—located in the relay bracket on the right side of the firewall.

High Speed Coolant Fan Relay—located on the left front side of the engine.

Horn Relay—located under the instrument panel, in the convenience center.

Low Speed Coolant Fan Relay—located near the battery, on the left side of the radiator shroud.

Rear Wiper Relay—located in the top center of the tailgate.

Starter Interrupt Relay—taped to the instrument panel harness, above the right side ashtray.

Computers

Location

Electronic Control Module—located on the right side of the vehicle. It is positioned under the instrument panel. In order to gain access to the electronic control module, it will be necessary to first remove the trim panel.

Cruise Control Module—located behind the instrument panel, above the accelerator pedal.

Daytime Running Lamp Control Module—located at the right side behind the instrument panel.

NOTE: The daytime running lamp control module is in Canadian vehicles only.

Anti-lock Brake Control Module—located in the center behind the instrument panel.

Flashers

Location

Hazard—located in the convenience center. The convenience center is a swing down type, located under the instrument panel near the fuse block.

Turn Signal—located behind the instrument panel, to the right of the steering column.

Cruise Control

For further information, please refer to Chilton's Chassis Electronics Service Manual.

NOTE: To keep the vehicle under control and to prevent possible vehicle damage, it is not advisable to use the cruise control on slippery roads. Disengage the cruise control in conditions such as varying or heavy traffic or when traveling down a steep graded hill.

Adjustments

1. Adjust the throttle lever to the idle position with the engine **OFF**. If equipped with the idle control solenoid, the solenoid must be de-energized.

2. Pull the servo assembly end of the cable towards the servo blade.

3. Align the holes in the servo blade with the cable pin. Install the cable pin.

4. If equipped with the 2.8L engine, it will be necessary to position the ball of the chain assembly into the chain retainer. This will allow a slight slack to occur not to exceed one ball diameter. Remove the excess chain outside of the chain retainer.

Bonneville, Delta 88, DeVille, Electra, Fleetwood, LeSabre, Ninety-Eight, Park Avenue, Park Avenue Ultra and 88 Royale

Location

FUSES

The fuse panel is located on the left side of the vehicle. It is under the instrument panel assembly. In order to gain access to the fuse panel, it may be necessary to first remove the under dash padding.

UNDERHOOD FUSE PANEL

On some vehicles there is also a fuse panel under the hood on the right side of the engine. It is located along the vehicle firewall.

CIRCUIT BREAKERS

The convenience center is located on the underside of the instrument panel near the fuse panel. It provides a central location for various relays, hazard flasher units and warning buzzers/chimes. All units are replaced with plug-in modules.

RELAYS

The relay center is located on the right side of the instrument panel. The relay center is mounted behind the glove box assembly.

Computers

Location

ECM

The electronic control module is located on the right side of the vehicle. It is positioned under the instrument panel. In order to gain access to electronic control module, it will be necessary to first remove the trim panel.

BCM

The body control module is located on the right side of the vehicle and positioned under the instrument panel. In order to gain access to body control module, it will be necessary to first remove the trim panel.

EBCM

The electronic brake control module is located on the right side of the vehicle and positioned under the right sound insulator panel. In order to gain access to electronic brake control module, it will be necessary to first remove the trim panel.

OLM

The oil life module is located on the right side of the vehicle, under the glove compartment. In order to gain access to the oil life module, the lower dash trim panel must first be removed.

HVAC PROGRAMMER

The heating and air conditioner controller (HVAC programmer) is located in the center of the vehicle below the dashboard. Access to the unit can be obtained from beneath the dashboard.

Flashers

Location

The turn signal flasher unit is located behind the instrument panel near the steering column, along with the hazard flasher. It is secured in place with a plastic retainer. In order to gain access to components, it may first be necessary to remove certain under dash padding.

The hazard flasher is located on the fuse block. It is positioned on the lower right side corner of the fuse block assembly. In order to gain access to the turn signal flasher it may be necessary to first remove the under dash padding.

Cruise Control

For further information, please refer to Chilton's Chassis Electronics Service Manual.

Adjustment

1. Turn the ignition switch **OFF**.
2. Fully retract the idle speed control motor plunger.

NOTE: The throttle lever must not touch the idle speed control plunger.

3. Connect the cruise control cable to the hole in the servo blade that leaves the minimum slack.
4. Install the retainer at the servo.

Allante, DeVille, DeVille Concours, Eldorado, Reatta, Riviera, Seville, Toronado and Trofeo

Location

FUSE PANELS

1990

Riviera and Reatta—front left side of console
Allante—center console, under ash tray
Eldorado and Seville—glove box
Toronado and Trofeo—right side of instrument panel

1991–92

Toronado and Trofeo—glove box

1991–94

Riviera and Reatta—front left side of console

Allante—center console, under ash tray
Eldorado and Seville—glove box

CIRCUIT BREAKERS

A circuit breaker is an electrical switch which breaks the circuit during an electrical overload. Some circuit breakers are designed to automatically reset after a specified period of time. Others must be manually reset after the electrical malfunction causing the overload has been corrected.

The majority of circuit breakers can be found in the fuse panel. Some, however, are installed in-line near the device they are intended to protect.

RELAYS

Relays are generally mounted in the vicinity of the device(s) they are intended to control. On the vehicles listed below, there is an Interior Relay Center (IRC).

Riviera and Reatta—below center of instrument panel, right front of console
Eldorado and Seville—behind right side of instrument panel, below glove box
Toronado and Trofeo—behind right side of instrument panel, behind instrument panel compartment

Computers

Location

ELECTRONIC CONTROL MODULE

Riviera and Reatta—behind right side of instrument panel, left of heater and air conditioning programmer
Allante—behind right side of instrument panel, near shroud
Eldorado and Seville—behind right side of instrument panel
Toronado and Trofeo—behind right side of instrument panel, left of heater and air conditioner programmer

BODY COMPUTER MODULE

Riviera and Reatta—behind upper right side of instrument panel, behind glove box
Allante—behind center of instrument panel
Eldorado and Seville—behind instrument panel, behind glove box
Toronado and Trofeo—behind instrument panel, above and right of fuse panel

Turn Signal/Hazard Flashers

Location

Riviera and Reatta (1990–93)—right side of steering column
Allante—the turn signals and hazard warning lights are controlled by the Body Computer Module (BCM). Therefore, individual turn signal and hazard flasher units are not used
Eldorado and Seville—behind center of instrument panel, below radio
Toronado and Trofeo—behind instrument panel, right side of steering column support

Cruise Control

For further information, please refer to Chilton's Chassis Electronics Service Manual.

Adjustment

REATTA, RIVIERA, TORANADO AND TROFEO

With the engine off, adjust the cable or rod length to obtain the minimum slack.

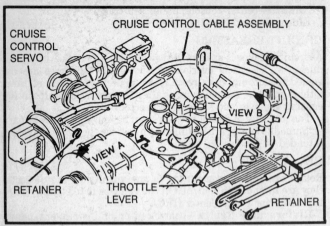

Adjusting cruise control cable — Allante, Eldorado and Seville

ALLANTE, ELDORADO AND SEVILLE

1. With the engine **OFF**, ensure that the idle speed motor has retracted until the throttle body lever contacts the minimum throttle angle adjusting screw.

2. Select the servo blade hole that will result in minimum cable slack.

Cavalier and Sunbird

Location
FUSIBLE LINKS

Fusible links are used to prevent major wire harness damage in the event of short circuit or an overload condition in the wiring circuits which are normally not fused, due to carrying high amperage loads or because of their locations within the wiring harness. Each fusible link is of a fixed value for a specific electrical load and should a link fail, the cause of failure must be determined and repaired prior to installing a new fusible link of the same value. Fusible links are located in the engine harness at the starter solenoid and the left hand front of the dash at the battery junction block.

CIRCUIT BREAKERS

Circuit breakers are used along with the fusible links to protect the various components of the electrical system, such as headlights, the windshield wipers and electric windows. The circuit breakers are located either in the switch or mounted on or near the lower lip of the instrument panel, to the right or left of the steering column.

FUSE PANELS

The fuse panel is located on the left side of the vehicle. It is under the instrument panel assembly. In order to gain access to the fuse panel, it may be necessary to first remove the under dash padding.

CONVENIENCE CENTER AND VARIOUS RELAYS

The convenience center is located on the underside of the instrument panel near the fuse panel. It provides a central location for various relays, hazard flasher units and buzzers. All units are easily replaced with plug-in modules.

Computer

Location

The Electronic Control Module (ECM) is located on the right

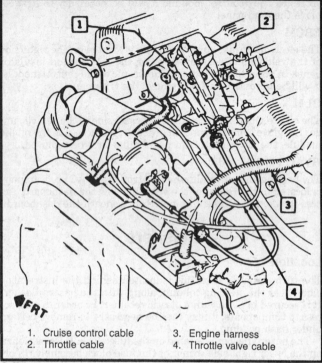

1. Cruise control cable
2. Throttle cable
3. Engine harness
4. Throttle valve cable

Adjusting cruise control cable — Reatta, Riviera, Toronado and Trofeo

side of the vehicle. It is positioned in front of the right side kick panel. In order to gain access to the assembly, remove the trim panel.

Flashers

Location
TURN SIGNAL FLASHER

The turn signal flasher is located directly under the steering column of the vehicle. It is secured in place by means of a plastic retainer. In order to gain access to the component, it may be necessary to remove the underdash padding panel.

HAZARD FLASHER

The hazard flasher is located in the fuse block. It is positioned on the lower right side corner of the fuse block assembly. In order to gain access to the turn signal flasher, it may be necessary to first remove the under dash padding.

Cruise Control

For further information, please refer to Chilton's Chassis Electronics Service Manual.

Adjustment
RELEASE SWITCH AND VALVE

1. Depress the brake pedal and insert the vacuum release valve into the retainer until a click is heard indicating that the valve switch is seated.

2. Allow the brake pedal to travel rearward to the positive stop.

3. The valve switch will be moved through the retainer into the proper position.

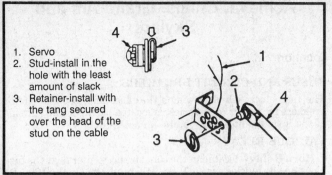

1. Servo
2. Stud-install in the hole with the least amount of slack
3. Retainer-install with the tang secured over the head of the stud on the cable

Servo cable adjustment

NOTE: **Audible clicks can be heard as threaded portion of switch is pushed through the clip toward the brake pedal. Vacuum release valve and stoplight switch are self-adjusting.**

SERVO CABLE

1. Install the cable into the engine bracket. Route the cable assembly to the servo bracket.
2. Pull the servo end of the cable towards the servo assembly without moving the throttle lever.
3. Line up the pin in the end of the cable with 1 of the holes in the servo assembly tab.
4. Insert the cable pin into 1 of the 6 holes in the servo bracket. Install the retainer.

NOTE: **Do not stretch the cable to make a certain connection as this will prevent the engine from returning to idle. Use the next closest hole.**

Beretta and Corsica

Location

FUSE PANEL

The fuse panel is located on the left side of the instrument panel assembly. In order to gain access to the fuse panel, it is necessary to first remove the lower trim panel.

FUSIBLE LINKS

Fusible links—A and E are located rear of the engine compartment, at the battery junction box.

Fusible links—B, C and D are located at the front section of the engine at the starter solenoid.

Fusible link—F is located on the left side of the engine compartment, near the battery.

CIRCUIT BREAKERS

Circuit breakers No. 12 and No. 15 are located in fuse block.

VARIOUS RELAYS

The coolant fan, air conditioning compressor, air conditioning high blower speed and fuel pump relays are all located in the engine compartment mounted to the center of the firewall on the relay bracket.

Computers

Location

The electronic control module is located on the right side of the vehicle. It is positioned up behind the glove box. In order to gain access to the electronic control module, remove the right side

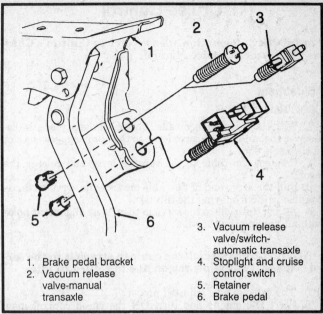

1. Brake pedal bracket
2. Vacuum release valve-manual transaxle
3. Vacuum release valve/switch-automatic transaxle
4. Stoplight and cruise control switch
5. Retainer
6. Brake pedal

Cruise control vacuum valve/switch installation

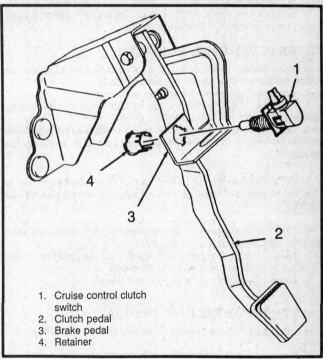

1. Cruise control clutch switch
2. Clutch pedal
3. Brake pedal
4. Retainer

Cruise control clutch switch installation

trim panel and/or glove box assembly.

Flashers

Location

TURN SIGNAL FLASHER

The turn signal flasher is located behind the lower left side of the instrument panel on the steering column.

HAZARD WARNING FLASHER

The hazard flasher is located behind the lower left side of the instrument panel on the steering column.

Cruise Control

For further information, please refer to Chilton's Chassis Electronics Service Manual.

Adjustment
CONTROL CABLE

1. With the servo cable installed on the brackets, place the cable over the stud on the servo lever so the stud engages the slot in the cable end.
2. Connect the cable to the throttle lever and release the lever.
3. Pull the servo end of the cable towards the servo as far as possible without moving the throttle.
4. Attach the cable to the servo in the closest alignment holes without moving the throttle.

NOTE: Do not stretch the cable to attach it to the servo. This will not allow the engine to return to idle.

5. The cable is now adjusted properly.
6. Start the engine and turn ON the speed control main switch.
7. Drive the vehicle above 25 mph.
8. Engage the speed control and check the following functions: set, disengage, coast and resume.

BRAKE PEDAL RELEASE SWITCH

The brake pedal release switch is located at the top of the brake pedal, directly above the brake pedal switch.
1. Remove the lower steering column cover.
2. Pull the brake pedal release switch from the mounting bracket.
3. Depress the brake pedal and insert the brake pedal release switch into the tubular retainer bracket until it seats on the retainer.

NOTE: Clicks can be heard as the threaded portion of the valve passes through the retainer toward the brake pedal.

4. Pull the brake pedal rearward against the pedal stop until audible clicks can no longer be heard.
5. Release the brake pedal and again, pull the pedal rearward to make sure no more clicks can be heard.
6. Install the lower steering column panel.

CLUTCH PEDAL RELEASE SWITCH

The clutch pedal release switch is located at the top of the clutch pedal.
1. Remove the lower steering column cover.
2. Pull the clutch pedal release switch from the mounting bracket.
3. Depress the clutch pedal and insert the clutch pedal release switch into the tubular retainer bracket until it seats on the retainer.

NOTE: Clicks can be heard as the threaded portion of the valve passes through the retainer toward the clutch pedal.

4. Pull the clutch pedal rearward against the pedal stop until audible clicks can no longer be heard.
5. Release the clutch pedal and again, pull the pedal rearward to make sure no more clicks can be heard.
6. Reinstall the lower steering column panel.

Achieva, Calais, Grand Am and Skylark

Location

FUSES AND CIRCUIT BREAKERS

The fuse block, which contains the fuses and also the circuit breakers for power accessories, is located on the lower left side of the instrument panel, behind an access door.

VARIOUS RELAYS

Horn Relay—located in the convenience center near the fuse block on all vehicles except 1990–91 Grand Am. On the 1990–91 Grand Am, it is taped to the wiring harness near the fuse block.

Power Antenna Relay—located on the right side of the instrument panel, below the speaker.

Rear Window Defogger Relay—located on the right side of the instrument panel on all vehicles except the 1990–91 Grand Am. On the 1990–91 Grand Am, it is located near the fuse panel.

Fuel Pump Relay—located in the engine compartment on the relay bracket on the firewall. This relay is closest to the blower.

A/C Compressor Cut Out Relay—located in the engine compartment on the relay bracket on the firewall. This relay is next to the fuel pump relay.

Cooling Fan Relay—located in the engine compartment on the relay bracket on the firewall. This relay is next to the blower speed relay.

Blower Speed Relay—located in the engine compartment on the relay bracket on the firewall. This relay is closest to the master cylinder.

Electronic Brake Control Relay—located in the engine compartment on the relay bracket on the firewall.

Fog Light Relay—located in the engine compartment on the relay bracket on the firewall.

Ignition Key, Seat Belt, Light and Turn Signal Warning Alarm—located in the convenience center near the fuse block in all vehicles except the 1990–91 Grand Am. On the 1990–91 Grand Am, it is mounted to a bracket above the glove box.

Cruise Control Module—mounted to a bracket on the left side of the instrument panel.

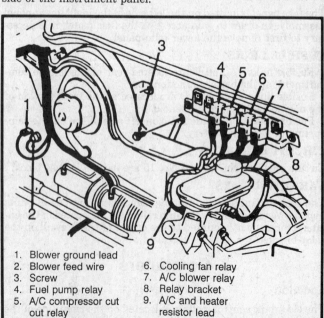

1. Blower ground lead
2. Blower feed wire
3. Screw
4. Fuel pump relay
5. A/C compressor cut out relay
6. Cooling fan relay
7. A/C blower relay
8. Relay bracket
9. A/C and heater resistor lead

Firewall mounted relay identification

Instrument Panel Light Dimmer Module—located on the lower left tie bar on all vehicles except the 1990–91 Grand Am. On the 1990–91 Grand Am, it is either mounted to a bracket to the right of the glove box or on the right side of the console front extension bracket.

ABS Enable Relay—located on the engine compartment side of the firewall, inside of the relay bracket and to the right.

Flashers

Location

TURN SIGNAL

The turn signal flasher is clipped to the instrument panel near the fuse block.

HAZARD

On all vehicles except 1990–91 Grand Am, the hazard flasher is in the convenience center, located near the fuse block. On the 1990–91 Grand Am, the hazard flasher is clipped to the console front extension bracket.

Computer

Location

The ECM is located on the right side of the instrument panel, near the glove box.

Cruise Control

Adjustment

1. Make sure the throttle lever is in the idle position with the engine OFF.

2. Pull the servo assembly end of the cable toward the servo without moving the throttle lever.

3. If 1 of the 6 holes in the servo assembly tab aligns with the cable pin, connect the pin to the tab and install the retainer with the tang over the stud.

4. If the pin does not align with a hole, install it to the next hole closest to the throttle lever and install the retainer.

5. Make sure the cable is not stretched in such a way that the throttle lever has been moved of its idle position.

LeMans

Location

FUSIBLE LINKS

Fusible link **A** is located to the lower rear of the engine, at the starter solenoid. Fusible link **B** is located at the left side of the engine compartment, at the battery.

CIRCUIT BREAKERS

Circuit breakers **12** and **15** are located in the fuse panel.

FUSE PANEL

The fuse panel is located at the left side of the instrument panel and is reached by pulling the release handle and swinging the panel downward. Always return the fuse panel to its full upward, latched position before driving the vehicle.

VARIOUS RELAYS

All relays for this vehicle are located on the fuse block, under the left side of the instrument panel.

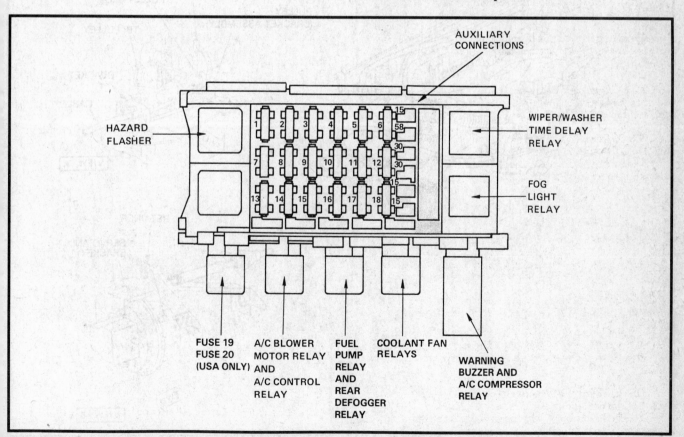

Typical fuse panel and relay pack

Computers

Location

ELECTRONIC CONTROL MODULE

The Electronic Control Module (ECM) is located behind the kick panel at the passenger-side door jam (under the dash).

MEMORY CALIBRATION UNIT

The memory calibration unit is located inside the ECM. It contains programmed information tailored to the vehicle's weight, engine, transmission, axle ratio and etc. Even though a single ECM unit can be used for various vehicles, a specific memory calibration unit must be used for each application.

Flashers

Location

MULTI-FUNCTION FLASHER

The turn signal/hazard flasher is a single multi-function flasher located on the fuse block, under the left side of the instrument panel.

Cruise Control

For further information, please refer to Chilton's Chassis Electronics Service Manual.

Adjustment

CONTROL CABLE

1. Disconnect the negative battery cable.
2. Pull the cable end of the servo assembly toward the servo without moving the idler pulley cam.
3. If 1 of the 6 holes in the servo assembly tab lines up with the cable pin, connect the pin to the tab with retainer 7.
4. If a tab hole does not line up with the pin, move the cable

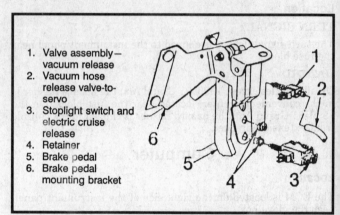

1. Valve assembly—vacuum release
2. Vacuum hose release valve-to-servo
3. Stoplight switch and electric cruise release
4. Retainer
5. Brake pedal
6. Brake pedal mounting bracket

Vacuum release switch mounting—cruise control

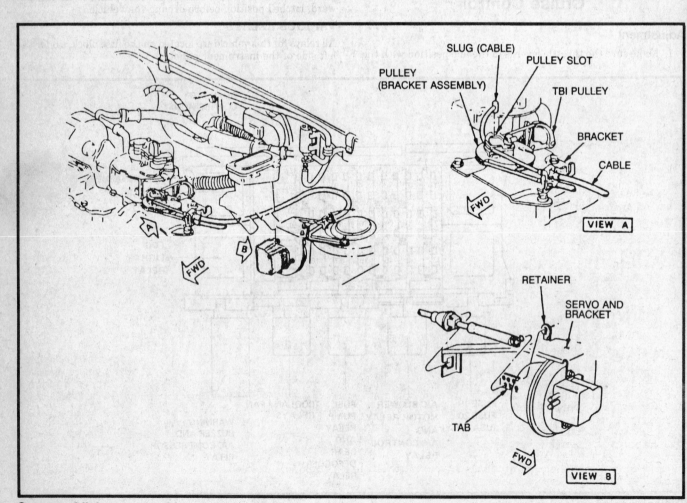

Servo and linkage assembly—cruise control

away from the servo assembly until the next closest tab hole lines up. Connect the pin-to-tab with retainer 7.

NOTE: Do not stretch the cable so as to make a particular tab hole connect to the pin. This could prevent the engine from returning to idle.

5. Connect the battery cable and test operation.

VACUUM RELEASE VALVE

1. Disconnect the negative battery cable.
2. With the brake pedal depressed, insert the valve into the tubular retainer until the valve seats on the retainer.

NOTE: Audible clicks can be heard as the threaded portion of the valve is pushed through the retainer toward the brake pedal.

3. Pull the brake pedal fully rearward against the pedal stop until the audible click sounds can no longer be heard. The valve will be moved in the tubular retainer providing the adjustment.
4. Release the brake pedal and repeat Step 3 to insure that no audible click sounds remain.
5. Connect the battery cable and test operation.

Cutlass Supreme, Grand Prix, Lumina and Regal

Location
FUSIBLE LINKS

The fuse links are in the following locations on the vehicle:
  Starter solenoid terminal
  Wiring harness near the battery
  Electrical center in the engine compartment.
  Fusible links are used to protect wiring in circuits that are not normally fused, such as the ignition circuit. In the event of an electrical overload, the fuse link will melt and create an open in the circuit. The fuse link is smaller than the wire it is to protect. The gauge size is marked on the insulation. The replacement fuse link must be the same size as the original link. To replace a damaged fuse link remove the wire section beyond the splice and splice the replacement link into the wiring harness.

CIRCUIT BREAKERS

The majority of the circuit breakers are located in the fuse block. There are a few circuit breakers located in the convenience center, which is located under the right side of the instrument panel behind right sound insulator.

FUSE PANEL

The fuse panel is located on the right side of the instrument panel under the lower storage compartment on Cutlass Supreme or in the glove box on the remaining models.

VARIOUS RELAYS

Coolant Fan Relay—located in the engine compartment mounted to the right side of the firewall on the relay bracket.
Air Conditioner Compressor Relay—located in the engine compartment mounted to the right side of the firewall on the relay bracket.
High Blower Speed Relay—located in the engine compartment mounted to the right side of the firewall on the relay bracket.
Fuel Pump Relay—located in the engine compartment mounted to the right side of the firewall on the relay bracket.
Power Door Lock Relay—located on the left side, behind the instrument panel.

Horn Relay—located in the engine compartment mounted to the forward lamp electrical center.

Computers and Modules

Location

Electronic Control Module (ECM)—located in the engine compartment forward of right strut tower.
Electronic Brake Control Module (EBCM)—located on left side of engine compartment in the fender.
Daytime Running Lights (DRL) module—located behind instrument panel on brake pedal support.
Computer Controlled Coil Ignition (C³I) module—located on right front of engine.

Flashers

Location

Hazard Warning Flasher—in the convenience center located under the right side of the instrument panel behind right sound insulator.
Turn Signal Flasher—located under the instrument panel to the right of the steering column.

Cruise Control

For further information, please refer to Chilton's Chassis Electronics Service Manual.

Adjustment

1. With cable installed in cable brackets, install cable end to throttle linkage.
2. Pull the servo end of the cable towards the servo as far as possible without moving the throttle.
3. Attach the cable to the servo in the closest alignment holes without moving the throttle.

NOTE: Do not stretch the cable to attach it to the servo. This will not allow the engine to return to idle.

4. Check the system operation and repeat the adjustment as necessary.

Saturn—SC1, SC2, SL, SL1, SL2, SW1 and SW2

Location
UNDERHOOD JUNCTION BLOCK

The block is located next to the battery on the left inner fender. It houses maxifuses, minifuses, relays and 1 circuit breaker. There are two 30 amp maxifuses for the ignition and 1 each for the battery, ABS and cooling fan. The circuit breaker is a 30 amp unit for the power windows and/or sunroof.

The horn, air conditioning control, cooling fan and automatic transaxle relays are located in the underhood junction block.

INSTRUMENT PANEL JUNCTION BLOCK

The block is located under the instrument panel, behind the center console. It houses minifuses and relays. The relays for the power window, fuel pump, flasher, rear defogger and blower motor are located in the block.

Computers

Location

ABS Electronic Brake Control Module (EBCM)—located on the carrier assembly behind the left kickpanel. The EBCM is in the bracket behind the PCM in the carrier assembly.

Cruise Control Module—located on the steering column support bracket, above the accelerator pedal.

Powertrain Control Module (PCM)—located on the carrier assembly behind the left kickpanel. The PCM contains the Engine Controller (EC) for all vehicles and the Transaxle Controller (TC) for vehicles with automatic transaxles.

Flashers

Location

The turn signal/hazard flasher unit is located in the instrument panel junction block, under the instrument panel and behind the center console.

Cruise Control

For further information, please refer to Chilton's Chassis Electronics Service Manual.

Adjustment

NOTE: The cable and adjuster are not repairable or replaceable. Do not attempt to remove the cable and adjuster from the cruise control module or damage to the module could result.

1. Disconnect the air intake tube at the throttle body.
2. Observe the position of the throttle blade.
3. Adjust the cable by pulling forward and turning the ring on the adjuster, located at the module, until the throttle blade is fully closed.
4. Loosen the adjuster ½ turn to allow approximately 0.040–0.079 inch (1–2mm) of slack in the cable.
5. Connect the air intake tube and check for proper operation.

Brougham and Fleetwood Brougham

Location

FUSIBLE LINKS

Fusible links are used to prevent major wire harness damage in the event of a short circuit or an overload condition in the wiring circuits which are normally not fused, due to carrying high amperage loads or because of their locations within the wiring harness. Each fusible link is of a fixed value for a specific electrical load and should a link fail, the cause of the failure must be determined and repaired prior to installing a new fusible link of the same value.

CIRCUIT BREAKERS

Various circuit breakers are located under the instrument panel. In order to gain access to these components, it may be necessary to first remove the under dash padding. Circuit breakers function by creating an open circuit if a short or overload condition occurs within the circuit which might damage other components.

Circuit breakers of 2 types can be found in these vehicles. The standard breaker is used, which will continue to cycle open and closed until the high current is removed. Also used is the Positive Temperature Coefficient (PTC) type breaker which will not reset until the circuit is manually opened by removing voltage from its terminals. The PTC breaker should reset within a few seconds after the open circuit condition is manually created.

FUSE PANEL

The fuse panel is located on the left side of the vehicle. It is under the instrument panel assembly. In order to gain access to the fuse panel, it may be necessary to first remove the under dash padding.

RELAYS

All vehicles use a combination of the following electrical relays in order to function properly.

Air Condition Compressor Control Relay—located on the left side of the firewall in the engine compartment.

Brake Modulator Pump Motor Relay—incorporated into the electronic brake modulator located in left hand front of the engine compartment, ahead of the engine.

Brake Modulator Solenoid Relay—incorporated into the electronic brake modulator located in left hand front of the engine compartment, ahead of the engine.

Defogger Relay—located in the accessory relay panel under the left side dash panel, to the left of the fuse block.

Door Lock Relay—attached to the lower right shroud panel behind the kick panel.

Electronic Level Control Relay—located in the accessory relay panel under the left side dash panel, to the left of the fuse block.

Fuel Pump Relay—located in the accessory relay panel under the left side dash panel, to the left of the fuse block.

Horn Relay—located in the convenience center, under the left side of the dash panel, to the left of the steering column.

Moon Roof Relay—located in the center of the windshield header, to the right of the moon roof actuator assembly.

Over-Voltage Protection Relay—located on the ABS harness near the EBCM under the glove box.

Power Antenna Relay—located in the accessory relay panel under the left side of the dash panel, to the left of the fuse box.

Reverse Light Relay—located in the accessory relay panel under the left side of the dash panel, to the left of the fuse box.

Starter Interrupt Relay—located in the accessory relay panel under the left side of the dash panel, to the left of the fuse box.

Theft Deterrent Relay—located behind the left side of the instrument panel to the right of the steering column.

Wiper/Washer Park and Pulse Relays—incorporated into the wiper/washer assembly on the firewall in the engine compartment.

Computers

Location

ECM

The Electronic Control Module (ECM) is located on the right side of the vehicle. It is positioned in front of the right kick panel. In order to gain access to the assembly the trim panel and, if necessary, the glove box must be removed.

EBCM

The Electronic Brake Control Module (EBCM) is located under the right side of the dash. In order to gain access to the module, the trim panel must first be removed.

Flashers

Location

TURN SIGNAL

The turn signal flasher is located at the base of the steering column to the right of the steering column support. In order to gain access to the turn signal flasher, it may be necessary to first remove the under dash padding.

HAZARD FLASHER

The hazard flasher is located in the fuse block. It is positioned on the lower right corner of the fuse block assembly. In order to gain access to the turn signal flasher, it may be necessary to first remove the under dash padding.

Caprice, Custom Cruiser, Estate Wagon and Roadmaster

Location
FUSIBLE LINKS

Fusible links are used to prevent major wire harness damage in the event of a short circuit or an overload condition in the wiring circuits which are normally not fused. Each fusible link is of a fixed value for a specific electrical load and should a link fail, the cause of the failure must be determined and repaired prior to installing a new fusible link of the same value.

CIRCUIT BREAKERS

Various circuit breakers are located under the instrument panel. In order to gain access to these components it may be necessary to first remove the under dash padding.

FUSE PANEL

The fuse panel is located on the left side of the vehicle. It is under the instrument panel assembly on the left front hinge pillar. Access is gained through a removable panel on the instrument panel carrier.

VARIOUS RELAYS

ABS Solenoid valve relay—integrated into the brake pressure modulator located in the left side of the engine compartment left of the generator.

A/C Blower Relay—integrated into the brake pressure modulator located in the left side of the engine compartment left of the generator.

A/C Blower Relay—located in the right rear of the engine compartment, near the blower motor on 1989–90 vehicles. For 1991–93 vehicles, it is near the blower which has been relocated to access from under the right hand side of the dash.

A/C Compressor Relay—located in the right rear of the engine compartment on the multi-use relay bracket.

Antenna Relay—located under the instrument panel compartment near the convenience center.

Choke Heater Relay—located on the left side front of the firewall, beside the brake booster.

Early Fuel Evaporation Relay—located in the right side of the engine compartment, top of the wheel house.

Electronic Level Control Relay—located in the engine compartment, on the fender next to the electronic level control compressor.

Fuel Pump Relay—located on a bracket in the right side of the engine compartment.

Headlight Relay—located at the front side of the engine compartment, near the headlight.

Horn Relay—is in the convenience center, behind the instrument panel to the left of the steering column.

Power Door Locks Relay—located behind the lower right kick panel.

Power Seat Relay—located on under the right or left seat.

Rear Glass Release Relay—located in the convenience center under the dash, left of the steering column.

Tailgate Release Relay—located at the base of the left side A pillar.

Theft Deterrent Relay—located behind the instrument panel to the left of the steering column.

Wiper Motor Relay—incorporated in the connector, on the wiper/washer assembly.

Control Modules

Location

Air Bag Diagnostic Energy Reserve Module (DERM)—located behind the left side instrument panel, left of the brake pedal bracket.

Cruise Control System Module—located in the left side rear of the engine compartment next to the master cylinder.

Electronic Brake Control Module (EBCM)—located behind the left side instrument panel, left of the brake pedal bracket.

Engine Electronic Control Module (ECM)—located behind the front right side kick panel.

Keyless Entry Control Module—mounted to left rear side under-shelf between delco-bose amplifier and left rear speaker.

Flashers

Location
TURN SIGNAL

The turn signal flasher is located inside the convenience center. In order to gain access to the turn signal flasher it may be necessary to first remove the under dash padding.

HAZARD

The hazard flasher is located in the convenience center and is positioned on the lower right side corner of the fuse block assembly.

Camaro and Firebird

Location
FUSE PANEL

The fuse panel is located on the left side of the vehicle, under the instrument panel assembly. In order to gain access to the fuse panel it may be necessary to first remove the under dash padding.

CIRCUIT BREAKERS

The circuit breakers are located at the fuse panel.

RELAYS

All vehicles use a combination of the following electrical relays:

Air Conditioner/Heater Blower High Speed Relay—located near the blower module on the air conditioner module.

Air Conditioner Compressor Relay—located on the left side engine cowl on the relay bracket.

Cooling Fan Relay—located on the left side of the engine cowl on the relay bracket.

Extend Relay—taped back to body rear harness near breakout to hatch pull-down/release unit.

Fog Light Relay (1990)—located in the left rear corner of the engine compartment; (1991–94)—located behind the left side instrument panel, near the fuse panel block.

Fuel Pump Relay—located on the left side of the engine cowl on the relay bracket.

Hatch Release Relay—located under the right side console, beside the gear selector.

Horn Relay—located in the convenience center, behind the instrument panel to the right of the steering column.

Power Antenna Relay—located behind the right side of the

...ment panel lower cover near the ECM.

Power Door Lock Relay Assembly — located on the left shroud near door jamb conduit.

Radio Amplifier Relay — located behind right side of instrument panel.

Starter Enable Relay — located below the left side instrument panel, on the kick panel.

Computers

Location

The engine Electronic Control Module (ECM), cruise control module, PASS key theft deterrent module and the SIR Diagnostic/Energy Reserve Module (DERM) for air bag equipped vehicles are all located under the right side of the instrument panel.

Flashers

Location

Hazard Flasher — located in the convenience center, behind the instrument panel to the right of the steering column.

Turn Signal Flasher — located in the convenience center.

Corvette

Location

FUSIBLE LINKS

Fusible links are located in various positions, including at the jump start junction block. Fusible links, which are normally not fused, are used to prevent wire harness damage in the event of a short circuit or an overload condition. Each fusible link is of a fixed value for a specific electrical load. Should a link fail, the cause of the failure must be determined and repaired prior to installing a new fusible link of the same value.

CIRCUIT BREAKERS

There are 3 different style circuit breakers used. A standard heat activated circuit breaker is used which will cycle open and closed until the overload condition is corrected. There is a mechanical type breaker and a solid state design called a Positive Temperature Coefficient (PTC) circuit breaker, both will not reset until the current source is removed for a few seconds. Various circuit breakers are located throughout the vehicle and the fuse block.

FUSE BLOCK

The main fuse block assembly is located behind the far right side of the instrument panel. The 2 auxiliary fuse blocks are found below the right of the instrument panel, next to the radio receiver box.

RELAYS

ABS Control Module Relay (1990) — located under the corner of the rear floor, in storage compartment.

ABS ACTIVE Indicator Relay — located under the left side of the cargo compartment.

ABS Pump Motor Relay — located under the corner of the rear floor on the ABS modulator assembly, in the storage compartment.

ABS Valve Solenoid Relay — located under the corner of the rear floor on the ABS modulator assembly, in the storage compartment.

Air Conditioning Clutch Relay — located in the left side of the engine compartment, in front of the battery.

Air Pump Relay — located in the left hand front of the engine compartment, on top of the air pump.

Amplifier Relay — located behind the left side of the instrument panel, to the right of the instrument cluster.

Blower Relays (High and Low) — located in the left side of the engine compartment, on the wheelhouse.

Cruise Control Cut-Off Relay — located below the instrument panel, left of the steering column.

Deck Lid Release Relay — located on the right front of the cargo compartment.

Delayed Accessory Bus (DAB) Relay — located below the left side of the instrument panel.

Dome Lamp Relay — located on the multi-use relay bracket to the bottom right side of the instrument panel.

Engine Cooling Fan Relays (Primary and Secondary) — located in the front of the engine compartment on the left side of the radiator shroud.

Fuel Pump Relays (1990–92) — located below right side of the instrument panel, left of the glove compartment on the multi-use relay bracket. The 5.7L (VIN J) engine uses a second relay located below the left side of the instrument panel.

Fog Lamp Relay — located on the multi-use relay bracket to the bottom right side of the instrument panel.

Hatch Release Relay — located in the rear of the cargo compartment, on the end panel.

Horn Relay — located on the multi-use relay bracket to the bottom right of the instrument panel.

Power Antenna Relay (Convertible and Coupe) — located on the left side of the cargo compartment above the rear of the wheel house.

Rear Defogger Relay — located on the multi-use relay bracket to the bottom right of the instrument panel.

Secondary Injector Relays (VIN J) — located rear of the left hand front wheelhouse, in front of the battery and behind the battery near the left hand door hinges.

Starter Enable Relay — located below the left side of the instrument panel, left of the steering column.

Shift-Up Relay — located in the left hand middle of the engine compartment, near the frame rail.

Computers

Location

Electronic Brake Control Module (EBCM) — located under the left corner of cargo compartment, behind the driver's seat.

Central Control Module (CCM, 1990–94) — located behind the middle of the instrument panel.

Diagnostic Energy Reserve (DERM) Module — located in the middle of the instrument panel, in front of and below the CCM.

Electronic Control Module (ECM) 1990–92 — located in the engine compartment, above the battery.

Electronic Spark Control Module (1990) — located on the right side of air conditioning heater blower housing.

Select Ride Control Module (SRCM) — located rear of the cargo compartment, under the cargo deck.

Flashers

Location

Turn Signal — located below left side of instrument panel, to the left of the steering column.

Hazard Flasher — located near the radio on the right side of the instrument panel.